The VNR Desktop Word Divider/Speller and Area Code Directory

The VNR Desktop Word Divider/Speller and Area Code Directory

Craig T. Norback

 VAN NOSTRAND REINHOLD COMPANY

NEW YORK   CINCINNATI   ATLANTA   DALLAS   SAN FRANCISCO
LONDON   TORONTO   MELBOURNE

Telephone Area Code Directory
© American Telephone and Telegraph Company

Van Nostrand Reinhold Company Regional Offices:
New York   Cincinnati   Atlanta   Dallas   San Francisco

Van Nostrand Reinhold Company International Offices:
London   Toronto   Melbourne

Copyright © 1980 by Litton Educational Publishing Inc.

Library of Congress Catalog Card Number: 79-21891
ISBN: 0-442-26338-4

Manufactured in the United States of America

Published by Van Nostrand Reinhold Company
135 West 50th Street, New York, N.Y. 10020

Published simultaneously in Canada by Van Nostrand Reinhold Ltd.

15 14 13 12 11 10 9 8 7 6 5 4 3 2 1

Library of Congress Cataloging in Publication Data

Norback, Craig T
    The VNR desktop word divider/speller and area code
directory.

    1. Secretaries—Handbooks, manuals, etc.   2. English
language—Syllabication.   3. Telephone—United States—
Area codes.   I. Title.
HF5547.5.N66   428'.1   79-21891
ISBN 0-442-26338-4

WORDBREAK RULES

1. Division of words should be minimized in leaded matter and avoided in double-leaded matter.

2. Wordbreaks should be avoided at the ends of more than two lines. Similarly, no more than two consecutive lines should end with the same word, symbol, group of numbers, etc.

3. In two-line centerheads, the first line should be centered and set as full as possible, but it should not be set to fill the measure by using unduly wide spacing. Wordbreaks should be avoided. Flush sideheads should be set full measure and wordbreaks used only if unavoidable. They should not be set ragged unless so indicated on the copy.

4. The final word of a paragraph should not be divided.

5. Words should be divided according to pronunciation; and to avoid mispronunciation, they should be divided so that the part of the word left at the end of the line will suggest the whole word: e.g., capac-ity, not capa-city; extraor-dinary, not extra-ordinary; Wednes-day, not Wed-nesday).

6. Under no circumstances are words to be divided on a single-letter syllable, whether it appears at the beginning or at the end of the word (e.g., usu-al-ly, not u-su-al-ly).

7. Division of short words (of five or fewer letters) should always be avoided; two-letter divisions, including the carryover of two-letter endings (ed, el, en, er, es, et, fy, ic, in, le, ly, or, and ty) should also be avoided. In narrow measure, however, a sounded suffix (e.g., paint-ed; not rained) or syllable of two letters may be carried over—only if unavoidable (See Rule 10.).

8. Words of two syllables should be split at the end of the first syllable: dis-pelled, con-quered; words of three or more syllables, with a choice of division possible, should be divided on the vowel: particu-lar, sepa-rate.

9. Words with short prefixes should be divided on the prefix; e.g., ac, co, de, dis, ex, in, non, on, pre, pro, re, un, etc. (e.g., non-essential, not nones-sential).

If possible, prefixes and combining forms of more than one syllable should be preserved intact: anti, infra, macro, micro, multi, over, retro, semi, etc. (e.g., anti-monopoly, not antimo-nopoly; over-optimistic; not overop-timistic). (For chemical prefixes, see Rule 30.)

10. Words ending in -er. Except in narrow measure and only if unavoidable, the -er words should not be divided unless division can be made on a prefix; e.g., per-ceiver.

11. Words ending in -or. Generally, -or words with a consonant preceding the -or should be divided before the preceding consonant; e.g., advi-sor (legal), fabrica-tor; but bail-or, con-sign-or.

12. The following suffixes should not be divided: ceous, cial, cient, cion, cious, scious, geous, gion, gious, sial, tial, tion, tious, and sion.

13. The suffixes -able and -ible should usually be carried over intact; but when the stem word loses its original form, these suffixes should be divided according to pronunciation: comfort-able, corrupt-ible, but dura-ble, audi-ble.

14. Words ending in -ing, with stress on the primary syllable, should be divided on the base word; e.g., appoint-ing, process-ing, etc. However, present participles, such as forbid-ding, refer-ring, with stress placed on the second syllable, should be divided between the doubled consonants (see also Rule 16.)

15. When the final consonant sound of a word belongs to a syllable ending with a silent vowel, the final consonant or consonants should become part of the added suffix: chuck-ling, han-dler, twin-kled, but rollick-ing.

16. When the addition of -ed, -er, -est, or of a similar ending, causes the doubling of a final consonant, the added consonant should be carried over: pit-ted, rob-ber; but dwell-er, gross-est.

17. Words with doubled consonants should usually be divided between these consonants: clas-sic, neces-sary; but call-ing, mass-ing.

18. If formation of a plural adds a syllable ending in an s sound, the plural ending should not be carried over by itself: hor-ses, voi-ces; but church-es, cross-es, thus not breaking the base word (see also Rule 7).

19. The digraphs ai, ck, dg, gh, gn, ng, oa, ph, sh, tch, and th should not be split.

20. Contractions should never be divided: e.g., doesn't, haven't.

21. Solid compounds should be divided between the members: bar-keeper, hand-kerchief, proof-reader, humming-bird.

22. A division which adds another hyphen to a hyphenated compound should be avoided: court-martial, not court-mar-tial; tax-supported, not tax-sup-ported.

23. A word of one syllable should never be split: tanned, shipped, quenched, through, chasm, prism.

24. Two consonants preceded and followed by a vowel should be divided on the first consonant: abun-dant, advan-tage, struc-ture.

25. When two adjoining vowels are sounded separately, the word should be divided between them: cre-ation, gene-alogy.

26. In breaking homonyms, distinction should be given to their relative functions: pro-ject (v.), proj-ect (n.); pro-duce (v.), prod-uce (n.)

27. Words ending in -meter. In the large group of words ending in -meter, distinction should be made between metric system terms and terms indicating a measuring instrument. When it is necessary to divide metric terms, the combining form -meter should be preserved; e.g., centi-meter, kil-meter. But measuring instruments should be divided after the m: al-tim-e-ter, ba-rom-e-ter, etc. Derivatives of these -meter terms follow the same form; e.g., bar-o-met-ric, ba-rom-e-try.

For orthographic reasons, however, several measuring instruments do not lend themselves to the general rule; e.g., volt-meter, water-meter, etc.

29. Chemical formulas. In chemical formulas, the hyphen has an important function. If a break is unavoidable in a formula, the division should be made after an original hyphen to avoid the introduction of a misleading hyphen. If it is impractical to break the word on a hyphen, division may be made after an original comma, and then no hyphen should be added to indicate a runover. The following formula shows original hyphens and commas where division may be made. No letterspacing is used in a chemical formula, but to fill a line, a space is permitted on both sides of a hyphen.

1-(2, 6, 6-trimethylcyclophex-1-en-1-yl)-3, 7, 12, 16

30. Chemical combining forms, prefixes, and suffixes. If possible, and subject to rules of good spacing, each of the combining forms which follow should be preserved as a unit:

aceto, anhydro, benzo bromo, chloro, chromo, cincho, cyclo, dehydro, diazo, flavo, fluora, glyco, hydroxy, iso, keto, methyl, naphtho, phospho, poly, silica, tetra, triaze.

The following suffixes are used in chemical printing. For patent and narrow measure composition, two-letter suffixes may be carried over.

al, an, ane, ase, ate, ene, ic, id, ide, in, ine, ite, ol, ole, on, one, ose, ous, oyl, yl, yne.

31. Mineral elements. When it is necessary to break mineral constituents, division should be made before a center period and beginning parenthesis, and after inferior figures following a closing parenthesis; but elements within parentheses should not be separated. In cases of unavoidable breaks, a hyphen should not be added to indicate a runover.

Mg (UO2) 2 (SiO3) 2(OH)2 6H2O

32. The em dash should not be used at the beginning of any line of type, unless it is required before a credit line or signature, or in lieu of opening quotation marks in foreign languages.

33. Neither periods nor asterisks used as an ellipsis should be run over alone at the end of a paragraph. If necessary, enough preceding lines should be run over to provide a short word or part of a word to accompany the ellipsis. If a runback is possible, subject to rules of good spacing and word division, this method may be adopted.

34. Abbreviations and symbols should not be broken at the end of a line: A.F. of L., A.T. & T., C. Cis. R., f.o.b., n.o.i.b.n., R. & D., r.p.m., WMAL. Where unavoidable, long symbols may be broken after letters denoting a complete word. No hyphens should be used. COM SUB A C LANT (Commander Submarine Allied Command Atlantic).

35. Figures of less than six digits, decimals, and closely connected combinations of figures and abbreviations should not be broken at the end of a line: $15,000, 34, 575, 31.416, L8 4s. 7d., $10.25, 5,000 kw-hr., A.D. 1952, 9 p.m., 18°F., NW¼. If a break in six digits or over is unavoidable, the figure should be divided on the comma or period, which should then be retained; or a hyphen should be used.

36. Closely related abbreviations and initials in proper names and accompanying titles should not be separated, nor should titles, such as Rev., Mr., Esq., Jr., 2d, be separated from surnames.

37. Proper names should not be divided, but if division is inescapable, the general rules for word division should be followed.

38. Divisional and subdivisional paragraph reference signs and figures, such as 18, section (a) (1), page 363(b), should not be divided, nor should such references be separated from the matter to which they pertain.

In case of an unavoidable break in a lengthy reference (e.g., 7(B) (1) (a) (i)), division should be made after elements in parentheses, and no hyphen should be used.

39. In dates, the month and day should not be divided, but the year may be carried over.

40. In case of an unavoidable break in a land-description symbol, it is necessary to group at the end of a line. No hyphen should be used, and the break should be made after a fraction.

41. Longitude and latitude figures should not be broken at the end of a line; the line should be spaced out instead. In case of an unavoidable break at the end of a line, a hyphen should be used.

Word Division

A

ab-a-ca
ab-a-cus
aban-don
abase
abate
abate-ment
abbey
abbot
ab-bre-vi-ate
ab-bre-vi-a-tion
ab-bre-vi-a-tor
ab-di-cate
ab-di-ca-tor
ab-do-men
ab-dom-i-nal
ab-duct
ab-duc-tor
ab-er-rant
ab-er-ra-tion
abet
abet-ter
abet-tor (law)
abey-ance
abhor
ab-hor-rence
abid-ance
abide
abid-ing
abil-i-ty
abi-ot-ic
ab-ject
ab-ju-ra-tion
ab-la-tion

ab-la-tive
ablaze
able
abloom
ab-lu-tion
ab-ne-gate
ab-ne-ga-tor
ab-nor-mal
ab-nor-mal-i-ty
aboard
abode
abol-ish
ab-o-li-tion-ist
abom-i-na-ble
ab-o-rig-i-nes
abort
abor-tion
abor-tive
abound
above
ab-ra-ca-dab-ra
ab-ra-sion
ab-ra-sive
abreast
abridge
abridge-ment
abroad
ab-ro-gate
ab-ro-ga-tion
abrupt
ab-scess
ab-scis-sa
ab-scis-sion
ab-scond

ab-sence
ab-sent
ab-sen-tee-ism
ab-so-lute
ab-so-lute-ly
ab-so-lu-tion
ab-so-lut-ism
ab-so-lu-tize
ab-solve
ab-solv-er
ab-sorb
ab-sorb-ent
ab-sorp-tion
ab-stain
ab-ste-mi-ous
ab-sten-tion
ab-sti-nence
ab-stract
ab-strac-tion
ab-struse
ab-surd
ab-surd-i-ty
abun-dance
abun-dant
abuse
abu-sive
abut
abut-ting
abut-ment
abys-mal
abyss
abys-sal
ac-a-de-mia
ac-a-dem-ic

ac-a-de-mi-cian
acad-e-my
acap-pel-la
ac-cede
ac-ced-ence
ac-cel-er-an-do
ac-cel-er-ate
ac-cel-er-a-tion
ac-cel-er-a-tor
ac-cel-er-om-e-ter
ac-cent
ac-cen-tu-ate
ac-cen-tu-a-tion
ac-cept
ac-cept-able
ac-cep-tance
ac-cep-ta-tion
ac-cept-ed
ac-cep-tor (law)
ac-cess
ac-ces-sible
ac-ces-sion
ac-ces-so-ry
ac-ces-so-ri-al
ac-ci-dent
ac-ci-den-tal
ac-claim
ac-cla-ma-tion
ac-cli-mate
ac-cli-ma-tion
ac-cli-ma-ti-za-
  tion
ac-cliv-i-ty
ac-co-lade

1

ac-com-mo-date
ac-com-mo-da-
   ting
ac-com-mo-da-
   tion
ac-com-pa-ni-
   ment
ac-com-pa-nist
ac-com-pa-ny
ac-com-plice
ac-com-plish
ac-com-plished
ac-com-plish-
   ment
ac-cord
ac-cord-ance
ac-cord-ing-ly
ac-cost
ac-count
ac-count-able
ac-coun-tan-cy
ac-count-ant
ac-count-ing
ac-cou-ter
ac-cou-ter-ment
ac-cred-it
ac-cred-i-ta-tion
ac-cre-tion
ac-crue
ac-cul-tur-ate
ac-cu-mu-late
ac-cu-mu-la-tion
ac-cu-mu-la-tive
ac-cu-mu-la-tor
ac-cu-ra-cy
ac-cu-rate
ac-cursed
ac-cus-al
ac-cu-sa-tion
ac-cu-sa-tive
ac-cus-a-to-ry
ac-cuse
ac-cus-er
ac-cus-tom
ac-cus-tomed

ac-et-al-de-hyde
ac-e-tate
ace-tic
ac-e-tone
ac-e-tyl
ac-e-tyl-cho-line
achieve-ment
Achil-les
ach-ro-mat-ic
ach-ro-ma-tic-i-ty
acid
acid-i-ty
ac-knowl-edge
ac-knowl-edge-
   able
ac-knowl-edg-
   ment
acme
acne
ac-o-ni-tum
acorn
acous-tic
ac-ous-ti-cian
ac-quaint
ac-quaint-ance
ac-quaint-ed
ac-qui-esce
ac-qui-es-cence
ac-quire
ac-qui-si-tion
ac-quis-i-tive
ac-quit
ac-quit-tal
acre
acre-age
ac-ri-mo-ni-ous
ac-ri-mo-ny
ac-ro-bat
ac-ro-bat-ics
ac-ro-nym
ac-ro-pho-bia
acrop-o-lis
across
acryl-ic
act-ing

ac-tion
ac-ti-vate
ac-ti-va-tion
ac-ti-va-tor
ac-tive
ac-tiv-ism
ac-tiv-ist
ac-tiv-i-ty
ac-to-my-o-sin
ac-tor
ac-tress
ac-tu-al
ac-tu-al-i-ty
ac-tu-al-ize
ac-tu-ar-y
ac-tu-ate
acu-i-ty
ac-u-punc-ture
a-cute
ad ab-sur-dum
adage
ada-gio
ad-a-mant
adapt
adapt-able
adapt-a-bil-i-ty
ad-ap-ta-tion
adapt-er
adap-tive
adap-tor
add-able
added
ad-den-da
ad-den-dum
adder
ad-dic-ted
ad-dic-tion
ad-di-tion
ad-di-tive
addle
ad-dress
ad-dress-ee
ad-dress-er
ad-dres-sor (law)
ad-duce

ad-e-nine
ad-e-noid
ad-e-noi-dal
adept
adept-ness
ad-e-quate
ad-e-qua-cy
ad-here
ad-her-ence
ad-her-ent
ad-he-sion
ad-he-sive
adieu
ad in-fi-ni-tum
adios
ad-i-pose
ad-ja-cent
ad-jec-ti-val
ad-jec-tive
ad-join
ad-join-ing
ad-journ
ad-ju-di-cate
ad-junct
ad-junc-tive
ad-ju-ra-tion
ad-jure
ad-jur-er
ad-just
ad-just-able
ad-just-er
ad-just-ment
ad-ju-tant
ad-min-is-ter
ad-min-is-trate
ad-min-is-tra-tion
ad-min-is-tra-tor
ad-min-is-tra-trix
ad-mi-ra-ble
ad-mi-ral
ad-mi-ral-ty
ad-mi-ra-tion
ad-mire
ad-mir-er
ad-mis-si-ble

ad-mis-sion
ad-mit
ad-mit-tance
ad-mit-ted-ly
ad-mon-ish
ad-mo-ni-tion
ad-mon-i-to-ry
ad nau-se-am
ado
adobe
ad-o-les-cence
ad-o-les-cent
adopt
adopt-er
adop-tive
ador-able
ad-o-ra-tion
adore
ador-er
adorn
adorn-ment
ad-re-nal
ad-ren-a-lin
adrift
adroit
adroit-ness
ad-sorb
ad-sorb-ate
ad-sor-bent
ad-sorp-tion
ad-sorp-tive
ad-u-late
ad-u-la-tion
adult
adul-ter-ate
adul-ter-er
adul-ter-ess
adul-ter-ous
adul-tery
ad-vance
ad-vance-ment
ad-vanc-er
ad-van-tage
ad-van-ta-geous
ad-vent

Ad-vent-ist
ad-ven-ture
ad-ven-tur-er
ad-ven-tur-ous
ad-verb
ad-ver-bi-al
ad-ver-sary
ad-verse
ad-ver-si-ty
ad-ver-tise
ad-ver-tise-ment
ad-ver-tis-er
ad-ver-tis-ing
ad-vice
ad-vis-able
ad-vise
ad-vised
ad-vis-ed-ly
ad-vis-er
ad-vi-sor (law)
ad-vi-so-ry
ad-vo-ca-cy
ad-vo-cate
ad-vo-ca-tor
aer-i-al
aer-i-al-ist
aerie
aer-o-bat-ics
aer-obe
aer-o-bic
aer-o-dy-nam-ic
aer-o-gram
aer-o-naut
aer-o-nau-tics
aer-o-sol
aes-thet-ic
afar
af-fa-ble
af-fair
af-fect
af-fec-ta-tion
af-fec-ted
af-fec-ting
af-fec-tion
af-fec-tion-ate

af-fec-tive
af-fer-ent
af-fi-da-vit
af-fil-i-ate
af-fin-i-ty
af-firm
af-fir-ma-tion
af-fir-ma-tive
affix
af-flict
af-flic-tion
af-flu-ence
af-flu-ent
af-ford
af-fray
af-front
af-ghan
Af-ghan-i-stan
afi-ci-o-na-do
afield
afire
afloat
afoot
afore-said
afor-ti-o-ri
afraid
afresh
Af-ri-ca
Af-ri-can
Afro
after
af-ter-care
af-ter-ef-fect
af-ter-life
af-ter-math
af-ter-noon
af-ter-taste
af-ter-thought
af-ter-ward
again
against
agape
agate
aged
age-less

agen-cy
agen-da
agent
ag-glom-er-ate
ag-glom-er-a-tion
ag-glu-ti-nate
ag-glu-ti-na-tion
ag-gran-dize
ag-gra-vate
ag-gra-va-tion
ag-gre-gate
ag-gress
ag-gres-sion
ag-gres-sive
ag-gres-sor
agile
agil-i-ty
aging
ag-i-tate
ag-i-ta-tion
ag-i-ta-tor
aglow
ag-nos-tic
ag-nos-ti-cism
ago
ag-o-nize
ag-o-niz-ing
agony
ag-o-ra-pho-bia
agrar-i-an
agree
agree-able
agreed
agree-ment
ag-ri-cul-ture
ag-ri-cul-tur-al
agron-o-mist
agron-o-my
ahead
ai-le-ron
ail-ment
aim-less
air-borne
air con di tion
air-con-di-tion-er

air-con-di-tion-ing
air-craft
air-field
air-flow
air-i-ly
air-i-ness
air-line
air-lin-er
air-mail
air-plane
air-port
air-sick
air-sick-ness
air-tight
airy
aisle
ajar
akin
Al-a-bam-a
al-a-bas-ter
alac-ri-ty
alamo
a la mode
alarm
alarm-ist
Alas-ka
Al-ba-nia
Al-ba-ny
al-ba-tross
al-bi-nism
al-bi-no
album
Al-bu-quer-que
al-bu-men (egg)
al-bu-min
   (chemical)
Al-ca-traz
al-che-mist
al-che-my
al-co-hol
al-co-hol-ism
al-cove
al-de-hyde
alert
alert-ness

al-fal-fa
algae
al-ge-bra
al-ge-bra-ic
al-ge-bra-i-cal
Al-ge-ria
Al-ge-ri-an
al-go-rism
al-go-rithm
alias
alibi
alien
al-ien-ate
al-ien-a-tion
alight
align
align-ment
alike
al-i-men-ta-ry
al-i-mo-ny
alive
al-ka-li
al-ka-line
al-ka-loid
allay
al-le-ga-tion
al-lege
al-leged
Al-le-ghe-ny
al-le-giance
al-le-gor-i-cal
al-le-go-ry
al-le-gro
al-lele
al-le-lu-ia
al-ler-gen
al-ler-gic
al-ler-gy
al-le-vi-a-tion
alley
al-li-ance
al-lied
Al-lies
al-li-ga-tor
al-lit-er-a-tion
al-lo-cate

al-lo-cu-tion
allot
al-lot-ted
al-lot-ting
al-lot-ment
al-lo-trope
al-lo-troph-ic
allow
al-low-ance
alloy
all-spice
al-lude
al-lure
al-lur-ing
ally
al-ma-nac
al-mighty
al-mond
al-most
alo-ha
alone
along
along-side
aloof
aloud
alpha
al-pha-bet
al-pha-bet-i-cal
al-pha-bet-ize
al-ready
al-right
also
altar
alter
al-ter-able
al-ter-a-tion
al-ter-cate
al-ter-ca-tion
al-ter-nate
al-ter-nate-ly
al-ter-na-tive
al-ter-na-tor
al-though
al-tim-e-ter
al-tim-e-try

al-ti-tude
alto
al-to-geth-er
al-tru-ism
alum
alu-mi-nize
alu-mi-num
alum-na
alum-nus
al-ve-o-lar
al-ve-o-lus
al-ways
amal-gam
amal-ga-mate
amal-ga-ma-tion
am-a-ryl-lis
amass
am-a-teur
am-a-teur-ish
amaze
amaze-ment
amaz-ing
Am-a-zon
Am-a-zo-ni-an
am-bas-sa-dor
am-bas-sa-do-ri-al
amber
am-ber-gris
am-bi-ance
am-bi-dex-trous
am-bi-ent
am-bi-gu-i-ty
am-big-u-ous
am-bi-tion
am-bi-tious
am-biv-a-lence
am-biv-a-lent
amble
am-bling
am-bro-sia
am-bro-sial
am-bu-lance
am-bu-la-to-ry
am-bush
ame-lio-rate

ame-lio-ra-tive
amen
ame-na-ble
amend
amend-a-to-ry
amend-ment
amen-i-ty
amen-or-rhea
Amer-i-ca
Amer-i-can
Amer-i-can-ism
Amer-i-can-ize
am-e-thyst
ami-able
am-i-ca-ble
amid
amid-ships
amigo
amine
amino
amity
am-me-ter
am-mo-nia
am-mu-ni-tion
am-ne-sia
am-nes-ty
amoe-ba
among
amor-al
amor-phism
amor-phous
amount
am-per-age
am-pere
am-per-sand
am-phet-a-mine
am-phib-i-an
am-phib-i-ous
am-pho-ter-ic
ample
am-pli-fi-ca-tion
am-pli-fi-er
am-pli-fy
am-pli-tude
amply

am-pu-tate
am-pu-ta-tion
am-pu-ta-tor
am-pu-tee
am-u-let
amuse
amuse-ment
amus-ing
amyg-da-line
An-a-bap-tist
an-a-bi-ot-ic
anach-ro-nism
an-aer-obe
an-aer-o-bic
an-a-gram
anal
an-al-ge-sia
an-al-ge-sic
an-a-log-i-cal
anal-o-gous
an-a-logue
anal-o-gy
anal-y-sand
anal-y-sis
ana-lyst
an-a-lyt-ic
an-a-lyt-i-cal
an-a-lyz-able
an-a-lyze
an-ar-chic
an-ar-chism
an-ar-chist
an-ar-chy
anath-e-ma
an-a-tom-i-cal
anat-o-mist
anat-o-my
an-ces-tor
an-ces-tral
an-ces-try
an-chor
an-chor-age
an-chor-man
an-chor-wom-an
an-cho-vy

an-cient
an-cil-lary
and-i-ron
an-dro-gen
an-drog-y-nous
an-droid
an-ec-dot-al
an-ec-dote
ane-mia
ane-mic
anem-o-ne
an-es-the-sia
an-es-the-si-ol-
   o-gist
an-es-the-si-ol-
   o-gy
an-es-thet-ic
an-es-the-tist
an-es-the-tize
an-eu-rysm
anew
angel
an-gel-ic
anger
an-gi-o-sperm
angle
an-gler
An-gli-can
an-gli-cize
an-gling
An-go-la
An-go-lese
An-go-ra
angry
angst
ang-strom
an-guish
an-gu-lar
an-gu-lar-i-ty
an-gu-la-tion
an-hy-drous
anima
an-i-mal
an-i-mal-ism
an-i-mal-ize

an-i-mate
an-i-mat-ed
an-i-ma-tion
an-i-ma-tor
an-i-mism
an-i-mos-i-ty
anion
an-i-on-ic
anise
an-is-ette
ankle
an-kle-bone
an-klet
an-nals
an-nex
an-nex-a-tion
an-ni-hi-late
an-ni-hi-la-tion
an-ni-ver-sa-ry
an-no-tate
an-no-ta-tion
an-no-ta-tor
an-nounce
an-nounce-ment
an-nounc-er
annoy
an-noy-ance
an-noy-ing
an-nu-al
an-nu-i-ty
annul
an-nul-ment
an-nun-ci-ate
an-nun-ci-a-tion
anode
anoint
anoint-ment
anom-a-lous
anom-a-ly
anon
an-o-nym-i-ty
anon-y-mous
an-o-rex-ia
an-oth-er
an-swer

an-swer-able
an-swer-er
an-swer-ing
ant-ac-id
an-tag-o-nism
an-tag-o-nist
an-tag-o-nize
Ant-arc-tic
Ant-arc-ti-ca
an-te-cede
an-te-ce-dence
an-te-ce-dent
an-te-cham-ber
an-te-date
an-te-di-lu-vi-an
an-te-lope
an-ten-na
an-te-ri-or
an-te-room
an-them
an-tho-log-i-cal
an-thol-o-gy
an-thra-cite
an-thrax
an-thro-po-cen-
    tric
an-thro-poid
an-thro-po-log-
    i-cal
an-thro-pol-o-gy
an-thro-po-met-
    ric
an-thro-po-mor-
    phism
an-thro-po-mor-
    phize
an-thro-po-mor-
    phous
an-ti-air-craft
an-ti-bal-lis-tic
an-ti-bi-ot-ic
an-ti-body
an-ti-christ
an-tic-i-pant
an-tic-i-pate

an-tic-i-pa-tion
an-tic-i-pa-to-ry
an-ti-cli-max
an-ti-co-ag-u-lant
an-ti-dot-al
an-ti-dote
an-ti-freeze
an-ti-gen
an-ti-he-ro
an-ti-his-ta-mine
an-ti-his-ta-min-ic
an-ti-mag-net-ic
an-ti-mat-ter
an-ti-mo-ni-al
an-ti-mo-ny
an-ti-par-ti-cle
an-ti-pas-to
an-tip-a-thy
an-ti-per-spi-rant
an-tiph-o-nal
an-tiph-o-ny
an-ti-pope
an-ti-quar-i-an
an-ti-quate
an-ti-quat-ed
an-tique
an-tiq-ui-ty
an-ti-sep-tic
an-ti-slav-ery
an-ti-so-cial
an-tith-e-sis
an-ti-thet-i-cal
an-ti-tox-ic
an-ti-tox-in
an-ti-trust
ant-ler
an-to-nym
an-u-re-sis
anvil
anx-i-e-ty
anx-ious
any
an-y-body
an-y-how
an-y-more

an-y-one
an-y-place
an-y-thing
an-y-way
an-y-where
aorta
a-or-tic
apart
apart-heid
apart-ment
ap-a-thet-ic
ap-a-thy
aper-i-tif
ap-er-ture
ap-er-tur-al
apex
apha-gia
apha-sia
aph-o-rism
aph-ro-dis-i-ac
api-ary
apiece
apla-sia
aplomb
Apoc-a-lypse
apoc-a-lyp-tic
Apoc-ry-pha
apoc-ry-phal
ap-o-gee
apo-lit-i-cal
apol-o-get-ic
ap-o-lo-gia
apol-o-gist
apol-o-gize
apol-o-gy
ap-o-plec-tic
ap-o-plexy
a pos-te-ri-o-ri
apos-tle
apos-to-late
ap-os-tol-ic
apos-tro-phe
apoth-e-cary
apoth-e-o-sis
Ap-pa-la-chian

ap-pall
ap-pall-ing
ap-pa-loo-sa
ap-pa-ra-tus
ap-par-el
ap-par-ent
ap-pa-ri-tion
ap-peal
ap-pear
ap-pear-ance
ap-pease
ap-pease-ment
ap-pel-lant
ap-pel-ate
ap-pel-la-tion
ap-pel-la-tive
ap-pend
ap-pend-age
ap-pen-dec-to-my
ap-pen-di-ci-tis
ap-pen-dix
ap-per-ceive
ap-per-cep-tion
ap-per-tain
ap-pe-tite
ap-pe-tiz-er
ap-pe-tiz-ing
ap-plaud
ap-plause
apple
ap-ple-sauce
ap-pli-ance
ap-pli-ca-ble
ap-pli-cant
ap-pli-ca-tion
ap-pli-ca-tive
ap-pli-ca-tor
ap-plied
ap-pli-que
ap-ply
ap-point
ap-point-ing
ap-point-ment
ap-por-tion
ap-por-tion-ment

ap-po-si-tion
ap-pos-i-tive
ap-prais-al
ap-praise
ap-pre-cia-ble
ap-pre-ci-ate
ap-pre-ci-a-tion
ap-pre-ci-a-tive
ap-pre-hend
ap-pre-hen-si-ble
ap-pre-hen-sion
ap-pre-hen-sive
ap-pren-tice
ap-prise
ap-proach
ap-proach-able
ap-proach-ing
ap-pro-bate
ap-pro-ba-tion
ap-pro-pri-ate
ap-pro-pri-a-tion
ap-pro-pri-a-tive
ap-prov-al
ap-prove
ap-prox-i-mate
ap-prox-i-ma-tion
aprax-ia
apri-cot
April
a pri-o-ri
apron
ap-ro-pos
ap-ti-tude
aqua
aq-ua-ma-rine
aq-ua-naut
aq-ua-plane
aquar-i-um
aquat-ic
aq-ue-duct
aque-ous
Arab
ar-a-besque
Ara-bia
Ara-bi-an

Ar-a-bic
ar-a-ble
arach-noid
ar-ach-noi-dal
arag-o-nite
Ar-a-ma-ic
ar-bi-ter
ar-bi-tra-ble
ar-bi-trary
ar-bi-trate
ar-bi-tra-tion
ar-bi-tra-tor
arbor
ar-bo-re-al
ar-bo-re-tum
ar-bor-ist
ar-bor-i-za-tion
ar-bo-rize
ar-cade
Ar-ca-dia
Ar-ca-di-an
ar-cane
ar-chae-ol-o-gist
ar-chae-ol-o-gy
ar-cha-ic
ar-cha-ism
arch-an-gel
arch-bish-op
arch-bish-op-ric
arch-dea-con
arch-dea-con-ry
arch-di-o-cese
arch-du-cal
arch-duch-ess
arch-duchy
arch-duke
arch-en-e-my
ar-che-o-log-i-cal
ar-che-ol-o-gy
arch-er
arch-ery
ar-che-typ-al
ar-che-type
ar-chi-pel-a-go
ar-chi-tect

ar-chi-tec-ture
ar-chi-tec-tur-al
ar-chi-val
ar-chives
ar-chi-vist
arch-priest
arch-way
Arc-tic
ar-dent
ardor
ar-du-ous
area
arena
Ar-gen-ti-na
ar-gen-tine
argon
ar-go-sy
ar-gu-able
argue
ar-gu-ment
ar-gu-men-ta-tive
ar-gyle
aria
Ar-i-an
arid
arid-i-ty
arise
ar-is-toc-ra-cy
aris-to-crat
aris-to-crat-ic
Ar-is-to-te-li-an
Ar-is-tot-le
ar-ith-met-ic
ar-ith-met-i-cal
Ar-i-zo-na
Ar-kan-sas
ar-ma-da
ar-ma-dil-lo
ar-ma-ment
arm-band
arm-chair
Ar-me-nia
Ar-me-ni-an
arm ful
ar-mi-stice

armor
ar-mored
ar-mor-er
ar-mo-ry
army
aroma
ar-o-mat-ic
ar-o-ma-ti-za-tion
aro-ma-tize
around
arous-al
arouse
arous-ing
ar-peg-gio
ar-raign
ar-raign-ment
ar-range
ar-range-ment
array
ar-rear
ar-rest
ar-res-ting
ar-riv-al
ar-rive
ar-ro-gance
ar-ro-gant
arrow
ar-row-head
ar-row-root
ar-se-nal
ar-se-nic (n.)
ar-sen-ic (adj.)
arson
ar-son-ist
ar-te-ri-al
ar-te-ri-ole
ar-te-ri-o-scle-ro-
   sis
ar-tery
ar-te-sian
art-ful
ar-thrit-ic
ar-thri-tis
ar-ti-choke
ar-ti-cle

ar-tic-u-late
ar-tic-u-la-tion
ar-tic-u-la-tor
ar-ti-fact
ar-ti-fice
ar-ti-fi-cial
ar-til-lery
ar-ti-san
art-ist
ar-tis-tic
ar-tist-ry
art-less
arty
Ar-y-an
Ar-y-an-ize
as-bes-tos
as-cend
as-cen-dan-cy
as-cen-dant
as-cend-er
as-cend-ing
as-cen-sion
as-cent
as-cer-tain
as-cet-ic
as-cet-i-cism
ascor-bic
ascot
as-cribe
as-crip-tion
asex-u-al
ashamed
ashen
ashore
Asia
Asian
Asi-at-ic
aside
as-i-nine
as-i-nin-i-ty
askance
askew
asleep
aso-cial
as-par-a-gus

as-pect
aspen
as-perse
as-per-sion
as-phalt
as-phyx-ia
as-phyx-i-ant
as-phyx-i-ate
aspic
as-pi-rant
as-pi-ra-tion
as-pi-ra-tor
as-pire
as-pi-rin
as-sail
as-sail-ant
as-sas-sin
as-sas-si-nate
as-sault
assay
as-sem-blage
as-sem-ble
as-sem-bler
as-sem-bly
as-sent
as-sen-ter
as-sent-ing-ly
as-sert
as-sert-ible
as-ser-tion
as-ser-tive
as-sess
as-sess-ment
as-ses-sor
asset
as-sid-u-ous
as-sign
as-sign-able
as-sign-ment
as-sign-or
as-sim-i-la-ble
as-sim-i-late
as-sim-i-la-tion
as-sist
as-sis-tance

as-sis-tant
as-so-ci-able
as-so-ci-ate
as-so-ci-a-tion
as-so-ci-a-tive
as-so-nance
as-sort
as-sort-ed
as-sort-ment
as-suage
as-sume
as-sum-ing
as-sump-tion
as-sump-tive
as-sur-ance
as-sure
aster
astat-ic
as-ter-isk
astern
as-ter-oid
as-ter-oi-dal
asth-ma
asth-mat-ic
as-tig-mat-ic
astig-ma-tism
astir
as-ton-ish
as-ton-ish-ment
as-tound
as-tound-ing
astray
as-trin-gent
as-trol-o-ger
as-tro-log-i-cal
as-trol-o-gy
as-tro-naut
as-tro-nau-tics
as-tron-o-mer
as-tro-nom-i-cal
as-tron-o-my
as-tro-phys-ics
as-tro-sphere
as-tute
asun-der

asy-lum
asym-met-ric
asym-met-ri-cal
asym-me-try
asymp-to-mat-ic
as-ymp-tote
as-ymp-tot-ic
atem-po-ral
athe-ism
athe-ist
athe-is-tic
Ath-ens
ath-lete
ath-let-ic
ath-let-i-cal-ly
At-lan-tic
atlas
at-mos-phere
at-mos-pher-ic
at-mos-pher-i-cal
atom
atom-ic
at-om-ism
at-om-ize
at-om-iz-er
aton-al
ato-nal-i-ty
atone
atone-ment
atop
atri-o-ven-tric-
  u-lar
atri-um
atro-cious
atroc-i-ty
at-ro-phy
at-tach
at-ta-che
at-tach-ment
at-tack
at-tain
at-tain-able
at-tain-ment
at-tempt
at-tend

at-ten-dance
at-ten-dant
at-ten-tion
at-ten-tive
at-ten-u-ate
at-ten-u-a-tor
at-test
at-tes-ta-tion
at-test-er
attic
at-tire
at-ti-tude
at-ti-tu-di-nal
at-ti-tu-di-nize
at-tor-ney
at-tract
at-trac-tion
at-trac-tive
at-trac-tor
at-trib-ut-able
at-trib-ute
at-trib-ut-er
at-tri-bu-tion
at-trib-u-tive
at-tri-tion
at-tune
atyp-i-cal
au-burn
auc-tion
auc-tion-eer
au-da-cious
au-dac-i-ty
au-di-bil-i-ty
au-di-ble
au-di-ence
au-di-o-vis-u-al
audit
au-di-tion
au-di-tor
au-di-to-ri-um
au-di-to-ry
aug-ment
aug-men-ta-tion
aug-men-ta-tive
aug-men-ted

au gra-tin
Au-gust
aura
aural
auric
au-ri-cle
au-ric-u-lar
au-ro-ra
au-ro-ra bo-re-
    al-is
aus-pice
aus-pi-ces
aus-pi-cious
aus-tere
aus-ter-i-ty
Aus-tra-lia
Aus-tra-lian
Aus-tria
Aus-tri-an
au-tar-chy
au-then-tic
au-then-ti-cal-ly
au-then-ti-cate
au-then-ti-ca-tor
au-then-tic-i-ty
au-thor
au-thor-ess
au-thor-i-tar-i-an
au-thor-i-ta-tive
au-thor-i-ty
au-thor-i-za-tion
au-thor-ize
au-thor-iz-er
au-tism
auto
au-to-bi-og-ra-
    phi-cal
au-to-bi-og-ra-phy
au-toc-ra-cy
au-to-crat
au-to-gen-e-sis
au-to-ge-net-ic
au-to-gen-ic
au-tog-e-nous
au-to-graph

au-to-harp
au-to-mat-ic
au-to-ma-tic-i-ty
au-to-ma-tion
au-tom-a-ton
au-to-nom-ic
au-ton-o-mous
au-ton-o-my
au-top-sy
au-to-troph
au-to-troph-ic
au-tumn
au-tum-nal
aux-il-ia-ry
auxin
avail
avail-able
av-a-lanche
avant-garde
av-a-rice
av-a-ri-cious
avenge
av-e-nue
av-er-age
aver-sion
avert
avi-ary
avi-a-tion
avi-a-tor
avi-a-trix
avid
avid-i-ty
av-o-ca-dos
av-o-ca-tion
avoid
avoid-ance
av-oir-du-pois
avow
avow-al
awake
awak-en
awak-en-ing
award
aware
away

awe-some
awe-strick-en
awful
awhile
awk-ward
awn-ing
awry
axial
ax-il-lar-y
axiom
ax-i-o-mat-ic
axon
azal-ea
az-i-muth
azon-ic
Aztec
azure

B

bab-ble
bab-bling
babka
ba-boon
ba-boon-ery
baby
ba-by-ish
Bab-y-lon
Bab-y-lo-nia
Bab-y-lo-ni-an
ba-by-sit
bac-ca-lau-re-ate
bach-e-lor
ba-cil-li
ba-cil-lus
back-bone
back-break-ing
back-door
back-er
back-fire
back-gam-mon
back-ground
back-ing
back-lash
back-list
back-log
back-pack

back-stage
back-stroke
back-track
back-up
back-ward
bacon
bac-te-ria
bac-te-ri-cide
bac-te-ri-ol-o-gist
bac-te-ri-ol-o-gy
bac-te-ri-um
badg-er
badly
bad-min-ton
baf-fle
baf-fling
bagel
bag-ful
bag-gage
baggy
bag-pipe
Ba-ha-ma
bail-er
bai-liff
bai-li-wick
bail-or
baker
bak-ery
bak-ing
bal-ance
bal-anc-er
bal-co-ny
bal-der-dash
bald-faced
bald-head-ed
bald-ing
Bal-kan
bal-lad
bal-lad-eer
bal-last
bal-le-ri-na
bal-let
bal-lis-tic
bal-loon
bal-loon-ist

bal-lot
ball-park
ball-play-er
ball-point
ball-room
balmy
ba-lo-ney
balsa
bal-sam
Bal-tic
Bal-ti-more
bam-bi-no
bam-boo
bam-boo-zle
banal
ba-nal-i-ty
ba-nana
band-age
ban-dan-na
ban-deau
ban-dit
band-stand
band-wag-on
bandy
ban-dy-ing
bane-ful
ban-gle
ban-ish
ban-is-ter
banjo
bank-book
bank-er
bank-ing
bank-rupt
bank-rupt-cy
ban-ner
ban-quet
ban-quet-er
ban-shee
ban-tam
ban-ter
bap-tism
bap-tis-mal
Bap-tist
bap-tize

bap-tiz-er
bar-bar-i-an
bar-bar-ic
bar-ba-rism
bar-bar-i-ty
bar-ba-rous
bar-be-cue
bar-bell
bar-ber
bar-ber-shop
bar-bi-tu-rate
bare-back
bare-foot
bare-hand-ed
bare-ly
bar-gain
bar-gain-er
bar-ing
bar-i-tone
bar-i-um
bark-er
bar-ley
bar-maid
bar mitz-vah
bar-na-cle
barn-yard
bar-o-graph
ba-rom-e-ter
bar-o-met-ric
ba-rom-e-try
baron
bar-on-ess
bar-on-et
ba-roque
bar-rack
bar-ra-cu-da
bar-rage
bar-rel
bar-reled
bar-ren
bar-rette
bar-ri-cade
bar-ring
bar-ris-ter
bar-room

bar-tend-er
bar-ter
ba-salt
ba-sal-tic
base-ball
base-board
base-less
base-ment
bash-ful
basic
ba-si-cal-ly
basil
ba-sil-i-ca
basin
basis
bas-ket
bas-ket-ball
bas-ket-ry
bas-set
bas-si-net
bas-soon
bas-tard
bas-tar-dize
bas-tille
bast-ing
bast-ion
bath-house
bath-robe
bath-room
batik
ba-tiste
baton
bat-tal-ion
bat-ten
bat-ter
bat-tery
bat-ting
bat-tle
bat-tle-field
bat-tle-ship
baux-ite
Ba-var-ia
Ba-var-i-an
bawdy
bay-o-net

bayou
ba-zaar
ba-zoo-ka
beach-comb-er
bea-con
bead-ing
bea-dle
bead-work
beady
bea-gle
beak-er
bean-pole
bean-stalk
bear-able
bear-er
bear-ing
Bé-ar-naise
bear-skin
beast-ly
beat-en
beat-er
be-a-tif-ic
be-at-i-fi-ca-tion
be-at-i-fy
beat-ing
be-at-i-tude
beau-te-ous
beau-ti-cian
beau-ti-ful
beau-ti-fy
beau-ty
bea-ver
be-came
be-cause
beck-on
be-come
be-com-ing
be-daz-zle
bed-ding
be-deck
be-dev-il
bed-lam
Bed-ou-in
be-drag-gle
bed-rid-den

bed-room
bed-side
bed-spread
bed-time
beech-nut
beef-steak
bee-hive
bee-keep-er
bees-wax
Bee-tho-ven
bee-tle
be-fall
befit
be-fit-ting
be-fore
be-fore-hand
be-friend
be-fud-dle
began
beg-gar
beg-gary
begin
be-gin-ner
be-gin-ning
be-grudge
be-guile
be-half
be-have
be-hav-ior
be-hav-ior-al
be-hav-ior-ism
be-head
be-hind
be-hold
be-hold-en
being
be-la-bor
be-lat-ed
be-lea-guer
bel-fry
Bel-gian
Bel-gium
be-lie
be-lief ·
be-lieve

be-liev-er
be-lit-tle
bell-boy
bel-li-cose
bel-li-cos-i-ty
bel-lig-er-ence
bel-lig-er-en-cy
bel-lig-er-ent
bel-low
belly
be-long
be-long-ing
be-lov-ed
below
bel-ve-dere
be-moan
be-muse
be-mused
be-neath
ben-e-dict
ben-e-dic-tion
ben-e-fac-tion
ben-e-fac-tor
ben-e-fac-tress
be-nef-ic
ben-e-fice
be-nef-i-cence
be-nef-i-cent
ben-e-fi-cial
ben-e-fi-ci-ary
ben-e-fit
ben-e-fit-ed
be-nev-o-lence
be-nev-o-lent
be-nign
be-nig-ni-ty
be-numb
ben-zene
ben-zo-ic
be-queath
be-rate
be-reave
beret
ber-i-beri
Berke-ley

berke-li-um
Ber-lin
Ber-mu-da
berry
ber-serk
be-ryl-li-um
be-seech
beset
be-side
be-siege
be-spec-ta-cled
bes-tial
bes-ti-al-i-ty
be-stow
be-stride
beta
be-tray
be-troth
be-troth-al
be-trothed
bet-ter
bet-ter-ment
bet-tor
be-tween
bevel
bev-er-age
bevy
be-ware
be-wil-der
be-wil-der-ing
be-wil-der-ment
be-witch
be-witch-ing
be-yond
bialy
bi-an-nu-al
bias
bi-ased
Bible
Bib-li-cal
bib-li-og-ra-pher
bib-li-o-graph-ic
bib-li-og-ra-phy
bib li o phile
bi-cam-er-al

bi-car-bon-ate
bi-cen-ten-a-ry
bi-cen-ten-ni-al
bi-ceps
bick-er
bick-er-ing
bi-cus-pid
bi-cy-cle
bi-cy-cling
bi-cy-clist
bid-ding
bi-en-ni-al
bi-en-ni-um
bi-fo-cal
big-a-mous
big-a-my
bigot
big-ot-ed
big-ot-ry
bi-ki-ni
bi-lat-er-al
bi-lin-gual
bi-lin-gual-ism
bil-ious
bill-board
bill-fold
bil-liards
bil-ling
bil-lion
bil-lion-naire
bil-lionth
bil-low
bi-man-u-al
bi-mo-dal
bi-month-ly
bi-na-ry
bin-au-ral
bind-er
bind-ery
bind-ing
bingo
bin-oc-u-lar
bi-no-mi-al
bi-o-chem-i-cal
bi-o-chem-ist

bi-o-chem-is-try
bi-o-de-grad-able
bi-o-feed-back
bi-og-ra-pher
bi-o-graph-i-cal
bi-og-ra-phy
bi-o-log-i-cal
bi-ol-o-gist
bi-ol-o-gy
bi-o-phys-ics
bi-op-sy
bi-o-sphere
bi-o-syn-the-sis
bi-ot-ic
bi-par-ti-san
bi-par-tite
biped
bipod
bi-po-lar
bi-ra-cial
bird-cage
bird-house
bird-seed
Bir-ming-ham
birth-day
birth-mark
birth-place
birth-rate
birth-right
birth-stone
bis-cuit
bi-sect
bi-sex-u-al
bish-op
bish-op-ric
bison
bis-tro
biter
bit-ing
bit-ter
bi-tu-men
bi-tu-mi-nous
bi-var-i-ate
bi-week-ly
bi-year-ly

bi-zarre
blab-ber
black-ber-ry
black-bird
black-board
black-en
black-ened
black-ish
black-list
black-mail
black-out
black-smith
black-top
blad-der
blad-ed
blam-able
blame-less
blame-wor-thy
blan-ket
blar-ney
blase
blas-pheme
blas-phe-mous
blas-phe-my
bla-tant
blaz-er
blaz-ing
bleach-er
bleed-er
bleed-ing
blem-ish
blend-er
blessed
bless-ing
blind-er
blind-fold
blind-ing
blink-er
blis-ter
bliz-zard
block-ade
block-age
block-bus-ter
blood-cur-dling
blood-less

blood-let-ting
blood-line
blood-shed
blood-shot
blood-thirsty
bloody
bloom-er
bloom-ing
bloop-er
blos-som
blot-ter
blow-er
bludg-eon
blue-ber-ry
blue-bird
blue-fish
blue-grass
blue-print
bluff-ing
blu-ish
blun-der
blun-der-er
blun-der-ing
blus-ter
boa
board-er
board-ing
boast-ful
boat-swain
bob-bin
bob-bi-net
bob-cat
bob-sled
bo-cac-cio
bo-da-cious
bod-ice
bod-i-ly
bod-y-guard
bo-gey
bog-gle
bo-gie (cart)
bo-gus
boil-er
boil-ing
bois-ter-ous

bold-face	bor-der-line	bow-leg	bread-win-ner
bo-le-ro	bore-dom	bow-leg-ged	break-able
Bo-liv-ia	bor-ing	bowl-er	break-age
Bol-she-vik	Bor-neo	bowl-ing	break-down
Bol-she-vism	boron	box-car	break-er
Bol-she-vist	bor-ough	box-er	break-fast
bol-ster	bor-row	box-ing	break-in
bom-bard	bosom	box-wood	break-ing
bom-bard-ier	bossy	boy-cott	break-through
bom-bast	Bos-ton	boy-friend	breast-bone
bom-bas-tic	Bos-to-ni-an	boy-ish	breast-feed
bom-bas-ti-cal	bo-tan-i-cal	boy-sen-ber-ry	breath-er
Bom-bay	bot-a-nist	brace-let	breath-ing
bomb-er	bot-a-ny	brac-ing	breath-less
bona fide	both-er	brack-et	breath-tak-ing
bo-nan-za	both-er-some	brack-ish	breed-er
Bo-na-parte	Bot-swa-na	brag-ga-do-cio	breed-ing
bon-bon	bot-tle	brag-gart	breezy
bond-age	bot-tle-neck	braid-ed	breth-ren
bond-ing	bot-tom	braid-ing	bre-vi-ary
bond-ser-vant	bot-tom-less	brain-stem	brev-i-ty
bonds-man	bot-u-lin	brain-storm	brew-er-y
bon-fire	bot-u-lism	brain-wash	brew-ing
bon-go	bou-doir	brain-wash-ing	briar
bon-net	bouf-fant	brainy	brib-ery
bon-us	bouil-la-baisse	brak-ing	brick-lay-er
bony	bouil-lon	bram-ble	bri-dal
book-bind-ing	boul-der	brand-er	bride-groom
book-case	bou-le-vard	bran-dish	brides-maid
book-ing	bounc-er	bran-dy	bri-dle
book-keep-ing	bounc-ing	bras-siere	bri-dling
book-let	bound-a-ry	brassy	brief-case
book-mak-er	boun-te-ous	brat-wurst	brief-ing
book-mark	boun-ti-ful	braun-schwei-ger	brier
book-stand	boun-ty	bra-va-do	bri-gade
book-store	bou-quet	brave-ly	brig-a-dier
boo-mer-ang	bour-bon	brav-er-y	brig-and
boor-ish	bour-geois	bravo	brig-and-age
boost-er	bour-geoi-sie	bra-vu-ra	brig-an-tine
boo-tie	bou-tique	brawny	bright-en
boot-leg	bou-ton-niere	bra-zen	bright-ness
boo-ty	bo-vine	Bra-zil	bril-liance
bo-rax	bowd-ler-ize	Bra-zil-ian	bril-lian-cy
Bor-deaux	bowie	bread-bas-ket	bril-liant
bor-der	bow-knot	bread-board	brim-ful

bri-oche
bri-quet
bris-ket
brisk-ly
bris-tle
bris-tly
Brit-ain
Bri-tan-nia
Brit-ish
Brit-ta-ny
brit-tle
broad-cast
broad-cast-er
broad-cloth
broad-en
broad-loom
broad-mind-ed
broad-side
Broad-way
bro-cade
broc-co-li
bro-chette
bro-chure
broil-er
bro-ken
bro-ker
bro-ker-age
bro-mine
bron-chia
bron-chi-al
bron-chi-ole
bron-chi-tis
bron-co
bron-co-bus-ter
brood-er
brood-ing-ly
broody
broth-el
broth-er
broth-er-hood
broth-er-ly
brow-beat
brown-stone
brows-er
bruis-er

bru-nette
bru-tal
bru-tal-i-ty
bru-tal-ize
brut-ish
bub-ble
bub-bler
bu-bon-ic
buc-ca-neer
buck-et
buck-et-ful
buck-le
buck-ler
buck-ling
buck-shot
buck-skin
buck-wheat
bu-col-ic
Bu-da-pest
Bud-dha
Bud-dhism
buddy
budg-et
budg-et-ary
buf-fa-lo
buff-er
buf-fet
buff-ing
buf-foon
buf-foon-ery
buggy
bugle
build-er
build-ing
Bul-gar-ia
Bul-gar-ian
bulg-i-ness
bulk-age
bulk-head
bulky
bull-dog
bull-doze
bull-doz-er
bullet
bul-le-tin

bul-let-proof
bull-fight
bull-head-ed
bul-lies
bul-lion
bull-ish
bull-mas-tiff
bul-lock
bully
bul-ly-ing
bul-rush
bul-work
bum-ble
bum-ble-bee
bump-er
bump-i-ness
bun-dle
bun-dler
bun-ga-low
bun-gle
bun-gler
bun-ion
bun-ker
bunk-house
bunk-mate
bunny
bunt-ing (v.)
bun-ting (n.)
buoy-an-cy
buoy-ant
bur-den
bur-dock
bu-reau
bu-reauc-ra-cy
bu-reau-crat
bu-reau-crat-ic
bur-geon
bur-gher
bur-glar
bur-glar-ize
bur-glar-proof
bur-gla-ry
bur-gle
bur-gun-dy

bur-i-al
bur-ied
bur-lap
bur-lesque
Burma
burn-er
burn-ing
bur-nish
burro
bur-row
bur-sar
bur-si-tis
bur-y-ing
buses
bush-el
bush-whack
bushy
bus-i-ly
busi-ness
busi-ness-like
busi-ness-man
busi-ness-wom-an
bus-ing
bust-er
bus-tle
bus-tling
busy
bu-tane
butch-er
butch-ery
but-ler
but-ter
but-ter-fat
but-ter-fly
but-ter-milk
but-ter-scotch
but-tery
but-tock
but-ton
but-tress
buxom
buyer
buz-zard
buzz-er
by-gone

by-law
by-path
by-prod-uct
by-stand-er

C

cab-a-ret
cab-bage
cab-in
cab-i-net
cab-i-net-mak-er
cable
ca-ble-gram
ca-boose
ca-chet
cack-le
cack-ling
ca-coph-o-nous
ca-coph-o-ny
cac-tus
ca-dav-er
ca-dav-er-ous
cad-die
ca-dence
ca-den-za
cadet
cad-mi-um
Cae-sar
Cae-sar-e-an
cafe
caf-e-te-ria
caf-feine
cagey
Cairo
ca-jole
ca-jol-ery
cal-a-mine
ca-lam-i-tous
ca-lam-i-ty
cal-ci-fi-ca-tion
cal-ci-fy
cal-ci-um
cal-cu-la-ble
cal-cu-late
cal-cu-lat-ed
cal-cu-lat-ing

cal-cu-la-tion
cal-cu-la-tor
cal-cu-lus
cal-dron
cal-en-dar
ca-len-dri-cal
calf-skin
Cal-ga-ry
cal-i-ber
cal-i-brate
cal-i-bra-tion
cal-i-bra-tor
cal-i-co
Cal-i-for-nia
cal-i-for-ni-um
ca-liph
cal-is-then-ics
call-er
cal-li-graph-ic
cal-lig-ra-phy
call-ing
cal-lous
calm-ing
calm-ly
ca-lor-ic
cal-o-rie
ca-lum-ni-ate
ca-lum-ni-ous
cal-um-ny
Cal-va-ry
Cal-vin-ism
ca-lyp-so
ca-ma-ra-de-rie
cam-bi-um
Cam-bo-dia
Cam-bo-di-an
cam-bric
Cam-bridge
camel
cam-el-eer
Cam-em-bert
cameo
cam-era
cam-er-al
cam-i-sole

cam-ou-flage
cam-paign
camp-er
camp-fire
camp-ground
cam-phor
camp-site
cam-pus
Ca-naan
Can-a-da
Ca-na-di-an
ca-nal
ca-nal-i-za-tion
ca-na-pe
ca-nard
ca-nary
ca-nas-ta
can-cel
can-celed
can-cel-ing
can-cel-la-tion
can-cer
can-cer-ous
can-de-la-brum
can-did
can-di-date
can-died
can-dle
can-dle-light
can-dle-stick
can-dor
can-dy
ca-nine
can-is-ter
can-ker
can-ker-ous
can-nery
can-ni-bal
can-ni-bal-ize
can-ning
can-non
can-non-ball
can-non-ry
can-not
canny

canoe
ca-noe-ist
canon
ca-non-i-cal
can-on-i-za-tion
can-on-ize
can-o-py
can-ta-loupe
can-tan-ker-ous
can-ta-ta
can-teen
can-ter
can-ti-cle
can-ti-na
Can-ton-ese
can-vas
can-vass
can-vass-er
can-yon
ca-pa-bil-i-ty
ca-pa-ble
ca-pac-i-tance
ca-pac-i-tate
ca-pac-i-tor
ca-pac-i-ty
caper
cap-il-lary
cap-i-tal
cap-i-tal-ism
cap-i-tal-ist
cap-i-tal-is-tic
cap-i-tal-i-za-tion
cap-i-tal-ize
ca-pit-u-la-tion
ca-pit-u-la-tor
capon
ca-price
ca-pri-cious
cap-size
cap-su-lar
cap-su-late
cap-sule
cap-tain
cap-tion
cap-ti-vate

cap-ti-va-tor
cap-tive
cap-tiv-i-ty
cap-tor
cap-ture
cap-ti-va-tor
ca-rafe
car-a-mel
carat
car-a-van
car-a-way
car-bine
car-bo-hy-drate
car-bol-ic
car-bon
car-bon-i-za-tion
car-bon-ize
car-box-yl
car-bu-re-tor
car-cass
car-cin-o-gen
car-cin-o-gen-ic
car-di-ac
Car-diff
car-di-gan
car-di-nal
card-ing
car-di-o-gram
car-di-o-graph
car-di-og-ra-phy
car-di-o-res-pir-a-
   to-ry
car-di-o-vas-cu-lar
ca-reen
ca-reer
care-free
care-ful
care-ful-ly
care-less
ca-ress
ca-ress-ing
care-tak-er
cargo
Car-ib-be-an
car-i-bou

car-i-ca-ture
car-i-ca-tur-ist
car-load
car-mine
car-nage
car-nal
car-nal-i-ty
car-na-tion
car-nau-ba
car-ne-lian
car-ni-val
car-ni-vore
car-niv-o-rous
carob
carol
car-oled
car-ol-er
Car-o-li-na
ca-rous-al
ca-rouse
car-ou-sel
car-pen-ter
car-pen-try
car-pet
car-pet-bag-ger
carp-ing
car-port
car-rel
car-riage
car-ri-er
car-ri-on
car-rot
carry
car-tel
Car-te-sian
Car-thage
car-ti-lage
car-tog-ra-phy
car-ton
car-toon
car-toon-ist
car-tridge
cart-wheel
carv-er
carv-ing

Ca-sa-blan-ca
cas-cade
case-ment
case-work
cash-ew
cash-ier
cash-mere
cas-ing
ca-si-no
cas-ket
cas-se-role
cas-sette
cas-sock
cas-ta-net
cast-a-way
cast-er
cas-ti-gate
cas-ti-ga-tor
cast-ing
cast-i-ron
cas-tle
cas-u-al
cas-u-al-ty
cas-u-ist
cas-u-ist-ry
cat-a-bol-ic
ca-tab-o-lism
ca-tab-o-lize
cat-a-clys-mic
cat-a-lep-sy
cat-a-log
cat-a-log-er
cat-a-log-ing
ca-tal-y-sis
cat-a-lyst
cat-a-lyze
cat-a-pult
cat-a-ract
ca-tas-tro-phe
cat-a-stroph-ic
catch-er
cat-e-che-sis
cat-e-chet-i-cal
cat-e-chism
cat-e-chist

cat-e-gor-i-cal
cat-e-go-rize
cat-e-go-ry
cater
ca-ter-er
cat-er-pil-lar
ca-thar-sis
ca-thar-tic
ca-the-dral
ca-thex-is
cath-ode
Cath-o-lic
Ca-thol-i-cism
cat-i-on
cat-i-on-ic
cat-sup
cat-tle
Cau-ca-sian
cau-cus
cau-dal
cau-date
cau-li-flow-er
caus-al
cau-sal-i-ty
cau-sa-tion
caus-a-tive
cause ce-le-bre
caus-tic
cau-ter-i-za-tion
cau-ter-ize
cau-tion
cau-tious
cav-al-cade
cav-a-lier
cav-al-ry
ca-ve-at
cav-ern
cav-ern-ous
cav-i-ar
cav-i-ty
ca-vort
cay-enne
cease-less
cedar
ceil-ing

cel-e-brant
cel-e-brate
cel-e-brat-ed
ce-leb-ri-ty
cel-ery
ce-les-tial
cel-i-ba-cy
cel-lar
cello
cel-lo-phane
cel-lu-lar
cel-lu-lose
Cel-si-us
Celt-ic
ce-ment
ce-ment-er
cem-e-tery
Ce-no-zo-ic
cen-sor
cen-so-ri-ous
cen-sor-ship
cen-sur-able
cen-sure
cen-sus
cen-taur
cen-ta-vo
cen-te-nar-i-an
cen-te-nary
cen-ten-ni-al
cen-ter
cen-ter-piece
cen-tes-i-mal
cen-tes-i-mo
cen-ti-grade
cen-time
cen-ti-me-ter
cen-ti-pede
cen-tral
cen-tral-i-ty
cen-tral-ize
cen-tral-ly
cen-trif-u-gal
cen-tri-fuge
cen-trip-e-tal
cen-tu-ri-al

cen-tu-ry
ce-phal-ic
ce-ram-ic
ce-ram-ist
ce-re-al
cer-e-bel-lum
ce-re-bral
cer-e-brum
cer-e-mo-ni-al
cer-e-mo-ni-ous
cer-e-mo-ny
ce-ri-um
cer-tain
cer-tain-ly
cer-tain-ty
cer-tif-i-cate
cer-ti-fi-ca-tion
cer-ti-fied
cer-ti-fy
cer-ti-tude
cer-vi-cal
cer-vix
Ce-sar-e-an
ce-si-um
ces-sa-tion
ces-sion
Cey-lon
Cha-blis
chaf-er
chaff-er (one who
    chaffs or
    banters)
chaf-fer (trade
    term - buying
    & selling)
cha-grin
chair-man
chair-man-ship
chair-per-son
chair-wom-an
chaise longue
chal-dron
cha-let
chal-ice
chalk-i-ness

chalky
chal-lah
chal-lenge
cham-ber
cham-ber-lain
cham-bray
cha-me-le-on
cham-ois
cham-pagne
cham-pi-gnon
cham-pi-on
cham-pi-on-ship
chan-cel
chan-cel-lery
chan-cel-lor
chancy
chan-de-lier
chan-dler
chan-dlery
change-able
chan-nel
chan-neled
chan-son
chan-teur
chan-ti-cleer
Cha-nu-kah
chaos
cha-ot-ic
chap-ar-ral
cha-peau
chap-el
chap-er-on
chap-lain
chap-ter
char-ac-ter
char-ac-ter-is-tic
char-ac-ter-i-za-
    tion
char-ac-ter-ize
cha-rades
char-coal
charge-able
char-ge d'af-faires
charg-er
char-i-ly

char-i-ness
char-i-ot
char-i-ot-eer
cha-ris-ma
char-is-mat-ic
char-i-ta-ble
char-i-ty
char-la-tan
Char-le-magne
charm-er
char-nel
char-ter
char-treuse
chas-er
chas-sis
chas-ten
chas-tise
chas-tise-ment
chas-tis-er
chas-ti-ty
cha-teau
cha-teau-bri-and
chat-ter
chat-ty
chauf-feur
chau-vin-ism
chau-vin-is-tic
cheap-en
check-book
check-ered
check-ers
check-mate
check-up
Ched-dar
cheeky
cheer-ful
cheery
cheese-burg-er
cheese-cake
cheese-cloth
chee-tah
chem-i-cal
che-mise
chem-ist
chem-is-try

chem-o-ther-a-py
che-mot-ro-pism
cher-ish
cher-ry
cher-ub
cher-vil
chess-board
chest-nut
chev-a-lier
chev-ron
Chey-enne
Chi-an-ti
Chi-ca-go
chi-cane
chi-ca-nery
chick-en
chic-o-ry
chid-ing
chid-ing-ly
chief-ly
chief-tain
chif-fon
chi-gnon
child-bear-ing
child-birth
child-hood
child-ish
chil-dren
Chile
chili
chilly
chi-me-ra
chi-mer-i-cal
chim-ney
chim-pan-zee
China
chin-chil-la
Chi-nese
chip-munk
chip-per
chi-rog-ra-pher
chi-rog-ra-phy
chi-rop-o-dy
chi-ro-prac-tic
chi-ro-prac-tor

chis-el
chis-eled
chis-el-ing
chiv-al-rous
chiv-al-ry
chlo-ride
chlo-ri-na-tion
chlo-rine
chlo-ro-form
chlo-ro-phyll
chlo-ro-plast
choc-o-late
choic-est
chok-er
chol-era
cho-les-ter-ol
cho-lic
choos-i-ness
choosy
chop-per
chop-py
cho-ral
cho-rale
cho-re-o-graph
cho-re-og-ra-pher
cho-re-og-ra-phy
cho-rog-ra-pher
cho-ro-graph-ic
cho-rog-ra-phy
chor-tle
cho-rus
cho-sen
chow-der
Christ-li-ness
Christ-ly
chris-ten
Chris-ten-dom
chris-ten-ing
Chris-tian
Chris-ti-an-i-ty
Christ-like
Christ-mas
chro-mate
chro-mat-ic
chro-ma-tic-i-ty

chro-mat-ics
chro-ma-tid
chro-ma-tin
chro-mi-um
chro-mo-plast
chro-mo-som-al
chro-mo-some
chron-ic
chron-i-cle
chron-i-cler
chron-o-graph
chro-nol-o-ger
chron-o-log-i-cal
chron-o-log-i-
    cal-ly
chro-nol-o-gy
chrys-an-the-mum
chub-by
chuck-le
chuck-ling
chum-my
chunky
church-go-er
church-war-den
church-yard
churl-ish
churn-ing
chut-ney
chutz-pah
ci-bo-ri-um
ci-ca-da
cider
cigar
cig-a-rette
cil-ia
cil-i-ary
cil-i-um
Cin-cin-nati
cinc-ture
cin-der
Cin-der-el-la
cin-e-ma
cin-e-mat-o-graph
cin-e-ma-tog-
    ra-pher

cin-e-ma-tog-ra-
    phy
cin-na-mon
cin-que-cen-to
ci-pher
circa
cir-ca-di-an
cir-cle
cir-cling
cir-cuit
cir-cuit-al
cir-cu-i-tous
cir-cuit-ry
cir-cu-lar
cir-cu-late
cir-cu-la-tion
cir-cu-la-to-ry
cir-cum-cise
cir-cum-ci-sion
cir-cum-fer-ence
cir-cum-fer-en-tial
cir-cum-lo-cu-tion
cir-cum-scrib-able
cir-cum-scribe
cir-cum-scrip-tion
cir-cum-spect
cir-cum-stance
cir-cum-stan-tial
cir-cum-stan-ti-al-
    i-ty
cir-cum-stan-ti-ate
cir-cum-vent
cir-cus
cir-rho-sis
cir-rus
cis-tern
cit-a-del
ci-ta-tion
ci-ta-to-ry
cit-i-fied
cit-i-fy
cit-i-zen
cit-i-zen-ry
cit-i-zen-ship
cit-ric

cit-ron
cit-ron-el-la
cit-rus
city
civic
civ-i-cism
civil
ci-vil-ian
ci-vil-i-ty
civ-i-li-za-tion
civ-i-lize
claim-ant
clair-voy-ance
clair-voy-ant
clam-bake
clam-my
clam-or
clam-or-ous
clan-des-tine
clang-or
clan-nish
clans-man
clans-wom-an
clar-i-fi-ca-tion
clar-i-fy
clar-i-net
clar-i-ty
clas-sic
clas-si-cal
clas-si-cism
clas-si-cist
clas-si-fi-able
clas-si-fi-ca-tion
clas-si-fy
class-mate
class-room
clat-ter
claus-tro-pho-bia
claus-tro-pho-bic
clav-i-chord
clav-i-cle
clean-er
cleans-er
cleans-ing
clear-ance

clear-head-ed
clear-ing
cleav-age
clem-en-cy
clem-ent
cler-gy
cler-gy-man
cler-gy-wom-an
cler-ic
cler-i-cal
Cleve-land
clev-er
cli-che
click-er
cli-ent
cli-en-tele
cli-mac-tic
cli-mate
cli-mat-ic
cli-ma-to-log-i-cal
cli-ma-tol-o-gy
cli-max
climb-er
clin-ic
clin-i-cal
cli-ni-cian
Clio
clip-board
clip-per
clip-ping
cliqu-ish
cloak-room
clock-wise
clock-work
clois-ter
clos-et
clo-sure
cloth-bound
cloth-ier
cloth-ing
clo-ture
cloudy
clo-ven
clo-ver
clown-ish

clum-si-ly
clum-si-ness
clum-sy
clus-ter
clut-ter
co-ad-ju-tant
co-ad-ju-tor
co-ag-u-lant
co-ag-u-late
co-ag-u-la-tion
co-ag-u-la-tor
co-a-lesce
co-a-li-tion
coars-en
coast-al
coast-er
coat-ed
coat-ing
co-ax-i-al
co-balt
co-bal-tic
cob-ble
cob-bler
cob-ble-stone
cobra
cob-web
co-caine
coc-cus
coch-lea
coch-le-ar
cock-ade
cock-er-el
cock-tail
cocky
cocoa
co-co-nut
co-coon
co-deine
cod-i-fy
co-ed-u-ca-tion
co-ef-fi-cient
co-erce
co-erc-ible
co-er-cion
co-er-cive

co-ex-ist
co-ex-is-tence
co-ex-tend
cof-fee
cof-fee-pot
cof-fer
cof-fin
co-gen-cy
co-gent
cog-i-tate
cog-i-ta-tion
cog-i-ta-tive
co-gnac
cog-nate
cog-ni-tion
cog-ni-tive
cog-ni-za-ble
cog-ni-zance
cog-ni-zant
co-hab-it
co-here
co-her-ence
co-her-ent
co-he-si-ble
co-he-sion
co-he-sive
co-hort
coif-feur
coif-fure
coin-age
co-in-cide
co-in-ci-dence
co-in-ci-den-tal
col-an-der
cole-slaw
colic
col-icky
col-i-se-um
col-lab-o-rate
col-lab-o-ra-tion
col-lab-o-ra-tor
col-lage
col-la-gen
col-lapse
col-laps-ible

col-lar
col-late
col-lat-er-al
col-la-tion
col-la-tor
col-league
col-lect
col-lect-ible
col-lect-ed
col-lec-tion
col-lec-tive
col-lec-tiv-i-ty
col-lec-tiv-ize
col-lec-tor
col-lege
col-le-gi-ate
col-lide
col-lie
co-lin-e-ar
col-li-sion
col-loid
col-loi-dal
col-lo-qui-al
col-lo-qui-al-ism
col-lo-qui-um
col-lo-quy
col-lu-sion
col-lu-sive
co-logne
Co-lum-bia
Co-lum-bi-an
colon
colo-nel
co-lo-ni-al
co-lo-ni-al-ism
co-lo-nist
col-o-ni-za-tion
col-o-nize
col-o-ny
color
Col-o-ra-do
col-or-a-tion
col-or-ing
col-or-less
co-los-sal

Col-os-se-um
co-los-sus
colt-ish
Co-lum-bia
col-um-bine
col-umn
co-lum-nar
col-um-nist
coma
co-ma-tose
com-bat
com-bat-ant
com-bat-ed
com-bat-ing
com-bat-ive
com-bat-ive-ness
comb-er
com-bi-na-tion
com-bi-na-tive
com-bine
combo
com-bust
com-bus-ti-ble
com-bus-tion
come-back
co-me-di-an
co-me-di-enne
com-e-dy
come-ly
comet
com-fort
com-fort-able
com-fort-a-bly
com-fort-er
comic
com-i-cal
com-ing
comma
com-mand
com-man-dant
com-man-deer
com-mand-er
com-mand-ing
com-mand-ment
com-man-do

com-mem-o-rate
com-mem-o-ra-
   tion
com-mem-o-ra-
   tive
com-mem-o-ra-tor
com-mence
com-mend
com-mend-able
com-men-da-tion
com-mend-a-to-ry
com-men-su-ra-
   ble
com-ment
com-men-tary
com-men-tate
com-men-ta-tor
com-merce
com-mer-cial
com-mer-cial-ize
com-mis-er-ate
com-mis-er-a-tion
com-mis-sar-i-at
com-mis-sary
com-mis-sion
com-mis-sion-er
com-mis-sur-al
com-mis-sure
com-mit
com-mit-ta-ble
com-mit-ment
com-mit-tee
com-mo-di-ous
com-mod-i-ty
com-mo-dore
com-mon
com-mon-er
com-mon-place
com-mon-wealth
com-mo-tion
com-mu-nal
com-mune
com-mu-ni-ca-
   ble
com-mu-ni-cate

com-mu-ni-ca-
   tion
com-mu-ni-ca-tive
com-mu-ni-ca-tor
com-mun-ion
com-mu-ni-que
Com-mu-nism
Com-mu-nist
com-mu-nis-tic
com-mu-ni-ty
com-mut-able
com-mu-ta-tion
com-mute
com-mut-er
com-pact
com-pan-ion
com-pan-ion-ship
com-pa-ny
com-pa-ra-ble
com-par-a-tive
com-pare
com-par-i-son
com-part-ment
com-part-men-tal-
   ize
com-pass
com-pas-sion
com-pas-sion-ate
com-pat-ible
com-pel
com-pel-ling
com-pen-di-um
com-pen-sa-ble
com-pen-sate
com-pen-sa-tion
com-pen-sat-ing
com-pen-sa-to-ry
com-pete
com-pe-tence
com-pe-tent
com-pe-ti-tion
com-pet-i-tive
com-pet-i-tor
com-pi-la-tion
com-pile

com-pil-er
com-pla-cen-cy
com-pla-cent
com-plain
com-plain-ant
com-plaint
com-plai-sance
com-plai-sant
com-ple-ment
com-ple-men-ta-
  ry
com-plete
com-ple-tion
com-plex
com-plex-ion
com-plex-i-ty
com-pli-ance
com-pli-ant
com-pli-cate
com-pli-cat-ed
com-pli-ca-tion
com-plice
com-plic-i-ty
com-pli-men-ta-ry
com-ply
com-po-nent
com-port
com-port-ment
com-pose
com-pos-er
com-pos-ite
com-po-si-tion
com-pos-i-tor
com-po-sure
com-pound
com-pound-er
com-pre-hend
com-pre-hend-ible
com-pre-hen-si-
  ble
com-pre-hen-sion
com-pre-hen-sive
com-press
com-press-ible
com-pres-sion

com-pres-sive
com-pres-sor
com-prise
com-pro-mise
comp-trol-ler
com-pul-sion
com-pul-sive
com-pul-so-ry
com-punc-tion
com-pu-ta-tion
com-pute
com-put-er
com-put-er-ize
com-rade
con-cat-e-nate
con-cat-e-na-tion
con-cave
con-ceal
con-ceal-able
con-ceal-ment
con-cede
con-ceit
con-ceit-ed
con-ceiv-a-bil-i-ty
con-ceiv-able
con-ceiv-a-bly
con-ceive
con-cen-trate
con-cen-tra-tion
con-cen-tra-tive
con-cen-tra-tor
con-cen-tric
con-cen-tri-cal
con-cen-tric-i-ty
con-cept
con-cep-tu-al
con-cep-tu-al-ize
con-cern
con-cerned
con-cern-ing
con-cert
con-cert-ed
con-cer-ti-na
con-cer-to
con-ces-sion

con-ces-sion-aire
con-ces-sion-ary
con-ci-erge
con-cil-i-ate
con-cil-i-a-to-ry
con-cise
con-clave
con-clude
con-clu-sion
con-clu-sive
con-com-i-tance
con-com-i-tant
con-cord
con-cord-ance
con-cord-ant
con-course
con-crete
con-cu-pis-cence
con-cur
con-cur-rence
con-cur-rent
con-cus-sion
con-demn
con-dem-na-tion
con-dem-na-to-ry
con-den-sa-ble
con-den-sa-tion
con-dense
con-dens-er
con-de-scend
con-de-scen-dence
con-de-scend-ing
con-de-scen-sion
con-di-ment
con-di-tion
con-di-tion-al
con-di-tioned
con-di-tion-er
con-di-tion-ing
con-dole
con-do-lence
con-do-min-i-um
con-done
con-du-cive
con-duct

con-duc-tance
con-duct-ed
con-duct-ible
con-duc-tive
con-duc-tiv-i-ty
con-duc-tor
con-fect
con-fec-tion
con-fec-tion-ery
con-fed-er-a-cy
con-fed-er-a-tion
con-fer
con-fer-ence
con-fess
con-fes-sion
con-fes-sion-al
con-fes-sor
con-fi-dant (n.)
con-fide
con-fi-dence
con-fi-dent (adj.)
con-fi-den-tial
con-fid-ing
con-fig-u-ra-tion
con-fine
con-fine-ment
con-fin-er
con-firm
con-firm-a-ble
con-fir-ma-tion
con-firm-a-to-ry
con-firmed
con-fis-cate
con-fis-ca-tion
con-fis-ca-to-ry
con-fla-gra-tion
con-flict
con-flic-tive
con-flu-ent
con-form
con-for-ma-tion
con-form-ist
con-form-i-ty
con-found
con-found-ed

con-front
Con-fu-cian-ism
Con-fu-cius
con-fuse
con-fus-ed-ly
con-fus-ing-ly
con-fu-sion
con-fut-able
con-fu-ta-tion
con-fute
con-ge-nial
con-ge-ni-al-i-ty
con-gen-i-tal
con-gest
con-ges-tion
con-glom-er-ate
con-glom-er-a-
   tion
Congo
con-grat-u-late
con-grat-u-la-tion
con-grat-u-la-to-ry
con-gre-gate
con-gre-ga-tion
con-gre-ga-tor
con-gress
con-gres-sion-al
con-gru-ence
con-gru-ent
con-gru-i-ty
con-gru-ous
conic
con-i-cal
con-i-fer
co-nif-er-ous
con-jec-tur-al
con-jec-ture
con-joint
con-ju-gal
con-ju-gate
con-ju-ga-tion
con-junct
con-junc-tion
con-junc-tive
con-junc-ture

con-jure
con-jur-er
con-nect
con-nect-able
Con-nect-i-cut
con-nec-tion
con-nec-tive
con-niv-ance
con-nive
con-nois-seur
con-no-ta-tion
con-note
con-nu-bi-al
con-quer
con-quered
con-quer-or
con-quest
con-quis-ta-dor
con-san-guin-e-
   ous
con-san-guin-i-ty
con-science
con-sci-en-tious
con-scion-able
con-scious
con-scious-ness
con-script
con-scrip-tion
con-se-crate
con-se-cra-tion
con-se-cra-tor
con-sec-u-tive
con-sen-sus
con-sent
con-se-quence
con-se-quent
con-se-quen-tial
con-se-quent-ly
con-ser-va-tion
con-ser-va-tion-ist
con-ser-va-tism
con-ser-va-tive
con-ser-va-to-ry
con-serve
con-sid-er

con-sid-er-able
con-sid-er-ate
con-sid-er-a-tion
con-sid-ered
con-sid-er-ing
con-sign
con-sign-ment
con-sign-or
con-sist
con-sis-ten-cy
con-sis-tent
con-so-la-tion
con-sole
con-sol-i-date
con-sol-i-da-tion
con-som-me
con-so-nance
con-so-nant
con-sort
con-sor-ti-um
con-spic-u-ous
con-spir-a-cy
con-spi-ra-tor
con-spire
con-sta-ble
con-stan-cy
con-stant
con-stel-la-tion
con-ster-nate
con-ster-na-tion
con-sti-pa-tion
con-stit-u-en-cy
con-stit-u-ent
con-sti-tute
con-sti-tu-tion
con-sti-tu-tion-al
con-sti-tu-tive
con-strain
con-strained
con-straint
con-strict
con-stric-tion
con-struct
con-struc-tion
con-struc-tive

con-strue
con-sul
con-sul-ar
con-sul-ate
con-sult
con-sult-ant
con-sul-ta-tion
con-sult-a-tive
con-sume
con-sum-er
con-sum-er-ism
con-sum-mate
con-sum-ma-to-ry
con-sum-ma-tion
con-sump-tion
con-tact
con-ta-gion
con-ta-gious
con-tain
con-tain-er
con-tam-i-nate
con-tam-i-na-tion
con-tam-i-na-tor
con-tem-plate
con-tem-pla-tion
con-tem-pla-tive
con-tem-po-ra-ne-
   ous
con-tem-po-rary
con-tempt
con-tempt-ible
con-temp-tu-ous
con-tend
con-tend-er
con-tent
con-tent-ed
con-ten-tion
con-ten-tious
con-tent-ment
con-test
con-test-ant
con-text
con-tex-tu-al
con-ti-gu-i-ty
con-tig-u-ous

con-ti-nence
con-ti-nent
con-ti-nen-tal
con-tin-gen-cy
con-tin-gent
con-tin-u-al
con-tin-u-a-tion
con-tin-ue
con-ti-nu-i-ty
con-tin-u-ous
con-tin-u-um
con-tort
con-tort-ed
con-tour
con-tra-band
con-tract
con-tract-ible
con-trac-tion
con-trac-tor
con-trac-tu-al
con-tra-dict
con-tra-dic-tion
con-tra-dic-to-ry
con-tra-ry
con-trast
con-trib-ute
con-trib-ut-ing
con-tri-bu-tion
con-trib-u-tor
con-trib-u-to-ry
con-triv-ance
con-trive
con-trol
con-trol-la-ble
con-trol-ler
con-tro-ver-sial
con-tro-ver-sy
con-tu-sion
co-nun-drum
con-va-lesce
con-va-les-cence
con-vene
con-ven-ience
con-ven-ien-cy
con-ven-ient

con-vent
con-ven-tion
con-ven-tion-al
con-ven-tion-al-
    i-ty
con-verge
con-ver-gence
con-ver-gent
con-verg-ing
con-ver-sa-tion
con-ver-sa-tion-al
con-ver-sa-tion-al-
    ist
con-verse
con-ver-sion
con-vert
con-vert-er
con-vert-ible
con-vex
con-vey
con-vey-ance
con-vey-er
con-vict
con-vic-tion
con-vince
con-vin-ci-ble
con-vinc-ing
con-viv-i-al
con-vo-ca-tion
con-vo-lute
con-vo-lut-ed
con-vul-sion
con-vul-sive
cook-ie
cool-ant
cool-er
co-op-er-ate
co-op-er-a-tion
co-op-er-a-tive
co-or-di-nate
co-or-di-na-tion
co-or-di-na-tor
Co-pen-ha-gen
cop-i-er
cop-ies

co-pi-ous
cop-per
copy
cop-y-right
cop-y-writ-er
co-quet-ry
co-quette
co-quet-tish
coral
cord-age
cor-date
cord-ed
cor-dial
cor-dial-i-ty
cor-do-van
cor-du-roy
Cor-inth
Co-rin-thi-an
cor-nea
cor-ne-al
cor-ner
cor-nered
cor-ner-stone
cor-net
cor-net-ist
cor-nice
corn-stalk
corn-starch
cor-nu-co-pia
cor-ol-lary
co-ro-na
cor-o-nal
cor-o-nary
cor-o-na-tion
cor-o-ner
cor-o-net
cor-po-ral
cor-po-ra-tion
cor-po-ra-tive
cor-po-re-al
cor-pu-lence
cor-pu-lent
cor-pus-cle
cor-ral
cor-rect

cor-rect-able
cor-rec-tion
cor-rec-tive
cor-rec-tor
cor-re-late
cor-re-la-tion
cor-rel-a-tive
cor-re-spond
cor-re-spon-dence
cor-re-spon-dent
cor-re-spond-ing
cor-ri-dor
cor-ri-gi-ble
cor-rob-o-rate
cor-rob-o-ra-tive
cor-rode
cor-ro-si-ble
cor-ro-sion
cor-ro-sive
cor-rupt
cor-rupt-ible
cor-rup-tion
cor-rup-tive
cor-sage
cor-tex
cor-ti-cal
cor-ti-sone
co-sign
co-sine
cos-met-ic
cos-me-ti-cian
cos-me-tol-o-gy
cos-mic
cos-mol-o-gy
cos-mo-naut
cos-mo-pol-i-tan
cos-mop-o-lite
cos-mos
co-star
Cos-ta Ri-ca
cost-ly
cos-tume
cos-tum-er
co-til-lion
cot-tage

cot-tag-er
cot-ton
cot-tony
cou-gar
cou-lomb
coun-cil
coun-cil-or
coun-sel
coun-seled
coun-sel-or
coun-te-nance
count-er (to oppose)
coun-ter (other meanings)
coun-ter-act
coun-ter-bal-ance
coun-ter-clock-wise
coun-ter-feit
coun-ter-part
coun-ter-pro-duc-tive
coun-ter-sign
count-ess
coun-try
coun-ty
cou-ple
cou-pler
cou-plet
cou-pling
cou-pon
cour-age
cou-ra-geous
cou-ri-er
cour-te-ous
cour-te-sy
cour-tier
court-mar-tial
court-room
court-yard
cous-in
cou-ture
cou-tu-ri-er
cov-e-nant

cov-e-nant-er
cov-e-nan-tor (law)
cover
cov-er-age
cov-ert
cov-ert-ly
covet
cov-et-ous
cow-ard
cow-ard-ice
cow-ard-ly
cow-boy
cower
co-wor-ker
coy-ote
co-zi-ness
cozy
crack-er
crack-ing
crack-le
crack-ling
cra-dle
cra-dling
crafty
crag-gy
cra-ni-al
cra-ni-ol-o-gy
cra-ni-um
cranky
cran-ny
cra-ter
cra-vat
crav-ing
crawl-er
cray-on
crazy
cream-er
cream-ery
creamy
cre-ate
cre-a-tion
cre-a-tive
cre-a-tiv-i-ty
cre-a-tor

crea-ture
cre-dence
cre-den-tial
cred-i-bil-i-ty
cred-ible
cred-it
cred-it-able
cred-i-tor
credo
cre-du-li-ty
cred-u-lous
creep-er
cre-mate
cre-ma-to-ry
Cre-ole
cre-scen-do
cres-cent
crest-fal-len
cre-tin
cre-tin-ism
cre-vasse
crev-ice
crib-bage
crick-et
crick-et-er
crier
Cri-me-an
crim-i-nal
crim-i-nal-i-ty
crim-son
crin-kle
crip-ple
crip-pling
cri-sis
crisp-er
cri-te-ria
cri-te-ri-on
crit-ic
crit-i-cal
crit-i-cism
crit-i-cize
cri-tique
cro-chet
cro-cheted
cro-chet-ing

croc-o-dile
cro-cus
crois-sant
crony
crook-ed
cro-quet
cross-ing
cross-ref-er-ence
crou-ton
cru-cial
cru-ci-ble
cru-ci-fix
cru-ci-fy
cru-di-ty
cruel
cru-el-ty
cruis-er
crul-ler
crum-ble
crum-bling
crum-ple
cru-sade
cru-sad-er
crus-ta-cean
crus-ta-ceous
crusty
cry-ing
cryp-tic
cryp-ti-cal
cryp-tog-ra-pher
cryp-to-gra-phy
crys-tal
crys-tal-line
crys-tal-lize
crys-tal-li-za-tion
crys-tal-liz-er
cubic
cu-bi-cal
cu-bi-cle (com-partment)
cub-ism
cub-ist
cuck-oo
cu-cum-ber
cud-dle

cudg-el
cudg-eled
cui-sine
cul-i-nary
cull-ing
cul-mi-nate
cul-mi-na-tion
cu-lotte
cul-pa-ble
cul-prit
cult-ism
cult-ist
cul-ti-vate
cul-ti-va-tion
cul-ti-va-tor
cul-tur-al
cul-ture
cum-ber
cum-ber-some
cu-mu-late
cu-mu-la-tion
cu-mu-la-tive
cu-mu-lus
cu-ne-i-form
cun-ning
cup-board
cup-cake
cup-ful
cu-pid-i-ty
cu-po-la
cur-able
cu-rate
cu-ra-tive
cu-ra-tor
cur-dle
cur-few
cu-ri-os-i-ty
cu-ri-ous
curl-er
curl-i-cue
curl-i-ness
curl-ing
curly
cur-rant (fruit)
cur-ren-cy

cur-rent
cur-ric-u-lum
curry
curs-ed
cur-so-ry
cur-tail
cur-tain
curt-sy
cur-va-ceous
cur-va-ture
cur-vi-lin-e-ar
cush-ion
cush-ioned
cus-pid
cus-tard
cus-to-di-an
cus-to-dy
cus-tom
cus-tom-ar-i-ly
cus-tom-ary
cus-tom-er
cus-tom-ize
cu-ta-ne-ous
cu-ti-cle
cut-lass
cut-lery
cut-let
cut-ter
cut-ting
cy-an-a-mide
cy-a-nide
cy-ber-net-ics
cyc-la-mate
cycle
cy-clic
cy-cli-cal
cy-cling
cy-clist
cy-clone
cyl-in-der
cy-lin-dri-cal
cym-bal
cynic
cyn-i-cal
cyn-i-cism

cy-press
Cyp-ri-an
Cyp-ri-ot (native
    of Cyprus)
Cy-prus
cys-tec-to-ny
cys-tic
cy-tol-o-gy
cy-to-plasm
czar-ism
Czech-o-slo-vak
Czech-o-slo-va-kia

D

dab-ble
dachs-hund
Da-cron
daf-fo-dil
dag-ger
dahl-ia
daily
dain-ti-ly
dain-ti-ness
dain-ty
Dai-qui-ri
dairy
daisy
Da-ko-ta
Dal-las
dal-li-ance
dally
Dal-ma-tian
dam-age
Da-mas-cus
damp-en
damp-er
danc-ing
dan-de-li-on
dan-druff
dan-ger
dan-ger-ous
dan-gle
dan-gling
Dan-ish
dap-per
dap-ple

dar-ing
dark-en
dark-ness
dar-ling
dash-ing
data
dated
date-line
datum
daub-er
daugh-ter
daunt-less
dau-phin
dav-en-port
daw-dle
daw-dler
day-break
day-dream
day-light
daz-zle
daz-zling
dea-con
dea-con-ess
dea-con-ry
de-ac-ti-vate
dead-en
dead-en-ing
dead-lock
dead-ly
deaf-en
deaf-en-ing
deal-er
deal-ing
dear-ly
death-ly
death-trap
de-bark
de-bar-ka-tion
de-base
de-bat-able
de-bate
de-bauch
deb-au-chee
de-bauch-ery
de-bil-i-tate

de-bil-i-tat-ed
de-bil-i-ty
debit
deb-o-nair
de-brief
de-brief-ing
de-bris
debt-or
debut
deb-u-tante
dec-ade
dec-a-dence
dec-a-dent
dec-a-gon
decal
de-cal-ci-fy
Dec-a-logue
dec-ane
dec-a-me-ter
de-cant
de-cant-er
de-cap-i-tate
de-cap-i-ta-tion
de-cap-i-ta-tor
de-cath-lon
decay
de-cease
de-ceased
de-ceit
de-ceit-ful
de-ceive
de-ceiv-er
de-cel-er-ate
de-cel-er-a-tion
de-cel-er-a-tor
De-cem-ber
de-cen-cy
de-cent
de-cen-tral-ize
de-cep-tion
de-cep-tive
dec-i-bel
de-cide
de-cid-ed
de-cid-u-ous

dec-i-mal
dec-i-mate
dec-i-ma-tion
dec-i-me-ter
de-ci-pher
de-ci-sion
de-ci-sive
de-claim
dec-la-ma-tion
de-clam-a-to-ry
de-clar-able
dec-la-ra-tion
de-clar-a-tive
de-clar-a-to-ry
de-clare
de-clas-si-fy
dec-li-na-tion
de-clin-a-to-ry
de-cline
de-code
de-cod-er
de-com-pose
de-com-po-si-tion
de-com-press
de-com-pres-sion
de-con-trol
decor
dec-o-rate
dec-o-ra-tion
dec-o-ra-tive
dec-o-ra-tor
dec-o-rous
de-co-rum
decoy
de-crease
de-cree
dec-re-ment
de-crep-it
de-crep-i-tude
de-cre-scen-do
de-cre-tal
dec-re-to-ry
de-crim-i-nal-ize
decry
ded-i-cate

ded-i-ca-tion
de-duce
de-duc-ible
de-duct
de-duct-ible
de-duc-tion
de-duc-tive
deep-en
de-es-ca-late
de-face
def-a-ma-tion
de-fam-a-to-ry
de-fame
de-fault
de-fea-si-ble
de-feat
de-feat-ism
de-fect
de-fec-tive
de-fec-tor
de-fend
de-fen-dant
de-fend-er
de-fense
de-fen-si-ble
de-fen-sive
def-er-ence
def-er-ent
def-er-en-tial
de-fer-ment
de-fer-ra-ble
de-ferred
de-fi-ance
de-fi-ant
de-fi-cien-cy
de-fi-cient
def-i-cit
de-file
de-fin-able
de-fine
def-i-nite
def-i-ni-tion
de-fin-i-tive
de-flate
de-fla-tion

de-flect
de-flec-tion
de-flec-tive
de-flec-tor
de-form
de-form-able
de-for-ma-tion
de-form-i-ty
de-fraud
de-frau-da-tion
de-fray
de-frost
de-frost-er
de-funct
defy
de-gen-er-ate
de-gen-er-a-tion
de-gen-er-a-tive
deg-ra-da-tion
de-grade
de-grad-ed
de-grad-ing
de-gree
de-hy-drate
de-hy-dra-tion
de-hy-dra-tor
de-if-ic
de-i-fi-ca-tion
deify
deism
de-is-tic
deity
de-ject
de-ject-ed
de-jec-tion
Del-a-ware
delay
de-lec-ta-ble
del-e-ga-cy
del-e-gate
del-e-ga-tion
de-lete
del-e-te-ri-ous
de-le-tion
de-lib-er-ate

de-lib-er-a-tion
de-lib-er-a-tive
del-i-ca-cy
del-i-cate
del-i-ca-tes-sen
de-li-cious
de-light
de-light-ed
de-light-ful
de-lim-it
de-lin-e-ate
de-lin-e-a-tion
de-lin-e-a-tor
de-lin-quen-cy
de-lin-quent
de-lir-i-ous
de-lir-i-um
de-liv-er
de-liv-er-ance
de-liv-er-y
delta
de-lude
del-uge
de-lu-sion
dem-a-gog-ic
dem-a-gogue
dem-a-gogu-ery
de-mand
de-mar-cate
de-mar-ca-tion
de-mean
de-mean-or
de-ment
de-ment-ed
de-men-tia
de-mer-it
dem-i-god
de-mise
dem-i-tasse
de-mo-bi-li-za-
    tion
de-mo-bil-ize
de-moc-ra-cy
dem-o-crat
dem-o-crat-ic

de-moc-ra-tize
de-mog-ra-pher
de-mo-graph-ic
de-mog-ra-phy
de-mol-ish
dem-o-li-tion
de-mon
de-mo-ni-ac
de-mon-ic
de-mon-ol-o-gy
de-mon-stra-ble
dem-on-strate
dem-on-stra-tion
de-mon-stra-tive
dem-on-stra-tor
de-mor-al-ize
de-note
demur (v.)
de-mure (adj.)
de-mys-ti-fy
de-na-ture
den-drite
den-drit-ic
de-ni-a-ble
de-ni-al
de-ni-er (one who
    denies)
de-nier (coin; silk)
den-i-grate
den-i-gra-tion
den-im
den-i-zen
Den-mark
de-nom-i-nate
de-nom-i-na-tion
de-nom-i-na-tive
de-nom-i-na-tor
de-no-ta-tion
de-no-ta-tive
de-note
de-noue-ment
de-nounce
den-si-ty
den-tal

den-tist
den-tist-ry
den-ture
de-nu-da-tion
de-nude
de-nun-ci-ate
de-nun-ci-a-tion
de-nun-ci-a-tive
de-nun-ci-a-to-ry
deny
de-o-dor-ant
de-o-dor-ize
de-o-dor-iz-er
de-part
de-part-ed
de-part-ment
de-part-men-tal
de-part-men-tal-
    ize
de-par-ture
de-pend
de-pend-able
de-pend-en-cy
de-pend-ent
de-per-son-al-ize
de-pict
de-plete
de-plor-able
de-plore
de-port
de-por-ta-tion
de-port-ment
de-pos-it
de-pos-i-tary
de-pos-it-ed
dep-o-si-tion
de-pos-i-to-ry
depot
de-prave
de-prav-i-ty
dep-re-cate
dep-re-ca-to-ry
de-pre-ci-ate
de-pre-ci-a-tion
de-pre-ci-a-to-ry

de-press
de-pres-sant
de-pressed
de-pres-sion
de-pres-sive
de-pres-sor
dep-ri-va-tion
de-prive
de-pro-gram
dep-u-ta-tion
dep-u-tize
dep-u-ty
de-rail
de-range
de-range-ment
derby
der-e-lict
der-e-lic-tion
de-ride
de-ri-sion
de-ri-sive
der-i-va-tion
de-riv-a-tive
de-rive
der-mal
der-ma-ti-tis
der-ma-tol-o-gy
der-nier
der-o-gate
de-rog-a-to-ry
der-ri-ere
der-rin-ger
der-vish
des-cant
de-scend
de-scend-ant
de-scend-er
de-scend-ible
de-scent
de-scrib-able
de-scribe
de-scrip-tion
de-scrip-tive
des-e-crate
de-seg-re-gate

de-seg-re-ga-tion
de-sen-si-tize
de-sert (n., that
  which is
  deserved; v.)
des-ert (n.; adj.,
  barren tract)
de-sert-er
de-ser-tion
de-serve
de-serv-ing
des-ic-cate
des-ic-ca-tor
de-sid-er-a-tum
de-sign
des-ig-nate
des-ig-na-tion
des-ig-na-tive
des-ig-na-tor
de-sign-ed-ly
des-ig-nee
de-sign-er
de-sign-ing
de-sir-able
de-sire
de-sist
des-o-late
des-o-la-tion
de-spair
des-per-a-do
des-per-ate
des-per-a-tion
des-pi-ca-ble
de-spis-able
de-spise
de-spis-er
de-spite
de-spoil
de-spo-li-a-tion
de-spond
de-spond-ence
de-spon-den-cy
de-spond-ent
des-pot

des-pot-i-cal
des-pot-ism
des-sert
des-ti-na-tion
des-tine
des-ti-ny
des-ti-tute
des-ti-tu-tion
de-stroy
de-stroy-er
de-struct
de-struc-ti-ble
de-struc-tion
de-struc-tive
des-ul-to-ry
de-tach
de-tach-ment
de-tail
de-tain
de-tain-er
de-tect
de-tect-able
de-tec-tion
de-tec-tive
de-tec-tor
de-tente
de-ten-tion
deter
de-ter-gent
de-te-ri-o-rate
de-te-ri-o-ra-tion
de-te-ri-o-ra-tive
de-ter-mi-na-ble
de-ter-mi-nant
de-ter-mi-nate
de-ter-mi-na-tion
de-ter-mine
de-ter-mined
de-ter-rence
de-ter-rent
de-test
de-test-able
det-o-nate
det-o-na-tion
det-o-na-tor

de-tour
de-tox-i-fy
de-tract
de-trac-tion
de-trac-tor
det-ri-ment
det-ri-men-tal
De-troit
deu-te-ri-um
Deu-ter-on-o-my
de-val-u-ate
dev-as-tate
dev-as-ta-tion
dev-as-ta-tor
de-vel-op
de-vel-op-er
de-vel-op-ment
de-vel-op-men-tal
de-vi-ant
de-vi-ate
de-vi-a-tion
de-vi-a-tor
de-vice
devil
dev-il-ish
de-vi-ous
de-vi-sa-ble
de-vise
de-void
de-vote
de-vot-ed
dev-o-tee
de-vo-tion
de-vo-tion-al
de-vour
de-vout
dex-ter-i-ty
dex-ter-ous
dex-trose
di-a-be-tes
di-a-bet-ic
di-a-bol-ic
di-a-bol-i-cal
di-a-dem
di-ag-nose

di-ag-no-sis
di-ag-nos-tic
di-ag-nos-ti-cian
di-ag-o-nal
di-a-gram
di-a-grammed
di-a-gram-mat-
  i-cal
dial
di-a-lect
di-a-lec-tic
di-a-logue
di-al-y-sis
di-am-e-ter
di-a-met-ri-cal
di-a-met-ri-cal-ly
di-a-mond
di-a-per
di-a-phragm
di-ar-rhea
diary
di-as-po-ra
di-a-spore
di-at-ro-pism
di-chot-o-mize
di-chot-o-mous
di-chot-o-my
Dic-ta-phone
dic-tate
dic-ta-tion
dic-ta-tor
dic-ta-to-ri-al
dic-ta-tor-ship
dic-tion
dic-tion-ary
di-dac-tic
die-sel
diet
di-e-tary
di-e-tet-ic
di-e-ti-tian
dif-fer
dif-fer-ence
dif-fer-ent
dif-fer-en-ti-able

dif-fer-en-tial
dif-fer-en-ti-ate
dif-fi-cult
dif-fi-cul-ty
dif-fi-dence
dif-fi-dent
dif-fract
dif-frac-tion
dif-fuse
dif-fus-er
dif-fus-ible
dif-fu-sion
dis-fu-sive
di-gest
di-gest-er
di-gest-ible
di-ges-tion
di-ges-tive
dig-ger
dig-gings
digit
dig-i-tal
dig-ni-fy
dig-ni-tary
dig-ni-ty
di-gress
di-gres-sion
di-gres-sive
di-lap-i-date
di-lap-i-dat-ed
dil-a-ta-tion
di-late
di-la-tion
di-la-tor
dil-a-to-ry
di-lem-ma
dil-i-gence
dil-i-gent
di-lute
di-lu-tion
di-men-sion
di-min-ish
di-min-u-tion
di-min-u-tive
dim-mer

dim-ple
diner
din-ghy
din-ner
di-no-saur
di-oc-e-san
di-o-cese
di-o-rama
di-o-ram-ic
di-ox-ide
diph-the-ria
diph-thong
dip-loid
di-plo-ma
di-plo-ma-cy
dip-lo-mat
dip-lo-mat-ic
dip-per
di-rect
di-rec-tion
di-rec-tion-al
di-rec-tive
di-rect-ly
di-rec-tor
di-rec-to-ry
dir-i-gi-ble
dirn-dl
dirt-i-ness
dirty
dis-a-bil-i-ty
dis-a-ble
dis-ac-cord
dis-ad-van-tage
dis-ad-van-ta-
  geous
dis-a-gree
dis-a-gree-able
dis-a-gree-ment
dis-ap-pear
dis-ap-pear-ance
dis-ap-peared
dis-ap-point
dis-ap-point-ed
dis-ap-point-ment
dis-ap-pro-val

dis-ap-prove
dis-arm
dis-ar-ma-ment
dis-arm-ing
dis-ar-ray
dis-as-ter
dis-as-trous
dis-band
dis-be-lief
dis-be-lieve
dis-burs-al
dis-burse
dis-burs-er
dis-burse-ment
dis-card
dis-cern
dis-cern-ible
dis-cern-ing
dis-cern-ment
dis-charge
dis-ci-ple
dis-ci-pli-nar-ian
dis-ci-pli-nary
dis-ci-pline
dis-ci-plin-er
dis-claim
dis-claim-er
dis-close
dis-clo-sure
dis-col-or
dis-col-or-a-tion
dis-com-fi-ture
dis-com-fort
dis-com-fort-able
dis-con-cert
dis-con-cert-ed
dis-con-nect
dis-con-nect-ed
dis-con-so-late
dis-con-tent
dis-con-tent-ed
dis-con-tin-ue
dis-con-ti-nu-i-ty
dis-con-tin-u-ous
dis-cord

dis-cor-dant
dis-co-theque
dis-count
dis-cour-age
dis-cour-age-ment
dis-course
dis-cour-te-ous
dis-cov-er
dis-cov-ery
dis-cred-it
dis-cred-it-able
dis-creet
dis-crep-an-cy
dis-crep-ant
dis-crete
dis-cre-tion
dis-cre-tion-ary
dis-crim-i-na-ble
dis-crim-i-nate
dis-crim-i-nat-ing
dis-crim-i-na-tion
dis-crim-i-na-tive
dis-crim-i-na-tor
dis-crim-i-na-to-ry
dis-cur-sive
discus
dis-cuss
dis-cuss-ant
dis-cuss-ible
dis-cus-sion
dis-dain
dis-dain-ful
dis-ease
dis-eas-es
dis-en-chant
dis-en-tan-gle
dis-fa-vor
dis-fig-ure
dis-fig-ure-ment
dis-grace
dis-grace-ful
dis-grun-tle
dis-guise
dis-gust
dis-gust-ed

dis-gust-ing
dis-ha-bille
dis-har-mony
dis-heart-en
di-shev-el
di-shev-eled
dis-hon-est
dis-hon-es-ty
dis-hon-or
dis-hon-or-able
dis-il-lu-sion
dis-in-cli-na-tion
dis-in-cline
dis-in-clined
dis-in-fect
dis-in-fec-tant
dis-in-her-it
dis-in-te-grate
dis-in-te-gra-tion
dis-in-ter-est
dis-in-ter-est-ed
dis-join
dis-joint
dis-joint-ed
dis-junct
dis-junc-tion
dis-junc-tive
dis-like
dis-lo-cate
dis-lodge
dis-mal
dis-man-tle
dis-may
dis-mem-ber
dis-miss
dis-mis-sal
dis-mount
dis-o-be-di-ence
dis-o-bey
dis-or-der
dis-or-dered
dis-or-der-ly
dis-or-gan-i-za-tion
dis-or-gan-ize
dis-o-ri-ent

dis-own
dis-par-age
dis-par-age-ment
dis-par-ag-er
dis-par-ate
dis-par-i-ty
dis-patch
dis-patch-er
dis-pel
dis-pelled
dis-pend
dis-pen-sa-ble
dis-pen-sa-ry
dis-pen-sa-tion
dis-pense
dis-pens-er
dis-per-sal
dis-perse
dis-pers-ible
dis-per-sion
dis-per-sive
dis-pir-it
dis-pir-it-ed
dis-place
dis-place-ment
dis-play
dis-please
dis-pleas-ure
dis-pos-able
dis-pos-al
dis-pose
dis-po-si-tion
dis-proof
dis-pro-por-tion
dis-pro-por-tion-al
dis-pro-por-tion-ate
dis-prove
dis-put-able
dis-pu-tant
dis-pu-ta-tion
dis-pu-ta-tious
dis-pute
dis-put-er

dis-qual-i-fi-ca-tion
dis-qual-i-fy
dis-qui-et
dis-re-gard
dis-re-pair
dis-rep-u-ta-ble
dis-re-pute
dis-rupt
dis-rupt-er
dis-rup-tive
dis-sat-is-fac-tion
dis-sat-is-fac-to-ry
dis-sat-is-fied
dis-sat-is-fy
dis-sect
dis-sect-ed
dis-sec-tion
dis-sec-tor
dis-sem-i-nate
dis-sen-sion
dis-sent
dis-sent-er
dis-ser-ta-tion
dis-ser-vice
dis-si-dence
dis-si-dent
dis-sim-i-lar
dis-sim-i-lar-i-ty
dis-sim-i-late
dis-sim-i-la-tion
dis-si-mil-i-tude
dis-si-pate
dis-si-pat-ed
dis-si-pa-tion
dis-so-ci-ate
dis-so-ci-a-tion
dis-sol-u-ble
dis-so-lute
dis-solv-able
dis-solve
dis-so-nance
dis-so-nant
dis-suade
dis-suad-er

dis-sua-sion
dis-sua-sive
dis-sym-me-try
dis-taff
dis-tance
dis-tant
dis-taste
dis-tem-per
dis-tend
dis-ten-si-ble
dis-ten-tion
dis-till
dis-til-la-tion
dis-tilled
dis-till-ery
dis-tinct
dis-tinc-tion
dis-tinc-tive
dis-tin-guish
dis-tin-guished
dis-tort
dis-tor-tion
dis-tract
dis-tract-ed
dis-tract-ible
dis-trac-tion
dis-trac-tive
dis-traught
dis-tress
dis-tress-ful
dis-tress-ing
dis-trib-ute
dis-tri-bu-tion
dis-trib-u-tive
dis-trib-u-tor
dis-trict
dis-trust
dis-turb
dis-turb-ance
dis-turb-er
dis-u-nite
dis-u-til-i-ty
ditto
di-ur-nal
divan

diver
di-verge
di-ver-gence
di-ver-gent
di-vers (several)
di-verse (unlike)
di-ver-si-fy
di-ver-sion
di-ver-si-ty
di-vert
di-ver-tisse-ment
di-vest
di-ves-ti-ture
di-vide
di-vid-ed
div-i-dend
di-vid-er
div-i-na-tion
di-vine
di-vin-i-ty
di-vis-ible
di-vi-sion
di-vi-sor
di-vorce
di-vor-cee
di-vulge
di-vul-gence
dizzy
doc-ile
doc-tor
doc-tor-al
doc-tor-ate
doc-tri-naire
doc-tri-nal
doc-trine
doc-u-ment
doc-u-ment-able
doc-u-men-ta-ry
doc-u-men-ta-tion
dodg-er
dogma
dog-mat-ic
dog-ma-tism
dog-ma tist
dog-ma-tize

dog-wood
doily
dol-drums
dole-ful
dol-lar
do-lo-rous
dol-phin
do-main
do-mes-tic
do-mes-ti-cate
do-mes-tic-i-ty
dom-i-cile
dom-i-cil-i-ary
dom-i-nance
dom-i-nant
dom-i-nate
dom-i-na-tion
dom-i-na-tor
dom-i-neer
Do-min-i-can
do-min-ion
dom-i-no
do-na-tion
don-key
donor
donut
doo-dle
door-way
Dopp-ler
dor-mant
dor-mer
dor-mi-to-ry
dor-sal
dos-age
dos-si-er
dot-ing
dou-ble
dou-bling
dou-bly
doubt-ful
doubt-less
dough-nut
dow-a-ger
dow dy
down-cast

down-fall
down-fall-en
down-right
down-stairs
down-town
down-ward
dowry
dox-o-log-i-cal
dox-ol-o-gy
doz-en
draft-ee
draft-ing
drafts-man
drafty
drag-net
drag-on
dra-goon
drain-age
drama
dra-mat-ic
dram-a-ti-za-tion
dram-a-tize
dram-a-turge
dram-a-tur-gy
drap-ery
dras-tic
draw-back
draw-er
draw-ing
dread-ful
dream-er
dreamy
drear-i-ness
dreary
dredg-er
dredg-ing
dres-sage
dress-er
dress-ing
dressy
drier
drift-age
drift-er
dril-ling
drip-ping
driv-en

driv-er
driv-ing
drom-e-dary
drop-per
drop-ping
drows-i-ness
drow-sy
drudg-ery
drum-mer
drunk-ard
drunk-en
drunk-en-ness
dryer
dual
du-al-ism
du-al-is-tic
du-bi-ous
du-bi-ta-ble
ducal
ducat
duch-ess
duchy
duck-ling
duc-tile
dudg-eon
duel
duet
duf-fel
dul-cet
dul-ci-mer
dul-lard
dul-ly
Du-luth
duly
dumb-found
dummy
dump-er
dump-ling
dumpy
dun-ga-ree
dun-geon
du-plex
du-pli-cate
du-pli-ca-tion
du-pli-ca-tive

du-pli-ca-tor
du-plic-i-ty
du-ra-bil-i-ty
du-ra-ble
du-ra-tion
du-ress
dur-ing
dust-er
dusty
du-te-ous
du-ti-ful
duty
dwarf-ish
dwell-er
dwell-ing
dwin-dle
dwin-dling
dyad
dy-ad-ic
dying
dy-nam-ic
dy-nam-i-cal
dy-na-mism
dy-na-mite
dy-na-mo
dy-nas-ty
dys-en-tery
dys-func-tion
dys-pep-sia
dys-pho-ria
dys-tro-phy

E

eager
eagle
ear-li-er
early
earn-er
ear-nest
earn-ings
ear-ring
earth-en
earth-en-ware
earth-ly
earth-quake
earth-shak-ing

easel
eas-i-ly
eas-i-ness
Eas-ter
eas-ter-ly
eas-tern
east-ern-er
easy
eaves-drop
ebony
ebul-lient
ec-cen-tric
ec-cen-tric-i-ty
Ec-cle-si-as-tes
ec-cle-si-as-tic
ec-cle-si-as-ti-cal
ech-e-lon
echo
eclair
eclat
ec-lec-tic
eclipse
eclip-tic
ec-o-log-i-cal
ecol-o-gy
ec-o-nom-ic
ec-o-nom-i-cal
ec-o-nom-ics
econ-o-mist
econ-o-mize
econ-o-my
eco-sphere
eco-sys-tem
ec-sta-sy
ec-stat-ic
ec-to-derm
Ec-ua-dor
Ec-ua-dor-an
ec-u-men-i-cal
ec-u-men-ism
ec-ze-ma
eddy
edel-weiss
Eden
edg-ing

edgy
ed-ible
edict
ed-i-fi-ca-tion
ed-i-fice
edify
edit
edi-tion
ed-i-tor
ed-i-to-ri-al
ed-i-to-ri-al-ize
ed-u-ca-ble
ed-u-cate
ed-u-ca-ted
ed-u-ca-tion
ed-u-ca-tion-al
ed-u-ca-tive
ed-u-ca-tor
eerie
ee-ri-ly
ef-face
ef-fac-ing
ef-fect
ef-fec-tive
ef-fec-tor
ef-fec-tu-al
ef-fem-i-nate
ef-fer-vesce
ef-fer-ves-cence
ef-fer-ves-cent
ef-fi-ca-cious
ef-fi-ca-cy
ef-fi-cien-cy
ef-fi-cient
ef-fi-gy
ef-flo-res-cence
ef-fort
ef-fort-less
egal-i-tar-i-an
egg-shell
ego
ego-cen-tric
ego-cen-tric-i-ty
ego-cen-trism
ego-ism

ego-ist
ego-is-ti-cal
ego-tism
ego-tist
ego-tis-ti-cal
Egypt
Egyp-tian
eight-een
eight-eenth
eight-i-eth
eighty
Ein-stein
ein-stein-i-um
Ei-sen-how-er
ei-ther
ejac-u-late
ejac-u-la-tion
ejac-u-la-to-ry
eject
ejec-tor
elab-o-rate
elab-o-ra-tion
elapse
elas-tic
elas-tic-i-ty
elate
elat-ed
ela-tion
elbow
elder
el-der-ly
el-dest
elect
elec-tion
elec-tion-eer
elec-tive
elec-tor
elec-tor-al
elec-tor-ate
elec-tric
elec-tri-cal
elec-tri-cian
elec-tri-ci-ty
elec-tri-fi-ca-tion
elec-tri-fy

elec-tro-car-di-o-
  gram
elec-tro-cute
elec-trode
elec-trol-y-sis
elec-tro-lyte
elec-tro-lyt-i-cal
elec-tro-lyze
elec-tro-mag-net
elec-tro-mag-net-
  ic
elec-tro-mag-net-
  ism
elec-tron
elec-tron-ic
elec-tron-i-cal-ly
elec-tron-ics
el-e-gance
el-e-gant
elegy
el-e-ment
el-e-men-tal
el-e-men-ta-ri-ly
el-e-men-ta-ry
el-e-phant
el-e-vate
el-e-vat-ed
el-e-va-tion
el-e-va-tor
elev-en
elev-enth
elfin
elf-ish
elic-it
el-i-gi-bil-i-ty
el-i-gi-ble
elim-i-nate
elim-i-na-tion
elim-i-na-tor
elite
elit-ism
elix-ir
el-lipse
el-lip-tic
el-lip-ti-cal

el-o-cu-tion
elon-gate
elon-ga-tion
elope
el-o-quence
el-o-quent
elu-ci-date
elu-ci-da-tion
elude
elu-sion
elu-sive
elu-so-ry
ema-ci-ate
em-a-nate
em-a-na-tion
eman-ci-pate
eman-ci-pa-tion
em-balm
em-bank-ment
em-bar-go
em-bark
em-bar-ka-tion
em-bar-rass
em-bar-rass-ment
em-bas-sy
embed
em-bed-ded
em-bel-lish
em-bel-lish-ment
ember
em-bez-zle
em-bit-ter
em-blem
em-bod-i-ment
em-body
em-bold-en
em-boss
em-boss-er
em-brace
em-brac-er
em-broi-der
em-broi-dery
em-bryo
em-bry-ol-o-gy
om-bry-on-ic
emcee

em-er-ald
emerge
emer-gence
emer-gen-cy
emer-gent
emer-i-tus
emersed
emer-sion
emery
emet-ic
em-i-grant
em-i-grate
em-i-gra-tion
emi-gre
em-i-nence
em-i-nent
em-is-sary
emis-sion
emis-sive
emit
emit-ter
Emmy
emol-lient
emote
emo-tion
emo-tion-al
emo-tion-al-i-ty
emo-tion-al-ize
emo-tion-less
em-path-ic
em-pa-thize
em-pa-thy
em-per-or
em-pha-sis
em-pha-size
em-phat-ic
em-phy-se-ma
em-pire
em-pir-i-cal
em-pir-i-cism
em-ploy
em-ploy-ee
em-ploy-er
em-ploy-ment
em-po-ri-um

em-pow-er
em-press
emp-ti-ness
empty
em-u-late
em-u-la-tion
emul-si-fi-er
emul-si-fy
emul-sion
en-able
en-a-bling
enact
en-am-el
en-am-el-ing
en-am-or
en-am-ored
en-camp
en-cap-su-late
en-case
en-chant
en-chant-ing
en-chant-ment
en-chi-la-da
en-cir-cle
en-clave
en-close
en-clo-sure
en-code
en-com-pass
en-core
en-coun-ter
en-cour-age
en-cour-age-ment
en-cour-ag-ing
en-croach
en-croach-ment
en-cum-ber
en-cum-brance
en-cyc-li-cal
en-cy-clo-pe-dia
en-cy-clo-pe-dic
en-dan-ger
en-dear
en-dear-ing
en-dear-ment

en-deav-or
en-deav-ored
en-dem-ic
end-ing
en-dive
end-less
en-do-crine
en-do-cri-nol-o-gy
en-do-derm
en-dog-e-nous
en-dors-able
en-dorse
en-dors-ee
en-dorse-ment
en-do-ther-mic
endow
en-dow-ment
en-dur-able
en-dur-ance
en-dure
en-dur-ing
enemy
en-er-get-ic
en-er-get-i-cal-ly
en-er-gize
en-er-giz-er
en-er-gy
en-er-vate
en-fold
en-force
en-force-able
en-fran-chise
en-gage
en-gaged
en-gage-ment
en-gag-ing
en-gine
en-gi-neer
en-gi-neer-ing
Eng-land
Eng-lish
en-gorge
en-grave
en-grav-er
en-grav-ing

en-gross
en-gross-ing
en-gulf
en-hance
enig-ma
enig-mat-ic
en-join
en-join-der
enjoy
en-joy-able
en-joy-ment
en-large
en-large-ment
en-light-en
en-light-en-ment
en-list
en-liv-en
en-mi-ty
ennui
enor-mi-ty
enor-mous
enough
en-rage
en-rich
en-rich-ment
en-roll
en-rolled
en-roll-ment
en-sconce
en-sem-ble
en-sign
en-slave
ensue
en-sure
en-tail
en-tan-gle
enter
en-ter-prise
en-ter-pris-ing
en-ter-tain
en-ter-tain-ing
en-ter-tain-ment
en-thrall
en-thuse
en-thu-si-asm

en-thu-si-ast
en-thu-si-as-tic
en-tice
en-tire
en-tire-ly
en-tire-ty
en-ti-tle
en-ti-ty
en-to-mo-log-i-cal
en-to-mol-o-gy
en-tou-rage
en-trails
en-trance
en-trant
en-treat
en-treaty
en-tree
en-trench
en-trench-ment
en-tre-pre-neur
en-tre-pre-neur-ial
en-tro-py
en-trust
entry
en-twine
enu-mer-ate
enu-mer-a-tion
enun-ci-ate
enun-ci-a-tion
en-vel-op (v.)
en-ve-lope (n.)
en-vel-op-ment
en-vi-able
en-vi-ous
en-vi-ron
en-vi-ron-ment
en-vi-ron-men-tal-
  ist
en-vi-rons
en-vis-age
en-vi-sion
envoy
envy
en-wrap
en-zyme

eon
ep-arch
ep-ar-chy
ephem-er-a
ephem-er-al
epic
ep-i-cure
ep-i-cu-re-an
ep-i-cu-re-an-ism
ep-i-dem-ic
ep-i-dem-i-cal
ep-i-de-mi-o-log-i-
  cal
ep-i-de-mi-ol-o-gy
ep-i-der-mis
ep-i-ge-al
ep-i-lep-sy
ep-i-lep-tic
ep-i-logue
ep-i-neph-rine
ep-i-phe-nom-e-
  nal-ism
ep-i-phe-nom-e-
  non
epis-co-pa-cy
epis-co-pal
Epis-co-pa-lian
epis-co-pal-ism
ep-i-sode
ep-i-sod-ic
epis-te-mol-o-gy
epis-tle
epis-to-lar-y
ep-i-taph
ep-i-thet
epit-o-me
epit-o-mize
epoch
ep-och-al
epoxy
ep-si-lon
eq-ua-ble
equal
equalled
equal-ly

equal-i-ty
equal-ize
equal-iz-er
equa-nim-i-ty
equate
equa-tion
equa-tor
equa-to-ri-al
eques-tri-an
equi-dis-tant
equi-lat-er-al
equi-li-brate
equil-i-bra-tion
equi-li-bra-tor
equi-lib-ri-um
equine
equi-nox
equip
equip-ment
equi-po-ten-tial
equipped
eq-ui-ta-ble
eq-ui-ta-tion
eq-ui-ty
equiv-a-lence
equiv-a-lent
equiv-o-cal
equiv-o-cate
equiv-o-ca-tion
equiv-o-ca-tor
era
erad-i-cate
erad-i-ca-tor
erase
eras-a-ble
eras-er
era-sure
er-bi-um
erect
erec-tile
erec-tion
erec-tor
ergo
Erie
er-mine

erode
ero-dent
erod-ible
erog-e-nous
ero-sion
ero-sive
erot-ic
erot-i-ca
erot-i-cism
er-rand
er-rat-ic
er-ro-ne-ous
error
er-u-dite
er-u-di-tion
erupt
erup-tion
es-ca-drille
es-ca-late
es-ca-la-tor
es-cal-lop
es-cal-loped
es-cap-able
es-ca-pade
es-cape
es-cap-ee
es-cape-ment
es-cap-ism
es-cap-ist
es-car-got
es-ca-role
es-chew
es-cort
es-crow
Es-ki-mos
esoph-a-gus
es-o-ter-ic
es-pa-drille
es-pe-cial
es-pe-cial-ly
es-pi-o-nage
es-pous-al
es-pouse
es-pous-er
es-pres-so

es-prit
es-quire
essay
es-say-ist
es-sence
es-sen-tial
es-tab-lish
es-tab-lish-ment
es-tate
es-teem
ester
es-thet-ic
es-thet-i-cism
es-ti-ma-ble
es-ti-mate
es-ti-ma-tion
es-ti-ma-tor
es-trange
es-tro-gen
es-tro-gen-ic
es-trus
es-tu-ary
et cet-era
etch-ing
eter-nal
eter-nal-ly
eter-ni-ty
eth-ane
eth-a-nol
ether
ethe-re-al
ethic
eth-i-cal
Ethi-o-pia
eth-nic
eth-ni-cal
eth-nic-i-ty
eth-no-cen-tric
eth-no-cen-trism
eth-no-log-i-cal
eth-nol-o-gy
ethos
ethyl
eti-o-log-i-cal
eti-ol-o-gy

et-i-quette
etude
et-y-mo-log-i-cal
et-y-mol-o-gy
eu-ca-lyp-tus
Eu-cha-rist
Eu-clid-e-an
eu-gen-i-cist
eu-gen-ics
eu-lo-gize
eu-lo-gy
eu-nuch
eu-phe-mism
eu-phe-mize
eu-phon-ic
eu-pho-ny
eu-pho-ria
Eu-phra-tes
Eur-a-sian
Eu-rope
Eu-ro-pe-an
eu-tha-na-sia
evac-u-ate
evac-u-a-tion
evac-u-ee
evade
eval-u-ate
ev-a-nes-cent
evan-gel-i-cal
evan-gel-ism
evan-ge-list
evan-ge-lize
evap-o-rate
eva-sion
eva-sive
even
eve-ning
event
event-ful
even-tu-al
even-tu-al-i-ty
ever
ev-er-glade
ev-er-green
ev-er-las-ting

ev-ery
ev-ery-body
ev-ery-day
ev-ery-one
ev-ery-thing
ev-ery-where
evict
evic-tion
evic-tor
ev-i-dence
ev-i-dent
ev-i-den-tial
ev-i-dent-ly
evil
evince
ev-o-ca-tion
evoc-a-tive
evoke
ev-o-lu-tion
ev-o-lu-tion-ary
ev-o-lu-tion-ism
ev-o-lu-tion-ist
evolve
ex-ac-er-bate
ex-ac-er-bat-ing
ex-ac-er-ba-tion
exact
ex-act-ing
ex-ac-ti-tude
ex-act-ly
ex-ag-ger-ate
ex-ag-ger-at-ed
ex-ag-ger-a-tion
exalt
ex-al-ta-tion
ex-alt-ed
ex-am
ex-am-i-na-tion
ex-am-ine
ex-am-in-er
ex-am-ple
ex-as-per-ate
ex-as-per-a-tion
ex-ca-vate
ex-ca-va-tion

ex-ca-va-tor
ex-ceed
ex-ceed-ing
ex-ceed-ing-ly
excel
ex-cel-lence
ex-cel-len-cy
ex-cel-lent
ex-cel-si-or
ex-cept
ex-cept-ing
ex-cep-tion
ex-cep-tion-able
ex-cep-tion-al
ex-cerpt
ex-cess
ex-ces-sive
ex-change
ex-change-able
ex-cise
ex-cit-able
ex-cit-ant
ex-ci-ta-tion
ex-ci-ta-tive
ex-cite
ex-cit-ed
ex-cite-ment
ex-cit-er
ex-cit-ing
ex-claim
ex-cla-ma-tion
ex-clam-a-to-ry
ex-clud-able
ex-clude
ex-clu-sion
ex-clu-sive
ex-com-mu-ni-
  cate
ex-com-mu-ni-ca-
  tion
ex-cre-ment
ex-crete
ex-cre-tion
ex-cre-to-ry
ex-cru-ci-ate

ex-cru-ci-at-ing
ex-cul-pate
ex-cul-pa-to-ry
ex-cur-sion
ex-cur-sive
ex-cus-able
ex-cus-a-to-ry
ex-cuse
ex-e-cute
ex-e-cut-ed
ex-e-cu-tion
ex-e-cu-tion-er
ex-ec-u-tive
ex-ec-u-tor
ex-ec-u-to-ry
ex-e-ge-sis
ex-em-plar
ex-em-pla-ry
ex-em-pli-fi-ca-
  tion
ex-em-pli-fy
ex-empt
ex-empt-ible
ex-empt-tion
ex-er-cise
ex-er-cis-er
exert
ex-er-tion
ex-ha-la-tion
ex-hale
ex-haust
ex-haust-ed
ex-haust-ible
ex-haus-tion
ex-haus-tive
ex-hib-it
ex-hi-bi-tion
ex-hi-bi-tion-er
ex-hib-i-tive
ex-hib-i-tor
ex-hib-i-to-ry
ex-hil-a-rate
ex-hil-a-rat-ing
ex-hil-a-ra-tion
ex-hort

ex-hor-ta-tion
ex-hor-ta-tive
ex-hu-ma-tion
ex-hume
ex-i-gen-cy
ex-i-gent
exile
exist
ex-ist-ence
ex-is-tent
ex-is-ten-tial
ex-is-ten-tial-ism
exit
ex-o-dus
ex-og-e-nous
ex-on-er-ate
ex-or-able
ex-or-bi-tance
ex-or-bi-tant
ex-or-cise
ex-or-cism
ex-o-ter-ic
ex-ot-ic
ex-pand
ex-pand-able
ex-panse
ex-pan-si-ble
ex-pan-sion
ex-pan-sive
ex-pa-tri-ate
ex-pect
ex-pect-an-cy
ex-pect-ant
ex-pec-ta-tion
ex-pect-a-tive
ex-pec-to-rate
ex-pe-di-en-cy
ex-pe-di-ent
ex-pe-dite
ex-pe-dit-er
ex-pe-ti-tion
ex-pe-di-tion-ary
ex-pe-di-tious
expel
ex-pel-ling

ex-pend
ex-pend-able
ex-pen-di-ture
ex-pense
ex-pen-sive
ex-pe-ri-ence
ex-pe-ri-en-tial
ex-per-i-ment
ex-per-i-men-tal
ex-per-i-men-ta-
    tion
ex-per-i-ment-er
ex-pert
ex-per-tise
ex-pi-ate
ex-pi-a-tion
ex-pi-ra-tion
ex-pir-a-to-ry
ex-pire
ex-plain
ex-pla-na-tion
ex-plan-a-to-ry
ex-ple-tive
ex-pli-ca-ble
ex-pli-cate
ex-pli-ca-tion
ex-pli-ca-tive
ex-plic-it
ex-plode
ex-ploit
ex-ploi-ta-tion
ex-ploit-a-tive
ex-ploit-er
ex-plo-ra-tion
ex-plor-a-to-ry
ex-plore
ex-plor-er
ex-plo-si-ble
ex-plo-sion
ex-plo-sive
ex-po-nent
ex-po-nen-tial
ex-port
ex-port-able
ex-por-ta-tion

ex-pose (v.)
ex-po-sé (n.)
ex-po-si-tion
ex-pos-i-to-ry
ex-po-sure
ex-press
ex-press-age
ex-press-ible
ex-pres-sion
ex-pres-sion-ism
ex-pres-sion-less
ex-pres-sive
ex-press-ly
ex-pul-sion
ex-pur-gate
ex-pur-ga-to-ry
ex-quis-ite
ex-scind
ex-tant
ex-tem-po-ra-ne-
    ous
ex-tem-po-rary
ex-tem-po-rize
ex-tend
ex-tend-ed
ex-tend-er
ex-tend-ible
ex-ten-si-bil-i-ty
ex-ten-si-ble
ex-ten-sion
ex-ten-sive
ex-tent
ex-ten-u-ate
ex-ten-u-at-ing
ex-ten-u-a-tion
ex-ten-u-a-tor
ex-te-ri-or
ex-te-ri-or-ize
ex-ter-mi-nate
ex-ter-mi-na-tion
ex-ter-mi-na-tor
ex-ter-nal
ex-ter-nal-i-ty
ex-ter-nal-ize
ex-tinct

ex-tinc-tion
ex-tinc-tive
ex-tin-guish
ex-tin-guish-er
extol
ex-tort
ex-tor-tion
ex-tor-tion-ist
extra
ex-tract
ex-tract-able
ex-trac-tion
ex-trac-tive
ex-trac-tor
ex-tra-cur-ric-
    u-lar
ex-tra-dit-able
ex-tra-dite
ex-tra-di-tion
ex-tra-mu-ral
ex-tra-ne-ous
ex-traor-di-nar-
    i-ly
ex-traor-di-nar-y
ex-trap-o-late
ex-trap-o-lat-ed
ex-trap-o-la-tion
ex-tra-sen-so-ry
ex-tra-ter-res-tri-al
ex-trav-a-gance
ex-trav-a-gant
ex-trav-a-gan-za
ex-treme
ex-trem-ism
ex-trem-ist
ex-trem-i-ty
ex-tri-cate
ex-trin-sic
ex-tro-ver-sion
ex-tro-vert
ex-tro-vert-ed
ex-trude
ex-tru-sion
ex-tu-ber-ance
ex-u-ber-ant

ex-u-da-tion
exude
exult
ex-ul-tant
ex-ul-ta-tion
eye-ful
eye-glass
eye-sight
eye-strain
eye-wit-ness
eye-ing

F

fable
fab-ric
fab-ri-cate
fab-ri-ca-tion
fab-ri-ca-tor
fab-u-lous
fa-cade
facet
fac-et-ed
fa-ce-tious
fa-cial
fac-ile
fa-cil-i-tate
fa-cil-i-ty
fac-ing
fac-sim-i-le
fac-tion
fac-tion-al
fac-tious
fac-tor
fac-tor-able
fac-to-ri-al
fac-to-ry
fac-tu-al
fac-ul-ty
fad-ing
Fahr-en-heit
fail-ing
fail-ure
Fair-banks
fair-ground
fairy
fair-y-land

fair-y-like
faith-ful
faith-less
fak-er
fal-con
fal-con-er
fal-con-ry
fal-la-cious
fal-la-cy
fall-en
fal-li-bil-i-ty
fal-li-ble
Fal-lo-pi-an
fall-out
fal-low
false-hood
fal-set-to
fal-si-fi-ca-tion
fal-si-fy
fal-ter
fa-mil-ial
fa-mil-iar
fa-mil-i-ar-i-ty
fa-mil-iar-ize
fam-i-ly
fam-ine
fam-ish
fam-ished
fa-mous
fa-nat-ic
fa-nat-i-cal
fa-nat-i-cism
fan-cied
fan-ci-er
fan-ci-ful
fancy
fan-fare
fan-ta-sia
fan-ta-size
fan-tas-tic
fan-ta-sy
farad
far-a-day
far-ci-cal
fare-well

fa-ri-na
farm-er
far-ri-er
far-sight-ed
far-ther
far-thest
far-thing
fas-ci-nate
fas-ci-nat-ing
fas-ci-na-tion
fas-ci-na-tor
fas-cism
fas-cist
fash-ion
fash-ion-able
fas-ten
fas-ten-er
fast-en-ing
fas-tid-i-ous
fatal
fa-tal-ism
fa-tal-ist
fa-tal-is-tic
fa-tal-i-ty
fa-tal-ly
fate-ful
fa-ther
fa-ther-hood
fa-ther-ly
fath-om
fath-om-able
fath-om-less
fat-i-ga-ble
fa-tigue
fa-tigued
fa-tigu-ing-ly
fat-ten
fatty
fa-tu-i-tous
fau-cet
fault-less
faulty
fauna
favor
fa-vor-able

fa-vored
fa-vor-ite
fa-vor-it-ism
fe-al-ty
fear-ful
fear-less
fear-some
fea-si-bil-i-ty
fea-si-ble
feath-er
feath-ery
fea-ture
fea-tured
Feb-ru-ar-y
fe-cund
fe-cun-di-ty
fed-er-a-cy
fed-er-al
fed-er-al-ism
fed-er-al-ist
fed-er-al-ly
fed-er-ate
fed-er-a-tion
fed-er-a-tive
fee-ble
feed-er
feel-er
feel-ing
feis-ty
feld-spar
fe-lic-i-tate
fe-lic-i-ta-tion
fe-lic-i-tous
fe-lic-i-ty
fe-line
fe-lin-i-ty
fel-low
fel-low-ship
felon
fe-lo-ni-ous
fel-o-ny
fe-male
fem-i-nine
fem-i-nin-i-ty
fem-i-nism
fem-o-ral

femur
fenc-er
fenc-ing
fend-er
fer-ment
fer-ment-able
fer-men-ta-tion
fer-ment-a-tive
fer-ment-er
fer-mi-um
fe-ro-cious
fe-roc-i-ty
fer-ret
fer-ric
ferry
fer-tile
fer-til-i-ty
fer-til-iz-able
fer-til-i-za-tion
fer-til-ize
fer-til-iz-er
fer-ven-cy
fer-vent
fer-vor
fes-ter
fes-ti-val
fes-tive
fes-tiv-i-ty
fes-toon
fetal
fetch-ing
fet-ish
fet-ish-ism
fet-ter
fetus
feu-dal
feu-dal-ism
fever
fe-ver-ish
fi-an-ce
fi-an-cee
fi-as-co
fiat
fiber
Fi-ber-glas (TM)
fi-ber-glass (n.)

fi-brous
fick-le
fick-le-ness
fic-tion
fic-tion-al
fic-ti-tious
fid-dle
fid-dler
fi-del-i-ty
fidg-et
fidg-ety
fi-du-ci-ary
field-er
fiend-ish
fi-ery
fi-es-ta
fif-teen
fif-teenth
fif-ti-eth
fifty
fight-er
fight-ing
fig-ment
fig-ur-al
fig-u-ra-tion
fig-u-ra-tive
fig-ure
fig-u-rine
fil-a-ment
fil-bert
filet
fil-i-al
fil-i-bus-ter
fil-ing
Fil-i-pi-no
fill-er (filled)
fil-ler (money unit)
fil-let
fil-ling
filly
film-strip
filmy
fil-ter
fil-ter-able

filth-i-ness
filthy
fil-trate
fil-tra-tion
fi-na-gle
final
fi-na-le
fi-nal-ist
fi-nal-i-ty
fi-nal-ize
fi-nal-ly
fi-nance
fi-nan-cial
fin-an-cier
fi-nanc-ing
find-er
find-ing
fin-ery
fi-nesse
fin-ger
fin-icky
fin-ish
fin-ished
fi-nite
fin-i-tude
Finn-ish
fire-arm
fire-box
fire-crack-er
fire-man
fire-place
fire-proof
fir-ing
fir-ma-ment
firm-er
fis-cal
fish-er-man
fish-ery
fish-ing
fishy
fis-sion
fis-sure
fit-ness
fit-ful
fit-ting

fix-ate
fix-a-tion
fix-a-tive
fix-ture
fiz-zle
flab-by
flac-cid
flac-cid-i-ty
fla-con
flag-el-lant
flag-el-late
flag-el-la-tion
fla-grant
flaky
flam-bee
flam-boy-ant
flam-ing
fla-min-go
flam-ma-ble
flank-er
flan-nel
flar-ing
flash-ing
flashy
flat-ten
flat-ter
flat-ter-ing
flat-tery
flau-tist
fla-vor
fla-vor-ing
fla-vor-less
flaw-less
fledg-ling
fleet-ing
Flem-ish
flex-ible
flex-or
flick-er
flier
flighty
flim-sy
flip-pant
flip-per
flir-ta-tious

float-er
float-ing
flood-light
floor-ing
flora
flo-ral
Flor-en-tine
flo-res-cence
flo-ri-cul-tur-al
flo-ri-cul-ture
Flor-i-da
flo-rist
flo-ta-tion
flot-sam
floun-der
flour-ish
flow-er
flow-ing
fluc-tu-ate
fluc-tu-a-tion
flu-en-cy
flu-ent
fluff-i-ness
fluffy
fluid
flu-id-i-ty
flu-o-res-cence
flu-o-res-cent
flu-o-ri-date
flu-o-ride
flu-o-rine
flu-o-ro-scope
flur-ry
flus-ter
flut-ed
flut-ing
flut-ist
flut-ter
flu-vi-al
fly-ing
foamy
focal
fo-cal-ize
focus
fo-cus-ing

fod-der
foggy
foi-ble
fold-er
fol-de-rol
fo-li-age
folic
folio
folk-lore
fol-li-cle
fol-lic-u-lar
fol-low
fol-low-er
fol-low-ing
folly
fo-ment
fo-men-ta-tion
fon-dant
fon-dle
fond-ling
fond-ness
fon-due
fool-ery
fool-ish
fool-proof
foot-age
foot-ball
foot-ing
foot-note
for-age
foray
for-bear
for-bear-ance
for-bear-ing
for-bid
for-bid-den
for-bid-ding
force-ful
for-ceps
forc-ible
forc-ing
fore-bode
fore-bod-ing
fore-cast
fore-close

fore-clo-sure
for-eign
for-eign-er
for-en-sic
fo-ren-si-cal
fore-run-ner
fore-see
fore-see-able
fore-sight
for-est
fore-stall
for-est-a-tion
for-est-er
for-est-ry
fore-tell
for-ev-er
fore-warn
fore-ward
for-feit
for-feit-er
for-feit-ure
for-gery
for-get
for-get-ful
for-give
for-give-ness
for-got
for-got-ten
for-lorn
for-mal
form-al-de-hyde
for-mal-i-ty
for-mal-ize
for-mat
for-ma-tion
form-a-tive
form-er (n.)
for-mer (adj.)
for-mic
For-mi-ca
for-mi-da-ble
for-mu-la
for-mu-lar-i-za-
   tion

for-mu-lar-y
for-mu-late
for-mu-la-tor
for-sake
for-syth-ia
forth-com-ing
for-ti-eth
for-ti-fi-ca-tion
for-ti-fy
for-ti-tude
for-tress
for-tu-i-tous
for-tu-i-ty
for-tu-nate
for-tune
forty
forum
for-ward
fos-sil
fos-sil-ize
fos-ter
foun-da-tion
found-er (n.)
foun-der (v.;
   n., act of
   foundering)
found-ling
found-ry
foun-tain
four-teen
four-teenth
foyer
fra-cas
frac-tion
frac-tion-al
frac-tious
frac-ture
frag-ile
fra-gil-i-ty
frag-ment
frag-men-tary
frag-men-ta-tion
fra-grance
fra-grant
frail-ty

fram-ing
fran-chise
fran-ci-um
frank-furt-er
fran-kin-cense
frank-ly
frank-ness
fran-tic
fran-ti-cal-ly
fra-ter-nal
fra-ter-ni-ty
frat-er-nize
fraud-u-lent
Frau-lein
fraz-zle
freck-le
freck-led
free-dom
freez-er
freight-er
fren-zied
fren-zy
fre-quence
fre-quen-cy
fre-quent
fre-quent-ly
fres-co
fresh-en
fret-ful
Freud-i-an
friar
fric-as-see
fric-tion
Fri-day
friend-less
friend-ly
friend-ship
fright-en
fright-ened
fright-en-ing
fright-ful
frig-id
fri-gid-i-ty
fril-ly
frisk-i-ly

frisk-y
frit-ter
fri-vol-i-ty
friv-o-lous
frol-ic
frol-icked
frol-ic-some
front-age
fron-tal
fron-tier
fron-tis-piece
frost-ed
frost-i-ness
frost-ing
frosty
frothy
fro-zen
fruc-tose
fru-gal
fru-gal-i-ty
fruit-ful
fru-i-tion
fruit-less
fruity
frus-trate
frus-tra-tion
fuch-sia
fuel
fu-gi-tive
fuh-rer
ful-crum
ful-fill
ful-fill-ing
ful-fill-ment
full-ness
fully
fu-ma-to-ry
fum-ble
fum-bler
fu-mi-gate
fu-mi-ga-tor
func-tion
func-tion-al
fun-da-men-tal
fu-ner-al

fu-ne-re-al
fun-gus (n.)
fun-nel
fun-neled
funny
fur-bish
fu-ri-ous
fur-lough
fur-nace
fur-nish
fur-nish-ing
fur-ni-ture
furor
fur-ri-er
fur-ring
fur-row
furry
fur-ther
fur-thest
fur-tive
fury
fu-se-lage
fu-si-bil-i-ty
fu-si-ble
fu-si-lier
fu-sil-lade
fu-sion
fussy
fu-tile
fu-til-i-ty
fu-ture
fu-tur-ism
fu-tur-ist
fu-tu-ri-ty
fuzz-i-ness
fuzzy

G

gab-ar-dine
gable
ga-bled
gadg-et
gadg-et-eer
gadg-et-ry
Gael-ic
gai-e-ty

gaily
gain-er
gait-ed
gala
ga-lac-tic
Ga-la-pa-gos
gal-ax-y
Gal-i-le-an
Gal-i-lee
gal-lant
gal-lant-ry
gal-le-on
gal-lery
gal-ley
Gal-lic
gal-li-um
gal-li-vant
gal-lon
gal-lop
gal-lop-ing
gal-lows
gall-stone
ga-lore
ga-losh
gal-van-ic
gal-va-nize
Gam-bia
gam-bit
gam-ble
gam-bling
game-ly
ga-mete
gam-ing
gamma
gamut
gan-der
Gan-dhi
gan-gling
gan-gli-on
gan-grene
gan-gre-nous
gang-ster
gan-try
gap-ing
ga-rage

gar-bage
gar-ble
gar-bling
gar-den
gar-den-er
gar-de-nia
gar-gan-tu-an
gar-gle
gar-gling
gar-goyle
gar-ish
gar-land
gar-lic
gar-licky
gar-ment
gar-ner
gar-net
gar-nish
gar-ni-ture
gar-ret
gar-ri-son
gar-ru-li-ty
gar-ru-lous
gar-ter
gas-e-ous
gas-ket
gas-o-line
gas-tric
gas-tri-tis
gas-tro-in-tes-ti-
  nal
gas-tro-nome
gas-tro-nom-ic
gas-tron-o-my
gath-er
gath-er-ing
gau-che-rie
gau-cho
gaudy
gaunt-let
gavel
ga-votte
gawk-i-ness
gawky
ga-zelle

ga-zette
gaz-et-teer
Gei-ger
gei-sha
gel-a-tin
ge-lat-i-nous
geld-ing
gem-i-nate
Gem-i-ni
gen-darme
gen-der
gen-e-al-o-gist
gen-e-al-o-gy
gen-er-al
gen-er-a-lis-si-mo
gen-er-al-ist
gen-er-al-i-ty
gen-er-al-i-za-tion
gen-er-al-ize
gen-er-al-ly
gen-er-ate
gen-er-a-tion
gen-er-a-tor
ge-ner-ic
ge-ner-i-cal
gen-er-os-i-ty
gen-er-ous
gen-e-sis
ge-net-i-cal
Ge-ne-va
ge-nial
ge-ni-al-i-ty
ge-nie
gen-i-tal
ge-nius
Gen-oa
gen-o-ci-dal
gen-o-cide
gen-o-type
genre
gen-teel
Gen-tile
gen-til-i-ty
gen-tle
gen-tle-man

gent-ly
gen-try
gen-u-flect
gen-u-flec-tion
gen-u-ine
genus
ge-o-cen-tric
ge-o-des-ic
ge-og-ra-pher
ge-o-graph-ic
ge-og-ra-phy
ge-o-log-i-cal
ge-ol-o-gist
ge-ol-o-gy
ge-o-met-ric
ge-o-met-ri-cal
ge-om-e-try
ge-o-phys-ics
Geor-gia
ge-o-tax-is
ge-o-trop-ic
ge-ot-ro-pism
ge-ra-ni-um
ger-bil
ger-i-at-ric
ger-i-a-tri-cian
ger-i-at-rics
Ger-man
ger-mane
Ger-man-ic
ger-ma-ni-um
Ger-ma-ny
ger-mi-ci-dal
ger-mi-cide
ger-mi-nate
ger-mi-na-tion
Ge-ron-i-mo
ge-ron-to-log-i-cal
ger-on-tol-o-gy
ger-und
Ge-stalt
Ge-sta-po
ges-tate
ges-ta-tion
ges-tic-u-late

ges-tic-u-la-tion
ges-ture
Ge-sund-heit
gey-ser
Ghana
ghast-ly
gher-kin
ghet-to
ghost-ly
ghost-writ-er
ghoul-ish
giant
gib-ber
gib-ber-ish
gib-let
Gi-bral-tar
giddy
gift-ed
gi-gan-tic
gig-gle
gild-er
gim-let
gim-mick
gim-micky
gin-ger
gin-ger-ly
ging-ham
gi-raffe
gird-er
gir-dle
gir-dling
girl-ish
given
giz-zard
glace
gla-cial
gla-ci-a-tion
gla-cier
glad-i-a-tor
glad-i-o-lus
glam-or-ize
glam-or-ous
glam-our
glan-du-lar
glar-ing

glass-i-ness
glassy
glau-co-ma
glid-er
glim-mer
glis-san-dro
glis-ten
glit-ter
glob-al
glob-al-ly
glob-u-lar
glob-ule
gloom-i-ly
gloomy
glo-ri-fi-ca-tion
glo-ri-fy
glo-ri-ous
glory
glos-sa-ry
gloss-i-ness
glossy
glov-er
glow-er
glow-ing
glox-in-ia
glu-cose
glu-ing
glu-ti-nous
glut-ton
glut-tony
glyc-er-in
glyc-er-ol
gly-co-gen
gnom-ish
gnos-tic
Gnos-ti-cism
goa-tee
gob-ble
gob-bler
gob-let
gob-lin
gog-gles
going
goi-ter
gold-en

gold-en-rod
gonad
gon-do-la
gon-or-rhea
good-ness
gooey
go-pher
gor-geous
go-ril-la
gory
gos-pel
gos-pel-er
gos-sip
Goth-am
Goth-ic
gour-mand
gour-mand-ise
gour-met
gov-ern
gov-ern-ance
gov-ern-ess
gov-ern-ment
gov-ern-men-tal
gov-er-nor
grace-ful
gra-cious
gra-cious-ness
gra-date
gra-da-tion
grad-er
gra-di-ent
grad-u-al
grad-u-ate
grad-u-a-tion
gra-ham
grainy
gram-mar
gram-mar-i-an
gram-mat-i-cal
gra-na-ry
grand-child
grand-dad
grand-daugh-ter
gran-deur
grand-fa-ther

gran-di-ose
grand-ma
grand-moth-er
grand-pa
grand-son
grang-er
gran-ite
grant-ee
grant-er
grant-or (law)
gran-u-lar
gran-u-lar-i-ty
gran-ule
grape-fruit
grape-vine
graph-ic
graph-ite
grap-ple
grap-pling
grasp-ing
grassy
grate-ful
grat-er
grat-i-fi-ca-tion
grat-i-fy
gra-tin
grat-ing
gra-tis
grat-i-tude
gra-tu-i-tous
gra-tu-i-ty
grav-en
grav-i-tate
grav-i-tat-er
grav-i-ta-tion
grav-i-ty
gravy
graz-ing
greas-i-ness
greasy
Gre-cian
greed-i-ness
greedy
green-ery
greet-ing

gre-gar-i-ous
Gre-go-ri-an
grem-lin
gre-nade
gren-a-dier
gren-a-dine
grey-hound
grid-dle
grid-i-ron
griev-ance
griev-ous
grim-ace
grimy
grind-er
grind-stone
grin-gos
grit-ty
griz-zly
gro-cer
gro-cer-ies
gro-cery
grog-gy
grom-met
gros-grain
gross-est
gro-tesque
gro-tes-que-rie
grot-to
grouchy
ground-ling
group-ing
grov-el
grov-el-er
growl-er
grub-by
gruel
gru-el-ing
grue-some
gruff-ly
grum-ble
grum-bler
grumpy
Gru-yere
gua-ca-mo-le
gua-ni-dine

gua-nine
guar-an-tee (n.; v.)
guar-an-ty (n.,
    law)
guard-ed
guard-i-an
Gua-te-ma-la
gu-ber-na-to-ri-al
gudg-eon
guern-sey
guer-ril-la
guess-work
guf-faw
guid-ance
guide-book
guide-line
guide-post
guile-less
guil-lo-tine
guilt-i-ly
guilt-less
guilty
Guin-ea
gui-tar
gul-li-ble
gully
gumbo
gummy
gump-tion
gun-fight
gun-fire
gun-man
gun-ner
gun-nery
gun-pow-der
gun-shot
gur-gi-ta-tion
gur-gle
gur-gling
gush-er
gus-ta-tion
gus-ta-to-ry
gusto
Gu-ten-berg
gut-ter

gut-tur-al
Guy-a-na
guz-zle
gym-kha-na
gym-na-si-um
gym-nast
gym-nas-tic
gy-ne-col-o-gy
gyp-sum
Gyp-sy
gy-rate
gy-ra-tion

H

ha-be-as
hab-er-dash-er
hab-er-dash-ery
ha-bil-i-tate
habit
hab-it-able
hab-i-tant
hab-i-tat
hab-i-ta-tion
ha-bit-u-al
ha-bit-u-ate
ha-bit-u-a-tion
ha-ci-en-da
hack-ney
had-dock
Ha-des
haf-ni-um
hag-gard
hag-gle
hairy
Hai-fa
Hai-ti
hal-cy-on
half-back
half-way
hal-i-but
hal-i-to-sis
hal-le-lu-jah
hall-mark
hal-low
hal-lowed
Hal-low-een

hal-lu-ci-nate
hal-lu-ci-na-tion
hal-lu-ci-na-to-ry
hal-lu-cin-o-gen
hall-way
halo
hal-o-gen
hal-ter
halt-ing
ham-burg-er
ham-let
ham-mer
ham-mock
ham-per
ham-ster
hand-book
hand-ed
hand-ful
hand-i-cap
hand-i-capped
hand-i-craft
hand-i-work
hand-ker-chief
han-dle
han-dler
han-dling
hand-made
hand-shake
hand-some
hand-som-est
hand-writ-ing
hang-ar
hang-er
han-ker
Ha-noi
Ha-nuk-kah
hap-haz-ard
hap-pen
hap-pen-ing
hap-pi-ness
happy
har-a-kiri
ha-rangue
har-ass
har-assed

har-ass-ment
har-bin-ger
har-bor
hard-en
hard-en-er
hard-en-ing
har-di-ness
Har-ding
hard-ly
hard-ship
hard-ware
hardy
harem
har-le-quin
harm-ful
harm-less
har-mon-ic
har-mon-i-ca
har-mo-ni-ous
har-mo-nize
har-mo-ny
har-ness
harp-ist
har-poon
harp-si-chord
har-row
har-row-ing
har-vest
har-vest-er
hash-ish
has-sle
has-sled
has-ten
hast-i-ly
hasty
hatch-ery
hatch-et
hate-ful
ha-tred
haugh-ti-ly
haugh-ti-ness
haugh-ty
haunt-ed
haunt-ing
hau-teur

Ha-vana
haven
havoc
Ha-waii
haz-ard
haz-ard-ous
hazel
head-ache
head-ing
head-line
head-lin-er
head-quar-ters
head-way
heal-er
health-i-est
health-y
heap-ing
hear-ing
heart-en
heart-i-ly
heat-er
hea-then
heath-er
heav-en
heav-en-ly
heav-i-ly
heavy
heav-y-weight
He-bra-ic
He-brew
heck-le
heck-ler
hec-tic
he-don-ics
he-do-nism
he-don-ist
he-do-nis-tic
heed-less
hefty
heif-er
height-en
hei-nous
heir-ess
heir-loom
hel-i-cop-ter

hel-i-port
he-li-um
Hel-len-ic
Hel-le-nism
Hel-le-nis-tic
hel-met
help-ful
help-ing
help-less
he-ma-tol-o-gy
hem-i-sphere
hem-i-spher-ic
he-mo-glo-bin
he-mo-phil-ia
he-mo-phil-i-ac
hem-or-rhage
hem-or-rhoid
hem-or-rhoi-dal
hence-forth
henna
hep-a-ti-tis
hep-ta-gon
hep-tag-o-nal
hep-tane
her-ald
her-ba-ceous
herb-al
her-bi-ci-dal
her-bi-cide
her-bi-vore
her-biv-o-rous
her-cu-le-an
he-red-i-tary
he-red-i-ty
Her-e-ford
her-e-sy
her-e-tic
he-ret-i-cal
her-it-age
her-me-neu-tics
her-met-ic
her-met-i-cal
her-mit
her-mit-age
her-nia

hero
he-ro-ic
her-o-in
her-o-ine
her-o-ism
heron
her-ring
her-self
hes-i-tan-cy
hes-i-tate
hes-i-tat-er
hes-i-ta-tion
Hes-sian
het-er-o-dox
het-er-o-doxy
het-er-o-ge-ne-i-ty
het-er-o-ge-ne-ous
het-er-og-e-nous
het-er-o-sex-u-al
het-er-o-sex-u-al-
  i-ty
heu-ris-tic
hex-a-gon
hex-ag-o-nal
hi-a-tus
hi-ber-nate
hi-ber-na-tion
hi-ber-na-tor
hick-o-ry
hid-den
hid-e-ous
hi-er-ar-chy
hi-er-o-glyph-ic
high-light
high-way
hi-jack
hi-lar-i-ous
hi-lar-i-ty
hilly
Hi-ma-la-yas
him-self
hin-der
hin-drance
hind-sight
Hin-du

Hin-du-ism
hin-ter-land
Hip-po-crat-ic
hip-po-pot-a-mus
Hir-o-shi-ma
His-pan-ic
his-ta-mine
his-to-gram
his-to-ri-an
his-tor-ic
his-tor-i-cal
his-to-ry
his-tri-on-ic
hith-er
hoard-ing
hob-ble
hobby
hock-ey
hold-er
hold-ing
hol-i-day
ho-li-ness
hol-lan-daise
Hol-land
Hol-land-er
hol-low
holly
hol-mi-um
hol-o-caust
Hol-stein
hol-ster
holy
hom-age
home-ly
home-made
ho-me-o-sta-sis
Ho-mer-ic
home-sick
home-stead
home-work
hom-i-ci-dal
hom-i-cide
hom-i-ly
hom-i-ny
ho-mo-ge-ne-i-ty

ho-mo-ge-ne-ous
ho-mog-e-ni-za-
  tion
ho-mog-e-niz-er
ho-mog-e-nize
ho-mol-o-gous
hom-o-nym
ho-mo-sex-u-al
ho-mo-sex-u-al-
  i-ty
Hon-du-ras
hon-est
hon-est-ly
honey
hon-ey-moon
hon-ey-suck-le
Hon-o-lu-lu
honor
hon-or-able
hon-o-rar-i-um
hon-or-ary
hon-or-if-ic
hood-ed
Hoo-ver
hope-ful
hope-ful-ly
hope-less
ho-ri-zon
hor-i-zon-tal
hor-mo-nal
hor-mone
hor-net
hor-o-scope
ho-ros-co-py
hor-ren-dous
hor-ri-ble
hor-rid
hor-ri-fy
hor-ror
horse-man
horse-shoe
horse-wom-an
hor-ta-tive
hor-ta-to-ry
hor-ti-cul-tur-al

hor-ti-cul-ture
ho-san-na
ho-siery
hos-pi-ta-ble
hos-pi-tal
hos-pi-tal-i-ty
hos-pi-tal-i-za-tion
hos-pi-tal-ize
hos-tage
hos-tel
hos-tel-er
hos-tel-ry
host-ess
hos-tile
hos-til-i-ty
hour-ly
house-hold
house-wife
house-work
hous-ing
Hous-ton
hovel
hover
how-ev-er
howl-er
howl-ing
hub-bub
huck-ster
hud-dle
Hu-gue-not
human
hu-mane
hu-man-ism
hu-man-ist
hu-man-ize
hu-man-i-tar-i-an-
 ism
hu-man-i-ty
hu-man-ize
hum-ble
hum-bling
humid
hu-mid-i-fi-er
hu-mid-i-fy
hu-mid-i-ty

hu-mil-i-ate
hu-mil-i-a-tion
hu-mil-i-ty
hum-ming-bird
humor
hu-mor-less
hu-mor-ous
hu-mus
hun-dred
hun-dredth
Hun-gar-i-an
Hun-ga-ry
hun-ger
hun-gry
hunt-er
hunt-ing
hur-dle
hur-dler
hurl-er
Huron
hur-ri-cane
hur-ried
hur-ried-ly
hurry
hur-tle
hur-tling
hus-band
hus-band-ry
husk-i-ness
husky
hus-tle
hy-a-cinth
hy-brid
hy-brid-ize
hy-drant
hy-drau-lic
hy-dro-car-bon
hy-dro-chlo-ric
hy-dro-e-lec-tric
hy-dro-gen
hy-drol-o-gy
hy-drol-y-sis
hy-dro-lyze
hy-dro-pho-bia
hy-dro-pho-bic

hy-dro-plane
hy-drox-ide
hyena
hy-giene
hy-gien-ic
hy-gien-ist
hymen
hym-nal
hy-per-ac-tive
hy-per-bo-le
hy-per-bol-ic
hy-per-crit-i-cal
hy-per-gly-ce-mia
hy-per-sen-si-tive
hy-per-ten-sion
hy-per-thy-roid
hy-per-thy-roid-
 ism
hy-per-ven-ti-la-
 tion
hy-phen
hy-phen-ate
hy-phen-at-ed
hyp-na-gog-ic
hyp-no-sis
hyp-no-ther-a-py
hyp-not-ic
hyp-no-tism
hyp-no-tist
hyp-no-tize
hy-po-chon-dria
hy-po-chon-dri-ac
hy-poc-ri-sy
hyp-o-crite
hy-po-der-mic
hy-po-sen-si-tiv-
 i-ty
hy-pot-e-nuse
hy-po-thal-a-mus
hy-poth-e-sis
hy-poth-e-size
hy-po-thet-i-cal
hy-po-thy-roid
hy-po-thy-roid-
 ism

hys-ter-ec-to-my
hys-te-ria
hys-ter-i-cal
hys-ter-ics

I

Ibe-ria
ice-berg
Ice-land
Ice-lan-dic
ici-cle
icing
icon
icon-o-clasm
icon-o-clast
icy
Ida-ho
idea
ideal
ide-al-ism
ide-al-ist
ide-al-is-tic
ide-al-i-za-tion
ide-al-ize
ide-al-ly
iden-ti-cal
iden-ti-fi-able
iden-ti-fi-ca-tion
iden-ti-fy
iden-ti-ty
ide-o-log-i-cal
ide-ol-o-gy
id-i-o-cy
id-i-om
id-i-o-mat-ic
id-i-o-syn-cra-sy
idiot
id-i-ot-ic
id-i-ot-i-cal-ly
idle
idler
idol
idol-a-ter
idol-a-trous
idol-a-try
idol-ize

idyl-lic	im-be-cil-i-ty	im-pal-pa-ble	im-plant
ig-loo	im-bibe	im-part	im-plan-ta-tion
ig-ne-ous	im-bro-glio	im-par-tial	im-plau-si-ble
ig-nit-able	im-i-tate	im-pass-able	im-ple-ment
ig-nite	im-i-ta-tion	im-passe	im-ple-men-ta-
ig-nit-er	im-i-ta-tive	im-pas-sive	tion
ig-ni-tion	im-mac-u-la-cy	im-pa-tience	im-pli-cate
ig-no-ble	im-mac-u-late	im-peach	im-pli-ca-tion
ig-no-min-i-ous	im-ma-nent	im-pec-ca-ble	im-plic-it
ig-no-miny	im-ma-te-ri-al	im-pede	im-plic-it-ly
ig-no-ra-mus	im-ma-ture	im-ped-i-ment	im-plied
ig-no-rance	im-meas-ur-able	im-ped-i-men-tal	im-plore
ig-no-rant	im-me-di-a-cy	impel	imply
ig-nore	im-me-di-ate	im-pel-ling	im-po-lite
igua-na	im-me-di-ate-ly	im-pend	im-port
il-le-gal	im-mense	im-pend-ing	im-por-tance
il-le-gal-i-ty	im-men-si-ty	im-pen-e-tra-bil-	im-por-tant
il-leg-ible	im-merse	i-ty	im-por-ta-tion
il-le-git-i-ma-cy	im-mers-ible	im-pen-e-tra-ble	im-port-er
il-le-git-i-mate	im-mers-ing	im-pen-i-tent	im-por-tu-nate
il-lic-it	im-mer-sion	im-per-a-tive	im-por-tune
Il-li-nois	im-mi-grant	im-per-cep-ti-ble	im-pose
il-lit-er-a-cy	im-mi-grate	im-per-fect	im-pos-ing
il-lit-er-ate	im-mi-gra-tion	im-per-fec-tion	im-po-si-tion
ill-ness	im-mi-nence	im-pe-ri-al	im-pos-si-bil-i-ty
il-log-i-cal	im-mi-nent	im-pe-ri-al-ism	im-pos-si-ble
il-lu-mi-nate	im-mis-ci-ble	im-per-il	im-pos-tor
il-lu-mi-na-tion	im-mo-bile	im-per-iled	im-po-tence
il-lu-mi-na-tive	im-mo-bi-lize	im-per-me-able	im-po-tent
il-lu-mi-na-tor	im-mod-est	im-per-mis-si-ble	im-pound
il-lu-sion	im-mor-al	im-per-son-al	im-pov-er-ish
il-lu-sive	im-mor-tal	im-per-son-ate	im-prac-ti-ca-ble
il-lu-so-ry	im-mor-tal-i-ty	im-per-son-a-tor	im-prac-ti-cal
il-lus-trate	im-mor-tal-ize	im-per-ti-nence	im-pre-cise
il-lus-tra-tion	im-mov-a-ble	im-per-ti-nent	im-preg-na-ble
il-lus-tra-tive	im-mune	im-per-turb-able	im-preg-nate
il-lus-tri-ous	im-mu-ni-ty	im-per-vi-ous	im-pre-sa-rio
image	im-mu-ni-za-tion	im-pet-u-os-i-ty	im-press
im-age-ry	im-mu-nize	im-pet-u-ous	im-press-ible
im-ag-i-na-ble	im-mu-nol-o-gy	im-pe-tus	im-pres-sion
im-ag-i-nary	im-mu-ta-ble	im-pinge	im-pres-sion-able
im-ag-i-na-tion	im-pact	im-ping-ing	im-pres-sion-ism
im-ag-i-na-tive	im-pact-ed	im-pi-ous	im-pres-sive
im-ag-ine	im-pair	imp-ish	im-pri-ma-tur
im-be-cile	im-pale	im-plac-able	im-print

im-print-ing
im-pris-on
im-prob-a-bil-i-ty
im-prob-able
im-promp-tu
im-prop-er
im-prove
im-prove-ment
im-prov-i-sa-tion
im-pro-vise
im-pru-dence
im-pru-dent
im-pu-dence
im-pu-dent
im-pulse
im-pul-sive
im-pu-ni-ty
im-pure
im-pu-ri-ty
im-pu-ta-tive
im-pute
in-ac-ces-si-ble
in-ac-cu-ra-cy
in-ac-cu-rate
in-ac-tive
in-ac-tiv-i-ty
in-ad-e-qua-cy
in-ad-e-quate
in-ad-mis-si-ble
in-ad-ver-tence
in-ad-vert-ent
in-ad-vis-able
in-al-ien-able
in-al-ter-able
inane
in-an-i-mate
in-ap-pli-ca-ble
in-ap-pre-cia-ble
in-ap-pre-cia-tive
in-ap-pro-pri-ate
in-ar-tic-u-late
in-au-di-ble
in-au-gu-ral
in-au-gu-rate
in-au-gu-ra-tion

in-cal-cu-la-ble
in-can-des-cence
in-can-des-cent
in-can-ta-tion
in-ca-pa-ble
in-ca-pac-i-tate
in-ca-pac-i-ty
in-car-cer-ate
in-car-cer-a-tion
in-car-nate
in-cen-di-ary
in-cense
in-cen-tive
in-cep-tion
in-cer-ti-tude
in-ces-sant
in-cest
in-ces-tu-ous
in-cho-ate
in-ci-dence
in-ci-dent
in-ci-den-tal
in-ci-den-tal-ly
in-cin-er-ate
in-cin-er-a-tor
in-cip-i-ent
in-ci-sion
in-ci-sive
in-ci-sor
in-ci-ta-tion
in-cite
in-cit-er
in-clem-ent
in-cli-na-tion
in-cline
in-clined
in-clud-able
in-clude
in-clud-ed
in-clu-sion
in-clu-sive
in-cog-ni-to
in-co-her-ence
in-co-her-ent
in-come

in-com-men-su-ra-
ble
in-com-men-su-
rate
in-com-mu-ni-ca-
ble
in-com-mu-ni-ca-
do
in-com-pa-ra-ble
in-com-pat-i-bil-
i-ty
in-com-pat-ible
in-com-pe-tent
in-com-plete
in-com-pre-hen-
si-ble
in-com-pre-hen-
sive
in-con-ceiv-able
in-con-clu-sive
in-con-gru-ent
in-con-gru-ous
in-con-se-quent
in-con-se-quen-
tial
in-con-sid-er-ate
in-con-sis-ten-cy
in-con-sis-tent
in-con-spic-u-ous
in-con-stan-cy
in-con-stant
in-con-ven-ience
in-con-ven-ient
in-con-vin-ci-ble
in-cor-po-rate
in-cor-po-rat-ed
in-cor-po-re-al
in-cor-rect
in-cor-ri-gi-ble
in-crease
in-cred-i-bil-i-ty
in-cred-ible
in-cre-du-li-ty
in-cred-u-lous
in-cre-ment

in-crim-i-nate
in-cu-bate
in-cu-ba-tion
in-cu-ba-tor
in-cum-ben-cy
in-cum-bent
incur
in-cur-able
in-cur-sion
in-debt-ed
in-debt-ed-ness
in-de-cen-cy
in-de-cent
in-de-ci-sion
in-de-ci-sive
in-deed
in-de-fat-i-ga-ble
in-de-fen-si-ble
in-de-fin-able
in-def-i-nite
in-del-ible
in-del-i-ca-cy
in-del-i-cate
in-dem-ni-fi-ca-
tion
in-dem-ni-fy
in-dem-ni-ty
in-de-mon-stra-ble
in-dent
in-den-ta-tion
in-den-ture
in-de-pen-dence
in-de-pen-den-cy
in-de-pend-ent
in-de-scrib-able
in-de-struct-ible
in-de-ter-mi-na-
ble
in-de-ter-mi-nate
index
In-dia
In-di-an
In-di-ana
In-di-an-ap-o-lis
in-di-cate

in-di-ca-tion
in-dic-a-tive
in-di-ca-tor
in-dict
in-dict-able
in-dict-er
in-dict-ment
In-dies
in-dif-fer-ence
in-dif-fer-ent
in-dig-e-nous
in-di-gent
in-di-gest-ible
in-di-ges-tion
in-dig-nant
in-dig-na-tion
in-dig-ni-ty
in-di-go
in-di-rect
in-dis-creet
in-dis-cre-tion
in-dis-crim-i-nate
in-dis-crim-i-na-
  tion
in-dis-pen-sa-ble
in-dis-pose
in-dis-pu-ta-ble
in-dis-sol-u-ble
in-dis-tin-guish-
  able
in-di-um
in-di-vi-du-al
in-di-vid-u-al-ist
in-di-vid-u-al-i-ty
in-di-vid-u-al-ize
in-di-vis-ible
in-doc-tri-nate
in-do-lent
in-dom-i-ta-ble
In-do-ne-sia
in-door
in-du-bi-ta-ble
in-duce
in-duc-er
in-duce-ment

in-duc-ible
in-duct
in-duct-ance
in-duc-tion
in-duc-tive
in-duc-tor
in-dulge
in-dul-gence
in-dul-gent
in-dus-tri-al
in-dus-tri-al-i-za-
  tion
in-dus-tri-al-ize
in-dus-tri-ous
in-dus-try
in-e-bri-ate
in-e-bri-at-ed
in-ed-ible
in-ef-fa-ble
in-ef-fec-tive
in-ef-fi-cien-cy
in-ef-fi-cient
in-el-i-gi-ble
inept
in-ep-ti-tude
in-e-qual-i-ty
in-eq-ui-ta-ble
in-eq-ui-ty
inert
in-er-tia
in-er-tial
in-es-cap-able
in-ev-i-ta-ble
in-ex-cus-able
in-ex-haust-ible
in-ex-o-ra-ble
in-ex-pen-sive
in-ex-pe-ri-enced
in-ex-pi-able
in-ex-pli-ca-ble
in-ex-press-ible
in-ex-tir-pa-ble
in-ex-tri-ca-ble
in-fal-li-ble
in-fa-mous

in-fa-my
in-fan-cy
in-fant
in-fan-tile
in-fan-try
in-fat-u-ate
in-fat-u-at-ed
in-fat-u-a-tion
in-fea-si-ble
in-fect
in-fec-tion
in-fec-tious
in-fe-lic-i-tous
in-fe-lic-i-ty
infer
in-fer-ence
in-fer-en-tial
in-fe-ri-or
in-fe-ri-or-i-ty
in-fer-nal
in-fer-no
in-fer-tile
in-fest
in-fes-ta-tion
in-fi-del
in-fi-del-i-ty
in-field
in-fil-trate
in-fil-tra-tion
in-fil-tra-tor
in-fi-nite
in-fin-i-tes-i-mal
in-fin-i-tive
in-fin-i-tude
in-fin-i-ty
in-firm
in-fir-ma-ry
in-fir-mi-ty
in-flame
in-flam-ma-ble
in-flam-ma-tion
in-flam-ma-to-ry
in-flate
in-flat-ed
in-fla-tion

in-flect
in-flec-tion
in-flex-ible
in-flict
in-flict-er
in-flic-tion
in-flo-res-cence
in-flu-ence
in-flu-en-tial
in-flu-en-za
in-flux
in-form
in-for-mal
in-for-mal-i-ty
in-form-ant
in-for-ma-tion
in-form-a-tive
in-form-er
in-fract
in-frac-tion
in-fran-gi-ble
in-fra-red
in-fre-quent
in-fringe
in-fring-er
in-fringe-ment
in-fu-ri-ate
in-fuse
in-fu-si-ble
in-fu-sion
in-ge-nious
in-ge-nue
in-ge-nu-i-ty
in-gen-u-ous
in-gest
in-grain
in-grained
in-grate
in-gra-ti-ate
in-grat-i-tude
in-gre-di-ent
in-grown
in-hab-it
in-hab-it-a-bil-i-ty
in-hab-i-tan-cy

in-hab-it-ant
in-hab-it-ed
in-ha-la-tion
in-ha-la-tor
in-hale
in-her-ent
in-her-it
in-her-it-able
in-her-i-tance
in-hib-it
in-hib-it-er
in-hi-bi-tion
in-hib-i-to-ry
in-hos-pit-able
in-hu-man
in-hu-mane
in-hu-man-i-ty
in-im-i-cal
in-im-i-ta-ble
in-iq-ui-tous
in-iq-ui-ty
ini-tial
ini-ti-ate
ini-ti-a-tion
ini-ti-a-tive
in-ject
in-jec-tion
in-ju-di-cious
in-junc-tion
in-junc-tive
in-jure
in-ju-ri-ous
in-ju-ry
in-jus-tice
in-kling
in-mate
in me-mo-ri-am
in-nate
inner
in-ner-most
in-ning
in-no-cence
in-no-cent
in-noc-u-ous
in-no-vate

in-no-va-tion
in-nu-en-do
in-nu-mer-able
in-oc-u-late
in-oc-u-la-tion
in-of-fen-sive
in-op-er-able
in-op-er-a-tive
in-op-por-tune
in-or-di-nate
in-or-gan-ic
in-pa-tient
input
in-quest
in-qui-e-tude
in-quire
in-quir-er
in-quiry
in-qui-si-tion
in-quis-i-tive
in-sane
in-san-i-tary
in-san-i-ty
in-sa-tia-ble
in-scribe
in-scrib-er
in-scrip-tion
in-scru-ta-ble
in-sect
in-sec-ti-ci-dal
in-sec-ti-cide
in-se-cure
in-se-cu-ri-ty
in-sem-i-nate
in-sem-i-na-tion
in-sen-sate
in-sen-si-ble
in-sen-si-tive
in-sep-a-ra-ble
in-sert
in-sert-ed
in-ser-tion
inset
in-side
in-sid-er

in-sid-i-ous
in-sight
in-sig-nia
in-sig-ni-fi-cance
in-sig-nif-i-cant
in-sin-cere
in-sin-u-ate
in-sin-u-at-ing
in-sin-u-a-tion
in-sip-id
in-si-pid-i-ty
in-sist
in-sis-tence
in-sis-tent
in-so-bri-e-ty
in-so-lence
in-so-lent
in-sol-u-ble
in-solv-able
in-sol-ven-cy
in-sol-vent
in-som-nia
in-som-ni-ac
in-sou-ci-ance
in-sou-ci-ant
in-spect
in-spec-tion
in-spec-tor
in-spi-ra-tion
in-spi-ra-tion-al
in-spire
in-sta-bil-i-ty
in-stal-la-tion
in-stalled
in-stall-ment
in-stance
in-stant
in-stan-ta-ne-ous
in-stant-ly
in-stead
in-step
in-sti-gate
in-sti-ga-tor
in-still
in-stinct

in-stinc-tive
in-sti-tute
in-sti-tu-tion
in-sti-tu-tion-al-
  ize
in-struct
in-struc-tion
in-struc-tive
in-struc-tor
in-stru-ment
in-stru-men-tal
in-stru-men-tal-ist
in-stru-men-tal-i-
  ty
in-sub-or-di-nate
in-sub-stan-tial
in-suf-fer-able
in-suf-fi-cient
in-su-lar
in-su-late
in-su-la-tion
in-su-la-tor
in-su-lin
in-sult
in-su-per-able
in-sup-port-a-ble
in-sur-ance
in-sure
in-sured
in-sur-er
in-sur-gence
in-sur-gen-cy
in-sur-gent
in-sur-mount-able
in-sur-rec-tion
in-tact
in-tan-gi-ble
in-te-ger
in-te-gral
in-te-grate
in-te-gra-tion
in-te-gra-tor
in-teg-ri-ty
in-tel-lect
in-tel-lec-tu-al

in-tel-li-gence
in-tel-li-gent
in-tel-li-gen-tsia
in-tel-li-gi-ble
in-tend
in-tend-ant
in-tend-ed
in-tense
in-ten-si-fy
in-ten-si-ty
in-ten-sive
in-tent
in-ten-tion
in-ten-tion-al
inter
in-ter-act
in-ter-cede
in-ter-cept
in-ter-cep-tor
in-ter-ces-sion
in-ter-change
in-ter-change-able
in-ter-col-le-gi-ate
in-ter-com
in-ter-con-nect
in-ter-con-ti-nen-
   tal
in-ter-dict
in-ter-dic-tion
in-ter-est
in-ter-est-ed
in-ter-est-ing
in-ter-face
in-ter-fere
in-ter-fer-ence
in-ter-ga-lac-tic
in-ter-im
in-te-ri-or
in-ter-ject
in-ter-jec-tion
in-ter-lude
in-ter-me-di-a-cy
in-ter-me-di-a-ry
in-ter-me-di-ate
in-ter mi na ble

in-ter-mis-sion
in-ter-mit-tent
in-tern
in-ter-nal
in-ter-nal-ize
in-ter-na-tion-al
in-ter-na-tion-al-
   ism
in-ter-plan-e-tary
in-ter-po-late
in-ter-po-la-tion
in-ter-pret
in-ter-pret-able
in-ter-pre-ta-tion
in-ter-pre-ta-tive
in-ter-pret-er
in-ter-ro-gate
in-ter-rog-a-tive
in-ter-ro-ga-tor
in-ter-rog-a-to-ry
in-ter-rupt
in-ter-rupt-ed
in-ter-rupt-er
in-ter-rupt-ing
in-ter-sect
in-ter-sec-tion
in-ter-sperse
in-ter-state
in-ter-stic-es
in-ter-twine
in-ter-val
in-ter-vene
in-ter-ven-er
in-ter-view
in-tes-ti-nal
in-tes-tine
in-ti-ma-cy
in-ti-mate
in-ti-mat-er
in-tim-i-date
in-tim-i-da-tion
in-tim-i-da-tor
into
in-tol-er-able
in-tol-er-ance

in-tol-er-ant
in-to-nate
in-to-na-tion
in-tox-i-cant
in-tox-i-cate
in-tox-i-ca-tion
in-trac-ta-ble
in-tra-mu-ral
in-tran-si-gent
in-tran-si-tive
in-tra-ve-nous
in-trep-id
in-tre-pid-i-ty
in-tri-ca-cy
in-trigue
in-trigu-er
in-trigu-ing
in-trin-sic
in-tro-duce
in-tro-duc-tion
in-tro-duc-to-ry
in-tro-spect
in-tro-spec-tion
in-tro-spec-tive
in-tro-vert
in-trude
in-trud-er
in-tru-sion
in-tru-sive
in-tu-it
in-tu-i-tion
in-tu-i-tive
in-un-date
in-un-da-tion
in-un-da-tor
in-vade
in-vad-er
in-va-lid (n.; v.;
   adj., not well)
in-val-id (adj., not
   valid)
in-val-i-date
in-va-lid-i-ty
in-val-u-able
in-var-i-able

in-va-sion
in-vent
in-ven-tion
in-ven-tive
in-ven-tor
in-ven-to-ry
in-verse
in-ver-sion
in-vert
in-ver-te-brate
in-vert-er
in-vest
in-ves-ti-gate
in-ves-ti-ga-tion
in-ves-ti-ga-tive
in-ves-ti-ga-tor
in-ves-ti-ture
in-vest-ment
in-ves-tor
in-vet-er-ate
in-vid-i-ous
in-vig-o-rate
in-vin-ci-ble
in-vi-o-la-ble
in-vi-o-late
in-vis-ible
in-vi-ta-tion
in-vi-ta-tion-al
in-vite
in-vit-ing
in-vo-ca-tion
in-voice
in-voke
in-vol-un-tary
in-volve
in-volved
in-vul-ner-able
in-ward
in-ward-ly
io-dine
io-dize
ion
ion-i-za-tion
ion-ize
ion-o-sphere

iota
Iowa
ipso facto
I-ran
I-raq
iras-ci-ble
irate
Ire-land
ir-i-des-cence
ir-i-des-cent
irid-i-um
iris
Irish
iron
iron-ic
irony
ir-ra-di-ate
ir-ra-di-a-tion
ir-rad-i-ca-ble
ir-ra-tion-al
ir-ra-tion-al-i-ty
ir-rec-on-cil-able
ir-re-deem-able
ir-re-duc-ible
ir-ref-u-ta-ble
ir-reg-u-lar
ir-reg-u-lar-i-ty
ir-rel-e-vance
ir-rel-e-vant
ir-re-me-di-able
ir-rep-a-ra-ble
ir-re-place-able
ir-re-press-ible
ir-re-sist-i-ble
ir-re-solv-able
ir-re-spon-si-ble
ir-rev-er-ence
ir-rev-er-ent
ir-re-vers-ible
ir-rev-o-ca-ble
ir-ri-ga-ble
ir-ri-gate
ir-ri-ta-bil-i-ty
ir-ri-ta-ble
ir-ri-tant

ir-ri-tate
ir-ri-ta-tion
Is-lam
Is-lam-ic
is-land
is-land-er
iso-la-ble
iso-late
iso-la-tion
iso-la-tion-ism
iso-mer
iso-met-ric
isos-ce-les
iso-tope
Is-ra-el
Is-rae-li
Is-ra-el-ite
is-su-able
is-su-ance
issue
isth-mus
Ital-ian
ital-ic
ital-i-cize
It-a-ly
item
item-i-za-tion
item-ize
itin-er-ary
it-self
ivo-ry
ivy

J

jack-al
jack-et
jack-knife
jack-pot
Jac-o-be-an
jaded
jag-uar
jai alai
Ja-mai-ca
jam-bo-ree
jan-gle
jan-gling

jan-i-tor
Jan-u-ary
Japan
Jap-a-nese
jar-gon
jas-mine
jas-per
jaun-dice
jaun-diced
jaunt-i-ly
jaun-ty
java
jav-e-lin
jeal-ous
jeal-ousy
Jef-fer-son
Jef-fer-so-ni-an
Je-ho-vah
Je-kyll
jel-lied
jelly
jeop-ard-ize
jeop-ardy
jer-sey
Je-ru-sa-lem
jest-er
Jes-u-it
Jesus
jet-ti-son
jetty
jewel
jew-eled
jew-el-er
Jew-ish
jez-e-bel
jig-gle
jin-gle
jin-gling
jingo
jock-ey
jo-cose
jo-cos-i-ty
joc-u-lar
joc-und
jo-cun-di-ty

jodh-pur
jog-ging
John-son
join-der
join-er
joint-ed
joker
jolly
jon-quil
Jor-dan
Jor-da-ni-an
jos-tle
jos-tling
jot-ting
jour-nal
jour-nal-ism
jour-nal-ist
jour-ney
jo-vi-al
jo-vi-al-i-ty
joy-ful
joy-ous
ju-bi-lant
ju-bi-la-tion
ju-bi-lee
Ju-da-ism
judg-ment
ju-di-ca-tive
ju-di-ca-tor
ju-di-ca-to-ry
ju-di-ca-ture
ju-di-cial
ju-di-ci-ary
ju-di-cious
judo
jug-gle
jug-gler
jug-gling
jug-u-lar
juicy
ju-jit-su
ju-jube
ju-li-enne
July
jum-ble

jum-bled
jumbo
jump-er (one who jumps)
jum-per (dress)
junc-tion
junc-ture
jun-gle
jun-ior
ju-ni-per
junta
Ju-pi-ter
ju-rid-i-cal
ju-ris-dic-tion
ju-ris-pru-dence
ju-rist
ju-ris-tic
juror
jury
jus-tice
jus-ti-fi-able
jus-ti-fi-ca-tion
jus-ti-fy
ju-ve-nile
ju-ve-nil-i-ty
jux-ta-pose
jux-ta-po-si-tion

K

ka-lei-do-scope
ka-lei-do-scop-ic
ka-mi-ka-ze
kan-ga-roo
Kan-sas
kappa
karat
ka-ra-te
ka-ty-did
kayak
keep-er
keep-ing
keep-sake
Kel-vin
Ken-ne-dy
ken-nel
Ken-tucky

Ken-ya
ker-chief
ker-nel
ker-o-sene
ketch-up
ke-tone
key-note
khaki
Khru-shchev
kib-butz
kib-itz
kib-itz-er
kick-off
kid-nap
kid-nap-er
kid-ney
kill-er
kill-ing
kil-o-gram
kil-o-me-ter
kil-o-watt
ki-mo-no
kin-der-gar-ten
kin-der-gart-ner
kin-dle
kind-li-ness
kin-dling
kind-ly
kind-ness
kin-dred
kin-e-scope
ki-net-ic
king-dom
kinky
kins-man
kiosk
kitch-en
kitch-en-ette
kit-ten
kitty
Klee-nex
klep-to-ma-nia
knap-sack
knav-ish
knick-ers

knock-out
knot-ted
knot-ty
know-ing
knowl-edge
knowl-edge-able
knuck-le
koala
Koran
Korea
ko-sher
Krem-lin
kryp-ton
ku-chen
kum-quat
Ku-wait

L

label
la-beled
labor
lab-o-ra-to-ry
la-bored
la-bor-er
la-bo-ri-ous
Lab-ra-dor
lab-y-rinth
lac-er-ate
lac-er-a-tion
lach-ry-mose
lac-ing
la-con-ic
lac-quer
la-crosse
lac-tase
lac-tic
lac-tose
lacy
lad-der
laden
ladle
lady
la-dy-like
La-fay-ette
la-goon
lais-sez faire

laity
lamb-da
la-ment
lam-en-ta-ble
lam-en-ta-tion
lam-i-nate
lam-i-nat-ed
lam-i-na-tion
lam-poon
land-ed
land-ing
land-la-dy
land-lord
land-mark
land-own-er
land-scape
land-slide
lan-guage
lan-guid
lan-guish
lan-guish-ing
lan-guor
lanky
lan-o-lin
lan-tern
Laos
lap-i-dary
La-o-tian
lar-ce-nist
lar-ce-ny
larg-er
large-ly
larg-est
lar-i-at
larva
lar-yn-gi-tis
lar-ynx
la-sag-na
las-civ-i-ous
laser
las-si-tude
lasso
last-ing
late-ly
la-ten-cy

la-tent
later
lat-er-al
lat-est
latex
lath-er
lath-er-ing
Latin
lat-i-tude
lat-i-tu-di-nal
lat-ter
lat-tice
laud-able
laud-a-to-ry
laugh-ter
launch-er
laun-der
laun-dress
Laun-dro-mat
laun-dry
lau-re-ate
lau-rel
lau-reled
lava
lav-a-to-ry
lav-en-der
lav-ish
law-break-er
law-ful
law-giv-er
law-less
law-mak-er
law-yer
layer
lay-ette
lay-man
lay-off
lay-out
lay-o-ver
la-zi-ly
la-zi-ness
lazy
lead-er
lead-er-ship
lead-ing

lea-guer
leak-age
leaky
lean-ing
learned (v.)
learn-ed (adj.)
learn-ing
leas-ing
leath-er
leav-en
Leb-a-nese
Leb-a-non
lech-er
lech-er-ous
lech-ery
lec-tern
lec-ture
lec-tur-er
ledg-er
lee-ward
left-hand-ed
leg-a-cy
legal
le-gal-i-ty
le-gal-ize
leg-ate
le-ga-tion
leg-end
leg-end-ary
leg-er-de-main
leg-ible
le-gion
le-gion-naire
leg-is-late
leg-is-la-tion
leg-is-la-tive
leg-is-la-tor
leg-is-la-ture
le-git-i-ma-cy
le-git-i-mate
leg-ume
lei-sure
lei-sure-ly
lemon
lem-on-ade
lem-ony

lend-er
length-en
length-wise
lengthy
le-ni-en-cy
le-ni-ent
Lent-en
len-til
leop-ard
le-o-tard
leper
lep-re-chaun
lep-ro-sy
lep-rous
les-bi-an
les-bi-an-ism
le-sion
les-see
less-en
less-er
les-son
les-sor
le-thal
le-thar-gic
leth-ar-gy
let-ter
let-ter-ing
let-tuce
leu-ke-mia
leu-ke-mic
level
lev-el-er
lever
le-ver-age
le-vi-a-than
lev-i-tate
lev-i-tat-ing
lev-i-ty
levy
lex-i-cal
lex-i-cog-ra-pher
lex-i-cog-ra-phy
lex-i-con
li-a-bil-i-ty
li-a-ble

li-ai-son
libel
li-bel-ant
li-bel-ous
lib-er-al
lib-er-al-ism
lib-er-al-i-ty
lib-er-al-ize
lib-er-ate
lib-er-a-tor
Li-be-ria
lib-er-tar-i-an
lib-er-tine
lib-er-ty
li-bi-do
li-brar-i-an
li-brary
Libya
li-cense
li-censed
li-cens-ee
li-cens-er
li-cen-tious
li-chen
lic-o-rice
Liech-ten-stein
lieu-ten-an-cy
lieu-ten-ant
life-less
life-long
life-sav-er
life-time
lig-a-ment
lig-a-ture
light-en
light-ened
light-er
light-ing
light-ly
light-ning
light-weight
lig-nite
lik-able
like-li-hood
like-ly

liken	Lis-bon	lob-by	Los An-ge-les
like-ness	lis-ten	lob-by-ist	loser
lilac	lis-ten-er	lo-bot-o-my	los-ing
lily	list-ing	lob-ster	lo-tion
lima	list-less	lo-cal	lot-tery
lim-ber	lit-a-ny	lo-cale	lo-tus
Lim-burg-er	liter	lo-cal-i-ty	Lou-i-si-ana
lime-ade	lit-er-a-cy	lo-cal-ize	Lou-is-ville
lime-light	lit-er-al	lo-cate	lous-i-ness
lim-er-ick	lit-er-al-ly	lo-ca-tion	lousy
lim-it	lit-er-ary	lo-ca-tor	lov-able
lim-i-ta-tion	lit-er-ate	lock-er	love-ly
lim-it-ed	lit-er-a-ture	lock-et	lov-ing
lim-it-less	lith-i-um	lo-co-mo-tion	lower
lim-ou-sine	lith-o-graph	lo-co-mo-tive	lowly
lim-pid	li-tho-gra-pher	lo-cus	loyal
lim-pid-i-ty	lith-o-graph-ic	lo-cust	loy-al-ist
Lin-coln	li-thog-ra-phy	lo-cu-tion	loy-al-ty
lin-e-age	Lith-u-a-nia	lodg-er	loz-enge
lin-e-al	lit-i-ga-ble	lodg-ing	lu-bri-cant
lin-e-a-ment	lit-i-gate	lofty	lu-bri-cate
lin-e-ar	lit-i-ga-tion	log-a-rithm	lu-bri-ca-tion
lin-e-ar-ly	lit-i-ga-tor	log-a-rith-mic	lu-bri-ca-tor
line-back-er	lit-mus	logic	lucid
linen	lit-ter	log-i-cal	lu-cid-i-ty
liner	lit-tle	lo-gi-cian	lu-cite
lin-ger	li-tur-gi-cal	lo-gis-ti-cian	luck-i-ly
lin-ge-rie	lit-ur-gy	lo-gis-tics	lucky
lin-gual	liv-able	loi-ter	lu-cra-tive
lin-guist	live-li-hood	lol-li-pop	lucre
lin-guis-tics	live-ly	Lon-don	lu-di-crous
lin-i-ment	liv-er	lone-li-ness	lug-gage
lin-ing	liv-ery	lone-ly	lu-gu-bri-ous
link-age	live-stock	lone-some	luke-warm
li-no-le-um	livid	lon-ger	lull-a-by
lin-seed	liv-ing	lon-gest	lum-ber
lint-er	liz-ard	lon-gev-i-ty	lu-mi-nes-cence
li-on	lla-ma	long-ing	lu-mi-nes-cent
li-on-ess	load-ed	lon-gi-tude	lu-mi-nos-i-ty
liq-ue-fy	load-er	lon-gi-tu-di-nal	lu-mi-nous
li-queur	load-ing	loos-en	lu-na-cy
liq-uid	loaf-er	loot-er	lunar
liq-ui-date	loath-ing	lop-sid-ed	lu-na-tic
liq-ui-da-tion	loath-some	lo-qua-cious	lunch-eon
liq-uor	lob-bied	lo-quac-i-ty	lurid

lus-cious
lus-ter
lus-trous
Lu-ther-an
Lux-em-bourg
Lux-em-bourg-er
lux-u-ri-ant
lux-u-ri-ous
lux-u-ry
ly-ce-um
lying
lym-phat-ic
lym-pho-cyte
lymph-oid
ly-on-naise
lyric
lyr-i-cal
lyr-i-cist

M

ma-ca-bre
mac-ad-am
mac-ad-am-ize
mac-a-ro-ni
mac-a-roon
Mac-ca-be-an
Mac-e-do-nia
ma-che-te
Mach-i-a-vel-li-an
mach-i-na-tion
ma-chine
ma-chin-ery
ma-chin-ist
macho
mack-er-el
mack-in-tosh
mac-ro-cosm
mac-ro-scop-ic
Madam
ma-dame
mad-den
Ma-dei-ra
ma-de-moi-selle
Mad-i-son
madly
mad-ness

ma-don-na
ma-dras
Ma-drid
mad-ri-gal
mae-stro
Mafia
mag-a-zine
ma-gen-ta
magic
mag-i-cal
ma-gi-cian
mag-is-te-ri-al
mag-is-trate
mag-na-nim-i-ty
mag-nan-i-mous
mag-ne-si-um
mag-net
mag-net-ic
mag-net-i-cal-ly
mag-net-ism
mag-ne-tize
mag-ni-fi-ca-tion
mag-nif-i-cence
mag-ni-fi-cent
mag-ni-fi-er
mag-ni-fy
mag-ni-tude
mag-no-lia
ma-hog-a-ny
maid-en
mail-er
mail-lot
Maine
main-ly
main-tain
main-te-nance
ma-jes-tic
maj-es-ty
major
ma-jor-i-ty
maker
mal-ad-just-ment
mal-a-droit
mal-a-dy
mal-aise

ma-lar-ia
ma-lar-i-al
Malay
Ma-lay-an
Ma-lay-sia
Ma-lay-sian
mal-con-tent
ma-lev-o-lence
ma-lev-o-lent
mal-for-ma-tion
mal-func-tion
mal-ice
ma-li-cious
ma-lign
ma-lig-nant
ma-lin-ger
mal-le-able
mal-let
mal-nour-ished
mal-nu-tri-tion
mal-prac-tice
mal-tend
mal-treat
mal-treat-ment
mam-mal
mam-ma-li-an
mam-mal-o-gy
mam-ma-ry
mam-moth
man-age
man-age-able
man-age-ment
man-ag-er
man-a-ge-ri-al
ma-ña-na
Man-chu-ria
man-da-rin
man-date
man-da-to-ry
man-do-lin
man-do-lin-ist
man-drake
ma-neu-ver
ma-neu-ver-a-bil-i-
ty

man-ga-nese
man-ger
man-gle
man-gler
mango
mangy
Man-hat-tan
man-hood
ma-ni-ac
ma-ni-a-cal
man-i-cot-ti
man-i-cure
man-i-cur-ist
man-i-fest
man-i-fes-ta-tion
man-i-fes-to
man-i-fold
man-i-kin
ma-nila
ma-nip-u-la-ble
ma-nip-u-late
ma-nip-u-la-tion
ma-nip-u-la-tor
manly
man-ner
man-nered
man-ner-ism
manor
man-sion
man-slaugh-ter
man-tel (arch.)
man-tle (garment)
man-u-al
man-u-fac-ture
man-u-fac-tur-er
ma-nure
man-u-script
many
maple
mar-a-schi-no
mar-a-thon
ma-raud
ma-raud-er
mar-ble
mar-bled

mar-ble-ize	Marx-ism	mat-ri-mo-ny	me-dal-lion
mar-ga-rine	Mar-y-land	ma-trix	med-dle
mar-gin	mar-zi-pan	ma-tron	med-dler
mar-gin-al	mas-cara	ma-tron-ly	med-dle-some
mar-i-gold	mas-cot	mat-ter	me-di-an
mar-i-jua-na	mas-cu-line	mat-tress	me-di-ate
ma-ri-na	mas-cu-lin-i-ty	mat-u-ra-tion	me-di-a-tion
mar-i-nade	mask-ing	ma-ture	me-di-a-tor
mar-i-nate	mas-och-ism	ma-tu-ri-ty	medic
ma-rine	mas-och-ist	matzo	me-di-ca-ble
mar-i-ner	mas-och-is-tic	maud-lin	Med-i-caid
mar-i-o-nette	mason	mau-so-le-um	med-i-cal
mar-i-tal	Ma-son-ic	mav-er-ick	Med-i-care
mar-i-time	ma-son-ry	mawk-ish	med-i-cate
mar-jo-ram	mas-quer-ade	maxim	med-i-ca-tion
mark-er	Mas-sa-chu-setts	max-i-mal	me-dic-i-nal
mar-ket	mas-sa-cre	max-i-mize	med-i-cine
mar-ket-able	mas-sa-cred	max-i-miz-er	me-die-val
mark-ing	mas-sage	max-i-mum	me-di-o-cre
mar-ma-lade	mass-ing	may-on-naise	me-di-oc-ri-ty
mar-mot	mas-sive	mayor	med-i-tate
ma-roon	mas-ter	may-or-al-ty	med-i-ta-tion
mar-quee (tent)	mas-ter-ful	ma-zur-ka	med-i-ta-tive
mar-que-try	mas-ter-mind	mead-ow	Med-i-ter-ra-ne-an
mar-quis (title)	mas-ter-piece	mea-ger	me-di-um
mar-riage	mas-tery	mealy	med-ley
mar-riage-able	mas-ti-cate	me-an-der	me-dul-la
mar-ried	mas-tiff	mean-ing	meet-ing
mar-row	mas-to-don	mean-ing-ful	meg-a-lop-o-lis
marry	mat-a-dor	mean-ing-less	meg-a-lo-pol-i-tan
mar-shal	ma-te-ri-al	mean-time	meg-a-phone
mar-shaled	ma-te-ri-al-ism	mean-while	mei-o-sis
marsh-mal-low	ma-te-ri-al-ize	mea-sles	mel-an-cho-lia
mar-su-pi-al	ma-ter-nal	meas-ur-able	mel-an-chol-ic
mar-tial	ma-ter-ni-ty	meas-ure	mel-an-choly
Mar-tian	math-e-mat-i-cal	meas-ured	me-lange
mar-tin	math-e-ma-ti-cian	meas-ure-ment	me-lee
mar-ti-net	math-e-mat-ics	mecca	me-lio-rate
mar-tin-gale	mat-i-nee	me-chan-ic	me-lio-ra-tion
mar-ti-ni	ma-tri-arch	me-chan-i-cal	me-lio-ra-tive
mar-tyr	ma-tri-ar-chal	mech-a-nism	mel-low
mar-tyr-dom	ma-tri-ar-chy	mech-a-nize	me-lo-de-on
mar-vel	mat-ri-ces	mech-a-ni-za-tion	me-lod-ic
mar-vel-ous	ma-tric-u-late	medal	me-lo-di-ous
	mat-ri-mo-ni-al	med-al-ist	mel-o-dra-ma

mel-o-dra-mat-ic
mel-o-dy
melon
melt-ing
mem-ber
mem-ber-ship
mem-brane
mem-bra-nous
me-men-to
me-men-tos
mem-oir
mem-o-ra-bil-ia
mem-o-ra-ble
mem-o-ran-dum
me-mo-ri-al
me-mo-ri-al-ize
me-mo-ri-al-iz-ing
mem-o-rize
mem-o-riz-er
mem-o-ry
men-ace
me-nage
me-nag-er-ie
men-da-cious
men-dac-i-ty
mend-er
men-di-cant
mend-ing
me-ni-al
men-in-gi-tis
Men-non-ite
men-o-pau-sal
men-o-pause
Me-no-rah
men-ses
men-stru-al
men-stru-ate
men-stru-a-tion
men-tal
men-tal-i-ty
men-thol
men-tion
men-tor
menu
mer-can-tile

mer-can-til-ism
mer-ce-nary
mer-cer-ize
mer-chan-dise
mer-chant
mer-ci-ful
mer-ci-less
mer-cu-ry
mercy
merg-er
me-rid-i-an
me-ringue
merit
mer-it-ed
mer-i-to-ri-ous
mer-maid
mer-ri-ment
merry
mesa
mes-ca-line
mes-en-ceph-a-lon
mes-mer-ism
mes-mer-ize
mes-o-derm
Mes-o-po-ta-mia
mes-o-sphere
Mes-o-zo-ic
mes-quite
mes-sage
mes-sen-ger
Mes-si-ah
messy
mes-ti-zo
met-a-bol-ic
me-tab-o-lism
me-tab-o-lize
metal
met-al-list
me-tal-lic
met-al-loid
met-al-lur-gi-cal
met-al-lur-gy
met-a-mor-phism
met-a-mor-phose
met-a-mor-pho-sis

met-a-phor
met-a-phor-i-cal
met-a-phys-i-cal
met-a-phys-ics
met-a-zo-an
me-te-or
me-te-or-ic
me-te-or-ite
me-te-or-ol-o-gist
me-te-or-ol-o-gy
meter
meth-ane
meth-od
me-thod-i-cal
Meth-od-ism
Meth-od-ist
meth-od-ize
meth-od-ol-o-gy
meth-yl
me-tic-u-lous
met-ric
met-ri-cal
met-ro-nome
me-trop-o-lis
met-ro-pol-i-tan
Mex-i-can
Mex-i-co
mez-za-nine
mez-zo-so-prano
mica
Mich-i-gan
mi-crobe
mi-cro-bi-ol-o-gy
mi-cro-cosm
mi-cro-fiche
mi-cro-film
mi-crom-e-ter
mi-cro-or-gan-ism
mi-cro-phone
mi-cro-phon-ic
mi-cro-scope
mi-cro-scop-ic
mi-cros-co-py
mid-brain
mid-day

mid-dle
mid-dling
midg-et
mid-night
mid-riff
mid-sum-mer
mid-way
mid-wife
mid-wife-ry
mid-win-ter
mid-year
mighty
mi-graine
mi-grate
mi-gra-tion
mi-gra-to-ry
mi-ka-do
mil-dew
mile-age
miler
mi-lieu
mil-i-tan-cy
mil-i-tant
mil-i-ta-rism
mil-i-ta-rist
mil-i-ta-rize
mil-i-tary
mi-li-tia
milky
mil-le-nary
mil-len-ni-um
mill-er
mil-let
mil-li-li-ter
mil-li-me-ter
mil-li-ner
mil-li-nery
mill-ing
mil-lion
mil-lion-aire
mil-lion-air-ess
mil-lionth
mil-li-pede
mim-e-o-graph
mimic

mim-ic-ry
min-a-ret
mind-less
miner
min-er-al
min-er-al-ize
min-e-stro-ne
min-gle
min-gling
min-i-a-ture
min-i-mal
min-i-mize
min-i-mum
min-ing
min-is-ter
min-is-te-ri-al
min-is-try
Min-ne-so-ta
min-now
minor
mi-nor-i-ty
Min-o-taur
min-strel
mint-age
min-u-et
mi-nus
min-us-cule
min-ute (time)
mi-nute (small)
min-ute-ly (every
   minute)
mi-nute-ly (pre-
   cisely)
mi-o-sis
mi-ot-ic
mir-a-cle
mi-rac-u-lous
mi-rage
mir-ror
mis-ad-ven-ture
mis-an-thrope
mis-an-throp-ic
mis-an-thro-py
mis-ap-pre-
   hend

mis-ap-pre-hen-
   sion
mis-ap-pro-pri-ate
mis-be-have
mis-be-hav-ior
mis-cal-cu-late
mis-car-riage
mis-car-ry
mis-cast
mis-cel-la-ne-ous
mis-cel-la-ny
mis-chief
mis-chie-vous
mis-con-ceive
mis-con-cep-tion
mis-con-duct
mis-con-strue
mis-de-mean-or
miser
mis-er-able
mi-ser-ly
mis-ery
mis-fea-sance
mis-fire
mis-fit
mis-for-tune
mis-give
mis-giv-ing
mis-guide
mis-hap
mis-in-ter-pret
mis-judge
mis-lay
mis-laid
mis-lead
mis-lead-ing
mis-match
mis-no-mer
mi-sog-y-nist
mi-sog-y-ny
mis-place
mis-print
mis-pro-nounce
mis-quote
mis-quo-ta-tion

mis-read
mis-rep-re-sent
mis-rep-re-sen-ta-
   tion
mis-sile
mis-sile-ry
miss-ing
mis-sion
mis-sion-ary
Mis-sis-sip-pi
mis-sive
Mis-sou-ri
mis-spell
mis-spelled
mis-tak-able
mis-take
mis-tak-en
Mis-ter
mis-tle-toe
mis-tral
mis-treat
mis-tress
mis-tri-al
mis-trust
misty
mis-un-der-stand
mis-un-der-stand-
   ing
mis-un-der-stood
mis-use
mit-i-gate
mit-i-ga-tion
mit-i-ga-tor
mi-to-chon-dri-a
mi-to-chon-dri-on
mi-to-sis
mi-tot-ic
mit-ten
mitz-vah
mixer
mix-ture
mne-mon-ic
mo-bile
mo-bil-i-ty
mo-bi-li-za-tion

mo-bil-ize
mob-ster
moc-ca-sin
mocha
mock-ery
mock-ing-bird
modal
model
mod-eled
mod-el-ing
mod-er-ate
mod-er-ate-ly
mod-er-a-tion
mod-er-a-tor
mod-ern
mod-ern-is-tic
mod-ern-ize
mod-est
mod-es-ty
mod-i-cum
mod-i-fi-ca-tion
mod-i-fi-er
mod-i-fy
mod-ish
mod-u-late
mod-u-la-tion
mod-u-la-tor
mod-ule
mod-u-lus
modus op-e-ran-di
mo-hair
Mo-ham-med
Mo-ham-med-an
mois-ten
mois-ten-er
mois-ture
molal
mo-lal-i-ty
mo-lar
mo-lar-i-ty
mo-las-ses
mold-er
mold-ing
moldy
mo-lec-u-lar

mol-e-cule
mo-lest
mo-les-ta-tion
mo-lest-er
mol-li-fy
mol-lusk
mol-ten
mo-lyb-de-num
mo-ment
mo-men-tar-i-ly
mo-men-tary
mo-men-tous
mo-men-tum
Mon-a-co
Mon-a-can
mo-nad
mo-nad-ic
mon-arch
mo-nar-chal
mon-ar-chism
mo-nar-chi-cal
mon-ar-chist
mon-ar-chy
mon-as-te-ri-al
mon-as-tery
mo-nas-tic
mo-nas-ti-cism
mon-a-tom-ic
Mon-day
mon-e-tar-y
money
mon-ger
Mon-go-lia
Mon-go-li-an
mon-gol-ism
Mon-gol-oid
mon-grel
mon-i-tor
mon-i-to-ry
mon-key
monk-ish
mon-o-chro-mat-
  ic
mon-o-cle
mo-nog-a-my

mon-o-gram
mon-o-grammed
mon-o-lith
mon-o-lith-ic
mon-o-logue
mo-nop-o-lize
mo-nop-o-ly
mon-o-rail
mon-o-the-ism
mon-o-tone
mo-not-o-nous
mo-not-o-ny
mon-ox-ide
Mon-sei-gneur
Mon-sieur
Mon-si-gnor
mon-soon
mon-ster
mon-stros-i-ty
mon-strous
mon-tage
Mon-tana
Mon-tes-so-ri
month-ly
mon-u-ment
mon-u-men-tal
moody
moon-light
moor-ing
Moor-ish
moral
mo-rale
mor-al-ist
mo-ral-i-ty
mor-al-ize
mor-al-ly
mor-a-to-ri-um
Mo-ra-via
Mo-ra-vi-an
mor-bid
mor-bid-i-ty
more-o-ver
mores
mor-i-bund
Mor-mon

Mor-mon-ism
morn-ing
Mo-roc-co
moron
mo-ron-ic
mo-rose
mor-phine
mor-pho-log-i-cal
mor-phol-o-gy
mor-pho-sis
mor-row
mor-sel
mor-tal
mor-tal-i-ty
mor-tar
mort-gage
mort-ga-gee
mort-ga-gor
mor-ti-cian
mor-ti-fi-ca-tion
mor-ti-fy
mor-tu-ary
mo-sa-ic
Mos-lem
mos-qui-to
mos-qui-toes
most-ly
motel
moth-er
moth-er-hood
moth-er-ly
mo-tif
mo-tion
mo-tion-less
mo-ti-vate
mo-ti-va-tion
mo-ti-va-tion-al
mo-tive
mot-ley
motor
mo-tor-ist
motto
moun-tain
moun-tain-eer
moun-tain-ous

mount-ed
mount-ing
mourn-er
mourn-ful
mourn-ing
mouth-ful
mouth-piece
mov-able
move-ment
mover
movie
mov-ing
Mo-zam-bique
moz-za-rel-la
mu-cous (adj.)
mu-cus (n.)
mud-dle
mud-dled
muddy
muf-fin
muf-fle
muf-fler
mug-ger
muggy
mu-lat-to
mu-lat-toes
mul-ish
mul-ti-col-ored
mul-ti-far-i-ous
Mul-ti-graph
mul-ti-me-dia
mul-ti-mil-lion-
  aire
mul-ti-ple
mul-ti-pli-able
mul-ti-pli-ca-tion
mul-ti-pli-ca-tive
mul-ti-plic-i-ty
mul-ti-pli-er
mul-ti-ply
mul-ti-tude
mul-ti-tu-di-nous
mum-ble
mum-bling
mum-mer

mum-mi-fy
mummy
mun-dane
mu-nic-i-pal
mu-nic-i-pal-i-ty
mu-ni-tion
mural
mur-der
mur-der-ous
murky
mur-mur
mur-mur-ous
mus-cat
mus-ca-tel
mus-cle
mus-cu-lar
mus-cu-la-ture
mu-se-um
mush-room
music
mu-si-cal
mu-si-cian
mus-ing
mus-ket
mus-ket-eer
musk-mel-on
Mus-lim
mus-lin
mus-sel
mus-tache
mus-tang
mus-tard
mus-ter
musty
mu-ta-bil-i-ty
mu-ta-ble
mu-tant
mu-ta-tion
mu-ti-late
mu-ti-neer
mu-ti-nous
mu-ti-ny
mut-ism
mut-ter
mut-ton

mu-tu-al
muz-zle
muz-zling
my-o-pia
my-op-ic
my-o-sin
myr-i-ad
myr-tle
my-self
mys-te-ri-ous
mys-tery
mys-tic
mys-ti-cal
mys-ti-cism
mys-ti-fi-ca-tion
mys-ti-fy
mys-tique
myth-i-cal
myth-o-log-i-cal
my-thol-o-gize
my-thol-o-gy

N

nadir
naive
na-ive-te
naked
name-less
name-sake
na-palm
nar-cis-sism
nar-cis-sis-tic
nar-cis-sus
nar-cot-ic
nar-rate
nar-ra-tion
nar-ra-tive
nar-ra-tor
nar-row
nar-thex
nasal
nas-ti-ly
nas-tur-tium
nasty
na-tion
na-tion-al

na-tion-al-ism
na-tion-al-ist
na-tion-al-i-ty
na-tion-al-ize
na-tion-wide
na-tive
na-tiv-is-tic
na-tiv-i-ty
nat-u-ral
nat-u-ral-ist
nat-u-ral-ize
nat-u-ral-ly
na-ture
naugh-ti-ness
naugh-ty
nau-sea
nau-se-ate
nau-se-at-ed
nau-seous
nau-ti-cal
naval
navel
nav-i-ga-ble
nav-i-gate
nav-i-ga-tion
nav-i-ga-tor
navy
Nazi
na-zism
Ne-an-der-thal
Ne-a-pol-i-tan
near-by
near-est
near-ly
near-sight-ed
Ne-bras-ka
neb-u-la
neb-u-lar
neb-u-lous
nec-es-sar-i-ly
nec-es-sary
ne-ces-si-tate
ne-ces-si-ty
neck-lace
ne-crop-o-lis

nec-tar
nec-tar-ine
need-i-ness
nee-dle
ne-far-i-ous
ne-gate
ne-ga-tion
neg-a-tive
neg-a-tiv-ism
ne-glect
ne-glect-er
ne-glect-ful
neg-li-gee
neg-li-gence
neg-li-gent
neg-li-gi-ble
ne-go-tia-ble
ne-go-ti-ate
ne-go-ti-a-tion
ne-go-ti-a-tor
Negro
Ne-groid
neigh-bor
neigh-bor-hood
neigh-bor-ing
neigh-bor-ly
nei-ther
nel-son
nem-e-sis
Ne-o-lith-ic
ne-ol-o-gism
ne-o-my-cin
neon
ne-o-phyte
neph-ew
ne-phri-tis
nep-o-tism
Nep-tune
nep-tu-ni-um
nerv-ous
nes-tle
nest-ling (n.)
nes-tling (v.)
net-tle
net-tled

net-work
Neuf-cha-tel
neu-ral
neu-rol-o-gy
neu-ron
neu-ro-psy-chi-a-
    try
neu-ro-sis
neu-ro-sur-gery
neu-rot-ic
neu-rot-i-cism
neu-ter
neu-tral
neu-tral-i-ty
neu-tral-ize
neu-tral-iz-er
neu-tri-no
neu-tron
Ne-vada
never
nev-er-the-less
new-com-er
New Hamp-shire
New Jer-sey
newly
New Mex-i-co
news-cast
news-pa-per
news-reel
news-stand
New-to-ni-an
New York
New Zea-land
nexus
Ni-ag-a-ra
nib-ble
nib-bling
Nic-a-ra-gua
nice-ly
ni-ce-ty
nick-el
nick-el-o-de-on
nick-name
nic-o-tine
nifty

Niger
Ni-ge-ria
night-fall
night-gown
night-in-gale
night-ly
night-mare
night-time
ni-hil-ism
ni-hi-list
nim-ble
nim-bly
nim-bus
nine-fold
nine-teen
nine-teenth
nine-ti-eth
nine-ty
ni-o-bi-um
nippy
nir-va-na
ni-trate
ni-tric
ni-tro-gen
Nix-on
No-bel
no-bel-i-um
no-bil-i-ty
noble
no-blesse
nobly
no-body
noc-tur-nal
nod-ule
noise-less
nois-i-ly
noisy
nomad
no-mad-ic
no-men-cla-ture
nom-i-nal
nom-i-nate
nom-i-nat-ed
nom-i-na-tion
nom-i-na-tive

nom-i-nee
non-a-ge-nar-i-an
non-cha-lance
non-cha-lant
non-com-mit-tal
non-com-pli-ance
non-con-duc-tor
non-con-form-ist
non-de-nom-i-na-
    tion-al
non-de-script
non-en-ti-ty
non-es-sen-tial
non-ex-ist-ence
non-ex-ist-ent
non-fic-tion
non-pa-reil
non-par-ti-san
non-plus
non-plused
non-pro-duc-tive
non-sense
non se-qui-tur
non-stop
non-vi-o-lence
non-vi-o-lent
non-white
noo-dle
nor-a-dren-a-lin
Nor-dic
nor-ep-i-neph-rine
nor-mal
nor-mal-cy
nor-mal-i-ty
nor-mal-ize
nor-mal-iz-er
Nor-man-dy
nor-ma-tive
North Car-o-li-na
North Da-ko-ta
north-east
north-east-ern
north-ern
north-ern-er
north-west

north-west-ern
Nor-way
Nor-we-gian
nos-tal-gia
nos-tril
nosy
no-ta-ble
no-ta-rize
no-ta-ry
no-ta-tion
note-book
note-wor-thy
noth-ing
no-tice
no-tice-able
no-ti-fi-ca-tion
no-ti-fy
no-tion
no-to-ri-e-ty
no-to-ri-ous
not-with-stand-
    ing
nou-gat
nour-ish
nour-ish-ment
nou-veau
nova
Nova Sco-tia
novel
nov-el-ette
nov-el-ist
nov-el-ty
No-vem-ber
nov-ice
no-vo-cain
nox-ious
noz-zle
nu-ance
nu-cle-ar
nu-cle-ic
nu-cle-o-lus
nu-cle-on
nu-cle-us
nud-ism
nu-di-ty

nu-ga-to-ry
nug-get
nui-sance
nul-li-fi-ca-tion
nul-li-fi-er
nul-li-fy
nul-li-ty
num-ber
num-bered
numb-ness
nu-mer-al
nu-mer-ate
nu-mer-a-tion
nu-mer-a-tor
nu-mer-i-cal
nu-mer-ol-o-gy
nu-mer-ous
nu-mis-mat-ics
nu-mis-ma-tist
nun-nery
nup-tial
nurs-ery
nur-ture
nut-crack-er
nut-meat
nut-meg
nu-tri-ent
nu-tri-ment
nu-tri-tion
nu-tri-tion-ist
nu-tri-tious
nu-tri-tive
nuz-zle
nylon

O

oak-en
oa-sis
oat-meal
obe-di-ence
obe-di-ent
obei-sance
obese
obe-si-ty
obey
ob-fus-cate

ob-fus-ca-tion
obit-u-ary
ob-ject
ob-jec-tion
ob-jec-tion-able
ob-jec-tive
ob-jec-tive-ly
ob-jec-tiv-i-ty
ob-la-tion
ob-li-gate
ob-li-ga-tion
o-blig-a-to-ry
oblige
ob-li-gee
oblig-ing
oblique
ob-liq-ui-ty
oblit-er-ate
obliv-i-on
obliv-i-ous
ob-long
ob-nox-ious
oboe
ob-scene
ob-scen-i-ty
ob-scure
ob-scu-ri-ty
ob-se-qui-ous
ob-serv-able
ob-ser-vance
ob-ser-vant
ob-ser-va-tion
ob-ser-va-to-ry
ob-serve
ob-serv-er
ob-sess
ob-ses-sion
ob-so-les-cence
ob-so-les-cent
ob-so-lete
ob-sta-cle
ob-ste-tri-cian
ob-stet-rics
ob-sti-na-cy
ob-sti-nate

ob-strep-er-ous
ob-struct
ob-struc-tion
ob-tain
ob-tru-sive
ob-tuse
ob-vi-ate
ob-vi-ous
ob-vi-ous-ly
oc-ca-sion
oc-ca-sion-al
oc-ca-sion-al-ly
oc-ci-dent
oc-ci-den-tal
oc-cip-i-tal
oc-clude
oc-clu-sion
oc-cult
oc-cult-ism
oc-cu-pan-cy
oc-cu-pant
oc-cu-pa-tion
oc-cu-pa-tion-al
oc-cu-py
occur
oc-curred
oc-cur-rence
ocean
ocean-ar-i-um
oce-an-ic
ocean-o-graph-ic
ocean-og-ra-pher
ocean-og-ra-phy
oc-e-lot
o'clock
oc-ta-gon
oc-tag-o-nal
oc-ta-he-dron
oc-tane
oc-tave
Oc-to-ber
oc-to-ge-nar-i-an
oc-to-pus
oc-tu-ple
oc-tup-let

oc-u-lar
oc-u-list
odd-i-ty
odom-e-ter
odor
odor-if-er-ous
odor-ous
od-ys-sey
oed-i-pal
of-fend
of-fend-er
of-fense
of-fen-sive
offer
of-fer-ing
of-fer-to-ry
of-fice
of-fi-cer
of-fi-cial
of-fi-ci-ary
of-fi-ci-ate
of-fi-cious
off-ing
off-set
off-spring
often
ogre
ogre-ish
Ohio
ohm-me-ter
oil-er
oily
oint-ment
Okla-ho-ma
okra
olden
old-ster
ol-fac-tion
ol-fac-to-ry
ol-i-garch
ol-i-gar-chi-cal
ol-i-gar-chy
olive
Olym-pi-an
Olym-pic

om-buds-man
omega
om-e-let
om-i-nous
omis-si-ble
omis-sion
omit
omit-ted
om-ni-bus
om-ni-far-i-ous
om-nip-o-tence
om-nip-o-tent
om-ni-pres-ence
om-ni-pres-ent
om-ni-science
om-nis-cient
om-ni-vore
om-niv-o-rous
on-com-ing
on-er-ous
one-self
one-sid-ed
on-go-ing
onion
on-look-er
only
on-o-mat-o-poe-ia
onset
on-slaught
On-tar-io
onto
on-tog-e-ny
on-to-log-i-cal
on-tol-o-gy
onus
onyx
opal
opaque
open
open-er
open-ing
op-era
op-er-able
op-er-and
op-er-ant

op-er-ate
op-er-at-ic
op-er-a-tion
op-er-a-tion-al
op-er-a-tive
op-er-a-tor
op-e-ret-ta
oph-thal-mic
oph-thal-mol-o-
  gist
oph-thal-mol-o-gy
opi-ate
opin-ion
opin-ion-at-ed
opium
opos-sum
op-po-nent
op-por-tune
op-por-tun-ism
op-por-tun-ist
op-por-tu-ni-ty
op-pos-able
op-pose
op-po-site
op-po-si-tion
op-press
op-pres-sion
op-pres-sive
op-pres-sor
optic
op-ti-cal
op-ti-cian
op-ti-mism
op-ti-mist
op-ti-mis-tic
op-ti-mize
op-ti-mum
op-tion
op-tion-al
op-tom-e-trist
op-tom-e-try
op-u-lent
opus
or-a-cle
orac-u-lar

oral
oral-ly
or-ange
or-ange-ry
or-ange-wood
orang-u-tan
orate
ora-tion
or-a-tor
or-a-tor-i-cal
or-a-to-ry
orbit
or-bit-al
or-bit-ed
or-bit-ing
or-chard
or-ches-tra
or-ches-trate
or-ches-tra-tion
or-chid
or-dain
or-deal
order
or-dered
or-der-ly
or-di-nal
or-di-nance
or-di-nar-i-ly
or-di-nary
oreg-a-no
Or-e-gon
organ
or-gan-dy
or-gan-ic
or-ga-nism
or-gan-ist
or-ga-niz-able
or-ga-ni-za-tion
or-ga-nize
or-ga-niz-er
orgy
ori-ent
Ori-en-tal
ori-en-ta-tion
or-i-fice

or-i-gin
orig-i-nal
orig-i-nal-i-ty
orig-i-nal-ly
orig-i-nate
orig-i-nat-ing
orig-i-na-tion
ori-ole
or-na-ment
or-na-men-tal
or-nate
or-nery
or-ni-thol-o-gy
or-phan
or-phan-age
or-tho-don-tia
or-tho-don-tist
or-tho-dox
or-tho-doxy
or-thog-o-nal
or-tho-pe-dic
or-tho-pe-dist
or-tho-psy-chi-a-
  try
os-cil-late
os-cil-la-tion
os-cil-la-tor
os-cil-la-to-ry
os-mo-sis
os-prey
os-si-cle
os-si-fi-ca-tion
os-si-fy
os-ten-si-ble
os-ten-sive
os-ten-ta-tion
os-ten-ta-tious
os-te-o-path
os-te-op-a-thy
os-tra-cism
os-tra-cize
os-trich
other
oth-er-wise
our-self

our-selves
oust-er
out-break
out-cast
out-come
out-date
out-dat-ed
out-dis-tance
outdo
out-door
outer
out-field
out-fit
outgo
out-go-ing
out-grow
out-guess
out-ing
out-land-ish
out-last
out-law
out-let
out-line
out-live
out-look
out-num-ber
out-pa-tient
out-put
out-rage
out-ra-geous
out-reach
out-ride
out-right
out-run
out-side
out-sid-er
out-skirts
out-smart
out-spo-ken
out-stand
out-stand-ing
out-ward
out-wit
oval
ovar-ian

ovary
ova-tion
oven
over
over-a-bun-dance
over-a-chieve
over-a-chiev-er
over-act
over-bear
over-bear-ing
over-board
over-bur-den
over-cast
over-charge
over-come
over-com-pen-sate
over-com-pen-sa-
    tion
over-de-vel-op
over-do
over-dose
over-draw
over-drawn
over-due
over-es-ti-mate
over-ex-ert
over-ex-pose
over-ex-tend
over-flow
over-haul
over-head
over-hear
over-in-dulge
over-joyed
over-lap
over-load
over-look
over-ly
over-night
over-play
over-pow-er
over-pow-er-ing
over-price
over-ride
over-rid-ing

over-rule
over-run
over-seas
over-see
over-se-er
over-sight
over-sim-pli-fy
over-sleep
over-slept
over-state
overt
over-take
over-throw
over-time
over-ture
over-turn
over-weight
over-whelm
over-whelm-ing
over-work
ovu-late
ovu-la-tion
ovum
owing
owner
own-er-ship
ox-al-ic
ox-i-da-tion
oxide
ox-i-diz-able
ox-i-dize
ox-i-diz-er
ox-y-gen
oys-ter
ozone

P

pac-er
pace-mak-er
pa-chi-si
pach-y-san-dra
Pa-cif-ic
pac-i-fi-ca-tion
pa-ci-fi-er
pa-ci-fism
pac-i-fist

pac-i-fy
pack-age
pack-ag-er
pack-ag-ing
pack-et
pack-ing
pad-ding
pad-dle
pad-dler
pad-dling
pad-dock
pad-lock
pagan
pa-gan-ism
pag-eant
pag-eant-ry
pag-i-nate
pag-i-na-tion
pag-ing
pa-go-da
pain-ful
pain-less
pains-tak-ing
paint-ed
paint-er
paint-ing
pais-ley
Pak-i-stan
Pak-i-stani
pal-ace
pal-at-a-bil-i-ty
pal-at-able
pal-ate (roof of
    mouth)
pa-la-tial
Pa-le-o-lith-ic
pa-le-on-tol-o-gy
Pa-le-o-zo-ic
Pal-es-tine
pal-ette (artist's
    board)
pal-i-sade
pal-la-di-um
pal-let (a bed)
pal-lette (armor)

pal-lid
pal-lor
pal-o-mi-no
pal-pa-ble
pal-pi-tate
pal-pi-ta-tion
palsy
pal-try
pam-per
pam-phlet
pam-phlet-eer
pan-a-cea
Pan-a-ma
pan-cake
pan-cre-as
panda
pan-dem-ic
pan-de-mo-ni-um
Pan-do-ra
pan-e-gyr-ic
pan-e-gy-rize
panel
pan-el-ing
pan-el-ist
panic
pan-icked
pan-o-rama
pan-o-ram-ic
pansy
pan-the-ism
pan-the-on
pan-ther
pan-to-mime
pan-to-mim-ist
pan-try
pa-pa-cy
papal
pa-pa-ya
paper
pa-per-back
pa-per-weight
pa-per-work
pa-pier ma-che
pa-pist
pa-poose

pa-pri-ka
pa-py-rus
par-able
pa-rab-o-la
par-a-bol-ic
par-a-bol-i-cal
par-a-chute
par-a-chut-ist
pa-rade
pa-rad-er
par-a-digm
par-a-dig-ma-tic
par-a-dise
par-a-dox
par-af-fin
par-a-gon
par-a-graph
Par-a-guay
Par-a-guay-an
par-a-keet
par-al-lel
par-al-leled
par-al-lel-ing
par-al-lel-ism
par-al-lel-o-gram
pa-ral-y-sis
par-a-lyt-ic
par-a-ly-za-tion
par-a-lyze
par-a-lyzed
pa-ram-e-ter
par-a-mount
par-a-noia
par-a-noi-ac
par-a-noid
par-a-pet
par-a-pet-ed
par-a-pher-na-lia
par-a-phrase
par-a-ple-gia
par-a-ple-gic
par-a-pro-fes-sion-
   al
par-a-psy-chol-o-
   gy

par-a-site
par-a-sit-ic
par-a-sit-ism
par-a-si-tize
par-a-si-tol-o-gy
par-a-sol
par-a-troop
par-a-troop-er
par-cel
par-celed
parch-ment
par-don
par-don-able
par-don-er
par-ent
par-ent-age
pa-ren-tal
pa-ren-the-sis
par-en-thet-i-cal
par ex-cel-lence
par-fait
pa-ri-ah
pa-ri-e-tal
par-ing
par-ish
pa-rish-ion-er
par-i-ty
parka
park-er
par-lance
par-lay (to bet)
par-lia-ment
par-lia-men-tar-
   i-an
par-lia-men-ta-ry
par-lor
Par-me-san
pa-ro-chi-al
par-o-dy
pa-role
pa-rol-ee
par-ri-cide
par-rot
parry
par-si-mo-ni-ous

par-si-mo-ny
pars-ley
pars-nip
par-son
par-son-age
par-take
par-tak-er
part-ed
par-tial
par-ti-al-i-ty
par-tial-ly
par-tic-i-pant
par-tic-i-pate
par-tic-i-pa-tion
par-tic-i-pa-tor
par-ti-cip-i-al
par-ti-ci-ple
par-ti-cle
par-tic-u-lar
par-tic-u-lar-i-ty
par-tic-u-lar-ly
part-ing
par-ti-san
par-ti-tion
part-ly
part-ner
part-ner-ship
par-tridge
par-tu-ri-tion
party
pass-able
pas-sage
passe
pas-sen-ger
pass-er
pas-si-ble
pass-ing
pas-sion
pas-sion-ate
pas-sive
pas-siv-ist
pas-siv-i-ty
Pass-o-ver
pass-port
pass-word

pasta
pas-tel
pas-tern
pas-teur-i-za-tion
pas-teur-ize
pas-time
pas-tor
pas-to-ral
pas-to-rale
pas-tra-mi
pas-try
pas-ture
patch-work
patchy
pat-ent
pat-ent-ee
pat-en-tor
pa-ter-nal
pa-ter-ni-ty
pa-thet-ic
path-o-gen
path-o-gen-ic
path-o-log-i-cal
pa-thol-o-gist
pa-thol-o-gy
pa-thos
pa-tience
pa-tient
pat-io
pa-tri-arch
pa-tri-ar-chal
pa-tri-ar-chy
pat-ri-cid-al
pat-ri-cide
pa-tri-ot
pa-tri-ot-ic
pa-tri-ot-ism
pa-tris-tic
pa-trol
pa-trolled
pa-trol-ling
pa-tron
pa-tron-age
pa-tron-ess
pa-tron-ize

pa-troon
pat-ter
pat-tern
pat-terned
pau-ci-ty
pau-per
pau-per-ize
paver
pave-ment
pa-vil-ion
pav-ing
Pav-lov-i-an
pay-check
payee
pay-ment
pay-off
pay-roll
peace-ful
peace-time
pea-cock
peaked (topped)
peak-ed (pale)
pea-nut
pearly
peas-ant
peas-ant-ry
peb-ble
pecan
pec-ca-ble
pec-ca-dil-lo
pec-tin
pec-to-ral
pe-cu-liar
pe-cu-li-ar-i-ty
pe-cu-ni-ary
ped-a-gog-ic
ped-a-gog-i-cal
ped-a-gogue
ped-a-go-gy
pedal
ped-aled
ped-ant
pe-dan-tic
ped-ant-ry
ped-dle

ped-dler
ped-es-tal
pe-des-tri-an
pe-di-at-ric
pe-di-a-tri-cian
ped-i-cure
ped-i-gree
peel-er
peel-ing
peep-er
peer-less
pee-vish
pe-jor-a-tive
pel-i-can
pel-let
pel-vic
pel-vis
pem-mi-can
penal
pe-nal-ize
pen-al-ty
pen-ance
pen-chant
pen-cil
pen-ciled
pend-ant (n.)
pend-ent (adj.)
pend-ing
pen-du-lum
pen-e-tra-ble
pen-e-trate
pen-e-trat-ing
pen-e-tra-tion
pen-e-tra-tive
pen-guin
pen-i-cil-lin
pen-in-su-la
pen-in-su-lar
pen-i-tent
pen-i-ten-tia-ry
pen-man-ship
pen-nant
pen-ni-less
Penn-syl-va-nia
penny

pe-nol-o-gy
pen-sion
pen-sion-er
pen-sive
pen-ta-gon
pen-tag-o-nal
pen-tane
pen-tar-chy
Pen-ta-teuch
Pen-te-cost
Pen-te-cos-tal
pe-nu-che
pe-nul-ti-mate
peon
peony
peo-ple
pep-per
pep-per-mint
pep-pery
pep-sin
pep-tic
pep-tide
pep-tone
per-ceiv-able
per-ceive
per-ceiv-er
per-cent-age
per-cent-ile
per-cept
per-cep-ti-ble
per-cep-tion
per-cep-tive
per-cep-tu-al
per-chance
per-co-late
per-co-la-tor
per-cus-sion
per-cus-sion-ist
per-cus-sive
pe-remp-to-ry
pe-ren-ni-al
per-fect
per-fect-ible
per-fec-tion
per-fec-tion-ism

per-fec-tion-ist
per-fect-ly
per-fid-i-ous
per-fi-dy
per-fo-rate
per-fo-ra-ted
per-fo-ra-tion
per-fo-ra-tor
per-form
per-form-ance
per-form-er
per-fume
per-fum-ery
per-func-to-ry
per-haps
per-i-gee
peril
per-il-ous
pe-rim-e-ter
pe-ri-od
pe-ri-od-ic (at
   intervals)
per-i-od-ic
   (chemistry)
pe-ri-od-i-cal
per-i-pa-tet-ic
pe-riph-er-al
pe-riph-er-al-ly
pe-riph-ery
per-i-scope
per-i-scop-ic
per-ish
per-ish-able
per-i-stal-tic
per-i-stal-sis
per-i-win-kle
per-jure
per-jur-er
per-ju-ri-ous
per-ju-ry
per-ma-nence
per-ma-nen-cy
per-ma-nent
per-man-ga-nate
per-me-a-bil-i-ty

per-me-able
per-me-ate
per-mis-si-ble
per-mis-sion
per-mis-sive
per-mit
per-mu-ta-tion
per-ni-cious
per-ox-ide
per-pen-dic-u-lar
per-pe-trate
per-pe-tra-tor
per-pet-u-al
per-pet-u-ate
per-plex
per-plexed
per-plex-i-ty
per-qui-site
per-se-cute
per-se-cu-tion
per-se-cu-tor
per-se-cu-to-ry
per-se-ver-ance
per-sev-er-a-tion
per-se-vere
Per-sia
Per-sian
per-sist
per-sis-tence
per-sis-tent
per-son
per-so-na
per-son-able
per-son-al
per-son-al-i-ty
per-son-al-ize
per-son-al-ly
per-son-i-fi-ca-
   tion
per-son-i-fy
per-son-nel
per-spec-tive
per-spi-cu-i-ty
per-spic-u-ous
per-spi-ra-tion

per-spire
per-suade
per-suad-er
per-sua-si-ble
per-sua-sion
per-sua-sive
per-tain
per-ti-nent
per-turb
per-turb-able
per-tur-ba-tion
pe-rus-al
pe-ruse
Peru
Pe-ru-vi-an
per-vade
per-va-sive
per-verse
per-ver-sion
per-ver-si-ty
per-vert
per-vert-ed
per-vert-ible
per-vi-ous
peso
pes-si-mism
pes-si-mist
pes-si-mis-tic
pes-ter
pes-tered
pes-ti-cide
pes-ti-lence
pes-ti-lent
petal
pet-al-ous
petit (law)
pe-tite
pe-ti-tion
pe-ti-tion-er
pet-ri-fy
pe-tro-chem-i-cal
pe-tro-le-um
pet-ti-coat
petty
pet-u-lant

pe-tu-nia
pew-ter
pfen-nig
phan-tom
Phar-aoh
phar-i-see
phar-ma-ceu-ti-cal
phar-ma-cist
phar-ma-col-o-gy
phar-ma-cy
phar-ynx
phas-er (one who
   phases)
pha-sor
   (electrical)
pheas-ant
phe-no-bar-bi-tal
phe-nom-e-nal
phe-nom-e-no-log-
   i-cal
phe-nom-e-nol-
   o-gy
phe-nom-e-non
phe-no-type
phi-lan-der
phil-an-throp-ic
phi-lan-thro-pist
phi-lan-thro-py
phil-a-tel-ic
phi-lat-e-list
phi-lat-e-ly
phil-har-mon-ic
Phil-ip-pines
phil-o-den-dron
phi-los-o-pher
phil-o-soph-i-cal
phi-los-o-phize
phi-los-o-phiz-er
phi-los-o-phy
phleg-mat-ic
pho-bia
phoe-be
Phoe-ni-cia
Phoe-ni-cian
pho-neme

pho-ne-mic
pho-net-ic
phon-ic
pho-no-graph
pho-no-graph-i-cal
pho-nog-ra-phy
phony
phos-phate
phos-phor
phos-pho-res-
   cence
phos-pho-res-cent
phos-phor-ic
phos-pho-rus
pho-to-cop-i-er
pho-to-copy
pho-to-e-lec-tric
pho-to-gen-ic
pho-to-graph
pho-tog-ra-pher
pho-to-graph-ic
pho-tog-ra-phy
pho-ton
Pho-to-stat
pho-to-syn-the-sis
pho-to-syn-the-
   size
pho-to-tax-is
pho-tot-ro-pism
phra-se-ol-o-gy
phras-ing
phy-log-e-ny
phy-lum
phys-ic
phys-i-cal
phy-si-cian
phys-i-cist
phys-ics
phys-i-o-log-i-cal
phys-i-ol-o-gy
phys-i-o-ther-a-py
pi-a-nis-si-mo
pi-an-ist
piano
pi-an-o-for-te

pica
pic-co-lo
pick-er-el
pick-et
pick-et-er
pick-ing
pick-le
pick-led
pick-ling
pic-nic
pic-nick-er
pic-to-graph
pic-to-graph-ic
pic-tog-ra-phy
pic-to-ri-al
pic-ture
pic-tur-esque
piece de re-sis-
   tance
piece-meal
pied-mont
pierc-er
piety
pi-geon
pig-ment
pig-men-tary
pig-men-ta-tion
pil-fer
pil-fer-age
pil-grim
pil-grim-age
pil-ing
pil-lage
pil-lag-er
pil-lar
pil-low
pilot
pi-lot-ing
pi-men-to
pim-ple
pim-ply
pin-cers
pin-e-al
pine-ap-ple
pin-ion

pink-ish
pin-na-cle
pi-noch-le
pi-non
pin-point
pin-stripe
pinto
pin-wheel
pi-o-neer
pi-o-neered
pious
pipe-line
piper
pip-ing
pi-quan-cy
pi-quant
pi-que (fabric)
pi-ra-cy
pi-ra-nha
pi-rate
pir-ou-ette
pis-tach-io
pis-tol
pis-ton
pitch-er
pit-e-ous
pit-fall
pithy
pit-i-able
pit-i-ful
pit-i-less
pit-tance
pit-ted
pi-tu-i-tary
pity
pivot
piv-ot-al
pizza
piz-ze-ria
plac-able
plac-ard
pla-cate
pla-cat-er
pla-ca-to-ry
pla-ce-bo

place-ment
pla-cen-ta
pla-cen-tal
plac-er
plac-id
pla-cid-i-ty
pla-gia-rism
pla-gia-rize
plain-tiff
plain-tive
pla-nar
plan-er
plan-et
plan-e-tar-i-um
plan-e-tary
plank-ton
plan-ta-tion
plant-er
plas-ma
plas-ter
plas-ter-board
plas-tic
plas-tic-i-ty
plas-tid
pla-teau
plat-ed
plate-ful
plat-form
plat-ing
plat-i-num
plat-i-tude
plat-i-tu-di-nous
pla-ton-ic
pla-toon
plat-ter
plat-y-pus
plau-si-ble
play-er
play-ful
play-house
plaza
plead-er
plead-ing
pleas-ant
pleas-ant-ry

pleas-ing
pleas-ur-able
pleas-ure
ple-be-ian
pleb-i-scite
pledg-ee
pledg-er
ple-na-ry
plen-i-tude
plen-te-ous
plen-ti-ful
plen-ty
ple-num
pleth-o-ra
ple-thor-ic
pleu-ra
pleu-ral
pleu-ri-sy
pli-able
pli-an-cy
pli-ant
pli-ers
plumb-er
plumb-ing
plum-met
plun-der
plu-ral
plu-ral-ism
plu-ral-i-ty
plu-ral-ize
Pluto
plu-to-ni-um
pneu-mo-nia
pneu-mon-ic
poach-er
pock-et
po-di-a-trist
po-di-a-try
po-di-um
poem
poet
po-et-ic
po-et-ry
poign-an-cy
poign-ant

poin-set-tia
point-ed
point-er
point-less
poi-son
poi-son-ous
poker
Po-land
polar
po-lar-i-ty
po-lar-i-za-tion
po-lar-ize
Po-lar-oid
po-lem-ic
po-lice
po-lice-man
po-lice-wom-an
po-lic-ing
pol-i-cy
polio
po-li-o-my-e-li-tis
Pol-ish
pol-ished
po-lit-bu-ro
po-lite
pol-i-tic
po-lit-i-cal
pol-i-ti-cian
pol-i-tics
pol-i-ty
polka
pol-len
pol-li-nate
pol-li-na-tion
pol-lock
pol-lut-ant
pol-lute
pol-lut-er
pol-lu-tion
polo
pol-o-naise
po-lo-ni-um
pol-y-chro-mat-ic
pol-y-es-ter
po-lyg-a-mist

po-lyg-a-my
pol-y-glot
pol-y-gon
pol-y-graph
pol-y-mer
Pol-y-ne-sia
Pol-y-ne-sian
pol-y-no-mi-al
polyp
pol-y-tech-nic
pol-y-the-ism
pome-gran-ate
pom-pa-dour
pom-pos-i-ty
pomp-ous
pon-cho
pon-der
pon-der-able
pon-der-o-sa
pon-der-ous
pon-tiff
pon-tif-i-cal
pon-tif-i-cate
pony
poo-dle
poor-ly
pop-lar
pop-lin
pop-ping
poppy
pop-u-lace
pop-u-lar
pop-u-lar-i-ty
pop-u-lar-ize
pop-u-late
pop-u-la-tion
pop-u-lous
por-ce-lain
por-cu-pine
por-no-graph-ic
por-nog-ra-phy
po-rous
por-poise
por-ridge
port-able

por-tage
por-tal
por-tend
por-tent
por-ten-tous
por-ter
por-ter-house
port-fo-lio
por-tion
por-trait
por-trait-ist
por-tray
por-tray-al
Por-tu-gal
Por-tu-guese
posit
po-si-tion
po-si-tion-er
pos-i-tive
pos-i-tive-ly
pos-i-tiv-ism
pos-i-tron
pos-sess
pos-sessed
pos-sess-es
pos-ses-sion
pos-ses-sive
pos-ses-sor
pos-si-bil-i-ty
pos-si-ble
post-age
post-al
post-er
pos-te-ri-or
pos-ter-i-ty
post-hu-mous
post-hyp-not-ic
post-lude
post-man
post-mark
post-mas-ter
post-op-er-a-tive
post-par-tum
post-pone
post-script

pos-tu-late
pos-tur-al
pos-ture
post-war
po-tas-si-um
po-ta-to
po-ten-cy
po-tent
po-ten-tial
po-ten-ti-al-i-ty
po-tion
pot-pour-ri
pot-ted
pot-ter
pot-tery
poul-tice
poul-try
pounc-er
pound-age
pov-er-ty
pow-der
pow-dered
pow-dery
power
pow-ered
pow-er-ful
pow-er-less
prac-ti-ca-ble
prac-ti-cal
prac-ti-cal-i-ty
prac-ti-cal-ly
prac-tice
prac-ticed
prac-tic-er
prac-ti-tion-er
prag-ma-tic
prag-ma-tism
prai-rie
praise-wor-thy
pra-line
pranc-er
prank-ster
prat-tle
pray-er
preach-er

pre-am-ble
pre-ar-range
Pre-cam-bri-an
pre-car-i-ous
pre-cau-tion
pre-cau-tion-ary
pre-cede
prec-e-dence
prec-e-dent
pre-ced-ing
pre-cept
pre-cep-tor
pre-cinct
pre-ci-os-i-ty
pre-cious
prec-i-pice
pre-cip-i-tant
pre-cip-i-tate
pre-cip-i-ta-tion
pre-cip-i-ta-tor
pre-cip-i-tous
pre-cise
pre-cise-ly
pre-ci-sion
pre-clude
pre-clu-sive
pre-co-cious
pre-co-cious-ly
pre-con-ceive
pre-con-cep-tion
pre-cur-sor
pre-cur-so-ry
pre-da-tion
pred-a-tor
pred-a-to-ry
pred-e-ces-sor
pre-des-ti-nate
pre-des-ti-na-tion
pre-des-tine
pre-de-ter-mi-na-
    tion
pre-de-ter-mine
pred-i-ca-ble
pre-dic-a-ment
pred-i-cate

pred-i-ca-tion
pred-i-ca-to-ry
pre-dict
pre-dict-a-bil-i-ty
pre-dict-able
pre-dic-tion
pre-dic-tor
pred-i-lec-tion
pre-dis-pose
pre-dom-i-nance
pre-dom-i-nant
pre-dom-i-nate
pre-em-i-nent
pre-empt
pre-emp-tion
pre-emp-tive
pre-emp-to-ry
pref-ace
pref-a-to-ry
pre-fer
pref-er-able
pref-er-ence
pref-er-en-tial
pre-fix
preg-nan-cy
preg-nant
pre-his-tor-ic
prej-u-dice
prej-u-di-cial
pre-lim-i-nary
prel-ude
pre-lu-di-al
pre-ma-ture
pre-med-i-cal
pre-med-i-tate
pre-med-i-tat-ed
pre-med-i-ta-tion
pre-mier (adj.)
pre-miere (n.)
prem-ise
pre-mi-um
pre-mo-ni-tion
pre-mon-i-to-ry
pre-oc-cu-pa-tion
pre-oc-cu-pied

pre-oc-cu-py
pre-op-er-a-tive
pre-or-dain
prep-a-ra-tion
pre-par-a-to-ry
pre-pare
pre-par-ed-ness
pre-par-er
pre-pon-der-ance
pre-pon-der-ant
prep-o-si-tion
prep-o-si-tion-al
pre-pos-ter-ous
pre-req-ui-site
pre-rog-a-tive
Pres-by-te-ri-an
pres-by-tery
pre-science
pre-scient
pre-scribe
pre-scrib-er
pre-scrip-ti-ble
pre-scrip-tion
pre-scrip-tive
pres-ence
pres-ent (adj.; n.)
pre-sent (v;
    n., military
    term)
pres-sent-able
pres-en-ta-tion
pre-sen-ti-ment
pres-ent-ly
pres-er-va-tion
pre-serv-a-tive
pre-serve
pre-serv-er
pre-side
pres-i-den-cy
pres-i-dent
pres-i-den-tial
press-ing
pres-sure
pres-sur-ize

pres-tige
pres-tig-ious
pre-sum-able
pre-sume
pre-sump-tion
pre-sump-tive
pre-sump-tu-ous
pre-sup-pose
pre-tend
pre-tend-ed
pre-tend-er
pre-tense
pre-ten-sion
pre-ten-tious
pre-ter-nat-u-ral
pre-test
pre-text
pret-ti-ness
pret-ty
pret-zel
pre-vail
pre-vail-ing
prev-a-lence
prev-a-lent
pre-var-i-cate
pre-var-i-ca-tion
pre-var-i-ca-tor
pre-vent
pre-vent-a-tive
pre-vent-er
pre-ven-tion
pre-ven-tive
pre-view
pre-vi-ous
price-less
prick-le
prick-ly
priest-hood
priest-ly
pri-ma-cy
prima donna
pri-mal
pri-mar-i-ly
pri-mary
pri-mate

prim-er
pri-me-val
prim-i-tive
prim-i-tiv-ism
pri-mo-gen-i-ture
pri-mor-di-al
prim-rose
prince-ly
prin-cess
prin-ci-pal
prin-ci-pal-i-ty
prin-ci-ple
prin-ci-pled
print-er
print-ing
prior
pri-or-i-ty
prism
pris-mat-ic
pris-on
pris-on-er
pris-tine
pri-va-cy
pri-vate
pri-va-tion
priv-i-lege
priv-i-leged
privy
prob-a-bil-i-ty
prob-able
prob-a-bly
pro-bate
pro-ba-tion
pro-ba-tion-er
pro-ba-tive
prob-lem
prob-lem-at-i-cal
pro-ce-dur-al
pro-ce-dure
pro-ceed
pro-ceed-ing
proc-ess (n.; v.)
proc-ess-ing
pro-ces-sion
pro-ces-sion-al

proc-es-sor
pro-claim
proc-la-ma-tion
pro-cliv-i-ty
pro-cras-ti-nate
pro-cras-ti-na-tion
pro-cras-ti-na-tor
pro-cre-ate
pro-cre-a-tor
pro-crus-te-an
proc-tor
pro-cure
pro-cure-ment
pro-cur-er
prod-i-gal
prod-i-gal-i-ty
pro-di-gious
prod-i-gy
pro-duce (v.)
prod-uce (n.)
pro-duc-er
prod-uct
pro-duc-tion
pro-duc-tive
pro-duc-tiv-i-ty
pro-fane
pro-fan-i-ty
pro-fess
pro-fessed
pro-fes-sion
pro-fes-sion-al
pro-fes-sion-al-ism
pro-fes-sor
pro-fes-so-ri-al
prof-fer
prof-fered
pro-fi-cien-cy
pro-fi-cient
pro-file
prof-it
prof-it-able
prof-i-teer
pro-found
pro-fun-di-ty
pro-fuse

pro-fu-sion
pro-gen-i-tor
prog-e-ny
prog-no-sis
prog-nos-tic
prog-nos-ti-cate
prog-nos-ti-ca-
tion
prog-nos-ti-ca-tor
pro-gram
pro-grammed
pro-gram-mer
pro-gram-ming
prog-ress (n.)
pro-gress (v.)
pro-gres-sion
pro-gres-sive
pro-hib-it
pro-hi-bi-tion
pro-hib-i-tive
proj-ect (n.)
pro-ject (v.)
pro-jec-tile
pro-jec-tion
pro-jec-tion-ist
pro-jec-tor
pro-le-tar-i-an
pro-le-tar-i-at
pro-lif-er-ate
pro-lif-er-a-tion
pro-lif-ic
pro-logue
pro-long
pro-lon-ga-tion
prom-e-nade
prom-e-nad-er
pro-me-thi-um
prom-i-nence
prom-i-nent
prom-is-cu-i-ty
pro-mis-cu-ous
prom-ise
prom-is-so-ry
pro-mote
pro-mot-er

pro-mo-tion
prompt-er
prom-ul-gate
pro-mul-ga-tion
pro-mul-ga-tor
pro-noun
pro-nounce
pro-nounced
pro-nounce-ment
pro-nun-ci-a-tion
proof-read
prop-a-gan-da
prop-a-gan-dist
prop-a-gan-dize
prop-a-gate
prop-a-ga-tion
prop-a-ga-tor
pro-pane
pro-pel
pro-pel-lant
pro-pel-ler
pro-pen-si-ty
prop-er
prop-er-ly
prop-er-ty
proph-e-cy (n.)
proph-e-sy (v.)
proph-et
pro-phet-ic
pro-pin-qui-ty
pro-po-nent
pro-por-tion
pro-por-tion-al
pro-por-tion-ate
pro-pos-al
pro-pose
prop-o-si-tion
pro-pri-e-tary
pro-pri-e-tor
pro-pri-e-ty
pro-pul-sion
pro-pul-sive
pro-rat-able
pro-rate
pro-sa-ic

pro-sa-i-cal-ly
pro-scribe
pro-scrip-tion
pro-scrip-tive
pros-e-cute
pros-e-cu-tion
pros-e-cu-tor
pros-e-lyte
pros-e-lyt-ize
pros-e-lyt-iz-er
pros-pect
pro-spec-tive
pros-pec-tor
pro-spec-tus
pros-per
pros-per-i-ty
pros-per-ous
pros-the-sis
pros-thet-ic
pros-ti-tute
pros-trate
pro-tag-o-nist
pro-te-an
pro-tect
pro-tec-tion
pro-tec-tive
pro-tec-tor
pro-te-ge
pro-tein
pro-test
Prot-es-tant
pro-test-er
pro-to-col
pro-ton
pro-to-plasm
pro-to-type
pro-to-typ-i-cal
pro-to-zoa
pro-to-zo-an
pro-tract
pro-tract-ible
pro-trac-tor
pro-trude
pro-tru-sion
pro-tru-sive

pro-tu-ber-ance
pro-tu-ber-ant
prov-able
prov-en
prov-erb
pro-ver-bi-al
pro-vide
pro-vid-ed
prov-i-dence
prov-i-dent
prov-i-den-tial
pro-vid-er
pro-vid-ing
prov-ince
pro-vin-cial
pro-vi-sion
pro-vi-sion-al
pro-vi-so
pro-vi-so-ry
prov-o-ca-tion
pro-voc-a-tive
pro-voke
pro-vost
prow-ess
prowl-er
prox-i-mal
prox-i-mate
prox-im-i-ty
proxy
pru-dence
pru-dent
pru-den-tial
prud-ish
psalm-ist
pseu-do
pseu-do-nym
pso-ri-a-sis
psy-che
psych-e-del-ic
psy-chi-at-ric
psy-chi-a-trist
psy-chi-a-try
psy-chic
psy-chi-cal
psy-cho-a-nal-y-sis

psy-cho-an-a-lyst
psy-cho-an-a-lyt-
  ic
psy-cho-an-a-lyze
psy-cho-dra-ma
psy-cho-dy-nam-
  ics
psy-cho-gen-ic
psy-cho-log-i-cal
psy-chol-o-gist
psy-chol-o-gy
psy-cho-met-rics
psy-cho-path
psy-cho-pa-thol-
  o-gy
psy-cho-sis
psy-cho-so-mat-ic
psy-cho-sur-ger-y
psy-cho-ther-a-py
psy-chot-ic
pto-maine
pu-ber-ty
pubic
pub-lic
pub-li-ca-tion
pub-li-cist
pub-lic-i-ty
pub-li-cize
pub-lic-ly
pub-lish
pub-lish-er
pud-ding
pud-dle
pudgy
pueb-lo
Puer-to Rico
pu-gi-lism
pu-gi-list
pu-gi-lis-tic
pug-na-cious
pug-nac-i-ty
Pul-it-zer
pul-ley
pul-mo-nary
pul-pit

pul-sate
pul-sa-tion
pul-ver-ize
pum-ice
pum-per-nick-el
pump-kin
punc-til-i-ous
punc-tu-al
punc-tu-al-i-ty
punc-tu-ate
punc-tu-a-tion
punc-tur-able
punc-ture
punc-tured
pun-gen-cy
pun-gent
pun-ish
pun-ish-able
pun-ish-er
pun-ish-ment
pu-ni-tive
pun-ster
pupa
pu-pil
pup-pet
pup-pet-eer
pup-pet-ry
puppy
pur-chas-able
pur-chase
pur-chas-er
pure-bred
puree
pure-ly
pur-ga-tive
pur-ga-to-ry
pu-ri-fi-ca-tion
pu-ri-fy
pur-ist
Pu-ri-tan
pu-ri-tan-i-cal
pu-ri-ty
pur-ple
pur-plish
pur-port

pur-port-ed-ly
pur-pose
pur-pose-ful
pur-pose-ly
pur-po-sive
pur-su-ance
pur-su-ant
pur-sue
pur-suit
pur-vey-or
pu-ta-tive
pu-tre-fy
pu-trid
put-ter
putty
puz-zle
putt-er (golf)
puz-zler
puz-zle-ment
Pyg-ma-li-on
pygmy
pylon
pyr-a-mid
py-ram-i-dal
Pyr-e-nees
Py-rex
py-rite
py-ro-ma-ni-a
py-thon

Q

quad-ran-gle
quad-rant
quad-ra-tic
quad-ri-lat-er-al
quad-ri-ple-gia
quad-ri-ple-gic
quad-ru-ped
quad-ru-ple
quad-ru-plet
quag-mire
Quak-er
qual-i-fi-ca-tion
qual-i-fied
qual-i-fi-er
qual-i-fy

qual-i-ta-tive
qual-i-ty
quan-da-ry
quan-ti-fy
quan-ti-ta-tive
quan-ti-ty
quan-tum
quar-an-tine
quar-rel
quar-reled
quar-rel-some
quar-ry
quar-ter
quar-ter-ly
quar-tet
quasi
quea-sy
query
ques-tion
ques-tion-able
ques-tion-naire
quib-ble
quick-en
quick-ly
quiet
qui-et-ly
qui-e-tude
quilt-ing
qui-nine
quin-tes-sence
quin-tet
quin-tu-ple
quin-tu-plet
quiv-er
quiv-ered
quiz-zi-cal
quo-rum
quota
quot-able
quo-ta-tion
quot-er
quo-tient

R

rabbi
rab-bit

rabid
ra-bid-i-ty
ra-bies
rac-coon
racer
race-way
ra-cial
ra-cial-ly
rac-ing
ra-cism
rac-ist
rack-et
rack-et-eer
racy
radar
ra-di-al
ra-di-ance
ra-di-ant
ra-di-ate
ra-di-a-tion
ra-di-a-tor
rad-i-cal
radio
ra-di-o-ac-tive
ra-di-o-ac-tiv-i-ty
ra-di-o-broad-cast
rad-ish
ra-di-um
ra-di-us
radon
raf-fle
raf-ter
rag-ged
rag-lan
raid-er
rail-ing
rail-ery
rail-road
rail-way
rain-bow
rain-fall
rain-storm
rais-er
rai-sin

rais-ing
ral-ly
ram-ble
ram-bler
ram-bling
ram-bunc-tious
ram-i-fi-ca-tion
ram-page
ram-pant
ram-part
ranch-er
ran-cid
ran-cor
ran-cor-ous
ran-dom
ran-dom-i-za-tion
ran-dom-ize
rang-er
ran-kle
ran-kled
ran-sack
ran-som
ran-som-er
rapid
ra-pid-i-ty
rap-pel
rap-port
rap-proche-ment
rap-ture
rap-tur-ous
rare-ly
rar-i-ty
ras-cal
ras-cal-i-ty
rasp-ber-ry
raspy
rater
rath-er
rat-i-fi-ca-tion
rat-i-fy
rat-ing
ratio
ra-tion
ra-tion-al
ra-tion-ale

ra-tion-al-i-ty
ra-tion-al-i-za-tion
ra-tion-al-ize
rat-tle
rat-tler
rat-tle-snake
rau-cous
rav-age
rav-ag-er
ravel
rav-eled
rav-el-ing
raven
rav-en-ous
ra-vine
rav-ing
ra-vi-o-li
rav-ish-ing
raw-hide
razor
react
re-ac-tance
re-ac-tion
re-ac-tion-ary
re-ac-ti-vate
re-ac-tive
re-ac-tor
read-er
read-er-ship
read-i-ness
read-ing
re-ad-just
ready
re-af-firm
re-a-gent
real
re-al-ism
re-al-ist
re-al-is-tic
re-al-i-ty
re-al-i-za-tion
re-al-ize
re-al-ly
re-al-tor
re-al-ty

reap-er
re-ar-range
rea-son
rea-son-able
rea-son-ing
re-as-sure
re-bate
re-bat-er
rebel
re-bel-lion
re-bel-lious
re-birth
re-born
re-bound
re-buff
re-build
re-buke
rebut
re-but-tal
re-cal-ci-trant
re-call
re-cant
re-ca-pit-u-la-tion
re-cede
re-ceipt
re-ceiv-able
re-ceive
re-ceiv-er
re-cent
re-cep-ta-cle
re-cep-tion
re-cep-tion-ist
re-cep-tive
re-cep-tor
re-cess
re-ces-sion-al
re-ces-sive
rec-i-pe
re-cip-i-ence
re-cip-i-ent
re-cip-ro-cal
re-cip-ro-cate
re-cip-ro-ca-tion
rec-i-proc-i-ty
re-ci-sion

re-cit-al
rec-i-ta-tion
re-cite
reck-less
reck-on
reck-on-ing
re-claim
rec-li-na-tion
re-cline
re-clin-er
rec-luse
re-clu-sion
re-clu-sive
rec-og-ni-tion
re-cog-ni-zance
rec-og-nize
re-coil
re-col-lect (collect
    again)
rec-ol-lect (re-
    member)
rec-om-mend
rec-om-men-da-
    tion
rec-om-pense
rec-on-cil-able
rec-on-cile
rec-on-cil-er
rec-on-cil-i-a-tion
re-con-nais-sance
rec-on-noi-ter
re-con-sid-er
re-con-struc-tion
rec-ord (adj., n.)
re-cord (v.)
re-cord-er
re-cord-ing
re-coup
re-course
re-cov-er
re-cov-ery
rec-re-ate
    (refresh)
re-cre-ate (create
    again)

rec-re-a-tion
re-cre-a-tion
re-cruit
re-cruit-er
re-cruit-ment
rec-tan-gle
rec-tan-gu-lar
rec-ti-fi-er
rec-ti-fy
rec-tor
rec-to-ry
rec-tum
re-cum-bent
re-cu-per-ate
re-cu-per-a-tion
re-cu-per-a-tive
recur
re-cur-rence
re-cur-rent
re-cy-cle
red-den
re-dec-o-rate
re-dec-o-ra-tion
re-deem
re-deem-er
re-demp-tion
re-dis-trib-ute
re-duce
re-duc-er
re-duc-ible
re-duc-tion
re-dun-dan-cy
re-dun-dant
reef-er
re-fec-to-ry
refer
ref-er-able
ref-er-ee
ref-er-ence
ref-er-en-dum
ref-er-ent
re-fer-ring
re-fine
re-fine-ment
re-fin-ery

re-fin-ish
re-flect
re-flec-tion
re-flec-tive
re-flec-tor
re-flex
re-flex-ive
re-flex-iv-i-ty
re-for-est
re-for-est-a-tion
re-form
ref-or-ma-tion
re-form-a-to-ry
re-formed
re-form-er
re-fract
re-frac-tion
re-frac-tive
re-frac-to-ry
re-frain
re-fresh
re-fresh-ing
re-fresh-ment
re-frig-er-ate
re-frig-er-at-ing
re-frig-er-a-tion
re-frig-er-a-tor
ref-uge
ref-u-gee
re-fund
re-fur-bish
re-fus-al
re-fuse (v.)
ref-use (adj.; n.)
ref-u-ta-tion
re-fute
re-fut-er
re-gain
regal
re-ga-lia
re-gard
re-gard-ing
re-gard-less
re-gard-less-ly
re-gat-ta

re-gen-cy
re-gen-er-ate
re-gen-er-a-tion
re-gen-er-a-tive
re-gen-er-a-tor
re-gent
re-gime
reg-i-men
reg-i-ment
reg-i-men-tal
reg-i-men-ta-ry
re-gion
re-gion-al
reg-is-ter
reg-is-tered
reg-is-tra-ble
reg-is-trar
reg-is-tra-tion
reg-is-try
re-gress
re-gres-sion
re-gres-sive
re-gret
re-gret-ful
re-gret-ta-ble
reg-u-lar
reg-u-lar-i-ty
reg-u-lar-ly
reg-u-late
reg-u-la-tion
reg-u-la-tive
reg-u-la-to-ry
re-gur-gi-tate
re-ha-bil-i-tate
re-ha-bil-i-ta-tive
re-hears-al
re-im-burse
re-in-car-nate
rein-deer
re-in-force
re-in-forced
re-in-force-ment
re-it-er-ate
re-ject
re-ject-er

re-joice
re-joic-ing
re-join
re-join-der
re-ju-ve-nate
re-ju-ve-na-tion
re-ju-ve-na-tor
re-lapse
re-late
re-lat-ed
re-la-tion
re-la-tion-ship
rel-a-tive
rel-a-tiv-ism
rel-a-tiv-i-ty
relax
re-lax-ant
re-lax-a-tion
relay
re-lease
re-leas-er
re-lent
re-lent-less
rel-e-vant
re-li-able
re-li-ance
re-li-ant
relic
re-lief
re-lieve
re-liev-er
re-li-gion
re-li-gi-os-i-ty
re-li-gious
re-lin-quish
rel-ish
re-lo-cate
re-luc-tance
rely
re-main
re-main-der
re-mark
re-mark-able
re-me-di-able

re-me-di-al
rem-e-dy
re-mem-ber
re-mem-brance
re-mind
re-mind-er
rem-i-nisce
rem-i-nis-cence
rem-i-nis-cent
re-miss
re-mis-sion
remit
re-mit-tance
rem-nant
re-mod-el
re-mod-eled
re-morse
re-morse-less
re-mote
re-mov-able
re-mov-al
re-move
re-moved
re-mu-ner-ate
re-mu-ner-a-tion
re-mu-ner-a-tive
ren-ais-sance
renal
ren-der
ren-dez-vous
ren-di-tion
ren-e-gade
re-nege
re-ne-go-ti-ate
renew
re-new-al
re-nounce
ren-o-vate
ren-o-va-tion
ren-o-va-tor
re-nown
re-nowned
rent-al
rent-er
re-nun-ci-a-tion

re-nun-ci-a-to-ry
re-o-pen
re-or-der
re-or-gan-i-za-tion
re-or-gan-ize
re-pair
re-pair-able
rep-a-ra-ble
rep-a-ra-tion
re-past
repay
re-peal
re-peat
re-peat-ed
re-peat-er
repel
re-pel-lant
re-pent
re-pen-tance
re-per-cus-sion
rep-er-toire
rep-er-to-ry
rep-e-ti-tion
rep-e-ti-tious
re-pet-i-tive
re-place
re-place-able
re-place-ment
re-plen-ish
re-plen-ish-er
re-plete
rep-li-ca
rep-li-cate
rep-li-ca-tion
reply
re-port
re-port-er
re-pose
re-pos-sess
rep-re-hend
rep-re-hen-si-ble
rep-re-hen-sion
rep-re-sent
rep-re-sen-ta-tion
rep-re-sen-ta-tive

re-press
re-press-ible
re-pres-sion
re-pres-sive
re-prieve
rep-ri-mand
re-print
re-pris-al
re-proach
re-proach-ful
re-pro-duce
re-pro-duc-ible
re-pro-duc-tion
re-prove
rep-tile
rep-til-i-an
re-pub-lic
Re-pub-li-can
re-pu-di-ate
re-pu-di-a-tion
re-pu-di-a-tor
re-pug-nance
re-pug-nant
re-pulse
re-pul-sion
re-pul-sive
rep-u-ta-ble
rep-u-ta-tion
re-pute
re-quest
re-qui-em
re-quire
re-quired
re-quire-ment
re-quir-er
req-ui-site
req-ui-si-tion
re-scind
re-scis-sion
res-cu-able
res-cue
res-cu-er
re-search
re-search-er
re-sem-blance

re-sem-ble
re-sent
re-sent-ful
re-sent-ment
res-er-va-tion
re-serve
re-served
res-er-voir
re-side
res-i-dence
res-i-den-cy
res-i-dent
res-i-den-tial
re-sid-u-al
res-i-due
re-sign
res-ig-na-tion
re-sil-ience
re-sil-ien-cy
resin
re-sist
re-sist-ance
re-sist-er (one who
   resists)
re-sist-ible
re-sis-tor (device)
re-sol-u-ble
res-o-lute
res-o-lu-tion
re-solve
res-o-nance
res-o-nant
res-o-nate
res-o-na-tor
re-sort
re-source
re-source-ful
re-spect
re-spect-a-bil-i-ty
re-spect-able
re-spec-tive
re-spec-tive-ly
res-pi-ra-tion
res-pi-ra-tor
res-pi-ra-to-ry

res-pite
re-splend-ent
re-spond
re-spon-dent
re-sponse
re-spon-si-bil-i-ty
re-spon-si-ble
re-spon-sive
res-tau-rant
res-tau-ra-teur
rest-ful
rest-ing
res-ti-tute
res-ti-tu-tion
res-tive
rest-less
res-to-ra-tion
re-stor-a-tive
re-store
re-strain
re-straint
re-strict
re-strict-ed
re-stric-tion
re-stric-tive
re-sult
re-sul-tant
re-sume (v.)
re-su-me (n.)
re-sump-tion
re-surge
re-sur-gent
res-ur-rec-tion
re-sus-ci-tate
re-sus-ci-ta-tor
re-tail
re-tain
re-tain-er
re-tal-i-ate
re-tal-i-a-tion
re-tal-i-a-to-ry
re-tard
re-tar-date
re-tar-da-tion
re-tard-ed

re-ten-tion
re-ten-tive
ret-i-cence
ret-i-cent
ret-i-na
re-tire
re-tired
re-tire-ment
re-tort
re-tort-er
re-tract
re-tract-able
re-trac-tion
re-treat
ret-ri-bu-tion
re-trib-u-tive
re-triev-able
re-triev-al
re-trieve
re-triev-er
ret-ro-ac-tive
ret-ro-spect
ret-ro-spec-tive
re-turn
re-turn-able
re-un-ion
re-u-nite
re-vamp
re-veal
rev-eil-le
revel
rev-e-la-tion
rev-eled
re-venge
rev-e-nue
re-ver-ber-ate
re-vere
rev-er-ence
rev-er-end
rev-er-ent
rev-er-ie
re-ver-sal
re-verse
re-vers-ible
re-vert

re-view
re-view-er
re-vise
re-vised
re-vis-er
re-vi-sion
re-viv-al
re-vive
rev-o-ca-ble
rev-o-ca-tion
re-voke
re-volt
re-volt-er
re-volt-ing
rev-o-lu-tion
rev-o-lu-tion-ary
rev-o-lu-tion-ize
re-volve
re-volv-er
re-vul-sion
re-ward
rhap-so-dy
rhe-ni-um
rhe-sus
rhet-o-ric
rhe-to-ri-cal
rheu-mat-ic
rheu-ma-tism
rhine-stone
rhi-noc-er-os
Rhode Is-land
Rho-de-sia
Rho-de-sian
rho-di-um
rho-do-den-dron
rhom-bus
rhu-barb
rhythm
rhyth-mi-cal
rib-bing
rib-bon
ri-bo-fla-vin
ri-bo-nu-cle-ic
ri-bose
ri-bo-some

rich-es
Rich-ter
rick-ets
ric-o-chet
ric-o-cheted
ri-cot-ta
rid-dle
rid-dled
rider
rid-i-cule
ri-dic-u-lous
rid-ing
rifle
ri-fle-ry
rig-ging
right-eous
right-ful
right-ly
rigid
ri-gid-i-ty
rig-id-ly
rigor
rig-or-ous
ring-er
ring-side
riot
ri-ot-er
ri-ot-ous
ripen
rip-ple
riser
ris-ing
risky
ris-que
rit-u-al
rit-u-al-is-tic
rival
ri-valed
ri-val-ry
river
rivet
roast-er
rob-ber
rob-bery
robin

robot
ro-bust
rock-er
rock-et
rock-et-eer
rock-et-ry
rocky
ro-dent
rodeo
ro-guish
roll-er
rol-lick-ing
ro-maine
Ro-man
ro-mance
Ro-man-esque
Ro-ma-nia
Ro-ma-ni-an
ro-man-tic
ro-man-ti-cism
ro-man-ti-cist
ro-man-ti-cize
roof-er
roof-ing
room-er
room-mate
roomy
Roo-se-velt
roost-er
roper
Roque-fort
Ror-schach
ro-sa-ry
rose
rose-mary
Rosh Ha-sha-na
rosin
ros-ter
rosy
ro-ta-ry
ro-tat-able
ro-tate
ro-ta-tion
ro-tis-se-rie
rot-ten

ro-tund
ro-tun-da
ro-tun-di-ty
rou-ble
rough-age
rough-er
rou-lette
round-up
rous-ing
rou-tine
rover
royal
Roy-al-ist
roy-al-ty
rub-ber
rub-bing
rub-bish
rub-ble
ru-bel-la
ru-bid-i-um
ru-bric
ruby
rud-der
rud-dy
rude-ly
rude-ness
ru-di-ment
ru-di-men-ta-ry
rue-ful
ruf-fi-an
ruf-fle
rug-by
rug-ged
ruin
ru-ined
ru-in-ous
ruler
rul-ing
rum-ble
ru-mi-nate
ru-mi-na-tion
rum-mage
rummy
rumor
rum-ple

rum-pled
run-a-way
run-ner
run-ning
run-way
rupee
rup-ture
rup-tured
rural
rus-set
Rus-sia
Rus-sian
rus-tic
rus-tle
rus-tler
rusty
ru-the-ni-um
ruth-less

S

Sab-bath
sab-bat-i-cal
saber
sab-o-tage
sab-o-teur
sac-cha-rine
sa-chet
sac-ra-ment
sac-ra-men-tal
sa-cred
sac-ri-fice
sac-ri-fi-cial
sac-ri-lege
sac-ri-le-gious
sac-ro-sanct
sad-den
sad-dle
sad-dlery
sa-dism
sa-dist
sa-dis-tic
sa-fa-ri
safe-guard
safe-keep-ing
safe-ty
saf-flow-er

saf-fron
saga
sa-ga-cious
sa-gac-i-ty
sage-brush
Sa-hara
sail-ing
sail-or
saint-ly
sal-able
salad
sal-a-man-der
sa-la-mi
sal-a-ried
sal-a-ry
sales-man
sales-per-son
sales-wom-an
sa-li-ence
sa-li-ent
sa-line
sa-lin-i-ty
sa-li-va
sal-i-vary
sal-i-vate
sal-i-va-tion
salm-on
salon
sa-loon
salty
sal-u-tary
sal-u-ta-tion
sa-lu-ta-to-ri-an
sa-lu-ta-to-ry
sa-lute
sal-va-ble
Sal-va-dor
sal-vage
sal-vage-able
sal-vag-er
sal-va-tion
Sa-mar-i-tan
samba
same-ness
Samoa

sam-ple
sam-pling
san-a-to-ri-um
sanc-ti-fi-ca-tion
sanc-ti-fied
sanc-ti-fy
sanc-tion
sanc-ti-ty
sanc-tu-ary
sanc-tum
san-dal
sand-er
sand-stone
sand-storm
sand-wich
sandy
San-for-ized
san-gria
san-guine
san-i-tar-i-an
san-i-tar-i-um
san-i-tary
san-i-ta-tion
san-i-ty
San-skrit
Santa Claus
Santo Do-min-go
sap-ling
sap-phire
sappy
sap-suck-er
sar-casm
sar-cas-tic
sar-coph-a-gus
sar-dine
sar-don-ic
sari
sa-rong
sas-sa-fras
sassy
Satan
sa-tan-ic
satch-el
sat-el-lite
sa-ti-ate

sa-ti-e-ty
satin
sat-ire
sa-tir-i-cal
sat-i-rize
sat-is-fac-tion
sat-is-fac-to-ri-ly
sat-is-fac-to-ry
sat-is-fy
sat-u-rate
sat-u-rat-ed
sat-u-ra-tion
Sat-ur-day
Sat-urn
sau-cer
saucy
Saudi A-ra-bia
sauer-bra-ten
sauer-kraut
sauna
saun-ter
sau-rel
sau-sage
saute
sau-teed
sau-terne
sav-age
sa-van-na
sa-vant
sav-ing
sav-ior
sa-voir faire
savor
sa-vory
sax-o-phone
say-ing
scaf-fold
scaf-fold-ing
scal-lion
scal-lop
scal-loped
scal-pel
scam-per
scam-pi
scan-dal

scan-dal-ize
scan-dal-ous
Scan-di-na-via
Scan-di-na-vi-an
scan-di-um
scan-ner
scan-ning
scanty
scape-goat
scarce-ly
scar-ci-ty
scar-let
scary
scath-ing
scat-ter
scat-tered
scat-ter-ing
scav-enge
scav-en-ger
sce-nar-io
scep-ter
sched-ule
sche-ma
sche-mat-ic
schil-ling
schiz-oid
schiz-o-phre-nia
schiz-o-phren-ic
schnau-zer
schnit-zel
schol-ar
schol-ar-ly
schol-ar-ship
scho-las-tic
school-ing
schoo-ner
sci-ence
sci-en-tif-ic
sci-en-tist
scin-til-late
scin-til-la-tion
scis-sors
scle-ro-sis
scold-ing
scoot-er

scorn-er
scorn-ful
scorn-ful-ly
scor-pi-on
Scot-land
Scots-man
Scot-tish
scoun-drel
scout-ing
scrab-ble
scram-ble
scram-bling
scrap-er
scrap-ing
scream-er
screen-er
screen-ing
scrib-ble
scrib-bler
scrim-mage
scrip-tur-al
Scrip-ture
scru-ple
scru-pu-lous
scru-ti-nize
scru-ti-ny
scuba
scuf-fle
sculp-tor
sculp-tur-al
sculp-ture
scur-ry
scur-vy
seal-ant
seal-er
seam-less
seam-stress
se-ance
search-light
sea-sick-ness
sea-son
sea-son-able
sea-son-al
sea-son-ing
seat-ing

se-ba-ceous
se-cant
se-cede
se-ces-sion
se-clude
se-clud-ed
se-clu-sion
sec-ond
sec-ond-ar-i-ly
sec-ond-ary
se-cre-cy
se-cret
sec-re-tar-i-al
sec-re-tar-i-at
sec-re-tary
se-crete
se-cre-tion
se-cre-tive
se-cre-to-ry
sec-tion
sec-tion-al
sec-tion-al-ize
sec-tor
sec-u-lar
sec-u-lar-ism
sec-u-lar-ize
se-cure
se-cu-ri-ty
sedan
se-date
se-da-tion
sed-a-tive
sed-en-tary
sed-i-ment
sed-i-men-ta-ry
se-duce
se-duc-tion
se-duc-tive
seed-ling
seep-age
seer-suck-er
seg-ment
seg-re-gate
seg-re-ga-tion
seign-ior

seis-mic
seis-mo-graph
seiz-ing
sei-zure
sel-dom
se-lect
se-lec-tion
se-lec-tive
se-lec-tiv-i-ty
se-le-ni-um
self-ish
selt-zer
sel-vage
se-man-tic
sem-blance
se-mes-ter
sem-i-an-nu-al
sem-i-fi-nal
sem-i-for-mal
sem-i-month-ly
sem-i-nar
sem-i-nary
sem-i-pri-vate
sem-i-pro-fes-sion-
    al
Se-mit-ic
Sem-i-tism
sem-i-week-ly
sem-i-year-ly
sen-ate
sen-a-tor
Sen-e-gal
Sen-e-gal-ese
se-nile
se-nil-i-ty
sen-ior
se-nior-i-ty
se-nor
se-no-ri-ta
sen-sa-tion
sen-sa-tion-al
sen-si-bil-i-ty
sen-si-ble
sen-si-tive
sen-si-tiv-i-ty

sen-si-tize
sen-so-ry
sen-su-al
sen-su-al-i-ty
sen-su-ous
sen-tence
sen-ti-ment
sen-ti-men-tal
sen-ti-men-tal-i-ty
sen-ti-nel
sen-try
sep-a-ra-ble
sep-a-rate
sep-a-ra-tion
sep-a-rat-ist
sep-a-ra-tor
Sep-tem-ber
sep-ten-ni-al
sep-tet
sep-tic
sep-tu-a-ge-nar-
    i-an
sep-tu-ple
sep-tu-plet
sep-ul-cher
se-pul-chral
se-quel
se-quence
se-quen-tial
se-ques-ter
se-ques-tered
se-quin
ser-aph
Ser-bia
Ser-bi-an
ser-e-nade
ser-e-nad-er
ser-en-dip-i-ty
se-rene
se-ren-i-ty
ser-geant
se-ri-al
se-ries
se-ri-ous
se-ri-ous-ly

ser-mon
ser-mon-ize
se-ro-ton-in
ser-pent
ser-vant
serv-er
ser-vice
ser-vice-able
ser-vile
serv-ing
ser-vi-tude
ses-a-me
ses-sion
set-ter
set-tle
set-tle-ment
set-tler
seven
sev-en-teen
sev-en-teenth
sev-enth
sev-en-ti-eth
sev-en-ty
sever
sev-er-al
sev-er-ance
se-vere
sev-ered
se-ver-i-ty
sew-age
sewer
sew-ing
sex-a-ge-nar-i-an
sex-en-ni-al
sex-ism
sex-tant
sex-tet
sex-ton
sex-tu-ple
sex-tu-plet
sex-u-al
sex-u-al-i-ty
sfor-zan-do
shack-le
shack-led

shad-ow
shady
shak-er
Shake-spear-e-an
shaky
shal-lot
shal-low
sham-bles
shame-ful
shame-less
shame-less-ly
sham-poo
sham-rock
shang-hai
shan-ty
shape-ly
sharp-en
sharp-en-ing
sharp-er
shat-ter
shat-tered
shav-er
shav-ing
sheep-ish
sheet-ing
shel-lac
shel-lack-ing
shel-ter
shel-tered
shelv-ing
shep-herd
sher-bet
sher-iff
sher-ry
Shet-land
shield-er
shil-ling
shin-gle
shin-gled
ship-ment
ship-ping
shiv-er
shiv-ered
shock-ing
shop-per

short-age
short-com-ing
short-en
short-ly
shot-gun
shoul-der
shoul-dered
shov-el
shov-eled
shov-el-er
show-case
show-er
show-ery
show-ing
showy
shrap-nel
shrewd-ness
shrink-age
shriv-el
shriv-eled
shrub-bery
shud-der
shuf-fle
shuf-fled
shut-ter
Si-a-mese
Si-be-ria
sib-ling
Si-cil-ian
Sic-i-ly
sick-en
sick-en-ing
sick-le
sick-ly
sick-ness
sided
side-walk
side-ways
sid-ing
si-er-ra
sight-see-ing
sigma
sig-nal
sig-naled
sig-na-ture

sig-nif-i-cance
sig-nif-i-cant
sig-ni-fy
si-gnor
si-gno-ra
si-lence
si-lenc-er
si-lent
sil-hou-ette
sil-i-con
silk-en
silky
silly
silo
sil-ver
sil-ver-ware
sil-very
sim-i-lar
sim-i-lar-i-ty
sim-i-le
si-mil-i-tude
sim-mer
si-mon-ize
sim-ple
sim-plic-i-ty
sim-pli-fy
sim-ply
sim-u-late
sim-u-la-tion
sim-u-la-tor
si-mul-ta-ne-ous
sin-cere
sin-cer-i-ty
sinew
sin-ewy
sing-er
sin-gle
sin-gly
sin-gu-lar
sin-gu-lar-i-ty
sin-is-ter
sin-ner
sin-u-ous
si-nus
si-phon

siren
sir-loin
sis-ter
sitar
sit-ting
sit-u-ate
sit-u-at-ed
sit-u-a-tion
six-teen
six-teenth
six-ti-eth
sixty
siz-able
siz-ing
siz-zle
siz-zled
skat-er
skel-e-tal
skel-e-ton
skep-tic
skep-ti-cal
skep-ti-cism
sketchy
skew-er
skil-let
skill-ful
skill-ful-ness
skip-per
skir-mish
skit-tish
sky-line
slack-en
slack-ened
sla-lom
slan-der
slan-der-ous
slaugh-ter
slaugh-ter-house
slav-ery
slav-ish
sleep-er
sleep-ing
sleepy
slen-der
slic-er

slid-ing
slight-ly
slip-per
sliv-er
slo-gan
sloth-ful
slov-en-ly
slug-gish
slum-ber
small-pox
smart-en
smat-ter
smock-ing
smoky
smok-er
smol-der
smol-dered
smor-gas-bord
smoth-er
smoth-ered
smug-gle
smug-gler
snap-per
snatch-er
sneak-er
sneak-i-ness
sneak-ing
snick-er-ing
snif-fle
snif-ter
snip-er
sniv-el
sniv-el-er
snob-bery
snob-bish
snor-kel
snow-ball
snow-fall
snow-flake
snow-mo-bile
snow-plow
snowy
snug-gle
snug-gled
soap-box

soapy
sober
so-bri-e-ty
soc-cer
so-cia-bil-i-ty
so-cia-ble
so-cial
so-cial-ism
so-cial-ist
so-cial-is-tic
so-cial-ite
so-cial-ize
so-cial-ly
so-ci-e-tal
so-ci-e-ty
so-ci-ol-o-gist
so-ci-ol-o-gy
so-ci-om-e-try
sock-et
So-crat-ic
soda
so-di-um
sofa
soft-ball
sof-ten
soft-en-er
soft-ware
soggy
soi-ree
so-journ
so-journ-er
sol-ace
solar
so-lar-i-um
sol-der
sol-dered
sol-dier
sole-ly
sol-emn
so-lem-ni-ty
sol-em-nize
so-lic-it
so-lic-i-ta-tion
so-lic-i-tor
so-lic-i-tous

so-lic-i-tude
solid
sol-i-dar-i-ty
so-lid-i-fy
so-lid-i-ty
so-lil-o-quy
sol-ip-sism
sol-i-taire
sol-i-tary
sol-i-tude
solo
so-lo-ist
sol-stice
sol-u-bil-i-ty
sol-u-ble
so-lu-tion
solv-able
sol-ven-cy
sol-vent
So-ma-lia
so-mat-ic
so-ma-to-gen-ic
som-ber
som-bre-ro
some-body
some-one
som-er-sault
some-thing
some-time
some-what
some-where
som-nam-bu-lism
som-nam-bu-list
som-no-lent
sonar
so-na-ta
sonic
son-net
soon-er
soon-est
sooth-say-er
soph-ist
so-phis-ti-cate
so-phis-ti-cat-ed
so-phis-ti-ca-tion

soph-ist-ry
soph-o-more
soph-o-mor-ic
sop-o-rif-ic
so-pra-no
sor-cer-er
sor-cery
sor-did
so-ror-i-ty
sor-rel
sor-row
sor-row-ful
sorry
souf-fle
sound-proof
sou-sa-phone
South Af-ri-ca
South Amer-i-ca
South Car-o-li-na
South Da-ko-ta
south-east
south-east-ern
south-er-ly
south-ern
south-ern-er
South Vi-et-nam
south-west
south-west-ern
sou-ve-nir
sov-er-eign
sov-er-eign-ty
So-vi-et Union
spac-ing
spa-cious
spa-ghet-ti
span-gle
span-gled
Span-iard
span-iel
Span-ish
spank-er
spank-ing
span-ner
spar-ing

spar-kle
spar-kler
spar-kling
spar-row
spar-si-ty
Spar-tan
spas-mod-ic
spas-tic
spa-tial
spat-ter
spat-u-la
speak-er
speak-ing
spear-mint
spe-cial
spe-cial-ist
spe-ci-al-i-ty
spe-cial-i-za-tion
spe-cial-ize
spe-cial-ty
spe-cies
spe-cif-ic
spe-cif-i-cal-ly
spec-i-fi-ca-tion
spec-i-fic-i-ty
spec-i-fy
spec-i-men
speck-le
speck-led
spec-ta-cle
spec-tac-u-lar
spec-ta-tor
spec-ter
spec-tro-scope
spec-tros-co-py
spec-trum
spec-u-late
spec-u-la-tion
spec-u-la-tive
spec-u-la-tor
speech-less
speed-er
speed-ing
speed-om-e-ter
spell-bound

spell-ing
spe-lunk-er
spe-lunk-ing
spend-er
spend-ing
spher-i-cal
spic-i-ness
spicy
spi-der
spig-ot
spin-ach
spi-nal
spin-dle
spin-et
spin-ner
spin-ning
spin-ster
spi-ral
spi-raled
spir-it
spir-it-ed
spir-i-tu-al
spir-i-tu-al-i-ty
spite-ful
splashy
splen-dent
splen-did
splen-dor
splic-er
splin-ter
splin-tered
split-ting
spoil-age
spoil-er
spo-ken
spon-gi-ness
spon-gy
spon-sor
spon-ta-ne-i-ty
spon-ta-ne-ous
spook-y
spoon-ful
spo-rad-ic
spo-rad-i-cal-ly
sport-ing

spor-tive
spot-less
spot-light
spot-ted
spot-ty
spread-er
spright-ly
spring-time
sprin-kle
sprin-kler
sprin-kling
sprint-er
spu-ri-ous
sput-ter
squad-ron
squal-id
squal-id-i-ty
squal-or
squan-der
squan-dered
squeaky
squeam-ish
squeez-er
squint-er
squir-rel
sta-bil-i-ty
sta-bi-li-za-tion
sta-bi-lize
sta-bi-liz-er
sta-ble
sta-bling
stac-ca-to
sta-di-um
stag-ger
stag-ing
stag-nant
stag-nate
stain-less
stair-way
sta-lac-tite
sta-lag-mite
stale-mate
stal-lion
stal-wart
sta-men

stam-i-na
stam-mer
stam-pede
stan-dard
stand-ard-i-za-tion
stan-dard-ize
stand-ing
Stan-ford Bi-net
stan-za
staph-y-lo-coc-cus
sta-ple
sta-pler
star-board
star-dom
star-let
star-ling
star-ry
start-er
star-tle
star-tling
star-va-tion
starv-ing
stat-ed
state-ly
state-ment
states-man
states-wom-an
stat-ic
sta-tion
sta-tion-ary
sta-tion-ery
sta-tis-tic
sta-tis-ti-cal
stat-is-ti-cian
stat-u-ary
stat-ue
stat-u-esque
stat-ure
stat-us
stat-ute
stat-u-to-ry
stead-fast
stead-i-ness
steady
stealth-i-ness

stealthy	sti-fling	strang-er (adj.)	stud-ied
steam-er	stig-ma	stran-gle	stu-dio
steep-er	stig-mat-ic	stran-gler	stu-di-ous
stee-ple	stig-ma-tism	stran-gu-late	study
stel-lar	stig-ma-tize	stran-gu-la-tion	stud-y-ing
stel-lu-lar	stim-u-lant	stra-te-gic	stuff-ing
sten-cil	stim-u-late	strat-e-gist	stuffy
sten-ciled	stim-u-la-tive	strat-e-gy	stul-ti-fy
sten-o-graph	stim-u-la-ter	strat-i-fi-ca-tion	stum-ble
ste-nog-ra-pher	stim-u-lus	strat-i-fy	stum-bling
sten-o-graph-ic	sting-er	strat-o-sphere	stun-ning
ste-nog-ra-phy	stin-gy	strat-o-spher-ic	stu-pe-fy
step-broth-er	sti-pend	stra-tum	stu-pen-dous
step-child	sti-pen-di-ary	stra-tus	stu-pid
step-daugh-ter	stip-u-late	straw-ber-ry	stu-pid-i-ty
step-fa-ther	stip-u-la-tion	streak-i-ness	stu-por
step-moth-er	stir-ring	streaky	stur-di-ly
step-sis-ter	stir-rup	stream-er	stur-dy
step-son	stock-ade	stream-line	stur-geon
ste-reo	stock-ing	strength-en	stut-ter
ster-e-o-phon-ic	stocky	strength-en-ing	stut-tered
ster-e-o-scope	stodgy	stren-u-ous	styl-ish
ster-e-o-scop-ic	stogy	strep-to-coc-cus	styl-ist
ster-e-os-co-py	stoic	strep-to-my-cin	sty-lis-tic
ster-e-o-type	sto-i-cal	stretch-er	styl-ize
ster-e-o-typed	sto-i-cism	stri-at-ed	sty-lus
ster-e-o-typ-er	stok-er	strick-en	sty-mie
ster-e-o-typy	sto-len	stri-dent	styp-tic
ster-ile	stom-ach	strik-er	sub-com-mit-tee
ste-ril-i-ty	stom-ach-ache	strik-ing	sub-con-tract
ster-i-li-za-tion	stony	strin-gent	sub-con-trac-tor
ster-i-lize	stop-per	strob-o-scope	sub-cul-ture
ster-i-liz-er	stor-age	stro-ga-noff	sub-di-vide
ster-ling	sto-ried	stron-ti-um	sub-di-vi-sion
ster-num	stormy	struc-tur-al	sub-due
ster-oid	story	struc-ture	sub-ject
steth-o-scope	stow-a-way	struc-tured	sub-jec-tive
Stet-son	strad-dle	stru-del	sub-jec-tiv-ism
stew-ard	strad-dler	strug-gle	sub-ju-gate
stew-ard-ess	strag-gle	strug-gled	sub-junc-tive
stick-er	strag-gler	strych-nine	sub-li-mate
stick-ler	straight-en	stub-born	sub-li-ma-tion
sticky	straight-for-ward	stub-born-ness	sub-lime
stiff-en	strain-er	stuc-co	sub-lim-i-nal
sti-fle	stran-ger (n.)	stu-dent	sub-ma-rine

sub-merge
sub-merged
sub-mer-gence
sub-merse
sub-mersed
sub-mers-ible
sub-mis-sion
sub-mis-sive
sub-mit
sub-nor-mal
sub-or-di-nate
sub-or-di-na-tion
sub-poe-na
sub-poe-naed
sub-scribe
sub-scrib-er
sub-script
sub-scrip-tion
sub-se-quent
sub-serve
sub-ser-vi-ent
sub-side
sub-sid-ence
sub-sid-i-ary
sub-si-dize
sub-si-dy
sub-sist
sub-sist-ence
sub-son-ic
sub-stance
sub-stan-tial
sub-stan-ti-ate
sub-stan-tive
sub-sti-tute
sub-sti-tu-tion
sub-sti-tu-tive
sub-sume
sub-ter-fuge
sub-ter-ra-ne-an
sub-ti-tle
sub-tle
sub-tle-ty
sub-tract
sub-tract-er
sub-trac-tion

sub-urb
sub-ur-ban
sub-ur-ban-ite
sub-ur-bia
sub-ver-sion
sub-ver-sive
sub-vert
sub-vert-er
sub-way
suc-ceed
suc-cess
suc-cess-ful
suc-ces-sion
suc-ces-sive
suc-ces-sor
suc-cinct
suc-co-tash
suc-cu-lence
suc-cu-lent
suc-cumb
su-crose
suc-tion
Su-dan
Su-da-nese
sud-den
sud-den-ly
Suez
suf-fer
suf-fer-ing
suf-fice
suf-fi-cien-cy
suf-fi-cient
suf-fix
suf-fo-cate
suf-fo-cat-ing
suf-fo-ca-tion
suf-frage
suf-fra-gist
sugar
sug-ared
sug-ary
sug-gest
sug-gest-i-bil-i-ty
sug-gest-ible
sug-ges-tion

sug-ges-tive
su-i-ci-dal
su-i-cide
suit-able
suit-or
su-ki-ya-ki
sul-fide
sul-fur
sul-fu-ric
sulk-i-ness
sulky
sul-len
sul-tan
sul-tan-ate
sul-try
sumac
sum-mar-i-ly
sum-ma-rize
sum-ma-ry
sum-ma-tion
sum-mer
sum-mit
sum-mon
sump-tu-ous
sun-burn
Sun-day
sun-dry
sunk-en
sunny
sun-rise
sun-set
super
su-per-a-bun-dant
su-perb
su-per-cil-i-ous
su-per-fi-cial
su-per-flu-ous
su-per-hu-man
su-per-in-tend
su-per-in-tend-ent
su-pe-ri-or
su-pe-ri-or-i-ty
su-per-la-tive
su-per-nat-u-ral
su-per-sede

su-per-son-ic
su-per-sti-tion
su-per-sti-tious
su-per-vene
su-per-vise
su-per-vi-sor
sup-per
sup-plant
sup-ple
sup-ple-ment
sup-pli-ant
sup-ply
sup-port
sup-port-er
sup-por-tive
sup-pose
sup-posed
sup-po-si-tion
sup-press
sup-pres-sor
sup-pres-sion
su-prem-a-cy
su-preme
sur-cease
sur-charge
sure-ly
sure-ty
sur-face
sur-fac-ing
sur-feit
surf-ing
sur-geon
sur-gery
sur-gi-cal
surly
sur-mise
sur-name
sur-pass
sur-pass-ing
sur-plice
sur-plus
sur-prise
sur-re-al
sur-re-al-ism
sur-re-al-ist

sur-ren-der
sur-rep-ti-tious
sur-rey
sur-ro-gate
sur-round
sur-round-ings
sur-veil-lance
sur-vey
sur-vey-ing
sur-viv-al
sur-vive
sur-vi-vor
sus-cep-ti-bil-i-ty
sus-cep-ti-ble
sus-pect
sus-pend
sus-pense
sus-pense-ful
sus-pen-sion
sus-pi-cion
sus-pi-cious
sus-tain
sus-te-nance
su-ture
swad-dle
swad-dled
swag-ger
Swa-hi-li
swal-low
swampy
swas-ti-ka
sweat-er
Swe-den
Swed-ish
sweep-er
sweep-ing
sweep-stakes
sweet-en
sweet-ened
sweet-en-ing
swell-ing
swel-ter
swel-ter-ing
swin-dle
swin-dler

swin-dling
switch-board
Swit-zer-land
swiv-el
swiv-eled
syc-a-more
syl-lab-ic
syl-la-bize
syl-la-ble
syl-la-bus
syl-lo-gism
syl-lo-gis-tic
syl-lo-gis-ti-cal
sym-bi-o-sis
sym-bi-ot-ic
sym-bol
sym-bol-ic
sym-bol-ism
sym-bol-ize
sym-met-ri-cal
sym-me-try
sym-pa-thet-ic
sym-pa-thize
sym-pa-thiz-er
sym-pa-thy
sym-phon-ic
sym-pho-ni-ous
sym-pho-ny
sym-po-si-um
symp-tom
symp-to-mat-ic
syn-a-gogue
syn-apse
syn-chro-nism
syn-chro-ni-za-
   tion
syn-chro-nize
syn-chro-niz-er
syn-chro-nous
syn-chro-ny
syn-co-pate
syn-co-pa-tion
syn-di-cate
syn-drome
syn-o-nym

syn-on-y-mous
syn-on-y-my
syn-op-sis
syn-op-size
syn-op-tic
syn-tax
syn-the-sis
syn-the-size
syn-the-siz-er
syn-thet-ic
Syr-ia
Syr-i-an
sy-ringe
syrup
sys-tem
sys-tem-at-ic
sys-tem-at-i-cal-ly
sys-tem-a-tize
sys-tem-ic
sys-tol-ic

T

Ta-bas-co
tabby
tab-er-na-cle
table
tab-leau
tab-leaux
tab-let
taboo
tab-u-lar
tab-u-lar-ize
tab-u-late
tab-u-la-tor
tacit
tac-i-turn
tac-i-tur-ni-ty
tack-le
taco
tact-ful
tac-tic
tac-ti-cal
tac-tile
tact-less
taf-fe-ta
taffy

Ta-hi-ti
Ta-hi-tian
tail-or
tai-lored
Tai-wan
Tai-wan-ese
tak-ing
tal-cum
tal-ent
tal-is-man
talk-a-tive
talk-er
tally
Tal-mud
Tal-mud-ic
ta-ma-le
tam-bou-rine
tam-per
tan-dem
tan-ge-lo
tan-ge-los
tan-gent
tan-gen-tial
tan-ger-ine
tan-gi-ble
tan-gle
tan-gled
tango
tank-er
tan-ning
tan-ta-lize
tan-ta-liz-er
tan-ta-lum
tan-ta-mount
tan-trum
Tan-za-nia
Tao-ism
Tao-ist
taper
tap-es-try
tap-i-o-ca
tap-ping
tap-ster
tar-an-tel-la
ta-ran-tu-la

tar-di-ness
tardy
tar-get
tar-iff
tar-nish
tar-pau-lin
tar-ra-gon
tarry
tar-tan
tar-tar
tas-sel
tas-seled
taste-less
tast-er
tasty
tat-tered
tat-tle
tat-too
tat-too-er
tau-to-log-i-cal
tau-tol-o-gy
tav-ern
tawny
tax-a-tion
taxi
tax-i-cab
tax-i-der-mist
tax-i-der-my
tax-ied
tax-i-ing
tax-on-o-my
tax-pay-er
teach-er
teach-ing
team-mate
team-ster
team-work
tear-drop
tear-ful
tea-sel
teas-er
tea-spoon
tech-ne-ti-um
tech-ni-cal
tech-ni-cal-i-ty

tech-ni-cian
tech-nique
tech-no-log-ical
tech-nol-o-gy
te-di-ous
teem-ing
teen-age
teen-ag-er
tee-ter
tee-to-tal-er
Tef-lon
tel-e-cast
tel-e-com-mu-ni-
    ca-tion
tel-e-gram
tel-e-graph
te-leg-ra-pher
tel-e-graph-ic
te-leg-ra-phy
tel-e-o-log-i-cal
tel-e-ol-o-gy
tel-e-path-ic
te-lep-a-thy
tel-e-phone
tel-e-phon-er
tel-e-pho-to
tel-e-scope
tel-e-scop-ic
te-les-co-py
tel-e-thon
Tel-e-type
tel-e-vise
tel-e-vi-sion
tell-er
tell-ing
tell-tale
tel-lu-ri-um
te-mer-i-ty
tem-per
tem-per-a-ment
tem-per-a-men-tal
tem-per-ance
tem-per-ate
tem-per-a-ture
tem-pered

tem-pest
tem-pes-tu-ous
tem-plate
tem-ple
tempo
tem-po-ral
tem-po-rar-i-ly
tem-po-rar-y
temp-ta-tion
tempt-er
tempt-ing
tempt-ress
ten-able
te-na-cious
te-nac-i-ty
ten-an-cy
ten-ant
tend-en-cy
tend-er (one who
    attends; ship)
ten-der (soft;
    offer)
ten-der-ize
ten-der-iz-er
ten-der-loin
ten-don
ten-dril
ten-e-ment
tenet
ten-fold
Ten-nes-see
ten-nis
tenor
ten-sion
ten-ta-cle
ten-ta-tive
ten-u-ous
ten-ure
tepee
tepid
te-qui-la
ter-bi-um
ter-i-ya-ki
ter-mi-na-ble
ter-mi-nal

ter-mi-nate
ter-mi-na-tion
ter-mi-na-tor
ter-mi-nol-o-gy
ter-mi-nus
ter-mite
ter-race
ter-rain
ter-rar-i-um
ter-res-tri-al
ter-ri-ble
ter-ri-bly
ter-ri-er
ter-rif-ic
ter-ri-fy
ter-ri-to-ri-al
ter-ri-to-ry
ter-ror
ter-ror-ism
ter-ror-ize
terry
tes-ta-ment
tes-ta-men-ta-ry
tes-ti-fy
tes-ti-mo-ni-al
tes-ti-mo-ny
tes-ti-ness
tes-tos-ter-one
testy
tet-a-nus
teth-er
teth-ered
tet-ra-he-dral
tet-ra-he-dron
Texas
text-book
tex-tile
tex-tu-al
tex-ture
tex-tured
Thai-land
thal-a-mus
thal-li-um
thank-ful
Thanks-giv-ing

the-a-ter
the-at-ri-cal
the-ism
the-mat-ic
the-mat-i-cal-ly
them-selves
the-o-lo-gian
the-o-log-i-cal
the-ol-o-gy
the-o-rem
the-o-ret-i-cal
the-o-re-ti-cian
the-o-rize
the-o-ry
ther-a-peu-tic
ther-a-peu-ti-cal-
  ly
ther-a-pist
ther-a-py
there-fore
ther-mal
ther-mo-dy-nam-
  ics
ther-mom-e-ter
ther-mos
ther-mo-sphere
ther-mo-stat
the-sau-rus
the-sis
thes-pi-an
theta
thi-a-mine
thick-en
thick-en-ing
thick-et
thick-ness
thim-ble
think-er
think-ing
thin-ner
thirst-y
thir-teen
thir-teenth
thir-ti-eth
thir-ty

this-tle
tho-rax
tho-ri-um
thorny
thor-ough
thor-ough-bred
thor-ough-fare
thought-ful
thought-less
thou-sand
thou-sandth
threat-en
threat-en-ing
thresh-er
thresh-old
thrift-i-ness
thrifty
thrill-er
throaty
throt-tle
throt-tled
through-out
thu-li-um
thumb-nail
thumb-tack
thump-ing
thun-der
thun-der-cloud
thun-der-ous
thun-der-show-er
thun-der-storm
Thurs-day
thy-roid
thy-rox-in
tiara
Tibet
Ti-bet-an
tibia
tick-et
tick-ing
tick-le
tick-lish
tid-al
ti-di-ness
tid-ings

tidy
tiger
tight-en
tight-en-er
ti-gress
tilde
til-ing
till-age
tim-bale
tim-ber
tim-bered
time-less
time-ly
timer
timid
ti-mid-i-ty
tim-ing
tim-o-rous
tim-o-thy
tim-pa-ni
tim-pa-nist
tinc-ture
tin-der
tin-gle
tin-gled
tin-ker
tin-kling
tin-sel
tiny
tip-toe
ti-rade
tire-less
tire-some
tis-sue
titan
ti-tan-ic
ti-ta-ni-um
tith-ing
tit-il-late
title
ti-tled
ti-trate
ti-tra-tion
tit-u-lar
toast-er

to-bac-co
to-bac-co-nist
to-bog-gan
to-bog-gan-er
today
tod-dle
tod-dler
toddy
toe-nail
tof-fee
toga
to-geth-er
tog-gle
toi-let
toi-let-ry
token
tol-er-able
tol-er-ance
tol-er-ant
tol-er-ate
tol-er-a-tion
tom-a-hawk
to-ma-to
tomb-stone
to-mor-row
tonal
to-nal-i-ty
tonic
to-night
ton-nage
ton-sil
ton-sil-lec-to-my
ton-sil-li-tis
tooth-ache
topaz
topic
top-i-cal
to-pog-ra-pher
top-o-graph-i-cal
to-pog-ra-phy
top-ping
top-ple
top-soil
tor-ment
tor-men-tor

tor-na-do
tor-pe-do
tor-rent
tor-ren-tial
tor-rid
torso
tor-ti-lla
tor-toise
tor-toise-shell
tor-tu-ous
tor-ture
tor-tur-er
tor-tur-ous
total
to-tal-i-tar-i-an
to-tal-i-tar-i-an-
   ism
to-tal-i-ty
to-tal-ly
totem
tot-ter
touch-down
touch-ing
touch-up
touchy
tough-en
tou-pee
tour-ism
tour-ist
tour-na-ment
tour-ni-quet
tou-sle
tou-sled
to-ward
towel
tower
tow-ered
tow-er-ing
town-ship
towns-peo-ple
toxic
toxin
trace-able
trac-er

tra-chea
trac-ing
trac-tion
trac-tor
trade-mark
trad-er
trades-man
tra-di-tion
tra-di-tion-al
traf-fic
trag-e-dy
trag-ic
trail-er
train-ee
train-er
trai-tor
trai-tor-ous
tra-ject
tra-jec-to-ry
tram-ple
tram-po-line
tran-quil
tran-quil-ize
tran-quil-iz-er
tran-quil-li-ty
trans-act
trans-ac-tion
trans-at-lan-tic
trans-ceiv-er
tran-scend
tran-scend-ent
tran-scen-den-tal
trans-con-ti-nen-
   tal
tran-scribe
tran-scrib-er
tran-script
tran-scrip-tion
trans-fer
trans-fer-able
trans-fer-ee
trans-fer-ence
trans-ferred
trans-fix
trans-fixed

trans-form
trans-for-ma-tion
trans-form-er
trans-fuse
trans-fu-sion
trans-gress
trans-gres-sion
trans-gres-sor
tran-science
tran-sient
tran-sis-tor
tran-sit
tran-si-tion
tran-si-tive
tran-si-to-ry
trans-late
trans-la-tion
trans-la-tor
trans-lu-cen-cy
trans-lu-cent
trans-mis-si-ble
trans-mis-sion
trans-mit
trans-mit-ter
trans-par-en-cy
trans-par-ent
tran-spire
trans-plant
trans-plan-ta-tion
trans-port
trans-por-ta-tion
trans-pose
trans-po-si-tion
trans-ver-sal
trans-verse
trap-e-zoid
trap-per
trap-pings
trau-ma
trau-mat-ic
trau-ma-tism
trau-ma-tize
tra-vail
trav-el
trav-eled

trav-el-er
trav-erse
trawl-er
treacher-ous
treach-ery
trea-son
trea-son-ous
treas-ur-able
treas-ur-er
treas-ury
trea-tise
treat-ment
trea-ty
treb-le
tre-bled
trel-lis
trel-lised
trem-ble
trem-bling
tre-men-dous
trem-or
trem-u-lous
trench-ant
trendy
tre-phine
trep-id
trep-i-da-tion
tres-pass
tres-pass-er
tres-tle
triad
trial
tri-an-gle
tri-an-gu-lar
trib-al
trib-al-ism
tribes-man
trib-u-la-tion
tri-bu-nal
trib-une
trib-u-tary
trib-ute
trick-ery
trick-le
tricky

tri-cot
tri-cy-cle
tri-en-ni-al
tri-fle
tri-fling
trig-ger
trig-o-nom-e-try
tril-lion
tril-lionth
tril-li-um
tril-o-gy
tri-mes-ter
trim-mer
trim-ming
trin-i-ty
trin-ket
tri-no-mi-al
trio
tri-par-tite
tri-ple
trip-let
trip-li-cate
tri-pod
tri-umph
tri-um-phant
triv-ia
triv-i-al
triv-i-al-i-ty
trol-ley
trom-bone
troop-er
tro-phy
trop-ic
trop-i-cal
tro-pism
trot-ter
trou-ba-dour
trou-ble
trou-bled
trou-ble-some
trou-sers
trous-seau
trow-el
tru-an-cy
tru-ant

truck-er
truck-load
truc-u-lence
truc-u-lent
trudg-en
tru-ism
truly
trum-pet
trum-pet-er
trun-cate
trun-cat-ed
trust-ee
trust-ee-ship
trust-wor-thy
truth-ful
try-ing
tuba
tu-ber-cu-lo-sis
tub-ing
Tudor
Tues-day
tu-i-tion
tulip
tum-ble
tum-bler
tum-bling
tumor
tu-mult
tu-mul-tu-ous
tuna
tun-dra
tuner
tung-sten
tu-nic
Tu-ni-sia
Tu-ni-sian
tun-nel
tun-neled
tur-ban
tur-bine
tur-bo-charg-er
tur-bo-jet
tur-bot
tur-bu-lence
tur-bu-lent

tur-key
Turk-ish
tur-moil
turn-ing
tur-nip
turn-out
turn-o-ver
turn-pike
turn-ta-ble
tur-pen-tine
tur-quoise
tur-tle
tus-sle
tu-te-lage
tutor
tu-tored
tu-to-ri-al
tux-e-do
tweez-ers
twen-ti-eth
twen-ty
twid-dle
twi-light
twin-kle
twin-kled
twin-kling
twist-er
two-di-men-sion-
   al
two-some
ty-coon
tying
tym-pan-ic
tym-pa-nist
type-cast
type-face
type-set-ter
type-write
type-writ-er
type-writ-ing
ty-phoid
ty-phoon
ty-phus
typ-i-cal
typ-i-fy

typ-ist
ty-pog-ra-pher
ty-po-graph-ic
ty-po-graph-i-cal
ty-pog-ra-phy
ty-ran-ni-cal
tyr-an-nize
tyr-an-ny
ty-rant

U

ubiq-ui-tous
ubiq-ui-ty
udder
Ugan-da
Ugan-dan
ugly
Ukrai-ni-an
uku-le-le
ulcer
ul-cer-a-tion
ul-cer-ous
ul-te-ri-or
ul-ti-mate
ul-ti-ma-tum
ul-tra-con-ser-va-
   tive
ul-tra-mod-ern
ul-tra-son-ic
ul-tra-vi-o-let
um-bil-i-cal
um-bil-i-cus
um-brel-la
um-pire
un-able
un-a-bridged
un-ac-cus-tomed
un-a-dul-ter-at-ed
un-af-fec-ted
un-al-ien-able
una-nim-i-ty
unan-i-mous
un-an-swer-able
un-ap-proach-able
un-arm
un-armed

un-as-sist-ed
un-as-sum-ing
un-at-tached
un-a-void-able
un-a-ware
un-bear-able
un-beat-able
un-beat-en
un-be-liev-able
un-bro-ken
un-buck-le
un-but-ton
un-can-ny
un-cer-tain
un-cer-tain-ty
un-class-i-fied
uncle
un-clear
un-com-fort-able
un-con-di-tion-al
un-con-nect-ed
un-con-quer-able
un-con-scious
un-con-sti-tu-tion-al
un-con-trol-lable
un-con-ven-tion-al
un-cov-er
un-cov-ered
uncut
un-daunt-ed
un-de-cid-ed
un-de-ni-able
under
un-der-a-chieve
un-der-age
un-der-cov-er
un-der-cut
un-der-de-vel-oped
un-der-es-ti-mate
un-der-ex-pose
un-der-go
un-der-grad-u-ate
un-der-ground

un-der-line
un-der-ling
un-der-ly-ing
un-der-mine
un-der-neath
un-der-nour-ish
un-der-priv-i-leged
un-der-score
un-der-stand
un-der-stand-ing
un-der-state
un-der-state-ment
un-der-stood
un-der-study
un-der-take
un-der-tak-er
un-der-tak-ing
un-der-wa-ter
un-der-weight
un-der-world
un-der-writ-er
un-de-serv-ed-ly
un-de-sir-able
un-de-ter-mined
undo
un-dress
un-du-late
un-du-la-tion
un-du-ly
un-dy-ing
un-easy
un-ed-u-cat-ed
un-em-ployed
un-e-qual
un-e-qualed
un-e-quiv-o-cal
un-es-sen-tial
un-e-ven
un-e-vent-ful
un-ex-cep-tion-al
un-ex-pec-ted
un-fair
un-faith-ful
un-fa-mil-iar
un-fas-ten

un-fa-vor-able
un-fin-ished
un-fit
un-fold
un-for-get-ta-ble
un-for-tu-nate
un-found-ed
un-friend-ly
un-glued
un-grate-ful
un-hap-py
un-healthy
uni-corn
uni-cy-cle
uni-fi-ca-tion
uni-form
unify
uni-lat-er-al
un-in-hib-i-ted
un-in-ter-es-ted
union
un-ion-ism
un-ion-ize
unique
uni-son
unit
Uni-tar-i-an
uni-tary
unite
unit-ed
unity
uni-ver-sal
uni-ver-sal-i-ty
uni-verse
uni-ver-si-ty
univ-o-cal
un-just
un-kempt
un-kind
un-known
un-lead-ed
un-less
un-like
un-like-li-hood
un-like-ly

un-lim-it-ed
un-list-ed
un-load
un-lock
un-lucky
un-marked
un-men-tion-able
un-mis-tak-able
un-mit-i-gat-ed
un-nat-u-ral
un-nec-es-sary
un-oc-cu-pied
un-of-fi-cial
un-pack
un-pleas-ant
un-plug
un-pop-u-lar
un-prec-e-dent-ed
un-pre-dict-able
un-pre-pared
un-pro-duc-tive
un-pro-fes-sion-al
un-ques-tion-able
un-rav-el
un-rea-son-able
un-re-lent-ing
un-re-li-able
un-re-spon-sive
un-rest
un-re-strained
un-ru-ly
un-sad-dle
un-screw
un-sel-fish
un-set-tled
un-skilled
un-so-cia-ble
un-so-phis-ti-cat-ed
un-sound
un-spe-cial-ized
un-sta-ble
un-steady
un-struc-tured
un-suc-cess-ful

un-suit-able
un-sus-pect-ing
un-ten-able
un-ti-dy
untie
until
un-time-ly
un-ti-tled
un-touch-able
un-true
un-u-su-al
un-veil
un-war-rant-ed
un-whole-some
un-wieldy
un-wind
up-com-ing
up-date
up-heav-al
up-hold
up-hol-ster
up-hol-ster-er
up-hol-stery
upper
up-right
up-roar
up-roar-i-ous
up-set
up-stairs
up-stand-ing
up-ward
ura-ni-um
Ura-nus
urban
ur-chin
urea
ur-gen-cy
ur-gent
uri-nary
uri-nate
urine
Uru-guay
usage
use-ful
use-less

user
usher
usu-al
usu-al-ly
usu-rer
usurp
usur-pa-tion
usurp-er
Utah
uten-sil
uter-us
util-i-tar-i-an
util-i-tar-i-an-ism
util-i-ty
uti-li-za-tion
util-ize
ut-most
Uto-pia
uto-pi-an
utter
ut-ter-ance
ut-ter-ly

V

va-can-cy
va-cant
va-cate
va-ca-tion
vac-ci-nate
vac-ci-na-tion
vac-ci-na-tor
vac-cine
vac-u-ous
vac-u-um
vag-a-bond
va-gary
va-gi-na
vag-i-nal
va-gran-cy
va-grant
val-ance
val-e-dic-to-ri-an
va-lence
Val-en-tine
valet
val-iant

valid
val-i-date
val-i-da-tion
va-lid-i-ty
va-lise
val-ley
valor
val-or-ous
val-u-able
value
val-ued
vam-pire
va-na-di-um
van-dal
van-dal-ism
van-dal-ize
van-guard
va-nil-la
van-ish
van-i-ty
van-quish
van-tage
vapor
va-por-i-za-tion
va-por-ize
va-por-iz-er
var-i-a-bil-i-ty
var-i-able
var-i-ance
var-i-ant
var-i-a-tion
var-i-cose
var-ied
var-i-e-gate
var-i-e-gat-ed
va-ri-e-ty
var-i-ous
var-nish
var-si-ty
vary
vas-ec-to-my
Vas-e-line
Vat-i-can
vaude-ville
vaude-vil-lian

vault-ing
veg-e-ta-ble
veg-e-tar-i-an
veg-e-ta-tion
ve-he-mence
ve-he-ment
ve-hi-cle
ve-hic-u-lar
ve-loc-i-ty
ve-lour
vel-vet
vel-vet-een
vender
ven-det-ta
ven-dor
ve-neer
ven-er-able
ve-ne-re-al
Ven-e-zue-la
venge-ance
ve-ni-al
ven-i-son
venom
ven-om-ous
ven-ti-late
ven-ti-la-tion
ven-ti-la-tor
ven-tri-cle
ven-tric-u-lar
ven-tril-o-quism
ven-tril-o-quist
ven-ture
ven-tur-er
ven-tur-ous
Venus
Ve-nu-si-an
ve-ra-cious
ve-rac-i-ty
ve-ran-da
ver-bal
ver-bal-i-za-tion
ver-bal-ize
ver-ba-tim
ver-bi-age
ver-bose

ver-bos-i-ty
ver-bo-ten
ver-dict
ve-rid-i-cal
ver-i-fi-able
ver-i-fi-ca-tion
ver-i-fy
ver-i-ta-ble
ver-mil-ion
ver-min
Ver-mont
ver-mouth
ver-nac-u-lar
ver-sa-tile
ver-sa-til-i-ty
ver-sion
ver-sus
ver-te-bra
ver-te-brate
ver-tex
ver-ti-cal
very
ves-i-cle
ves-per
ves-sel
vest-ed
ves-ti-bule
ves-tige
vest-ment
ves-try
vet-er-an
vet-er-i-nar-i-an
vet-er-i-nary
veto
vex-a-tion
vi-a-bil-i-ty
vi-able
vi-a-duct
vi-brant
vi-brate
vi-bra-tion
vic-ar-age
vi-car-i-ous
vice versa
vi-chys-soise

vi-cin-i-ty
vi-cious
vi-cis-si-tude
vic-tim
vic-tim-ize
vic-tor
Vic-to-ri-an
vic-to-ri-ous
vic-to-ry
video
Vi-et-cong
Vi-et-nam
Vi-et-nam-ese
view-point
vigil
vig-i-lance
vig-i-lant
vig-i-lan-te
vi-gnette
vigor
vig-or-ous
vi-king
villa
vil-lage
vil-lag-er
vil-lain
vil-lain-ous
vil-lainy
vin-di-cate
vin-di-ca-tion
vin-dic-tive
vin-e-gar
vin-ery
vine-yard
vin-tage
vinyl
viola
vi-o-la-ble
vi-o-late
vi-o-la-tion
vi-o-la-tor
vi-o-lence
vi-o-lent
vi-o-let
vi-o-lin

vi-o-lin-ist
vi-o-lon-cel-lo
viper
vi-per-ous
vir-gin
vir-gin-al
Vir-gin-ia
Virgin Is-lands
vir-gin-i-ty
vir-ile
vi-ril-i-ty
vir-tu-al
vir-tu-al-ly
vir-tue
vir-tu-o-so
vir-tu-ous
virus
visa
vis-age
vis-cous
vis-i-bil-i-ty
vis-i-ble
vi-sion
vis-it-a-tion
vis-i-tor
visor
vista
vis-u-al
vis-u-al-ize
vital
vi-tal-i-ty
vi-tal-ize
vi-ta-min
vi-va-cious
vi-vac-i-ty
vivid
viv-id-ly
viv-i-fy
viv-i-sec-tion
vixen
vo-cab-u-lary
vocal
vo-cal-ist
vo-cal-ize
vo-ca-tion

vo-ca-tion-al
vo-cif-er-ous
vodka
void-ed
vol-a-tile
vol-a-til-i-ty
vol-can-ic
vol-ca-no
vo-li-tion
vol-ley
vol-ley-ball
volt-age
volt-me-ter
vol-ume
vo-lu-mi-nous
vol-un-tar-i-ly
vol-un-tary
vol-un-teer
vol-un-teered
vo-lup-tu-ous
vomit
voo-doo
vo-ra-cious
vo-rac-i-ty
voter
vouch-er
vowel
voy-age
voy-ag-er
vul-can-ize
vul-gar
vul-gar-i-ty
vul-ner-able
vul-ture

W

wad-dle
wad-dled
wader
wafer
waf-fle
wager
wagon
wait-er
wait-ing
wait-ress

waiv-er
waken
wal-let
wal-nut
wal-rus
wam-pum
wan-der
wan-der-lust
want-ing
wan-ton
war-ble
war-bler
war-den
ward-robe
ware-house
war-fare
warm-er
warn-ing
war-rant
war-ran-ty
war-ri-or
wary
wash-able
wash-er
wash-ing
Wash-ing-ton
waste-bas-ket
wast-ed
wast-er
waste-ful
waste-land
wast-ing
wast-rel
watch-dog
watch-man
water
wa-ter-fall
Wa-ter-gate
wa-ter-mel-on
wa-ter-me-ter
wa-ter-proof
wa-tery
watt-age
wave-length
waver

wavy
waxen
waxy
way-far-ing
weak-en
weak-ened
weak-ling
weak-ness
wealthy
weap-on
weap-on-ry
wear-able
wea-ri-ness
wea-ri-some
wea-ry
wea-sel
wea-seled
weath-er
weath-ered
weath-er-man
weav-er
web-bing
wed-ding
wed-lock
Wednes-day
weed-er
week-day
week-end
week-ly
weep-ing
weight-less
wel-come
wel-fare
Wes-ley-an
west-er-ly
west-ern
west-ern-er
West Ger-ma-ny
West Indies
West Vir-gin-ia
whal-er
whal-ing
what-ev-er
whee-dle

whee-dled
wheel-er
when-ev-er
where-as
wher-ev-er
wheth-er
which-ev-er
whim-per
whim-pered
whim-si-cal
whim-sy
whin-ny
whip-lash
whip-ping
whirl-wind
whisk-er
whisk-ered
whis-key
whis-per
whis-pered
whis-tle
whis-tler
whis-tling
whit-en
white-wash
whit-ing
whit-tle
whit-tled
who-ev-er
whole-heart-ed
whole-heart-ed-ly
whole-sale
whole-some
whol-ly
whoop-ing
whop-per
whop-ping
wick-ed
wick-ed-ly
wick-ed-ness
wick-er
wick-et
widen
widow
wid-ow-er

wie-ner schnit-zel
wig-gle
wig-wam
wil-der-ness
wild-flow-er
wild-life
will-ing
wil-low
wind-ing
win-dow
wind-shield
windy
win-ery
win-ner
win-ning
win-some
win-ter
win-ter-green
win-ter-ize
win-try
wiper
wir-ing
wiry
Wis-con-sin
wish-ful
wist-ful
witch-craft
witch-ery
with-draw
with-draw-al
with-drawn
with-er
with-ered
with-ers
with-hold
with-in
with-stand
wit-ness
wit-ti-cism
wiz-ard
wiz-ard-ry
wob-ble
wob-bly
woo ful
wol-ver-ine

woman
wom-an-hood
wom-an-ly
women
won-der
won-dered
won-der-ful
won-drous
wood-chuck
wood-ed
wood-en
wood-peck-er
wood-wind
wood-work
wool-en
wool-ly
word-ing
wordy
work-er
work-ing
world-ly
world-wide
wor-ri-some
worry
wors-en
wor-ship
wor-shiped
wor-ship-er
wor-ship-ful

wor-sted
worth-less
worth-while
wor-thy
woven
wran-gle
wran-gler
wrap-per
wrap-ping
wreck-age
wres-tle
wres-tler
wres-tling
wretch-ed
wrig-gle
wrin-kle
wrin-kled
writ-er
writ-ing
writ-ten
Wy-o-ming

X

xenon
Xerox
x ray
xy-lo-phone

Y

yacht-ing

Yan-kee
yard-age
yard-stick
yar-mul-ke
yawn-ing
year-book
year-ling
year-ly
yearn-ing
yel-low
Yemen
Yem-en-ite
yeo-man
yes-ter-day
Yid-dish
yield-ing
yodel
yo-del-er
yoga
yo-gurt
yokel
yon-der
young-ster
your-self
youth-ful
yt-ter-bi-um
Yu-go-slav
Yu-go-sla-
via

Z

Zam-bia
Zam-bi-an
zany
zeal-ot
zeal-ous
zebra
ze-nith
zeph-yr
zero
zin-nia
Zion
Zi-on-ism
zip-per
zir-co-ni-um
zo-di-ac
zom-bie
zonal
zo-o-log-i-cal
zo-ol-o-gist
zo-ol-o-gy
Zo-ro-as-tri-
an
Zo-ro-as-tri-
an-ism
zuc-chi-ni
Zulu
zy-gote
zwie-back

Area Code

TELEPHONE AREA CODE DIRECTORY

INDEX

NUMBERING PLAN AREAS WITH CODES

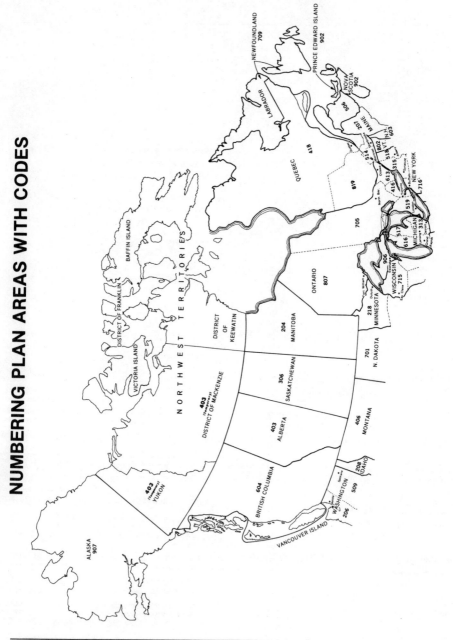

NUMBERING PLAN AREAS WITH CODES

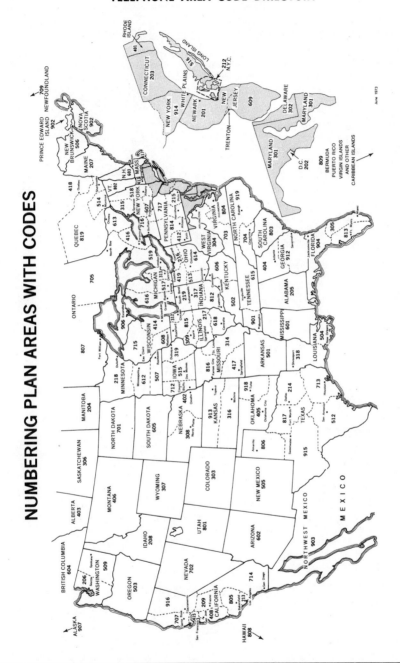

THE USE OF AREA CODES ASSURES FASTER LONG DISTANCE SERVICE

This Telephone Area Code Directory contains a list of cities, towns and localities in the United States, Canada, Mexico, Bahamas, Bermuda, Dominican Republic, Jamaica, Puerto Rico and the Virgin Islands with their associated Area Codes. The Directory is arranged alphabetically by states for the United States. The provinces of Canada follow the states, and Mexico, Bahamas, Bermuda, Dominican Republic, Jamaica, Puerto Rico and the Virgin Islands follow Canada. Within each state, province, country or island, places are listed alphabetically.

Where a single NPA covers an entire state or province, specific locations are not listed. Pages for these states or provinces contain a single statement indicating the NPA for all points in that state or province, e.g., Alabama, All Points—Area Code 205.

WHAT ARE AREA CODES AND HOW ARE THEY USED

The United States, Canada, Mexico, Bahamas, Bermuda, Dominican Republic, Jamaica, Puerto Rico and the Virgin Islands have been divided into more than 123 telephone areas, each identified by a 3-digit Area Code number. (See illustrative maps.)

Area codes are used for calling from one telephone area to another. They are not used when calling another telephone having the same Area Code.

DIRECT DISTANCE DIALING

With Direct Distance Dialing (DDD) it is possible to dial station-to-station long distance calls, by using the proper Area Code listed in this directory. Introductory pages of the local telephone directories indicate if DDD service is available. Since variations exist in the dialing of long distance calls, the introductory pages of the local telephone directory also provide information on how to dial calls. Even on calls which must be placed with an operator, providing the Area Code will get long distance calls through faster.

LONG DISTANCE DIRECTORY ASSISTANCE (AREA CODE PLUS 555-1212)

If you don't know the out-of-town number, DDD makes it possible to obtain Long Distance Directory Assistance service. Just dial the Area Code serving the locality of the desired called points plus 555-1212.

LONG DISTANCE CALLS WHICH CAN NOT BE DIALED

On calls which can not be dialed, simply give the long distance operator the Area Code (if it is different from the Area Code of the telephone being used) and the telephone number.

SPECIAL AREA CODE 800 (INWARD WATS)

Station-to-Station long distance calls to customers who have Inward Wide Area Telephone Service (WATS) may be direct dialed from specified locations without charge to the calling party. Dial as you would any DDD call using the prefix, if appropriate, and the special Area Code 800 plus the number. To obtain the Inward WATS number of a customer who offers this service, dial the prefix, if appropriate, and special Area Code 800 plus 555-1212.

TELEPHONE AREA CODE DIRECTORY

ALPHABETICAL LIST OF LOCATIONS WITH AREA CODES

State or Province	Area Code
Alabama	205
Alaska	907
Arizona	602
Arkansas	501
California	209, 213, 408, 415, 707, 714, 805, 916
Colorado	303
Connecticut	203
Delaware	302
District of Columbia	202
Florida	305, 813, 904
Georgia	404, 912
Hawaii	808
Idaho	208
Illinois	217, 309, 312, 618, 815
Indiana	219, 317, 812
Iowa	319, 515, 712
Kansas	316, 913
Kentucky	502, 606
Louisiana	318, 504
Maine	207
Maryland	301
Massachusetts	413, 617
Michigan	313, 517, 616, 906
Minnesota	218, 507, 612
Mississippi	601
Missouri	314, 417, 816
Montana	406
Nebraska	308, 402
Nevada	702
New Hampshire	603
New Jersey	201, 609
New Mexico	505
New York	212, 315, 516, 518, 607, 716, 914
North Carolina	704, 919
North Dakota	701
Ohio	216, 419, 513, 614
Oklahoma	405, 918
Oregon	503

TELEPHONE AREA CODE DIRECTORY

ALPHABETICAL LIST OF LOCATIONS WITH AREA CODES

State or Province	Area Code
Pennsylvania	215, 412, 717, 814
Rhode Island	401
South Carolina	803
South Dakota	605
Tennessee	615, 901
Texas	214, 512, 713, 806, 817, 915
Utah	801
Vermont	802
Virginia	703, 804
Washington	206, 509
West Virginia	304
Wisconsin	414, 608, 715
Wyoming	307

Alberta	403
British Columbia	604
Manitoba	204
New Brunswick	506
Newfoundland	709
Northwest Territories (Dist. of Mackenzie) (Temp.)	403
Nova Scotia	902
Ontario	416, 519, 613, 705, 807
Prince Edward Island	902
Quebec	418, 514, 819
Saskatchewan	306
Yukon (Temp.)	403

Mexico	903
Bahamas	809
Bermuda	809
Dominican Republic	809
Jamaica	809
Puerto Rico	809
Virgin Islands	809
Inward WATS	800

TELEPHONE AREA CODE DIRECTORY

NUMERICAL LIST OF AREA CODES

Area Code	Location	Area Code	Location
201	New Jersey	401	Rhode Island
202	District of Columbia	402	Nebraska
203	Connecticut	403	Alberta
204	Manitoba	403	Northwest Territories
205	Alabama		(Dist. of Mackenzie) (Temp.)
206	Washington	403	Yukon (Temp.)
207	Maine	404	Georgia
208	Idaho	405	Oklahoma
209	California	406	Montana
212	New York	408	California
213	California	412	Pennsylvania
214	Texas	413	Massachusetts
215	Pennsylvania	414	Wisconsin
216	Ohio	415	California
217	Illinois	416	Ontario
218	Minnesota	417	Missouri
219	Indiana	418	Quebec
		419	Ohio
301	Maryland	501	Arkansas
302	Delaware	502	Kentucky
303	Colorado	503	Oregon
304	West Virginia	504	Louisiana
305	Florida	505	New Mexico
306	Saskatchewan	506	New Brunswick
307	Wyoming	507	Minnesota
308	Nebraska	509	Washington
309	Illinois	512	Texas
312	Illinois	513	Ohio
313	Michigan	514	Quebec
314	Missouri	515	Iowa
315	New York	516	New York
316	Kansas	517	Michigan
317	Indiana	518	New York
318	Louisiana	519	Ontario
319	Iowa		

TELEPHONE AREA CODE DIRECTORY

NUMERICAL LIST OF AREA CODES

Area Code	Location	Area Code	Location
601	Mississippi	800	Inward WATS
602	Arizona	801	Utah
603	New Hampshire	802	Vermont
604	British Columbia	803	South Carolina
605	South Dakota	804	Virginia
606	Kentucky	805	California
607	New York	806	Texas
608	Wisconsin	807	Ontario
609	New Jersey	808	Hawaii
612	Minnesota	809	Bahamas
613	Ontario	809	Bermuda
614	Ohio	809	Dominican Republic
615	Tennessee	809	Jamaica
616	Michigan	809	Puerto Rico
617	Massachusetts	809	Virgin Islands
618	Illinois	812	Indiana
		813	Florida
		814	Pennsylvania
		815	Illinois
		816	Missouri
		817	Texas
		819	Quebec
701	North Dakota	901	Tennessee
702	Nevada	902	Nova Scotia
703	Virginia	902	Prince Edward Island
704	North Carolina	903	Mexico
705	Ontario	904	Florida
707	California	906	Michigan
709	Newfoundland	907	Alaska
712	Iowa	912	Georgia
713	Texas	913	Kansas
714	California	914	New York
715	Wisconsin	915	Texas
716	New York	916	California
717	Pennsylvania	918	Oklahoma
		919	North Carolina

ALL POINTS—AREA CODE 205

ALL POINTS—AREA CODE 907

ALL POINTS—AREA CODE 602

ALL POINTS—AREA CODE 501

Place Name	Area Code	Place Name	Area Code	Place Name	Area Code	Place Name	Area Code	Place Name	Area Code
Acampo	209	Avenal	209	Bogue	916	Cantil	714	Colma	415
Adelaida	805	Avila	805	Bohemian Grove	707	Cantua Creek	209	Coloma	916
Adelanto	714	Avon	415	Bolinas	415	Canyon Country	805	Colton	714
Adin	916	Azusa	213	Boonville	707	Capay (Glenn Co.)	916	Columbia	209
Aetna Springs	707			Boron	714	Capay (Yolo Co.)	916	Colusa	916
Agnew	408			Borrego	714	Capistrano Beach	714	Compton	213
Agoura	213	Baden	415	Borrego Springs	714	Capistrano Valley	714	Concord	415
Aguanga	714	Badger	209	Boulder Creek	408	Capitola	408	Copperopolis	209
Ahwahnee	209	Baker	714	Bowles	209	Cardiff	714	Corcoran	209
Alameda	415	Bakersfield	805	Boyes Hot Springs	707	Carlotta	707	Cordelia	707
Alameda Naval Air		Balboa	714	Bradbury	213	Carlsbad	714	Corning	916
Station	415	Baldwin Park	213	Bradley	805	Carmel	408	Corona	714
Alamo	415	Ballard	805	Brawley	714	Carmel Highlands	408	Corona del Mar	714
Albany	415	Ballico	209	Bray	916	Carmel Valley	408	Coronado	714
Alberhill	714	Balls Ferry	916	Brea	714	Carmichael	916	Corte Madera	415
Albion	707	Bangor	916	Brentwood	415	Carnelian Bay	916	Costa Mesa	714
Alcatraz	415	Banning	714	Bridgeport	714	Carpinteria	805	Cotati	707
Alderpoint	707	Bard	714	Bridgeville	707	Carrisa Plains	805	Cottonwood	916
Alder Springs	209	Barstow	714	Brisbane	415	Carson	213	Coulterville	209
Alhambra	213	Bassett	213	Brockway	916	Cartago	714	Courtland	916
Alisal	408	Bass Lake	209	Broderick	916	Caruthers	209	Covelo	707
Alleghany	916	Bayliss	916	Brookdale	408	Casmalia	805	Covina	213
Alma	408	Baywood Park	805	Brooks	916	Castaic	805	Cowell	415
Almaden	408	Beale Air Force Base	916	Browns Valley	916	Castle Air Force Base	209	Coyote	408
Alpaugh	209	Bear Valley	209	Bryn Mawr	714	Castro Valley	415	Crescent City	707
Alpine (Alpine Co.)	916	Beaumont	714	Bryte	916	Castroville	408	Crescent Mills	916
Alpine		Beckwourth	916	Buelton	805	Cathedral City	714	Crestline	714
(San Diego Co.)	714	Bell	213	Buena Park	714	Catheys Valley	209	Crockett	415
Alta	916	Bellflower	213	Buntingville	916	Cayucos	805	Cromberg	916
Altadena	213	Bell Gardens	213	Burbank		Cazadero	707	Crowley Lake	714
Al Tahoe	916	Belmont	415	(Los Angeles Co.)	213	Cedar Glen	714	Crows Landing	209
Alta Loma	714	Belmont Shore	213	Burbank		Cedar Pines Park	714	Cucamonga	714
Altaville	209	Belridge	805	(Santa Clara Co.)	408	Cedarville	916	Cudahy	213
Alton	707	Belvedere		Burlingame	415	Centerville		Culver City	213
Alturas	916	(Los Angeles Co.)	213	Burney	916	(Alameda Co.)	415	Cupertino	408
Alvarado	415	Belvedere (Marin Co.)	415	Burrel	209	Centerville		Cutler	209
Alviso	408	Ben Hur	209	Butte City	916	(Fresno Co.)	209	Cuyama	805
Amador City	209	Benicia	707	Buttonwillow	805	Central Valley	916	Cypress	714
Anaheim	714	Ben Lomond	408	Byron	415	Ceres	209		
Anderson	916	Benton	714			Cerritos	213		
Angel Island	415	Berkeley	415			Challenge	916		
Angels Camp	209	Berkeley Recreation		Cabazon	714	Chambers Lodge	916	Daggett	714
Angwin	707	Camp	209	Calabasas	213	Charter Oak	213	Dairyville	916
Annapolis	707	Bermuda Dunes	714	Calaveras Big Trees	209	Chatsworth	213	Daly City	415
Antelope	916	Berrenda Mesa	805	Calexico	714	Cherry Valley		Dana	916
Antioch	415	Berry Creek	916	California City	714	(Riverside Co.)	714	Dana Point	714
Anza	714	Berryessa	707	California Hot Springs	805	Chester	916	Danville	415
Applegate	916	Bethel Island	415	Calimesa	714	Chicago Park	916	Darwin	714
Apple Valley	714	Betteravia	805	Calipatria	714	Chico	916	Davenport	408
Aptos	408	Beverly Hills	213	Calistoga	707	China Lake	714	Davis	916
Aqueduct	805	Bidwell Bar	916	Callahan	916	Chino	714	Death Valley	714
Arboga	916	Bieber	916	Calpella	707	Chowchilla	209	Decoto	415
Arbuckle	916	Big Basin	408	Calwa	209	Chualar	408	Deer Park	707
Arcadia	213	Big Bear City	714	Camanche	209	Chula Vista	714	Delano	805
Arcata	707	Big Bear Lake	714	Camarillo	805	Citrus Heights	916	Delhi	209
Argus	714	Big Bend	916	Cambria	805	Claremont	714	Del Mar	714
Arleta	213	Big Bend Hot Springs	916	Camino	916	Clarksburg	916	Del Monte	408
Arlington	714	Big Creek	209	Campbell	408	Clayton	415	Delpiedra	209
Armona	209	Biggs	916	Camp Cooke	805	Clearlake Highlands	707	Del Rey	209
Aromas	408	Big Pine	714	Camp Ducey	209	Clearlake Oaks	707	Del Rey Oaks	408
Arrowbear	714	Big Springs	916	Camp Kaweah	209	Clearlake Park	707	Del Rosa	714
Arrowhead	714	Big Sur	408	Campo	714	Clements	209	Descanso	714
Arrowhead Springs	714	Big Wheels	916	Camp Pendleton	714	Clio	916	Desert Beach	714
Arroyo Grande	805	Bijou	916	Camp Richardson	916	Cloverdale	707	Desert Center	714
Artesia	213	Biola	209	Camp Roberts	805	Clovis	209	Desert Hot Springs	714
Artois	916	Birds Landing	707	Camp San Luis		Coachella	714	Desert Shores	714
Arvin	805	Bishop	714	Obispo	805	Coalinga	209	Desmont	714
Asti	707	Black Point	415	Camp Seeley	714	Coarsegold	209	Devore	714
Atascadero	805	Blairsden	916	Camp Sierra	209	Coast Guard Airbase	415	Diablo	415
Atherton	415	Bloomington	714	Camptonville	916	Coast Guard District		Diamond Bar	714
Atwater	209	Blue Lake	707	Camp Wishon	209	Hdqrs.	415	Diamond Springs	916
Auberry	209	Blythe	714	Cana	916	Cobb Mountain	707	Dillon Beach	707
Auburn	916	Bodega	707	Canby	916	Coleville	916	Dinuba	209
Aukum	209	Bodega Bay	707	Canoga Park	213	Colfax	916	Dixon	916
Avalon	213	Bodfish	714			Collinsville	707	Dobbins	916

Place Name	Area Code
Donner City	916
Dorris	916
Dos Palos	209
Douglas City	916
Downey	213
Downieville	916
Drytown	209
Duarte	213
Dublin	415
Ducor	209
Dulzura	714
Dumbarton	415
Dunlap	209
Dunnigan	916
Dunsmuir	916
Durham	916
Dutch Flat	916
Eagle Lake	916
Eagle Mountain	714
Eagle Rock	213
Eagleville	916
Earlimart	805
Earp	714
East Bakersfield	805
East Bay	415
East Contra Costa	415
East Highland	714
East Montebello	213
East Nicolaus	916
Easton	209
Eden Hot Springs	714
Edgemar	415
Edgemont	714
Edison	805
Edwards	805
Edwards Air Force Base	805
El Cajon	714
El Centro	714
El Cerrito	415
Elderwood	209
El Dorado	916
Eldridge	707
Elk	707
Elk Creek	916
Elk Grove	916
Elmira	707
El Mirage	714
El Modena	714
El Monte	213
El Rio	805
El Segundo	213
Elsinore	714
El Sobrante	415
El Toro Marine Base	714
El Verano	707
Elverta	916
Emeryville	415
Emigrant Gap	916
Emmet	408
Empire	209
Encinitas	714
Encino	213
Enterprise	916
Escalon	209
Escondido	714
Esparto	916
Estrella	805
Etiwanda	714
Etna	916
Eureka	707
Exchequer	209
Exeter	209
Fairfax	415
Fairfield	707
Fairfield-Suisun	707
Fairmead	209
Fair Oaks (Sacramento Co.)	916
Fair Oaks (San Luis Obispo Co.)	805
Fallbrook	714
Fallen Leaf Lake	916
Fall River	916
Fall River Mills	916
Falls Vale	714
Farmersville	209
Farmington	209
Fawnskin	714
Feather Falls	916
Felix	209
Fellows	805
Felton	408
Fern	916
Fernbridge	707
Ferndale	707
Fiddletown	209
Fields Landing	707
Fillmore	805
Finley	707
Firebaugh	209
Firestone Park	213
Fish Camp	209
Fish Canyon	213
Florin	916
Flournoy	916
Folsom	916
Fontana	714
Foresthill	916
Forest Home	714
Forestville	707
Fort Baker	415
Fort Bidwell	916
Fort Bragg	707
Fort Irwin	714
Fort Jones	916
Fort MacArthur	213
Fort Mason	415
Fort McDowell	415
Fort Miley	415
Fort Ord	408
Fort Ord Village	408
Fort Point Coast Guard Light Sta.	415
Fort Ross	707
Fort Scott	415
Fortuna	707
Foster City	415
Fountain Valley	714
Fowler	209
Franklin	916
Frazier Park	805
Fredericksburg	916
Freedom	408
Freeport	916
Fremont	415
Fremont-Newark	415
French Camp	209
French Gulch	916
Fresno	209
Friant	209
Fullerton	714
Fulton	707
Furnace Creek	714
Galt	209
Garberville	707
Gardena	213
Garden Grove	714
Gas Point	916
Gasquet	707
Gazelle	916
George Air Force Base	714
Georgetown	916
Gerber	916
Geyserville	707
Gilman Hot Springs	714
Gilroy	408
Glen Alpine	916
Glenburn	916
Glencoe	209
Glendale	213
Glendora	213
Glen Ellen	707
Glenn	916
Glennville	805
Globins Al Tahoe	916
Goldstone	714
Goleta	805
Gonzales	408
Gorman	805
Goshen	209
Graeagle	916
Granada Hills	213
Grangeville	209
Grant Grove	209
Grass Lake	916
Grass Valley	916
Greenbrae	415
Greenfield (Kern Co.)	805
Greenfield (Monterey Co.)	408
Green Valley Lake	714
Greenview	916
Greenville	916
Grenada	916
Gridley	916
Grimes	916
Groveland	209
Grover City	805
Guadalupe	805
Gualala	707
Guasti	714
Guerneville	707
Guernsey	209
Guinda	916
Gustine	209
Hacienda Heights	213
Halcyon	805
Half Moon Bay	415
Hamburg	916
Hamilton	916
Hamilton Air Force Base	415
Hamilton City	916
Hanford	209
Happy Camp	916
Happy Camp Ranger Station	916
Harbor City	213
Hardwick	209
Hatchet	916
Hat Creek	916
Havasu Lake	714
Hawaiian Gardens	213
Hawthorne	213
Hayfork	916
Hayward	415
Healdsburg	707
Heber	714
Helendale	714
Hemet	714
Herald	209
Hercules	415
Herlong	916
Hermosa Beach	213
Hesperia	714
Hickman	209
Highgrove	714
Highland	714
Highland Park	213
Hillsborough	415
Hilmar	209
Hinkley	714
Hiouchi	707
Hobart Mills	916
Hollister	408
Hollydale	213
Hollywood	213
Hollywood Beach	805
Holt	209
Holtville	714
Homeland	714
Homestead Valley	714
Homewood	916
Honeydew	707
Hood	916
Hoopa	916
Hopland	707
Hornbrook	916
Hornitos	209
Horse Creek	916
Hueneme	805
Hughson	209
Hume Lake	209
Hunter Liggett Military Reservation	408
Hunter's Point Drydock (Navy)	415
Hunters Valley	209
Huntington Beach	714
Huntington Lake	209
Huntington Park	213
Huron	209
Hydesville	707
Idlewild (Placer Co.)	916
Idria	408
Idyllwild (Riverside Co.)	714
Ignacio	415
Igo	916
Imola	707
Imperial	714
Imperial Beach	714
Independence	714
Indian Gulch	209
Indian Wells	714
Indio	714
Industry	213
Inglewood	213
Ingot	916
Inverness	415
Inwood	916
Inyokern	714
Ione	209
Iowa Hill	916
Iron Mountain	916
Irvine	714
Irvington	415
Irwin	209
Irwindale	213
Isleton	916
Ivanhoe	209
Jackson	209
Jacumba	714
Jamestown	209
Jamul	714
Janesville	916
Jenny Lind	209
Jerseydale	209
Johannesburg	714
Johnsondale	714
Johnstonville	916
Jolon	408
Joshua Tree	714
Jovista	805
Julian	714
June Lake	714
Keddie	916
Kelseyville	707
Kensington	415
Kentfield	415
Kenwood	707
Kerman	209
Kernvale	714
Kernville	714
Keyes	209
Keystone	209
King City	408
Kings Beach	916
Kingsburg	209
Kings Canyon	209
Kirkwood Meadows	209
Klamath	707
Klamath River	916
Knightsen	415
Knights Ferry	209
Knights Landing	916
Knowles	209
Korbel	707
La Canada	213
La Crescenta	213
Lafayette	415
La Grange	209
Laguna Beach	714
Laguna Hills	714
Lagunitas	415
La Habra	213
La Honda	415
La Jolla	714
Lake Almanor	916
Lake Arrowhead	714
Lake Berryessa	707
Lake City	916
Lake Hughes	805
Lake Isabella	714
Lakeport	707
Lakeside	714
Lakeview	714
Lake View Terrace	213
Lakewood	213
Lamanda Park	213
La Mesa	714
La Mirada	714
Lamont	805
Lancaster	805
Landers	714
La Puente	213
La Quinta	714
Larkspur	415
La Selva Beach	408
Lathrop	209
Laton	209

Place Name	Area Code	Place Name	Area Code	Place Name	Area Code	Place Name	Area Code	Place Name	Area Code
Laurel Canyon	213	Malibu	213	Montague	916	North Highlands	916	Pacific Beach	714
La Verne	714	Mammoth Lakes	714	Montalvo	805	North Hollywood	213	Pacific Grove	408
Lawndale	213	Manchester	707	Montara	415	North Palm Springs	714	Pacific Manor	415
Laws	714	Manhattan Beach	213	Monta Vista	408	Northridge	213	Pacific Palisades	213
Laytonville	707	Manteca	209	Montclair	714	North Sacramento	916	Pacoima	213
Lebec	805	Manton	916	Montebello	213	North San Juan	916	Paicines	408
Lee Vining	714	March Air Force Base	714	Montecito	805	North Shore	714	Pala	714
Leggett	707	Mare Island	707	Monterey	408	North Yuba	916	Palmdale	805
Le Grand	209	Mare Island		Monterey Park	213	Norton Air Force		Palm Desert	714
Lemon Cove	209	Navy Yard	707	Monte Rio	707	Base	714	Palms	213
Lemon Grove	714	Maricopa	805	Monte Sereno	408	Norwalk	213	Palm Springs	714
Lemoore	209	Marina	408	Montgomery Creek	916	Novato	415	Palo Alto	415
Lennox	213	Marina Del Rey	213	Montrose	213	Nubieber	916	Palo Cedro	916
Lenwood	714	Marin City	415	Moorpark	805	Nuevo	714	Palomar Mountain	714
Leucadia	714	Marine Depot of		Moraga	415	Nut Tree	707	Palos Verdes	213
Lewiston	916	Supplies	714	Moreno	714			Palo Verde	714
Lick Observatory	408	Mariposa	209	Morgan Hill	408			Panoche	408
Likely	916	Markleeville	916	Morongo Valley	714			Panorama City	213
Lincoln	916	Marshalls	415	Morro Bay	805	Oakdale	209	Paradise	916
Linden	209	Martell	209	Morro del Mar	805	Oakhurst	209	Paramount	213
Lindsay	209	Martinez	415	Moss Beach	415	Oak Knoll	916	Parker Dam	714
Litchfield	916	Mar Vista	213	Moss Landing	408	Oak Knoll		Parkfield	805
Littlerock	805	Marysville	916	Mountain Center	714	Ranger Station	916	Parlier	209
Little Shasta	916	Mather Air Force		Mountain Pass	714	Oakland	415	Pasadena	213
Live Oak		Base	916	Mountain Ranch	209	Oakland Army Base	415	Paskenta	916
(San Benito Co.)	408	Matilija Hot Springs	805	Mountain View	415	Oakland Recreation		Paso Robles	805
Live Oak (Sutter Co.)	916	Maxwell	916	Mount Baldy	714	Camp	209	Patterson	209
Livermore	415	Maywood	213	Mount Bullion	209	Oakley	415	Patton	714
Livingston	209	McClellan		Mount Eden	415	Oak Run	916	Patton Village	916
Locke	916	Air Force Base	916	Mount Hamilton	408	Oak View	805	Pauma Valley	714
Lockeford	209	McCloud	916	Mount Hebron	916	Oakville	707	Paynes Creek	916
Lodi	209	McFarland	805	Mount Hermon	408	Oasis (Riverside Co.)	714	Pebble Beach	408
Loleta	707	McKittrick	805	Mount Laguna	714	O'Brien	916	Pedro Valley	415
Loma Linda	714	Meadowview	916	Mount Shasta	916	Occidental	707	Penngrove	707
Loma Rica	916	Mecca	714	Mount Wilson	213	Ocean Cove	707	Pennington	916
Lomita	213	Meeks Bay	916	Muir Woods	415	Oceano	805	Penryn	916
Lomita Park	415	Mendocino	707	Mulberry	408	Ocean Park	213	Pepperwood	707
Lomo	916	Mendota	209	Murphys	209	Oceanside	714	Permanente	408
Lompoc	805	Menifee	714	Murray	209	Ocotillo	714	Perris	714
Lone Pine	714	Menlo Park	415	Murray Park	415	Oil Center	805	Pescadero	415
Long Beach	213	Mentone	714	Murrieta	714	Oil City	805	Petaluma	707
Lookout	916	Merced	209	Muscoy	714	Oildale	805	Petrolia	707
Loomis	916	Meridian	916	Myers Flat	707	Ojai	805	Phelan	714
Los Alamitos	213	Mesa Del Rey	408			Olancha	714	Philo	707
Los Alamos	805	Mesa Grande	714			Old River	805	Pickle Meadows	
Los Altos	415	Meyers	916			Oleander	209	Marine Base	714
Los Angeles	213	Michigan Bar	916	Napa	707	Oleum	415	Pico Rivera	213
Los Angeles Harbor		Middletown	707	National City	714	Olinda	916	Piedmont	415
Coast Guard Light		Midpines	209	Naval Ordnance		Olive	714	Piedra	209
Sta.	213	Midway	916	Test Station	714	Omo	209	Piercy	707
Los Banos	209	Midway City	714	Navarro	707	O'Neals	209	Pigeon Point Coast	
Los Gatos	408	Milford	916	Needles	714	Ono	916	Guard Light Sta.	415
Los Laureles	408	Millbrae	415	Nevada City	916	Ontario	714	Pilot Hill	916
Los Molinos	916	Milbrae Highlands	415	Newark	415	Onyx	714	Pine Creek	714
Los Nietos	213	Mill Valley	415	New Auberry	209	Ophir	916	Pine Crest (San	
Los Olivos	805	Millville	916	Newberry	714	Orange	714	Bernardino Co.)	714
Los Serranos	714	Milpitas	408	Newbury Park	805	Orange Cove	209	Pinecrest	
Lost Hills	805	Milton	209	Newcastle	916	Orangevale	916	(Tuolumne Co.)	209
Lost Lake	714	Mineral	916	New Cuyama	805	Orcutt	805	Pinedale	209
Lovelock	916	Mira Loma	714	Newell	916	Oregon House	916	Pine Grove	
Lower Lake	707	Miramonte-Pinehurst	209	Newhall	805	Orick	707	(Amador Co.)	209
Loyalton	916	Miranda	707	Newman	209	Orinda	415	Pine Grove	
Lucerne	707	Mission Hills	213	New Pine Creek	916	Orland	916	(Shasta Co.)	916
Lucerne Valley	714	Mission San Jose	415	Newport Beach	714	Orleans	916	Pine Ridge	209
Lynwood	213	Mission Viejo	714	Nicasio	415	Oro Grande	714	Pine Valley	714
Lytle Creek	714	Moccasin	209	Nice	707	Orosi	209	Pinnacles	408
		Modesto	209	Nicolaus	916	Oroville	916	Pinole	415
		Moffett Field (Naval		Niland	714	Ostrom	916	Pinyon	714
Macdoel	916	Air Station)	415	Niles	415	Oswald	916	Pioneer	209
Madera	209	Mohawk	916	Nimbus	916	Oxnard	805	Pioneertown	714
Madison	916	Mojave	805	Nipinnawasee	209			Piru	805
Mad River	707	Mokelumne Hill	209	Nipomo	805			Pismo Beach	805
Madrone	408	Monmouth	209	Norco	714	Pacheco	415	Pittsburg	415
Magalia	916	Mono Lake	714	Nord	916	Pacifica	415	Pittville	916
Malaga	209	Monrovia	213	North Fork	209			Pixley	209

CALIFORNIA
Placentia—Upper Lake

Place Name	Area Code	Place Name	Area Code	Place Name	Area Code	Place Name	Area Code	Place Name	Area Code
Placentia	714	Rescue	916	San Juan Capistrano	714	Silverthorne	916	Taft	805
Placerville	916	Reseda	213	San Leandro	415	Simi Valley	805	Tahoe City	916
Planada	209	Reward	805	San Lorenzo	415	Sky Forest	714	Tahoe Pines	916
Plaster City	714	Rialto	714	San Lucas	408	Sloat	916	Tahoe Valley	916
Platina	916	Richardson Springs	916	San Luis Obispo	805	Sloughhouse	916	Tahoe Vista	916
Playa Del Rey	213	Richfield	916	San Luis Rey	714	Smartsville	916	Tahoma	916
Pleasant Grove	916	Richmond	415	San Marcos	714	Smith River	707	Talmage	707
Pleasant Hill	415	Richvale	916	San Marino	213	Smiths Center	916	Tanforan	415
Pleasanton	415	Ridgecrest	714	San Martin	408	Snelling	209	Tarzana	213
Plymouth	209	Rim Forest	714	San Mateo	415	Snow Valley	714	Taylorsville	916
Point Arena	707	Rio Dell	707	San Miguel	805	Soboba Hot Springs	714	Tecate	714
Point Mugu	805	Rio Del Mar	408	San Pablo	415	Soda Springs	916	Tecopa	714
Point Pinos	408	Rio Linda	916	San Pedro	213	Solana Beach	714	Tehachapi	805
Point Pleasant	916	Rio Nido	707	San Quentin	415	Soledad	408	Tehama	916
Point Reyes	415	Rio Oso	916	San Rafael	415	Solvang	805	Temecula	714
Point Reyes Coast Guard Light Sta.	415	Rio Vista	707	San Ramon	415	Somerset	916	Temple City	213
Point Reyes Coast Guard Sta.	415	Ripley	714	San Ramon Village	415	Somes Bar	916	Templeton	805
		Ripon	209	San Simeon	805	Somis	805	Tennant	916
Point Sur Coast Guard Light Sta.	408	Riverbank	209	Santa Ana	714	Sonoma	707	Terminal Island	213
Pollock Pines	916	Riverdale	209	Santa Anita Canyon	213	Sonora	209	Terminous	209
Pomona	714	Riverside	714	Santa Barbara	805	Soquel	408	Terra Bella	209
Pond	805	Robbins	916	Santa Clara	408	South Dos Palos	209	Thermal	714
Poplar	209	Robla	916	Santa Cruz	408	South Gate	213	Thermalito	916
Port Chicago	415	Robles del Rio	408	Santa Fe Springs	213	South Laguna	714	Thornton	209
Porterville	209	Rocklin	916	Santa Margarita	805	South Pasadena	213	Thousand Oaks	805
Port Hueneme	805	Rodeo	415	Santa Maria	805	South Placer	916	Thousand Palms	714
Portola	916	Rohnert Park	707	Santa Monica	213	South San Francisco	415	Thousand Pines	714
Portola Valley	415	Rolling Hills	213	Santa Paula	805	South Tahoe	916	Three Rivers	209
Port San Luis	805	Romoland	714	Santa Rosa	707	Spadra	714	Tiburon	415
Portuguese Bend	213	Rosamond	805	Santa Susana	805	Spreckels	408	Tierra Buena	916
Posey	805	Rosedale	805	Santa Venetia	415	Spring Valley	714	Timber Cove	707
Potrero	714	Rosemead	213	Santa Ynez	805	Springville	209	Tipton	209
Potrero Heights	213	Roseville	916	Santa Ysabel	714	Squaw Hill Ferry	916	Tivy Valley	209
Potter Valley	707	Ross	415	Santee	714	Squaw Valley (Fresno Co.)	209	Toll House	209
Poway	714	Rossmoor	213	San Ysidro	714			Tomales	707
Presidio of Monterey	408	Rough & Ready	916	Saratoga	408	Squaw Valley (Placer Co.)	916	Topanga	213
Presidio of San Francisco	415	Round Mountain	916	Saticoy	805	Standard	209	Topaz	916
Princeton	916	Rowland Heights	213	Saugus	805	Standish	916	Torrance	213
Princeton-by-the-Sea	415	Rumsey	916	Sausalito	415	Stanford	415	Toyon	916
Project City	916	Running Springs	714	Sawpit Canyon	213	Stanton	714	Tracy	209
		Rutherford	707	Scotia	707	Stateline	916	Tranquility	209
		Ryde	916	Scott Bar	916	Stevinson	209	Traver	209
				Scotts Valley	408	Stewarts Point	707	Travis Air Force Base	707
Quail Valley	714			Seacliff	408	Stinson Beach-Bolinas	415	Treasure Island	415
Quartz Hill	805	Sacramento	916	Seal Beach	213	Stirling City	916	Tres Pinos	408
Quincy	916	Sage	714	Sea Ranch	707	Stockton	209	Trevarno	415
		St. Helena	707	Seaside	408	Stockton Training Base	209	Trinidad	707
		Salida	209	Sebastopol	707	Stonyford	916	Trinity Center	916
		Salinas	408	Seeley	714	Storey (Madera Co.)	209	Trona	714
Rackerby	916	Salton	714	Seeley Flats	714	Stratford	209	Truckee	916
Railroad Flat	209	Salton Sea State Park	714	Seiad Valley	916	Strathmore	209	Tudor	916
Ramona	714	Samoa	707	Selby	415	Strawberry Flat	714	Tujunga	213
Rancho California	714	Sams Neck	916	Selma	209	Strawberry Inn	209	Tulare	209
Rancho Cordova	916	San Andreas	209	Sepulveda	213	Studio City	213	Tulelake	916
Rancho Mirage	714	San Anselmo	415	Sequoia	209	Sugar Loaf	714	Tuolumne	209
Rancho Santa Fe	714	San Ardo	408	Seven Oaks	714	Suisun	707	Tupman	805
Randsburg	714	San Benito	408	Shafter	805	Sultana	209	Turlock	209
Raymond	209	San Bernardino	714	Shandon	805	Summerland	805	Tustin	714
Red Bluff	916	San Bruno	415	Sharpe Army Depot	209	Summit Valley	714	Twain Harte	209
Redding	916	San Carlos-Belmont	415	Shasta Lake	916	Sun City	714	Twentynine Palms	714
Redlands	714	San Clemente	714	Shaver	209	Sunland	213	Twin Peaks	714
Red Mountain	714	Sand City	408	Sheldon	916	Sunland-Tujunga	213		
Redondo	213	San Diego	714	Shell Beach	805	Sunnymead	714		
Redondo Beach	213	San Dimas	714	Sherman Oaks	213	Sunnyvale	408		
Redway	707	San Fernando	213	Shingle Springs	916	Sunol	415	Ukiah	707
Redwood City	415	San Francisco	415	Shingletown	916	Sunset Beach	213	Union City	415
Redwood Valley	707	San Gabriel	213	Shoshone	714	Sun Valley	213	U.S. Naval Hdqrs.- Twelfth Naval Dist.	415
Reedley	209	Sanger	209	Sierra City	916	Surf	805	U.S. Naval Ordnance, Test Station	714
Relief Hot Springs	714	San Jacinto	714	Sierra Madre	213	Susanville	916	Universal City	213
Represa	916	San Joaquin	209	Sierra Ordnance Depot	916	Sutter City	916	Upland	714
		San Jose	408	Sierraville	916	Sutter Creek	209	Upper Lake	707
		San Juan	408	Signal Hill	213	Sylmar	213		
		San Juan Bautista	408	Silverado Canyon	714				

Place Name	Area Code	Place Name	Area Code	Place Name	Area Code	Place Name	Area Code	Place Name	Area Code
Vacaville	707	Villa Grande	707	Watsonville Junction	408	Whittier	213	Woodland Hills	213
Valinda	213	Vina	916	Watts	213	Wildomar	714	Woodside	415
Vallecito	209	Vineburg	707	Waukena	209	Williams	916	Woodville	209
Vallecitos Nuclear		Viola	916	Weaverville	916	Willits	707	Woody	805
Center	415	Visalia	209	Weed	916	Willow Creek		Wrightwood	714
Vallejo	707	Vista	714	Weimar	916	(Humboldt Co.)	916	Wyandotte	916
Valle Vista	714	Volcano	209	Weldon	714	Willow Creek		Wyntoon	916
Valley Acres	805			Wengler	916	(Lassen Co.)	916		
Valley Center	714			Weott	707	Willows	916		
Valley Ford	707			West Covina	213	Willow Springs	805		
Valley Home	209	Walker	916	Westhaven	209	Wilmington	213	Yerba Buena Island	415
Valley Springs	209	Walker Basin	805	Westlake Village	805	Wilseyville	209	Yermo	714
Val Verde	714	Wallace	209	Westley	209	Wilton	916	Yettem	209
Valyermo	805	Walnut	714	West Los Angeles	213	Winchester	714	Yorba Linda	714
Vandenberg Air		Walnut Creek	415	Westminster	714	Windsor	707	Yosemite	209
Force Base	805	Walnut Grove	916	Westmorland	714	Winterhaven	714	Youngstown	209
Van Nuys	213	Walnut Park	213	West Point	209	Winters	916	Yountville	707
Venice	213	Walteria	213	West Sacramento	916	Winton	209	Yreka	916
Ventura	805	Warm Springs	415	Westwood	916	Wishon	209	Yuba City	916
Verdugo City	213	Warner Springs	714	Westwood Village	213	Wofford Heights	714	Yucaipa	714
Vernon	213	Wasco	805	Wheatland	916	Woodbridge	209	Yucca Valley	714
Veterans Home	707	Washington	916	Wheeler Hot Springs	805	Woodfords	916		
Victor	209	Waterford	209	Whitethorn	707	Woodlake	209		
Victorville	714	Watsonville	408	Whitmore	916	Woodland	916	Zuma	213

ALL POINTS—AREA CODE 303

ALL POINTS—AREA CODE 203

ALL POINTS—AREA CODE 302

ALL POINTS—AREA CODE 202

Place Name	Area Code	Place Name	Area Code	Place Name	Area Code	Place Name	Area Code	Place Name	Area Code
Alachua	904	Bradenton	813	Coral Gables	305	Everglades	813	Gretna	904
Alford	904	Bradenton Beach	813	Coral Springs	305	Evinston	904	Grove City	813
Alligator Point	904	Bradley Junction	813	Coronado Beach	904			Groveland	904
Alligator Reef Coast		Brandon	813	Corry Field	904			Grove Park	904
Guard Light Sta.	305	Branford	904	Cortez	813	Fahkahatchee	813	Gulf Breeze	904
Altamonte Springs	305	Bratt	904	Cottage Hill	904	Fairfield	904	Gulf Hammock	904
Altha	904	Brewster	813	Cottondale	904	Felda	813	Gulf Port	813
Altoona	904	Brighton	813	Craig	305	Fellsmere	305	Gulfstream	305
Alturas	813	Bristol	904	Crawford	904	Fenholloway	904		
Alva	813	Bronson	904	Crawfordville	904	Fernandina Beach	904		
Amelia Island Coast		Brooker	904	Crescent City	904	Ferndale	305	Hague	904
Guard Light Sta	904	Brooksville	904	Crestview	904	Fern Park	305	Haines City	813
Anclote	813	Brownville	813	Cross City	904	Flagler Beach	904	Hallandale	305
Anclote Keys Coast		Bryceville	904	Crystal Beach	813	Flamingo	813	Hampton	904
Guard Light Sta.	813	Buchanan	813	Crystal River	904	Florahome	904	Hanson	904
Anna Maria	813	Buckingham	813	Crystal Springs	813	Floral City	904	Hastings	904
Anthony	904	Bunnell	904	Cudjoe Key	305	Florence Villa	813	Havana	904
Apalachicola	904	Bushnell	904	Cutler	305	Florida City	305	Hawthorne	904
Apollo Beach	813					Florida Sheriffs		Hernando	904
Apopka	305					Boys Ranch	904	Hialeah	305
Arcadia	813					Foley	904	Highland	904
Archer	904	Callahan	904	Dade City	904	Fort Denaud	813	Highland Beach	305
Argyle	904	Campbellton	904	Dania	305	Fort George	904	Highland City	813
Astatula	904	Camp Blanding	904	Davenport	813	Fort Lauderdale	305	High Springs	904
Astor	904	Camp E-chock-o-tee	904	Davie	305	Fort Lauderdale Coast		Hilliard	904
Astor Park	904	Canal Point	305	Davisville	904	Guard Sta. No. 208	305	Hillsboro Beach	305
Athena	904	Canaveral	305	Daytona Beach	904	Fort McCoy	904	Hobe Sound	305
Atlantic Beach	904	Candler	904	DeBary	305	Fort Meade	813	Holder	904
Auburndale	813	Cantonment	904	Deep Lake	813	Fort Myers	813	Holiday	813
Avon Park	813	Cape Canaveral	305	Deerfield Beach	305	Fort Myers Beach	813	Holley-Navarre	904
		Cape Coral	813	De Funiak Springs	904	Fort Ogden	813	Hollister	904
		Cape Haze	813	De Land	904	Fort Pierce	305	Holly Hill	904
		Cape Kennedy		De Leon Springs	904	Fort Walton Beach	904	Hollywood	305
Babson Park	813	AF Station	305	Delray Beach	305	Fort White	904	Holmes Beach	813
Bagdad	904	Cape Sable	813	Deltona	305	Fountain	904	Holopaw	305
Bahia Honda Key	305	Captiva Island	813	De Soto City	813	Fowey Rocks Coast		Holt	904
Baker	904	Carnestown	813	Destin	904	Guard Light Sta.	305	Homeland	813
Baldwin	904	Carol City	305	Disney World	305	Freeport	904	Homestead	305
Balm	813	Carrabelle	904	Doctors Inlet	904	Frontenac	305	Homosassa	904
Barberville	904	Carysfort Reef Coast		Dowling Park	904	Frostproof	813	Homosassa Springs	904
Barrineau Park	904	Guard Light Sta.	305	Drifton	904	Fruitland Park	904	Horseshoe Beach	904
Bartow	813	Caryville	904	Duck Key	305	Fruitville	813	Hosford	904
Bayard	904	Cassadaga	904	Dukes	904	Fullers	305	Howey-in-the-Hills	904
Bay Harbor Islands	305	Casselberry	305	Dundee	813			Hudson	813
Bay Pines	813	Caxambas	813	Dunedin	813			Hull	813
Bayshore Gardens	813	Cecil Field	904	Dunnellon	904	Gainesville	904	Hypoluxo	305
Beacon Hill	904	Cedar Keys	904	Dupont	813	Garden Cove	305		
Bean City	305	Center Hill	904			Gaskin	904		
Bell	904	Century	904			Gasparilla	813	Immokalee	813
Belleair	904	Chattahoochee	904	Eagle Lake	813	Geneva	305	Indialantic Beach	305
Belleair Beach	813	Cherry Lake	904	Eastlake Weir	904	Georgetown	904	Indian Harbor Beach	305
Belle Glade	305	Chiefland	904	East Orange	305	Gibsonton	813	Indian Lake	813
Belleview	904	Childs	813	East Palatka	904	Gifford	305	Indian Lake Estates	813
Bethel Creek Coast		Chipley	904	East Point	904	Gilberts Bar Coast		Indian River Inlet	
Guard Sta. No. 205	904	Chokoloskee	813	Eatonville	305	Guard Sta. No. 207	305	Coast Guard	
Beverly Hills	904	Chosen	305	Eau Gallie	305	Glendale	904	Sta. No. 206	305
Big Pine	305	Christmas	305	Edgar	904	Glen St. Mary	904	Indian Rocks Beach	813
Biscayne Bay Coast		Chuluota	305	Edgewater	904	Glenwood	904	Indiantown	305
Guard Sta. No. 209	305	Chumuckla	904	Eglin Air Force Base	904	Golden Beach	305	Indrio	305
Bithlo	305	Citra	904	Egmont Key	813	Gonzalez	904	Inglis	904
Blanton	904	Citrus Park	813	Eldred	305	Goodland	813	Interbay	813
Blountstown	904	Citrus Springs	904	Elfers	813	Goodno	813	Interlachen	904
Boca Chica	305	City Point	305	El Jobean	813	Goulds	305	Inverness	904
Boca Chica Auxiliary		Clearwater	813	Elkton	904	Graceville	904	Iona	813
Air Facilities	305	Clearwater Beach	813	Ellenton	813	Graham	904	Irvine	904
Boca Grande	813	Clermont	904	Ellyson Field	904	Grandin	904	Islamorada	305
Boca Raton	305	Cleveland	813	Eloise	813	Grand Island	904	Island Grove	904
Bonifay	904	Clewiston	813	Emporia	904	Grand Ridge	904		
Bonita Springs	813	Cocoa	305	Englewood	813	Grant	305		
Bostwick	904	Cocoa Beach	305	Enterprise	305	Grassy Key	305	Jacksonville	904
Boulogne	904	Coconut Grove	305	Estero	813	Green Cove Springs	904	Jacksonville Beach	904
Bowling Green	813	Coleman	904	Esto	904	Greensboro	904	Jasper	904
Boyd	904	Collier City	813	Eustis	904	Greenville	904	Jay	904
Boynton Beach	305	Conch Key	305	Eva	904	Greenwood	904		

FLORIDA
Jennings—South Bay

Place Name	Area Code
Jennings	904
Jensen Beach	305
Johnson	904
Juno Beach	305
Jupiter	305
Kathleen	813
Keaton Beach	904
Kenansville	305
Kendall	305
Kendrick	904
Kennedy, J. F. Space Center	305
Keuka	904
Key Biscayne	305
Key Colony Beach	305
Key Largo	305
Keystone Heights	904
Keysville	813
Key West	305
Killarney	305
Kingsley Lake	904
Kissimmee	305
La Belle	813
Lacoochee	904
Lacosta Island	813
LaCrosse	904
Lady Lake	904
Laguna Beach	904
Lake Alfred	813
Lake Buena Vista	305
Lake Butler	904
Lake City	904
Lake Como	904
Lake Garfield	813
Lake Hamilton	813
Lake Harbor	305
Lake Helen	904
Lake Jem	904
Lakeland	813
Lake Mary	305
Lake Monroe	305
Lakemont	813
Lake Park	305
Lake Placid	813
Lake Wales	813
Lake Weir	904
Lake Worth	305
Lamont	904
Lanark Village	904
Land O'Lakes	813
Lantana	305
Largo	813
Lauderdale-By-The-Sea	305
Lauderdale Lakes	305
Lauderhill	305
Laurel	813
Laurelhill	904
Lawtey	904
Lecanto	904
Lee	904
Leesburg	904
Lehigh Acres	813
Lighthouse Point	305
Limestone	813
Limona	813
Lithia	813
Little River	305
Little Torch Key	305
Live Oak	904
Lloyd	904
Lochloosa	904
Lockhart	305
Long Beach	813
Longboat Key	813
Long Key	305
Longwood	305
Loretto	904
Loughman	813
Lowell	904
Loxahatchee Farm	305
Lulu	904
Luraville	904
Lutz	813
Lynn Haven	904
Macclenny	904
MacDill Air Force Base	813
Madeira Beach	813
Madison	904
Maitland	305
Malabar	305
Malone	904
Manalapan	305
Manatee	813
Mandarin	904
Mango	813
Marathon	305
Marco Island	813
Margate	305
Marianna	904
Marietta	904
Marineland	904
Mary Esther	904
Masaryktown	904
Mascotte	904
Matecumbe	305
Maxville	904
Mayo	904
Mayport	904
Mayport U.S. Naval Air Sta.	904
McCoy Air Force Base	305
McIntosh	904
McMeekin	904
Melbourne	305
Melbourne Beach	305
Melrose	904
Memphis	813
Merritt Island	305
Mexico Beach	904
Miami	305
Miami Beach	305
Miami Shores	305
Miami Springs	305
Micanopy	904
Micco	305
Miccosukee	904
Middleburg	904
Milton	904
Mims	305
Minneola	305
Miramar	305
Molino	904
Monroe	813
Monticello	904
Montverde	305
Moore Haven	813
Mossyhead	904
Moultrie	904
Mountain Lake	813
Mount Dora	904
Mount Pleasant	904
Mount Plymouth	904
Mulberry	813
Munson	904
Murdock	813
Myakka	813
Myrtle Grove	904
Naples	813
Naranja	305
National Gardens	904
Navarre	904
Neptune Beach	904
Newberry	904
Newport	904
New Port Richey	813
New Smyrna Beach	904
Newtown	813
Niceville	904
Nichols	813
Nobleton	904
Nocatee	813
Nokomis	813
Noma	904
North Dade	305
North Fort Myers	813
North Key Largo	305
North Lakeland	813
North Miami Beach	305
North Naples	813
North Palm Beach	305
North Port	813
Oak	904
Oak Hill	904
Oakland	305
Oakland Park	305
O'Brien	904
Ocala	904
Ocean Breeze Park	305
Oceanway	904
Ochopee	813
Ocklocknee	904
Ocoee	305
Odessa	813
Ojus	305
Okahumpka	904
Okeechobee	813
Oklawaha	904
Oldsmar	813
Old Town	904
Olustee	904
Olympia	305
Ona	813
Oneco	813
Opa Locka	305
Orange City	904
Orange Lake	904
Orange Park	904
Orange Springs	904
Orlando	305
Ormond Beach	904
Osprey	813
Osteen	305
Otter Creek	904
Oviedo	305
Oxford	904
Ozona	813
Pace	904
Pahokee	305
Palatka	904
Palma Sola	813
Palm Bay	305
Palm Beach	305
Palm City	305
Palm Coast	904
Palmdale	813
Palmetto	813
Palm Harbor	813
Palm Shores	305
Palm Valley	904
Panacea	904
Panama City	904
Panama City Beach	904
Panama City Naval Sta.	904
Panasoffkee	904
Paola	305
Paolita	813
Parker	904
Parrish	813
Passagrille	813
Patrick Air Force Base	305
Paxton	904
Pembroke	813
Pembroke Pines	305
Penney Farms	904
Pensacola	904
Pensacola Naval Air Station	904
Perrine	305
Perry	904
Philips Camp	904
Pierce	813
Pierson	904
Pigeon Key	305
Pinecastle	305
Pinellas Park	813
Pine Island	813
Pinetta	904
Pirates Cove	305
Placida	813
Plantation	305
Plantation Key	305
Plant City	813
Plymouth	305
Point Washington	904
Polk City	813
Pomona Park	904
Pompano Beach	305
Ponce de Leon	904
Ponte Vedra	904
Ponte Vedra Beach	904
Port Charlotte	813
Port Everglades	305
Port Mayaca	305
Port Orange	904
Port Richey	813
Port St. Joe	904
Port St. Lucie	305
Port Sewall	305
Port Tampa	813
Princeton	305
Punta Gorda	813
Punta Rassa	813
Putnam Hall	904
Quay	305
Quincy	904
Quintette	904
Raiford	904
Raleigh	904
Reddick	904
Redington Beach	813
Reynolds Hill	904
Ridge Manor	904
River Junction	904
Riverview	813
Riviera Beach	305
Rocket City	305
Rock Harbor	305
Rockledge	305
Romeo	904
Roseland	305
Royal Palm Beach	305
Royal Palm Hammock	813
Rubonia	813
Ruskin	813
Safety Harbor	813
St. Andrew	904
St. Augustine	904
St. Augustine Beach	904
St. Catherine	904
St. Cloud	305
St. James City	813
St. Joe Beach	904
St. Leo	904
St. Marks	904
St. Petersburg	813
St. Petersburg Beach	813
Salem	904
Salerno	305
Salt Springs	904
Samoset	813
San Antonio	904
Sanderson	904
Sanford	305
Sanibel—Captiva Islands	305
San Mateo	904
Santa Rosa Beach	904
Santa Rosa Coast Guard Sta. No. 212	904
Sarasota	813
Satellite Beach	305
Satsuma	904
Saufley Field	904
Scottsmoor	305
Seagrove Beach	904
Sebastian	305
Sebring	813
Secotan	904
Seffner	813
Seminole	813
Seville	904
Sewalls Point	305
Shady Grove	904
Shalimar	904
Shamrock	904
Sharpes	305
Sherman	813
Shiloh	904
Sidney	813
Silver Springs	904
Silver Springs Shores	904
Slater	813
Snake Creek	305
Sneads	904
Sopchoppy	904
Sorrento	904
South Bay	305

Place Name	Area Code	Place Name	Area Code	Place Name	Area Code	Place Name	Area Code	Place Name	Area Code
South Miami	305	Tallahassee	904	Umatilla	904	Wauchula	813	Windermere	305
Southport	904	Tallavast	813	Union Park	305	Wausau	904	Winter Beach	305
Sparr	904	Tamarac	305			Waverly	813	Winter Garden	305
Springfield	904	Tamiami City	813			Webster	904	Winter Haven	813
Spring Hill	904	Tampa	813			Weekiwachee Springs	904	Winter Park	305
Spring Lake	**813**	Tangerine	904			Weirsdale	904	Winter Springs	305
Starke	904	Tarpon Springs	813	Valkaria	305	Wekiwa-Springs	305	Woodville	904
State Prison Farm	904	Tavares	904	Valparaiso	904	Welaka	904	Worthington Springs	904
Steinhatchee	904	Tavernier	305	Valrico	813	Wellborn	904		
Stuart	305	Temple Terrace	813	Venice	813	West Bay	904		
Sugarloaf Key	305	Ten Mile	305	Venus	813	West Palm Beach	305		
Sulphur Springs	813	Terra Ceia	813	Vernon	904	Westville	904		
Sumatra	904	The Beaches	904	Vero Beach	305	Wewahitchka	904		
Summerfield	904	Thonotosassa	813	Vilas	904	Whale Harbor	305	Yalaha	904
Summer Haven	904	Tice	813			White City (Gulf Co.)	904	Yankeetown	904
Summerland Key	305	Tildenville	305			White City		Yeehaw Junction	305
Sumterville	904	Titusville	305			(St. Lucie Co.)	305	Yelvington	904
Sun City	813	Trailer Estates	813			White Springs	904	Youngstown-Fountain	904
Sunny Hills	904	Treasure Island	813	Wabasso	305	Whitfield Estates	813	Yulee	904
Sunny Isles	305	Trenton	904	Wacissa	904	Whiting Field	904		
Sunny Side Beach	904	Trilby	904	Wakulla	904	Whitney	904		
Surfside	305	Trillacoochee	904	Wakulla Springs	904	Wildwood	904		
Suwannee	904	Twenty Mile Bend		Waldo	904	Williams Point	305		
Switzerland	904	(Palm Beach Co.)	305	Walnut Hill	904	Williston	904		
		Tyndall Air		Warm Mineral		Wilma	904	Zellwood	305
		Force Base	904	Springs	813	Wilton Manor	305	Zephyrhills	813
Taft	305	Tyndall Field	904	Warrington	904	Wimauma	813	Zolfo Springs	813

Place Name	Area Code	Place Name	Area Code	Place Name	Area Code	Place Name	Area Code	Place Name	Area Code
Abba	912	Bethlehem	404	Cartecay	404	Covington	404	Elberton	404
Abbeville	912	Between	404	Carters	404	Cox	912	Elko	912
Acree	912	Bibb City	404	Cartersville	404	Crabapple	404	Ellabelle	912
Acworth	404	Big Canoe	404	Caruso	404	Crandall	404	Ellaville	912
Adairsville	404	Bishop	404	Cassville	404	Cravey	912	Ellenton	912
Adel	912	Blackshear	912	Cataula	404	Crawford	404	Ellenwood	404
Adrian	912	Blairsville	404	Cave Spring	404	Crawfordville	404	Ellerslie	404
Ailey	912	Blakely	912	Cecil	912	Crescent	912	Ellijay	404
Alamo	912	Blitchton	912	Cedar Grove	912	Crest	404	Emerson	404
Alapaha	912	Bloomingdale	912	Cedar Point	912	Crosland	912	Emory	404
Albany	912	Blount	912	Cedar Springs	912	Culloden	912	English Eddy	912
Aline	912	Blue Ridge	404	Cedartown	404	Cumming	404	Enigma	912
Allenhurst	912	Bluffton	912	Centerville		Cusseta	404	Epworth	404
Allentown	912	Blundale	912	(De Kalb Co.)	404	Cuthbert	912	Erick	912
Alma	912	Blythe	404	Centerville				Esom Hill	404
Alpharetta	404	Bogart-Statham	404	(Houston Co.)	912			Eton	404
Alston	912	Bolton	404	Centerville				Eulonia	912
Alto	404	Bonaire	912	(Wilkes Co.)	404	Dacula	404	Evans	404
Alvaton	404	Boone Hill	912	Chalybeate Springs	404	Dahlonega	404	Everett City	912
Ambrose	912	Boston	912	Chamblee	404	Daisy	912	Experiment	404
Americus	912	Bostwick	404	Charles	912	Dallas	404		
Anderson	912	Bowdon	404	Charlotte	912	Dalton	404		
Andersonville	912	Bowersville	404	Chastain	404	Damascus	912		
Anguilla	912	Bowman	404	Chatsworth	404	Danielsville	404	Fairburn	404
Aonia	404	Boxspring	404	Chattahoochee	912	Danville	912	Fairmount	404
Appling	404	Boynton	404	Chauncey	912	Darien	912	Fair Oaks	404
Arabi	912	Bradley	912	Chester	912	Dasher	912	Fairyland	404
Aragon	404	Brantley	912	Chickamauga	404	Davisboro	912	Fargo	912
Argyle	912	Braselton	404	Chicopee	404	Dawnville	404	Farmington	404
Arlington	912	Bremen	404	Chipley	404	Dawson	912	Farrar	404
Armuchee	404	Brentwood	912	Chula	912	Dawsonville	404	Fayetteville	404
Arnoldsville	404	Brewton	912	Cisco	404	Dearing	404	Felton	404
Arp	912	Bristol	912	Clarkdale	404	Decatur	404	Fife	404
Ashburn	912	Bronwood	912	Clarkesville	404	Delray	404	Fincherville	404
Ashland	404	Brookfield	912	Clarks Bluff	912	Demorest	404	Finleyson	912
Ashton	912	Brooklet	912	Clarkston	404	De Soto	912	Fish	404
Atco	404	Brooklyn	912	Claxton	912	Devereux	404	Fitzgerald	912
Athens	404	Brooks	404	Clayton	404	Dewyrose	404	Fitzpatrick	912
Atlanta	404	Browning	912	Clermont	404	Dexter	912	Flemington	912
Attapulgus	912	Browns Crossing	912	Cleveland	404	Dial	404	Flintside	912
Auburn	404	Browns Station	912	Climax	912	Dickey	912	Flintstone	404
Augusta	404	Broxton	912	Clinchfield	912	Dillard-Mountain City	404	Flippen	404
Austell	404	Brunswick	912	Clito	912	Dixie	912	Florence	912
Autreyville	912	Buchanan	404	Cloudland	404	Dobbins Air		Flovilla	404
Avera	404	Buena Vista	912	Clyattville	912	Force Base	404	Flowery Branch	404
Avondale	912	Buffington	404	Cobb	912	Doerun	912	Floyd	404
Avondale Estates	404	Buford	404	Cobbham	404	Doles	912	Folkston	912
Axson	912	Bullards	912	Cobbtown	912	Donalsonville	912	Forest Glen	912
		Burnt Fort	912	Cochran	912	Dooling	912	Forest Park	404
		Burwell	404	Cochran Field	912	Doraville	404	Forest Pond	912
Baconton	912	Butler	912	Coffinton	912	Dorchester	912	Forsyth	912
Bainbridge	912	Butler Island	912	Cohutta	404	Double Branches	404	Fort Benning	404
Bairdstown	404	Byromville	912	Cohutta Springs	404	Doublehead	912	Fort Gaines	912
Baldview	404	Byron	912	Colbert	404	Douglas	912	Fort Gordon	404
Baldwin	404			Coleman	912	Douglas Lake	912	Fort McPherson	404
Ball Ground	404			Colesburg	912	Douglasville	404	Fort Oglethorpe	404
Banning	404			College Park	404	Dover	912	Fortson	404
Barnesville	404	Cadwell	912	Collins	912	Dry Branch	912	Fort Stewart	912
Barnett	404	Cairo	912	Colquitt	912	Dry Pond	404	Fort Valley	912
Barney	912	Calhoun	404	Columbus	404	Dublin	912	Franklin	404
Bartow	912	Calvary-Reno	912	Comer	404	Dudley	912	Franklin Springs	404
Barwick	912	Camak	404	Commerce	404	Duluth	404	Fry	404
Bascom	912	Camilla	912	Concord	404	Dunwoody	404	Funston	912
Batesville	404	Camp Civitania	404	Conley	912	DuPont	912		
Battey General		Camp Dixie	404	Conyers	404	Durand	404		
Hospital	404	Camp Ground	404	Cooktown	912				
Baxley	912	Campton	404	Coolidge	912			Gabbettville	404
Bayboro	912	Candler	404	Coosa	404			Gainesville	404
Beaverdale	404	Canon	404	Cordele	912	Eastanollee	404	Garfield	912
Beersheba	404	Canoochee	912	Cordray	912	Eastman	912	Gartrell	404
Bellton	404	Canton	404	Corinth	404	East Point	404	Gay	404
Benevolence	912	Carlton	404	Cornelia	404	Eatonton	404	Geneva	404
Ben Hill	404	Carnegie	912	Cortez	912	Edison	912	Georgetown	912
Berlin	912	Carnesville	404	Cotton	912	Egypt	912	Gibson	404
Berryton	404	Carrollton	404	Covena	912	Elam	912	Gillsville	404

Place Name	Area Code	Place Name	Area Code	Place Name	Area Code	Place Name	Area Code	Place Name	Area Code
Girard	912	Hunter Field	912	Lilburn	404	Millen	912	Omaha	912
Gladys	912			Lilly	912	Millhaven	912	Omega	912
Glennville	912			Lincolnton	404	Millwood	912	Osierfield	912
Glenwood	912	Ideal	912	Lindale	404	Milner	404	Oxford	404
Glynco Naval Air		Ila	404	Linwood	404	Milstead	404		
Station	912	Imlac	404	Lithia Springs	404	Mineral Bluff	404		
Goats Rock	404	Indian Springs	404	Lithonia	404	Mitchell	404		
Godfrey	404	Inman	404	Lizella	912	Mize	404	Palmetto	404
Goode	404	Iron City	912	Loco	404	Modoc	912	Panola	404
Good Hope	404	Irwinton	912	Locust Grove	404	Molena	404	Parrott	912
Gorday	912	Irwinville	912	Loganville	404	Monroe	404	Patterson	912
Gordon	912			Loneoak	404	Montezuma	912	Pavo	912
Gordy's Mill	404			Long Pond	912	Monticello	404	Peachtree City	404
Goshen	912			Louisville	912	Montrose	912	Pearson	912
Gough	404	Jackson	404	Lovejoys Station	404	Moody Field	912	Pelham	912
Gracewood	404	Jacksonville	912	Lovelace	404	Moreland	404	Pembroke	912
Graham	912	Jakin	912	Lovett	912	Morgan	912	Pendergrass	404
Grantville	404	Jasper	404	Ludowici	912	Morganton	404	Penfield	404
Graves Station	912	Jefferson	404	Lula	404	Morganville	404	Pennville	404
Gray	912	Jeffersonville	912	Lumber City	912	Morris Station	912	Perkins	912
Graymont	912	Jekyll Island	912	Lumpkin	912	Morrow	404	Perry	912
Grayson	404	Jenkinsburg	404	Luthersville	404	Morven	912	Phoenix	404
Greensboro	404	Jesup	912	Lyerly	404	Moultrie	912	Pickard	404
Greenville	404	Jewell	404	Lynchburg	404	Mountain City	404	Pine Harbor	912
Griffin	404	Johnson Corner	912	Lynn	912	Mountain Park	404	Pinehurst	912
Grovetown	404	Jonesboro	404	Lyons	912	Mount Airy	404	Pine Lake	404
Guyton	912	Jones Creek	912			Mount Pleasant	912	Pinelog	404
		Juliette	912			Mount Vernon	912	Pine Mountain	404
		Junction City	404	Mableton	404	Mountville	404	Pine Mountain	
Habersham	404	Juniper	404	Macland	404	Murray	912	State Park	404
Haddock	912			Macon	912	Musella	912	Pine Mountain Valley	404
Hagan	912			Madison	404			Pineview	912
Hahira	912			Madras	404			Pitts	912
Halcyondale	912	Kathleen	912	Madray Springs	912	Nacoochee	404	Plainfield	912
Hamilton	404	Keith	404	Manassas	912	Nahunta	912	Plains	912
Hampton	404	Keithsburg	404	Manchester	404	Nashville	912	Plainville	404
Hapeville	404	Keller	912	Manor	912	Naylor	912	Pleasant Hill	912
Haralson	404	Kelly	404	Mansfield	404	Nelson	404	Plowshare	404
Hardwick	912	Kennesaw	404	Marble Hill	404	Nesbit	912	Point Peter	404
Harlem	404	Kensington	404	Marietta	404	Nevils	912	Pooler	912
Harris	404	Kenwood	404	Marshallville	912	Newborn	404	Portal	912
Harrison	912	Kenzie	404	Martin	404	New England	404	Porterdale	404
Hartsfield	912	Keysville	404	Martinez	404	New Holland	404	Port Wentworth	912
Hartwell	404	Kibbee	912	Massee	404	New Hope	404	Poulan	912
Hastings Farm	404	Kingsland	912	Matthews	404	Newington	912	Powder Springs	404
Hawkinsville	912	Kingston	404	Maxeys	404	Newnan	404	Powersville	912
Hayston	404	Kite	912	Maxim	404	Newton	912	Prater	404
Hazlehurst	912	Knoxville	912	Mayfield	404	Nicholls	912	Preston	912
Helen	404	Kramer	912	Maysville	404	Nicholson	404	Pulaski	912
Helena	912			McBean	912	Noble	404	Putney	912
Henderson	912			McBrayer Station	404	Norcross	404	Pyne	404
Hephzibah	404			McCaysville	404	Norman	404		
Herod	912	La Cross	912	McDonough	404	Norman Park	912		
Hiawassee	404	La Fayette	404	McGregor	912	Norristown	912	Quitman	912
Hickory Flat	404	La Grange	404	McIntosh	912	Norwood	404		
High Point	404	Lake Blackshear	912	McIntyre	912				
Hillsboro	404	Lake Burton	404	McLendon's Place	912				
Hilltonia	912	Lakeland	912	McRae	912			Rabun Gap	404
Hinesville	912	Lakemont	404	Meansville	404	Oakfield	912	Racepond	912
Hinsonton	912	Lake Park	912	Meda	404	Oak Park	912	Raleigh	404
Hiram	404	Lake Sinclair	912	Meigs	912	Oakwood	404	Ranger	404
Hoboken	912	Lakewood	404	Mendes	912	Ocee	404	Ramhurst	404
Hogansville	404	Lathamtown	404	Menlo	404	Ochlocknee	912	Ray City	912
Hollonville	404	Lavonia	404	Meridian	912	Ocilla	912	Rayle	404
Holly Springs	404	Lawrenceville	404	Merrillville	912	Oconee	912	Raymond	404
Homer	404	Leah	404	Mershon	912	Odessadale	404	Rebecca	912
Homerville	912	Leary	912	Metasville	404	Odum	912	Redan	404
Hortense	912	Lee Pope	912	Metcalf	912	Offerman	912	Red Oak	404
Hoschton	404	Leesburg	912	Metter	912	Ogeechee	912	Register	912
Howard	912	Lenox	912	Midland	404	Oglethorpe	912	Reidsville	912
Howells	912	Leola	912	Midville	912	Ohoopee	912	Remerton	912
Huching	404	Leslie	912	Midway	912	Oliver	912	Renfroe	912
Hughland	912	Lexington	404	Milan	912	Oliver General		Reno	912
Hull	404	Lexsy	912	Milledgeville	912	Hospital	404	Rentz	912

Place Name	Area Code	Place Name	Area Code	Place Name	Area Code	Place Name	Area Code	Place Name	Area Code
Resaca	404	Schlatterville	912	Stonewall	404	Turin	404	Waverly Hall	404
Rex	404	Scotland	912	Suches	404	Turner Field	912	Waycross	912
Reynolds	912	Scott	912	Summertown	912	Turnerville	404	Waynesboro	404
Reynoldsville	912	Scottdale	404	Summerville	404	Twin City	912	Waynesville	912
Rhine	912	Screven	912	Summit	912	Tybee Island	912	Wayside	912
Riceboro	912	Sea Island	912	Sumner	912	Tyrone	404	West Brow	404
Richland	912	Senoia	404	Surrency	912	Ty Ty	912	Weston	912
Richmond Hill	912	Seville	912	Suwanee	404	Tyus	404	West Point	404
Ridgeville	912	Shady Dale	404	Swainsboro	912			Westville	404
Rincon	912	Shannon	404	Sycamore	912			Whigham	912
Ringgold	404	Sharon	404	Sylvania	912			White	404
Rising Fawn	404	Sharpsburg	404	Sylvester	912	Unadilla	912	Whitehall	404
Riverdale	404	Sharps Spur	912			Union City	404	White Oak	912
Roberta	912	Shawnee	912			Union Point	404	White Plains	404
Robertstown	404	Shellman	912			U. S. Army-Hdqrs.		Whitesburg	404
Robins Air Force		Shellmans Bluff	912	Talbotton	404	of Service Commands-		Whitestone	404
Base	912	Shiloh	404	Talking Rock	404	Third Army	404	Whitley	912
Rochelle	912	Shingler	912	Tallapoosa	404	Upatoie	404	Whitney	404
Rockmart	404	Sigsbee	912	Tallulah Falls	404	Upson	404	Wildwood	404
Rocky Face	404	Siloam	404	Talmo	404	Uvalda	912	Wiley	404
Rocky Ford	912	Silver Creek	404	Tarrytown	912			Willacoochee	912
Roderick	912	Smithsonia	404	Tate	404			Williamson	404
Rome	404	Smithville	912	Tattnall Prison	912			Winder	404
Roopville	404	Smyrna	404	Taylorsville	404			Winfield	404
Rossville	404	Snellville	404	Tazewell	912	Valdosta	912	Winston	404
Roswell	404	Social Circle	404	Temperance	912	Valdosta Air Force		Winterville	404
Round Oak	912	Sonoraville	404	Temple	404	Base	912	Woodbine	912
Rover	404	Soperton	912	Tennga	404	Valona	912	Woodbury	404
Royston	404	South Guyton	912	Tennille	912	Vanna	404	Woodcliff	912
Rupert	912	Sparks	912	Thalmann	912	Vidalia	912	Woodland	404
Rural Hill	912	Sparta	404	The Rock	404	Vidette	404	Woodstock	404
Rutledge	404	Spence Field	912	Thomasboro	912	Vienna	912	Woodville	404
Rydal	404	Springfield	912	Thomaston	404	Villanow	404	Woolsey	404
Rye Patch	912	Spring Place	404	Thomasville	912	Villa Rica	404	Worthville	404
		Springvale	912	Thompson's Store	912			Wray	912
		Stapleton	404	Thomson	404			Wrens	404
		Stark	404	Thunderbolt	912	Waco	404	Wrightsville	912
St. George	912	Starrsville	404	Tifton	912	Wadley	912	
St. Marys	912	Statenville	912	Tiger	404	Walden	912	
St. Simons Island	912	Statesboro	912	Tignall	404	Waleska	404	
Sale City	912	Statham	404	Toccoa	404	Walthourville	912	Yatesville	404
Salem Church	404	Stellaville	404	Toomsboro	912	Waresboro	912	Young Harris	404
Sandersville	912	Stephens Crossing	912	Toonigh	404	Waring	404	Youngs	404
Sandy Cross	912	Sterling	912	Tournapull	404	Warm Springs	404	
Sandy Springs	404	Stevens Pottery	912	Towns	912	Warner Robins	912	
Sapelo Island	912	Stillmore	912	Townsend	912	Warrenton	404	
Sardis	912	Stillwell	912	Trenton	404	Warthen	912	Zebulon	404
Sargent	404	Stilson	912	Trion	404	Warwick	912	Zeigler	912
Sasser	912	Stockbridge	404	Trion Mills	404	Washington	404	Zenith	912
Savannah	912	Stockton	912	Tucker	404	Watkinsville	404	Zetella	404
Savannah Beach	912	Stone Mountain	404	Tunnel Hill	404	Waverly	912	Zingara	404

ALL POINTS—AREA CODE 808

ALL POINTS—AREA CODE 208

Place Name	Area Code	Place Name	Area Code	Place Name	Area Code	Place Name	Area Code	Place Name	Area Code
Abingdon	309	Ashland	217	Bennett	217	Breeds	309	Calumet City	312
Adair	309	Ashley	618	Bensenville	312	Breese	618	Calumet Park	312
Adams	217	Ashmore	217	Benson	309	Brereton	309	Camargo	217
Addieville	618	Ashton	815	Bentley	217	Brewer	217	Cambria	618
Addison	312	Assumption	217	Benton	618	Bridgeport	618	Cambridge	309
Adeline	815	Astoria	309	Berger	312	Bridgeview	312	Camden	217
Adrian	217	Athens	217	Berkeley	312	Brighton	618	Cameron	309
Agnew	815	Athensville	217	Berlin	217	Brimfield	309	Campbell Hill	618
Akin	618	Atkinson	309	Bernice	312	Bristol	312	Campgrove	309
Albany	309	Atlanta	217	Berry	217	Broadlands	217	Camp Lincoln	217
Albers	618	Atlas	217	Berwick	309	Broadview	312	Camp Logan	312
Albion	618	Atterberry	217	Berwyn	312	Broadwell	217	Camp Point	217
Alden	815	Atwood	217	Bethalto	618	Brock	815	Campus	815
Aledo	309	Auburn	217	Bethany	217	Brocton	217	Canton	309
Alexander	217	Augusta	217	Beverly	217	Bronson	217	Cantrall	217
Alexis	309	Aurora	312	Bible Grove	618	Brookfield	312	Capron	815
Alfolkey	815	Ava	618	Big Foot Prairie	815	Brooklyn		Carbon Cliff	309
Algonquin	312	Avena	618	Biggs	309	(St. Clair Co.)	618	Carbondale	618
Alhambra	618	Avia	618	Biggsville	309	Brooklyn		Carbon Hill	815
Allen	309	Aviston	618	Bigneck	217	(Schuyler Co.)	309	Carlinville	217
Allendale	618	Avon	309	Big Rock	312	Brookport	618	Carlock	309
Allens Corner	312	Ayers	618	Birds	618	Brookville	815	Carlyle	618
Allentown	309			Birkbeck	217	Brothers	217	Carman	309
Allenville	217			Birkner	618	Broughton	618	Carmi	618
Allerton	217			Birmingham	309	Brownell	312	Carpenter	618
Alma	618			Bishop	309	Browning	217	Carpentersville	312
Almora	312	Babylon	309	Bishop Hill	309	Brown Mills	815	Carriers Mills	618
Alonzo	815	Bader	309	Bismarck	217	Browns	618	Carrollton	217
Alorton	618	Baileyville	815	Bixby	618	Brownstown	618	Carterville	618
Alpha	309	Baker	815	Blackhawk Heights	312	Brownsville	618	Carthage	217
Alpine	312	Bald Mound	312	Blackstone	815	Brubaker	618	Carthage Junction	309
Alsey	217	Baldwin	618	Blair	618	Bruce	217	Carthage Lake	309
Alsip	312	Ballard	815	Blairsville		Brussels	618	Cartter	618
Alta	309	Banner	309	(Hamilton Co.)	618	Bryant	309	Cary	312
Altamont	618	Bannockburn	312	Blairsville		Bryce	815	Cascade	217
Alton	618	Barclay	217	(Williamson Co.)	618	Buckhart	217	Casey	217
Altona	309	Bardolph	309	Blanding	815	Buckingham	815	Caseyville	618
Alton Summit	618	Barrington	312	Blandinsville	309	Buckley	217	Castleton	309
Alto Pass	618	Barrow	217	Block	217	Buckner	618	Catlin	217
Alvin	217	Barry	217	Bloomingdale	312	Buda	309	Cave In Rock	618
Amboy	815	Barstow	309	Bloomington	309	Budd	815	Cayuga	815
Ames	618	Bartelso	618	Blue Island	312	Buena Vista	815	Cazenovia	309
Anchor	309	Bartlett	312	Blue Mound	217	Buffalo	217	Cedar Lake	312
Ancona	815	Bartonville	309	Blue Ridge	217	Buffalo Grove	312	Cedar Point	815
Andalusia	309	Basco	217	Bluff City	618	Buffalo Hart	217	Cedarville	815
Andover	309	Batavia	312	Bluff Hall	217	Buffalo Prairie	309	Centerville	
Andres	815	Batchtown	618	Bluff Lake	312	Bulpitt	217	(St. Clair Co.)	618
Andrew	217	Bath	217	Bluffs	217	Bunker Hill	618	Centerville	
Anna	618	Baylis	217	Bluff Springs	217	Bureau	815	(White Co.)	618
Annapolis	618	Beach	312	Bluford	618	Burgess	309	Central	815
Annawan	309	Beardstown	217	Blyton	309	Burlington	312	Central City	
Antioch	312	Beason	217	Bolingbrook	312	Burnham	312	(Grundy Co.)	815
Appanoose	217	Beaucoup	618	Bolivia	217	Burnside	217	Central City	
Apple River	815	Beavercreek	618	Bondville	217	Burnt Prairie	618	(Marion Co.)	618
Appleton	309	Beaverville	815	Bone Gap	618	Burr Oak	312	Centralia	618
Aptakisic	312	Beckemeyer	618	Bonfield	815	Burton	217	Cerro Gordo	217
Arcadia	217	Bedford	217	Bongard	217	Burton's Bridge	815	Chadwick	815
Archer	217	Bedford Park	312	Bonnie	618	Burton View	217	Chain O Lakes	312
Arcola	217	Beecher	312	Borton	217	Bush	618	Chambersburg	217
Ardmore	312	Beecher City	618	Boulder	618	Bushnell	309	Champaign-Urbana	217
Arenzville	217	Beechville	618	Bourbon	217	Bushton	217	Chana	815
Argenta	217	Belle Prairie	618	Bourbonnais	815	Butler	217	Chandlerville	217
Argo	312	Belle Rive	618	Bowden	309	Byrneville	618	Channahon	815
Argo Fay	815	Belleville	618	Bowen	217	Byron	815	Channel Lake	312
Argonne	312	Bellevue	309	Bowes	312			Chanute Air Force	
Argyle	815	Bellflower	309	Boyd	618			Base	217
Arlington	815	Bellmont		Braceville	815			Chapin	217
Arlington Heights	312	(Wabash Co.)	618	Bradford	309	Cabery	815	Chappell	312
Armington	217	Bellwood	312	Bradley	815	Cable	309	Charleston	217
Armstrong	217	Belmont		Braidwood	815	Cache	618	Charlotte	815
Aroma	815	(Du Page Co.)	312	Breckenridge		Cadwell	217	Chatham	217
Aroma Park	815	Belmont Heights	312	(Hancock Co.)	217	Cahokia	618	Chatsworth	815
Arrowsmith	309	Beltrees	618	Breckenridge		Cairo	618	Chatton	217
Arthur	217	Belvidere	815	(Sangamon Co.)	217	Caledonia	815	Chauncey	618
Ashkum	815	Bement	217			Calhoun	618	Chautauqua	618
		Benld	217						

ILLINOIS
Chebanse—Fosterburg

Place Name	Area Code	Place Name	Area Code	Place Name	Area Code	Place Name	Area Code	Place Name	Area Code
Chebanse	815	Cottage Hills	618	Dennison	217	East Grove	312	Everett	312
Chemung	815	Cottonwood	618	Denver	217	East Hazel Crest	312	Evergreen Park	312
Cheneyville	217	Council Hill	815	Depue	815	East Louisiana	217	Ewing	618
Chenoa	815	Coulterville	618	Derinda Center	815	East Lynn	217	Exeter	217
Cherry	815	Country Club Hills	312	Deselm	815	East Moline	309	Exline	815
Cherry Valley	815	Countryside	312	De Soto	618	East Muscatine	309	Eylar	815
Chester	618	Covell	309	Des Plaines	312	Easton	309		
Chesterfield	618	Cowden	217	Detroit	217	East Peoria	309		
Chestervale	217	Cowling	618	Dewey	217	East St. Louis	618	Fairbanks	217
Chesterville	217	Coxeyville	618	Dewitt	217	East Stockton	815	Fairbury	815
Chestnut	217	Crab Orchard	618	Dexter	618	Eberle	217	Fairdale	815
Chicago	312	Craig (Dewitt Co.)	217	Diamond	815	Ebner	815	Fairfield	618
Chicago Heights	312	Crainville	618	Diamond Hill	815	Eckard	309	Fairgrange	217
Chicago Ridge	312	Cramer	309	Diamond Lake	312	Eddyville	618	Fairhaven	815
Chili	217	Cravat	618	Dieterich	217	Edelstein	309	Fairland	217
Chillicothe	309	Creal Springs	618	Dillsburg	217	Eden	309	Fairman	618
Chrisman	217	Crescent City	815	Dimmick	815	Edgemont	618	Fairmont City	618
Christopher	618	Creston	815	Diplar Springs	309	Edgewood	618	Fairmount	217
Cicero	312	Crestwood	312	Disco	217	Edgington	309	Fair View (Cook Co.)	312
Cisco	217	Crete	312	Diswood	618	Edinburg	217	Fairview (Fulton Co.)	309
Cisne	618	Creve Coeur	309	Divernon	217	Edwardsville	618	Fairview	
Cissna Junction	815	Crisp	618	Dix	618	Edwardsville Crossing	618	(St. Clair Co.)	618
Cissna Park	815	Crooked Lake	312	Dixmoor	312	Effingham	217	Fairview Heights	618
Clare	815	Cropsey	309	Dixon	815	Egan	815	Faithorn	312
Claremont	618	Cross Lake	312	Dixon Springs	618	Eileen	815	Fall Creek	217
Clarence	217	Crossville	618	Doddsville	309	Elburn	312	Falling Spring	618
Clarendon Hills	312	Crystal Lake	815	Dollville	217	Elco	618	Fandon	309
Clarksdale	217	Cuba	309	Dolton	312	El Dara	217	Farina	618
Clarksville	217	Cullom	815	Dongola	618	Eldena	815	Farmdale	309
Clay City	618	Cumberland	312	Donnellson	217	Elderville	217	Farmer City	217
Clayton	217	Curran	217	Donovan	815	Eldorado	618	Farmersville	217
Claytonville	815	Custer Park	815	Doran	217	Eldred	217	Farmington	309
Clearing	312	Cutler	618	Dorchester	618	Eleroy	815	Fayetteville	618
Cliffdale	618	Cutmer	815	Dorrisville	618	Elgin	312	Fayville	618
Clifton	815	Cypress	618	Dorsey	618	Eliza	309	Federal	618
Clinton	217			Douglas	309	Elizabeth	815	Feehanville	312
Clintonville	312			Dover	815	Elizabethtown	618	Fenton	815
Cloverdale	312			Dow	618	Elk Grove	312	Ferrin	618
Clyde	312	Daggetts	815	Dowell	618	Elk Grove Village	312	Ferris	217
Coal City	815	Dahinda	309	Downers Grove	312	Elkhart	217	Fiatt	309
Coalton	217	Dahlgren	618	Downey	312	Elkhorn Grove	815	Fidelity	618
Coal Valley	309	Dailey	217	Downs	309	Elkville	618	Fieldon	618
Coatsburg	217	Dakota	815	Dresden Heights	815	Ellery	618	Fillmore	217
Cobden	618	Dale	618	Druces Lake	312	Elliott	217	Filson	217
Coello	618	Dallas City	217	DuBois	618	Elliottstown	217	Findlay	217
Coffeen	217	Dalton City	217	Duck Island	309	Ellis	217	Fisher	217
Colchester	309	Dalzell	815	Duck Lake	312	Ellis Grove	618	Fishhook	217
Coleman	312	Damascus	815	Dudley	217	Ellisville	309	Fithian	217
Coles	217	Dana	815	Dunbar	815	Ellsworth	309	Flag Center	815
Coleta	815	Danforth	815	Duncans Mills	309	Elmhurst	312	Flanagan	815
Colfax	309	Danvers	309	Dundas	618	Elmira	309	Flat Rock	618
Collinsville	618	Danville	217	Dundee	312	Elmwood	309	Flatville	217
Collison	217	Danway	815	Dunfermline	309	Elmwood Park	312	Fletcher	309
Colmar	309	Darien	312	Dunkel	217	El Paso	309	Flora	618
Colona	309	Darmstadt	618	Dunlap	309	Elsah	618	Floraville	618
Colp	618	Davis	815	Du Page	312	Elva	815	Florence	217
Columbia	618	Davis Junction	815	Dupo	618	Elvaston	217	Florence Station	815
Columbus	217	Dawson	217	Du Quoin	618	Elwin	217	Florid	815
Colusa	217	Dawson Park	815	Durand	815	Elwood	815	Flossmoor	312
Como	815	Daysville	815	Durham	217	Emden	217	Foosland	217
Compton	815	Decatur	217	Dwight	815	Emerson	815	Ford Central	815
Concord	217	Deep Lake	312			Emington	815	Forest (Cook Co.)	312
Congerville	309	Deer Creek	309			Energy	618	Forest City	309
Congress Park	312	Deerfield	312			Enfield	618	Forest Lake	312
Conover	309	Deer Grove	815	Eaglepoint	815	Enterprise	618	Forest Park	312
Cooks Mills	217	Deer Park	815	Earlville	815	Eola	312	Forest View	312
Cooksville	309	Deer Plain	618	East Alton	618	Equality	618	Forrest	
Cooperstown	217	Deers	217	East Brooklyn	815	Erie	309	(Livingston Co.)	815
Copperas Creek	309	De Kalb	815	East Carondelet	618	Esmond	815	Forreston	815
Coral	815	De Land	217	East Chicago Heights	312	Essex	815	Fort Gage	618
Cordova	309	Delavan	309	East Clinton	815	Etna	217	Fort Hill	312
Cornell	815	Delhi	618	East Dubuque	815	Eureka	309	Fort Sheridan	312
Cornland	217	Delmar	815	East Dundee	312	Evanston	312	Foster	309
Cortland	815	De Long	309	East Fort Madison	217	Evansville	618	Fosterburg	618
Coster	815	Delrey	815	East Galesburg	309	Evarts	815		

Place Name	Area Code	Place Name	Area Code	Place Name	Area Code	Place Name	Area Code	Place Name	Area Code
Foster Pond	618	Glencoe	312	Haldane	815	Hicks	618	Inverness	312
Fountain Creek	217	Glendale	618	Half Day	312	High Lake	312	Iola	618
Fountain Green	217	Glen Ellyn	312	Hallock	815	Highland	618	Ipava	309
Fowler	217	Glenn	618	Hallsville	217	Highland Park	312	Irene	815
Fox	312	Glenridge	618	Hamburg	618	Highlands	312	Iroquois	815
Fox Lake	312	Glenview	312	Hamel	618	Highwood	312	Irving	217
Fox River	312	Glenwood	312	Hamilton	217	Hillcrest	815	Irvington	618
Fox River Grove	312	Glover	217	Hamlet	309	Hillery	217	Irwin	815
Fox River Heights	312	Godars Landing	618	Hammond	217	Hillsboro	217	Isabel	217
Fox River Valley Gardens	312	Godfrey	618	Hampshire	312	Hillsdale	309	Island Lake	312
Frankfort	815	Godley	815	Hampton	309	Hillside	312	Itasca	312
Frankfort Heights	618	Golconda	618	Haney	312	Hillview	217	Iuka	618
Franklin	217	Golden	217	Hanna City	309	Himrod	217	Ivanhoe (Cook Co.)	312
Franklin Grove	815	Golden Eagle	618	Hanover	815	Hinckley	815	Ivanhoe (Lake Co.)	312
Franklin Park	312	Goldengate	618	Hanover Park	312	Hindsboro	217	Ivesdale	217
Franklinville	815	Golf	312	Harco	618	Hines	312		
Frederick	217	Goodenow	312	Hardin	618	Hinsdale	312		
Freeburg	618	Goodfield	309	Harding	815	Hitt	815		
Freeman Spur	618	Good Hope	309	Hardinville	618	Hodges Park	618	Jacksonville	217
Freeport	815	Goodings Grove	312	Harkers Corners	309	Hodgkins	312	Jacob	618
Fremont Center	312	Goodrich	815	Harlem	815	Hoffman	618	Jamaica	217
French Village	618	Goodwine	815	Harmon	815	Hoffman Estates	312	Jamesburg	217
Fullersburg	312	Goreville	618	Harmony (Jefferson Co.)	618	Holbrook	312	Jamestown	618
Fullerton	217	Gorham	815	Harmony (McHenry Co.)	815	Holcomb	815	Janesville	217
Fulton	815	Gorman	217	Harness	309	Holder	309	Jeisyville	217
Fults	618	Gower	312	Harper	815	Holliday	217	Jenkins	217
Funkhouser	217	Grafton	618	Harpster	217	Hollis	309	Jerseyville	618
Funks Grove	309	Grand Detour	815	Harris	217	Hollywood	312	Jewett	217
		Grand Ridge	815	Harrisburg	618	Holton	309	Joetta	217
		Grand Tower	618	Harrison	815	Homer	217	Johnsburg	815
		Grandview	217	Harrisonville	618	Hometown	312	Johnsonville	618
		Granger	312	Harristown	217	Homewood	312	Johnston City	618
Gages Lake	312	Granite City	618	Harrisville	815	Hookdale	618	Joliet	815
Galatia	618	Grantfork	618	Hartford	618	Hoopeston	217	Jonesboro	618
Gale	618	Grant Park	815	Hartland	815	Hooppole	309	Joppa	618
Galena	815	Grant Works	312	Hartsburg	217	Hope	217	Joslin	309
Galesburg	309	Granville	815	Harvard	815	Hopedale	309	Joy	309
Galt	815	Grape Creek	217	Harvel	217	Hopkins Park	815	Junction	618
Galton	217	Grass Lake (East Side)	312	Harvey	312	Horse Shoe Lake	618	Justice	312
Galva	309	Graymont	815	Hastings Lake	312	Hoyleton	618		
Garber	217	Grays Lake	312	Havana	309	Hubbard Woods	312		
Gardenplain	309	Grayville	618	Hawthorne	312	Hudson	309		
Garden Prairie	815	Great Lakes Naval Training Station	312	Hayes	217	Huegely	618	Kaiser	309
Gardner	815	Greenfield	217	Hazel Crest	312	Huey	618	Kampsville	618
Garrett	217	Green River	309	Hazel Dell	217	Hull	217	Kane	217
Gaskin City	618	Green Rock	309	Hazelhurst	815	Humboldt	217	Kaneville	312
Gays	217	Greenup	217	Heathsville	618	Hume	217	Kangley	815
Geff	618	Green Valley	309	Heaton	217	Humphrey	217	Kankakee	815
Geneseo	309	Greenview	217	Hebron	815	Humrick	217	Kansas	217
Geneva	312	Greenville	618	Hecker	618	Hunt	815	Kappa	309
Genoa	815	Greenwood	815	Hegeler	217	Huntley	312	Karbers Ridge	618
Georgetown	217	Greer	815	Held	309	Huntsville	217	Karnak	618
Gerald	217	Gregs	312	Helmar	815	Hurst	618	Kaskaskia	618
Gerlaw	309	Gretna	312	Henderson	309	Hutsonville	618	Keeneyville	312
Germantown	618	Gridley	309	Henkel	815	Hutton	217	Keensburg	618
Germantown Hills	309	Griggsville	217	Hennepin	815			Keithsburg	309
German Valley	815	Griswold	815	Henning	217			Kell	618
Giant City State Park	618	Griswold Lake	815	Henry	309			Keller	309
Gibson City	217	Gross Point	312	Herald	618	Ideal	815	Kellerville	217
Gifford	217	Grove City	217	Herbert	815	Idlewild	312	Kelleyville	217
Gila	217	Groveland	309	Herborn	217	Illinois City	309	Kelsey	309
Gilberts	312	Guilford	815	Hermon	309	Illiopolis	217	Kemp	217
Gilchrist	309	Gulfport	309	Herrick	618	Ina	618	Kemper	618
Gilgal	217	Gurnee	312	Herrin	618	Indian Hill	312	Kempton	815
Gillespie	217	Guthrie	217	Herscher	815	Indian Oaks	815	Kenilworth	312
Gilman	815			Hersman	217	Indianola	217	Kenney	217
Gilmer	312			Hervey City	217	Indian Point (Lake Co.)	312	Kent	815
Gilmore	618			Hess	618	Indian Point (Menard Co.)	217	Kernan	815
Gilson	309			Hettick	618	Industry	309	Kewanee	309
Girard	217			Heyworth	309	Infirmary	309	Keyesport	618
Gladstone	309	Hagarstown	618	Hickman	815	Ingalton	312	Kickapoo	309
Glasford	309	Hagener	217	Hickory Hills	312	Ingleside	312	Kickapoo Junction	309
Glasgow	217	Hagensbend	312	Hickoryridge	217	Ingraham	618	Kilbourne	309
Glenarm	217	Hahnaman	815					Kincaid	217
Glen Carbon	618	Hainesville	312					Kinderhook	217

TELEPHONE AREA CODE DIRECTORY

ILLINOIS
Kingman—New Lenox

Place Name	Area Code	Place Name	Area Code	Place Name	Area Code	Place Name	Area Code	Place Name	Area Code
Kingman	217	Leland	815	Lynnville	217	McLeansboro	618	Morrison	815
Kings	815	Leland Grove	217	Lyons (Cook Co.)	312	McNabb	815	Morrisonville	217
Kingston		Lemont	312	Lyons (Vermilion Co.)	217	McQueens	312	Morton	309
(De Kalb Co.)	815	Lena	815			Meacham	312	Morton Grove	312
Kingston (Kingston		Lenzburg	618			Meadows	309	Morton Park	312
Mines) (Peoria Co.)	309	Leonore	815			Mechanicsburg	217	Mossville	309
Kinmundy	618	Lerna	217	Mabel	217	Media	309	Mound City	618
Kinsman	815	Le Roy	309	Macedonia	618	Medinah	312	Mounds	618
Kirkland	815	Leverett	217	Mackinaw	309	Medora	618	Mount Auburn	217
Kirksville	217	Lewistown	309	Macomb	309	Meeks	217	Mount Carmel	618
Kirkwood	309	Lexington	309	Macon	217	Melody	312	Mount Carroll	815
Knoxville	309	Liberty	217	Madison	618	Melrose Park	312	Mount Erie	618
Kolze	312	Libertyville	312	Maeystown	618	Melville	618	Mount Forest	312
Kumler	217	Lidice	815	Magnolia	815	Melvin	217	Mount Morris	815
		Lily Lake (Kane Co.)	312	Mahomet	217	Menard	618	Mount Olive	217
		Lily Lake		Makanda	618	Mendon	217	Mount Palatine	815
Lace	312	(McHenry Co.)	815	Mallard	217	Mendota	815	Mount Prospect	312
La Clede	618	Lilymoor	815	Malta	815	Menominee	815	Mount Pulaski	217
Lacon	309	Lima	217	Malvern	815	Meppen	618	Mount Sterling	217
Lacrosse	217	Limestone	309	Manchester	217	Meredosia	217	Mount Vernon	618
Ladd	815	Lincoln	217	Manhattan	815	Meriden	815	Mount Zion	217
La Fayette	309	Lincolnshire	312	Manheim	312	Merna	309	Moweaqua	217
Lafox	312	Lincoln's New Salem	217	Manito	309	Merrionette Park	312	Mozier	618
La Grange	312	Lincolnwood	312	Manlius	815	Metamora	309	Muddy	618
La Grange Park	312	Lindenhurst	312	Mansfield	217	Metcalf	217	Mulberry Grove	618
La Harpe	217	Lindenwood	815	Manteno	815	Metropolis	618	Mulkeytown	618
Lake Bluff	312	Linn	618	Manville	815	Meyer	217	Muncie	217
Lake Corner	312	Lisbon	815	Maple Park	312	Michael	618	Mundelein	312
Lake Forest	312	Lisbon Center	815	Maples Mill	309	Middlecreek	217	Munger	312
Lake Fork	217	Lisle	312	Mapleton	309	Middlegrove	309	Murdock	217
Lake in the Hills	312	Litchfield	217	Maplewood Park	618	Middlesworth	217	Murphysboro	618
Lake Katharin	312	Literberry	217	Maquon	309	Middletown	217	Murrayville	217
Lake Marie	312	Little Indian	217	Marblehead	217	Midland City	217	Mylith Park	312
Lakemoor	815	Little Rock	312	Marcelline	217	Midlothian	312	Myrtle	815
Lake Piano	312	Little Silver Lake	312	Marengo	815	Midway	815	
Lake Villa	312	Littleton	309	Marietta	309	Milan	309	
Lakewood		Little York	309	Marine	618	Milford	815	
(McHenry Co.)	815	Liverpool	309	Marion	618	Millbrook	312	Nachusa	815
Lakewood		Livingston	618	Marissa	618	Millburn	312	Nameoki	618
(Shelby Co.)	217	Loami	217	Mark	815	Milledgeville	815	Naperville	312
Lake Zurich	312	Lock Haven	618	Markham (Cook Co.)	312	Miller City	618	Naples	217
Lambert	312	Lockport	815	Markham		Millersburg		Nashville	618
La Moille	815	Loda	217	(Morgan Co.)	217	(Bond Co.)	618	Nason	618
Lanark	815	Lodge	217	Marley	815	Millersburg		National City	618
Lancaster		Logan	618	Maroa	217	(Mercer Co.)	309	Natrona	309
(Stephenson Co.)	815	Lomax	217	Marseilles	815	Millersville	217	Nauvoo	217
Lancaster		Lombard	312	Marshall	217	Millington	312	Naval Reserve
(Wabash Co.)	618	London Mills	309	Martinsburg	217	Mill Shoals	618	Aviation Base	312
Lane	217	Lone Tree	309	Martinsville	217	Millstadt	618	Neal	217
Lanesville	217	Long Branch	309	Martinton	815	Milton	217	Nebo	217
Langenheim	312	Long Grove	312	Maryland	815	Mindale	217	Nekoma	309
Langham	217	Long Lake (Lake Co.)	312	Maryville	618	Mineral	309	Nelson	815
Langleyville	217	Long Lake		Mascoutah	618	Minier-Armington	309	Neoga	217
Lansing	312	(Madison Co.)	618	Mason	618	Minonk	309	Neponset	309
La Place	217	Long Point	815	Mason City	217	Minooka	815	Nettlecreek	815
La Prairie	217	Longview	217	Massbach	815	Mitchell	618	Nevada	815
Larchland	309	Loogootee	618	Matanzas Beach	309	Mode	217	Newark	815
La Rose	309	Loon Lake	312	Matherville	309	Modesto	217	New Athens	618
La Salle	815	Loraine	217	Matteson	312	Modoc	618	New Baden	618
Latham	217	Loran	815	Mattoon	217	Mokena	312	New Bedford	815
Laura	309	Lorenzo	815	Maunie	618	Moline	309	New Berlin	217
Lavergne	312	Loretto	815	Mays Lake	312	Momence	815	New Boston	309
Lawndale	217	Lostant	815	Mayview	217	Monee	312	New Burnside	618
Lawrence	815	Lotus	217	Maywood	312	Moneyville	312	New Canton	217
Lawrenceville	618	Louden	618	Mazon	815	Monmouth	309	New City	217
Layton	217	Louisville	618	McBride's Grove	618	Monroe Center	815	New Dennison	618
Leaf River	815	Lovejoy	618	McCall	217	Monroe City	618	New Design	618
Leamington	312	Loves Park	815	McClure	618	Monterey	309	New Douglas	217
Lebanon	618	Lovington	217	McClusky	618	Montezuma	217	Newell	217
Ledford	618	Lowell	815	McConnell	815	Montgomery	312	New Hanover	618
Lee	815	Low Point	309	McCook	312	Monticello	217	New Hartford	217
Lee Center	815	Loxa	217	McCullom Lake	815	Montrose	217	New Haven	618
Lehigh	618	Ludlow	217	McDowell	815	Mooseheart	312	New Holland	217
Leithton	312	Lyndon	815	McHenry	815	Moro	618	New Lebanon	815
		Lynn Center	309	McLean	309	Morris	815	New Lenox	815

Place Name	Area Code	Place Name	Area Code	Place Name	Area Code	Place Name	Area Code	Place Name	Area Code
Newman	217	Olmsted	618	Pennington Point	309	Prospect	217	Rock City	815
Newmansville	217	Olney	618	Penrose	815	Prospect Heights	312	Rock Cut	815
New Memphis	618	Olympia Fields	312	Peoria	309	Proving Ground	815	Rockdale	815
New Milford	815	Omaha	618	Peoria Heights	309	Pulaski	618	Rock Falls	815
New Minden	618	Omega	618	Peotone	312	Pulleys Mill	618	Rockford	815
New Palestine	618	Onarga	815	Percy	618	Putnam	815	Rock Grove	815
New Philadelphia	309	Oneco	815	Perry	217			Rock Island	309
New Salem	217	Oneida	309	Perryville	815			Rockport	217
New Salem State Park	217	Ontarioville	312	Peru	815			Rockton	815
Newton	618	Opdyke	618	Pesotum	217	Qulqley	217	Rockwell	815
New Trier	312	Opheim	309	Petersburg	217	Quincy	217	Rockwood	618
New Windsor	309	Oquawka	309	Petite Lake	312			Rolling Meadows	312
Niantic	217	Orangeville	815	Philadelphia	217			Rollo	815
Niles	312	Orchard Mines	309	Philo	217			Rome	309
Niota	217	Orchard Place	312	Phoenix	312	Radford	217	Romeo	815
Noble	618	Orchardville	618	Piasa	618	Radnor	309	Romeoville	815
Nokomis	217	Ordill	618	Pierron	618	Radom	618	Romine	618
Noltings	618	Oreana	217	Pierson Station	217	Raleigh-Galatia	618	Rondout	312
Nora	815	Oregon	815	Pike	217	Ramsey	618	Roodhouse	217
Normal	309	Orient	618	Pinckneyville	618	Randolph	309	Rooks Creek	815
Normantown	815	Orion	309	Pinelands	618	Rankin	217	Rosamond	217
Norridge	312	Orland	312	Pingree Grove	312	Ransom	815	Roscoe	815
Norris	309	Orland Park	312	Pinkstaff	618	Rantoul	217	Rose Hill	618
Norris City	618	Orleans	217	Piper City	815	Rapatee	309	Rose Lake	618
North Aurora	312	Ormonde	309	Pistakee	815	Rapids City	309	Roselle	312
Northbrook	312	Osceola	309	Pistakee Bay	815	Rardin	217	Rosemont	312
North Chicago	312	Osco	309	Pistakee Highlands	312	Raritan	309	Roseville	309
North Chillicothe	309	Osman	217	Pistakee Lake	815	Ravinia	312	Rosiclare	618
North Crystal Lake	815	Ospur	217	Pittsburg		Ray	217	Roslyn	217
Northfield	312	Oswego	312	(Fayette Co.)	618	Raymond	217	Rossville	217
North Harvey	312	Ottawa	815	Pittsburg		Red Bud	618	Rossville Junction	217
North Henderson	309	Otterville	618	(Williamson Co.)	618	Reddick	815	Round Grove	815
Northlake	312	Otto	815	Pittsfield	217	Reddish	618	Round Knob	618
North Pekin	309	Owaneco	217	Pittwood	815	Redmon	217	Round Lake	312
North Riverside	312	Ozark	618	Plainfield	815	Red Oak	815	Round Lake Beach	312
Nortonville	217			Plainview	618	Reds Landing	618	Round Lake Heights	312
Norway	815			Plainville	217	Reeds Corners	309	Round Lake Park	312
Norwood Park	312			Plano	312	Renault	618	Rowe	815
Nunda	815	Palatine	312	Plato Center	312	Renshaw	618	Rowell	217
Nutwood	618	Palestine	618	Plattville	815	Rentchler	618	Roxana	618
		Palmer	217	Pleasant Hill	217	Reynolds	309	Roxbury	815
		Palmyra	217	Pleasant Mound	618	Rice	618	Royal	217
		Paloma	217	Pleasant Plains	217	Richfield	217	Royalton	618
Oak Brook	312	Palos Heights	312	Pleasantview	217	Richmond	815	Ruma	618
Oakbrook Terrace	312	Palos Hills	312	Plymouth	309	Richton Park	312	Ruma Convent	618
Oakdale	618	Palos Park	312	Poag	618	Richview	618	Rumpler	217
Oakford	217	Palos Springs	312	Pocahontas	618	Riddlehill	217	Rushville	217
Oak Forest	312	Pana	217	Polo	815	Ridge Farm	217	Russell	312
Oak Forest South	312	Panama	217	Pontiac	815	Ridgefield	815	Rutland	815
Oakglen	312	Panola	309	Pontoosuc	217	Ridgeville	815		
Oak Grove	309	Papineau	815	Poplar Camp	618	Ridgway	618		
Oak Hill	309	Paris	217	Poplar Grove	815	Ridott	815		
Oakhurst	815	Park City	312	Port Byron	309	Riggston	217	Sabina	309
Oakland	217	Parkersburg	618	Posen	312	Rinard	618	Sadorus	217
Oak Lawn	312	Park Forest	312	Posey	618	Ringwood	815	Sag Bridge	312
Oak Leaf	217	Park Forest South	312	Potawatomie	312	Rio	309	Saidora	217
Oak Park	312	Parkland	309	Potomac	217	Ripley	217	Sailor Springs	618
Oakwood	217	Park Ridge	312	Pottstown	309	Rising	217	St. Anne	815
Oblong	618	Parkville	217	Powellton	217	Ritchey	815	St. Charles	312
Oconee	217	Parnell	217	Prairie	618	Riverdale	312	St. David	309
Ocoya	815	Patoka	618	Prairie Center	815	River Forest	312	St. Elmo	618
Odell	815	Patterson	217	Prairie City	309	River Grove	312	Ste. Marie	618
Odin	618	Pauline	217	Prairie-du-Rocher	618	Riverside	312	St. Francisville	618
O'Fallon	618	Paulton	618	Prairie Garden	618	Riverton	217	St. George	815
Ogden	217	Pawnee	217	Prairietown	618	Riverview	312	St. Jacob	618
Oglesby	815	Paw Paw	815	Prairie View	312	River Wood	815	St. James	618
Ohio	815	Paxton	217	Prairieville	815	Roanoke	309	St. Joseph	217
Ohlman	217	Paynes Point	815	Preemption	309	Robbins	312	St. Libory	618
Okawville	618	Payson	217	Prentice	217	Robbs	618	St. Paul	618
Old Mill Creek	312	Pearl	217	Preston	618	Roberts	217	St. Peter	618
Old Ripley	618	Pearl City	815	Prince Crossing	312	Robinson	618	St. Rose	618
Olive Branch	618	Pecatonica	815	Princeton	815	Roby	217	Salem	618
Oliver (Edgar Co.)	217	Pekin	309	Princeville	309	Rochelle	815	Salisbury	217
Oliver (Whiteside Co.)	815	Pembroke	815	Proctor	217	Rochester	217	Sand Lake	312
Olivet	217	Penfield	217	Prophetstown	815	Rockbridge	217	Sandoval	618

ILLINOIS
Sands—White Hall

Place Name	Area Code	Place Name	Area Code	Place Name	Area Code	Place Name	Area Code	Place Name	Area Code
Sands	815	Sorento	217	Summum	309	Trenton	618	Wanda	618
Sandusky	618	South Bartonville	309	Sumner	618	Trilla	217	Wann	618
Sandwich	815	South Beloit	815	Sunnyland	309	Trimble	618	Wapella	217
San Jose	309	South Bergen	815	Sutter	217	Triumph	815	Warren	815
Sankoty	309	South Chicago		Sutton Station	312	Trivoli	309	Warrenhurst	312
Sauget	618	Heights	312	Swan Creek	309	Trowbridge	217	Warrensburg	217
Sauk Village	312	S. E. Shore		Swansea	618	Troy	618	Warrenville	312
Saunemin	815	Petite Lake	312	Swanwick	618	Troy Grove	815	Warsaw	217
Savanna	815	South Elgin	312	Swedona	309	Tunnel Hill	618	Wartburg	618
Savoy	217	South Holland	312	Swygert	815	Tuscola	217	Wasco	312
Saybrook	309	South Pekin	309	Sycamore	815			Washburn	309
Scales Mound	815	South Sharon	815	Sylvan Lake	312			Washington	309
Scarboro	815	South Standard	217	Symerton	815			Washington Park	618
Schapville	815	South Wilmington	815			Udina	312	Wataga	309
Schaumburg	312	Sparland	309			Ulah	309	Waterloo	618
Scheller	618	Sparta	618			Ullin	618	Waterman	815
Schiller Park	312	Spaulding (Cook Co.)	312	Table Grove	309	Union	815	Watertown	309
Schram City	217	Spaulding		Tabor	217	Union Grove	815	Watkins	217
Schuline	618	(Sangamon Co.)	217	Talbott	309	Union Hill	815	Watseka	815
Schwer	815	Specialville	312	Tallmadge	815	Unionville	815	Watson	217
Sciota	309	Speedbowl Park	815	Tallula	217	U. S. Lock & Dam		Wauconda	312
Scioto Mills	815	Speer	309	Tamalco	618	No. 53	618	Waukegan	312
Scott Air Force Base	618	Spencer	815	Tamaroa	618	Unity	618	Wauponsee	815
Scottville	217	Spillertown	618	Tamms	618	Upton	312	Waverly	217
Seaplane Port		Spring Bay	309	Tampico	815	Urbana	217	Wayne	312
(Great Lakes)	312	Springerton	618	Taylor Ridge	309	Urbandale	618	Wayne City	618
Seaton	309	Springfield	217	Taylors Lake	312	Ursa	217	Waynesville	217
Secor	309	Spring Forest	312	Taylor Springs	217	Ustick	815	Webster	217
Sefton	618	Spring Grove	815	Taylorville	217	Utica	815	Wedron	815
Sellers	217	Spring Hill	309	Techny	312			Weedman	217
Selmaville	618	Spring Lake	309	Tempest	217			Weir	217
Seneca	815	Springs Beach	312	Tennessee	309			Weldon	217
Sepo	309	Spring Valley	815	Terra Cotta	815	Valier	618	Wellington	815
Serena	815	Staleys	217	Terre Haute	217	Valmeyer	618	Wendelin	618
Sesser	618	Stallings	618	Teutopolis	217	Vandalia	618	Wenona	815
Seward	815	Standard	815	Texas City	618	Van Petten	815	Wesley Junction	309
Seymour	217	Standard City	217	Texico	618	Varna	309	West Brooklyn	815
Shabbona	815	Stanford	309	Thawville	217	Velma	217	Westchester	312
Shabbona Grove	815	Starks	312	Thebes	618	Venedy	618	West Chicago	312
Shaletown	309	Starved Rock	815	Third Lake	312	Venice	618	West City	618
Shannon	815	Staunton	618	Thomas (Bureau Co.)	309	Vergennes	618	West Dana	217
Sharpsburg	217	Stavenger	815	Thomas		Vermilion	217	West Dundee	312
Sharps Corners	312	Steeleville	618	(Vermilion Co.)	217	Vermilion Grove	217	Western Springs	312
Shattuc	618	Steelton	217	Thomasboro	217	Vermont	309	Westervelt	217
Shawneetown	618	Steger	312	Thomasville	217	Vernon	618	Westfield	217
Sheffield	815	Sterling	815	Thompson Lake	309	Vernon Hills	312	West Frankfort	618
Shelbyville	217	Stevens	815	Thompsonville	618	Verona	815	West Harvey	312
Sheldon	815	Steward	815	Thomson	815	Versailles	217	Westhaven	312
Sheridan	815	Stewardson	217	Thornton	312	Victoria	309	West Hinsdale	312
Sherman	217	Stickney	312	Thornton Junction	312	Vienna	618	West Jersey	309
Sherrard	309	Stillman Valley	815	Ticona	815	Villa Grove	217	West Junction	815
Shiloh	618	Stillwell	217	Tiedtville	312	Villa Park	312	West Kankakee	815
Shipman	618	Stockdale	815	Tilden	618	Villa Ridge	618	West Lake Forest	312
Shirland	815	Stockland	815	Tilton	217	Viola	309	West Liberty	618
Shirley	309	Stockton	815	Time	217	Virden	217	West McHenry	815
Shobonier	618	Stolle	618	Timewell	217	Virgil	312	Westmont	312
Shumway	217	Stonefort	618	Tinley Park	312	Virginia	217	Westmore	312
Sibley	217	Stone Gate	312	Tioga	217	Volo	815	West Newell	217
Sicily	217	Stone Park	312	Tipton	217	Vulcan	618	Weston (Du Page Co.)	312
Sidell	217	Stones	815	Tiskilwa	815			Weston (McLean Co.)	815
Sidney	217	Stonington	217	Todds Point	217			West Point	217
Sigel	217	Stoy	618	Toledo	217			Westport	618
Silvis	309	Strasburg	217	Tolono	217	Wacker	815	West Ridge	217
Simpson	618	Stratford	815	Toluca	815	Waddams Grove	815	West Salem	618
Skokie	312	Strawn	815	Tomlinson	217	Wadsworth	312	West Union	217
Slocum Lake	312	Streamwood	312	Tonica	815	Waggoner	217	Westview	618
Smithboro	618	Streator	815	Tonti	618	Wakefield	618	Westville	217
Smithfield	309	Stronghurst	309	Topeka	309	Walnut	815	Westwood	312
Smithshire	309	Stubblefield	618	Torino	815	Walnut Grove	618	West York	618
Smithton	618	Sublette	815	Toulon	309	Walnut Hill	618	Wheaton	312
Smithville	309	Sugar Grove	312	Tovey	217	Walpole	618	Wheeler	217
Snicarte	309	Sullivan	217	Towanda	309	Walsh	618	Wheeling	312
Sollitt	815	Summerfield	618	Tower Hill	217	Walton	815	Whitaker	815
Solon Mills	815	Summer Hill	217	Tower Lake	312	Waltonville	618	Whiteash	618
Somonauk	815	Summit	312	Tremont	309	Wamac	618	White Hall	217

Place Name	Area Code	Place Name	Area Code	Place Name	Area Code	Place Name	Area Code	Place Name	Area Code
White Heath	217	Willow Hill	618	Winterrowd	217	Woodside	217	Yale	618
White Pigeon	815	Willow Springs	312	Winthrop Harbor	312	Woodson	217	Yates City	309
White Pine		Wilmette	312	Wireton	312	Woodstock	815	York Center	312
State Park	815	Wilmington	815	Witt	217	Woodville	217	Yorkfield	312
Whittington	618	Wilson	312	Woburn	618	Woodworth	815	Yorktown	815
Wichert	815	Wilsonville	217	Wonder Lake	815	Woosung	815	Yorkville	312
Wilderman	618	Wilton Center	815	Woodbine	815	Worden	618	Youngsdale	312
Wildwood	312	Winchester	217	Woodburn	618	Worth	312	Youngstown	309
Willard	618	Windsor	217	Woodbury	217	Wrayville	309	Yuton	309
Willeys	217	Winfield	312	Wood Dale	312	Wyanet	815	
Williamsburg	217	Wing	815	Woodhull	309	Wyoming	309	
Williamsfield	309	Winnebago	815	Woodland	815			
Williamson	618	Winneburg	618	Woodlawn	618			
Williams Park	312	Winneshiek	815	Woodridge	312			Zearing	815
Williamsville	217	Winnetka	312	Wood River	618			Zeigler	618
Willisville	618	Winslow	815	Woods	618	Xenia	618	Zion	312

Place Name	Area Code	Place Name	Area Code	Place Name	Area Code	Place Name	Area Code	Place Name	Area Code
Acme	812	Beverly Shores	219	Cannelton	812	Craigville	219	Eaton	317
Acton	317	Bicknell	812	Carbon	812	Crandall	812	Eckerty	812
Adams	812	Big Lake	219	Carlisle	812	Crane	812	Economy	317
Adams Lake	219	Big Springs	317	Carlos City	317	Crane Naval		Eden	317
Ade	219	Billingsville	317	Carmel	317	Ordnance Depot	812	Edgewater Beach	219
Advance	317	Bippus	219	Cartersburg	317	Crawfordsville	317	Edinburg	812
Adyeville	812	Birdseye	812	Carthage	317	Creston	219	Edwardsport	812
Aetna	219	Blackhawk	812	Castleton	317	Crisman	219	Edwardsville	812
Ainsworth	219	Black Hawk Beach	219	Cates	317	Crocker	219	Effner	219
Akron	219	Blackoak	219	Catlin	317	Cromwell	219	Ekin	317
Alamo	317	Blanford	317	Cave	317	Cross Plains	812	Elberfeld	812
Albany	317	Blocher	812	Cayuga	317	Crothersville	812	Elizabeth	812
Albion	219	Bloomfield	812	Cedar Grove	317	Crown Center	317	Elizabethtown	812
Alexandria	317	Bloomingdale	317	Cedar Lake	219	Crown Point	219	Elizaville	317
Alfordsville-		Blooming Grove	317	Celestine	812	Crumstown	219	Elkhart	219
Glendale	812	Bloomington	812	Center	317	Culver	219	Ellettsville	812
Alpine	317	Blountsville	317	Centerpoint	812	Cumberland	317	Elliston	812
Altona	219	Blue Ridge	317	Centerville	317	Cutler	317	Elnora	812
Alvarado	219	Bluffton	219	Central	812	Cuzco	812	Elwood	317
Ambia	317	Boggstown	317	Central Barren	812	Cynthiana	812	Eminence	317
Amboy	317	Boone Grove	219	Chalmers	219			Emison	812
Americus	317	Boonville	812	Chandler	812			English	812
Amo	317	Borden	812	Charlestown	812			English Lake	219
Anderson	317	Boston	317	Charlottesville	317	Dale	812	Enos	219
Andrews	219	Boswell	317	Chesterfield	317	Daleville	317	Enterprise	812
Angola	219	Bourbon	219	Chesterton	219	Dam 43 (Ohio River)	812	Epsom	812
Apalona	812	Bowling Green	812	Chestnut Hill	812	Dana	317	Etna	219
Arcadia	317	Bradford	812	Chili	317	Danville	317	Etna Green	219
Arcola	219	Branchville	812	Chrisney	812	Darlington	317	Eureka	812
Ardmore	219	Brazil	812	Churubusco	219	Darmstadt	812	Evanston	812
Argos	219	Bremen	219	Cicero	317	Daylight	812	Evansville	812
Arlington	317	Bridgeport	317	Cincinnati	812	Dayton	317	Ewing	812
Armour	219	Bright	812	Circleville	317	Decatur	219		
Armstrong	812	Brimfield	219	Clarke Station	219	Decker	812		
Aroma	317	Bringhurst	219	Clarksburg	812	Deedsville	317		
Asherville	812	Bristol	219	Clarks Hill	317	Deep River	219		
Ashley	219	Bristow	812	Clarksville		Deer Creek	219	Fairbanks	812
Athens	219	Brook	219	(Clark Co.)	812	Delong	219	Fairfield	317
Atlanta	317	Brooklyn	317	Clarksville		Delphi	317	Fairland	317
Attica	317	Brookston	317	(Hamilton Co.)	317	Demotte	219	Fairmount	317
Atwood	219	Brookville	317	Clay City	812	Denham	219	Fair Oaks	219
Auburn	219	Brownsburg	317	Claypool	219	Denver	317	Falmouth	317
Aurora	812	Brownstown	812	Claysburg	812	Depauw	812	Farmersburg	812
Austin	812	Brownsville	317	Clayton	317	Deputy	812	Farmland	317
Avilla	219	Bruce Lake	219	Clear Creek	812	Derby	812	Fayetteville	812
Avoca	812	Bruceville	812	Clearlake	219	Desoto	317	Fenns	317
		Brunswick	219	Clear Spring	812	Dexter	812	Ferdinand	812
		Bryant	219	Clermont	317	Diamond	317	Ferndale	317
		Buck Creek	317	Clifford	812	Dillsboro	812	Fillmore	317
Babcock	219	Buffalo	219	Clinton	317	Dinwiddie	219	Fishers	317
Baileytown	219	Buffaloville	812	Cloverdale	317	Disko	219	Flat Rock	812
Bainbridge	317	Buffington	219	Cloverland	812	Doans	812	Flat Rock Cave	812
Bakers Corner	317	Bunker Hill	317	Clyde	812	Donaldson	219	Flint	219
Bandon	812	Burdick	219	Clymers	219	Doolittle Mills	812	Flint Lake	219
Barce	317	Burket	219	Coal Bluff	812	Dora	219	Flora	219
Bargersville	317	Burlington	317	Coal City	812	Dublin	317	Florence	812
Bass Lake	219	Burlington Beach	219	Coalmont	812	Dubois	812	Floyds Knobs	812
Batesville	812	Burnettsville	219	Coatesville	317	Dudleytown	812	Folsomville	812
Bath	317	Burney	812	Coburg	219	Dugger	812	Foraker	219
Battle Ground	317	Burns City	812	Coesse	219	Dune Acres	219	Forest	317
Bear Branch	812	Burr Oak	219	Colburn	317	Dunkirk	317	Fort Benjamin	
Beatrice	219	Burrows	219	Colfax	317	Dunlap	219	Harrison	317
Bedford	812	Butler	219	Columbia City	219	Dunnington	317	Fort Branch	812
Beech Grove	317	Butlerville	812	Columbus	812	Dunreith	317	Fort Ritner	812
Beechwood	812	Byrneville	812	Commiskey	812	Dupont	812	Fortville	317
Belle Union	317			Connersville	317	Dyer	219	Fort Wayne	219
Belleville	317			Converse	317			Foster	317
Bellmore	317			Cook	219			Fountain City	317
Belshaw	219	Cadiz	317	Cope	317			Fountaintown	317
Benham	812	Calumet	219	Cortland	812			Fowler	317
Bennettsville	812	Calvertville	812	Corunna	219	Earlham	317	Fowlerton	317
Bennington	812	Cambridge City	317	Cory	812	Earl Park	219	Francesville	219
Benton	219	Camby	317	Corydon	812	East Chicago	219	Francisco	812
Berne	219	Camden	219	Covington	317	East Enterprise	812	Frankfort	317
Bethlehem	812	Campbellsburg	812	Cowan	317	East Gary	219	Franklin	317
		Canaan	812			East Mount Carmel	812	Frankton	317

Place Name	Area Code	Place Name	Area Code	Place Name	Area Code	Place Name	Area Code	Place Name	Area Code
Fredericksburg	812	Hanover Center	219	Kansas	812	Lewis	812	Medora	812
Fredonia	812	Hardinsburg	812	Kempton	317	Lewisville		Mellott	317
Freedom	812	Harlan	219	Kendallville	219	(Henry Co.)	317	Memphis	812
Freeland Park	317	Harmony	812	Kennard	317	Lewisville		Mentone	219
Freelandville	812	Harrodsburg	812	Kent	812	(Morgan Co.)	317	Merom	812
Freeman	812	Hartford City	317	Kentland	219	Lexington	812	Merrillville	219
Freetown	812	Hartsdale	219	Kersey	219	Liberty	317	Metamora	317
Fremont	219	Hartsville	812	Kewanna	219	Liberty Center	219	Metz	219
French Lick	812	Hatfield	812	Keystone	317	Liberty Mills	219	Mexico	317
Frenchtown	812	Haubstadt	812	Kimmell	219	Libertyville	317	Miami	317
Friendship	812	Hayden	812	Kingman	317	Ligonier	219	Michiana Shores	219
Fritchton	812	Haysville	812	Kingsbury	219	Limedale	317	Michigan City	219
Fulda	812	Hazelrigg	317	Kingsford Heights	219	Lincoln	219	Michigantown	317
Fulton	219	Hazelwood	317	Kirklin	317	Lincoln City	812	Middlebury	219
Furnessville	219	Hazleton	812	Kitchel	317	Linden	317	Middletown	
		Hebron	219	Klaasville	219	Linngrove	219	(Henry Co.)	317
		Hedrick	219	Klondike	219	Linton	812	Middletown	
Galena	812	Helmer	219	Knightstown	317	Little York	812	(Shelby Co.)	317
Galveston	219	Helmsburg	812	Knightsville	812	Livonia	812	Midland	812
Garrett	219	Heltonville	812	Knox	219	Lizton	317	Midway	812
Gary	219	Hemlock	317	Kokomo	317	Lochiel	317	Milan	812
Garyton	219	Henryville	812	Koleen	812	Logansport	219	Milford	219
Gas City	317	Herbst	317	Koontz Lake	219	London	317	Milford Junction	219
Gaston	317	Hessville	219	Kouts	219	Long Beach	219	Mill Creek	219
Gatchell	812	Highland	219	Kramer	317	Long Lake	219	Miller	219
Geetingsville	317	Hillcrest	219	Kurtz	812	Loogootee	812	Millersburg	
Geneva (Adams Co.)	219	Hillisburg	317	Kyana	812	Losantville	317	(Elkhart Co.)	219
Geneva (Shelby Co.)	317	Hillsboro	317			Lowell	219	Millersburg	
Gentryville	812	Hillsdale	317			Lucerne	219	(Warrick Co.)	812
Georgetown	812	Hoagland	219			Lydick	219	Millhousen	812
Gerald	812	Hobart	219			Lynn	317	Milligan	317
Gessie	317	Hobbs	317	Laconia	812	Lynnville	812	Milltown	812
Gibson	219	Holland	812	La Crosse	219	Lyons	812	Millville	317
Gill	812	Hollandsburg	317	Ladoga	317			Millwood	219
Glendale	812	Holton	812	Lafayette	317			Milroy	317
Glen Park	219	Homer	317	La Fontaine	317			Milton	317
Glenwood	317	Honey Creek	317	Lagrange	219			Mineral Springs	219
Glezen	812	Hope	812	Lagro	219	Mace	317	Mishawaka	219
Goldsmith	317	Howe	219	Lake Cicott	219	Mackey	812	Mitchell	812
Goodland	219	Hudson	219	Lake Eliza	219	Macy	219	Modoc	317
Goshen	219	Hudson Lake	219	Lake Freeman	219	Madison	812	Mohawk	317
Gosport	812	Huntertown	219	Lake James	219	Magnet	812	Mongo	219
Grabill	219	Huntingburg	812	Lake Maxinkuckee	219	Majenica	219	Monitor	317
Grammer	812	Huntington	219	Lake Monroe	812	Malden	219	Monon	219
Grand View	812	Hurlburt	219	Lake-of-The-Woods	219	Manchester	812	Monroe	219
Granger	219	Huron	812	Lake Shafer	219	Manilla	317	Monroe City	812
Grasscreek	219	Hymera	812	Lakes of the Four		Manson	317	Monroeville	219
Grassell	219			Seasons	219	Marco	812	Monrovia	317
Graysville	812			Lake Station	219	Marengo	812	Monterey	219
Greencastle	317			Laketon	219	Mariah Hill	812	Montezuma	317
Greendale	812	Idaville	219	Lake Village	219	Marietta	317	Montgomery	812
Greenfield	317	Indiana Arsenal	812	Lakeville	219	Marion	317	Monticello	219
Greensboro	317	Indiana Harbor	219	Lake Wawasee	219	Mark	219	Montmorenci	317
Greensburg	812	Indianapolis	317	Lamar	812	Markland	812	Montpelier	317
Greens Fork	317	Indian Springs	812	Lancaster	219	Markle	219	Monument City	219
Greentown	317	Ingalls	317	Landess	317	Markleville	317	Mooreland	317
Greenville	812	Inglefield	812	Lanesville	812	Marshall	317	Moores Hill	812
Greenwood	317	Inwood	219	Laotto	219	Marshfield	317	Mooresville	317
Griffin	812	Ireland	812	Lapaz	219	Martinsville	317	Moran	317
Griffith	219			Lapel	317	Marysville	812	Morgantown	812
Grissom Air Force				La Porte	219	Matthews	317	Morocco	219
Base	317			Larwill	219	Mauckport	812	Morris	812
Grovertown	219	Jamestown	317	Laud	219	Maumee	812	Morristown	317
Guilford	812	Jasonville	812	Laurel	317	Maxwell	317	Morton	317
		Jasper	812	Lawrence	317	Maynard	219	Mount Ayr	219
		Jefferson	812	Lawrenceburg	812	Mays	317	Mount Carmel	812
		Jeffersonville	812	Leavenworth	812	McCool	219	Mount Comfort	317
Hagerstown	317	Johnsons Beach	219	Lebanon	317	McCordsville	317	Mount Etna	219
Hall	317	Jolletville	317	Leesburg	219	McCutchanville	812	Mount Meridian	317
Hamilton	219	Jonesboro	317	Leipsic	812	Mecca	317	Mount Pleasant	812
Hamlet	219	Jones Landing	219	Leiters Ford	219	Mechanicsburg		Mount Summit	317
Hammond	219	Jonesville	812	Leo	219	(Boone Co.)	317	Mount Vernon	812
Hancock Chapel	812	Jordan Village	812	Leopold	812	Mechanicsburg		Mulberry	317
Hanna	219	Judson	317	Leota	812	(Henry Co.)	317	Muncie	317
Hanover	812	Judyville	317	Leroy	219	Medaryville	219	Munster	219

Place Name	Area Code	Place Name	Area Code	Place Name	Area Code	Place Name	Area Code	Place Name	Area Code
Nabb	812	Ora	219	Queensville	812	Saltillo	812	Stinesville	812
Napoleon	812	Orestes	317	Quincy	317	Sandborn	812	Stockwell	317
Nappanee	219	Oriole	812			Sandford	812	Stonebluff	317
Nashville	812	Orland	219			Sandridge	812	Straughn	317
Navilleton	812	Orleans	812			San Jacinto	812	Stroh	219
Nebraska	812	Osborn	219	Radnor	317	San Pierre	219	Sullivan	812
Nevada	317	Osceola	219	Rainsville	317	Santa Claus	812	Sulphur	812
Nevada Mills	219	Osgood	812	Raleigh	317	Saratoga	317	Sulphur Springs	317
New Albany	812	Ossian	219	Ramsey	812	Sardinia	812	Summitville	317
New Alsace	812	Otis	219	Range Line	219	Saxony	219	Sunman	812
New Amsterdam	812	Otisco	812	Ranger	812	Schererville	219	Surprise	812
Newberry	812	Otterbein	317	Ravenswood	317	Schneider	219	Swan	219
New Bethel	317	Otwell	812	Ray	219	Schnellville	812	Swanington	317
New Boston	317	Owensburg	812	Raymond	317	Scipio	812	Swayzee	317
New Brunswick	317	Owensville	812	Rays Crossing	317	Scircleville	317	Sweetser	317
Newburgh	812	Oxford	317	Reddington	812	Scotland	812	Switz City	812
New Carlisle	219			Redkey	317	Scottsburg	812	Syracuse	219
New Castle	317			Reelsville	317	Sedalia	317		
New Chicago	219			Remington	219	Sedley	219		
New Corydon	219			Rensselaer	219	Seelyville	812		
New Goshen	812	Paisley	219	Reservoir	219	Sellersburg	812	Tab	317
New Harmony	812	Palmer	219	Reynolds	219	Selma	317	Talbot	317
New Haven	219	Palmyra	812	Richland	812	Servia	219	Tampico	812
New Lebanon	812	Paoli	812	Richmond	317	Seymour	812	Tangier	317
New Lisbon	317	Paragon	317	Richvalley	219	Shannondale	317	Taswell	812
New London	317	Paris Crossing	812	Ridgeville	317	Sharpsville	317	Taylorsville	812
New Market	317	Parker	317	Riley	812	Shelburn	812	Teegarden	219
New Middletown	812	Parker City	317	Rileysburg	317	Shelby	219	Tefft	219
New Palestine	317	Parkers Settlement	812	Rising Sun	812	Shelbyville	317	Tell City	812
New Paris	219	Parr	219	Roachdale	317	Shepardsville	317	Templeton	317
New Philadelphia	812	Patoka	812	Roann	317	Sheridan	317	Tennyson	812
New Point	812	Patricksburg	812	Roanoke	219	Shipshewana	219	Terre Coupee	219
Newport	317	Patriot	812	Robertsdale	219	Shirkieville	317	Terre Haute	812
New Richmond	317	Patronville	812	Roby	219	Shirley	317	Thayer	219
New Ross	317	Paxton	812	Rochester	219	Shoals	812	Thornhope	219
New Salisbury	812	Pekin	812	Rockcreek	219	Siberia	812	Thorntown	317
Newtonville	812	Pence	317	Rockfield	219	Sidney	219	Tippecanoe	219
Newtown	317	Pendleton	317	Rockford	812	Silver Lake	219	Tipton	317
New Trenton	812	Pennville	219	Rockport	812	Simpson	219	Tobinsport	812
New Washington	812	Peoria	812	Rockville	317	Sims	317	Tocsin	219
New Waverly	219	Perkinsville	317	Rolling Prairie	219	Smedley	812	Tolleston	219
New Whiteland	317	Perrysville	317	Rome	812	Smithville	812	Topeka	219
New Winchester	317	Pershing	219	Rome City	219	Solitude	812	Tower	812
Nineveh	317	Peru	317	Romney	317	Solsberry	812	Trafalgar	317
Noblesville	317	Petersburg	812	Rosedale	317	Somerset	317	Tremont	219
Norman	812	Petroleum	219	Roseland	219	Somerville	812	Trevlac	812
Normanda	317	Pickwick Park	219	Roselawn	219	South Bend	219	Trinity Springs	812
North Hayden	219	Pierceton	219	Ross	219	South Gary	219	Trinity-Williams	812
North Judson	219	Pilot Knob	812	Rossville	317	South Milford	219	Troy	812
North Liberty	219	Pimento	812	Royal Center	219	Southport	317	Tunnelton	812
North Madison	812	Pine	219	Rushville	317	South Raub	317	Turkey Run	317
North Manchester	219	Pine Village	317	Russellville	317	South Three Oaks	219	Twelve Mile	219
North Salem	317	Pittsboro	317	Russiaville	317	South Whitley	219	Tyner	219
North Vernon	812	Pittsburg	317			Spades	812		
North Webster	219	Plainfield	317			Sparksville	812		
Notre Dame	219	Plainville	812			Sparta	812		
		Pleasant Lake	219			Speed	812	Underwood	812
		Pleasant Mills	219	St. Anthony	812	Speedway City	317	Union	812
		Pleasantville	812	St. Bernice	317	Speicherville	219	Union City	317
		Plymouth	219	St. Croix	812	Spencer	812	Uniondale	219
Oak	219	Poe-Hoagland	219	St. Joe	219	Spencerville	219	Union Mills	219
Oakford	317	Pokagon	219	St. John	219	Spiceland	317	Uniontown	812
Oakland City	812	Poland	812	St. Joseph	812	Springport	317	Universal	317
Oaklandon	317	Poneto	219	St. Leon	812	Springville	812	Upland	317
Oaktown	812	Portage	219	St. Marks	812	Spurgeon	812	Urbana	219
Oakville	317	Port Chester	219	St. Mary-of-the-		Stanford	812	Utica	812
Ober	219	Porter	219	Woods	812	Stanley	812		
Odell	317	Portland	219	St. Marys	219	Star City	219		
Odon	812	Poseyville	812	St. Meinard	812	State Line	317		
Ogden Dunes	219	Prairie Creek	812	St. Paul	317	Staunton	812		
Old Bath	317	Prairleton	812	St. Philip	812	Stendal	812	Valley City	812
Oldenburg	812	Preble	219	St. Wendells	812	Stewart	317	Vallonia	812
Olean	812	Prescott	317	Salamonia	219	Stewartsville	812	Valparaiso	219
Onward	219	Princeton	812	Salem	812	Stilesville	317	Van Buren	317
Oolitic	812	Providence	317	Salem Center	219	Stillwell	219	Vawter Park	219
		Putnamville	317	Saline City	812			Veedersburg	317

INDIANA
Velpen—Zionsville

Place Name	Area Code	Place Name	Area Code	Place Name	Area Code	Place Name	Area Code	Place Name	Area Code
Velpen	812	Washington	812	West Hollansburg	317	Wicker Park	219	Woodland	219
Vernon	812	Waterford	219	West Lafayette	317	Wilkinson	317	Woodville	219
Versailles	812	Waterloo	219	West Lebanon	317	Williams	812	Worthington	812
Vevay	812	Water Valley	219	West Middleton	317	Williamsburg	317	Wyatt	219
Vienna	812	Wauhub Lake	219	West Newton	317	Williamsport	317		
Vincennes	812	Waveland	317	West Oxford	317	Willow Branch	317		
		Waverly	317	Westphalia	812	Willow Creek	219		
		Waverly Beach	219	West Point	317	Wilson	219		
		Wawaka	219	Westport	812	Winamac	219	Yankeetown	812
Wabash	219	Wawasee	219	West Terre Haute	812	Winchester	317	Yeddo	317
Wadena	219	Waynedale	219	Westville	219	Windfall	317	Yeoman	219
Wadesville	812	Waynetown	317	West Wabash	317	Winfield	219	Yoder	219
Wakarusa	219	Webster	317	Wheatfield	219	Wingate	317	Yorktown	317
Waldron	317	Weisburg	812	Wheatland	812	Winona Lake	219	Yorkville	812
Walkerton	219	West Antwerp	219	Wheeler	219	Winslow	812	Young America	219
Wallace	317	West Baden	812	Wheeling	812	Wolcott	219		
Walton	219	West College Corner	317	Whitcomb	317	Wolcottville	219		
Wanamaker	317	West Edon	219	Whiteland	317	Wolf Lake (Lake Co.)	219		
Wanatah	219	Westfield	317	Whitestown	317	Wolf Lake			
Warren	219	West Harrison	812	Whitesville	317	(Noble Co.)	219	Zanesville	219
Warsaw	219	West Hicksville	219	Whiting	219	Woodburn	219	Zionsville	317

Place Name	Area Code	Place Name	Area Code	Place Name	Area Code	Place Name	Area Code	Place Name	Area Code
Ackley	515	Bailey	515	Buck Grove	712	Cleves	515	Delta	515
Ackworth	515	Baldwin	319	Buckingham	319	Climbing Hill	712	Denison	712
Adair	515	Balltown	319	Buena Vista		Clinton	319	Denmark	319
Adaza	712	Bancroft	515	(Clayton Co.)	319	Clio	515	Denver	319
Adel	515	Bankston	319	Buena Vista		Clive	515	Derby	515
Afton	515	Barnes City	515	(Clinton Co.)	319	Clutier	319	Des Moines	515
Agency	515	Barnum	515	Buffalo	319	Coburg	712	De Soto	515
Ainsworth	319	Bartlett	712	Buffalo Center	515	Coggon	319	Dewar	319
Akron	712	Bassett	515	Bunch	515	Coin	712	De Witt	319
Albert City	712	Batavia	515	Burchinal	515	Colesburg	319	Dexter	515
Albia	515	Battle Creek	712	Burlington	319	Colfax	515	Diagonal	515
Albion	515	Baxter	515	Burnside	515	College Springs	712	Dickens	712
Alburnett	319	Bayard	712	Burr Oak	319	Collins	515	Dike	319
Alden	515	Beacon	515	Burt	515	Colo	515	Dinsdale	319
Alexander	515	Beaconsfield	515	Bussey	515	Columbia	515	Dixon	319
Algona	515	Beaman	515			Columbus City	319	Dodgeville	319
Alleman	515	Beaver	515			Columbus Junction	319	Dolliver	712
Allendorf	712	Bedford	712			Colwell	515	Donahue	319
Allerton	515	Beech	515	Calamus	319	Commerce	515	Donnan	319
Allison	319	Belknap	515	Callender	515	Conesville	319	Donnellson	319
Alpha	319	Belle Plaine	319	Calmar	319	Confidence	515	Doon	712
Alta	712	Bellevue	319	Calumet	712	Conrad	515	Dorchester	319
Alta Vista	515	Belmond	515	Camanche	319	Conroy	319	Douds	515
Alton	712	Beloit	712	Cambria	515	Conway	712	Dougherty	515
Altoona	515	Bennett	319	Cambridge	515	Coon Rapids	712	Dow City	712
Alvord	712	Bentley	712	Camp Dodge	515	Cooper	515	Downey	319
Amana	319	Benton	515	Cantril	319	Coppock	319	Dows	515
Amber	319	Berea	712	Carbon	515	Coralville	319	Drakesville	515
Ames	515	Berkley	515	Carl	515	Corley	712	Dubuque	319
Amund	515	Bernard	319	Carlisle	515	Cornell	712	Dumont	515
Anamosa	319	Bertram	319	Carnarvon	712	Corning	515	Dunbar	515
Anderson	712	Berwick	515	Carpenter	515	Correctionville	712	Duncombe	515
Andover	319	Bethesda	712	Carroll	712	Corwith	515	Dundee	319
Andrew	319	Bettendorf	319	Carrollton	712	Corydon	515	Dunkerton	319
Angus	515	Bevington	515	Carson	712	Cotter	319	Dunlap	712
Anita	712	Big Rock	319	Carter Lake	712	Coulter	515	Durango	319
Ankeny	515	Birmingham	515	Cartersville	515	Council Bluffs	712	Durant	319
Anthon	712	Bladensburg	515	Cascade	319	Craig	712	Dyersville	319
Aplington	319	Blairsburg	515	Casey	515	Cranston	319	Dysart	319
Arcadia	712	Blairstown	319	Castalia	319	Crawfordsville	319		
Archer	712	Blakesburg	515	Castana	712	Crescent	712		
Ardon	319	Blanchard	712	Cedar	515	Cresco	319	Eagle Grove	515
Aredale	515	Blencoe	712	Cedar Bluff	319	Creston	515	Earlham	515
Argo	319	Blockton	515	Cedar Falls	319	Cromwell	319	Earling	712
Argyle	319	Bloomfield	515	Cedar Rapids	319	Crystal Lake	515	Earlville	319
Arion	712	Blue Grass	319	Center Junction	319	Cumberland	712	Early	712
Arispe	515	Bode	515	Center Point	319	Cumming	515	East Amana	319
Arlington	319	Bonaparte	319	Centerville	515	Curlew	712	East Canton	712
Armstrong	712	Bondurant	515	Central City	319	Cushing	712	East Fairview	319
Arnolds Park	712	Boone	515	Centralia	319	Cylinder	712	East Harrisburg	712
Arthur	712	Booneville	515	Chapin	515			East Hudson	712
Asbury	319	Botna	712	Chariton	515			East Nebraska City	712
Ashgrove	515	Bouton	515	Charles City	515			East Pleasant Plain	319
Ashton	712	Boxholm	515	Charlotte	319	Dakota City	515	Eddyville	515
Aspinwall	712	Boyden	712	Charter Oak	712	Dallas	515	Edgewood	319
Atalissa	319	Boyer	712	Chatsworth	712	Dallas Center	515	Edna	712
Athelstan	515	Braddyville	712	Chelsea	515	Dana	515	Elberon	319
Atkins	319	Bradford	515	Cherokee	712	Danbury	712	Eldon	515
Atlantic	712	Bradgate	515	Chester	319	Danville	319	Eldora	515
Attica	515	Brandon	319	Chillicothe	515	Davenport	319	Eldorado	319
Auburn	712	Brayton	712	Church	515	Davis City	515	Eldridge	319
Audubon	712	Brazil	515	Churdan	712	Dawson	515	Elgin	319
Aurelia	712	Breda	712	Cincinnati	515	Dayton	515	Elkader	319
Aurora	319	Bremer	319	Clare	515	Dean	515	Elkhart	515
Austinville	515	Bridgewater	712	Clarence	319	Decatur	515	Elk Horn	712
Avery	515	Brighton	319	Clarinda	712	Decorah	319	Elkport	319
Avoca	712	Bristow	319	Clarion	515	Dedham	712	Elliott	712
Avon	515	Britt	515	Clarksville	319	Deep River	515	Ellston	515
Ayrshire	712	Bronson	712	Clayton	319	Defiance	712	Ellsworth	515
		Brooklyn	515	Clearfield	515	Delaware	319	Elma	515
		Brooks	515	Clear Lake	515	Delhi	319	Elon	319
		Brunsville	712	Cleghorn	712	Delmar	319	Elwood	319
Badger	515	Bryant	319	Clemons	515	Deloit	712	Ely	319
Bagley	515	Buckeye	515	Clermont	319	Delphos	515	Emeline	319

Place Name	Area Code	Place Name	Area Code	Place Name	Area Code	Place Name	Area Code	Place Name	Area Code
Emerson	712	Glasgow	319	Highlandville	319	Keswick	319	Lockridge	319
Emmetsburg	712	Glenwood	712	Hills	319	Keystone	319	Logan	712
Enterprise	515	Glidden	712	Hillsboro	319	Kilbourn	319	Lohrville	712
Epworth	319	Goldfield	515	Hinton	712	Killduff	515	Lone Rock	515
Essex	712	Goodell	515	Hiteman	515	Kimballton	712	Lone Tree	319
Estherville	712	Goose Lake	319	Holbrook	319	Kingsley	712	Long Grove	319
Everly	712	Gowrie	515	Holland	319	Kingston	319	Lorimor	515
Ewart	515	Graettinger	712	Holly Springs	712	Kinross	319	Lost Nation	319
Exira	712	Graf	319	Holmes	515	Kirkman	712	Loveland	712
Exline	515	Grafton	515	Holstein	712	Kirkville	515	Lovilia	515
		Grand Junction	515	Holy Cross	319	Kiron	712	Lowden	319
		Grand Mound	319	Homestead	319	Klemme	515	Lowell	319
		Grand River	515	Honey Creek	712	Knierim	712	Lower South Amana	319
Fairbank	319	Grandview	319	Hopeville	515	Knoke	712	Low Moor	319
Fairfax	319	Granger	515	Hopkinton	319	Knoxville	515	Luana	319
Fairfield	515	Grant	712	Hornick	712			Lucas	515
Fairport	319	Grant Center	712	Hospers	712			Ludlow	319
Farley	319	Granville	712	Houghton	319	Lacey	515	Luther	515
Farlin	515	Gravity	712	Hubbard	515	Lacona	515	Luton	712
Farmersburg	319	Gray	712	Hudson	319	Ladora	319	Luverne	515
Farmington	319	Greeley	319	Hull	712	Lake City	515	Luxemburg	319
Farnhamville	712	Greene	515	Humboldt	515	Lake Manawa	712	Luzerne	319
Farragut	712	Greenfield	515	Humeston	515	Lake Mills	515	Lyman	712
Farrar	515	Green Island	319	Huntington	712	Lake Okoboji	712	Lynnville	515
Farson	515	Green Mountain	515	Hurley	515	Lake Park	712	Lytton	712
Faulkner	515	Greenville	712	Hurstville	319	Lake View	712		
Fayette	319	Grimes	515	Hutchins	515	Lakota	515		
Fenton	515	Grinnell	515	Huxley	515	Lamoille	515		
Ferguson	515	Griswold	712			Lamoni	515	Macedonia	712
Fernald	515	Grundy Center	319			Lamont	319	Macksburg	515
Fertile	515	Gruver	712			LaMotte	319	Madrid	515
Festina	319	Guernsey	319	Iconium	515	Lanesboro	712	Magnolia	712
Floris	515	Guss	515	Ida Grove	712	Langdon	712	Malcom	515
Floyd	515	Guthrie Center	515	Imogene	712	Langworthy	319	Mallard	712
Fonda	712	Guttenberg	319	Independence	319	Lansing	319	Maloy	515
Fontanelle	515			Indianola	515	Lanyon	515	Malvern	712
Forest City	515			Inwood	712	La Porte City	319	Manchester	319
Fort Atkinson	319	Halbur	712	Ionia	515	Larchwood	712	Manilla	712
Fort Des Moines	515	Hale	319	Iowa City	319	Larrabee	712	Manly	515
Fort Dodge	515	Halfa	712	Iowa Falls	515	Latimer	515	Manning	712
Fort Madison	319	Hamburg	712	Ira	515	Laurel	515	Manson	712
Fostoria	712	Hamilton	515	Ireton	712	Laurens	712	Maple Hill	712
Frankville	319	Hamlin	712	Irvington	515	Lavinia	712	Maple River	712
Fraser	515	Hampton	515	Irwin	712	Lawler	515	Mapleton	712
Fredericksburg	319	Hancock	712	Ivy	515	Lawton	712	Maquoketa	319
Frederika	319	Hanlontown	515			Leando	515	Marathon	712
Fredonia	319	Hansell	515			Le Claire	319	Marble Rock	515
Fremont	515	Harcourt	515	Jackson Junction	319	Ledyard	515	Marcus	712
Froelich	319	Hardy	515	Jacksonville	712	Le Grand	515	Marengo	319
Fruitland	319	Harlan	712	Jamaica	515	Lehigh	515	Marion	319
		Harper	515	Janesville	319	Leighton	515	Mark	515
		Harpers Ferry	319	Jefferson	515	Leland	515	Marne	712
Galt	515	Harris	712	Jerico	319	Le Mars	712	Marquette	319
Galva	712	Hartford	515	Jerome	515	Lenox	515	Marshalltown	515
Garber	319	Hartley	712	Jesup	319	Leon	515	Martelle	319
Garden City	515	Hartwick	515	Jewell	515	Le Roy	515	Martensdale	515
Garden Grove	515	Harvard	515	Johnston	515	Lester	712	Martinsburg	515
Garnavillo	319	Harvey	515	Joice	515	Letts	319	Marysville	515
Garner	515	Haskins	319	Jolley	712	Lewis	712	Mason City	515
Garrison	319	Hastings	712	Jordan	515	Liberty Center	515	Masonville	319
Garwin	515	Havelock	712			Libertyville	515	Massena	712
Gaza	712	Haverhill	515			Lidderdale	712	Massillon	319
Geneva	515	Hawarden	712	Kalona	319	Lime Springs	319	Matlock	712
George	712	Hawkeye	319	Kamrar	515	Lincoln	515	Maurice	712
Gibson	515	Hayfield	319	Kanawha	515	Linden	515	Maxwell	515
Gifford	515	Hazleton	319	Kellerton	515	Lineville	515	May City	712
Gilbert	515	Hedrick	515	Kelley	515	Linn Grove	712	Maynard	319
Gilbertville	319	Henderson	712	Kellogg	515	Lisbon	319	Maysville	319
Gillett Grove	712	Herndon	515	Kensett	515	Liscomb	515	McCallsburg	515
Gilman	515	Herring	712	Kent	515	Little Cedar	515	McCausland	319
Gilmore City	515	Hesper	319	Keokuk	319	Littleport	319	McClelland	712
Gladbrook	515	Hiawatha	319	Keosauqua	319	Little Rock	712	McGregor	319
Gladwin	319	High Amana (High)	319	Keota	515	Little Sioux	712	McIntire	515
		Highland Center	515	Kesley	319	Livermore	515	McPaul	712

Place Name	Area Code	Place Name	Area Code	Place Name	Area Code	Place Name	Area Code	Place Name	Area Code
Mechanicsville	319	Neola	712	Oxford	319	Randall	515	Sanborn	712
Mediapolis	319	Nevada	515	Oxford Junction	319	Randolph	712	Sandyville	515
Melbourne	515	Nevinville	515	Oyens	712	Rands	712	Savannah	515
Melcher	515	New Albin	319			Rathbun	515	Scarville	515
Melrose	515	Newbern	515			Raymond	319	Schaller	712
Meltonville	515	New Boston	319			Readlyn	319	Schleswig	712
Melvin	712	Newburg	515	Pacific Junction	712	Reasnor	515	Scotch Grove	319
Menlo	515	Newell	712	Packwood	515	Redding	515	Scranton	712
Meriden	712	Newhall	319	Palmer	712	Redfield	515	Searsboro	515
Merrill	712	New Hampton	515	Palo	319	Red Oak	712	Selma	515
Merrimac	319	New Hartford	319	Panama	712	Red Rock	515	Sergeant Bluff	712
Meservey	515	New Haven	515	Panora	515	Reinbeck	319	Sewal	515
Middle Amana	319	New Liberty	319	Parkersburg	319	Rembrandt	712	Sexton	515
Middletown	319	New London	319	Parnell	319	Remsen	712	Seymour	515
Midland	712	New Market	712	Paton	515	Renwick	515	Shambaugh	712
Miles	319	New Providence	515	Patterson	515	Rhodes	515	Shannon City	515
Milford	712	New Sharon	515	Paullina	712	Riceville	515	Sharon Center	319
Miller	515	Newton	515	Payne	712	Richards	712	Sharpsburg	515
Millersburg	319	New Vienna	319	Pella	515	Richland	515	Sheffield	515
Millerton	515	New Virginia	515	Peoria	515	Richmond	319	Shelby	712
Millville	319	Nichols	319	Peosta	319	Ricketts	712	Sheldahl	515
Milo	515	Nodaway	712	Percival	319	Ridgeway	319	Sheldon	712
Milton	515	Nora Junction	515	Percy	515	Rinard	712	Shell Rock	319
Minburn	515	Nora Springs	515	Perry	515	Ringsted	712	Shellsburg	319
Minden	712	Nordness	319	Pershing	515	Rippey	515	Shenandoah	712
Mineola	712	Northboro	712	Persia	712	Riverside	319	Sherrill	319
Mingo	515	North Branch	319	Peru	515	River Sioux	712	Siam	712
Missouri Valley	712	North Buena Vista	319	Peterson	712	Riverton	712	Sibley	712
Mitchell	515	North English	319	Pierson	712	Robins	319	Sidney	712
Mitchellville	515	North Hopkins	712	Pilot Grove	319	Rochester	319	Sigourney	515
Modale	712	North Liberty	319	Pilot Mound	515	Rock Creek Lake	515	Silver City	712
Mona	515	North Sheridan	712	Pioneer	515	Rock Falls	515	Sioux Center	712
Mondamin	712	North Washington	515	Pisgah	712	Rockford	515	Sioux City	712
Moneta	712	Northwood	515	Pitzer	515	Rock Rapids	712	Sioux Rapids	712
Monmouth	319	Norwalk	515	Plainfield	319	Rock Valley	712	Slater	515
Monona	319	Norway	319	Plainview	319	Rockwell	515	Sloan	712
Monroe	515	Norwood	515	Plano	515	Rockwell City	712	Smithland	712
Monteith	515	Numa	515	Pleasanton	515	Rodman	515	Soldier	712
Monterey	515			Pleasant Plain	319	Rodney	712	Solon	319
Montezuma	515			Pleasant Prairie	319	Roland	515	Somers	712
Montgomery	712			Pleasant Valley	319	Rolfe	712	South Adams	515
Monticello	319	Oakland	712	Pleasantville	515	Rome	319	South Bigelow	712
Montour	515	Oakland Mills	319	Plover	712	Rose Hill	515	South Canton	319
Montpelier	319	Oakville	319	Plymouth	515	Ross	712	South Eitzen	319
Montrose	319	Ocheyedan	712	Pocahontas	712	Rossie	712	South Emmons	515
Moorhead	712	Odebolt	712	Polk City	515	Rossville	319	South English	319
Moorland	515	Oelwein	319	Pomeroy	712	Rowan	515	South Granger	319
Moravia	515	Ogden	515	Popejoy	515	Rowley	319	South Harmony	319
Morley	319	Okoboji	712	Port Louisa	319	Royal	712	South Jackson	319
Morning Sun	319	Olds	319	Portsmouth	712	Rubio	515	South Round Lake	712
Morrison	319	Olin	319	Postville	319	Rudd	515	South Spring Grove	319
Moscow	319	Ollie	515	Prairieburg	319	Runnells	515	South Valley Springs	712
Moulton	515	Onawa	712	Prairie City	515	Russell	515	Spaulding	515
Mount Auburn	319	Oneida	319	Prescott	515	Ruthven	712	Spencer	712
Mount Ayr	515	Onslow	319	Preston	319	Rutland	515	Sperry	319
Mount Hamill	319	Oran	319	Primghar	712	Ryan	319	Spillville	319
Mount Pleasant	319	Orange City	712	Primrose	319			Spirit Lake	712
Mount Sterling	319	Orchard	515	Princeton	319			Spragueville	319
Mount Union	319	Orient	515	Prole	515			Springbrook	319
Mount Vernon	319	Orleans	712	Promise City	515	Sabula	319	Springdale	319
Mount Zion	319	Orson	515	Protivin	319	Sac City	712	Spring Hill	515
Moville	712	Osage	515	Pulaski	515	Sageville	319	Springville	319
Munterville	515	Osceola	515			St. Ansgar	515	Stacyville	515
Murray	515	Osgood	712			St. Anthony	515	Stanhope	515
Muscatine	319	Oskaloosa	515			St. Benedict	515	Stanley	319
Mystic	515	Ossian	319	Quasqueton	319	St. Charles	515	Stanton	712
		Osterdock	319	Quimby	712	St. Donatus	319	Stanwood	319
		Otho	515			St. Joseph	515	State Center	515
Napier	515	Otley	515			St. Lucas	319	Steamboat Rock	515
Nashua	515	Oto	712			St. Marys	515	Stevens	515
Nashville	319	Otter Creek	319	Radcliffe	515	St. Olaf	319	Stiles	515
Nassett	319	Ottosen	515	Rake	515	Salem	319	Stockport	515
Nemaha	712	Ottumwa	515	Ralston	712	Salina	319	Stockton	319
		Owasa	515	Randalia	319	Salix	712	Storm Lake	712

Place Name	Area Code	Place Name	Area Code	Place Name	Area Code	Place Name	Area Code	Place Name	Area Code
Story City	515	Tiffin	319	Van Cleve	515	Waubeek	319	Whittemore	515
Stout	319	Tingley	515	Van Horne	319	Waucoma	319	Whitten	515
Strahan	712	Tipton	319	Van Meter	515	Waukee	515	Whittier	319
Stratford	515	Titonka	515	Van Wert	515	Waukon	319	Wick	515
Strawberry Point	319	Toddville	319	Varina	712	Waukon Junction	319	Williams	515
Struble	712	Toeterville	515	Ventura	515	Waupeton	319	Williamsburg	319
Stuart	515	Toledo	515	Victor	319	Waverly	319	Williamson	515
Sully	515	Toronto	319	Villisca	712	Wayland	319	Wilton	319
Sulphur Springs	712	Tracy	515	Vincennes	319	Webb	712	Wilton Junction	319
Sumner	515	Traer	319	Vincent	515	Webster	319	Winfield	319
Sunbury	319	Treynor	712	Vining	515	Webster City	515	Winterset	515
Superior	712	Tripoli	319	Vinton	319	Weldon	515	Winthrop	319
Sutherland	712	Troy	515	Viola	319	Wellman	319	Wiota	712
Swaledale	515	Troy Mills	319	Volga	319	Wellsburg	515	Woden	515
Swan	515	Truesdale	712	Voorhies	319	Welton	319	Woodbine	712
Swea City	515	Truro	515			Wesley	515	Woodburn	515
Swedesburg	319	Turin	712			West Amana (West)	319	Woodward	515
Swisher	319					West Bend	515	Woolstock	515
						West Branch	319	Worthington	319
				Wadena	319	West Burlington	319	Wright	515
				Wahpeton	712	West Chester	319	Wyman	319
				Walcott	319	West Des Moines	515	Wyoming	319
Tabor	712	Udell	515	Walford	319	Westfield	712		
Taintor	515	Ulmer	712	Walker	319	Westgate	515		
Tama	515	Underwood	712	Wallingford	712	West Grove	515		
Teeds Grove	319	Union	515	Wall Lake	712	West Liberty	319	Yale	515
Templeton	712	Unionville	515	Walnut	712	West Mitchell	515	Yarmouth	319
Tennant	712	University Park	515	Wapello	319	Westphalia	712	Yetter	712
Terril	712	Upper South Amana	319	Ware	712	West Point	319	Yorktown	712
Thayer	515	Urbana	319	Washburn	319	Westside	712		
Thompson	515	Ute	712	Washington	319	West Union	319		
Thor	515			Washta	712	Wever	319		
Thornburg	515			Waterloo	319	What Cheer	515		
Thornton	515	Vail	712	Waterville	515	Wheatland	319	Zearing	515
Thurman	712	Valeria	515	Watkins	319	Whiting	712	Zwingle	319

Place Name	Area Code	Place Name	Area Code	Place Name	Area Code	Place Name	Area Code	Place Name	Area Code
Abbyville-Plevna	316	Beeler	913	Caney	316	Damar	913	Fairway	913
Abilene	913	Bellaire	913	Canton	316	Danville	316	Fall River	316
Achilles	913	Belle Plaine	316	Carbondale-		Dearing	316	Falun	913
Acme	913	Belleville	913	Wakarusa	913	Deerfield	316	Fanning	913
Acres	316	Belmont	316	Carlton	913	Delavan	913	Farlington	316
Ada	913	Beloit	913	Cassoday	316	Delia	913	Farlinville	913
Admire	316	Belpre	316	Castleton	316	Dellvale	913	Faulkner	316
Agenda	913	Belvidere	316	Catherine	913	Delphos	913	Feterita	316
Agra	913	Belvue	913	Cave	316	Denison	913	Florence	316
Agricola	913	Bendena	913	Cawker City	913	Denmark	913	Flush	913
Alamota	316	Benedict	316	Cedar	913	Dennis	316	Fontana	913
Albert	316	Bennington	913	Cedar Point	316	Densmore	913	Forbes Air Force	
Alden	316	Benton	316	Cedar Vale	316	Denton	913	Base	913
Alexander	913	Bern	913	Centerville	913	Derby	316	Ford	316
Aliceville	913	Berryton	913	Centralia	913	De Soto	913	Forest Lake	913
Allen	316	Bethel	913	Centropolis	913	Devon	316	Formoso	913
Allison	913	Beverly	913	Chalk	316	Dexter	316	Fort Dodge	316
Alma	913	Big Bow	316	Chanute	316	Diamond Springs	913	Fort Leavenworth	913
Almena	913	Bigspring	913	Chapman	316	Dighton	316	Fort Riley	913
Altamont	316	Bird City	913	Charleston	316	Dillwyn	316	Fort Scott	316
Alta Vista	913	Bison	913	Chase	316	Dodge City	316	Fostoria	913
Alton	913	Blaine	913	Chatauqua	316	Doniphan	913	Fowler	316
Altoona	316	Blair	913	Cheney	316	Dorrance	913	Frankfort	913
Americus	316	Blakeman	913	Cherokee	316	Douglass	316	Franklin	316
Ames	913	Block	913	Cherryvale	316	Dover	913	Fredonia	316
Amy	316	Bloom	316	Chetopa	316	Downs	913	Freeport	316
Andale	316	Bloomington	913	Cheyenne	913	Dresden	913	Friend	316
Andover	316	Blue Mound	913	Chiles	913	Dunavant	913	Frisbie	913
Angola	316	Blue Rapids	913	Cimarron	316	Dunlap	316	Frizell	316
Anson	316	Bluff City	316	Circleville	913	Duquoin	316	Frontenac	316
Antelope	316	Bogue	913	Claflin	316	Durham	316	Fulton	316
Anthony	316	Boicourt	913	Clare	913	Dwight	913	Furley	316
Antonino	913	Boling	913	Clay Center	913				
Arcadia	316	Bonita	913	Clayton	913				
Argentine	913	Bonner Springs	913	Clearwater	316				
Argonia	316	Boyd	316	Clements	316	Earleton	316		
Arkansas City	316	Boyle	913	Clifton	913	Easton	913	Galatia	316
Arlington	316	Brantford	913	Climax	316	Edgerton	913	Galena	316
Arma	316	Brazilton	316	Clinton	913	Edmond	913	Galesburg	316
Arnold	913	Bremen	913	Clonmel	316	Edna	316	Galva	316
Arrington	913	Brenham	316	Clyde	913	Edson	913	Garden City	316
Asherville	913	Brenner	913	Coats	316	Edwardsville	913	Garden Plain	316
Ash Grove	913	Brewster	913	Codell	913	Effingham	913	Gardner	913
Ashland	316	Bridgeport	913	Coffeyville	316	Elbing	316	Garfield	316
Ashton	316	Bronson	316	Colby	913	El Dorado	316	Garland	316
Assaria	913	Brookville	913	Coldwater	316	Elgin	316	Garnett	913
Atchison	913	Broughton	913	Collyer	913	Elkader	316	Gas	316
Athol	913	Brownell	913	Colony	316	Elk City	316	Gaylord	913
Atlanta	316	Buckeye	913	Columbus	316	Elk Falls	316	Gem	913
Attica	316	Bucklin	316	Columbus Rural	316	Elkhart	316	Geneseo	316
Atwood	913	Bucyrus	913	Colwich-Bentley	316	Ellinwood	316	Geuda Springs	316
Auburn	913	Buffalo	316	Concordia	913	Ellis	913	Girard	316
Augusta	316	Buffalo Park	913	Conway	316	Ellsworth	913	Glade	913
Aulne	316	Buhler	316	Conway Springs	316	Elmdale	316	Glasco	913
Aurora	913	Bunker Hill	913	Coolidge	316	Elm Grove	913	Glen Elder	913
Axtell	913	Burden	316	Copeland	316	Elmo	913	Globe	913
		Burdett	316	Corbin	316	Elmont	913	Goddard	316
		Burdick	913	Corning	913	Elsmore	316	Goessel	316
Baileyville	913	Burlingame	913	Corwin	316	Elwood	913	Goff	913
Baldwin	913	Burlington	316	Cottonwood Falls	316	Elyria	316	Goodland	913
Banner	913	Burns	316	Council Grove	316	Emmett	913	Goodrich	913
Barclay	913	Burr Oak	913	Countryside	913	Emporia	316	Gordon	316
Barnard	913	Burrton	316	Courtland	913	Englewood	316	Gorham	913
Barnes	913	Bush City	913	Covert	913	Ensign	316	Gove	913
Bartlett	316	Bushong	316	Coyville	316	Enterprise	913	Grainfield	913
Basehor	913	Bushton	316	Craig	913	Erie	316	Grantville	913
Bavaria	913	Buxton	316	Crestline	316	Esbon	913	Gray	316
Baxter Springs	316	Byers	316	Croft	316	Eskridge	913	Great Bend	316
Bazaar	316			Crotty	316	Eudora	913	Greeley	913
Bazine	913			Crystal Springs	316	Eureka	316	Green	913
Beagle	913	Cadmus	913	Cuba	913	Everest	913	Greenleaf	913
Beardsley	913	Cairo	316	Cullison	316			Greensburg	316
Beattie	913	Caldwell	316	Culver	913			Greenwich	316
Beaumont	316	Calvert	913	Cummings	913	Fairport	913	Grenola	316
Beaver	316	Cambridge	316	Cunningham	316	Fairview	913	Gridley	316
		Canada	316					Grinnell	913

Place Name	Area Code	Place Name	Area Code	Place Name	Area Code	Place Name	Area Code	Place Name	Area Code
Gross	316	Idana	913	Lawton	316	McLouth	913	New Albany	316
Grove	913	Independence	316	Leavenworth	913	McPherson	316	New Almelo	913
Groveland	316	Industry	913	Leawood	913	Meade	316	New Cambria	913
Gypsum	913	Ingalls	316	Leawood South	913	Medicine Lodge	316	New Gottland	316
		Inman	316	Lebanon	913	Melrose		New Lancaster	913
		Iola	316	Lebo	316	(Cherokee Co.)	316	Newman	913
		Ionia	913	Lecompton	913	Melrose		New Salem	316
		Iowa Point	913	Lehigh	316	(Johnson Co.)	913	Newton	316
Haddam	913	Irving	913	Lenape	913	Melvern	913	Nickerson	316
Haggard	316	Isabel	316	Lenexa	913	Menlo	913	Niles	913
Halford	913	Iuka	316	Lenora	913	Mentor	913	Niotaze	316
Hallowell	316			Leon	316	Mercier	913	Nonchalanta	913
Halls Summit	316			Leona	913	Meriden	913	Norcatur	913
Halstead	316			Leonardville	913	Merriam	913	Northbranch	913
Hamilton	316	Jaggard	913	Leoti	316	Michigan Valley	913	North Manchester	316
Hamlin	316	Jamestown	913	Leoville	913	Milan	316	North Tyrone	316
Hammond	316	Jarbalo	913	LeRoy	316	Milberger	913	Norton	913
Hanover-Hollenberg	913	Jefferson	316	Levant	913	Mildred	316	Nortonville	913
Hanston	316	Jennings	913	Lewis	316	Milford	913	Norwich	316
Hardtner	316	Jetmore	316	Liberal	316	Miller	913	
Harlan	913	Jewell	913	Liberty	316	Milo	913	
Harper	316	Johnson	316	Liebenthal	913	Miltonvale	913	
Harris	913	Joy	316	Lillis	913	Minneapolis	913	Oak Hill	913
Hartford	316	Junction City	913	Lincoln	913	Minneola	316	Oakley	913
Harveyville	913			Lincolnville	316	Mission	913	Oak Mills	913
Havana	316			Lindsborg	913	Mission Hills	913	Oak Valley	316
Haven	316			Linn	913	Mission Woods	913	Oberlin	913
Havensville	913	Kackley	913	Linwood	913	Missler	316	Ocheltree	913
Haverhill	316	Kanona	913	Little River	316	Modoc	316	Odin	316
Haviland	316	Kanopolis	913	Logan	913	Moline	316	Offerle	316
Hays	913	Kanorado	913	Lone Star	913	Montezuma	316	Ogallah	913
Haysville	316	Kansas City	913	Longford	913	Monticello	913	Ogden	913
Hazelton	316	Kansas Ordnance		Long Island	913	Mont Ida	913	Oil Hill	316
Healy	316	Works	316	Longton	316	Montrose	913	Oketo	913
Hepler	316	Keats	913	Loring	913	Monument	913	Olathe	913
Herington	913	Kechi	316	Lorraine	913	Moonlight	913	Olivet	316
Herkimer	913	Keene	913	Lost Springs	913	Moran	316	Olmitz	316
Herndon	913	Keily	913	Louisburg	913	Morehead	316	Olpe	316
Hesston	316	Kendall	316	Louisville	913	Morganville	913	Olsburg	913
Hewins	316	Kensington	913	Lovewell	913	Morland	913	Onaga	913
Hiattville	316	Kimbal	316	Lucas	913	Morrill	913	Oneida	913
Hiawatha	913	Kincaid	316	Ludell	913	Morrowville	913	Opolis	316
Hickok	316	Kingman	316	Lund	913	Morse	913	Orohoque	913
Highland	913	Kingsdown	316	Luray	913	Moscow	316	Osage City	913
Hill City	913	Kinsley	316	Lydia	316	Mound City	913	Osawatomie	913
Hillsboro	316	Kiowa	316	Lyle	913	Moundridge	316	Osborne	913
Hillsdale	913	Kiro	913	Lyndon	913	Mound Valley	316	Oskaloosa	913
Hitchman	316	Kirwin	913	Lyons	316	Mount Hope	316	Oswald Oil Field	913
Hoisington	316	Kismet	316			Mulberry	316	Oswego	316
Holcomb	316	Kling	316			Mullinville	316	Otis	913
Hollenberg	913	Kossuth	913			Mulvane	316	Ottawa	913
Holliday	913			Macksville	316	Muncie	913	Otto	316
Hollis	913			Madison	316	Munden	913	Overbrook	913
Holton	913			Mahaska	913	Murdock	316	Overland Park	913
Holyrood	913	Labette	316	Maize	316	Muscotah	913	Oxford	316
Home	913	La Crosse	913	Manchester	913			Ozawkie	913
Homer	913	La Cygne	913	Manhattan	913			
Hope	913	Ladysmith	913	Mankato	913			
Hopewell	316	Lafontaine	316	Manning	316	Narka	913	Page City	913
Horace	316	La Harpe	316	Manter	316	Nashville	316	Palacky	913
Horton	913	Laird	913	Maple City	316	Natoma	913	Palco	913
Howard	316	Lake City	316	Maple Hill	913	Natrona	316	Palermo	913
Howell	316	Lakin	316	Mapleton	316	Naval Air Station		Palmer	913
Hoxie	913	Lamar	913	Marienthal	316	(Gardner)	913	Paola	913
Hoyt	913	Lamont	316	Marietta	913	Naval Air Station		Paradise	913
Hudson	316	Lancaster	913	Marion	316	(Hutchinson)	316	Park	913
Hugoton	316	Lane	913	Marquette	913	Navarre	913	Parker	913
Humboldt	316	Langdon	316	Marysville	913	Nekoma	913	Parkerville	913
Hunnewell	316	Langley	316	Matfield Green	316	Neodesha	316	Parsons	316
Hunter	913	Lansing	913	Mayetta	913	Neosho Falls	316	Partridge	316
Huntsville	316	Larkinburg	913	Mayfield	316	Neosho Rapids	316	Pauline	913
Huron	913	Larned	316	McCracken	913	Ness City	913	Pawnee Rock	316
Huscher	913	Latham	316	McCune	316	Netawaka	913	Paxico	913
Hutchinson	316	Latimer	913	McDonald	913	Nettleton	316	Peabody	316
		Lawrence	913	McFarland	913	Neutral	316	Peck	316

Place Name	Area Code	Place Name	Area Code	Place Name	Area Code	Place Name	Area Code	Place Name	Area Code
Penalosa	316	Rosalia	316	South Bloomington	913	Topeka	913	Weir City	316
Pendennis	913	Rose Hill	316	South Byron	913	Topeka-Greenfield	913	Welda	913
Penokee	913	Rossville	913	South Chester	913	Toronto	316	Wellington	316
Perry	913	Roxbury	913	South Danbury	913	Towanda	316	Wells	913
Peru	316	Rozel	316	South Du Bois	913	Trading Post	913	Wellsford	316
Petrolia	316	Rush Center	913	South Falls City	913	Traer	913	Wellsville	913
Pfeifer	913	Russell	913	South Franklin	913	Treece	316	Weskan	913
Phillipsburg	913	Russell Springs	913	South Haigler	913	Tribune	316	West Cleveland	913
Piedmont	316	Rydal	913	South Hardy	913	Trousdale	316	West Drexel	913
Pierceville	316	Ryus	316	South Haven	316	Troy	913	Westfall	913
Pilsen	316			South Hubbell	913	Troy Junction	913	West Hume	913
Piper	913			South Inavale	913	Turner	913	West Mineral	316
Piqua	316			South Liberty	913	Turon	316	Westmoreland	913
Pittsburg	316			South Mound	316	Tyro	316	Westphalia	913
Plains	316	Sabetha	913	South Naponee	913			Westwood	913
Plainville	913	Saffordville	316	South Odell	913			Westwood Hills	913
Pleasanton	913	St. Francis	913	South Pawnee City	913			Wetmore	913
Pomona	913	St. George	913	South Red Cloud	913	Udall	316	Wheaton	913
Portis	913	St. John	316	South Republican		Ulysses	316	Wheeler	913
Potter	913	St. Marys	913	City	913	Uniontown	316	White City	913
Potwin	316	St. Paul	316	South Riverton	913	Upland	913	White Cloud	913
Powhattan	913	Salemsburg	913	South Stratton	913	Urbana	316	White Water	316
Prairie View	913	Salina	913	South Superior	913	Utica	913	Whiting	913
Prairie Village	913	Sanford	316	South Wilsonville	913			Whitman	316
Pratt	316	Satanta	316	Sparks	913			Wichita	316
Prescott	913	Saunders	316	Spearville	316			Wichita-Jackson	316
Preston	316	Savonburg	316	Speed	913			Wichita-Parkview	316
Pretty Prairie	316	Sawyer	316	Spivey	316	Valeda	316	Wilbur	316
Princeton	913	Saxman	316	Spring Hill	913	Valencia	913	Wilburton	316
Protection	316	Scammon	316	Springvale	316	Valley Center	316	Wilder	913
		Scandia	913	Stafford	316	Valley Falls	913	Willard	913
		Schilling Air Force		Stanley	913	Varner	316	Williamsburg	913
		Base	913	Stark	316	Vermillion	913	Williamstown	913
Quenemo	913	Schoenchen	913	Sterling	316	Vesper	913	Willis	913
Quincy	316	Scott City	316	Stickney	316	Victoria	913	Wilmore	316
Quinter	913	Scottsville	913	Stilwell	913	Victory Highway		Wilsey	913
		Scranton	913	Stockton	913	Junction	913	Wilson	913
		Sedan	316	Strawn	316	Vilas	316	Winchester	913
		Sedgwick	316	Strickler	316	Vinland	913	Windom	316
Rago	316	Selden	913	Strong City	316	Viola	316	Winfield	316
Ramona	913	Selkirk	316	Studley	913	Virgil	316	Winifred	913
Randall	913	Seneca	913	Stull	913	Vliets	913	Winona	913
Ransom	913	Severance	913	Stuttgart	913	Voda	913	Wolcott	913
Rantoul	913	Severy	316	Sublette	316			Woodbine	913
Ray	316	Seward	316	Summerfield	913			Woodruff	913
Raymond	316	Shady Bend	913	Sun City	316			Woodston	913
Reading	316	Shaffer	316	Sunflower	913			Worden	913
Reager	913	Shallow Water	316	Sunflower Ordnance		Wabaunsee	913	Wright	316
Redfield	316	Sharon	316	Works	913	Wadsworth	913		
Redwing	316	Sharon Springs	913	Susank	316	Wagstaff	913		
Reece	316	Shawnee	913	Sycamore	316	Wakarusa	913		
Reno	913	Shawnee Mission	913	Sylvan Grove	913	WaKeeney	913		
Republic	913	Sherman	316	Sylvia	316	Wakefield	913		
Reserve	913	Sherwin	316	Syracuse	316	Waldo	913	Xavier	913
Rexford	913	Shields	316			Waldron	316		
Richfield	316	Silica	316			Walker	913		
Richland (Miami Co.)	913	Silverdale	316			Wallace	913		
Richland		Silver Lake	913			Walnut	316		
(Shawnee Co.)	913	Simpson	913	Talmage	913	Walton	316	Yates Center	316
Richmond	913	Sitka	316	Talmo	913	Wamego	913	Yocemento	913
Riley	913	Smith Center	913	Tampa	913	Washington	913		
Riverdale	316	Smolan	913	Tecumseh	913	Waterville	913		
Riverton	316	Soldier	913	Television City	316	Wathena	913		
Robinson	913	Solomon	913	Tescott	913	Watson	913		
Robinson Station	316	Solomon Rapids	913	Thayer	316	Wauneta	316	Zarah	913
Rock	316	Somerset	913	Timken	913	Waverly	913	Zeandale	913
Rock Creek	913	South Alma	913	Tipton	913	Wayne	913	Zenda	316
Roeland Park	913	South Barneston	913	Tonganoxie	913	Wayside	316	Zenith	316
Rolla	316	South Benkelman	913			Webber	913	Zurich	913

Place Name	Area Code	Place Name	Area Code	Place Name	Area Code	Place Name	Area Code	Place Name	Area Code
Aberdeen	502	Belfry	606	Brooksville	606	Chambers	502	Cumberland	606
Absher	502	Bellefonte	606	Broughtontown	606	Chapel Hill	502	Cumberland Falls	606
Acton	502	Bellevue	606	Browder	502	Chapeze	502	Cunningham	502
Adair	502	Bells	502	Brownsboro	502	Chaplin	502	Custer	502
Adairville	502	Belmont	502	Browns Grove	502	Chapman	606	Cynthiana	606
Addison	502	Belton	502	Brownsville	502	Chavies	606		
Adolphus	502	Bengal	502	Bruce	502	Chenoa	606		
Aflex	606	Benge	606	Brumfield	606	Chestnut Grove	502	Dade Park	502
Aiax	606	Benham-Lynch	606	Brush Creek	606	Chevrolet	606	Daisy	606
Albany	606	Benton	502	Bryant	606	Chilesburg	606	Dant	502
Alberta	502	Berea	606	Bryantsville	606	Chilton	606	Danville	606
Alcalde	606	Berkeley (Burkley)	502	Buckhorn	606	Christianburg	502	Darfork	606
Alexandria	606	Bernstadt	606	Buckner	502	Churchill	502	David	606
Allegre	502	Berry	606	Buechel	502	Clark	502	Dawson Springs	502
Allen	606	Bessie Bend	502	Buena Vista	606	Clarkson	502	Dayton	606
Allendale	502	Bethel	606	Buffalo	502	Clarksville Army Air		Deane	606
Allen Springs	502	Bethlehem		Bulan	606	Base	502	Deatsville	502
Allensville	502	(Hardin Co.)	502	Burdick	606	Clay	502	Defoe	502
Allock	606	Bethlehem		Burdine	606	Clay City	606	Delaware	502
Almo	502	(Henry Co.)	502	Burgin	606	Clayhole	606	Dema	606
Alphoretta	606	Beulah	502	Burkesville	502	Claymour	502	De Mossville	606
Alton Station	502	Beverly	606	Burlington	606	Clay Village	502	Depoy	502
Altro	606	Bevier	502	Burna	502	Clear Creek Springs	606	Derrick	606
Alvaton	502	Big Clifty	502	Burning Springs	606	Clearfield	606	Dexter	502
Anchorage	502	Big Creek	606	Burnside	606	Cleaton	502	Diamond Springs	502
Anco	606	Biggs	606	Butler	606	Clermont	502	Dishman Springs	606
Anneta	502	Bighill	606	Butterfly	606	Cleveland	606	Disputanta	606
Annville	606	Big Spring	502	Bybee	606	Cliff	606	Dix Dam	606
Arjay	606	Black Cross Roads	606	Bypro	606	Clinton	502	Dixon	502
Arlington	502	Blackey	606			Clintonville	606	Dizney	606
Artemus	606	Blackford	502			Cloverport	502	Domino	606
Asher	606	Blaine	606			Coalgood	606	Donerail	606
Ashland	606	Blandville	502			Coal Run	606	Donithon	606
Atchison	502	Blaze	606	Cadiz	502	Coburg	502	Dorton	606
Athens	606	Bledsoe	606	Calhoun	502	Cody	606	Dot	502
Athertonville	502	Bloomfield	502	California	606	Cold Spring	606	Dover	606
Atomic Area	502	Blue Diamond	606	Callaway	502	Colesburg	502	Draffin	606
Auburn	502	Bluegrass		Calvert City	502	College Hill	606	Drakesboro	502
Augusta	606	Ordnance Depot	606	Camargo	606	Collins	606	Drennon Springs	502
Aurora	502	Bluff Springs	502	Camden	502	Colson	606	Dreyfus	606
Austerlitz	606	Boaz	502	Campbellsburg	502	Columbia	502	Drift	606
Avoca	502	Bonanza	606	Campbellsville	502	Columbus	502	Dry Ridge	606
Avon	606	Bonayr	502	Camp Breckinridge	502	Combs	606	Duff	502
Axtel	502	Bondville	606	Camp Daniel Boone	606	Confederate	502	Dukedom	502
		Bonnieville	502	Camp Nelson	606	Conkling	606	Dulaney	502
		Bonnyman	606	Campton	606	Conley	606	Duncan	606
Bagdad	502	Booneville	606	Canada	606	Constance	606	Dundee	502
Balkan	606	Boonsboro	606	Cane Valley	502	Cooper	606	Dunham	606
Bancroft	502	Boons Camp	606	Caney	606	Coral Hill	502	Dunlap	606
Bandana	502	Bordley	502	Caneyville	502	Corbin	606	Dunmor	502
Banner	606	Boreing	606	Canmer	502	Corinth (Grant Co.)	606	Dunnville	606
Barbourville	606	Bourne	606	Cannel City	606	Corinth (Logan Co.)	502	Dwarf	606
Bardo	606	Bow	502	Canoe	606	Cornishville	606	Dycusburg	502
Bardstown	502	Bowen	606	Canton	606	Cornwell	606		
Bardstown Junction	502	Bowling Green	502	Capito	606	Corydon	502		
Bardwell	502	Bowman Field	502	Cardinal	606	Cottle	606	Eagle	502
Barlow	502	Boyd	606	Cardwell	502	Cottonburg	502	Earles	502
Bartles	502	Bracktown	606	Carlisle	606	Covington	606	Earlington	502
Barton	606	Bradfordsville	502	Carpenter	606	Cowcreek	606	Earnestville	606
Baskett	502	Bradley	606	Carrollton	502	Coxs Creek	502	East Bernstadt	606
Bass	502	Bradshaw	606	Carrs	606	Coxton	606	East Hickman	606
Battletown	502	Brandenburg	502	Cartersville	606	Crab Orchard	606	East Point	606
Baxter	606	Brannon	606	Cary	606	Creelsboro	502	East Texas	606
Beattyville	606	Braxton	606	Casey Creek	502	Crescent Springs	606	Eastview	502
Beaver Dam	502	Bremen	502	Catlettsburg	606	Crestwood	502	Eastwood	502
Beckton	502	Bridgeport	502	Cave City	502	Crider	502	Ebenezer	606
Bedford	502	Brighton	606	Cawood	606	Crittenden	606	Eddyville	502
Beech Creek	502	Brights Bend	606	Cayce	502	Crocus	606	Edgoten	502
Beech Grove		Bristletown	502	Cecilia	502	Crofton	502	Edmonton	502
(Bullitt Co.)	502	Brodhead	606	Cedar Bluff	502	Cromwell	502	Edwards	502
Beech Grove		Bromley	606	Center	502	Cropper	502	Egypt	606
(McLean Co.)	502	Bronston	606	Centertown	502	Crossland	502	Eighty Eight	502
Bee Spring	502	Brooks	502	Central City	502	Crummies	606	Ekron	502
				Cerulean	502	Crutchfield	502	Elamton	606

Place Name	Area Code	Place Name	Area Code	Place Name	Area Code	Place Name	Area Code	Place Name	Area Code
Elihu	606	Fordsville	502	Gray	606	Highsplint	606	Kensee	606
Elizabethtown	502	Fort Campbell	502	Gray Hawk	606	Highway	606	Kenton	606
Elizaville	606	Fort Knox	502	Grays Knob	606	Hi Hat	606	Kenvir	606
Elkatawa	606	Fort Mitchell	606	Grayson	606	Hillsboro	606	Kenwood	606
Elk Chester	606	Fort Spring	606	Greasy Creek	502	Hillspring	502	Kettle	502
Elk Creek	502	Fort Thomas	606	Greenbrier	502	Hima	606	Kettle Island	606
Elk Horn	502	Fort Wright	606	Greendale	606	Himlerville	606	Kevil	502
Elkhorn City	606	Foster	606	Green Hall	606	Hindman	606	Kidds Store	606
Elkton	502	Fountain Run	502	Greensburg	502	Hinesdale	502	Kings Mountain	606
Ellisburg	606	Fourmile	606	Greenup	606	Hinkleville	502	Kingswood	502
Elliston	606	Fox Creek	502	Greenville	502	Hiseville	502	Kirbyton	502
Elmendorf	606	Fox Ridge	606	Greenwood		Hitchins	606	Kirk	502
Elsmere	606	Frankfort	502	(McCreary Co.)	606	Hobbs	502	Kirkmansville	502
Eminence	502	Franklin	502	Greenwood		Hobson	502	Kirksey	502
Emlyn	606	Franklin Crossroads	502	(Pendleton Co.)	606	Hodgenville	502	Kirksville	606
Emma	606	Franklinton	502	Grethel	606	Hollybush	606	Kirkwood	606
English	502	Frazer	606	Grider	502	Hopkinsville	502	Kitts	606
Ennis	502	Fredericktown	606	Grundy	606	Horse Branch	502	Kona	606
Ensor	502	Fredonia	502	Gum Sulphur	606	Horse Cave	502	Kosmosdale	502
Enterprise	606	Freeburn	606	Guthrie	502	Howard	502	Kuttawa	502
Erlanger	606	Freedom	502			Howardstown	502		
Esco	606	Frenchburg	606			Howe	502		
Estill	606	Frys Hill	502			Howe Valley	502		
Eubank	606	Fulgham	502	Habit	502	Hubers	502	La Center	502
Evanston	606	Fullerton	606	Hadley	502	Hueysville	606	Lacie	502
Evarts	606	Fulton	502	Hager	606	Huff	502	Lackey	606
Eveleigh	502			Hagerhill	606	Hustonville	606	La Fayette	502
Ewing	606			Haldeman	606	Hyden	606	La Grange	502
Exie	502			Halfway	502			Lakeland	502
Ezel	606	Gabe	502	Halls Gap	606			Lakeville	606
		Gadberry	502	Handy Bend	606			Lamb	606
		Gage	502	Hanly	606	Ice	606	Lancaster	606
		Gamaliel	502	Hansbrough	502	Independence	606	Lancer	606
Fairdale	502	Garfield	502	Hansford	606	Index	606	Langnau	606
Fairdealing	502	Garlin	502	Hanson	502	Indian Fields	606	Latonia	606
Fair Field	502	Garner	606	Happy	606	Inez	606	Lawrenceburg	502
Fairplay	502	Garrett (Floyd Co.)	606	Hardburly	606	Insko	606	Lawton	606
Fairview		Garrett (Meade Co.)	502	Hardin	502	Irvine	606	Leafdale	502
(Fleming Co.)	606	Garrettsburg	502	Hardinsburg	502	Irvington	502	Leander	606
Fairview (Todd Co.)	502	Garrison	606	Hardyville	502	Island	502	Leatherwood	606
Falcon	606	Gatliff	606	Harlan	606	Island City	606	Lebanon	502
Fallsburg	606	Geneva	606	Harned	502	Iuka	502	Lebanon Junction	502
Falls of Rough	502	Georgetown	502	Harold	606			Leburn	606
Falmouth	606	Germantown	606	Harrisonville	502			Leckieville	606
Fancy Farm	502	Gethsemane	502	Harrodsburg	606			Lecta	502
Farmers	606	Ghent	502	Harrods Creek	502	Jackson	606	Leeco	606
Farmersville	502	Gilbertsville	502	Hartford	502	Jackson Store	606	Leitchfield	502
Farmington	502	Gilpin	606	Harveyton	606	Jacksonville	502	Lenarue	606
Faubush	606	Glasgow	502	Hatcher	606	Jamestown	502	Lenore	606
Fedscreek	606	Glenarm	502	Hawesville	502	Jeff	606	Lenox	606
Fern Creek	502	Glencoe	502	Hayward (Carter Co.)	606	Jeffersontown	502	Lerose	606
Ferndale	606	Glendale	502	Haywood (Barren Co.)	502	Jeffersonville	606	Levi	606
Fernleaf	606	Glen Dean	502	Hazard	606	Jellico	606	Lewisburg (Logan Co.)	502
Finchville	502	Glens Fork	502	Hazel	502	Jenkins	606	Lewisburg	
Finley	502	Glenview	502	Hazel Green	606	Jenson	606	(Mason Co.)	606
Firebrick	606	Glo	606	Heath	502	Jeptha	502	Lewisport	502
Fisherville	502	Glomawr	606	Hebbardsville	502	Jericho	502	Lewistown	502
Fisty	606	Godman Field	502	Hebron	606	Jett	502	Lexington	606
Flaherty	502	Goldbug	606	Hedgeville	606	Johnson Junction	606	Liberty	606
Flat Creek	606	Golden Pond	502	Heflin	502	Johnsontown	502	Lickburg	606
Flat Gap	606	Golds	502	Heidelberg	606	Johnsville	606	Lick Skillet	502
Flat Lick	606	Goodnight	502	Helena	606	Jonancy	606	Lida	606
Flat Rock	606	Goshen	502	Hellier	606	Jonesville	606	Liggett	606
Flatwoods	606	Gracey	502	Hempridge	502	Jordan	606	Ligon	606
Fleming	606	Gradyville	502	Henderson	502	Junction City	606	Lilac	502
Flemingsburg	606	Graham (Green Co.)	502	Hendricks	606			Lily	606
Fletcher	606	Graham		Henshaw	502			Lincoln Ridge	502
Florence	606	(Muhlenberg Co.)	502	Herd	606			Lisman	502
Florida Heights	502	Grahn	606	Herndon	502	Kayjay	606	Litsey	502
Floydsburg	502	Grand Rivers	502	Hickman	502	Keavy	606	Little Hickman	606
Folsomdale	502	Grant	606	Hickory	502	Keene	606	Little Rock	606
Fonde	606	Grassy Creek	606	High Bridge	606	Kelly	502	Livermore	502
Ford	606	Gratz	502	Highgrove	502	Ken Lake	502	Livia	502
Fords Branch	606	Gravel Switch	502	Highland Heights	606	Kennedy	502	Livingston	606

Place Name	Area Code	Place Name	Area Code	Place Name	Area Code	Place Name	Area Code	Place Name	Area Code
Lock E	502	McGaha	502	Mullikin	502	Packard	606	Raceland	606
Lock No. 8	606	McGowan	502	Mullins	606	Paducah	502	Radcliff	502
Lodiburg	502	McHenry	502	Munfordville	502	Paint Lick	606	Ravenna	606
Logana	606	McKee	606	Murray	502	Paintsville	606	Raywick	502
Logansport	502	McKinney	606	Myers	606	Panther	502	Ready	502
Lola	502	McNary	502	Myra	606	Paris	606	Red Ash	606
London	606	McQuady	502			Park City	502	Redbud	606
Loneoak	502	McRoberts	606			Parkers Lake	606	Redwine	606
Long Branch	502	McWhorter	606			Park Hills	606	Reed	502
Long Ridge	502	Meadowlawn	502			Parksville	606	Regina	606
Longrun	502	Meads	606			Patesville	502	Reidland	502
Longview	502	Means	606	Nada	606	Paynes Depot	606	Renfro Valley	606
Lookout	606	Medora	502	Nancy	606	Payneville	502	Repton	502
Loretto	502	Meeting Creek	502	Napfor	606	Peabody	606	Reynoldsville	606
Lost Creek	606	Melber	502	Narrows	502	Pellville	502	Rice Station	606
Lot	606	Melbourne	606	Natural Bridge	606	Pembroke	502	Ricetown	606
Lothair	606	Melvin	606	Nazareth	502	Pendleton	502	Richardsville	502
Louellen	606	Memphis Junction	502	Nealton	502	Penrod	502	Richmond	606
Louisa	606	Mentor	606	Nebo	502	Perkins	606	Rich Pond	502
Louisville	502	Meredith	502	Needmore	606	Perry Park	502	Riley	502
Louisville Coast Guard Sta. No. 276	606	Merrimac	502	Neon	606	Perryville	606	Rineyville	502
Lovelaceville	502	Middleburg	606	Nepton	502	Petersburg	606	Riverview	606
Lowes	502	Middlesboro	606	Nerinx	502	Petersville	606	Roaring Spring	502
Lowmansville	606	Middletown	502	Netty	606	Pewee Valley	502	Robards	502
Loyall	606	Midway	606	Nevada	606	Phillipsburg	502	Robinson Creek	606
Lucas	502	Milburn	606	Nevisdale	606	Philpot	502	Rochester	502
Ludlow	606	Milford	606	New Castle	502	Pikeville	606	Rockbridge	502
Luzerne	502	Millard	606	New Concord	502	Pilot Oak	502	Rockfield	502
Lykins	606	Mill Creek	606	New Haven	502	Pilot View	606	Rock Haven	502
Lynch	606	Millersburg	606	New Hope	502	Pinckard	606	Rockholds	606
Lyndon	502	Millerstown (Grayson Co.)	502	New Liberty	502	Pine Hill	606	Rock House	606
Lynn Grove	502	Millerstown (Logan Co.)	502	Newman	502	Pine Knot	606	Rockport	502
Lynnville	502	Millport	502	New Market	502	Pine Ridge	606	Rockvale	502
		Millstone	606	Newport	606	Pineville	606	Rocky Hill	502
		Milltown	502	Nicholasville	606	Piney	502	Rogersville	502
		Millville	606	Nigh	606	Pink	606	Romine	502
		Millwood	606	Nigh Station	606	Pippa Passes	606	Rose Hill	606
		Milton	606	Nina	606	Pisgah	606	Rose Terrace	502
		Minerva	606	Noble	606	Pittsburg	606	Rosine	502
Mac	502	Minnie	606	Nolin	502	Place	606	Roseville	502
Maceo	502	Mitchellsburg	606	North Fork	606	Pleasant Ridge	502	Ross	606
Mackville	606	Modoc	502	North Garrett	606	Pleasant View	606	Rosslyn	606
Maddoxtown	606	Monterey	502	North Middletown	606	Pleasure Ridge Park	502	Rothwell	606
Madisonville	502	Montgomery	502	North Pleasureville	502	Pleasureville	502	Roundhill (Edmonson Co.)	502
Magnolia	502	Monticello	606	Nortonville	502	Point Leavell	606	Roundhill (Madison Co.)	606
Majestic	606	Moorefield	606	Norwood	606	Point Pleasant	502	Round Tree	606
Malone	606	Mooresville	606	Nuckols	502	Polin	606	Rowletts	502
Mammoth Cave	502	Moorman	502			Pollard	606	Roxana	606
Manchester	606	Morehead	606			Pollys Bend	606	Royal	502
Mannsville	502	Moreland	606			Pomp	606	Royalton	606
Marcellus	606	Morganfield	502	Oak Grove	502	Poole	502	Ruddles Mills	606
Marion	502	Morgantown	606	Oakland	502	Poplar Plains	606	Rumsey	502
Marksbury	606	Morning View	606	O'Bannon	502	Port Royal	502	Russell	606
Marrowbone	502	Mortons Gap	502	Offutt	606	Potter	606	Russell Springs	502
Martin	606	Mortonsville	502	Oil City	502	Pottertown	502	Russellville	502
Martindale	502	Mount Aerial	502	Oil Springs	606	Pottsville	502	
Martwick	502	Mountain Ash	606	Oil Valley	606	Powderly	502	
Mary Helen	606	Mount Carmel	606	Oklahoma	502	Premium	606	
Mashfork	606	Mount Eden	502	Okolona	502	Prentiss	502	
Mason	606	Mount Gilead	606	Olive Hill	606	Preston	606	
Maud	606	Mount Lebanon	606	Olmstead	502	Prestonsburg	606	
Mayfield	502	Mount Olivet	606	Oneida	606	Price	606	Sacramento	502
Mayking	606	Mount Salem	606	Onyx Cave	502	Priceville	502	Sadieville	502
Mayo	606	Mount Sterling	606	Orell	502	Princeton	502	St. Catherine	502
Mays Lick	606	Mount Vernon	606	Orinoco	606	Prospect	502	St. Charles	502
Maysville	606	Mount Washington	502	Orkney	502	Providence	502	St. Elmo	502
Maywood	606	Mousie	606	Ottawa	606	Pryorsburg	502	St. Francis	502
McAfee	606	Mouthcard	606	Outwood	502	Pryse	606	St. Helens (Jefferson Co.)	502
McAndrews	606	Muir	606	Owensboro	502			St. Helens (Lee Co.)	606
McCall P. O.	606	Muldraugh	502	Owenton	502			St. John	502
McCarr	606			Owingsville	606	Quincy	606	St. Joseph	502
McDaniels	502								
McDowell	606								

Place Name	Area Code	Place Name	Area Code	Place Name	Area Code	Place Name	Area Code	Place Name	Area Code
St. Mary	502	Skylight	502	Sulphur	502	Uniontown	502	West Liberty	606
St. Matthews	502	Slade	606	Sulphur Well	502	U. S. Government Dam		West Louisville	502
St. Paul	606	Slaughters	502	Summer Shade	502	No. 31	606	West Plains	502
St. Vincent	502	Slaughterville	502	Summersville	502	Upland	502	West Point	502
Salem	502	Sligo	502	Summit	502	Upton	502	West Van Lear	606
Salmons	502	Sloans Valley	606	Sumpter	606	Utica	502	Wheatcroft	502
Saloma	502	Smithfield	502	Sunnyside	502	Utility	502	Wheatley	502
Salt Lick	606	Smithland	502	Sunrise	606			Wheelwright	606
Salt River	502	Smith Mills	502	Susie	606			Wheelwright Junction	606
Salubria Springs	502	Smiths Grove	502	Sutton	606			Whitehouse	606
Salvisa	606	Smiths Switch	502	Sweethome	502			White Lily	606
Salyersville	606	Snow	606	Symsonia	502	Valley Hill	606	White Oak	606
Samuels	502	Soldier	606			Valley Station	502	White Plains	502
Sanders	502	Solitude	502			Vanburen	502	Whitesburg	606
Sandersville	606	Solway	502			Vanceburg	606	Whitesville	502
Sandgap	606	Somerset	606			Vancleve	606	Whitewood	502
Sandy Hook	606	Sonora	502	Talmage	606	Vanderburg	502	Whitley City	606
Saratoga	502	Sorgho	502	Tanner	502	Van Lear	606	Wickliffe	502
Sardis	606	South Carrollton	502	Tateville	606	Varilla	606	Wilder Station	606
Saxton	606	South Elkhorn	606	Tatham Springs	606	Varnarsdell	606	Williamsburg	606
Schley	502	South Fort Mitchell	606	Taylors Station	606	Veechdale	502	Williamson	606
Science Hill	606	Southgate	606	Taylorsville	502	Verda	606	Williamsport	606
Scotts Station	502	South Hardin	502	Tejay	606	Verona	606	Williamstown	606
Scottsville	502	South Pleasureville	502	Temple Hill	502	Versailles	606	Willisburg	606
Scuddy	606	South Portsmouth	606	Texas	606	Vicco	606	Willow Shade	502
Sebree	502	South Ripley	606	Thealka	606	Victory	606	Willowtown	502
Seco	606	South Shore	606	Thelma	606	Viley	606	Wilmore	606
Sedalia	502	South Union	502	Thompsonville	502	Vine Grove	502	Winchester	606
Semiway	502	Southville	502	Threeforks	606	Viola	502	Wingo	502
Sergent	606	South Williamson	606	Three Point	606	Viper	606	Wiscoal	606
Seven Hills	502	Sparksville	502	Tiline	502	Virgie	606	Wisemantown	606
Seventy Six	606	Sparta	606	Tinsley	606			Wofford	606
Shakertown	606	Spears	606	Toler	606			Woodbine	606
Sharon	606	Speck	502	Tollesboro	606			Woodburn	502
Sharondale	606	Spottsville	502	Tomahawk	606			Woodbury	502
Sharon Grove	502	Springdale	606	Tompkinsville	502	Waco	606	Woodside	606
Sharpe	502	Springfield	606	Tonieville	502	Waddy	502	Wooton	606
Sharpsburg	606	Springlake	606	Topmost	606	Wales	606	Worth	502
Sharpsville	606	Spring Lick	502	Tousey	502	Wallace	606	Worthington	
Shawhan	606	Spring Station	606	Travellers Rest	606	Wallingford	606	(Greenup Co.)	606
Shelbiana	606	Springville	606	Trenton	502	Wallins Creek	606	Worthington	
Shelby City	606	Spurlington	502	Tribbey	606	Wallsend	606	(Jefferson Co.)	502
Shelbyville	502	Stacy Fork	606	Trinity	606	Walnut Hill	606	Worthville	502
Shepherdsville	502	Staffordsville	606	Tuckahoe	606	Walton	606	Wrigley	606
Sherburne	606	Stamping Ground	502	Tucker	502	Waneta	606	Wurtland	606
Sheridan	502	Stanford	606	Tunnel Hill	502	Warfield	606		
Sherman	606	Stanley	502	Turners	502	Warsaw	606		
Shiloh	502	Stanton	606	Tutor Key	606	Washington	606		
Shively	502	Station Camp	606	Twila	606	Wasioto	606		
Shopville	606	Stearns	606	Twin Springs	502	Waterford	502	Yancey	606
Short Creek	502	Stearns-Whitley City	606	Twin Tunnels	606	Watergap	606	Yarbro	502
Shrewsbury	502	Stephensburg	502	Tygart	606	Water Valley	502	Yarnallton	606
Sidney	606	Stepstone	606	Tyner	606	Waverly	502	Yeager	606
Siloam	606	Steubenville	606	Tyrone	502	Wayland	606	Yeaman	502
Silva	502	Stewart	606			Waynesburg	606	Yocum	606
Silver Grove	606	Stinnett	606			Wayside	502	Yosemite	606
Simpsonville	502	Stone	606			Webster	502	Yuma	502
Sinking Fork	502	Straight Creek	606	Ulvah	606	Weeksbury	606		
Sirocco	502	Sturgeon	606	Union	606	Weir	502		
Skillman	502	Sturgis	502	Union City	502	West Clifty	606		
Skinnersburg	502	Sullivan	502	Union Mills	606	West Fork	502	Zoneton	502

Place Name	Area Code	Place Name	Area Code	Place Name	Area Code	Place Name	Area Code	Place Name	Area Code
Abbeville	318	Bourg	504	Crowville	318	Folsom	504	Harrisonburg U. S.	
Abita Springs	504	Boutte	504	Cullen	318	Fordoche	504	Government Sta.	318
Ada	318	Boyce	318	Curtis	318	Forest	318	Harvey	504
Addis	504	Braithwaite	504	Cut Off	504	Forest Hill	318	Haughton	318
Aimwell	318	Branch	318	Cypress	318	Forked Island	318	Hayes	318
Albany	504	Breaux Bridge	318			Fort Necessity	318	Haynesville	318
Alexandria	318	Bridge City	504			Fort Pike	504	Head of Island	504
Algiers	504	Bristol	318			Fort Polk	318	Hebert	318
Allendale	504	Broussard	318	Darnell	318	Franklin	318	Hebron	318
Alluvial City	504	Brusly	504	Darrow	504	Franklinton	504	Heflin	318
Alsatia	318	Bryceland	318	Davant	504	French Settlement	504	Henderson	318
Alto	318	Bunkie	318	Delacroix	504	Frierson	318	Hessmer	318
Ama	504	Buras	504	Delcambre	318	Frost	504	Hester	504
Amelia	504	Burnside	504	Delhi	318	Fullerton	318	Hineston	318
Amite	504	Burr Ferry	318	Delta	318			Hodge	318
Amite City	504	Bush	504	Deltabridge	318			Holden	504
Anacoco	318			Denham Springs	504			Holly Ridge	318
Angie	504			De Quincy	318	Gahagan	318	Homer	318
Angola	504			De Ridder	318	Galliano	504	Hopedale	504
Anse La Butte	318	Calcasieu	318	Derry	318	Gallion	318	Hornbeck	318
Arabi	504	Calhoun	318	Des Allemands	504	Galvez	504	Hosston	318
Arcadia	318	Calumet	504	Destrehan	504	Garden City	318	Hot Wells	318
Archibald	318	Calvin	318	Deville	318	Garland	318	Houma	504
Archie	318	Cameron	318	Dixie	318	Garyville	504	
Arcola	504	Camp Beauregard	318	Dodson	318	Gayle	318	
Arnaudville	318	Campti	318	Donaldsonville	504	Geismar	504	
Ashland	318	Cane River	318	Donner	504	Gentilly	504	Ida	318
Atchafalaya	318	Cankton	318	Downsville	318	Georgetown	318	Independence	504
Athens	318	Carencro	318	Doyline	318	Gheens	504	Innis	504
Avery Island	318	Carlisle	504	Dry Creek	318	Gibsland	318	Iota	318
Avondale	504	Carlyss	318	Dry Prong	318	Gibson	504	Iowa	318
		Carville	504	Dubach	318	Gilbert	318	Irish Bayou	504
		Caspiana	318	Dubberly	318	Gilliam	318	
		Castor	318	Dubuisson	318	Glencoe	318	
Bains	504	Cecelia	318	Dulac	504	Glenmora	318	
Baker	504	Cedar Grove	318	Duplessis	504	Gloster	318	Jackson	504
Baldwin	318	Centerville	318	Duson	318	Golden Meadow	504	Jamestown	318
Barataria	504	Chacahoula	504	Dutch Town	504	Goldonna	318	Jarreau	504
Barksdale Air Force		Chackbay	504			Gonzales	504	Jeanerette	318
Base	318	Chalmette	504			Good Hope	504	Jefferson Island	318
Basile	318	Charenton	318	Eagle Lake	318	Good Pine	318	Jena	318
Baskin	318	Chase	318	Easton	318	Gorum	318	Jennings	318
Bastrop	318	Chataignier	318	East Point	318	Goudeau	318	Jesuit Bend	504
Batchelor	504	Chatham	318	Echo	318	Grambling	318	Johnsons Bayou	318
Baton Rouge	504	Chauvin	504	Edgard	504	Gramercy	504	Jones	318
Bayou Blue	504	Chef Menteur	504	Egan	318	Grand Bayou	318	Jonesboro	318
Bayou Bouef	504	Cheneyville	318	Elizabeth	318	Grand Caillou	504	Jonesville	318
Bayou Corne	504	Chesbrough	504	Ellendale	504	Grand Cane	318	Joyce	318
Bayou Goula	504	Chestnut	318	Elmer	318	Grand Chenier	318	
Bayou Pigeon	504	Choudrant	318	Elton	318	Grand Coteau	318	
Bayou Sale	318	Church Point	318	Empire	504	Grand Isle	504	
Bayou Vista	504	Cinclare	504	Epps	318	Grangeville	504	Kaplan	318
Belcher	318	Clarence	318	Erath	318	Gray	504	Keatchie	318
Bell City	318	Clarks	318	Eros	318	Grayson	318	Keithville	318
Belle Chasse	504	Clay	318	Erwinville	504	Greensburg	504	Kelly	318
Belledeau	318	Clayton	318	Esler Field	318	Greens Ditch	504	Kenner	504
Belle River	504	Clinton	504	Esterwood	318	Greenwell Springs	504	Kentwood	504
Bellerose	504	Cloutierville	318	Ethel	504	Greenwood	318	Kickapoo	318
Belmont	318	Colfax	318	Eunice	318	Gretna	504	Kilbourne	318
Benson	318	Collinston	318	Evangeline	318	Grosse Tete	504	Killian	504
Bentley	318	Columbia	318	Evergreen	318	Gueydan	318	Killona	504
Benton	318	Convent	504					Kinder	318
Bermuda	318	Converse	318					Kingston	318
Bernice	318	Cottonport	318					Kingsville	318
Berwick	504	Cotton Valley	318	Farmerville	318	Hackberry	318	Klotzville	504
Bienville	318	Couchwood	318	Fenton	318	Hahnville	504	Koran	318
Big Cane	318	Coushatta	318	Ferriday	318	Hall Summit	318	Krotz Springs	318
Blanchard	318	Covington	504	Fillmore	318	Hamburg	318	
Blanks	504	Cow Island	318	Fisher	318	Hammond	504	
Bogalusa	504	Cravens	318	Fishville	318	Hanna	318	
Bonita	318	Creole	318	Flatwoods	318	Happy Jack	504	Labadieville	504
Boothville	504	Creston	318	Flora	318	Harahan	504	Labarre	504
Bordelonville	318	Crowley	318	Florien	318	Harmon	318	Lacamp	318
Bossier City	318	Crown Point	504	Fluker	504	Harrisonburg	318	Lacassine	318

Place Name	Area Code	Place Name	Area Code	Place Name	Area Code	Place Name	Area Code	Place Name	Area Code
Lacombe	504	Mathews	504	Paincourtville	504	Rosepine	318	Taylor	318
Lafayette	318	Maurepas	504	Palmetto	318	Rosewood	318	Taylortown	318
Lafitte	504	Maurice	318	Panola	318	Rougon	504	Terry	318
Lafourche Crossing	504	McDade	318	Paradis	504	Ruston	318	Theriot	504
Lagan	504	McManus	504	Parks	318			Thibodaux	504
La Grange	504	Meeker	318	Patterson	504			Thomas	504
Lake Arthur	318	Melder	318	Pearlington	504			Thornwell	318
Lake Bruin	318	Melrose	318	Pearl River	504	St. Amant	504	Tickfaw	504
Lake Catherine	504	Melville	318	Pecan Island	318	St. Bernard	504	Tioga	318
Lake Charles	318	Mermenteau	318	Peck	318	St. Francisville	504	Toca	504
Lakeland	504	Mer Rouge	318	Pelican	318	St. Gabriel	504	Trees	318
Lake Providence	318	Merryville	318	Perry	318	St. James	504	Triumph	504
Lake St. John	318	Metairie	504	Pierre Part	504	St. Joseph	318	Trout	318
Lamourie	318	Midland	318	Pine	504	St. Landry	318	Tullos	318
Laplace	504	Milton	318	Pine Grove	504	St. Martinville	318	Tunica	504
Larose	504	Minden	318	Pine Prairie	318	St. Maurice	318	Turkey Creek	318
Lavacca	318	Mira	318	Pineville	318	St. Rose	504		
Lawtell	318	Mix	504	Pioneer	318	Saline	318		
Leander	318	Monroe	318	Pitkin	318	Sarepta	318		
Le Beau	318	Montegut	504	Plain Dealing	318	Schriever	504	Urania	318
Lecompte	318	Monterey	318	Plains	504	Scotlandville	504	Utility	318
Lee Bayou	318	Montgomery	318	Plaquemine	504	Scott	318		
Leesville		Monticello	318	Plattenville	504	Seabrook	504		
(Vernon Par.)	318	Montpelier	504	Plaucheville	318	Shady Grove	504		
Leeville		Montrose	318	Pleasant Hill	318	Shell Beach	504	Vacherie	504
(Lafourche Par.)	504	Mooringsport	318	Point Blue	318	Shongaloo	318	Valentine	504
Le Moyen	318	Mora	318	Pointe a la Hache	504	Shreveport	318	Valverda	504
Leonville	318	Moreauville	318	Pollock	318	Sibley (Lincoln Par.)	318	Varnado	504
Leton	318	Morgan City	504	Ponchatoula	504	Sibley (Webster Par.)	318	Venice	504
Lettsworth	504	Morganza	504	Port Allen	504	Sicily Island	318	Ventress	504
Lewisburg	318	Morrow	318	Port Barre	318	Sikes	318	Verdonville	318
Linville	318	Morse	318	Port Hudson	504	Simmesport	318	Vick	318
Lisbon	318	Mound	318	Port Sulphur	504	Simpson	318	Vidalia	318
Little Creek	318	Mount Airy	504	Port Vincent	504	Simsboro	318	Ville Platte	318
Little Woods	504	Mount Hermon	504	Powhatan	318	Singer	318	Vinton	318
Livingston	504	Myrtle Grove	504	Prairieville	504	Slaughter	504	Violet	504
Livonia	504			Pride	504	Slidell	504	Vivian	318
Lobdell	504			Princeton	318	Sligo	318		
Lockport	504			Provencal	318	Smithfield	504		
Locust Ridge	318	Napoleonville	504			Sondheimer	318	Waddell	318
Logansport	318	Natchitoches	318			Sorrento	504	Walker	504
Longleaf	318	Nebo	318			South Dodge City	318	Walters	318
Longstreet	318	Negreet	318	Quitman	318	South Junction City	318	Washington	318
Longville	318	Newellton	318			South Osyka	504	Water Proof	318
Loranger	504	New Iberia	318			Spearsville	318	Watson	504
Loreauville	318	Newllano	318			Spencer	318	Waverly	318
Lottie	504	New Orleans	504			Springfield	504	Weeks Island	318
Louisa	318	New Roads	504	Raceland	504	Springhill		Welsh	318
Lucerne	318	New Sarpy	504	Ragley	318	(Washington Par.)	504	Westlake	318
Lucky	318	Noble	318	Ramah	504	Springhill		West Monroe	318
Lucy	504	Norco	504	Rapides	318	(Webster Par.)	318	Westwego	504
Luling	504	North Baton Rouge	504	Rayne	318	Starks	318	Weyanoke	504
Lutcher	504	North Cornor	504	Rayville	318	Start	318	White Castle	504
		North Shore	504	Readheimer	318	Sterlington	318	Whitehall	504
		Norwood	504	Reddell	318	Stonewall	318	Whiteville	318
				Reeves	504	Sugartown	318	Wilson	504
Madisonville	504			Reserve	504	Sulphur	318	Winnfield	318
Mamou	318			Rhinehart	318	Summer Grove	318	Winnsboro	318
Manchac	504			Ridgecrest	318	Summerville	318	Wisner	318
Mandeville	504	Oak Alley	504	Ringgold	318	Sun	504		
Mangham	318	Oakdale	318	Rita	504	Sunset	318		
Manifest	318	Oak Grove	318	Riverside	318	Sunshine	504		
Mansfield	318	Oak Ridge	318	Riverton	318	Supreme	504	Youngsville	318
Mansura	318	Oakville	504	Roanoke	318	Sweet Lake	318	Yscloskey	504
Many	318	Oberlin	318	Robeline	318				
Maplewood	318	Oil City	318	Robert	504				
Maringouin	504	Olla	318	Rochelle	318				
Marion	318	Oneonta	318	Rodessa	318			Zachary	504
Marksville	318	Opelousas	318	Rosa	318	Taft	504	Zenoria	318
Marrero	504	Oscar	504	Rosedale	504	Tallulah	318	Zimmerman	318
Marthaville	318	Oxford	318	Roseland	504	Tangipahoa	504	Zwolle	318

ALL POINTS—AREA CODE 207

ALL POINTS—AREA CODE 301

Place Name	Area Code	Place Name	Area Code	Place Name	Area Code	Place Name	Area Code	Place Name	Area Code
Abington	617	Bradford	617	Cotuit (Highlands)	617	Elmwood	617	Hadley	413
Accord	617	Braintree	617	Craigville	617	Erving	617	Halifax	617
Acoaxet	617	Brant Rock	617	Cummaquid	617	Essex	617	Hamilton	617
Acton	617	Brant Rock		Cummington	413	Everett	617	Hampden	413
Acushnet	617	Coast Guard Sta.	617	Cushman	413			Hancock	413
Adams	413	Breckwood Park	413	Cuttyhunk	617			Hanover	617
Adamsville	413	Brewster	617	Cuttyhunk Coast		Fairhaven	617	Hanson	617
Agawam	413	Bridgewater	617	Guard Sta.	617	Fairview	413	Harding	617
Aldenville	413	Brier Neck	617			Fall River	617	Hardwick	413
Alford	413	Brighton	617	Dalton	413	Falmouth	617	Hartsville	413
Allerton	617	Brimfield	413	Danvers	617	Falmouth Heights	617	Harvard	617
Allston	617	Brockton	617	Dartmouth	617	Farnams	413	Harwich	617
Amesbury	617	Brookfield	617	Dedham	617	Farnumsville	617	Harwich Port	617
Amherst	413	Brookline	617	Deerfield	413	Fayville	617	Hatchville	617
Andover	617	Brookville	617	Deer Island	617	Feeding Hills	413	Hatfield	413
Annisquam	617	Bryantville	617	Dennis	617	Fields Corner	617	Hathorne	617
Arlington	617	Buckland	413	Dennisport	617	First Naval		Haverhill	617
Army Hdqrs. First Naval		Burlington	617	Dighton	617	District Hdqrs.	617	Hawley	413
District Hdqrs.	617	Buzzards Bay	617	Dodgeville	617	Fisherville	617	Haydenville	413
Ashburnham	617	Byfield	617	Dorchester	617	Fiskdale	617	Heath	413
Ashby	617			Douglas	617	Fitchburg	617	Hebronville	617
Ashfield	413			Dover	617	Florence	413	Hingham	617
Ashland	617	Cambridge	617	Dracut	617	Florida	413	Hingham (Ammunition	
Ashley Falls	413	Camp Edwards	617	Dudley	617	Fore River	617	Depot)	617
Ashmont	617	Campello	617	Dunstable	617	Forestdale	617	Hingham (Marine	
Assinippi	617	Camp Myles Standish	617	Duxbury	617	Forest Hills	617	Barracks)	617
Assonet	617	Canal Boat House		Dwight	413	Forge Village	617	Hinsdale	413
Athol	617	Coast Guard Sta.	617			Fort Andrews	617	Holbrook	617
Attleboro	617	Canton	617			Fort Banks	617	Holden	617
Attleboro Falls	617	Carlisle	617	East Acton	617	Fort Dawes	617	Holland	413
Auburn	617	Carver	617	East Boston	617	Fort Devens	617	Holliston	617
Auburndale	617	Caryville	617	East Boxford	617	Fort Duvall	617	Holyoke	413
Avon	617	Cataumet	617	East Brewster	617	Fort Heath	617	Hopedale	617
Ayer	617	Centerville		East Bridgewater	617	Fort Revere	617	Hopkinton	617
		(Barnstable Co.)	617	East Brookfield	617	Fort Rodman	617	Houghs Neck	617
		Centerville (Essex Co.)	617	East Charlemont	413	Fort Standish	617	Housatonic	413
Babson Park	617	Chaffin	617	East Dedham	617	Fort Strong	617	Hubbardston	617
Bakers Island	617	Charlemont	413	East Deerfield	413	Fort Warren	617	Hudson	617
Bakers Island		Charles River		East Dennis	617	Foxboro	617	Hull	617
Coast Guard Sta.	617	(Village)	617	East Douglas	617	Framingham	617	Humarock	617
Baldwinville	617	Charlestown	617	East Falmouth	617	Franklin	617	Huntington	413
Ballardvale	617	Charlton	617	East Foxboro	617	Freetown	617	Hyannis	617
Barnstable	617	Chartley	617	East Freetown	617			Hyannis Port	617
Barre	617	Chatham	617	Eastham	617			Hyde Park	617
Barrowsville	617	Chatham Coast		Easthampton	413				
Bass River	617	Guard Sta.	617	East Harwich	617	Gardner	617		
Bass Rocks	617	Chathamport	617	East Holliston	617	Gay Head	617		
Becket	413	Chelmsford	617	East Lexington	617	Gay Head Coast		Indian Orchard	413
Bedford	617	Chelsea	617	East Longmeadow	413	Guard Sta.	617	Interlaken	413
Belchertown	413	Cherry Valley	617	East Lynn	617	Georgetown	617	Ipswich	617
Bellingham	617	Cheshire	413	East Mansfield	617	Gilbertville	413	Island Creek	617
Belmont	617	Chester	413	East Millbury	617	Gill	413	Islington	617
Berkley	617	Chester Center	617	East Milton	617	Gleasondale	617		
Berkshire	413	Chesterfield	413	Easton	617	Glendale	413		
Berlin	617	Chestnut Hill	617	Eastondale	617	Gloucester	617		
Bernardston	413	Chicopee	413	East Orleans	617	Gloucester Coast		Jamaica Plain	617
Beverly	617	Chicopee Falls	413	East Otis	413	Guard Sta.	617	Jefferson	617
Beverly Farms	617	Chilmark	617	East Pembroke	617	Goshen	413		
Billerica	617	Clarksburg	413	East Pepperell	617	Gosnold	617		
Blackstone	617	Clifton	617	East Phillipston	617	Grafton	617		
Blandford	413	Cliftondale	617	East Princeton	617	Granby	413	Kingston	617
Bolton	617	Clinton	617	East Sandwich	617	Graniteville	617		
Bondsville	413	Cochesett	617	East Taunton	617	Granville	413		
Boston	617	Cochituate	617	East Templeton	617	Great Barrington	413		
Boston Air and		Cohasset	617	East Upton	617	Greenbush	617	Lake Attitash	617
Seaplane Port	617	Collinsville	617	East Walpole	617	Greenfield	413	Lake Boon	617
Boston Light		Colrain	413	East Wareham	617	Green Harbor	617	Lake Pearl	617
Coast Guard Sta.	617	Concord	617	East Watertown	617	Greenwood	617	Lake Pleasant	413
Boston Navy Yard	617	Conway	413	East Weymouth	617	Griswoldville	413	Lakeville	617
Bourne	617	Coolidge Corner	617	Edaville	617	Groton	617	Lancaster	617
Bournedale	617	Coonamessett	617	Edgartown	617	Grove Hall	617	Lanesboro	413
Boxboro	617	Cordaville	617	Egremont	413	Groveland	617	Lanesville	617
Boxford	617	Coskata Coast Guard		Egypt	617	Gurnet Coast Guard		Lawrence	617
Boylston	617	Sta.	617	Ellisville	617	Sta.	617	Lee	413

MASSACHUSETTS
Leeds–Swampscott

Place Name	Area Code	Place Name	Area Code	Place Name	Area Code	Place Name	Area Code	Place Name	Area Code
Leeds	413	Millis	617	North Eastham	617	Point Independence	617	Shirley	617
Leicester	617	Mill River		North Easton	617	Pondville	617	Shrewsbury	617
Lenox	413	(Berkshire Co.)	413	North Egremont	413	Popponesset	617	Shutesbury	413
Lenox Dale	413	Mill River		North Falmouth	617	Prides Crossing	617	Siasconset	617
Leominster	617	(Franklin Co.)	413	Northfield	413	Princeton	617	Silver Lake	
Leverett	413	Millville	617	North Hadley	413	Provincetown	617	(Middlesex Co.)	617
Lexington	617	Milton	617	North Hanover	617			Silver Lake	
Leyden	413	Minot	617	North Hanson	617			(Plymouth Co.)	617
Lincoln	617	Monponsett	617	North Harwich	617			Somerset (Village)	617
Linwood	617	Monroe Bridge	413	North Hatfield	413	Quincy	617	Somerville	617
Lithia	413	Monson	413	North Leverett	413	Quinsigamond Lake	617	South Acton	617
Littleton	617	Montague	413	North Marshfield	617	Quissett	617	Southampton	413
Lockwoods Basin		Montague City	413	North Orange	617			South Ashburnham	617
(Naval Section		Montello	617	North Oxford	617			South Ashfield	413
Base)	617	Monterey	413	North Pembroke	617			South Attleboro	617
Long Beach		Montgomery	413	North Plymouth	617			South Barre	617
(Essex Co.)	617	Montserrat	617	North Reading	617	Race Point		South Bellingham	617
Long Beach		Montville	413	North Scituate	617	Coast Guard Sta.	617	Southboro	617
(Plymouth Co.)	617	Moores Corner	413	North Scituate Coast		Randolph	617	South Boston	617
Long Island	617	Morningdale	617	Guard Sta.	617	Raynham (Center)	617	South Braintree	617
Longmeadow	413	Mount Auburn	617	North Shirley	617	Reading	617	Southbridge	617
Lowell	617	Mount Hermon	413	North Sudbury	617	Readville	617	South Bridgewater	617
Lowell Junction	617	Mount Tom	413	North Swansea	617	Rehoboth	617	South Byfield	617
Ludlow	413	Mount Washington	413	North Truro	617	Revere	617	South Carver	617
Lunenburg	617			North Uxbridge	617	Richmond	413	South Chatham	617
Lynn	617			North Westport	617	Rings Island	617	South Chelmsford	617
Lynnfield	617			North Weymouth	617	Riverside		South Dartmouth	617
Lynnfield Center	617	Nabnasset	617	North Wilbraham	413	(Franklin Co.)	413	South Deerfield	413
Lyonsville	413	Nahant	617	North Wilmington	617	Riverside		South Dennis	617
		Nahant Coast Guard		Norton	617	(Middlesex Co.)	617	South Duxbury	617
		Sta.	617	Norwell	617	Riverview Station	617	South Easton	617
		Nantasket Beach	617	Norwood	617	Rochdale	617	South Egremont	413
Maddaket Coast Guard		Nantucket	617	Nutting Lake	617	Rochester	617	Southfield	413
Sta.	617	Natick	617			Rockland	617	Southgate	617
Magnolia	617	Naushon Island	617			Rockport	617	South Hadley (Falls)	413
Malden	617	Naval Reserve				Rocky Neck	617	South Hamilton	617
Manchaug	617	Air Sta.	617	Oak Bluffs	617	Roslindale	617	South Hanover	617
Manchester	617	Needham	617	Oakdale	617	Rowe	413	South Hanson	617
Manomet	617	Neponset	617	Oakham	617	Rowley	617	South Harwich	617
Mansfield	617	New Ashford	413	Ocean Bluff	617	Roxbury	617	South Lee	413
Marblehead	617	New Bedford	413	Ocean Grove	617	Roxbury Crossing	617	South Lincoln	617
Marion	617	New Boston	413	Onset	617	Royalston	617	South Lynnfield	617
Marivista	617	New Braintree	617	Orange	617	Russell	413	South Middleboro	617
Marlboro	617	Newbury	617	Orient Heights	617	Rutland	617	South Natick	617
Marshfield	617	Newburyport	617	Orleans	617			South Orleans	617
Marstons Mills	617	New Marlboro	413	Osterville	617			South Peabody	617
Martha's		New Salem	617	Otis	413			South Royalston	617
Vineyard Island	617	Newton	617	Otis Air Force Base	617	Sagamore	617	South Sandwich	617
Mashpee	617	Newton Center	617	Oxford	617	Salem	617	South Sudbury	617
Matfield	617	Newton Highlands	617			Salisbury	617	South Sutton	617
Mattapan	617	Newton Lower Falls	617			Salisbury Beach		South Swansea	617
Mattapoisett	617	Newton Upper Falls	617			Coast Guard Sta.	617	South Tewksbury	617
Maynard	617	Newtonville	617	Palmer	413	Sandisfield	413	Southville	617
Maynard Ammunition		Nonatum	617	Paxton	617	Sandwich	617	South Walpole	617
Back-up Storage		Nonquitt	617	Peabody	617	Sankaty	617	South Wellfleet	617
Point	617	Norfolk	617	Pelham	413	Sankaty Light Coast		South Westport	617
Medfield	617	North Abington	617	Pemberton	617	Guard Sta.	617	South Weymouth	617
Medford	617	North Adams	413	Pembroke	617	Santuit	617	Southwick	413
Medway	617	North Agawam	413	Pepperell	617	Saugus	617	South Yarmouth	617
Megansett	617	North Amherst	413	Peru	413	Saundersville	617	Spencer	617
Melrose	617	Northampton	413	Petersham	617	Savoy	413	Springfield	413
Mendon	617	North Andover	617	Phillipston	617	Saxonville	617	Squantum	617
Menemsha	617	North Attleboro	617	Pigeon Cove	617	Scituate	617	State Line	413
Merrimac	617	North Billerica	617	Pinehurst	617	Seekonk	617	Sterling	617
Merrimac River Coast		Northboro	617	Pittsfield	413	Segregansett	617	Still River	617
Guard Sta.	617	North Brookfield	617	Plainfield	413	Sharon	617	Stockbridge	413
Methuen	617	North Cambridge	617	Plainville	617	Shattuckville	413	Stoneham	617
Middleboro	617	North Carver	617	Pleasant Lake	617	Shawsheen Village	617	Stoughton	617
Middlefield	413	North Chatham	617	Plum Island	617	Sheffield	413	Stow	617
Middleton	617	North Chelmsford	617	Plymouth	617	Shelburne	413	Sturbridge	617
Milford	617	North Chester	413	Plympton	617	Shelburne Falls	413	Sudbury	617
Millbrook	617	North Cohasset	617	Pocasset	617	Sheldonville	617	Sunderland	413
Millbury	617	North Dartmouth	617	Point Allerton Coast		Sherborn	617	Sutton	617
Millers Falls	413	North Dighton	617	Guard Sta.	617			Swampscott	617

Place Name	Area Code	Place Name	Area Code	Place Name	Area Code	Place Name	Area Code	Place Name	Area Code
Swansea	617	Waban	617	West Brewster	617	Weston	617	Williamsville	
Swift River	413	Wakefield	617	West Bridgewater	617	Westover Air Force		(Worcester Co.)	617
		Wales	413	West Brimfield	413	Base	413	Willimansett	413
		Walpole	617	West Brookfield	617	West Peabody	617	Wilmington	617
		Waltham	617	West Chatham	617	Westport	617	Winchendon	617
Taunton	617	Waquoit	617	West Chelmsford	617	Westport Harbor	617	Winchester	617
Teaticket	617	Ward Hill	617	West Chop	617	Westport Point	617	Windsor	413
Templeton	617	Ware	413	West Concord	617	West Roxbury	617	Wingaersheek	617
Tewksbury	617	Wareham	617	West Cummington	413	West Somerville	617	Winter Hill	617
Thorndike	413	Warren	413	Westdale	617	West Springfield	413	Winter Island Air Sta.	
Three Rivers	413	Warwick	617	West Deerfield	413	West Stockbridge	413	Coast Guard Sta.	617
Tisbury	617	Washington	413	West Dennis	617	West Tisbury	617	Winthrop	617
Tolland	413	Watertown	617	West Dudley	617	West Townsend	617	Woburn	617
Topsfield	617	Waterville	617	West Duxbury	617	West Upton	617	Wollaston	617
Touisset	617	Waverly Center	617	West Falmouth	617	West Wareham	617	Woods Hole (Naval	
Townsend	617	Wayland	617	Westfield	413	West Warren	413	Section Base)	617
Truro	617	Webster	617	Westford	617	Westwood	617	Woodville	617
Turners Falls	413	Wedgemere	617	West Groton	617	West Wrentham	617	Worcester	617
Tyngsboro	617	Wellesley	617	Westhampton	413	West Yarmouth	617	Woronoco	413
Tyringham	413	Wellfleet	617	West Hanover	617	Weymouth	617	Worthington	413
		Wellington	617	West Harwich	617	Whately	413	Wrentham	617
		Wendell	617	West Hawley	413	Wheelwright	413	Wyoming	617
		Wenham	617	West Hyannisport	617	Whitinsville	617		
Uphams Corner	617	Wequaquet Lake	617	West Lynn	617	Whitman	617		
Upton	617	West Acton	617	West Mansfield	617	Wianno	617		
Uxbridge	617	West Andover	617	West Medford	617	Wilbraham	413	Yarmouth	
		West Barnstable	617	West Medway	617	Wilkinsonville	617	(Yarmouthport)	617
		West Berlin	617	West Millbury	617	Williamsburg	413		
		Westboro	617	Westminster	617	Williamstown	413		
		West Boxford	617	West Newbury	617	Williamsville			
Vineyard Haven	617	West Boylston	617	West Newton	617	(Berkshire Co.)	413	Zoar	413

Place Name	Area Code	Place Name	Area Code	Place Name	Area Code	Place Name	Area Code	Place Name	Area Code
Ackerson Lake	517	Baldwin	616	Bloomfield Hills	313	Caseville	517	Coopersville	616
Acme	616	Baldwin Lake	616	Bloomingdale	616	Casnovia	616	Copemish-	
Ada	616	Ballards	616	Bogie Lake	313	Caspian	906	Thompsonville	616
Adamsville	616	Baltic Mine	906	Bois Blanc	616	Cass City	517	Copper City	906
Addison	517	Banat	906	Boon	616	Cassopolis	616	Copper Harbor	906
Adrian	517	Bancroft	517	Borculo	616	Castle Park	616	Coral	616
Advance	616	Banfield	616	Bowers Harbor	616	Cathro	517	Corey Lake	616
Afton	616	Bangor	616	Bowne Center	616	Cedar	616	Cornell	906
Agate Falls	906	Bankers	517	Boyne City	616	Cedar Lake	517	Corning	616
Ahmeek	906	Bannister	517	Boyne Falls	616	Cedar River	906	Corunna	517
Akron	517	Baptist Lake	616	Bradley	616	Cedar Run	616	Coryell Island	906
Alabaster	517	Baraga	906	Brampton	906	Cedar Springs	616	Covert	616
Alanson	616	Barbeau	906	Branch	616	Cedarville	906	Covington	906
Alba	616	Bard	517	Brant	517	Cement City	517	Crawford	517
Albion	517	Bark River	906	Breckenridge	517	Center Line	313	Cross Village	616
Alden	616	Barlow Lake	616	Brethren	616	Central Lake	616	Croswell	313
Alger	517	Baroda	616	Brevort	906	Centreville	616	Croton Dam	616
Algonac	313	Barron Lake	616	Brice	517	Ceresco	616	Crump	517
Allegan	616	Barryton	517	Bridgeport	517	Champion	906	Crystal	517
Allen	517	Barton City	517	Bridgeton	616	Channing	906	Crystal Falls	906
Allendale	616	Bass Lake	616	Bridgman	616	Chapin	517	Crystal Lake	517
Allen Park	313	Bass River	616	Brighton	313	Charles	906	Crystal Valley	616
Allenton	313	Batavia	517	Brimley	906	Charlesworth	517	Curtis	906
Allouez	906	Batcheller	616	Brinton	517	Charlevoix	616	Curtisville	517
Alma	517	Bath	517	Britton	517	Charlevoix U. S. Coast		Custer	616
Almont	313	Battle Creek	616	Brohman	616	Guard Sta. No. 258	616	Custer Air Force	
Aloha	616	Baw Beese Lake	517	Bronson	517	Charlotte	517	Sta.	616
Alpena	517	Bay City	517	Brooklyn	517	Chase	616	Cutlerville	616
Alpha	906	Bay Mills	906	Brown City	313	Chassell	906		
Alston	906	Bay Port	517	Bruce Crossing	906	Chatham	906		
Alto	616	Bay View	616	Brunswick	616	Cheboygan	616		
Alverno	616	Beacon	906	Brutus	616	Chelsea	313	Dafter	906
Amasa	906	Beacon Hill	906	Buchanan	616	Chemung Lake	517	Daggett	906
Amber	616	Beal City	517	Buckley	616	Cheneaux Islands	906	Dalton	616
Amble	616	Bear Lake	616	Budd Lake	517	Chesaning	517	Dansville	517
Amsden	517	Beaver Island	906	Bundy Hill	517	Chester	517	Davisburg	313
Anchorville	313	Beaverton	517	Burdickville	616	Chesterfield	313	Davison	313
Ann Arbor	313	Bedford	616	Burlington	517	Chief	616	Dearborn	313
Antlers	906	Belding	616	Burnips Corners	616	Childsdale	616	Decatur	616
Antrim	616	Bellaire	616	Burnside	313	Chippewa Lake	616	Decker	313
Applegate	313	Belle Isle Coast		Burr Oak	616	Christie Lake	616	Deckerville	313
Arcadia	616	Guard Sta.	313	Burt Lake	616	Christmas	906	Deerfield	517
Argenta	616	Belleville	313	Butternut	517	Clam River	616	Deer Park	906
Argentine	313	Bellevue	616	Byron	313	Clare	517	Deerton	906
Argyle	517	Bell Oak	517	Byron Center	616	Clarion	616	Deford	517
Armada	313	Belmont	616			Clarklake	517	Delton	616
Arnheim	906	Bendon	616			Clarkston	313	Delwin	517
Ashley	517	Bennington	517	Cadillac	616	Clarksville	616	De Tour	906
Assinins	906	Benona	517	Cadmus	517	Clawson	313	Detroit	313
Athens	517	Benton Harbor	616	Caledonia	616	Clayton	517	Devils Lake	517
Atlanta	517	Benton Heights	616	Calumet	906	Clifford	517	De Witt	517
Atlantic Mine	906	Benzonia	616	Cambria	517	Climax	616	Dexter	313
Atlas	313	Bergland	906	Cambridge	517	Clinton	517	Dimondale	517
Attica	313	Berkley	313	Camden	517	Clio-Mount Morris	313	Diorite	906
Atwood	616	Berlamont	616	Camp Grayling	517	Cloverdale	616	Dixboro	313
Auburn	517	Berrien Center	616	Camp Lake	616	Cobmoosa	616	Dodgeville	906
Auburn Heights	313	Berrien Springs	616	Camp Lucas	906	Cohoctah	517	Dollar Bay	906
Au Gres	517	Berville	313	Camp Nissokone	517	Coldwater	517	Dollarville	906
Augusta	616	Bessemer	906	Canal	906	Coldwater Lake	517	Donken	906
Aurelius	517	Beulah	616	Canandaigua	517	Coleman	517	Dorr	616
Au Sable	517	Beverly Hills	313	Cannonsburg	616	Collins	517	Doster	616
Austin Mine	906	Big Bay	906	Capac	313	Coloma	616	Douglas	616
Au Train	906	Big Pine Island Lake	616	Carland	517	Colon	517	Dowagiac	616
Averill	517	Big Rapids	616	Carleton	313	Columbiaville	313	Dowling	616
Avoca	313	Billings	517	Carlshend	906	Columbus	313	Drayton Plains	313
Avondale	616	Birch Creek	906	Carney	906	Commerce	313	Drenthe	616
Azalia	313	Birch Run	517	Caro	517	Comstock	616	Drummond Island	906
		Birmingham	313	Carp Lake	616	Comstock Park	616	Dryburg	906
		Biteley	616	Carp River	906	Concord	517	Dryden	313
		Black River	517	Carr	616	Conklin	616	Ducklake	517
Bad Axe	517	Blaine	313	Carrollton	517	Constantine	616	Dukes	906
Bagley	906	Blanchard	517	Carson City	517	Conway	517	Dundee	313
Bailey	616	Bliss	616	Carsonville	313	Cooks	906	Dunham	906
Bakertown	616	Blissfield	517	Cascade	616	Cooks Corners	616	Durand	517

MICHIGAN
Dutton—Laporte

Place Name	Area Code	Place Name	Area Code	Place Name	Area Code	Place Name	Area Code	Place Name	Area Code
Dutton	616	Ferrysburg	616	Goodrich	313	Hazel Park	313	Jackson	517
		Fibre	906	Gould City	906	Helena	517	Jacobsville	906
		Fife Lake	616	Gowen	616	Hell	313	Jamestown	616
		Filer City	616	Graafschap	616	Hemlock	517	Jasper	517
Eagle Harbor	906	Filion	517	Grace Harbor	517	Henderson	517	Jeddo	313
Eagle River	906	Findley	616	Grand Beach	616	Henrietta	517	Jenison	616
East Dayton	517	Fisher Lake	616	Grand Blanc	313	Henry	616	Jerome	517
East Detroit	313	Fisherville	517	Grand Haven	616	Hermansville	906	Johannesburg	517
East Grand Rapids	616	Fitchburg	517	Grand Junction	616	Hersey	616	Jones	616
East Jordan	616	Flat Rock	313	Grand Ledge	517	Ilesperia	616	Jonesville	517
East Lake	616	Flint	313	Grand Marais	906	Hessel	906	
East Lansing	517	Flushing	313	Grand Marais Coast		Hess Lake	616	
East Leroy	616	Forest Grove	616	Guard Sta. No. 296	906	Hiawatha Forest	906	
Eastmanville	616	Forest Hill	517	Grand Rapids	616	Hickory Corners	616	Kalamazoo	616
East Paris	616	Forest Lake	906	Grandville	616	Higgins Lake	517	Kaleva	616
Eastport	616	Forestville	517	Grant	616	Highland	313	Kalkaska	616
East Tawas	517	Fort Custer	616	Grant Center	616	Highland Park	313	Karlin	616
Eaton Rapids	517	Foster City	906	Grass Lake	517	Highwood	517	Kawkawlin	517
Eau Claire	616	Fostoria	517	Grattan	616	Hillman	517	Kearsarge	906
Eben	906	Fountain	616	Grawn	616	Hillsdale	517	Keego Harbor	313
Eckerman	906	Fowler-Pewamo	517	Grayling	517	Hobart	616	Kelden	906
Ecorse	313	Fowlerville	517	Green	906	Holland	616	Kelloggsville	616
Eden	517	Fox	906	Greenbush	517	Holland Coast Guard		Kent City	616
Edenville	517	Frankenmuth	517	Greenfield Mills	616	Sta. No. 271	616	Kenton	906
Edgerton	616	Frankfort	616	Green Lake	616	Holly	313	Kewadin	616
Edmore	517	Frankfort Coast Guard		Greenland	906	Holt	517	Keweenaw	906
Edwardsburg	616	Sta. No. 263	616	Green Oak	313	Holton	616	Keweenaw Bay	906
Elba	313	Franklin	313	Greenville	616	Homer	517	Kincheloe Air	
Elberta	616	Franklin Mine	906	Gregory	313	Honor	616	Force Base	906
Elbridge	616	Fraser	313	Gresham	517	Hooper	616	Kinde	517
Elk Rapids	616	Freda	906	Grind Stone City	517	Hope	517	Kingsford	906
Elkton	517	Frederic	517	Groos	906	Hopkins	616	Kingsley	616
Ellsworth	616	Freeland	517	Grosse Ile	313	Horton	517	Kingston	517
Elmdale	616	Freeport	616	Grosse Ile (Naval		Horton Bay	616	Kinross	906
Elm Hall	517	Freesoil	616	Air Station)	313	Houghton	906	Kipling	906
Elmira	616	Fremont	616	Grosse Pointe	313	Houghton Heights	517	
Elo	906	Frontier	517	Gulliver	906	Houghton Lake	517	
Elsie	517	Fruitport	616	Gull Lake	616	Houghton Point	517	
Elwell	517	Fulton	616	Gun Lake	616	Howard City	616	La Branche	906
Emmett	313			Gwinn	906	Howell	517	Lacey	616
Empire	616					Howlandsburg	616	Lachine	517
Engadine	906					Hoxeyville	616	Lacota	616
Englishville	616	Gaastra	906			Hubbard Lake	517	Laingsburg	517
Ensley	616	Gagetown	517	Hadley	313	Hubbardston	517	Lake	517
Epoufette	906	Gaines	517	Hale	517	Hubbell	906	Lake Angelus	313
Epsilon	616	Galesburg	616	Halfway Lake	906	Hudson	517	Lake Ann	616
Erie	313	Galien	616	Hamburg	313	Hudsonville	616	Lake City	616
Escanaba	906	Ganges	616	Hamilton	616	Hulbert	906	Lake George	517
Essexville	517	Garden	906	Hamlin Lake	616	Huntington Woods	313	Lake Harbor	616
Evans	616	Garden City	313	Hamtramck	313	Huron City	517	Lakeland	313
Evans Lake	517	Gay	906	Hancock	906	Huron Heights	313	Lake Lansing	517
Evart	616	Gaylord	517	Hanover	517			Lake Leelanau	616
Ewen	906	Genesee	313	Harbert	616			Lake Linden	906
		Geneva	517	Harbor Beach	517			Lake Michigan Beach	616
		Gera	517	Harbor Beach Coast				Lake Mine	906
		Germfask	906	Guard Sta. No. 247	517	Ida	313	Lake Oakland	313
Fairfield	517	Gibbs City	906	Harbor Point	616	Idlewild	616	Lake Odessa	616
Fairgrove	517	Gibraltar	313	Harbor Springs	616	Imlay City	313	Lake of the North	616
Fair Haven	313	Gilford	517	Hardwood	906	Indian Lake	616	Lake Orion	313
Fairplain	616	Gladstone	906	Harlem	616	Indian River	616	Lakeport	313
Fairview	517	Gladwin	517	Harper Woods	313	Ingalls	906	Lake Roland	906
Faithorn	906	Glen Arbor	616	Harrietta	616	Inkster	313	Lakeside	616
Falmouth	616	Glenco	517	Harris	906	Interlochen	616	Lakeview	517
Fargo	313	Glendora	616	Harrisburg	616	Ionia	616	Lakeville	313
Farmington	313	Glen Haven	616	Harrison	517	Irish Hills	517	Lakewood	
Farwell	517	Glen Lake	616	Harrisville	517	Iron Mountain	906	(Monroe Co.)	313
Felch	906	Glenlord	616	Harsens Island	313	Iron River	906	Lakewood	
Fence River	906	Glenn	616	Hart	616	Irons	616	(Muskegon Co.)	616
Fennville	616	Glennie	517	Hartford	616	Ironwood	906	Lambertville	313
Fenton	313	Gobles	616	Hartland	313	Isabella	906	Lamont	616
Fenton Lake	313	Goetzville	906	Harvey	906	Ishpeming	906	L'Anse	906
Fenwick	517	Golden Lake	906	Haslett	517	Island Lake	313	Lansing	517
Ferndale	313	Goodells	313	Hastings	616	Islington	906	Lapeer	313
Ferry	616	Goodhart	616	Hawks	517	Ithaca	517	Laporte	517

Place Name	Area Code	Place Name	Area Code	Place Name	Area Code	Place Name	Area Code	Place Name	Area Code
La Salle	313	Mapleton	616	Moorestown	616	Northville	313	Pearl	616
Lathrop	906	Marcellus	616	Moorland	616	Norton Shores	616	Pearl Beach	313
Lathrup Village	313	Marengo	616	Moran	906	Norvell	517	Pearline	616
Laurium	906	Marenisco	906	Morenci	517	Norwalk	616	Peck	313
Lawrence	616	Marine City	313	Morgan	517	Norway	906	Pelkie	906
Lawton	616	Marion	616	Morley	616	Norwood	616	Pellston	616
Leach Lake	616	Marion Springs	517	Morrice	517	Nottawa	616	Penfield	616
Leaton	517	Marlette	517	Morrison Lake	616	Novi	313	Pentecost	517
Leetsville	616	Marne	616	Moscow	517	Nunica	616	Pentwater	616
Leland	616	Marquette	906	Mosherville	517			Perkins	906
Lemon Lake	616	Marquette Coast Guard		Mottville	616			Perrinton	517
Lennon	313	Sta. No. 297	906	Mount Clemens	313	Oak Grove	517	Perronville	906
Leonard	313	Marshall	616	Mount Forest	517	Oakley	517	Perry	517
Leonidas	616	Martin	616	Mount Morris	313	Oak Park	313	Petersburg	313
Le Roy	616	Marysville	313	Mount Pleasant	517	Ocqueoc	616	Petoskey	616
Les Cheneaux	906	Mason	517	Muir	517	Oden	616	Petreville	517
Leslie	517	Masonville	906	Mullett Lake	616	Ogden Center	517	Pewamo	517
Levering	616	Mass	906	Mulliken	517	Okemos	517	Pickford	906
Lewiston	517	Matherton	517	Munger	517	Old Mission	616	Pierport	616
Lexington	313	Mattawan	616	Munising	906	Old Port	313	Pierson	616
Liberty	517	Maybee	313	Munith	517	Olivet	616	Pigeon	517
Lickleys Corners	517	Mayfair	313	Munson	517	Olney	517	Pilgrim	616
Limestone	906	Mayfield	616	Munuscong	906	Omena	616	Pinckney	313
Lincoln	517	Mayville	517	Muskegon	616	Omer	517	Pinconning	517
Lincoln Lake	616	McBain	616	Muskegon Heights	616	Onaway	517	Pine Lake	616
Lincoln Park	313	McBrides	517			Onekama	616	Pine River	517
Linden	313	McGregor	313			Onondaga	517	Pine Run	313
Linkville	517	McKinley	517			Onota	906	Pine Stump Junction	906
Linwood	517	McMillan	906	Nadeau	906	Onsted	517	Pinnebog	517
Litchfield	517	Mears	616	Nahma	906	Ontonagon	906	Pioneer	616
Little Lake	906	Mecosta	616	Napoleon	517	Orangeville	616	Pittsburg	517
Little Long Lake	616	Medina	517	Nashville	517	Orchard Lake	313	Pittsford	517
Little Point Sable	616	Melita	517	Nathan	906	Orleans	616	Plainfield	517
Livonia	313	Melstrand	906	National City	517	Ortonville	313	Plainwell	616
Long Lake		Melvin	313	National Mine	906	Oscoda	517	Pleasant Lake	
(Alpena Co.)	517	Melvindale	313	Naubinway	906	Oshtemo	616	(Jackson Co.)	517
Long Lake (Iosco Co.)	517	Memphis	313	Neely	616	Oskar	906	Pleasant Lake	
Loretto	906	Mendon	616	Negaunee	906	Osseo	517	(Washtenaw Co.)	313
Lost Peninsula	313	Menominee	906	Nessen City	616	Ossineke	517	Pleasant Ridge	313
Lovells	517	Merrill	517	Nestor	517	Otia	616	Plymouth	313
Lowell	616	Merritt	616	Nestoria	906	Otisville	313	Point Au Gres	517
Lucas	616	Merriweather	906	Newaygo	616	Otsego	616	Point Aux Barques	517
Ludington	616	Merson	616	New Baltimore	313	Otsego Lake	517	Point Betsie Coast	
Ludington Coast		Mesick	616	Newberry	906	Ottawa Beach	616	Guard Sta. No. 262	616
Guard Sta.	616	Metamora	313	New Boston	313	Ottawa Lake	313	Pointe Aux Pins	616
Lum	313	Meyers Lake	616	New Buffalo	616	Otter Lake	313	Point Lookout	517
Luna Pier	313	Michiana	616	New Era	616	Overisel	616	Point Nip-i-gon	616
Lupton	517	Michigamme	906	New Haven	313	Oviatt	517	Pokagon	616
Luther	616	Michigamme Forest	906	New Holland	616	Ovid	517	Pompeii	517
Lyon Manor	517	Michigan Center	517	New Hudson	313	Owasippi	616	Pontiac	313
Lyons	517	Michillinda	616	New Lothrop	313	Owendale	517	Portage	
		Middleton	517	Newport	313	Owosso	517	(Kalamazoo Co.)	616
		Middleville	616	New Swanzy	906	Oxford	313	Portage	
Macatawa Lake	616	Midland	517	New Troy	616			(Manistee Co.)	616
Mackinac Island	906	Mikado	517	Niles	616			Portage Coast Guard	
Mackinaw City	616	Milan	313	Nisula	906			Sta. No. 300	906
Macon	517	Milford-White Lake	313	North Adams	517	Painesdale	906	Portage Lake	313
Madison	517	Millbrook	517	North Bradley	517	Palmer	906	Port Austin	517
Madison Heights	313	Millburg	616	North Branch	313	Palms	517	Port Hope	517
Mancelona	616	Millersburg	517	North Detroit	313	Palmyra	517	Port Huron	313
Manchester	313	Millett	517	North Dorr	616	Palo	517	Port Huron Coast	
Manistee	616	Millington	517	North Fayette	517	Paradise	906	Guard Sta.	313
Manistee Coast Guard		Milnes	517	North Land O'Lakes	906	Parchment	616	Portland	517
Sta. No. 264	616	Minden City	517	North Manitou		Paris	616	Port Sanilac	313
Manistique	906	Mio	517	Island	616	Parisville	517	Posen	517
Manitou Beach	517	Misery Bay	906	North Morenci	517	Parkville	616	Potterville	517
Manitou Island Coast		Mohawk	906	North Muskegon	616	Parma	517	Powers	906
Guard Light Sta.	906	Moline	616	North Orland	517	Parmelee	616	Prairieville	616
Manning	616	Mona Lake	616	North Phelps	906	Pavilion	616	Prattville	517
Manton	616	Monroe	313	Northport	616	Paw Paw	616	Prescott	517
Maple City	616	Montague	616	Northport Point	616	Paw Paw Lake	616	Presque Isle	517
Maplegrove	517	Monterey	616	Northstar	517	Paynesville	906	Princeton	906
Maple Rapids	517	Montgomery	517	North Street	313	Peacock	616	Prosper	616
Maple Ridge	517	Montrose	313	North Sylvania	313			Prudenville	517

TELEPHONE AREA CODE DIRECTORY

Place Name	Area Code	Place Name	Area Code	Place Name	Area Code	Place Name	Area Code	Place Name	Area Code
Pulaski	517	Round Lake		Shelby	616	Sugar Island	906	Vandalia	616
Pullman	616	(Oakland Co.)	313	Shelbyville	616	Summit City	616	Vanderbilt	517
		Round Lake		Shelldrake	906	Sumner	517	Vandercook Lake	517
		(Shiawassee Co.)	517	Shelter Bay	906	Sumnerville	616	Vassar	517
		Rousseau	906	Shepardsville	517	Sundell	906	Vermontville	517
		Royal Oak	313	Shepherd	517	Sunfield	517	Vernon	517
Quanicassee	517	Rudyard	906	Sheridan	517	Suttons Bay	616	Vestaburg	517
Quimby	616	Rumely	906	Sherman Lake	616	Swartz Creek	313	Vickeryville	517
Quincy	517	Rustford	616	Sherwood	517	Sylvan Lake	313	Vicksburg	616
Quinnesec	906	Ruth	517	Shields	517			Vineland	616
				Shingleton	906			Vriesland	616
				Sidnaw	906			Vulcan	906
				Sidney	517				
				Silver City	906	Talbot	906		
Raber	906	Saginaw	517	Silver Lake	616	Tapiola	906		
Raco	906	Saginaw River Coast		Silverwood	517	Tawas City	517		
Ramsay	906	Guard Sta.	517	Sister Lakes	616	Tawas City Coast Guard		Wabaningo	616
Rankin	313	Sagola	906	Sitka	616	Sta. No. 250	517	Wabasis Lake	616
Ransom	517	St. Charles	517	Six Lakes	517	Taylor	313	Wacousta	517
Rapid City	616	St. Clair	313	Sixty Lakes	517	Tecumseh	517	Wahjamega	517
Rapid River	906	St. Clair Flats Coast		Skandia	906	Tekonsha	517	Wakefield	906
Rapson	517	Guard Sta.	313	Skanee	906	Temperance	313	Waldron	517
Ravenna	616	St. Clair Shores	313	Skeels	517	Thompson	906	Walhalla	616
Rawsonville	313	St. Clair Shores Coast		Slocum	616	Three Oaks	616	Walkerville	616
Reading	517	Guard Sta.	313	Smiths Creek	313	Three Rivers	616	Wallace	906
Redman	517	St. Helen	517	Smyrna	616	Tipton	517	Walled Lake	313
Redridge	906	St. Ignace	906	Snover	313	Toivola	906	Wallin	616
Reed City	616	St. James	616	Sodus	616	Tompkins Center	517	Walloon Lake	616
Reeman	616	St. Johns	517	Solon	616	Topinabee	616	Walnut Lake	313
Reese	517	St. Joseph	616	Somerset Center	517	Torch Lake Village	616	Wamplers Lake	517
Remus	517	St. Joseph Coast Guard		South Boardman	616	Torch River Bridge	616	Warren	313
Republic	906	Sta. No. 273	616	Southbranch	517	Tower	517	Washington	313
Rexton	906	St. Louis	517	Southfield	313	Traunik	906	Waterford	313
Rhodes	517	Salem	313	Southgate	313	Traverse City	616	Waters	517
Richland	616	Saline	313	South Haven	616	Traverse City Coast		Watersmeet	906
Richland Junction	616	Samaria	313	South Haven Coast		Guard Sta.	616	Watervliet	616
Richmond	313	Sand Creek	517	Guard Sta. No. 272	616	Trenary	906	Watson (Allegan Co.)	616
Richville	517	Sand Lake (Kent Co.)	616	South Lyon	313	Trenton	313	Watson	
Ridgeway	517	Sand Lake		South Manitou		Trimountain	906	(Marquette Co.)	906
Riga	517	(Lenawee Co.)	517	Island	616	Trout Creek	906	Watton	906
Riverdale	517	Sand Lake Heights	517	South Range	906	Trout Lake	906	Wayland	616
River Rouge	313	Sand River	906	South Rockwood	313	Troy	313	Wayne	313
Riverside	616	Sandusky	313	Spalding	906	Trufant	616	Webberville	517
Riverview	313	Sanford	517	Sparta	616	Turner	517	Weidman	517
Rives Junction	517	Sans Souci	313	Spinks Corners	616	Tuscola	517	Wells	906
Rochester	313	Saranac	616	Spring Arbor	517	Tustin	616	Wellston	616
Rock	906	Saugatuck	616	Springfield	616	Twining	517	Wequetonsing	616
Rockford	616	Sault Ste. Marie	906	Spring Lake	616	Twin Lake		West Bloomfield	313
Rockland	906	Sawyer	616	Springport	517	(Muskegon Co.)	616	West Branch	517
Rock River	906	Sawyer Air Force Base	906	Springville	517	Twin Lakes	906	Westland	313
Rockwood	313	Schaffer	906	Springwells	313	Tyre	517	West Olive	616
Rogers City	517	Schomberg	616	Stalwart	906			Weston	517
Rogers Dam	616	Schoolcraft	616	Stambaugh	906			Westphalia	517
Rollin	517	Schultz	616	Standish	517			Wetmore	906
Rome Center	517	Scott Point	906	Stanton	517			Wheeler	517
Romeo	313	Scotts	616	Stanwood	616			White Cloud	616
Romulus	313	Scottville	616	Steiner	313	Ubly	517	Whitefish Lake	616
Roosevelt Park	616	Sears	517	Stephenson	906	Union	616	Whitefish Point	906
Roscommon	517	Sebewaing	517	Sterling	517	Union City	517	Whitefish Point Coast	
Rosebush	517	Selfridge Air Force		Sterling Heights	313	Union Lake	313	Guard Lifeboat	
Rose City	517	Base	313	Stevensville	616	Union Pier	616	Station	906
Roseville	313	Selfridge Coast		Stockbridge	517	Unionville	517	Whiteford Center	313
Rothbury	616	Guard Sta.	313	Stony Creek	313	U. S. War Department		Whitehall	616
Round Lake		Seneca	517	Stony Lake	616	Detroit Ordnance Plant		White Lake	
(Jackson Co.)	517	Seney	906	Stronach	616	Center Line	313	(Muskegon Co.)	616
Round Lake		Senter	906	Strongs	906	Urbandale	616	White Lake	
(Lenawee Co.)	517	Shaftsburg	517	Sturgis	616	Utica	313	(Oakland Co.)	313

Place Name	Area Code	Place Name	Area Code	Place Name	Area Code	Place Name	Area Code	Place Name	Area Code
White Pigeon	616	Willis	313	Wolf Lake		Woodland	616	Yale	313
White Pine	906	Willow Run	313	(Jackson Co.)	517	Woodland Park	616	Yorkville	616
White Rock	517	Wilson	906	Wolf Lake		Woodville	616	Ypsilanti	313
White Stone Point	517	Winegars	517	(Muskegon Co.)	616	Wooster	616		
Whitmore Lake	313	Wing Lake	313	Wolverine	616	Wurtsmith		Zeeland	616
Whittemore	517	Winn	517	Wolverine Lake	313	Air Force Base	517	Zilwaukee	517
Wilkinson Lake	616	Winona	906	Woodbury	616	Wyandotte	313	Zutphen	616
Williamsburg	616	Wise	517	Woodhaven	313	Wyoming	616		
Williamston	517	Wixom	313						

Place Name	Area Code	Place Name	Area Code	Place Name	Area Code	Place Name	Area Code	Place Name	Area Code
Ada	218	Baxter	218	Bruno	612	Coast Guard Sta.		Dennison	507
Adams	507	Bayport	612	Brushvale	218	No. 304	218	Dent	218
Adolph	218	Beardsley	612	Buckman	612	Coates	612	Detroit Lakes	218
Adrian	507	Bear River	218	Buffalo	612	Cobden	507	Dexter	507
Afton	612	Beaulieu	218	Buffalo Lake	612	Cohasset	218	Dilworth	218
Ah-gwah-ching	218	Beaver Bay	218	Buhl	218	Cokato	612	Dodge Center	507
Airlie	507	Beaver Creek	507	Burchard	507	Cold Spring	612	Donaldson	218
Aitkin	218	Becida	218	Burnett	218	Coleraine	218	Donnelly	612
Akeley	218	Becker	612	Burnsville	612	Collegeville	612	Doran	218
Albany	612	Bejou	218	Burr	507	Collis	612	Dorothy	218
Alberta	612	Belgrade	612	Burtrum	612	Cologne	612	Dorset	218
Albert Lea	507	Bellechester	612	Butler	218	Columbia Heights	612	Dotson	507
Albertville	612	Belle Plaine	612	Butterfield	507	Comfrey	507	Douglas	507
Alborn	218	Bellingham	612	Buyck	218	Comstock	218	Dover	507
Alden	507	Beltrami	218	Bygland	218	Conger	507	Dovray	507
Aldrich	218	Belview	507	Byron	507	Constance	612	Downer	218
Alexandria	612	Bemidji	218			Cook	218	Dresbach	507
Allen Junction	218	Bena	218			Cooley	218	Dudley	507
Alma City	507	Benedict	218			Coon Creek	612	Duluth	218
Almelund	612	Bennettville	218	Caledonia	507	Coon Rapids	612	Dundas	507
Almora	218	Benson	612	Callaway	218	Copas	612	Dundee	507
Alpha	507	Beroun	612	Calumet	218	Cormorant	218	Dunnell	507
Altura	507	Bertha	218	Cambria	507	Corning	507	Duquette	218
Alvarado	218	Bethany	507	Cambridge	612	Correll	612	
Alwwood	218	Bethel	612	Campbell	218	Corvuso	612	
Amboy	507	Big Bend City	612	Camp Ripley	612	Cosmos	612	
Amiret	507	Bigelow	507	Canby	507	Cottage Grove	612	
Andover	612	Big Falls	218	Cannon Falls	507	Cotton	218	Eagle Bend	218
Angora	218	Bigfork	218	Canton	507	Cottonwood	507	Eagle Lake	507
Angus	218	Big Lake	612	Canyon	218	Courtland	507	East Abercrombie	218
Annandale	612	Bingham Lake	507	Carlisle	218	Craigville	218	East Chain	507
Anoka	612	Birchdale	218	Carlos	612	Crane Lake	218	East Drayton	218
Appleton	612	Birchwood	612	Carlton	218	Cromwell	218	East Elkton	507
Apple Valley	612	Bird Island	612	Carson Lake	218	Crookston	218	East Fairmount	218
Arago	218	Biscay	612	Carver	612	Crosby	218	East Garretson	507
Arco	507	Biwabik	218	Cass Lake	218	Cross Lake	218	East Gary	507
Arendahl	507	Bixby	507	Castle Rock	507	Crow Wing	218	East Grand Forks	218
Argyle	218	Blackberry	218	Cazenovia	507	Crystal	612	Easton	507
Arlington	612	Blackduck	218	Cedar	612	Crystal Bay	612	East Valley Springs	507
Armstrong	507	Blakely	612	Cedar Mills	612	Culver	218	Ebro	218
Asbury	612	Blomkest	612	Center City	612	Currie	507	Echo	507
Ashby	218	Blooming Prairie	507	Centerville	612	Cushing	612	Echols	507
Ash Lake	218	Bloomington	612	Cerro Gordo	612	Cusson	218	Eden Prairie	612
Ash River	218	Blue Earth	507	Ceylon	507	Cuyuna	218	Eden Valley	612
Askov	612	Bluffton	218	Champlin	612	Cyphers	218	Edgerton	507
Atkinson	218	Bock	612	Chandler	507	Cyrus	612	Edina	612
Atwater	612	Bombay	507	Chanhassen	612			Effie	218
Audubon	218	Bongards	612	Charlesville	218			Eitzen	507
Augusta	612	Borup	218	Chaska	612			Elba	507
Aure	218	Bovey	218	Chatfield	507			Elbow Lake	218
Aurora	218	Bowlus	612	Cherry Grove	507	Dakota	507	Elcor	218
Austin	507	Bowstring	218	Chester	507	Dalbo	612	Eldred	218
Automba	218	Boyd	612	Chisago City	612	Dale	218	Elgin	507
Averill	218	Boy River	218	Chisholm	218	Dalton	218	Elizabeth	218
Avoca	507	Braham	612	Chokio	612	Danube	612	Elko	612
Avon	612	Brainerd	218	Circle Pines	612	Danvers	612	Elk River	612
		Brandon	218	Clara City	612	Darfur	507	Elkton	507
		Bratsberg	507	Claremont	507	Darling	612	Ellendale	507
		Breckenridge	218	Clarissa	218	Darwin	612	Ellsworth	507
Babbitt	218	Breezy Point	218	Clarkfield	612	Dassel	612	Elmdale	612
Backus	218	Brevik	218	Clarks Grove	507	Dawson	612	Elmer	218
Badger	218	Brewster	507	Claybank	612	Day	612	Elmore	507
Bagley	218	Bricelyn	507	Clearbrook	218	Dayton	612	Elrosa	612
Baker	218	Brimson	218	Clear Lake	612	Deephaven	612	Ely	218
Balaton	507	Brooklyn Center	612	Clearwater	612	Deer Creek	218	Elysian	507
Bald Eagle	612	Brook Park	612	Clements	507	Deer River	218	Embarrass	218
Ball Club	218	Brooks	218	Clementson	218	Deerwood	218	Emily	218
Barnesville	218	Brookston	218	Cleveland	507	De Graff	612	Emmons	507
Barnum	218	Brooten	612	Climax	218	Delano	612	Enfield	612
Barrett	612	Browerville	218	Clinton	612	Delavan	507	Erdahl	218
Barrows	218	Brownsdale	507	Clitherall	218	Delft	507	Erhard	218
Barry	612	Browns Valley	612	Clontarf	612	Delhi	507	Ericsburg	218
Battle Lake	218	Brownsville	507	Cloquet	218	Dellwood	612	Erskine	218
Baudette	218	Brownton	612	Cloverton	612	Denham	218	Esko	218

MINNESOTA
Essig—Maple Grove

Place Name	Area Code	Place Name	Area Code	Place Name	Area Code	Place Name	Area Code	Place Name	Area Code
Essig	507	Georgetown	218	Hastings	612	Jackson	507	Lawler	218
Euclid	218	Georgeville	612	Hasty	612	Jacobson	218	Lawndale	218
Eureka	612	Gheen	218	Hatfield	507	Janesville	507	Leader	218
Eureka Center	612	Ghent	507	Havana	507	Jasper	507	Le Center	612
Evan	507	Gibbon	507	Hawick	612	Jeffers	507	Leech Lake	218
Evansville	218	Giese	612	Hawley	218	Jenkins	218	Leetonia	218
Eveleth	218	Gilbert	218	Hay Creek	612	Jessie Lake	218	Lengby	218
Everdell	218	Gilman	612	Haydenville	612	Johnson	612	Leonard	218
Excelsior	612	Glen	612	Hayfield	507	Johnsville	612	Leonidas	218
Eyota	507	Glencoe	612	Hayward	507	Jordan	612	Leota	507
		Glendorado	612	Hazel	218	Judson	507	Lerdal	507
		Glen Lake	612	Hazel Run	612			LeRoy	507
		Glenville	507	Hector	612			Lester Prairie	612
Fairfax	507	Glenwood	612	Heidelberg	612			Le Sueur	612
Fairhaven	612	Gluek	612	Helena	612	Kabetogama	218	Lewiston	507
Fairmont	507	Glyndon	218	Henderson	612	Kanaranzi	507	Lewisville	507
Faribault	507	Godahl	507	Hendricks	507	Kandiyohi	612	Libby	218
Farmington	612	Golden Valley	612	Hendrum	218	Karlstad	218	Lime Creek	507
Farwell	612	Gonvick	218	Henning	218	Kasota	507	Lincoln	218
Fayal	218	Goodhue	612	Henriette	612	Kasson	507	Lindstrom	612
Federal Dam	218	Goodland	218	Herman	612	Keewatin	218	Lismore	507
Felton	218	Goodridge	218	Heron Lake	507	Kelliher	218	Litchfield	612
Fergus Falls	218	Good Thunder	507	Hewitt	218	Kellogg	507	Little Falls	612
Fertile	218	Gordonsville	507	Hibbing	218	Kelly Lake	218	Little Fork	218
Fifty Lakes	218	Gowan	218	Highland	218	Kelsey	218	Little Marais	218
Finland	218	Graceton	218	Hill City	218	Kennedy	218	Little Sauk	612
Finlayson	612	Graceville	612	Hillman	612	Kenneth	507	Lockhart	218
Fisher	218	Granada	507	Hills	507	Kensington	612	Loman	218
Flaming	218	Grand Lake	218	Hinckley	612	Kent	218	London	507
Flensburg	612	Grand Marais	218	Hines	218	Kenyon	507	Long Beach	612
Flom	218	Grand Meadow	507	Hitterdal	218	Kerkhoven	612	Long Lake	612
Floodwood	218	Grand Portage	218	Hoffman	612	Kerrick	218	Long Prairie	612
Florence	507	Grand Rapids	218	Hokah	507	Kettle River	218	Long Siding	612
Florenton	218	Grandy	612	Holdingford	612	Kiester	507	Longville	218
Foley	612	Granger	507	Holland	507	Kilkenny	507	Lonsdale	507
Forada	612	Granite Falls	612	Hollandale	507	Kimball	612	Loretto	612
Forbes	218	Grasston	612	Holloway	612	Kimberly	218	Louisburg	612
Forest Lake	612	Greaney	218	Holmes City	612	Kinbrae	507	Louriston	612
Foreston	612	Greenbush	218	Holt	218	Kinney	218	Lowry	612
Fort Snelling	612	Green Isle	612	Holyoke	218	Klossner	507	Lucan	507
Fosston	218	Greenland	507	Homer	507	Knife River	218	Luna	218
Fountain	507	Green Valley	507	Hope	507	Kragnes	218	Lutsen	218
Foxhome	218	Greenwald	612	Hopkins	612			Luverne	507
Fox Lake	507	Grey Eagle	612	Hopper	218			Lydia	612
Franconia	612	Grogan	507	Houston	507			Lyle	507
Franklin	507	Groningen	612	Hovland	218	Lac Qui Parle	612	Lynd	507
Fraser	218	Grove City	612	Howard Lake	612	La Crescent	507	Lyndale	612
Frazee	218	Grygla	218	Hoyt Lakes	218	Lafayette	507		
Freeborn	507	Guckeen	507	Hubbard	218	Lake Benton	507		
Freedhem	612	Gully	218	Hugo	612	Lake Bronson	218		
Freeport	612	Gunflint Trail	218	Humboldt	218	Lake City	612	Mabel	507
French River	218	Guthrie	218	Huntley	507	Lake Crystal	507	Madelia	507
Fridley	612			Hutchinson	612	Lake Elmo	612	Madison	612
Friesland	612					Lakefield	507	Madison Lake	507
Frontenac	612					Lake George	218	Magnolia	507
Frost	507					Lake Henry	612	Mahnomen	218
Fulda	507	Hackensack	218	Ideal Corners	218	Lake Hubert	218	Mahtomedi	612
Funkley	218	Hadley	507	Idington	218	Lakeland	612	Mahtowa	218
		Hallock	218	Ihlen	507	Lakeland Shores	612	Maine	218
		Halma	218	Imogene	507	Lake Lillian	612	Makinen	218
		Halstad	218	Inger-Wirt	218	Lake Minnetonka	612	Malcolm	218
Garden City	507	Hamburg	612	International Falls	218	Lake Park	218	Mallory	218
Garfield	612	Hamel	612	Invergrove	612	Lakeville	612	Malmo	612
Garrison	612	Hammond	507	Iona	507	Lake Wilson	507	Malung-Wannaska	218
Garvin	507	Hampton	612	Iron Junction	218	Lamberton	507	Manchester	507
Gary	218	Hancock	612	Ironton	218	Lamoille	507	Manganese	218
Gateway	218	Hanley Falls	507	Irving	612	Lancaster	218	Manhattan Beach	218
Gatzke	218	Hanover	612	Isabella	218	Lanesboro	507	Mankato	507
Gaylord	612	Hanska	507	Isanti	612	Lansing	507	Manley	507
Gemmell	218	Harding	612	Island Park	612	Laporte	218	Mantorville	507
Geneva	507	Hardwick	507	Isle	612	La Prairie	218	Manyaska	507
Genola	612	Harmony	507	Itasca	218	Larsmont	218	Maple	612
Gentilly	218	Harris	612	Ivanhoe	507	La Salle	507	Maple Bay	218
		Hartland	507			Lastrup	612	Maple Grove	612

Place Name	Area Code	Place Name	Area Code	Place Name	Area Code	Place Name	Area Code	Place Name	Area Code
Maple Lake	612	Murdock	612	Okabena	507	Prosit	218	Russell	507
Maple Plain	612	Muskoda	218	Oklee	218	Prosper	507	Rustad	218
Mapleton	507	Myrtle	507	Olivia	612	Puposky	218	Ruthton	507
Marble	218			Onamia	612			Rutledge	612
Marcell	218			Orleans	218				
Margie	218			Ormsby	507				
Marietta	612	Nashua	218	Orono	612	Quamba	612		
Markville	612	Nashwauk	218	Oronoco	507			Sabin	218
Marna	507	Nassau	612	Orr	218			Sacred Heart	612
Marshall	507	Navarre	612	Ortonville	612			Saginaw	218
Matawan	507	Nay-Ta-Waush	218	Osage	218	Racine	507	St. Anthony	612
Max	218	Nebish	218	Osakis	612	Radium	218	St. Bonifacius	612
Mayer	612	Nelson	612	Oshawa	507	Rainy Junction	218	St. Charles	507
Maynard	612	Nemadji	218	Oslo	218	Ramey	612	St. Clair	507
Mazeppa	507	Nerstrand	507	Osseo	612	Randall	612	St. Cloud	612
McComber	218	Nett Lake	218	Ostrander	507	Randolph	507	St. Croix Beach	612
McGrath	612	Nevis	218	Otisco	507	Ranger	218	St. Francis	612
McGregor	218	New Auburn	612	Ottawa	612	Ranier	218	St. Hilaire	218
McHugh	218	New Brighton	612	Ottertail	218	Rapidan	507	St. James	507
McIntosh	218	Newfolden	218	Outing	218	Ray	218	St. Joseph	612
McKinley	218	New Germany	612	Owatonna	507	Raymond	612	St. Leo	507
Meadowlands	218	New Hope	612			Reading	507	St. Louis Park	612
Medford	507	Newhouse	507			Reads Landing	612	St. Martin	612
Medicine Lake	612	New London	612			Redby	218	St. Michael	612
Meire Grove	612	New Market	612	Palisade	218	Red Lake	218	St. Paul	612
Melby	218	New Munich	612	Palmers	218	Red Lake Falls	218	St. Paul Park	612
Melrose	612	Newport	612	Palmyra	612	Redore	218	St. Peter	507
Melrude	218	New Prague	612	Palo	218	Red Top	612	St. Rosa	612
Menahga	218	New Prairie	612	Parent	612	Red Wing	612	St. Stephens	612
Mendota	612	New Richland	507	Parkers Prairie	218	Redwood	507	St. Vincent	218
Mentor	218	New Sweden	507	Park Rapids	218	Redwood Falls	507	Salol	218
Meriden	507	New Trier	612	Paupores	218	Regal	612	Sanborn	507
Merrifield	218	New Ulm	507	Payne	218	Remer	218	Sandstone	612
Mesaba	218	New York Mills	218	Paynesville	612	Renova	507	Santiago	612
Middle River	218	Nickerson	218	Pease	612	Renville	612	Sargeant	507
Miesville	612	Nicollet	507	Pelican Lake	218	Reservation River	218	Sartell	612
Milaca	612	Nielsville	218	Pelican Rapids	218	Revere	507	Sauk Centre	612
Milan	612	Nimrod	218	Pemberton	507	Rice	612	Sauk Rapids	612
Mildred	218	Nisswa	218	Pencer	218	Richfield	612	Saum	218
Millerville	612	Nodine	507	Pengilly	218	Richmond	612	Savage	612
Millville	507	Nokay Lake	218	Pennington	218	Richville	218	Sawyer	218
Miloma	507	Nopeming	218	Pennock	612	Richwood	218	Scandia-Marine	612
Milroy	507	Norcross	612	Pequot Lakes	218	Ridge	218	Scanlon	218
Miltona	218	North Branch	612	Perham	218	Ridgeway	507	Schley	218
Minerva	218	North Burr Oak	507	Perley	218	Robbinsdale	612	Schroeder	218
Minneapolis	612	North Chester	612	Peterson	507	Robinson	218	Seaforth	507
Minneiska	507	Northcote	218	Philbrook	218	Rochert	218	Searles	507
Minneota	507	North Estherville	507	Pierz	612	Rochester	507	Sebeka	218
Minnesota City	507	Northfield	507	Pigeon River	218	Rock Creek	612	Sedan	612
Minnesota Falls	612	North Lake Park	507	Pike	218	Rock Dell	507	Shafer	612
Minnesota Lake	507	North Lime Springs	507	Pillager	218	Rockford	612	Shakopee	612
Minnetonka	612	North Little Rock	507	Pine Bend	612	Rockville	612	Shaw	218
Minnetonka Beach	612	North New Albin	507	Pine City	612	Rogers	612	Shelly	218
Mission	218	Northome	218	Pine Creek	507	Rollag	218	Sherburn	507
Mizpah	218	North Rake	507	Pine Island	507	Rollingstone	507	Sherman	612
Monterey	507	North Redwood	507	Pine River	218	Rollins	218	Shevlin	218
Montevideo	612	North Rock Rapids	507	Pinewood	218	Ronneby	612	Shooks	218
Montgomery	612	Northrop	507	Pipestone	507	Roosevelt	218	Shovel Lake	218
Monticello	612	North St. Paul	612	Pitt	218	Roscoe	612	Silver Bay	218
Montrose	612	North Spirit Lake	507	Plainview	507	Roseau	218	Silver Creek	612
Moorhead	218	North Swea City	507	Plato	612	Rose Creek	507	Silver Lake	612
Moose Lake	218	Norwood	612	Plummer	218	Roseland	612	Simpson	507
Mora	612	Noyes	218	Point Douglas	612	Rosemount	612	Skibo	218
Morgan	507			Ponemah	218	Roseville	612	Skime	218
Morningside	612			Ponsford	218	Rosewood	218	Skyberg	612
Morris	612			Porter	507	Ross	218	Slayton	507
Morristown	507			Pratt	507	Rossburg	218	Sleepy Eye	507
Morton	507	Oakland	507	Predmore	507	Rothsay	218	Smith Mill	507
Motley	218	Oak Park	612	Preston	507	Round Lake	507	Sobieski	612
Mound	612	Oak Terrace	612	Priam	612	Round Prairie	612	Soderville	612
Mound Prairie	507	Odessa	612	Princeton	612	Royalton	612	Solway	218
Mountain Iron	218	Odin	507	Prinsburg	612	Rush City	612	Soudan	218
Mountain Lake	507	Ogema	218	Prior Lake	612	Rushford	507	South Burnsville	612
Munger	218	Ogilvie	612	Proctor	218	Rushmore	507	South Haven	612

MINNESOTA
South St. Paul–Zumbrota

Place Name	Area Code	Place Name	Area Code	Place Name	Area Code	Place Name	Area Code	Place Name	Area Code
South St. Paul	612	Taconite Harbor	218	U. S. Naval		Wanda	507	Willmar	612
Spicer	612	Talmoon	218	Radio Sta.	218	Wannaska	218	Willow River	218
Spooner	218	Tamarack	218	Upsala	612	Warba	218	Wilmont	507
Springfield	507	Taopi	507	Urbank	218	Warren	218	Wilton	218
Spring Grove	507	Taunton	507	Utica	507	Warroad	218	Windom	507
Spring Hill	612	Taylors Falls	612			Warsaw	507	Winger	218
Spring Lake	218	Ten Mile Lake	218			Waseca	507	Winnebago	507
Spring Lake Park	612	Tenney	218			Washkish	218	Winona	507
Spring Park	612	Tenstrike	218			Wastedo	507	Winsted	612
Spring Valley	507	Terrace	612	Vasa	612	Waterford	507	Winthrop	507
Squaw Lake	218	Theilman	612	Verdi	507	Watertown	612	Winton	218
Stacy	612	Thief River Falls	218	Vergas	218	Waterville	507	Wirock	507
Stanchfield	612	Thomson	218	Vermillion	612	Watkins	612	Wirt	218
Stanton	507	Tintah	218	Verndale	218	Watson	612	Withrow	612
Staples	218	Tobique	218	Vernon Center	507	Waubun	218	Witoka	507
Starbuck	612	Tofte	218	Veseli	507	Waverly	612	Wolf Lake	218
Steen	507	Toivola	218	Vesta	507	Wawina	218	Wolverton	218
Stephen	218	Tonka Bay	612	Victoria	612	Wayzata	612	Wood Lake	507
Stewart	612	Tower	218	Viking	218	Weaver	507	Woodstock	507
Stewartville	507	Tower Junction	218	Villard	612	Webster	507	Worthington	507
Stillwater	612	Tracy	507	Vining	218	Wegdahl	612	Wrenshall	218
Stockton	507	Trail	218	Viola	507	Welch	612	Wright	218
Storden	507	Traverse	507	Virginia	218	Welcome	507	Wykoff	507
Strandquist	218	Trimont	507	Vlasaty	507	Wells	507	Wyoming	612
Strathcona	218	Triumph	507			Wendell	218		
Stubbs Bay	612	Trommald	218			Westbrook	507		
Sturgeon Lake	218	Trosky	507			Westbury	218		
Sullivan Lake	612	Trout Brook	612			West Concord	507		
Sumter	612	Truman	507	Wabasha	612	West Danbury	612		
Sunburg	612	Turtle River	218	Wabasso	507	Westport	612		
Sunrise	612	Twig	218	Waconia	612	West St. Paul	612		
Svea	612	Twin Lakes	507	Wacouta	612	West Union	612	Young America	612
Swan River	218	Twin Valley	218	Wadena	218	Whalan	507		
Swanville	612	Two Harbors	218	Wahkon	612	Wheaton	612		
Swatara	218	Two Islands	218	Wahlsten	218	Whipholt	218		
Swift	218	Tyler	507	Waite Park	612	White Bear Lake	612		
Swift Falls	612			Waldorf	507	White Earth	218		
Syre	218			Walker	218	White Rock	612		
				Walnut Grove	507	Whitman	507	Zim	218
				Walters	507	Wilder	507	Zimmerman	612
		Ulen	218	Waltham	507	Willernie	507	Zumbro Falls	507
Taconite	218	Underwood	218	Wanamingo	507	Williams	218	Zumbrota	507

ALL POINTS—AREA CODE 601

Place Name	Area Code	Place Name	Area Code	Place Name	Area Code	Place Name	Area Code	Place Name	Area Code
Adrian	816	Bearcreek	417	Breckenridge	816	Centertown	314	Crystal City	314
Advance	314	Beaufort	314	Brentwood	314	Centerview	816	Cuba	314
Affton	314	Bedison	816	Bridgeton	314	Centerville	314	Curryville	314
Agency	816	Belgique	314	Brighton	417	Centralia	314	Cyrene	314
Alanthus	816	Belgrade	314	Brimson	816	Chadwick	417		
Alba	417	Bell City	314	Brinktown	314	Chaffee	314		
Albany	816	Belle	314	Brock	816	Chamois	314		
Aldrich	417	Belleview	314	Bronaugh	417	Charleston	314	Dadeville	417
Alexandria	314	Bellflower	314	Brookfield	816	Cherryville	314	Daisy	314
Allendale	816	Bel Nor	314	Brookline	417	Chesapeake	417	Dalton	816
Allenton	314	Belton	816	Brooklyn	816	Chesterfield	314	Damsel	314
Allenville	314	Benbow	314	Broseley	314	Chilhowee	816	Danby	314
Alley Spring	314	Bennett Spring		Browning	816	Chillicothe	816	Danville	314
Alma	816	State Park	417	Browningtown	417	Chula	816	Dardenne	314
Altamont	816	Benton	314	Browns Station	314	Civil Bend	816	Darlington	816
Altenburg	314	Benton City	314	Brownwood	314	Clarence	816	Davis	314
Alton	417	Berger	314	Brumley	314	Clark	314	Davisville	314
Amazonia	816	Berkeley	314	Bruner	417	Clarksburg	314	Dawn	816
Americus	314	Berlin	816	Brunswick	816	Clarksdale	816	Dean Lake	816
Amity	816	Bernie	314	Brush Creek	417	Clarksville	314	Dearborn	816
Amoret	816	Bertrand	314	Buckhorn	314	Clarkton	314	Decaturville	314
Amsterdam	816	Bethany	816	Bucklin	816	Claryville	314	Dederick	417
Ancell	314	Bethel	816	Buckner	816	Claycomo	816	Deepwater	816
Anderson	417	Beulah	314	Bucyrus	417	Clayton	314	Deerfield	417
Andover	816	Beverly	816	Buell	314	Clearmont	816	Deering	314
Annada	314	Bevier	816	Buffalo	417	Clearwater Lake	314	Defiance	314
Annapolis	314	Biehle	314	Bunceton	816	Cleveland	816	De Kalb	816
Anniston	314	Bigelow	816	Bunker	314	Clever	417	Delta	314
Antonia	314	Big Piney	314	Burfordville	314	Clifton City	816	Denton (Johnson Co.)	816
Appleton City	816	Bigspring	314	Burlington Junction	816	Clifton Hill	816	Denton	
Arbela	816	Big Spring State Park	314	Butler	816	Climax Springs	314	(Pemiscot Co.)	314
Arbyrd	314	Billings	417	Butterfield	417	Clinton	816	Denver	816
Arcadia	314	Birch Tree	314	Bynumville	816	Cliquot	417	Des Arc	314
Archie	816	Birmingham	816			Clubb	314	Desloge	314
Arcola	417	Bismarck	314			Clyde	816	De Soto	314
Argyle	314	Bixby	314	Cabool	417	Coal	816	Desperes	314
Arkoe	816	Black	314	Cadet	314	Coatesville	816	Devils Elbow	314
Armstrong	816	Blackburn	816	Cainesville	816	Coffey	816	De Witt	816
Arnold	314	Black Jack	314	Cairo	816	Cole Camp	816	Dexter	314
Arrow Rock	816	Blackwater	816	Caledonia	314	College Mound	816	Diamond	417
Asbury	417	Blackwell	314	Calhoun	816	Collins	417	Diehlstadt	314
Ashburn	314	Blairstown	816	California	314	Columbia	314	Diggins	417
Ash Grove	417	Bland	314	Callao	816	Commerce	314	Dillard	314
Ashland	314	Bliss	314	Camden	816	Conception	816	Dillon	314
Ashley	314	Blodgett	314	Camden Point	816	Conception Junction	816	Dixon	314
Ashton	816	Bloomfield	314	Camdenton	314	Concordia	816	Dodson	816
Athens	816	Bloomsdale	314	Cameron	816	Connelsville	816	Doe Run	314
Atherton	816	Blue Eye	417	Campbell	314	Conran	314	Doniphan	314
Atlanta	816	Blue Springs	816	Canalou	314	Converse	314	Dora	417
Augusta	314	Blythedale	816	Canton	314	Conway	417	Dorena	314
Aullville	816	Boaz	417	Cantwell	314	Cook Station	314	Dover	816
Aurora	417	Bogard	816	Cape Fair	417	Cooper Hill	314	Downing	816
Auxvasse	314	Bois D'Arc	417	Cape Girardeau	314	Cooter	314	Drake	314
Ava	417	Bolckow	816	Caplinger Mills	417	Cora	314	Dresden	816
Avalon	816	Bolivar	417	Cardwell	314	Corder	816	Drexel	816
Avenue City	816	Bonne Terre	314	Carl Junction	417	Corning	816	Drynob	417
Avilla	417	Bonnots Mill	314	Carrollton	816	Cornwall	314	Dudenville	417
Avondale	816	Boonesboro	816	Carsonville	314	Corso	314	Dudley	314
		Boonville	816	Carterville	417	Cosby	816	Duenweg	417
		Boss	314	Carthage	417	Cottleville	314	Duke	314
Babler State Park	314	Bosworth	816	Caruth	314	Cottonwood Point	314	Dunlap	816
Bagnell	314	Bourbon	314	Caruthersville	314	Couch	417	Dunnegan	417
Bakersfield	417	Bowen	816	Cassville	417	Courtney	816	Durham	314
Ballwin	314	Bowling Green	314	Castlewood	314	Cowgill	816	Dutchtown	314
Baring	816	Boynton	816	Catawissa	314	Craig	816	Dutzow	314
Barnard	816	Bradleyville	417	Catron	314	Crane	417		
Barnett	314	Braggadocio	314	Caulfield	417	Creighton	816		
Barnhart	314	Bragg City	314	Cedar City	314	Crescent	314	Eagle Rock	417
Bates City	816	Brandsville	417	Cedar Creek	417	Crestwood	314	Eagleville	816
Baxter Point	417	Branson	417	Cedar Gap	417	Creve Coeur	314	East Arcadia	314
Bay	314	Brashear	816	Cedar Hill	314	Crocker	314	East Atchison	816
Beach	417	Braymer	816	Cedar Springs	417	Cross Timbers	417	East Fort Scott	417
Beaman	816	Brazeau	314	Centaur	314	Crosstown	314	East Galena	417
Bean Lake	816	Brazito	314	Center	314	Crowder	314	East Garland	417

MISSOURI
East Independence—Lamar

Place Name	Area Code	Place Name	Area Code	Place Name	Area Code	Place Name	Area Code	Place Name	Area Code
East Independence	816	Flat River	314	Gobler	314	Hermann	314	Jamestown	816
East Leavenworth	816	Flemington	417	Golden	417	Hermitage	417	Jane	417
East Lynne	816	Fletcher	314	Golden City	417	Hermondale	314	Japan	314
East Mulberry	417	Flinthill	314	Goodman	417	Hickman Mills	816	Jasper	417
Easton	816	Florence	816	Gordonville	314	Higbee	816	Jedburg	314
East Opolis	417	Florida	314	Gore	314	Higginsville	816	Jefferson Barracks	314
East Pittsburg	417	Florissant	314	Gorin	816	High Gate	314	Jefferson City	314
East Pleasanton	816	Foley	314	Goss	816	High Hill	314	Jenkins	417
East Prairie	314	Folk	314	Gower	816	Highlandville	417	Jennings	314
Edgar Springs	314	Forbes	816	Graham	816	High Point	816	Jerico Springs	417
Edgerton	816	Ford City	816	Grain Valley	816	High Ridge	314	Jerome	314
Edgewood	314	Fordland	417	Granby	417	Hillsboro	314	Johnson City	816
Edina	816	Forest City	816	Grandin	314	Hillsdale	314	Jonesburg	314
Edwards	816	Forest Green	816	Grand Pass	816	Hinch	314	Joplin	417
Eldon	314	Foristell	314	Grandview	816	Hoberg	417	
El Dorado Springs	417	Fornfelt	314	Granger	816	Hodge	816	
Elijah	417	Forsyth	417	Graniteville	314	Holcomb	314	Kahoka	816
Elk Creek	417	Fort Crowder	417	Grant City	816	Holden	816	Kaiser	314
Elkland	417	Fortescue	816	Granville	816	Holland	314	Kansas City	816
Ellington	314	Fort Leonard Wood	314	Gravois Mills	314	Holliday	816	Kearney	816
Ellisville	314	Fortuna	816	Grayridge	314	Hollister	417	Kelso	314
Ellsinore	314	Foster	816	Grayson	816	Hollywood	314	Kennett	314
Elm	816	Frankclay	314	Gray Summit	314	Holmes Park	816	Kenoma	417
Elmer	816	Frankenstein	314	Greenbrier	314	Holstein	314	Kewanee	314
Elmira	816	Frankford	314	Green Castle	816	Holt	816	Keyes Summit	314
Elmo	816	Franklin	314	Green City	816	Holts Summit	314	Keysville	314
Elsberry	314	Fredericktown	314	Greenfield	417	Hooker	314	Keytesville	816
Elsey	417	Freeburg	314	Green Ridge	816	Hope	314	Kidder	816
Elston	314	Freedom	314	Greensburg	816	Hopkins	816	Kimberling City	417
Elvins	314	Freeman	816	Greentop	816	Hornersville	314	Kimmswick	314
Elwood	417	Freistatt	417	Greenville	314	Horton	417	Kinder	314
Emden	314	Fremont	314	Greenwood	816	House Springs	314	Kinderpost	314
Eminence	314	Friedheim	314	Grover	314	Houston	417	King City	816
Emma	816	Frisbee	314	Grovespring	417	Houstonia	816	Kingdom City	314
Enon	314	Fristoe	417	Grubville	314	Hughesville	816	Kings Lake	314
Eolia	314	Frohna	314	Guilford	816	Humansville	417	Kingston	816
Essex	314	Fruitland (Cape		Gunn City	816	Hume	816	Kingsville	816
Esther	314	Girardeau Co.)	314	Guthrie	314	Humphreys	816	Kinloch	314
Ethel	816	Fruitland				Hunnewell	314	Kinsey	314
Ethlyn	314	(Greene Co.)	417	Hale	816	Hunter	314	Kirbyville	417
Etterville	314	Fulton	314	Half Way	417	Huntleigh	314	Kirksville	816
Eudora	417			Halls	816	Huntsdale	314	Kirkwood	314
Eugene	314			Hallsville	314	Huntsville	816	Kissee Mills	417
Eureka	314	Gainesville	417	Halltown	417	Hurdland	816	Knob Lick	314
Eve	417	Galena	417	Hamilton	816	Hurley	417	Knob Noster	816
Everton	417	Galesburg	417	Hannibal	314	Hutton Valley	417	Knox City	816
Ewing	314	Gallatin	816	Hardin	816	Huzzah	314	Knoxville	816
Excello	816	Galt	816	Harris	816			Koch	314
Excelsior Springs	816	Garden City	816	Harrisburg	314			Koeltztown	314
Exeter	417	Garrison	417	Harrisonville	816	Iantha	417	Koshkonong	417
		Garwood	314	Hartford	816	Iatan	816	Krakow	314
		Gasconade	314	Hartsburg	314	Iberia	314	
Fagus	314	Gashland	816	Hartshorn	417	Iconium	417	
Fairdealing	314	Gaynor	816	Hartville	417	Idalia	314	Labadie	314
Fairfax	816	Gazette	314	Hartwell	816	Ilasco	314	La Belle	816
Fairfield	816	Gentry	816	Harvester	314	Ilmo	314	Lackland	314
Fair Grove	417	Gentryville	816	Harviell	314	Imperial	314	Laclede	816
Fair Play	417	Gerald	314	Harwood	417	Independence	816	Laddonia	314
Fairport	816	Gerster	417	Haseville	816	Indian Grove	816	La Due (Henry Co.)	816
Fairview	417	Gibbs	816	Hatfield	816	Indian Point	417	Ladue (St. Louis Co.)	314
Fanning	314	Gideon	314	Hatton	314	Ionia	314	La Grange	314
Farber	314	Gifford	816	Hawk Point	314	Irondale	314	Lake City	816
Farley	816	Gilliam	816	Haytl	314	Iron Mountain	314	Lake City Arsenal	816
Farmington	314	Gilman City	816	Hazelwood	314	Ironton	314	Lake Lotawana	816
Farrar	314	Gilmore	314	Hazlegreen	314	Irwin	417	Lakenan	314
Faucett	816	Ginger Blue	417	Helena	816			Lake Ozark	314
Fayette	816	Gladstone	816	Helwig	816			Lake St. Louis	314
Fenton	314	Glasgow	816	Hematite	314	Jacket	417	Lakeside	314
Ferguson	314	Glenallen	314	Hemple	816	Jackson	314	Lake Sherwood	314
Ferrelview	816	Glencoe	314	Hendrickson	314	Jacksonville	816	Lake Tapawingo	816
Festus	314	Glendale	314	Henley	314	Jadwin	314	Lake Tarsney	816
Filley	417	Glensted	314	Henrietta	816	Jameson	816	Lakeview Heights	816
Fillmore	816	Glenwood	816	Herculaneum	314	Jamesport	816	Lake Waukomis	816
Fisk	314	Glover	314			James River	417	Lamar	417

Place Name	Area Code	Place Name	Area Code	Place Name	Area Code	Place Name	Area Code	Place Name	Area Code
Lambert Airport	314	Malta Bend	816	Montauk	314	Northview	417	Pierce City	417
La Mine	816	Manchester	314	Montauk Park	314	Norwood	417	Pilot Grove	816
La Monte	816	Manes	417	Montevallo	417	Novelty	816	Pilot Knob	314
Lampe	417	Mano	417	Montgomery City	314	Novinger	816	Pine Lawn	314
Lanagan	417	Mansfield	417	Monticello	314			Pineville	417
Lancaster	816	Mapaville	314	Montier	314			Pittsburg	417
Langdon	816	Maplegrove	417	Montreal	314	Oak Grove	816	Pittsville	816
La Plata	816	Maplewood	314	Montrose	816	Oak Ridge	314	Plato	417
Laredo	816	Marble Hill	314	Montserrat	816	Oakville	314	Platte City	816
Latham	816	Marceline	816	Mooresville	816	Oakwood	314	Platte Woods	816
Lathrop	816	Marionville	417	Morehouse	314	Oates	314	Plattsburg	816
Latour	816	Marquand	314	Morley	314	Odessa	816	Pleasant Green	816
Lawson	816	Marshall	816	Morrellton	314	O'Fallon	314	Pleasant Hill	816
Leadington	314	Marshall Junction	816	Morrison	314	Ohio	816	Pleasant Hope	417
Leadwood	314	Marshfield	417	Morrisville	417	Old Appleton	314	Plevna	816
Leasburg	314	Marston	314	Morse Mill	314	Oldfield	417	Pocahontas	314
Leavenworth	816	Marthasville	314	Mosby	816	Old Mines	314	Point Lookout	417
Lebanon	417	Martin City	816	Moscow Mills	314	Old Monroe	314	Point Pleasant	314
Leeper	314	Martinsburg	314	Moselle	314	Olean	314	Polk	417
Lees Summit	816	Martinstown	816	Mound City	816	Olive	417	Pollock	816
Leeton	816	Martinsville	816	Moundville	417	Olney	314	Polo	816
Leewood	816	Maryland Heights	314	Mountain Grove	417	Omaha	816	Pomona	417
Lemay	314	Marys Home	314	Mountain View	417	Oran	314	Ponce de Leon	417
Lemons	816	Maryville	816	Mount Leonard	816	Orchardfarm	314	Pond	314
Lenox	314	Matson	314	Mount Moriah	816	Oregon	816	Ponder	314
Leonard	816	Matthews	314	Mount Sterling	314	Oronogo	417	Poplar Bluff	314
Leopold	314	Maxville	314	Mount Vernon	417	Orrick	816	Portage Des Sioux	314
Leora	314	Maysville	816	Myrick	816	Orrsburg	816	Portageville	314
Leslie	314	Mayview	816	Myrtle	417	Osage Beach	314	Portland	314
Lesterville	314	Maywood	314			Osage City	314	Postoak	816
Levasy	816	McBaine	314			Osborn	816	Potosi	314
Lewistown	314	McCredie	314	Napoleon	816	Osceola	417	Powell	417
Lexington	816	McDowell	417	Nashua	816	Osgood	816	Powersite	417
Liberal	417	McFall	816	Nashville	417	Oskaloosa	417	Powersville	816
Liberty	816	McGirk	314	Naylor	314	Otterville	816	Prairie Hill	816
Licking	314	McKittrick	314	Nebo	417	Otto	314	Prairie Home	816
Liege	314	Meadville	816	Neck City	417	Overland	314	Preston	417
Liguori	314	Mehlville	314	Neelyville	314	Owensville	314	Princeton	816
Lilbourn	314	Melbourne	816	Neeper	314	Oxly	314	Protem	417
Lincoln	816	Memphis	816	Nelson	816	Ozark	417	Purcell	417
Linden (Christian Co.)	417	Mendon	816	Neongwah	314	Ozark Beach	417	Purdin	816
Linden (Clay Co.)	816	Mendota	816	Neosho	417	Ozark Dam	417	Purdy	417
Linn	314	Menfro	314	Netherlands	314			Purvis	314
Linn Creek	314	Meramec State		Nevada	417			Puxico	314
Linneus	816	Park	314	Newark	816	Pacific	314		
Lithium	314	Mercer	816	New Bloomfield	314	Palmyra	314		
Livonia	816	Merwin	816	New Boston	816	Palopinto	816	Queen City	816
Lock Springs	816	Meta	314	Newburg	314	Papinsville	417	Quincy	417
Lockwood	417	Metz	417	New Cambria	816	Paris	816	Quitman	816
Logan	417	Mexico	314	New Florence	314	Parkville	816	Qulin	314
Lohman	314	Miami	816	New Franklin	816	Parma	314		
Lone Elm	816	Middle Brook	314	New Hamburg	314	Parnell	816		
Lonejack	816	Middletown	314	New Hampton	816	Pascola	314	Racine	417
Lonestar	816	Mike	816	New Hartford	314	Passaic	816	Ravanna	816
Long Lane	417	Milan	816	New Haven	314	Patterson	314	Ravenwood	816
Longtown	314	Milford	417	New London	314	Patton	314	Raymondville	417
Loose Creek	314	Miller	417	New Madrid	314	Pattonsburg	816	Raymore	816
Louisburg	417	Millersburg	314	New Market	816	Pattonville	314	Raytown	816
Louisiana	314	Mill Grove	816	New Melle	314	Paynesville	314	Rayville	816
Lowry City	417	Mill Spring	314	New Offenburg	314	Peace Valley	417	Rea	816
Lucerne	816	Milo	417	New Point	816	Peach Orchard	314	Readsville	314
Ludlow	816	Mindenmines	417	Newtonia	417	Pea Ridge	314	Red Bird	314
Lupus	816	Mine La Motte	314	Newtown	816	Peculiar	816	Redford	314
Luray	816	Mineola	314	New Truxton	314	Perrin	417	Reeds	417
Lutesville	314	Mineral Point	314	New Wells	314	Perry	314	Reeds Spring	417
Lynchburg	417	Mingo	314	Niangua	417	Perryville	314	Reform	314
Lyon	314	Mirabile	816	Nixa	417	Pershing	314	Regal	816
		Missouri City	816	Nodaway	816	Pevely	314	Reger	816
		Moberly	816	Noel	417	Phelps	417	Renick	816
Macks Creek	314	Modena	816	Norborne	816	Phelps City	816	Rensselaer	314
Macon	816	Mokane	314	Normandy	314	Philadelphia	314	Republic	417
Madison	816	Molino	314	North Blytheville	314	Phillipsburg	417	Revere	816
Maitland	816	Monett	417	North Kansas City	816	Pickering	816	Reynolds	314
Malden	314	Monroe City	314	Northmoor	816	Piedmont	314	Rhineland	314

Place Name	Area Code	Place Name	Area Code	Place Name	Area Code	Place Name	Area Code	Place Name	Area Code
Richards	417	Salem	314	Spring City	417	Tracy	816	Wayne	417
Richards-Gebaur Air		Salisbury	816	Springfield	417	Treloar	314	Waynesville	314
Force Base	816	San Antonio	816	Spruce	816	Trenton	816	Weatherby	816
Rich Fountain	314	Sandyhook	816	Squires	417	Trimble	816	Weaubleau	417
Rich Hill	417	Santa Fe	314	Stanberry	816	Triplett	816	Webb City	417
Richland	314	Santa Rosa	816	Stanton	314	Troy	314	Webster Groves	314
Richmond	816	Sappington	314	Stark City	417	Truesdale	314	Weingarten	314
Richmond Heights	314	Sarcoxie	417	Steedman	314	Truxton	314	Weldon Spring	314
Richwoods	314	Savannah	816	Steele	314	Tunas	417	Wellington	816
Ridgedale	417	Saverton	314	Steelville	314	Turney	816	Wellston	314
Ridgeway	816	Schell City	417	Steffenville	816	Tuscumbia	314	Wellsville	314
Risco	314	Scott City	314	Stella	417			Wentworth	417
Ritchey	417	Sedalia	816	Stephens				Wentzville	314
Rivermines	314	Sedalia Air Force		(Callaway Co.)	314	Ulman	314	Wesco	314
Riverside	816	Base	816	Stet	816	Union	314	Westalton	314
Riverview	314	Sedgewickville	314	Stewartsville	816	Union Star	816	Westboro	816
Rives	314	Seligman	417	Stockton	417	Uniontown	314	West Line	816
Roach	314	Senath	314	Stolpe	314	Unionville	816	Weston	816
Roads	816	Seneca	417	Stony Hill	314	University City	314	Westphalia	314
Roanoke	816	Seventy-Six	314	Stotesbury	417	Urbana	417	West Plains	417
Roaring River		Seymour	417	Stotts City	417	Urich	816	West Quincy	314
State Park	417	Shamrock	314	Stoutland	417	Utica	816	Wheatland	417
Robertson	314	Shawnee Mound	816	Stoutsville	314			Wheaton	417
Robertsville	314	Shawneetown	314	Stover	314			Wheeling	816
Robins	816	Shelbina	314	Strafford	417	Valles Mines	314	Whiteman Air Force
Roby	417	Shelby	816	Strasburg	816	Valley Park	314	Base	816
Rocheport	314	Shelbyville	314	Sturdivant	314	Van Buren	314	Whiteoak	314
Rockaway Beach	417	Sheldon	417	Sturgeon	314	Vandalia	314	Whiteside	314
Rockbridge	417	Shell Knob	417	Success	417	Vanduser	314	Whitesville	816
Rock Hill	314	Sheridan	816	Sugar Creek	816	Vanzant	417	Whitewater	314
Rock Port	816	Sherman	314	Sugar Lake	816	Verona	417	Wilcox	816
Rockville	816	Sherrill	314	Sullivan	314	Versailles	314	Wilhelmina	314
Rocky Comfort	417	Shirley	314	Sulphur Springs	314	Vibbard	816	Willard	417
Rocky Mount	314	Sibley	816	Summerfield	314	Viburnum	314	Willhoit	417
Rogersville	417	Sikeston	314	Summersville	417	Vichy	314	Williamsburg	314
Rolla	314	Silex	314	Sumner	816	Victoria	314	Williamstown	314
Romance	417	Siloam Springs	417	Sunnen Lake	314	Vienna	314	Williamsville	314
Rombauer	314	Silva	314	Sunrise Beach	314	Villa Ridge	314	Willow Springs	417
Rosati	314	Silver Dollar City	417	Swedeborg	314	Vineland	314	Windsor	816
Rosebud	314	Simmons	417	Sweet Springs	816	Virginia	816	Windyville	417
Roselle	314	Skidmore	816	Swiss	314	Vista	417	Winfield	314
Rosendale	816	Slater	816	Syracuse	816	Vulcan	314	Winigan	816
Rothville	816	Sleeper	417					Winona	314
Round Spring	314	Sligo	314					Winston	816
Rush Hill	314	Smithton	816	Taberville	816	Waco	417	Winthrop	816
Rushville	816	Smithville	816	Tallapoosa	314	Wakenda	816	Wisdom	816
Russellville	314	South Athelstan	816	Taneycomo Park	417	Waldron	816	Wishart	417
Rutledge	816	South Braddyville	816	Taneyville	417	Walker	417	Withers Mill	314
		South Davis City	816	Taos	314	Wallace	816	Wittenberg	314
		South Gifford	816	Tarkio	816	Walnut Grove	417	Woodlandville	314
Safe	314	South Greenfield	417	Taylor	314	Walnut Shade	417	Wooldridge	816
St. Albans	314	South Hamburg	816	Tebbetts	314	Wappapello	314	Worland	816
St. Ann	314	South Kansas City	816	Tecumseh	417	Wappapello Park	314	Worth	816
St. Catherine	816	South Lineville	816	Thayer	417	Wardell	314	Worthington	816
St. Charles	314	South Mount Sterling	816	Theodosia	417	Ware	314	Wright City	314
St. Clair	314	South Nixa	417	Thomas Hill	816	Warren	314	Wyaconda	816
St. Elizabeth	314	South Redding	816	Thomasville	417	Warrensburg	816	Wyatt	314
Ste. Genevieve	314	South St. Joseph	816	Thompson	314	Warrenton	314		
St. James	314	South Seymour	816	Tiff	314	Warsaw	816		
St. Joseph	816	South West City	417	Tiffany Springs	816	Washburn	417	Yarrow	816
St. Louis	314	Spalding	314	Tiff City	417	Washington	314	Yukon	417
St. Marys	314	Spanish Lake	314	Tiffin	417	Washington Center	816		
St. Patrick	816	Sparta	417	Timber	314	Wasola	417		
St. Paul	314	Speed	816	Tina	816	Waterloo	816		
St. Peters	314	Spickard	816	Tindall	816	Watson	816	Zalma	314
St. Robert	314	Spokane	417	Tipton	816	Waverly	816	Zebra	314
St. Thomas	314	Spring Bluff	314	Tobin Creek	816	Wayland	816	Zion	314

ALL POINTS—AREA CODE 406

Place Name	Area Code	Place Name	Area Code	Place Name	Area Code	Place Name	Area Code	Place Name	Area Code
Abbott	308	Boelus	308	Creston	402	Fairmont	402	Herman	402
Abie	402	Boone	402	Crete	402	Falls City	402	Hershey	308
Adams	402	Bostwick	402	Crofton	402	Farnam	308	Hickman	402
Agnew	402	Boys Town	402	Crookston	402	Farwell	308	Hildreth	308
Ainsworth	402	Bradshaw	402	Culbertson	308	Filley	402	Hoag	402
Albion	402	Brady	308	Curtis	308	Finchville	308	Holbrook	308
Alda	308	Brainard	402	Cushing	308	Firth	402	Holdrege	308
Alexandria	402	Brandon	308			Fontanelle	402	Holland	402
Allen	402	Brewster	308			Fordyce	402	Holmesville	402
Alliance	308	Bridgeport	308	Dakota City	402	Fort Calhoun	402	Holstein	402
Alma	308	Bristow	402	Dalton	308	Fort Crook	402	Homer	402
Almeria	308	Broadwater	308	Danbury	308	Fort Robinson	308	Hooper	402
Alvo	402	Brock	402	Dannebrog	308	Foster	402	Hordville	402
Ames	402	Brocksburg	402	Darr	308	Franklin	308	Hoskins	402
Amherst	308	Broken Bow	308	Davenport	402	Fremont	402	Houston	402
Andrews	308	Brownlee	308	Davey	402	Friend	402	Howe	402
Angora	308	Brownville	402	David City	402	Fullerton	308	Howells	402
Angus	402	Brule	308	Dawson	402	Funk	308	Hubbard	402
Anoka	402	Bruning	402	Daykin	402			Hubbell	402
Anselmo	308	Bruno	402	Decatur	402			Humboldt	402
Ansley	308	Brunswick	402	Denman	308	Garland	402	Humphrey	402
Antioch	308	Burchard	402	Denton	402	Garrison	402	Huntley	308
Arapahoe	308	Burr	402	Deshler	402	Gates	308	Huskerville	402
Arcadia	308	Burton	402	De Soto	402	Geneva	402	Hyannis	308
Archer	308	Burwell	308	De Soto Bend	402	Genoa	402		
Arlington	402	Bushnell	308	Deweese	402	Gering	308		
Arnold	308	Butte	402	De Witt	402	Gibbon	308	Imperial	308
Arnold Heights	402	Byron	402	Dickens	308	Gilead	402	Inavale	402
Arthur	308			Diller	402	Giltner	402	Indianola	308
Ashby	308			Dix	308	Gladstone	402	Ingleside	402
Ashland	402	Cairo	308	Dixon	402	Glen	308	Inland	402
Ashton	308	Calhoun	402	Dodge	402	Glenvil	402	Inman	402
Atkinson	402	Callaway	308	Doniphan	402	Goehner	402	Irvington	402
Atlanta	308	Cambridge	308	Dorchester	402	Goodwin	402	Ithaca	402
Auburn	402	Campbell	402	Douglas	402	Gordon	308		
Aurora	402	Carleton	402	DuBois	402	Gothenburg	308		
Avoca	402	Carroll	402	Dunbar	402	Grafton	402	Jackson	402
Axtell	308	Cedar Bluffs	402	Duncan	402	Grainton	308	Jansen	402
Ayr	402	Cedar Creek	402	Dunning	308	Grand Island	308	Johnson	402
		Cedar Rapids	308	Dwight	402	Grant	308	Johnstown	402
		Center	402			Greeley	308	Joy	402
Bancroft	402	Central City	308			Greenwood	402	Julian	402
Barada	402	Ceresco	402	Eagle	402	Gresham	402	Juniata	402
Barneston	402	Chadron	308	East Albin	308	Gretna	402		
Bartlett	308	Chalco	402	East La Grange	308	Gross	402		
Bartley	308	Chambers	402	Eddyville	308	Guide Rock	402	Kearney	308
Bassett	402	Champion	308	Edgar	402	Gurley	308	Keene	308
Battle Creek	402	Chapman	402	Edison	308			Kenesaw	402
Bayard	308	Chappell	308	Elba	308			Kennard	402
Beatrice	402	Chester	402	Elgin	402	Hadar	402	Keystone	308
Beaver City	308	Clarks	308	Eli	308	Haig	308	Kilgore	402
Beaver Crossing	402	Clarkson	402	Elk City	402	Haigler	308	Kimball	308
Bee	402	Clatonia	402	Elk Creek	402	Hallam	402	Kimball City	308
Beemer	402	Clay Center	402	Elkhorn	402	Halsey	308	Koshopah	402
Belden	402	Clearwater	402	Ellis	402	Hamlet	308	Kramer	402
Belgrade	308	Clinton	308	Ellsworth	308	Hampton	402		
Bellevue	402	Closter	402	Elm Creek	308	Hansen	402		
Bellwood	402	Cody	308	Elmwood	402	Harbine	402	Lakeside	308
Belvidere	402	Coleridge	402	Elsie	308	Hardy	402	Lamar	308
Benedict	402	College View	402	Elsmere	308	Harrisburg	308	Lanham	402
Benkelman	308	Colon	402	Elwood	308	Harrison	308	La Platte	402
Bennet	402	Columbus	402	Elyria	308	Hartington	402	Laurel	402
Bennington	402	Comstock	308	Emerson	402	Harvard	402	La Vista	402
Bertrand	308	Concord	402	Emmet	402	Hastings	402	Lawrence	402
Berwyn	308	Cook	402	Enders	308	Havelock	402	Lebanon	308
Bethany	402	Cordova	402	Endicott	402	Havens	308	Leigh	402
Big Springs	308	Cornlea	402	Enola	402	Hayes Center	308	Lemoyne	308
Bingham	308	Cortland	402	Ericson	308	Hay Springs	308	Leshara	402
Bladen	402	Cotesfield	308	Eustis	308	Hazard	308	Lewellen	308
Blair	402	Cowles	402	Ewing	402	Heartwell	308	Lewiston	402
Bloomfield	402	Cozad	308	Exeter	402	Hebron	402	Lexington	308
Bloomington	308	Crab Orchard	402			Hemingford	308	Liberty	402
Blue Hill	402	Craig	402			Henderson	402	Lincoln	402
Blue Springs	402	Crawford	308	Fairbury	402	Hendley	308	Lincoln Air Park	
Bluevale	402	Creighton	402	Fairfield	402	Henry	308	West	402

Place Name	Area Code	Place Name	Area Code	Place Name	Area Code	Place Name	Area Code	Place Name	Area Code
Lindsay	402	Nebraska City	402	Phillips	402	Shelton	308	Trumbull	402
Linwood-Morse Bluff	402	Nehawka	402	Pickrell	402	Shestak	402	Tryon	308
Lisco	308	Neligh	402	Pierce	402	Shickley	402		
Litchfield	308	Nelson	402	Pilger	402	Sholes	402		
Lodgepole	308	Nemaha	402	Plainview	402	Shubert	402	Uehling	402
Loma	402	Nenzel	402	Platte Center	402	Sidney	308	Ulysses	402
Long Pine	402	Newark	308	Plattsmouth	402	Silver Creek	308	Unadilla	402
Loomis	308	Newcastle	402	Pleasant Dale	402	Smithfield	308	Union	402
Loretto	402	Newman Grove	402	Pleasanton	308	Snyder	402	Upland	308
Lorton	402	Newport	402	Plymouth	402	Sodtown	308	Utica	402
Louisville	402	Nickerson	402	Polk	402	South Ardmore	308		
Loup City	308	Niobrara	402	Ponca	402	South Bend	402		
Lushton	402	Nora	402	Poole	308	South Bonesteel	402	Valentine	402
Lyman	308	Norfolk	402	Potter	308	South Burke	402	Valley	402
Lynch	402	Norman	308	Powell	402	South Gregory	402	Valparaiso	402
Lyons	402	North Bend	402	Prague	402	South Oelrichs	308	Venango	308
		North Herndon	308	Preston	402	South Omaha	402	Verdel	402
		North Hollenberg	308	Primrose	308	South Sioux City	402	Verdigre	402
		North Julesburg	308	Princeton	402	South Yankton	402	Verdon	402
Macon	308	North Long Island	308	Prosser	402	Spalding	308	Verona	402
Macy	402	North Loup	308	Purdum	308	Spencer	402	Virginia	402
Madison	402	North Mahaska	402			Sprague	402		
Madrid	308	North Peetz	308			Springfield	402		
Magnet	402	North Platte	308			Springview	402	Wabash	402
Malcolm	402	Northport	308	Raeville	402	Stamford	308	Waco	402
Malmo	402	North Sabetha	402	Ragan	308	Stanton	402	Wahoo	402
Manley	402	North Summerfield	402	Ralston	402	Staplehurst	402	Wakefield	402
Marion	308	North Woodruff	308	Randolph	402	Stapleton	308	Wallace	308
Marquette	402			Ravenna	308	Star	402	Walnut	402
Marsland	308			Raymond	402	Steele City	402	Walthill	402
Martell	402			Redbird	402	Steinauer	402	Walton	402
Martinsburg	402	Oak	402	Red Cloud	402	Stella	402	Wann	402
Mascot	308	Oakdale	402	Redington	308	Sterling	402	Washington	402
Maskell	402	Oakland	402	Republican City	308	Stockham	402	Waterbury	402
Mason City	308	Obert	402	Reynolds	402	Stockville	308	Waterloo	402
Max	308	Oconto	308	Richfield	402	Strang	402	Wauneta	308
Maxwell	308	Octavia	402	Ringgold	308	Strategic Air Command		Wausa	402
Maywood	308	Odell	402	Rising City	402	Offutt Air Force		Waverly	402
McCook	308	Odessa	308	Riverdale	308	Base	402	Wayne	402
McCool Junction	402	Offutt Air Force Base	402	Riverton	402	Stratton	308	Wayside	308
McGrew	308	Ogallala	308	Roca	402	Stromsburg	402	Webster	402
McLean	402	Ohiowa	402	Rockford	402	Stuart	402	Weeping Water	402
Mead	402	Omaha	402	Rockville	308	Sumner	308	Weissert	308
Meadow	402	O'Neill	402	Rosalie	402	Sunol	308	Wellfleet	308
Meadow Grove	402	Ong	402	Roscoe	308	Superior	402	Western	402
Melbeta	308	Orchard	402	Roseland	402	Surprise	402	Westerville	308
Memphis	402	Ord	308	Rosemont	402	Sutherland	308	West Hamburg	402
Merna	308	Ordville	308	Royal	402	Sutton	402	Weston	402
Merriman	308	Orleans	308	Ruby	402	Swanton	402	West Point	402
Milburn	308	Osceola	402	Rulo	402	Swedeburg	402	Whiteclay	308
Milford	402	Oshkosh	308	Rushville	308	Swedehome	402	Whitman	308
Millard	402	Osmond	402	Ruskin	402	Sweetwater	308	Whitney	308
Miller	308	Otoe	402			Syracuse	402	Wilber	402
Milligan	402	Overton	308					Wilcox	308
Mills	402	Ovina	308					Willis	402
Minatare	308	Oxford	308	St. Bernard	402			Willow Island	308
Minden	308			St. Edward	402	Table Rock	402	Wilsonville	308
Mirage Flats	308			St. Helena	402	Talmage	402	Winnebago	402
Mitchell	308			St. Libory	308	Tamora	402	Winnetoon	402
Monowi	402	Page	402	St. Mary	402	Tarnov	402	Winside	402
Monroe	402	Palisade	308	St. Paul	308	Taylor	308	Winslow	402
Moorefield	308	Palmer	308	Salem	402	Tecumseh	402	Wisner	402
Morrill	308	Palmyra	402	Santee	402	Tekamah	402	Wolbach	308
Motala	308	Panama	402	Sarben	308	Thayer	402	Wood Lake	402
Mullen	308	Papillion	402	Sargent	308	Thedford	308	Wood River	308
Murdock	402	Parks	308	Schuyler	402	Thompson	402	Wymore	402
Murray	402	Paul	402	Scotia	308	Thurston	402	Wynot-Fordyce-	
		Pauline	402	Scottsbluff	308	Tilden	402	St. Helena	308
		Pawnee City	402	Scribner	402	Tobias	402	Wyoming	402
		Paxton	308	Sedan	402	Touhy	402		
Nacora	402	Pender	402	Seneca	308	Trenton	308	York	402
Naper	402	Peru	402	Seward	402	Tri-City	402	Yutan	402
Naponee	308	Petersburg	402	Shelby	402				

ALL POINTS—AREA CODE 702

ALL POINTS—AREA CODE 603

Place Name	Area Code	Place Name	Area Code	Place Name	Area Code	Place Name	Area Code	Place Name	Area Code
Ablett Village	609	Basking Ridge	201	Brass Castle	201	Cedarwood Park	201	Cranberry Lake	201
Absecon	609	Batsto	609	Breton Woods	201	Center Grove	201	Cranbury	609
Absecon Inlet Coast		Bay Head	201	Brick Town	201	Centerton		Cranford	201
Guard Sta. No. 124	609	Bay Head Coast Guard		Bridgeboro	609	(Burlington Co.)	609	Crawfords Corner	201
Adamston	201	Sta. No. 106	201	Bridgepoint	201	Centerton		Creamridge	609
Adelphia	201	Bayonne	201	Bridgeport	609	(Salem Co.)	609	Cresskill	201
Albion	609	Bayonne U. S. Naval		Bridgeton	609	Centerville		Cross Keys	609
Albion Place	609	Supply Depot	201	Bridgeville	201	(Hunterdon Co.)	201	Crosswicks	609
Aldine	609	Bay Point	609	Bridgewater		Centerville		Croton	201
Allaire	201	Bayside	609	Township	201	(Monmouth Co.)	201	Culvers Lake	201
Allamuchy	201	Bayville	201	Brielle	201	Central Park	609	Cupsaw Lake	201
Allendale	201	Bayway	201	Brigantine	609	Centre Grove			
Allenhurst	201	Beach Glen	201	Brigantine Coast Guard		(Cumberland Co.)	609		
Allentown	609	Beach Haven	609	Sta. No. 121	609	Chadwick	201		
Allenwood	201	Beach Haven Crest	609	Broadway	201	Changewater	201	Daretown	609
Allerton	201	Beach Haven Terrace	609	Brooklawn	609	Chapel Hill	201	Darlington	201
Alliance	609	Beachwood	201	Brookside	201	Chapel Hill Coast		Dayton	201
Alloway	609	Bear Pond	201	Brotmanville	609	Guard Light Sta.	201	Deal	201
Allwood	201	Beatyestown	201	Browns Mills	609	Chatham	201	Deal Coast Guard	
Almonesson	609	Beaver Brook	609	Browntown	201	Chatsworth	609	Sta. No. 102	201
Alpha	201	Beaver Dam	609	Budd Lake	201	Cheesequake	201	Deans	201
Alphano	201	Beaver Lake	201	Buddtown	609	Cherry Hill	609	Deepwater	609
Alpine	201	Bedminster	201	Buena	609	Cherryville	201	Deerfield	609
Amsterdam	201	Beesley's Point	609	Bunvale	201	Chesilhurst	609	Delair	609
Ancora	609	Belcoville	609	Burleigh	609	Chester	201	Delanco	609
Anderson	201	Belford	201	Burlington	609	Chesterfield	609	Delawanna	201
Andover	201	Belle Mead	201	Burnt Mills	201	Chestnut Point	201	Delaware	201
Annandale	201	Belle Plain	609	Bushkill	201	Chews Landing	609	Delaware Sub Post	
Anthony	201	Belleville	201	Butler	201	Churchtown	609	Raritan Arsenal	
Applegarth	609	Bellmawr		Buttzville	201	Cinnaminson	609	U. S. Army	609
Aqueduct	609	(Camden Co.)	609	Byram	609	Clark	201	Delaware Water Gap	201
Arbor	201	Bell's Lake	609	Byram Cove	201	Clarksboro	609	Del Haven	609
Arcola	201	Belmar		Byram Township	201	Clarksburg	609	Delmont	609
Ardena	201	(Monmouth Co.)	201			Clark's Pond	609	Delran	609
Arlington	201	Belvidere	201			Clarksville	609	Demarest	201
Asbury	201	Bergenfield	201			Clayton	609	Dennisville	609
Asbury Park	201	Berkeley Heights	201	Caldwell	201	Clementon	609	Denville	201
Ashland	609	Berkshire Valley	201	Califon	201	Clermont		Deptford	609
Atco	609	Berlin	609	Camden	609	(Burlington Co.)	609	Devonshire	609
Athenia	201	Bernardsville	201	Campbells Junction	201	Clermont		Dias Creek	609
Atlantic City	609	Bertrand Island	201	Camp Charles Wood	201	(Cape May Co.)	609	Dilts Corner	609
Atlantic City Coast		Bevans	201	Camp Coles	201	Cliffside	201	Direction Finder	
Guard Sta. No. 123	609	Beverly	609	Camp Edison	201	Cliffside Park	201	Station U. S. Coast	
Atlantic City U. S.		Birmingham	609	Camp Evans	201	Cliffwood	201	Guard	609
Naval Air Sta.	609	Bissell	201	Campgaw	201	Cliffwood Beach	201	Dividing Creek	609
Atlantic Highlands	201	Bivalve	609	Camp Kilmer	201	Cliffwood Lake	201	Dorchester	609
Atsion	609	Blackwells Mills	201	Canton	609	Clifton	201	Dorothy	609
Auburn	609	Blackwood	609	Cape Breton	201	Clinton	201	Dover	201
Audubon	609	Blackwood Terrace	609	Cape May	609	Closter	201	Downer	609
Augusta	201	Blairstown	201	Cape May Court		Clover Hill	201	Drakestown	201
Aura	609	Blawenburg	609	House	609	Coffins Corner	201	Duke Farms	201
Avalon	609	Blenheim	609	Cape May Point	609	Cohansey	609	Dumont	201
Avalon Coast Guard		Bloomfield	201	Cape May Point Coast		Cokesbury	201	Dunbarton	609
Sta. No. 131	609	Bloomingdale	201	Guard Sta. No. 137	609	Cold Spring	609	Dunellen	201
Avenel	201	Bloomsbury	201	Cardiff	609	Collingswood	609	Dunhams Corner	201
Avon-by-the-Sea	201	Bloomsbury Heights	201	Carlstadt	201	Collingswood Park	201	Dutch Neck	609
Awosting	201	Blue Anchor	609	Carlton Hill	201	Cologne	609	Dutchtown	201
		Blue Lake	609	Carmel	609	Colonia	201		
		Bogota	201	Carneys Point	609	Colonial Gardens	201		
		Bonds Coast Guard		Carpentersville	201	Colonial Manor	609		
Bailey's Corner	201	Sta. No. 118	609	Carteret	201	Colonial Terrace	201	Earle U. S. Naval	
Baleville	201	Bonhamtown	201	Cassville	201	Colts Neck	201	Ammunition Depot	201
Baptistown	201	Boonton	201	Castle Rock Park	201	Columbia	201	East Bound Brook	201
Barber	201	Boonton Lakes	201	Cecil	609	Columbus	609	East Brunswick	201
Barbertown	201	Bordentown	609	Cedar Brook	201	Colwick	201	Easthampton	
Bargaintown	609	Bound Brook	201	Cedarcroft	201	Conovertown	609	Township	609
Barnegat	609	Bowerstown	201	Cedar Grove		Convent Station	201	East Hanover	
Barnegat Coast Guard		Bradley Beach	201	(Essex Co.)	201	Cookstown	609	Township	201
Sta. No. 113	609	Bradley Gardens	201	Cedar Grove		Corbin City	609	East Keansburg	201
Barnegat Light	609	Brady Park	201	(Mercer Co.)	609	Cornell Heights	609	East Milford	201
Barnegat Pines	609	Brainards	201	Cedar Knolls	201	Cornell Heights	609	East Millstone	201
Barnsboro	609	Branchburg	201	Cedar Lake	201	Cow Tongue Point	201	East Newark	201
Barrington	609	Branchville	201	Cedar Run	609	Coytesville	201	East Orange	201
Bartley	201	Brant Beach	609	Cedarville	609	Cozy Lake	201	East Rutherford	201
						Cragmere	201		

NEW JERSEY
East Shore Estates—Lake View

Place Name	Area Code	Place Name	Area Code	Place Name	Area Code	Place Name	Area Code	Place Name	Area Code
East Shore Estates	201	Flatbrookville	201	Great Cove	201	Hazen	201	Jacksonville	609
East Vineland	609	Flemington	201	Great Egg Coast		Hazlet	201	Jacobstown	609
East Windsor		Flemington Junction	201	Guard Sta. No. 125	609	Heislerville	609	Jamesburg	201
Township	609	Florence		Great Meadows	201	Helmetta	201	Janvier	609
Eatontown	201	(Burlington Co.)	609	Great Notch	201	Henderson Cove	201	Jefferson	609
Echo Lake	201	Florence		Green Bank	609	Herberts Corner	201	Jefferson Lake	201
Edgewater	201	(Camden Co.)	609	Green Brook	201	Herbertsville	201	Jefferson Township	201
Edgewater Park	609	Florham Park	201	Green Creek	609	Hereford Inlet Coast		Jericho	609
Edgewood	609	Folsom	609	Greendell	201	Guard Light Sta.	609	Jersey City	201
Edinburg	609	Fords	201	Greenfield		Hereford Inlet Coast		Jobstown	609
Edison	201	Forked River	609	(Cape May Co.)	609	Guard Sta. No. 133	609	Johnsonburg	201
Egg Harbor	609	Forked River Coast		Green Fields		Hewitt	201	Jones Island	609
Elberon	201	Guard Sta. No.		(Gloucester Co.)	609	Hibernia	201	Juliustown	609
Eldora	609	112	201	Green Grove	201	High Bridge	201	Jutland	201
Eldridges Hill	609	Fort Dix	609	Green Pond	201	Highland Lakes	201		
Elizabeth	201	Fort Elfsborg	609	Green Village	201	Highland Park			
Elizabethport	201	Fortescue	609	Greenwich	609	(Camden Co.)	609	Karrsville	201
Ellisburg	609	Fort Hancock	201	Greenwood Lake	201	Highland Park		Keansburg	201
Ellisdale	609	Fort Lee	201	Grenloch	609	(Middlesex Co.)	201	Kearny	201
Elmer	609	Fort Monmouth	201	Greystone Park	201	Highlands	201	Keasbey	201
Elmora	201	Foul Rift	201	Griggstown	201	Hightstown	609	Kendall Park	201
Elmwood Park	201	Franklin	201	Grovers Mill	609	Hillsdale	201	Kenilworth	201
Elsinboro	609	Franklin Boro	201	Groveville	609	Hillside	201	Kenilworth Lakes	609
Elwood	609	Franklin Lakes	201	Guttenberg	201	Hilltop	609	Kenvil	201
Emerson	201	Franklin Park	201			Hillwood Lakes	609	Keyport	201
Englewood	201	Franklin Township				Hi-Nella	609	Kings Cove	201
Englewood Cliffs	201	(Glouster Co.)	609	Hackensack	201	Hoboken	201	Kingston	609
English Creek	609	Franklin Township		Hackettstown	201	Hoffmans	201	Kingwood	201
Englishtown	201	(Somerset Co.)	201	Hacklebarney	201	Hohokus	201	Kinnelon	201
Erial	609	Franklinville	609	Haddonfield	609	Holland	201	Kirkwood	609
Erlton	609	Fredon	201	Haddon Heights	609	Holly Park	201	Klinesville	201
Erma	609	Freehold	201	Haddon Hills	609	Holmdel	201	Knowlton	201
Erskine Lakes	201	Freewood Acres	201	Haddonleigh	609	Holmeson	609	Kresson	609
Essex Fells	201	Frenchtown	201	Haddon Township	609	Homestead Park	201	Kunaths Corner	201
Estell Manor City	609	Freneau	201	Hainesburg	201	Hopatcong	201		
Estelle	609	Friesburg	609	Hainesport	201	Hopatcong Shores	201		
Etra	609	Fries Mill	609	Hainesville	201	Hope	201	Lafayette	201
Everett	201			Haledon	201	Hopelawn	201	Lake Arrowhead	201
Everittstown	201			Haleyville	609	Hopewell		Lake Cotoxen	609
Evesboro	609	Gandy's Beach	609	Halltown	201	(Cumberland Co.)	609	Lake Denmark	201
Ewan	609	Gardenville Center	609	Halsey	201	Hopewell		Lake Denmark U. S.	
Ewansville	609	Garfield	201	Halsey Island	201	(Mercer Co.)	609	Naval Ammunition	
Ewing	609	Garwood	201	Hamburg	201	Hopewell Township	609	Depot	201
Ewingville	609	Germania	609	Hamden	201	Hornerstown	609	Lake Erskine	201
		Gessler Cove	201	Hamilton Square	609	Houses	201	Lake Forest	201
		Gibbsboro	609	Hamilton Township	609	Howell	201	Lake Garrison	609
Fairfield	201	Gibbstown	609	Hammonton	609	Hudson Heights	201	Lake Gilman	609
Fair Haven	201	Gillette	201	Hampton	201	Hughesville	201	Lake Hiawatha	201
Fair Lawn	201	Gladstone	201	Hancocks Bridge	609	Huntington	201	Lake Hopatcong	201
Fairmount	201	Glassboro	609	Hanover Township	201	Huntsville	201	Lakehurst	201
Fairton	609	Glasser	201	Harbourton	609	Hurdtown	201	Lakehurst U. S. Naval	
Fairview		Glendale	609	Hardingville	609	Hurffville	609	Air Station	201
(Bergen Co.)	201	Glendola	201	Hardyston Township	201	Hutchinsons Mills	609	Lake Intervale	201
Fairview		Glendora	609	Hardystonville	201			Lake Iosco	201
(Camden Co.)	609	Glen Gardner	201	Harlingen	201			Lake Lackawanna	201
Fairview		Glen Moore	609	Harmersville	609	Imlaystown	609	Lakeland	609
(Gloucester Co.)	609	Glen Ridge	201	Harmony	201	Indian Lake	201	Lake Lenape	201
Fairview		Glen Rock	201	Harmony Station	201	Indian Mills	609	Lake Lookover	201
(Monmouth Co.)	201	Glenside	609	Harrington Park	201	Interlaken	201	Lake Mohawk	201
Fanwood	201	Glen Wild Lake	201	Harrison	201	Iona	609	Lake Nelson	201
Far Hills	201	Glenwood	201	Harrisonville		Ironia	201	Lake Owassa	201
Farmersville	201	Gloucester	609	(Gloucester Co.)	609	Irvington	201	Lake Parsippany	201
Farmingdale	201	Gloucester Township	609	Harrisonville		Iselin	201	Lake Pine	609
Farmington	609	Golf Manor	609	(Salem Co.)	609	Island Beach	201	Lake Rogerene	201
Fayson Lakes	201	Golfview Park	609	Hartford	201	Island Beach Coast		Lake Saginaw	201
Fellowship	609	Gooseneck Point	609	Harvey Cedars	609	Guard Sta. No. 110	201	Lake Shawnee	201
Ferrell	609	Gordon Lake	201	Harvey Cedars Coast		Island Heights	201	Lakeside Park	609
Fieldsboro	609	Gordons Corner	201	Guard Sta. No. 115	609			Lake Swannanoa	201
Finderne	201	Goshen	609	Hasbrouck Heights	201			Lake Tamarack	201
Finesville	201	Gouldtown	609	Haskell	201	Jackson	201	Lake Telemark	201
Fishing Creek	609	Grantwood	201	Haven Beach	609	Jacksonburg	201	Lake Valhalla	201
Flagtown	201	Grasselli	201	Haworth	201	Jacksons Mills	201	Lake View	201
Flanders	201	Grassy Sound	609	Hawthorne	201				

Place Name	Area Code
Lake Winona	201
Lakewood	201
Lambertville	609
Lambs Terrace	609
Landing	201
Landisville	609
Lanoka Harbor	609
Larison's Corner	201
Laureldale	609
Laurel Hill	201
Laurel Lake	609
Laurel Springs	609
Laurelton	201
Laurence Harbor	201
Lavallette	201
Lawnside	609
Lawrence Station	609
Lawrence Township	609
Lawrenceville	609
Layton	201
Layton's Lake	609
Lebanon	201
Lebanon Township	201
Ledgewood	201
Leeds Point	609
Leesburg	609
Legler	201
Lenola	609
Leonardo	201
Leonardville	201
Leonia	201
Liberty Corner	201
Lincoln	201
Lincoln Park	201
Lincroft	201
Linden	201
Lindenwold	609
Lindys Lake	201
Linwood	609
Lions Head Lake	201
Little Beach Coast Guard Sta. No. 120	609
Little Brook	201
Little Egg Coast Guard Sta. No. 119	609
Little Falls	201
Little Ferry	201
Little Silver	201
Little York	201
Livingston	201
Llewellyn Park	201
Loch Arbour	201
Locktown	201
Locust	201
Lodi	201
Long Beach Coast Guard Sta. No. 117	609
Long Beach Township	609
Long Branch	201
Longport	609
Long Valley	201
Longwood Lake	201
Longwood Valley	201
Lopatcong	201
Loveladies	609
Lower Alloways Creek	609
Lower Bank	609
Lower Berkshire Valley	201
Lower Valley	201
Low Moor	201
Lucaston	609
Ludlow	201

Place Name	Area Code
Lumberton	609
Lyndhurst	201
Lyons	201
Lyonsville	201
Macopin	201
Madison	201
Madison Township	201
Magnolia	609
Magnolia Heights	609
Mahwah	201
Malaga	609
Manahawkin	609
Manalapan Township	201
Manasquan	201
Manasquan Inlet Coast Guard Sta. No. 105	201
Manasquan Park	201
Manasquan Radio Compass Station U. S. Navy	201
Mannington Township	609
Mansfield Township	201
Mantoloking	201
Mantoloking Coast Guard Sta. No. 107	201
Mantua	609
Manunkachunk	201
Manville	201
Maple Shade	609
Maplewood	201
Marcella	201
Margate City	609
Marksboro	201
Marlboro	201
Marlton	609
Marmora	609
Marshall's Corner	609
Martinsville	201
Masonville	609
Matawan	201
Mauricetown	609
Mayetta	609
Mays Landing	609
Mayville	609
Maywood	201
McAfee	201
McGuire Air Force Base	609
McKee City	609
Medford	609
Medford Lakes	609
Mendham	201
Menlo Park	201
Mercerville	609
Merchantville	609
Meriden	201
Metedeconk	201
Metuchen	201
Meyersville	201
Miami Beach	609
Mickleton	609
Middlebush	201
Middlesex	201
Middletown	201
Middle Valley	201
Middleville	201
Midland Park	201
Midstreams	201
Midvale	201
Milford	201

Place Name	Area Code
Millbrook	201
Milburn	201
Millington	201
Millstone	201
Millstone Township	201
Milltown (Middlesex Co.)	201
Milltown (Morris Co.)	201
Millville	609
Milmay	609
Milton	201
Mine Brook	201
Mine Hill	201
Mine Mount	201
Minotola	609
Mizpah	609
Monmouth Beach	201
Monmouth Beach Coast Guard Sta. No. 100	201
Monmouth Hills	201
Monmouth Junction	201
Monroe	201
Monroeville	609
Montague	201
Montana	201
Montclair	201
Montgomery Corner	201
Montvale	201
Montville	201
Moonachie	201
Moorestown	609
Morgan	201
Morganville	201
Morris Plains	201
Morristown	201
Morrisville	201
Morse Lakes	201
Mountain Lake (Warren Co.)	201
Mountain Lakes (Morris Co.)	201
Mountainside	201
Mountain View	201
Mountainville	201
Mount Airy	609
Mount Arlington	201
Mount Bethel	201
Mount Ephraim	609
Mount Fern	201
Mount Freedom	201
Mount Hermon	201
Mount Holly	609
Mount Hope	201
Mount Horeb	201
Mount Horeb Park	201
Mount Joy	201
Mount Kemble Lake	201
Mount Kipp	201
Mount Laurel	609
Mount Laurel Lakes	609
Mount Olive	201
Mount Pleasant	201
Mount Rose	609
Mount Royal	609
Mount Tabor	201
Mullica Hill	609
Murray Hill	201
National Park	609
Naughright	201
Navesink	201

Place Name	Area Code
Navesink Coast Guard Light Sta.	201
Neptune	201
Neptune City	201
Neshanic	201
Neshanic Station	201
Netcong	201
Netherwood	201
Newark	201
New Bedford	201
New Brooklyn	609
New Brunswick	201
New Egypt	609
Newfield	609
Newfoundland	201
New Gretna	609
New Hampton	201
New Lisbon	609
New Market	201
New Milford	201
New Monmouth	201
Newport	609
New Providence	201
New Sharon	609
New Shrewsbury	201
Newton	201
Newtonville	609
New Vernon	201
New Village	201
Nixon	201
Nolan's Point	201
Norma	609
Normandie	201
Normandy Beach	201
Normandy Heights	201
North Arlington	201
North Beach	609
North Bergen	201
North Branch	201
North Brunswick	201
North Caldwell	201
North Cape May	609
North Church	201
Northfield	609
North Haledon	201
North Newark	201
North Paterson	201
North Plainfield	201
Northvale	201
North Wildwood	609
Northwood	201
Nortonville	609
Norwood	201
Nummytown	609
Nutley	201
Oak Hill	201
Oak Hills	201
Oakhurst	201
Oakland	201
Oaklyn	609
Oak Ridge	201
Oak Tree	201
Oak Valley	609
Oak View Park	201
Ocean City	609
Ocean City Coast Guard Sta. No. 126	609
Ocean Gate	201
Ocean Grove	201
Oceanport	201
Ocean Township	201

Place Name	Area Code
Ocean View	609
Oceanville	609
Ogdensburg	201
Old Bridge	201
Old Bridge Township	201
Old Tappan	201
Oldwick	201
Oradell	201
Orange	201
Ortley	201
Osage	609
Osbornville	201
Othello	609
Outcalt	201
Oxford	201
Packanack Lake	201
Palatine	609
Palermo	609
Palisade	201
Palisades Park	201
Palmyra	609
Panther Lake	201
Paradise Lakes	609
Paramus	201
Parker	201
Parkertown	609
Park Ridge	201
Parkside	201
Parlin	201
Parry	609
Parsippany	201
Passaic	201
Paterson	201
Pattenburg	201
Paulinskill Lake	201
Paulsboro	609
Peapack	201
Pedricktown	609
Pelican Island	201
Pemberton	609
Penbryn	609
Penn Beach	609
Pennington	609
Pennsauken	609
Penns Grove	609
Penns Neck	609
Pennsville	609
Penton	609
Penwell	201
Pequannock	201
Perkintown	609
Perrineville	201
Perth Amboy	201
Petersburg	609
Petty's Island	609
Phalanx	201
Phillipsburg	201
Picatinny	201
Picatinny U. S. Army Arsenal	201
Pierces	609
Pine Beach	201
Pine Brook (Monmouth Co.)	201
Pine Brook (Morris Co.)	201
Pinecliff Lake	201
Pine Grove	609
Pine Hill	609
Pine Lake Park	201
Pines Lake	201

NEW JERSEY
Pine Tree Point—West Allenhurst

Place Name	Area Code	Place Name	Area Code	Place Name	Area Code	Place Name	Area Code	Place Name	Area Code
Pine Tree Point	201	Ridgefield	201	Sea Isle City	609	Stanton Station	201	Union Lake	609
Pine Valley	609	Ridgefield Park	201	Sea Isle City Coast		Steelmanville	609	Uniontown	201
Pinewald	201	Ridgewood	201	Guard Sta.	609	Stelton	201	Union Valley	609
Piscataway	201	Riegel Ridge	201	Seaside Heights	201	Stephensburg	201	Union VIllage	201
Pitman	609	Riegelsville	201	Seaside Park	201	Stewartsville	201	Unionville	
Pittsgrove	609	Ringoes	201	Seaville	609	Still Valley	201	(Hunterdon Co.)	201
Pittstown	201	Ringwood	201	Secaucus	201	Stillwater	201	Unionville (Union Co.)	201
Plainfield	201	Rio Grande	609	Sergeantsville	609	Stirling	201	Upper Berkshire	
Plainsboro	609	Riverdale	201	Sewaren	201	Stockholm	201	Valley	201
Pleasant Grove	201	River Edge	201	Sewell	609	Stockton	609	Upper Deerfield	
Pleasant View	201	River Plaza	201	Shady Lake	201	Stone Harbor	609	Township	609
Pleasantville	609	Riverside	609	Shark River Coast Guard		Stone Harbor Coast		Upper Greenwood	
Pluckemin	201	Riverside Heights	201	Sta. No. 103	201	Guard Sta. No. 132	609	Lake	201
Point Pleasant	201	River Styx	201	Shark River Hills	201	Stoutsburg	609	Upper Midvale	201
Point Pleasant Beach	201	Riverton	609	Sharptown	609	Stow Creek	609	Upper Montclair	201
Pole Tavern	609	River Vale	201	Shiloh	609	Stratford	609	Upper Penns Neck	609
Pomona	609	Riverview	201	Shimer Manor	201	Strathmere	609	Upper Saddle River	201
Pompton Lakes	201	Riviera Beach	609	Ship Bottom	609	Stroudsburg	201	
Pompton Plains	201	Roadstown	609	Ship Bottom Coast		Succasunna	201	
Port-au-Peck	201	Roamer Shoal Coast		Guard Sta. No. 116	609	Summit	201	Vail	201
Port Colden	201	Guard Sta.	201	Shirley	609	Sunny Side	201	Vanderburgh	201
Port Elizabeth	609	Robbinsville	609	Shongum	201	Sunset Lake	609	Van Hiseville	201
Port Mercer	609	Robertsville	201	Shore Acres	201	Surf City	609	Vauxhall	201
Port Monmouth	201	Rochelle Park	201	Shore Hills Estates	201	Sussex	201	Ventnor City	609
Port Morris	201	Rockaway	201	Short Hills	201	Swainton	609	Ventnor Heights	609
Port Murray	201	Rockaway Neck	201	Shrewsbury	201	Swartswood	201	Verga	609
Port Newark	201	Rockaway Township	201	Shrewsbury Township	201	Swartswood Lake	201	Vernon	201
Port Norris	609	Rockaway Valley	201	Sicklerville	609	Swedesboro	609	Vernon Township	201
Port Reading	201	Rockleigh	201	Sidney	201	Sykesville	609	Verona	201
Port Republic	609	Rockport	201	Silver Bay	201			Victory Gardens	201
Potterstown	201	Rock Ridge Lake	201	Silverton	201			Vienna	201
Pottersville	201	Rocky Hill	609	Singac	201			Villas	609
Powerville	201	Rocky Run	201	Skillman	609			Vincentown	609
Preakness	201	Roebling	609	Smithville		Tabernacle	609	Vineland	609
Princeton	609	Roosevelt	609	(Atlantic Co.)	609	Tanners Corner	201	Voorhees Corner	201
Princeton Junction	609	Roseland	201	Smithville		Tansboro	609	Voorhees Township	609
Prospect Heights	609	Roselle	201	(Burlington Co.)	609	Taunton Lakes	609	
Prospect Park	201	Roselle Park	201	Smoke Rise	201	Tavistock	609	
Prospect Plains	609	Rosemont	609	Somerdale	609	Taylortown	201	Wading River	609
Prospect Point	201	Rosenhayn	609	Somerset	201	Teaneck	201	Waldwick	201
		Roseville	201	Somers Point	609	Teetertown	201	Wall	201
		Rossmoor	609	Somerville	201	Tenafly	201	Wallington	201
		Round Valley	201	South Amboy	201	Tennent	201	Walnut Valley	201
Quakertown	201	Roxburg	201	Southard	201	Teterboro	201	Walpack	201
Quinton	609	Roxbury Township	201	South Belmar	201	Thompsons Beach	609	Walpack Center	201
		Roycefield	201	South Bound Brook	201	Thorofare	609	Wanamassa	201
		Royce Valley	201	South Branch	201	Three Bridges	201	Wanaque	201
		Rumson	201	South Brunswick	201	Tinton Falls	201	Waretown	609
Raccoon Island	201	Runnemede	609	South Dennis	609	Titusville	609	Warren	201
Radburn	201	Rutherford	201	South Hackensack	201	Toms River	201	Warren Glen	201
Rahway	201			South Orange	201	Toms River Coast		Warren Grove	609
Rainbow Lakes	201			South Plainfield	201	Guard Sta. No. 109	201	Warren Point	201
Ramapo Park	201			South River	201	Totowa	201	Warren Township	201
Ramsey	201	Saddle Brook	201	South Seaville	609	Towaco	201	Warrenville	201
Rancocas	609	Saddle River	201	South Somerville	201	Town Bank	609	Washington	201
Rancocas Heights	609	Sadlertown	609	South Toms River	201	Townsbury	201	Washington Crossing	609
Rancocas Woods	609	Salem	609	South Vineland	609	Townsends Inlet	609	Washington Township	
Randolph Township	201	Salem Cove	609	Sparta	201	Townsends Inlet Coast		(Bergen Co.)	201
Raritan	201	Sand Brook	201	Sperry Springs	201	Guard Sta. No. 130	609	Washington Township	
Raritan Arsenal	201	Sandy Hook	201	Spotswood	201	Tranquility	201	(Gloucester Co.)	609
Raven Rock	609	Sandy Hook Coast Guard		Spray Beach	609	Tremley	201	Watchung	201
Readington	201	Sta. No. 97	201	Springdale	201	Tremley Point	201	Waterford	609
Reaville	201	Saxton Falls	201	Springfield	201	Trenton	609	Waterloo	201
Red Bank	201	Sayres Neck	609	Spring Lake	201	Troy Hills	201	Water Witch	201
Red Lion	609	Sayreville	201	Spring Lake Coast		Tuckahoe	609	Watsontown	609
Red Mill	201	Schellenger's Landing	609	Guard Sta. No. 104	201	Tuckerton	609	Wayne	201
Red Valley	201	Schooleys Mountain	201	Spring Lake Heights	201	Turnersville	609	Wayside	201
Reed's Beach	609	Scobeyville	201	Spring Mills	201	Tuttle's Corner	609	Weehawken	201
Reevytown	201	Scotch Plains	201	Springtown	201			Weekstown	609
Repaupo	609	Scullville	609	Spruce Run	201			Wenonah	609
Retreat	201	Sea Breeze	609	Staffordville	609			Wertsville	609
Richfield	201	Sea Bright	201	Stanhope	201	Union	201	West Allenhurst	201
Richland	609	Seabrook	609	Stanton	201	Union Beach	201	
Richwood	609	Sea Girt	201			Union City	201	
						Union Hill	201	

Place Name	Area Code	Place Name	Area Code	Place Name	Area Code	Place Name	Area Code	Place Name	Area Code
West Atlantic City	609	West New York	201	Whitehouse	201	Williamstown				
West Bank Coast Guard		Weston	201	Whitehouse Station	201	Junction	609	Wood-Ridge	201
Light Sta.	201	West Orange	201	White Meadow Lake	201	Willingboro	609	Woodruff	609
West Belmar	201	West Paterson	201	Whitesbog	609	Willow Grove	609	Woodruff Gap	201
West Berlin	609	West Point Island	201	Whitesboro	609	Windsor	609	Woods Tavern	201
West Caldwell	201	West Point Pleasant	201	Whitesville	201	Winfield	201	Woodstown	609
West Cape May	609	West Portal	201	Whiting	201	Winslow Crossing	609	Woodsville	609
West Collingswood	609	West Trenton	609	Wickatunk	201	Winslow Township	609	Wortendyke	201
West Collingswood		Westville	609	Wilburtha	609	Wolf Lake	201	Wrightstown	609
Heights	609	Westville Grove	609	Wildwood	609	Woodbine	609	Wyckoff	201
West Creek	609	West Wildwood	609	Wildwood Coast Guard		Woodbridge	201		
West Deal	201	West Windsor		Lookout Tower	609	Woodbury	609		
West End	201	Township	609	Wildwood Coast Guard		Woodbury Heights	609	Yardville	609
West Englewood	201	Westwood	201	Sta. No. 134	609	Woodcliff Lake	201	Yardville Heights	609
Westfield	201	Weymouth	609	Wildwood Crest	609	Woodcrest	609	Yellow Frame	201
West Keansburg	201	Whale Beach	609	Wildwood Shores	201	Woodfern	201	Yorktown	609
West Long Branch	201	Wharton	201	Wildwood Villas	609	Woodglen	201		
West Milford	201	Whippany	201	Williamstown	609	Woodlynne	609	Zarephath	201
Westmont	609	White Horse	609			Woodport	201	Zion	201

ALL POINTS—AREA CODE 505

Place Name	Area Code	Place Name	Area Code	Place Name	Area Code	Place Name	Area Code	Place Name	Area Code
Accord	914	Ardsley	914	Barre Center	716	Bergen	716	Brantingham Lake	315
Acidalia	914	Ardsley-on-Hudson	914	Barrington	607	Bergholtz	716	Brant Lake	518
Acra	518	Arena	914	Barrytown	914	Berkshire	607	Brasher Falls	315
Adams	315	Argusville	518	Barryville	914	Berlin	518	Brasie Corners	315
Adams Basin	716	Argyle	518	Barton	607	Berne	518	Breakabeen	518
Adams Center	315	Arletta	518	Basom	716	Bernhards Bay	315	Breesport	607
Adams Corners	914	Arkport	607	Batavia	716	Besemer	607	Breezy Point	212
Adamsville	518	Arkville	914	Batchellerville	518	Bethany	716	Brentwood	516
Addison	607	Arlington	914	Bates	518	Bethel	914	Brewerton	315
Aden	914	Armonk Village	914	Datesville	518	Bethpage	516	Brewster	914
Adirondack	518	Armor	716	Bath	607	Big Brook	518	Briarcliff	914
Adrian	607	Arshamogue	516	Battenville	518	Big Creek	607	Briarcliff Manor	914
Afton	607	Arthur	315	Bayberry Point	516	Big Flats	607	Bridgehampton	516
Akron	716	Arthursburg	914	Bay Crest	516	Big Indian	914	Bridgeport	315
Alabama	716	Arverne	212	Bayport	516	Big Moose	315	Bridgeville	914
Albany	518	Asharoken	516	Bay Shore	516	Billings	914	Bridgewater	315
Albertson	516	Ashford	716	Bayside	212	Billsboro	315	Brier Hill	315
Albion	716	Ashford Hollow	716	Bayswater	212	Binghamton	607	Brighton	716
Alcove	518	Ashland	518	Bayview	716	Binnewater	914	Brighton Beach	212
Alden	716	Ashokan	914	Bayville	516	Birchwood	914	Brightwaters	516
Alder Creek	315	Ashville	716	Beach Hampton	516	Birdsall	607	Brinckerhoff	914
Alexander	716	Ashwood	716	Beachville	607	Bisby Lake	315	Brisben	607
Alexandria Bay	315	Assembly Point	518	Beacon	914	Bishopville	607	Bristol	315
Alfred	607	Astoria	212	Bear Mountain Park	914	Black Creek	716	Bristol Center	716
Algona	315	Athens	518	Bear Pond	518	Black River	315	Bristol Springs	716
Allaben	914	Athol	518	Bearsville	914	Blaine	518	Broadalbin	518
Allegany	716	Athol Springs	716	Beaver Brook	914	Blasdell	716	Broad Channel	212
Allenshill	716	Atlanta	716	Beaver Dams	607	Blauvelt	914	Brockport	716
Allentown	716	Atlantic	516	Beaver Dam Station	914	Bleecker	518	Brockway	914
Alligerville	914	Atlantic Beach	516	Beaver Falls	315	Bliss	716	Brocton	716
Alloway	315	Attica	716	Beaver Meadow	315	Blockville	716	Brodhead	914
Alma	716	Atwaters	315	Beaver River	315	Blodgett Mills	607	Bronx	212
Almond	607	Atwell	315	Beckers Corners	518	Bloomingburg	914	Bronxville	914
Aloquin	315	Atwood	914	Bedell	914	Bloomingdale	518	Brookfield	315
Alpine	607	Auburn	315	Bedford Hills	914	Blooming Grove	914	Brookhaven	516
Alplaus	518	Auburndale	212	Bedford Village	914	Bloomington	914	Brooklyn	212
Alps	518	Aurelius (Station)	315	Beechhurst	212	Bloomville	607	Brookman's Corners	518
Alsen	518	Aurlesville	518	Beechwood	716	Blossom	716	Brooksburg	518
Altamont	518	Aurora	315	Beekmantown	518	Blossvale	315	Brooktondale	607
Altay	607	Ausable Chasm	518	Beerston	607	Blue Mountain Lake	518	Brookview	518
Altmar	315	Au Sable Forks	518	Beixedon	914	Blue Point	516	Brookville	516
Alton	315	Austerlitz	518	Belfast	716	Blue Ridge	518	Broome Center	518
Altona	518	Ava	315	Belfort	315	Bluff Point	315	Brownville	315
Amagansett	516	Averill Park	518	Belgium	315	Bohemia	516	Brunswick	518
Amawalk	914	Avoca	607	Bellaire	212	Boiceville	914	Brushton	518
Amber	315	Avon	716	Belle Harbor	212	Bolivar	716	Bruynswick	914
Amboy	315			Belle Isle	315	Bolton Landing	518	Buchanan	914
Amenia	914			Bellerose	516	Bombay	518	Buckbrook	914
Ames	518			Belle Terre	516	Boomertown	716	Buck Pond	716
Amity	914			Belleview	716	Boonville	315	Buckton	315
Amityville	516	Babcock Lake	518	Belleville	315	Borden	607	Buel	518
Amsterdam	518	Babylon	516	Bellevue	518	Border City	315	Buffalo	716
Ancram	518	Bainbridge	607	Bellmore	516	Borodino	315	Buffalo Coast Guard	
Ancramdale	518	Baiting Hollow	516	Bellona	315	Boston	716	Sta. No. 235	716
Andes	914	Bakers Falls	518	Bellport	516	Boston Corner	518	Buffalo U.S. Naval	
Andover	607	Bakers Mills	518	Bellport Coast Guard		Bouckville	315	Radio Sta.	716
Angelica	716	Bald Mountain	315	Sta. No. 79	516	Bouquet	518	Bulls Head	516
Angola	716	Baldwin	516	Bellvale	914	Bovina (Center)	607	Bullville	914
Annadale	212	Baldwin Place	914	Bellwood	315	Bowens Corners	315	Burden Lake	518
Annadale-on-Hudson	914	Baldwinsville	315	Belmont	716	Bowmansville	716	Burdett	607
Antwerp	315	Balfour Lake	518	Belmont Park	516	Boyleston	315	Burke	518
Apalachin	607	Ballston Lake	518	Belvidere	716	Boyntonville	518	Burlingham	914
Apex	607	Ballston Spa	518	Bemis Heights	518	Braddocks Bay	716	Burlington Flats	607
Applegate	607	Balmville	914	Bemus Point	716	Bradford	607	Burnhams	716
Appleton	716	Bangall	914	Benedict	518	Bradley	914	Burns	607
Apulia	315	Bangor	518	Bennett Bridge	315	Brainard (Station)	518	Burnside	914
Apulia Station	315	Banksville	914	Bennettsburg	607	Brainardsville	518	Burnt Hills	518
Aquebogue	516	Barberville	518	Bennetts Creek	607	Braman Corners	518	Burt	716
Aqueduct		Barcelona	716	Bennettsville	607	Bramanville	518	Burtonsville	518
(Queens Co.)	212	Bardonia	914	Bennington	518	Branch	914	Bushnell Basin	716
Aqueduct		Barker	716	Benson	716	Branchport	315	Bushnellsville	914
(Schenectady Co.)	518	Barkersville	518	Benson Mines	315	Brandreth Lake	315	Bushville	
Arcade	716	Barkertown	716	Benton	315	Brant	716	(Genesee Co.)	716
Arden	914	Barnerville	518	Benton Center	315	Brantingham	315	Bushville	
Ardonia	914	Barneveld	315					(Sullivan Co.)	914

TELEPHONE AREA CODE DIRECTORY

Place Name	Area Code	Place Name	Area Code	Place Name	Area Code	Place Name	Area Code	Place Name	Area Code
Buskirk	518	Cayuta	607	Chestertown	518	Collamer	315	Crooked Lake	518
Busti	716	Cayutaville	607	Cheviot	518	College Point	212	Cropseyville	518
Butler Center	315	Caywood	607	Chichester	914	Colliersville	607	Crosby	315
Butterfly	315	Cazenovia	315	Childwold	518	Collins	716	Cross River	914
Byersville	716	Cedarcliff	914	Chili (Center)	716	Collinsville	315	Croton Falls	914
Byron	716	Cedar Hill	518	Chili Station	716	Colonie	518	Croton-on-Hudson	914
		Cedarhurst	516	Chippewa Bay	315	Colosse	315	Crown Point	518
		Cedar Lake	315	Chittenango	315	Colton	315	Crugers	914
		Cedar River	518	Chittenango Falls	315	Columbiaville	518	Crumcreek	518
		Cedarville	315	Chodikee Lake	914	Commack	516	Crystal Dale	315
Cadosia	607	Celoron	716	Churchtown	518	Commander Squadron		Crystal Lake	
Cadyville	518	Cementon	914	Churchville	716	Coast Guard		(Cattaraugus Co.)	716
Cahoonzie	914	Center Brunswick	518	Churubusco	518	Sta. No. 2	212	Crystal Lake	
Cairo	518	Centereach	516	Cicero	315	Como	315	(Lewis Co.)	315
Calcium	315	Center Falls	518	Cincinnatus	607	Comstock	518	Crystal Lake	
Caldwell	518	Center Lisle	607	Circleville	914	Concord	212	(Schoharie Co.)	518
Caledonia	716	Center Moriches	516	City Island	212	Conesus	716	Crystal Run	914
Callicoon	914	Centerport		Clarence	716	Conesville	607	Cuba	716
Calverton	516	(Cayuga Co.)	315	Clarence Center	716	Conewango	716	Cuddebackville	914
Cambria Heights	212	Centerport		Clarenceville	212	Coney Island	212	Cumminsville	716
Cambridge	518	(Suffolk Co.)	516	Clarendon	716	Congers	914	Curriers	716
Camden	315	Center Village	607	Clarks Mills	315	Conklin	607	Curry	914
Cameron	607	Centerville		Clarkson	716	Conklingville	518	Currytown	518
Camillus	315	(Allegany Co.)	716	Clarksville	518	Connelly	914	Curtis	607
Campbell	607	Centerville		Claryville	914	Conquest	315	Cutchogue	516
Campbell Hall	914	(Oswego Co.)	315	Claverack	518	Constable	518	Cuyler	607
Campbell's Point	315	Central Bridge	518	Clay	315	Constableville	315	Cuylerville	716
Camp Smith	914	Central Islip	516	Clayburg	518	Constantia	315		
Canaan	518	Central Square	315	Clayton	315	Constantia Center	315		
Canaan Lake	516	Central Valley	914	Clayville	315	Cooksburg	518		
Canada Lake	518	Centre Island	516	Clearview	315	Cooks Corners	518		
Canadice	716	Ceres	716	Clemons	518	Cooks Falls	607	Dairyland	914
Canadice Lake	716	Chadwicks	315	Clermont	518	Coopers Plains	607	Dale	716
Canajoharie	518	Chaffee	716	Cleveland	315	Cooperstown	607	Dalton	716
Canandaigua	716	Chambers	607	Cleverdale	518	Coopersville	518	Danby	607
Canaseraga	607	Champion	315	Cliff Haven	518	Copake	518	Dannemora	518
Canastota	315	Champlain	518	Clifton (Monroe Co.)	716	Copake Lake	518	Dansville	716
Candor	607	Chapin	716	Clifton		Copenhagen	315	Darien	716
Caneadea	716	Chappaqua	914	(Richmond Co.)	212	Copiague	516	Darien Center	716
Canisteo	607	Charleston (Charleston		Clifton Park	518	Coram	516	Darts	315
Canoe Place	516	Four Corners)		Clifton Springs	315	Corbett	607	Davenport	607
Canoga	315	(Montgomery Co.)	518	Climax	518	Corbettsville	607	Davis Park	516
Canton	315	Charleston		Clinton	315	Corfu	716	Davis Pond	914
Cape Vincent	315	(Richmond Co.)	212	Clinton Corners	914	Corinth	518	Daysville	315
Cardiff	315	Charlotte Center	716	Clintondale	914	Corning	607	Dayton	716
Carle Place	516	Charlotte Coast		Clinton Heights	518	Cornwall	914	Deansboro	315
Carlisle	518	Guard Sta. No. 233	716	Clinton Hollow	914	Cornwallville	518	Decatur	607
Carlton (Station)	716	Charlotteville	607	Clintonville	518	Corona	212	Deerfield	516
Carman	518	Charlton	518	Clockville	315	Cortland	607	Deerhead	518
Carmel	914	Chase Mills	315	Clove	914	Cossayuna	518	Deerland	518
Caroga Lake	518	Chasm Falls	518	Clover Bank	914	Cottekill	914	Deer Park	516
Caroline (Center)		Chateaugay	518	Clums Corners	518	Cove Neck	516	Deer River	315
(Depot)	607	Chateaugay Lake	518	Clyde	315	Coventry	607	Deferiet	315
Carson	607	Chatham	518	Clymer	716	Coventry Station	607	De Freestville	518
Carthage	315	Chatham Center	518	Cobleskill	518	Covert	607	Degrasse	315
Cascade	315	Chaumont	315	Cochecton	914	Covington	716	De Kalb Junction	315
Cascade Lake	315	Chauncey	914	Cochecton Center	914	Cowlesville	716	De Lancey	607
Cascade Mills	315	Chautauqua	716	Coeymans	518	Coxsackie	518	Delanson	518
Cassadaga	716	Chazy	518	Coeymans Hollow	518	Cragsmoor	914	Delevan	716
Cassville	315	Chazy Lake	518	Cohocton	716	Craig Colony	716	Delhi	607
Castile	716	Cheektowaga	716	Cohoes	518	Craigsville	914	Delmar	518
Castle Creek	607	Chelsea	914	Cold Brook		Cranberry Creek	518	Delphi Falls	315
Castle Point	914	Chemung	607	(Herkimer Co.)	315	Cranberry Lake	315	Demster	315
Castleton	518	Chenango Bridge	607	Cold Brook		Cranberry Pond	716	Denault Corners	518
Castorland	315	Chenango Forks	607	(Ulster Co.)	914	Crary Mills	315	Denley	315
Catawba	607	Chenango Lake	607	Colden	716	Craryville	518	Denmark	315
Catherine	607	Cheneys Point	716	Coldenham	914	Craterclub	518	Denning	914
Catlin	607	Cheningo	607	Cold Spring		Creek Locks	914	Denton	914
Cato	315	Chepachet	315	(Putnam Co.)	914	Crescent	518	Denver	607
Caton	607	Cherry Creek	716	Cold Spring Harbor	516	Crestwood	914	Depauville	315
Catskill	518	Cherry Grove	516	Cold Springs		Crittenden	716	Depew	716
Cattaraugus	716	Cherryplain	518	(Steuben Co.)	607	Croghan	315	De Peyster	315
Cayuga	315	Cherry Valley	607	Cold Water	716	Crompond	914	Deposit	607
Cayuga Heights	607	Chester	914	Coleman Station	518	Cronomer Valley	914	Derby	716

Place Name	Area Code	Place Name	Area Code	Place Name	Area Code	Place Name	Area Code	Place Name	Area Code
Dering Harbor	516	East Aurora	716	Eatons Neck Coast		Falconer	716	Forks	716
De Ruyter	315	East Avon	716	Guard Sta. No. 94	516	Fallsburg	914	Fort Ann	518
Devon	516	East Berne	518	Ebenezer	716	Fancher	716	Fort Covington	518
Dewey's Bridge	518	East Bethany	716	Eddyville	914	Farleys	315	Fort Drum	315
Dewitt	315	East Bloomfield	716	Eden	716	Farmersville (Station)	716	Fort Edward	518
Dewittville	716	East Branch	607	Edgemere	212	Farmingdale	516	Fort Hamilton	212
Dexter	315	East Caroga Lake	518	Edinburg	518	Farmington	716	Fort Hunter	518
Diamond	315	East Chatham	518	Edmeston	607	Farmingville	516	Fort Jackson	315
Diamond Point	518	Eastchester	914	Edwards	315	Farnham	716	Fort Johnson	518
Dickinson	518	East Clarence	716	Edwardsville	315	Far Rockaway	212	Fort Michle	516
Dickinson Center	518	East Cobleskill	518	Eggertsville	716	Fayette	315	Fort Miller	518
District Headquarters		East Concord	716	Egypt	716	Fayetteville	315	Fort Montgomery	914
Coast Guard Light		East Corning	607	Elba	716	Felts Mills	315	Fort Ontario	315
Sta.	212	East Durham	518	Elbridge	315	Fenimore	518	Fort Plain	518
District Headquarters		East Elmhurst	212	Eldred	914	Fentonville	716	Fort Salonga	516
Coast Guard Sta.	212	East Fire Island	516	Elizabethtown	518	Fergusonville	607	Fort Slocum	914
District Headquarters		East Freetown	607	Elizaville	914	Ferndale	914	Fortsville	518
U.S. Naval Radio		East Gaines	716	Elk Creek	607	Fernwood	315	Fort Tilden	212
Sta.	212	East Galway	518	Elkdale	716	Feura Bush	518	Fort Totten	212
Ditch Plain Coast		East Greenbush	518	Ellenburg Center	518	Fillmore	716	Fort Wadsworth	212
Guard Sta. No. 65	516	East Greenville	518	Ellenburg Corners	518	Findley Lake	716	Fort Wright, H. G.	516
Divine Corners	914	East Greenwich	518	Ellenburg Depot	518	Fine	315	Foster	607
Dix Hills	516	East Hampton	516	Ellenville	914	Fineview	315	Fosterdale	914
Dobbs Ferry	914	East Hills	516	Ellery Center	716	Fire Island	516	Fostertown	914
Dolgeville	315	East Homer	607	Ellicottville	716	Fire Island Coast		Fosterville	315
Dongan Hills	212	East Hoosick	518	Ellington	716	Guard Light Sta.	516	Fourth Lake	315
Dorloo	518	East Islip	516	Ellis	607	Fire Island Coast		Fowlerville	716
Dormansville	518	East Ithaca	607	Ellisburg	315	Guard Sta. No. 83	516	Fox Hollow	518
Douglaston	212	East Jewett	518	Ellistown	607	Fire Island Pines	516	Frankfort	315
Dover Furnace	914	East Kingston	914	Elma	716	Fire Island U.S.		Franklin	607
Dover Plains	914	East Maine	607	Elmgrove	716	Naval Radio Sta.	516	Franklin Falls	518
Downsville	607	East Marion	516	Elmhurst	212	First Lake	315	Franklin Springs	315
Doyle	716	East Martinsburg	315	Elmira	607	Firthcliffe	914	Franklin Square	
Dresden	315	East Meadow	516	Elmont	516	Fish Creek		(Nassau Co.)	516
Dresden Station	518	East Meredith	607	Elmsford	914	(Lewis Co.)	315	Franklin Square	
Dresserville	315	East Moriches	516	Elm Valley	607	Fish Creek		(Orange Co.)	914
Driftwood	716	East Nassau	518	Elnora	518	(Oneida Co.)	315	Franklinton	518
Dryden	607	East Northport	516	Elsmere	518	Fishers	716	Franklinville	716
Duane	518	East Norwich	516	Eltings Corners	914	Fishers Island	516	Fraser	607
Duanesburg	518	Easton	518	Eltingville	212	Fishers Island Coast		Fredonia	716
Dugway	315	East Otto	716	Elton	716	Guard Sta. No. 59	516	Freedom	716
Dundee	607	East Palmyra	315	Elwood	516	Fishers Landing	315	Freedom Plains	914
Dunham Hollow	518	East Park	914	Emerson	315	Fishkill	914	Freehold	518
Dunhams Basin	518	East Patchogue	516	Emeryville	315	Fishkill Plains	914	Freeman	607
Dunkirk	716	East Pembroke	716	Endicott	607	Fishs Eddy	607	Freeport	516
Dunkirk Coast Guard		East Penfield	716	Endwell	607	Five Corners	315	Freetown Corners	607
Light Sta.	716	East Pharsalia	607	Enfield Center		Flackville	315	Freeville	607
Dunnsville	518	East Poestenkill	518	(Enfield Falls)	607	Flanders	516	Fremont Center	914
Dunraven	914	Eastport	516	Ensenore	315	Flatbush	914	French Creek	716
Dunsbach Ferry	518	East Quogue	516	Ephratah	518	Flatcreeks	518	French Woods	914
Dunton	212	East Randolph	716	Erieville	315	Fleets Neck	516	Fresh Meadows	212
Durham	518	East Rochester	716	Erin	607	Fleetwood	914	Frewsburg	716
Durhamville	315	East Rockaway	516	Erwins	607	Fleischmanns	914	Freysbush	518
Durkeetown	518	East Rodman	315	Esopus	914	Fleming	315	Friend	315
Durlandville	914	East Schaghticoke	518	Esperance	518	Flint	315	Friendship	716
Dutchess Junction	914	East Schodack	518	Essex	518	Floral Park	516	Friends Lake	518
Duttonville	914	East Seneca	716	Etna	607	Florence	315	Frisbee Street	518
Dwaar Kill	914	East Setauket	516	Euclid	315	Florida	914	Frost Valley	914
		East Shelby	716	Evans	716	Flowerfield	516	Fruitland	315
		East Springfield	607	Evans Mills	315	Flower Hill	516	Fruit Valley	315
		East Steamburg	607			Floyd	315	Fulton	315
		East Steuben	315			Flushing	212	Fultonham	518
Eagle (Onondaga Co.)	315	East Syracuse	315			Fluvanna	716	Fultonville	518
Eagle (Wyoming Co.)	716	East Taghkanic	518	Fabius	315	Fly Creek	607	Furnaceville	315
Eagle Bay	315	East Troupsburg	607	Fairfield	315	Folsomdale	716	Furniss	315
Eagle Bridge	518	Eastview	914	Fair Harbor	516	Fonda	518	Fyler Settlement	315
Eagle Harbor	716	East Wattsburg	716	Fair Haven		Forestburg	914		
Eagle Lake	518	East Williamson	315	(Cayuga Co.)	315	Forest Hills	212		
Eagle Mills	518	East Williston	516	Fair Haven		Forest Home	607		
Eagle Nest	518	East Windham	518	(Orleans Co.)	716	Forest Lawn	716	Gabriels	518
Eagle Valley	914	East Windsor	607	Fairmount	315	Forestport	315	Gage	315
Earlton	518	East Worcester	607	Fair Oaks	914	Forestville	716	Gaines	716
Earlville	315	Eaton	315	Fairport	716	Forge River Coast		Gainesville	716
East Amherst	716	Eatons Neck	516	Fairville	315	Guard Sta. No. 77	516	Galena	607

NEW YORK
Galeville—Irishtown

Place Name	Area Code	Place Name	Area Code	Place Name	Area Code	Place Name	Area Code	Place Name	Area Code
Galeville	914	Glen Wild		Groveland (Station)	716	Hartwood	914	Homer	607
Galloo Island Coast		(Sullivan Co.)	914	Grovenor Corners	518	Harvard	607	Honeoye	716
Guard Sta. No. 231	315	Glenwood (Erie Co.)	716	Groveville	914	Hasbrouck	914	Honeoye Falls	716
Gallupville	518	Glenwood		Grymes Hill	212	Haskinville	607	Honeyville	315
Galway	518	(Nassau Co.)	516	Guilderland	518	Hastings (Oswego Co.)	315	Honnedaga	315
Gang Mills	607	Glenwood		Guilderland Center	518	Hastings		Hook Creek	212
Gansevoort	518	(Tompkins Co.)	607	Guilford	607	(Westchester Co.)	914	Hoosick Falls	518
Garbutt	716	Glenwood Landing	516	Gulfport	212	Hastings-on-Hudson	914	Hope	518
Garden	716	Gloversville	518	Gulf Summit	607	Hauppauge	516	Hope Falls	518
Garden City	516	Godeffroy	914	Gull Island	516	Haverstraw	914	Hope Farm	914
Gardenville	716	Goldens Bridge	914	Guyanoga	315	Hawkinsville	315	Hopewell Center	716
Gardiner	914	Goose Creek	212	Guymard	914	Hawleyton	607	Hopewell Junction	914
Gardiners Island	516	Gordon Heights	516			Hawthorne	914	Hopkinton	315
Gardners Corners	315	Gorham	315			Haynersville	518	Horicon	518
Gardnertown	914	Goshen	914			Hayts Corners	607	Hornby	607
Gardnersville	518	Gouldtown	315	Hadley	518	Head of the Harbor	516	Hornell	607
Garfield	518	Gouverneur	315	Hagaman	518	Hector	607	Horseheads	607
Garland	716	Governors Island	212	Hagedorns Mills	518	Heddens	607	Horseshoe	518
Garnerville	914	Gowanda	716	Hagerman	516	Hedgesville	607	Horseshoe Lake	716
Garnet	518	Gracie	607	Hague	518	Helena	315	Horton	607
Garoga	518	Grafton	518	Hailesboro	315	Helmuth	716	Hortonville	914
Garrattsville	607	Grahamsville	914	Haines Falls	518	Hemlock	716	Houghton	716
Garrison	914	Grand Gorge	607	Halcott Center	914	Hempstead	516	Howard	607
Garwoods	607	Grand Island	716	Halcottsville	518	Henderson	315	Howardsville	315
Gasport	716	Grand View-on-		Hale Eddy	607	Henrietta	716	Howes Cave	518
Gates	716	Hudson	914	Halesite	516	Hensonville	518	Hubbardsville	315
Gayhead	518	Granite	914	Halfmoon	518	Herkimer	315	Hudson	518
Geddes	315	Granite Springs	914	Halfmoon Lake	914	Hermitage	716	Hudson Falls	518
Geneseo	716	Grant	315	Halfway	315	Hermon	315	Hughsonville	914
Geneva	315	Grant City	212	Hall	315	Herrings	315	Huguenot	
Genoa	315	Granton	607	Halliday's Corners	315	Heuvelton	315	(Orange Co.)	914
George Junior		Granville	518	Hallsville	518	Hewittsville	315	Huguenot	
Republic	607	Grapeville	518	Halsey Valley	607	Hewlett	516	(Richmond Co.)	212
Georgetown	315	Grasmere	212	Halseyville	607	Hibernia	914	Hulburton	716
Georgica Coast Guard		Gravesend	212	Hambletville	607	Hickling Heights	607	Huletts Landing	518
Sta. No. 69	516	Gravesville	315	Hamburg	716	Hicksville	516	Hume	716
Germantown	518	Gray	315	Hamburg-on-Lake	716	High Bridge	315	Humphrey	716
Gerry	716	Great Bend	315	Hamden	607	High Falls	914	Humphrey Center	716
Getzville	716	Great Kills	212	Hamilton	315	Highland	914	Hungerford Corners	315
Ghent	518	Great Neck	516	Hamilton Mountain	518	Highland Falls	914	Hunns Lake	914
Gibson (Nassau Co.)	516	Great River	516	Hamlet	716	Highland Lake	914	Hunter	518
Gibson (Steuben Co.)	607	Great Valley	716	Hamlin	716	Highland Mills	914	Huntersland	518
Gibson Landing	607	Greece	716	Hammels	212	Highmarket	315	Huntington	516
Gilbert Lake	607	Greendale	518	Hammond	315	High Mills	518	Huntington Bay	516
Gilbertsville	607	Greene	607	Hammondsport	607	Highmount	914	Hunts	716
Gilboa	518	Greenfield Center	518	Hampton	315	High View	914	Hunts Corners	607
Gilgo Beach	516	Greenfield Park	914	Hampton Bays	516	Higleys Falls	315	Hurley	914
Girarde	914	Green Haven	914	Hamptonburgh	914	Hillburn	914	Hurleyville	914
Glasco	914	Greenhurst	716	Hancock	607	Hill Crest	607	Huron	315
Glass Lake	518	Green Island	518	Hankins	914	Hillsdale	518	Hyde Park	914
Glen	518	Green Lake	518	Hannacroix	518	Hillside	212	Hyndsville	518
Glen Aubrey	607	Greenlawn	516	Hannawa Falls	315	Hillside Heights	516		
Glencairn	607	Greenport		Hannibal	315	Hilton	716		
Glenco Mills	518	(Columbia Co.)	518	Hardys	716	Hiltonville	607		
Glen Cove	516	Greenport		Harford (Mills)	607	Himrod	607	Idle Hour	516
Glendale	212	(Suffolk Co.)	516	Harkness	518	Hinckley	315	Igerna	518
Glenfield	315	Greenvale (Station)	516	Harlemville	518	Hinsdale	716	Ilion	315
Glenford	914	Greenville		Harmon	914	Hoag Corners	518	Independence	607
Glenham	914	(Greene Co.)	518	Harmony Corners	518	Hobart	607	Indian Falls	716
Glen Haven	716	Greenville		Harpersfield	607	Hoffman	716	Indian Lake	518
Glen Head	516	(Orange Co.)	914	Harpursville	607	Hoffman Island	212	Indian River	315
Glen Island	518	Greenwich	518	Harriman	914	Hoffmans	518	Indian Village	315
Glen Lake	518	Greenwood	607	Harris	914	Hoffmeister	315	Industry	716
Glenmere	914	Greenwood Lake	914	Harrisburg	315	Hogansburg	518	Ingham Mills	315
Glenmont	518	Greig	315	Harris Hill	716	Holbrook	516	Ingleside	716
Glenmore	315	Greigsville	716	Harrison	914	Holcomb	716	Ingraham	518
Glenora	607	Greycourt	914	Harrisville	315	Holland	716	Inlet	315
Glenpark	315	Griffis Air Force		Hartfield	716	Holland Patent	315	Interlaken	315
Glens Falls	518	Base	315	Hartford	518	Holley	716	Inwood	516
Glenside	315	Groom Corners	518	Hartman	518	Hollis	212	Iona Island	914
Glen Spey	914	Grossinger	914	Hartsdale	914	Hollowville	518	Ionia	716
Glenville	518	Groton	607	Harts Island	212	Holmes	914	Ira	315
Glen Wild		Groton City	607	Hartsville	607	Holmesville	607	Ireland Corners	914
(Saratoga Co.)	518	Grove	607	Hartwick	607	Holtsville	516	Irishtown	518

Place Name	Area Code	Place Name	Area Code	Place Name	Area Code	Place Name	Area Code	Place Name	Area Code
Irona	518	Kelsey	607	Lake Hill	914	Lewis	518	Long Pond	
Irondequoit	716	Kendaia	315	Lake Huntington	914	Lewisboro	914	(Monroe Co.)	716
Iroquois	716	Kendall	716	Lake Kanawauke	914	Lewiston	716	Loon Lake	
Irvine Mills	716	Kendall Mills	716	Lake Katrine	914	Lewisville	518	(Franklin Co.)	518
Irving	716	Kenmore	716	Lakeland	914	Lexington	518	Loon Lake	
Irvington	914	Kennedy	716	Lake Luzerne	518	Liberty	914	(Warren Co.)	518
Ischua	716	Kennedys Corners	607	Lake Minnewaska	914	Lido Beach	516	Lordville	607
Island Park	516	Kenoza Lake	914	Lake Mohonk	914	Lilly Dale	716	Lorraine	315
Islip	516	Kensington	516	Lakemont	607	Lima	716	Loudonville	518
Islip Terrace	516	Kent	716	Lake Ozonia	315	Lime Kiln	315	Louisville	315
Italy (Hill)	607	Kent Cliffs	914	Lake Panamoka	516	Lime Lake	716	Lounsberry	607
Ithaca	607	Kenwood (Albany Co.)	518	Lake Peekskill	914	Limerick	315	Lower Jay	518
		Kenwood		Lake Placid	518	Limestone	716	Low Hampton	518
		(Madison Co.)	315	Lake Pleasant	518	Lincklaen	315	Lowman	607
		Kenyonville	716	Lakeport	315	Lincoln	315	Lowville	315
Jackson Heights	212	Kerhonkson	914	Lake Rondaxe	315	Lincolndale	914	Ludingtonville	914
Jacksonville	607	Keuka	607	Lake Ronkonkoma	516	Linden	716	Ludlowville	607
Jack's Reef	315	Keuka Park	315	Lake Sebago	914	Lindenhurst	516	Lummisville	315
Jamaica	212	Kew Gardens	212	Lakeside	315	Lindley	607	Luther	518
Jamaica South	212	Kiamesha	914	Lake Stahahe	914	Linlithgo	518	Lutheranville	518
Jamaica Square	516	Kiantone	716	Lake Success	516	Linwood	716	Luzerne	518
Jamesport	516	Kidders	607	Lake Tiorati	914	Lisbon	315	Luzon	914
Jamestown	716	Killawog	607	Lake Titus	518	Lishaskill	518	Lycoming	315
Jamesville	315	Kill Buck	716	Lakeview (Erie Co.)	716	Lisle	607	Lykers	518
Jamison Road	716	Kinderhook	518	Lakeview		Litchfield		Lynbrook	516
Jasper	607	King Ferry	315	(Nassau Co.)	516	(Oneida Co.)	315	Lyndon	315
Java	716	Kingsbury	518	Lakeville	716	Litchfield (Tioga Co.)	607	Lyndonville	716
Jay	518	Kings Park	516	Lakewood	716	Little Britain	914	Lynn	607
Jeddo	716	Kings Point	516	Lambs Corners	518	Little Falls	315	Lyon Mountain	518
Jefferson	607	Kingston	914	Lamont	716	Little Genesee	716	Lyons	315
Jefferson Valley	914	Kirchnerville	315	Lancaster	716	Little Gull Island		Lyons Falls	315
Jeffersonville	914	Kirkland	315	Lanesville	914	Coast Guard Light		Lysander	315
Jenkinstown	914	Kirkville	315	Langford	716	Sta.	516		
Jericho (Clinton Co.)	518	Kirkwood	607	Lansing	607	Little Moose (Lake)	315		
Jericho (Nassau Co.)	516	Kiskatom	518	Lansingburg	518	Little Neck			
Jewell	315	Kismet	516	Lansingville	607	(Nassau Co.)	516		
Jewett	518	Kitchawan	914	Laona	716	Little Neck		Mabbettsville	914
Jewettville	716	Knapp Creek	716	La Peer	607	(Queens Co.)	212	MacDougall	315
Joe Indian Pond	315	Knowelhurst	518	Larchmont	914	Little Tupper Lake	518	Macedon	315
Johnsburg	518	Knowlesville	716	Lassellsville	518	Little Valley	716	Machias	716
Johnson	914	Knox	518	Latham	518	Little York	607	Mackey	518
Johnsonburg	716	Knoxboro	315	Latintown	914	Liverpool	315	Macomb	315
Johnson City	607	Kosterville	315	Lattingtown	516	Livingston	518	Madalin	914
Johnson Creek	716	Kringsbush	518	Laurel	516	Livingston Lake	518	Madison	315
Johnsonville	518	Kripplebush	914	Laurel Hollow	516	Livingston Manor	914	Madrid	315
Johnstown	518	Krums Corners	607	Laurelton	212	Livingstonville	518	Mahopac	914
Jones Beach	516	Krumville	914	Laurens	607	Livonia	716	Maine	607
Jones Beach Coast		Kyserike	914	Lava	914	Lloyd	914	Malba	212
Guard Sta. No. 86	516			Lawrence	516	Lloyd Harbor	516	Malden Bridge	518
Jonesville	518			Lawrenceville		Lloyd Neck	516	Malden-on-Hudson	914
Jordan	315	Lackawack	914	(Greene Co.)	518	Lobdell	518	Mallory	315
Jordanville	315	Lackawanna	716	Lawrenceville		Loch Berlin	315	Malloryville	607
Joy	315	Lacona	315	(St. Lawrence Co.)	315	Loch Sheldrake	914	Malone	518
Junius	315	Ladleton	914	Lawton Station	716	Locke	315	Malta (Maltaville)	518
		La Fargeville	315	Lawyersville	518	Lockport	716	Malverne	516
		LaFayette	315	Lebanon	315	Locksley Park	716	Mamakating	914
Kaaterskill Junction	518	LaFayette Corners	607	Lebanon Springs	518	Lockwood	607	Mamakating Park	914
Kanes Falls	518	Lafayetteville	914	Ledyard	315	Locust Valley	516	Mamaroneck	914
Kanona	607	La Grange		Lee Center	315	Lodi	607	Manchester	716
Karner	518	(Dutchess Co.)	914	Leeds	518	Logan	607	Mandana	315
Kashong	315	Lagrange		Leedsville	914	Logtown	914	Manhasset	516
Kast Bridge	315	(Wyoming Co.)	716	Le Fever Falls	914	Lomontville	914	Manhattan Beach	212
Katonah	914	La Grangeville	914	Leibhardt	914	Long Beach	516	Manheim	315
Katrine	914	Lake	914	Leicester	716	Long Beach Coast		Manitou Beach	716
Kattskill Bay	518	Lake Amenia	914	Lenape Lake	914	Guard Sta. No. 90	212	Manlius	315
Kauneonga Lake	914	Lake Bluff	315	Leon	716	Long Island City	212	Manlius Center	315
Kecks Center	518	Lake Bonaparte	315	Leonardsville	315	Long Lake		Manning	716
Keene	518	Lake Carmel	914	Leptondale	914	(Hamilton Co.)	518	Mannsville	315
Keene Valley	518	Lake Clear (Junction)	518	Le Roy	716	Long Lake		Manny's Corners	518
Keeseville	518	Lake Cohasset	914	Lester	607	(Oneida Co.)	315	Manorhaven	516
Kelleys Station	518	Lake Cossayuna	518	Levanna	315	Long Lake West	518	Manorkill	607
Kelloggsville	315	Lake Delaware	607	Levant	716	Long Point	716	Manorton	518
Kelly Corners	914	Lake George	518	Levittown	516	Long Pond		Manorville	516
		Lake Grove	516	Lewbeach	914	(Lewis Co.)	315	Maplecrest	518

NEW YORK
Maple Springs—Northville

Place Name	Area Code	Place Name	Area Code	Place Name	Area Code	Place Name	Area Code	Place Name	Area Code
Maple Springs	716	Merriewold	914	Montezuma	315	Navarino	315	Nissequogue	516
Mapleton	315	Merrill	518	Montgomery	914	Nedrow	315	Niverville	518
Mapletown	518	Messengerville	607	Monticello	914	Needhamville	518	Norfolk	315
Maple View	315	Mettacahonts	914	Montour Falls	607	Nehasane	315	Northampton	518
Maplewood	914	Mexico	315	Montrose	914	Nelliston	518	North Babylon	516
Marathon	607	Middleburgh	518	Montville	315	Nelson	315	North Bangor	518
Marbletown		Middle Falls	518	Mooers	518	Nelsonville	914	North Bay	315
(Ulster Co.)	914	Middlefield	607	Mooers Forks	518	Neponsit	212	North Bellmore	516
Marbletown		Middlefield Center	607	Moores Mill	914	Nesconset	516	North Bergen	716
(Wayne Co.)	315	Middle Granville	518	Moose River	315	Netherwood	914	North Blenheim	518
Marcellus	315	Middle Grove	518	Moravia	315	Neversink	914	North Bloomfield	716
Marcy	315	Middle Hope	914	Morehouseville	315	Nevis	914	North Boston	716
Marengo	315	Middle Island	516	Moreland	607	New Albion	716	North Branch	914
Margaretville	914	Middleport	716	Morganville	518	Newark	315	North Brookfield	315
Mariaville	518	Middlesex	315	Moriah Center	518	Newark Valley	607	Northbush	518
Marietta	315	Middletown	914	Moriches	516	New Baltimore		North Cameron	607
Marilla	716	Middle Village	212	Morley	315	(Station)	518	North Chatham	518
Marilla Station	716	Middleville		Morris	607	New Berlin	607	North Chemung	607
Marion	315	(Herkimer Co.)	315	Morrisonville	518	New Boston	315	North Chili	716
Marlboro	914	Middleville		Morristown	315	New Bremen	315	North Clove	914
Marshfield	716	(Suffolk Co.)	516	Morrisville	315	New Brighton	212	North Clymer	716
Marshville	518	Midland	516	Morton	716	Newburgh	914	North Cohocton	716
Martindale	518	Milan	914	Moseskill	518	New City	914	North Collins	716
Martinsburg	315	Mileses	914	Mosherville	518	Newcomb	518	North Creek	518
Martinsville	716	Milford	607	Mossyglen	607	New Concord	518	Northeast	914
Martville	315	Milford Center	607	Motor Island	716	New Dorp	212	North Evans	716
Maryland	607	Millbrook	914	Mottville	315	Newfane	716	North Fenton	607
Mason	518	Miller Place	516	Mountaindale	914	Newfield	607	North Germantown	518
Masonville	607	Millers	716	Mountain Lake	518	New Hackensack	914	North Granville	518
Maspeth	212	Millers Mills	315	Mountain View	518	New Hamburg	914	North Greece	716
Massapequa	516	Millerton	518	Mountainville	914	New Hampton	914	North Greenbush	518
Massena	315	Millgrove	716	Mount Hope	914	New Hartford	315	North Harford	607
Mastens Lake	914	Mill Neck	516	Mount Ivy	914	New Haven	315	North Harpersfield	607
Mastic	516	Mill Point	518	Mount Kisco	914	New Hope	315	North Haven	516
Matinecock	516	Mill Port	607	Mount Lebanon	518	New Hurley	914	North Hebron	518
Mattituck	516	Mills Mills	716	Mount Marion	914	New Hyde Park	516	North Hector	607
Maybrook	914	Millville	716	Mount McGregor	518	New Kingston	914	North Hills	516
Mayfield	518	Millwood	914	Mount Meenagha	914	Newkirk (Mills)	315	North Hoosick	518
Mays Mills	315	Milo	315	Mount Morris	716	New Lebanon (Center)	518	North Hornell	607
Mays Point	315	Milton	914	Mount Pleasant	914	New London	315	North Hudson	518
Mayville	716	Minden	518	Mount Sinai	516	New Milford	914	North Huron	315
Maywood	518	Mindenville	518	Mount Tremper	914	New Oregon	716	North Jasper	607
McClure Settlement	607	Mineola	516	Mount Upton	607	New Paltz	914	North Java	716
McConnellsville	315	Mineral Springs	518	Mount Vernon	914	Newport	315	North Lake	315
McDonough	607	Minerva	518	Mount Vision	607	New Rochelle	914	North Lansing	607
McGraw	607	Minetto	315	Mud Lake	315	New Russia	518	North Lawrence	315
McKeever	315	Mineville	518	Mumford	716	New Salem		North Manlius	315
McKinley	518	Minisink	914	Munnsville	315	(Albany Co.)	518	North Massapequa	516
McKinneys	607	Minnewaska	914	Munsey Park	516	New Salem		North Merrick	516
McLean	607	Minoa	315	Munson	914	(Ulster Co.)	914	North Norwich	607
McPherson Point	716	Minstead	315	Munsonville	518	New Scotland	518	North Pelham	914
Meadow Brook		Mitchell Air Force		Murray	716	New Suffolk	516	North Petersburg	518
(Nassau Co.)	516	Base	516	Muttontown	516	Newton Falls	315	North Pharsalia	607
Meadow Brook		Mitchellville	607	Mycenae	315	Newton Hollow	607	North Pitcher	607
(Orange Co.)	914	Model City	716	Myers	607	Newton Hook	518	Northport	516
Meadowmere Park	516	Modena	914	Myers Point	607	Newtonville	518	Northport Coast Guard	
Mechanicstown	914	Moffittsville	518			New Vernon	914	Light Sta.	516
Mechanicville	518	Mohawk	315			New Windsor	914	North River	518
Mecklenburg	607	Mohawk Hill	315			New Woodstock	315	North Rose	315
Medford	516	Mohawk View	518	Nanticoke	607	New York City	212	North Roslyn	516
Medina	716	Mohegan	914	Nanuet	914	New York Mills	315	North Rush	716
Medusa	518	Mohonk Lake	914	Napanoch	914	New York		North Salem	914
Medway	518	Moira	518	Napeague Coast Guard		Ordnance Works	315	North Sanford	607
Mellenville	518	Mombaccus	914	Sta. No. 67	516	Niagara Coast Guard		North Scriba	315
Melrose	518	Mongaup	914	Naples	716	Sta. No. 234	716	North Sea	516
Melville	516	Mongaup Valley	914	Napoli	716	Niagara Falls	716	Northside	518
Memphis	315	Monroe	914	Narrowsburg	914	Nichols	607	North Spencer	607
Menands	518	Monsey	914	Nassau		Nicholville	315	North Sterling	315
Mendon (Center)	716	Montague	315	(Rensselaer Co.)	518	Nile	716	North Stockholm	315
Meredith	607	Montauk Coast Guard		Nassau Lake	518	Niles	315	North Syracuse	315
Meridale	607	Light Sta.	516	Nassau Point	516	Nineveh	607	North Tarrytown	914
Meridian	315	Montauk Point	516	Natural Bridge	315	Nineveh Junction	607	North Tonawanda	716
Merrick	516	Montela	914	Natural Dam	315	Niobe	716	North Van Etten	607
Merrickville	607	Monterey	607	Naumburg	315	Niskayuna	518	Northville	518

Place Name	Area Code	Place Name	Area Code	Place Name	Area Code	Place Name	Area Code	Place Name	Area Code
North Western	315	Oscawana	914	Pellets Island	914	Pleasantville	914	Pulteney	607
North White Plains	914	Osceola	315	Pembroke	716	Plessis	315	Pultneyville	315
North Wolcott	315	Ossian	716	Pendleton	716	Plymouth	607	Purchase	914
Norton Hill	518	Ossining	914	Penfield	716	Pocantico Hills	914	Purdy Creek	607
Norway	315	Oswegatchie	315	Pennellville	315	Poestenkill	518	Purdys	914
Norwich	607	Oswego	315	Penn Yan	315	Point au Roche	518	Purdy's Mills	518
Norwich Corners	315	Oswego Coast Guard		Peoria	716	Point Breeze	716	Purdy Station	914
Norwood	315	Light Sta.	315	Pepacton	607	Point Chautauqua	716	Purling	518
Noyack	516	Oswego Coast Guard		Perkinsville	716	Point Lookout	516	Putnam	518
Number Four	315	Sta. No. 232	315	Perry	716	Point O'Woods	516	Putnam Lake	914
Nunda	716	Otego	607	Perry City	607	Point Peninsula	315	Putnam Valley	914
Nyack	914	Otisco	315	Perrysburg	716	Point Salubrious	315	Pyrites	315
		Otisco Valley	315	Perrys Mills	518	Point Vivian	315		
		Otisville	914	Perryville	315	Poland	315		
Oak Beach	516	Otsdawa	607	Peru	518	Poland Center	716	Quackenkill	518
Oakdale	516	Otselic	315	Peruville	607	Pomona	914	Quaker Basin	315
Oakfield	716	Otter Creek	315	Peterboro	315	Pompey	315	Quaker Bridge	716
Oak Hill	518	Otter Lake	315	Petersburg	518	Pond Eddy	914	Quaker Hill	914
Oakland	716	Otto	716	Petersburg Junction	518	Ponquogue	516	Quaker Street	518
Oakland Gardens	212	Ouaquaga Lake	607	Petries Corners	315	Pontiac	716	Quarantine	212
Oakland Valley	914	Overlook	914	Petrolia	716	Poolville	315	Quarryville	914
Oak Orchard	716	Ovid	607	Pharsalia	607	Pope Mills	315	Queechy	518
Oakpoint	315	Ovid Center	607	Phelps	315	Poplar Ridge	315	Queens	212
Oak Ridge	914	Owasco	315	Philadelphia	315	Poquott	516	Queensbury	518
Oaks Corners	315	Owasco Lake	315	Phillipsburg	914	Portage	716	Queens Village	212
Oaksville	607	Owego	607	Phillipsport	914	Portageville	716	Quinneville	607
Oakwood (Cayuga Co.)	315	Owls Head	518	Philmont	518	Port Benjamin	914	Quiogue	516
Oakwood		Oxbow	315	Phoenicia	914	Port Byron	315	Quogue	516
(Richmond Co.)	212	Oxford	607	Phoenix	315	Port Chester	914	Quogue Coast Guard	
Obernburg	914	Oxford Depot	914	Piercefield	518	Port Crane	607	Sta. No. 74	516
Obi	716	Oyster Bay	516	Piermont	914	Port Dickinson	607		
Ocean Beach	516	Oyster Bay Cove	516	Pierrepont	315	Port Douglas	518		
Oceanside	516	Ozone Park	212	Pierrepont Manor	315	Porters Corners	518		
Odessa	607			Piffard	716	Porterville	716	Raceville	518
Ogden (Center)	716			Pike	716	Port Ewen	914	Rainbow Lake	518
Ogdensburg	315	Painted Post	607	Pike Five Corners	716	Port Gibson	315	Ramapo	914
Ohio	315	Palatine Bridge	518	Pillarpoint	315	Port Henry	518	Ram Island	516
Ohioville	914	Palatine Church	518	Pilot Knob	518	Port Ivory	212	Randall	518
O'Kara Lake	315	Palenville	518	Pine Aire	516	Port Jefferson	516	Randallsville	315
Olcott	716	Palisades	914	Pine Bush	914	Port Jervis	914	Randolph	716
Old Brookville	516	Palmer Falls	518	Pine City	607	Port Kent	518	Ransomville	716
Old Chatham	518	Palmyra	315	Pine Hill (Erie Co.)	716	Portland	716	Raquette Lake	315
Old Field	516	Panama	716	Pine Hill (Ulster Co.)	914	Portland Point	607	Rathbone	607
Old Forge	315	Panther Lake	315	Pine Island	914	Portlandville	607	Ravena	518
Old Quogue	516	Paradise Point	516	Pinelawn	516	Port Leyden	315	Ray Brook	518
Old Westbury	516	Paradox	518	Pine Neck	516	Port Ontario	315	Raymertown	518
Olean	716	Paris	315	Pine Plains	518	Port Orange	914	Raymondville	315
Olive	914	Parish	315	Pine Valley	607	Port Richmond	212	Reading	607
Oliverea	914	Parishville	315	Pineville	315	Port Socony	212	Reading Center	607
Olmstedville	518	Paris Station	315	Piseco	518	Portville	716	Reber	518
Omar	315	Parksville	914	Pitcairn	315	Port Washington	516	Rector	315
Onativia	315	Parma	716	Pitcher	607	Post Creek	607	Red Creek	315
Onchiota	518	Partlow	315	Pittsford	716	Potsdam	315	Redfield	315
Oneida	315	Pataukunk	914	Pittstown	518	Potter	315	Redford	518
Oneonta	607	Patchin	716	Plainedge	516	Potter Hill	518	Red Hook	914
Onondaga Hill	315	Patchinville	716	Plainfield	315	Potter Hollow	518	Red Rock	518
Onoville	716	Patchogue	516	Plainview	516	Pottersville	518	Redwood	315
Ontario	315	Pattens Mills	518	Plainville	315	Poughkeepsie	914	Reeds Corners	315
Onteora Park	518	Patterson	914	Plandome	516	Poughquag	914	Rego Park	212
Oppenheim	518	Pattersonville	518	Platte Clove	518	Pound Ridge	914	Reichard's Lake	518
Oquaga Lake	607	Paul Smiths	518	Plattekill	914	Prattham	315	Remsen	315
Oramel	716	Pavilion	716	Plattsburgh	518	Prattsburg	607	Remsenburg	516
Oran	315	Pawling	914	Pleasant Brook	607	Pratts Hollow	315	Rensselaer	518
Orangeburg	914	Peach Lake	914	Pleasantdale	518	Prattsville	518	Rensselaer Falls	315
Orange Lake	914	Peakville	607	Pleasant Lake	315	Preble	607	Rensselaerville	518
Orchard Park	716	Pearl Creek	716	Pleasant Plains		Presho	607	Resort	315
Orient	516	Pearl River	914	(Dutchess Co.)	914	Preston Hollow	518	Result	518
Orient Point Coast Guard		Peasleeville	518	Pleasant Plains		Prince's Bay	212	Retsof	716
Light Sta.	518	Peconic	516	(Richmond Co.)	212	Promised Land	516	Rex	518
Oriskany	315	Peekskill	914	Pleasant Point	315	Prospect	315	Rexford	518
Oriskany Falls	315	Pekin (Niagara Co.)	716	Pleasant Valley		Prospect Heights	518	Rexford Falls	607
Orrs Mills	914	Pekin (Oswego Co.)	315	(Dutchess Co.)	914	Protection	716	Rexville	607
Orwell	315	Pelham	914	Pleasant Valley		Providence	518	Reydon Shores	516
				(Steuben Co.)	914	Pulaski	315		

Place Name	Area Code	Place Name	Area Code	Place Name	Area Code	Place Name	Area Code	Place Name	Area Code
Reynoldsville	607	Rose	315	Sandusky	716	Shady	914	Sodus Point Coast	
Rheims	607	Rosebank	212	Sandy Creek	315	Shandaken	914	Guard Light Sta.	315
Rhinebeck	914	Roseboom	607	Sandy Pond	315	Shandelee Lake	914	Solon	607
Rhinecliff	914	Rosedale	212	Sanfordville	315	Shanks Village	914	Solsville	315
Rices	315	Rose Hill	315	Sangerfield	315	Sharon Springs	518	Solvay	315
Riceville		Rosendale	914	Sanitaria Springs	607	Sharon Station	914	Somers	914
(Cattaraugus Co.)	716	Roseton	914	Santa Clara	518	Shavertown	914	Somerville	315
Riceville		Rosiere	315	Saranac	518	Shawnee	716	Sonora	607
(Fulton Co.)	518	Roslyn	516	Saranac Lake	518	Sheds	315	Sonyea	716
Richburg	716	Rossburg	716	Saratoga Springs	518	Sheepshead Bay	212	South Alabama	716
Riches Corners	716	Rossie	315	Sardinia	716	Shelby	716	South Albion	315
Richfield Junction	315	Rossman	518	Saugerties	914	Sheldon	716	South Amenia	914
Richfield Springs	315	Ross Mill	716	Sauquoit	315	Shelldrake (Springs)	607	Southampton	516
Richford	607	Rossville	212	Savannah	315	Shelter Island	516	South Apalachin	607
Richland	315	Rotterdam	518	Savilton	914	Shenorock	914	South Bay	315
Richmond Hill	212	Rotterdam Junction	518	Savona	607	Sherburne	607	South Berne	518
Richmond Mills	716	Round Lake	518	Sawkill	914	Sheridan	716	South Bethlehem	518
Richmondville	518	Round Pond	716	Saxton	518	Sherman	716	South Bradford	607
Richville	315	Round Top	518	Sayles Corners	315	Sherrill	315	South Buffalo Coast	
Rickard	315	Rouses Point	518	Sayville	516	Sherwood	315	Guard Light Sta.	716
Ridge	516	Roxbury		Scarborough	914	Shinnecock	516	South Butler	315
Ridgebury	914	(Delaware Co.)	607	Scaroon Manor	518	Shirley (Suffolk Co.)	516	South Byron	716
Ridgeway	716	Roxbury (Queens Co.)	212	Scarsdale	914	Shirly (Erie Co.)	716	South Cairo	518
Ridgewood	212	Ruby	914	Schaghticoke	518	Shokan	914	South Cambridge	518
Rifton	914	Rural Grove	518	Schenectady	518	Shoreham	516	South Cameron	607
Riga	716	Rural Hill	315	Schenevus	607	Short Beach Coast		South Canisteo	607
Rio	914	Rush	716	Schodack Center	518	Guard Sta. No. 88	516	South Centerville	914
Riparius	518	Rushford	716	Schodack Landing	518	Shortsville	716	South Colton	315
Ripley	716	Rushville	315	Schoharie	518	Short Tract	716	South Columbia	315
Ripley Point	518	Russell	315	Schroon Lake	518	Shrub Oak	914	South Corning	607
Risingville	607	Russia	315	Schultzville	914	Shuetown	315	South Cortland	607
Riverhead	516	Rutsonville	914	Schuyler Falls	518	Shushan	518	South Dansville	607
Riverside		Rye	914	Schuyler Lake	315	Sidney	607	South Dayton	716
(Broome Co.)	607			Schuylerville	518	Sidney Center	607	South Durham	518
Riverside				Scio	716	Silver Bay	518	South Edmeston	607
(Steuben Co.)	607			Sciota	518	Silver Creek	716	South Fallsburg	914
Riverside				Scipio Center	315	Silver Lake		Southfields	914
(Warren Co.)	518	Sabael	518	Scipioville	315	(Clinton Co.)	518	South Floral Park	516
Riverview	518	Sabattis	518	Scotch Bush	518	Silver Lake		South Gilboa	607
Roanoke Heights	516	Sabbath Day Point	518	Scotchtown	914	(Dutchess Co.)	914	South Glens Falls	518
Robert Corners	315	Sacandaga	518	Scotia	518	Silver Lake		South Hammond	315
Robins Rest	516	Sackets Harbor	315	Scott	607	(Richmond Co.)	212	South Hartford	518
Rochester	716	Sackett Lake	914	Scott Corners	607	Silver Lake		South Haven	516
Rochester Junction	716	Saddle Rock	516	Scottsburg	716	(Wyoming Co.)	716	South Hempstead	516
Rockaway	212	Sagaponack	516	Scottsville	716	Silver Springs	716	South Horicon	518
Rockaway Point Coast		Sagetown	607	Scout Haven	716	Simpsonville	607	South Jamesport	516
Guard Sta. No. 92	212	Sag Harbor	516	Scranton	716	Sinclairville	716	South Kortright	607
Rock City		St. Albans	212	Scriba	315	Skaneateles	315	South Lansing	607
(Cattaraugus Co.)	716	St. Andrew	914	Sea Breeze	716	Skinners Falls	914	South Lima	716
Rock City		St. Bonaventure	716	Sea Cliff	516	Slate Hill	914	South Livonia	716
(Dutchess Co.)	914	St. George	212	Seaford	516	Slaterville Springs	607	South Millbrook	914
Rock City Falls	518	St. Huberts	518	Sea Gate	212	Sleightsburg	914	South New Berlin	607
Rockdale	607	St. James	516	Seager	914	Slingerlands	518	South Nyack	914
Rock Glen	716	St. Johnsburg	716	Searingtown	516	Sliters	518	South Salem	914
Rock Hill	914	St. Johnsville	518	Searsburg	607	Sloan	716	South Schenectady	518
Rock Lake	914	St. Josen	914	Searsville	914	Sloansville	518	South Schodack	518
Rockland	607	St. Josephs	914	Seaside	212	Sloatsburg	914	South Scriba	315
Rockland Lake	914	St. Regis Falls	518	Seaview	516	Smallwood	914	South Sodus	315
Rock Rift	607	St. Remy	914	Second Milo	315	Smartville	315	South Spafford	607
Rock Stream	607	Salamanca	716	Selden	516	Smithboro	607	South Stockton	716
Rock Tavern	914	Salem	518	Selkirk (Albany Co.)	518	Smiths Basin	518	South Troupsburg	607
Rockville Centre	516	Salem Center	914	Selkirk (Oswego Co.)	315	Smiths Mills	716	South Valley	607
Rockwells Mills	607	Salisbury Center	315	Sempronius	315	Smithtown	516	South Wales	716
Rockwood	518	Salisbury Mills	914	Seneca Castle	315	Smithtown Branch	516	South Westerlo	518
Rocky Point	516	Salmon River	518	Seneca Falls	315	Smithtown Landing	516		
Rodman	315	Saltaire	516	Seneca Hill	315	Smithville	315		
Rogersville	716	Salt Point	914	Seneca Ordnance		Smithville Flats	607		
Rome	315	Salt Springville	518	Depot	315	Smyrna	607		
Romulus	607	Sammonsville	518	Sennett	315	Snowshoe Bay	315		
Rondout	914	Sampson	315	Setauket	516	Snyder	716		
Ronkonkoma	516	Samsonville	914	Seventh Lake	315	Snyders Corners	518		
Roosevelt	516	Sanborn	716	Severance	518	Snyders Lake	518		
Roosevelttown	315	Sand Lake	518	Seward	518	Sodom	518		
Roscoe	607	Sands Point	516	Shackleton Point	315	Sodus	315		

Place Name	Area Code
South West Hoosick	518
Southwest Oswego	315
South Worcester	607
Spafford	607
Sparkill	914
Sparrow Bush	914
Speculator	518
Speigletown	518
Spencer	607
Spencer Hill	607
Spencerport	716
Spencertown	518
Speonk	516
Spier Falls	518
Split Rock	315
Spragueville	315
Sprakers	518
Spring Brook	716
Springfield	212
Springfield Center	315
Spring Glen	914
Springlake	315
Springs	516
Springtown	914
Spring Valley	914
Springville	716
Springwater	716
Springwood Village	914
Sprout Brook	518
Spruceton	518
Spy Lake	518
Staatsburg	914
Stafford	716
Stamford	607
Standards	716
Standish	518
Stanfordville	914
Stanley	315
Stanwix	315
Stapleton	212
Starbuckville	518
Starkey	607
Starkville	518
Star Lake	315
State Line	518
Staten Island	212
Staten Island Coast Guard Light Sta.	212
Steamburg	716
Stedman	716
Stella	914
Stephens Mills	607
Stephentown	518
Sterling	315
Sterling Forest	914
Steuben	315
Stevensville	914
Stewart Air Force Base	914
Stilesville	607
Stillwater (Center)	518
Stissing	914
Stittville	315
Stockport	518
Stockton	716
Stone Arabia	518
Stoneco	914
Stone Ridge	914
Stoner Lake	518
Stony Brook	516
Stony Brook Glen	716
Stony Creek (Jefferson Co.)	315
Stony Creek (Warren Co.)	518
Stony Point (Jefferson Co.)	315
Stony Point (Rockland Co.)	914
Stormville	914
Stottville	518
Stow	716
Straits Corners	607
Stratford	315
Strykersville	716
Sturgeon Point	716
Stuyvesant (Falls)	518
Suffern	914
Sugar Loaf	914
Sullivan	315
Sullivanville	607
Summerville	716
Summit	518
Summitville	914
Sundown	914
Sunnyside	212
Sunside	518
Surprise	518
Swain	716
Swancott Mill	315
Swan Lake	914
Swartwood	607
Swastika	518
Sweden	716
Swormville	716
Sycaway	518
Sylvan Beach	315
Sylvan Lake	914
Syosset	516
Syracuse	315
Taberg	315
Taborton	518
Tahawas	518
Talcottville	315
Talcville	315
Tallman	914
Tannersville	518
Tappan	914
Tarrytown	914
Taughannock (Falls)	607
Taunton	315
Taylor	607
Taylor Center	607
Tenantville	518
Ten Mile River	914
Terryville	516
Texas	315
Texas Valley	607
The Branch	516
The Glen	518
The Landing	516
Thendara	315
The Raunt	212
Theresa	315
Thiells	914
Third Lake	315
Thirteenth Lake	518
Thirty Mile Point Coast Guard Light Sta.	716
Thomaston	516
Thompson Ridge	914
Thompsons Lake	518
Thompsonville	914
Thomson	518
Thornwood	914
Three Mile Bay	315
Throop	315
Throopsville	315
Thurman Station	518
Thurston	607
Tiana Coast Guard Sta. No. 73	516
Tiashoke	518
Ticonderoga	518
Tillson	914
Tilly Foster	914
Tioga Center	607
Titusville	914
Tivoli	914
Tomhannock	518
Tomkins Cove	914
Tompkins Corners	914
Tompkinsville	212
Tonawanda	716
Tottenville	212
Towlesville	607
Towners	914
Town Line	716
Townsend	607
Townsendville	607
Travis	212
Treadwell	607
Trenton	315
Triangle	607
Tribes Hill	518
Tripp Lake	518
Troupsburg	607
Troutburg	716
Trout Creek	607
Trout Pond	914
Trout River	518
Troy	518
Trumansburg	607
Trumbull Corners	607
Truthville	518
Truxton	607
Tuckahoe	914
Tuckers Corners	914
Tully	315
Tunnel	607
Tupper Lake	518
Turin	315
Tuscarora	716
Tusten	914
Tuttles	716
Tuxedo	914
Twin Harbors	516
Tyre	315
Tyrone	607
Ulster Heights	914
Ulster Park	914
Ulsterville	914
Unadilla	607
Unadilla Forks	315
Underwood	518
Union	607
Union Center	607
Union Course	212
Uniondale	516
Union Falls	518
Union Grove	914
Union Hill	716
Union Springs	315
Union Valley (Chenango Co.)	607
Union Valley (Cortland Co.)	315
Unionville (Albany Co.)	518
Unionville (Orange Co.)	914
Unionville (Sullivan Co.)	914
Upper Brookville	516
Upper Jay	518
Upper Lisle	607
Upper Red Hook	914
Upton	516
Upton Lake	914
Urbana	607
Urlton	518
Ushers	518
Utica	315
Vail Mills	518
Vails Gate	914
Valatie	518
Valcour	518
Valhalla	914
Valley Cottage	914
Valley Falls	518
Valley Junction	914
Valley Road	914
Valley Stream	516
Valois	607
Van Buren	716
Vandalia	716
Van Etten	607
Van Hornesville	315
Van Wies Point	518
Varna	607
Varysburg	716
Vaughan's Corners	518
Vega	607
Venice	315
Venice Center	315
Verbank	914
Verdoy	518
Vermillion	315
Vermontville	518
Vernon	315
Verona	315
Verplanck	914
Versailles	716
Vesper	315
Vestal	607
Vestal Center	607
Vetaran	914
Victor	716
Victoria	716
Victory	315
Victory Mills (Victory) (Saratoga Co.)	518
Viewmont	518
Vincent	716
Vine Valley	315
Virgil	607
Vista	914
Voorheesville	518
Waccabuc	914
Waddington	315
Wadhams	518
Wading River	516
Wadsworth	716
Wainscott	516
Wakefield	212
Walden	914
Wales	716
Walker	716
Walker Valley	914
Wallace	607
Wallington	315
Wallkill	914
Walloomsac	518
Walton	607
Walworth	315
Wampsville	315
Wanakah	716
Wanakena	315
Wantagh	516
Wappingers Falls	914
Warner	315
Warner's Lake	518
Warnerville	518
Warren	315
Warrensburg	518
Warsaw	716
Warwick	914
Washington Hollow	914
Washington Mills	315
Washingtonville	914
Wassaic	914
Waterburg	607
Waterford	518
Water Island	516
Waterloo	315
Water Mill	516
Waterport	716
Watertown	315
Watervale	315
Water Valley	716
Waterville	315
Watervliet	518
Watkins Glen	607
Watson	315
Watts Flats	716
Wave Crest	212
Waverly	607
Wawarsing	914
Wayland	716
Wayne	607
Wayne Center	315
Wayneport	315
Webatuck	914
Webster	716
Webster Crossing	716
Weedsport	315
Welch Hill	315
Welfare Island	212
Wellesley Island	315
Wells	518
Wells Bridge	607
Wellsburg	607
Wellsville	716
Wemple	518
Wende	716
Wendelville	716
Wesley	716
West Albany	518
West Alden	716
West Almond	607
West Amboy	315
West Athens	518
West Babylon	516
West Bangor	518
West Barre	716
West Batavia	716
West Bellerose	516

Place Name	Area Code	Place Name	Area Code	Place Name	Area Code	Place Name	Area Code	Place Name	Area Code
West Berne	518	Westhampton	516	West Stockholm	315	Willet	607	Woodstock	914
West Bloomfield	716	West Harpersfield	607	West Stony Creek	518	Williamson	315	Woodville	
West Branch	315	West Haverstraw	914	West Taghkanic	518	Williamstown	315	(Jefferson Co.)	315
West Brighton	212	West Hempstead	516	Westtown	914	Williamsville	716	Woodville	
Westbrookville	914	West Henrietta	716	West Union	607	Willing	716	(Ontario Co.)	716
West Burlington	607	West Hills		West Valley	716	Williston	716	Worcester	607
Westbury		(Nassau Co.)	516	West Vienna	315	Williston Park	516	Worth	315
(Cayuga Co.)	315	Westbury		Westville		Willow	914	Wrights Corners	518
Westbury		(Rensselaer Co.)	518	(Franklin Co.)	518	Willow Creek	607	Wurlitzer	716
(Nassau Co.)	516	West Hoosick	518	Westville (Otsego Co.)	607	Willowemoc	914	Wurtemburg	914
West Bush	518	West Hurley	914	West Walworth	315	Willow Glen	518	Wurtsboro	914
West Cameron	607	West Islip	516	West Webster	716	Willow Point	607	Wyandanch	516
West Camp	914	West Kill	518	West Windsor	607	Willowvale	315	Wyckoff	315
West Caroga Lake	518	West Laurens	607	West Winfield	315	Willsboro	518	Wynantskill	518
West Caton	607	West Lebanon	518	West Yaphank	516	Willseyville	607	Wyoming	716
West Charlton	518	West Leyden	315	Wethersfield	716	Wilmington	518		
West Chazy	518	West Martinsburg	315	Wethersfield Springs	716	Wilson	716		
West Chenango	607	West Milton	518	Wevertown	518	Wilton	518		
West Clarksville	716	West Monroe	315	Whaley Lake	914	Winchester	716		
West Commack	516	Westmoreland	315	Whallonsburg	518	Windham	518		
West Copake	518	West Newark	607	Wheatfield	716	Windom	716	Yankee Lake	914
West Coxsackie	518	West New Brighton	212	Wheatley Hills	516	Windsor	607	Yaphank	516
Westdale	315	West Nyack	914	Wheatville	716	Wingdale	914	Yates	716
West Danby	607	Weston	607	Wheeler	607	Winterton	914	Yatesville	315
West Davenport	607	West Oneonta	607	Wheelerville	518	Winthrop	315	Yonkers	914
West Day	518	Westons Mills	716	Whippleville	518	Wiscoy	716	York	716
West Dryden	607	West Park	914	White Church	518	Witherbee	518	Yorkshire	716
West Durham	518	West Perth	518	White Creek	518	Wittenberg	914	Yorktown	914
West Eaton	315	West Plattsburgh	518	Whiteface Mountain	518	Wolcott	315	Yorktown Heights	315
West Edmeston	315	West Point	914	Whitehall	518	Wolcottsburg	716	Yorkville	315
Westerleigh	212	Westport	518	White Lake	914	Wolf Creek	518	Yosts	518
Westerlo	518	West Portland	716	White Lake Station	315	Woodbourne	914	Young Hickory	607
Westernville	315	West Richmondville	518	White Plains	914	Woodbury	516	Youngstown	716
West Exeter	315	West Rodman	315	Whiteport	914	Woodbury Falls	914	Youngsville	914
West Falls	716	West Rush	716	Whitesboro	315	Woodgate	315	Yulan	914
Westfield	716	West Sand Lake	518	White Sulphur Springs	914	Woodhaven	212		
Westford	607	West Saugerties	914	Whitesville	607	Woodhull	607		
West Fort Ann	518	West Sayville	516	Whitney Crossings	607	Woodland	914		
West Fulton	518	West Seneca	716	Whitney Point	607	Woodmere	516		
West Glens Falls	518	West Shelby	716	Wiccopee	914	Woodridge	914		
West Greece	716	West Shokan	914	Wildcat Pond	914	Woodsburgh	516	Zena	914
West Greenville	518	West Sparta	716	Wildwood	516	Woodside	212	Zoar	315
West Greenwood	607	West Stephentown	518	Willard	607	Woods Lake	315	Zurich	315
West Groton	607								

Place Name	Area Code
Abbottsburg	919
Aberdeen	919
Acme	919
Addor	919
Advance	919
Ahoskie	919
Airlie	919
Alamance	919
Albemarle	704
Alexander	704
Allenton	919
Alliance	919
Almond	704
Altamahaw	919
Altamont	704
Alton	704
Amity Hill	704
Anderson	919
Andrews	704
Angier	919
Ansonville	704
Antioch	704
Apex	919
Arapahoe	919
Arcadia-Midway	704
Archdale	919
Arcola	919
Arden	704
Ash	919
Asheboro	919
Asheville	704
Ashford	704
Atkinson	919
Atlantic	919
Atlantic Beach	919
Auburn	919
Aulander	919
Aurora	919
Autryville	919
Avon	919
Ayden	919
Aydlett	919
Badin	704
Badin Lake	919
Bahama	919
Bailey	919
Bakersville	704
Bald Creek	704
Bald Head Coast Guard Light Sta.	919
Baldwin	919
Balfour	704
Balsam	704
Balsam Grove	704
Banner Elk	704
Barco	919
Barium Springs	704
Barnardsville	704
Barnesville	919
Bat Cave	704
Bath	919
Battleboro	919
Bayboro	919
Bear Creek	919
Bear Poplar	704
Beaufort	919
Beech Mountain	704
Belcross	919
Belews Creek	919
Belhaven	919
Bellarthur	919
Belmont	704
Belvidere	919
Belwood	704
Bennett	919
Benson	919
Bertha	919
Bessemer City	704
Bethania	919
Bethel	919
Bethlehem	704
Beulah	919
Beulaville	919
Biltmore	704
Biscoe	919
Black Creek	919
Black Mountain	704
Bladenboro	919
Blanche	919
Blowing Rock	704
Blue Ridge	704
Boardman	919
Bodie Island	919
Boger City	704
Bogue	919
Boiling Springs	704
Bolivia	919
Bolton	919
Bonlee	919
Bonnerton	919
Boomer	919
Boone	704
Boonville	704
Bostic	704
Bowdens	919
Brasstown	704
Brevard	704
Bridgeton	919
Broadway	919
Brookford	704
Brooks	919
Brooks Cross Roads	919
Browns Summit	919
Brunswick	919
Bryson City	704
Bules Creek	919
Bullock	919
Bunn	919
Bunnlevel	919
Burgaw	919
Burlington	919
Burnsville	704
Butner	919
Buxton	919
Bynum	919
Calabash	919
Calypso	919
Camden	919
Cameron	919
Camp Le Jeune	919
Candler	704
Candor	919
Canton	704
Cape Fear Coast Guard Light Sta.	919
Cape Fear Coast Guard Sta. No. 193	919
Cape Fear Power Station	919
Cape Hatteras Coast Guard Sta.	919
Cape Lookout Coast Guard Sta.	919
Caroleen	704
Carolina Beach	919
Carrboro	919
Carrowinds	704
Carthage	919
Cary	919
Casar	704
Cash Corner	919
Cashiers	704
Castalia	919
Castle Hayne	919
Catawba	704
Ca-Vel	919
Cedar Falls	919
Cedar Grove	919
Cedar Mountain	704
Celo	704
Centerville	919
Cerro Gordo	919
Chadbourn	919
Champion	919
Chapanoke	919
Chapel Hill	919
Charlotte	704
Cherokee	704
Cherry Point	919
Cherryville	704
Chicod	919
Chimney Rock	704
China Grove—Landis	704
Chinquapin	919
Chocowinity	919
Churchland	704
Claremont	704
Clarendon	919
Clarkton	919
Clayton	919
Clemmons	919
Cleveland	704
Cliffside	704
Climax	919
Clingman	919
Clinton	919
Clyde	704
Coats	919
Cofield	919
Coharie	919
Coinjock	919
Colerain	919
Coleridge	919
Colfax	919
Columbia	919
Columbus	704
Como	919
Concord	704
Conetoe	919
Connellys Springs	704
Conover	704
Conway	919
Cooleemee	704
Corapeake	919
Cordova	704
Cornelius	704
Council	919
Courtney	919
Cove City	919
Cramerton	704
Cranberry	704
Creedmoor	919
Creston	704
Creswell	919
Crisp	919
Crossnore	704
Crouse	704
Crutchfield	919
Culberson	704
Cullowhee	704
Currie	919
Currituck	919
Cypress Creek	919
Dallas	704
Danbury	919
Davidson	704
Davis	919
Deep Run	919
Delco	919
Denton	704
Denver	704
Derita	704
Dillon	919
Dillsboro	704
Dixon	919
Dobson	919
Dover	919
Draper	919
Drexel	704
Dublin	919
Dunn	919
Durham	919
Eagle Springs	919
Earl	704
East Arcadia	919
East Bend	919
East Laport	704
Eden	919
Edenton	919
Edgemont	704
Edneyville	704
Edward	919
Efland	919
Ela	704
Elberon	919
Elizabeth City	919
Elizabethtown	919
Elkin	919
Elk Park	704
Ellenboro	704
Ellerbe	919
Elm City	919
Elmwood	704
Elon College	919
Emerald Isle	919
Enfield	919
Engelhard	919
Enka-Candler	704
Erwin	919
Etowah	704
Eureka	919
Everetts	919
Evergreen	919
Fair Bluff	919
Fairmont	919
Fairview	704
Faison	919
Faith	704
Falcon	919
Falkland	919
Fallston	704
Farmer	919
Farmville	919
Fayetteville	919
Flat Rock	704
Fletcher	704
Florence	919
Folkston	919
Fontana Village	704
Forbush	919
Forest City	704
Fort Bragg	919
Fort Caswell	919
Fort Macon Coast Guard Sta. No. 191	919
Fountain	919
Four Oaks	919
Franklin	704
Franklinton	919
Franklinville	919
Freeman	919
Fremont	919
Fuquay Springs	919
Fuquay-Varina	919
Garden City	704
Garland	919
Garner	919
Garysburg	919
Gaston	919
Gastonia	704
Gatesville	919
Gatewood	919
Germanton	919
Gibson	919
Gibsonville	919
Gilkey	704
Glade Creek	919
Glen Alpine	704
Glendale Springs	919
Glendon	919
Glen Raven	919
Glenville	704
Glenwood Providence	704
Gliden	919
Gloucester	919
Godwin	919
Gold Hill	704
Goldsboro	919
Goldston	919
Goose Creek	704
Graham	919
Grandy	919
Granite Falls	704
Granite Quarry—Rockwell	704
Grantham	919
Grantsboro	919
Green Creek	704
Green Mountain	704
Greensboro	919
Greenville	919
Gregory	919
Grifton	919
Grimesland	919
Grover	704
Guilford College	919
Gulf	919
Gumberry	919
Guntertown	704

NORTH CAROLINA
Halifax—Roanoke Rapids

Place Name	Area Code	Place Name	Area Code	Place Name	Area Code	Place Name	Area Code	Place Name	Area Code
Halifax	919	Julian	919	Lowesville	704	Mountain View	704	Parmele	919
Hallsboro	919			Lowgap	919	Mount Airy	919	Patterson	704
Hamilton	919			Lucama	919	Mount Gilead	919	Patterson Springs	704
Hamlet	919			Lucia	704	Mount Holly	704	Paw Creek	704
Hampstead	919	Kannapolis	704	Lumber Bridge	919	Mount Mourne	704	Peachland—Polkton	704
Hamptonville	919	Kelford	919	Lumberton	919	Mount Olive	919	Pelham	919
Harbinger	919	Kelly	919	Lynn	704	Mount Pleasant	704	Pembroke	919
Harkers Island	919	Kenansville	919			Mount Ulla	704	Penland	704
Harmony	704	Kenly	919			Mount Vernon Springs	919	Penrose	704
Harrells	919	Kernersville	919			Moyock	919	Pfafftown	919
Harrellsville	919	Kill Devil Hills	919	Macclesfield	919	Mulberry	919	Pike Road	919
Harris	704	Kill Devil Hills		Mackeys	919	Murfreesboro	919	Pikeville	919
Harrisburg	704	Coast Guard Sta.	919	Macon	919	Murphy	704	Pilot	919
Hassell	919	Kimesville	919	Madison	919			Pilot Mountain	919
Hatteras	919	King	919	Maggie Valley	704			Pinebluff	919
Havelock	919	Kings Mountain	704	Magnolia	919			Pine Hall	919
Haw River	919	Kinston	919	Maiden	704	Nags Head	919	Pinehurst	919
Hayesville	704	Kipling	919	Mamie	919	Nantahala	704	Pine Level	919
Hays	919	Kittrell	919	Manchester	919	Naples	704	Pineola	704
Hazelwood	704	Kitty Hawk	919	Manley	919	Nashville	919	Pinetops	919
Hedricks Grove	704	Knightdale	919	Manns Harbor	919	Nathans Creek	919	Pinetown	919
Hemby Bridge	704	Knotts Island	919	Mansfield	919	Nebo	704	Pineville	704
Henderson	919	Kure Beach	919	Manson	919	Neuse	919	Piney Woods	919
Hendersonville	704			Manteo	919	New Bern	919	Pink Hill	919
Henrietta	704			Maple Hill	919	Newell	704	Pinnacle	919
Herring	919			Marble	704	Newhill	919	Pisgah	919
Hertford	919	La Grange	919	Margarettsville	919	New Holland	919	Pisgah Forest	704
Hickory	704	Lake Junaluska	704	Maribel	919	New Hope	704	Pittsboro	919
Hiddenite	704	Lake Lure	704	Marietta	919	Newland	704	Pleasant Garden	919
Highfalls	919	Lake Toxaway	704	Marion	704	New London	704	Pleasant Hill	919
High Hampton	704	Lakeview	919	Marshall	704	Newport	919	Plumtree	704
Highlands	704	Lake Waccamaw	919	Marshallberg	919	New Salem	704	Plymouth	919
High Point	919	Landis	704	Mars Hill	704	Newton	704	Point Harbor	919
High Shoals	704	Lansing	919	Marshville	704	Newton Grove	919	Polkton	704
Hildebran	704	Lattimore	704	Marston	919	New Topsail Beach	919	Polkville	704
Hillsborough	919	Laurel Hill	919	Matthews	704	Nixonton	919	Pollocksville	919
Hobbsville	919	Laurinburg	919	Maury	919	Norlina	919	Pope Air Force Base	919
Hobgood	919	Lawndale	704	Maxton	919	Norman	919	Poplar Branch	919
Hobucken	919	Leaksville	919	Mayodan	919	North Cove	704	Potecasi	919
Hoffman	919	Leaman	919	Maysville	919	North Wilkesboro	919	Powells Point	919
Holden Beach	919	Leasburg	919	McAdenville	704	Norwood	704	Powellsville	919
Hollister	919	Ledger	704	McCain	919			Price	919
Holly Ridge	919	Leechville	919	McDonalds	919			Princeton	919
Holly Springs	919	Leggett	919	McFarlan	704			Proctorville	919
Hookerton	919	Leicester	704	Mebane	919	Oakboro	704	Prospect Hill	919
Hope Mills	919	Leland	919	Merritt	919	Oak City	919	Providence	919
Horse Shoe	704	Lemon Springs	919	Merry Hill	919	Oak Island Coast Guard		Purvis	919
Hot Springs	704	Lenoir	704	Mesic	919	Sta. No. 194	919		
Hudson	704	Level Cross	919	Micaville	704	Oak Ridge	919		
Huntersville	704	Lewiston	919	Micro	919	Ocean Isle Beach	919		
Hurdle Mills	919	Lewisville	919	Middlesex	919	Ocracoke	919	Quaker Gap	919
		Lexington	704	Midland	704	Old Fort	704		
		Liberty		Millboro	919	Oldtown	919		
Icard	704	(Cherokee Co.)	704	Millers Creek	919	Old Trap	919		
Ijames	704	Liberty		Milton	919	Olivia	919	Raeford	919
Indian Trail	704	(Randolph Co.)	919	Mineral Springs	704	Oregon Inlet	919	Raleigh	919
Inez	919	Lilesville	704	Minneapolis	704	Oregon Inlet Coast		Ramseur	919
Ingleside	919	Lillington	919	Misenheimer	704	Guard Sta.	919	Randleman	919
Ivanhoe	919	Lincolnton	704	Mocksville	704	Oriental	919	Ranlo	704
		Linville	704	Momeyer	919	Orrum	919	Raynham	919
		Linville Falls	704	Moncure	919	Ossipee	919	Red Brush	919
		Linwood	704	Monroe	704	Oswalt	704	Red Springs	919
Jackson	919	Lisbon	919	Monticello	919	Oteen	704	Reeds	704
Jackson Creek	919	Little Switzerland	704	Montreat	704	Otto	704	Reidsville	919
Jackson Springs	919	Littleton	919	Mooresboro	704	Otway	919	Research	
Jacksonville	919	Locust	704	Mooresville	704	Oxford	919	Triangle Park	919
James City	919	Lomax	919	Moravian Falls	919			Rhodhiss	704
Jamestown	919	Long Beach	919	Morehead City	919			Richfield	704
Jamesville	919	Longhurst	919	Morganton	704			Richlands	919
Jarvisburg	919	Longview	704	Morrisville	919	Pactolus	919	Rich Square	919
Jefferson	919	Longwood	919	Morven	704	Pamlico	919	Ridgecrest	704
Johns	919	Loray	704	Moss Hill	919	Pantego	919	Ridgeway	919
Jonesville	919	Louisburg	919	Mountain Home	704	Parkton	919	Riegelwood	919
		Lowell	704	Mountain Park	919	Parkwood	919	Roanoke Rapids	919

Place Name	Area Code	Place Name	Area Code	Place Name	Area Code	Place Name	Area Code	Place Name	Area Code
Roaring Gap	919	Shallotte	919	Stony Point	704	Valdese	704	White Lake	919
Roaring River	919	Sharpsburg	919	Stovall	919	Vale	704	White Oak	919
Robbins	919	Shawboro	919	Stumpy Point	919	Valle Crucis	704	White Plains	919
Robbinsville	704	Sheffield	704	Sugar Grove	704	Vanceboro	919	Whiteville	919
Robersonville	919	Shelby	704	Suit	704	Vandemere	919	Whitnel	704
Rockingham	919	Sherrills Ford	704	Summerfield	919	Varina	919	Whitsett	919
Rockwell	704	Sherwood	704	Sunbury	919	Vass	919	Whittier	704
Rocky Mount	919	Shiloh	919	Sunset Beach	919	Vaughan	919	Wildwood	919
Rocky Point	919	Shoals	919	Supply	919	Verona	919	Wilgrove	704
Rodanthe	919	Shooting Creek	704	Surf City	919	Vilas	704	Wilkesboro	919
Roduco	919	Sidney Cross Roads	919	Swannanoa	704	Virgilina	919	Willard	919
Rolesville	919	Siler City	919	Swanquarter	919			Williamston	919
Ronda	919	Siloam	919	Swansboro	919			Williston	919
Roper	919	Sims	919	Swepsonville	919			Willow Spring	919
Roseboro	919	Six Run	919	Swiss	704			Wilmington	919
Rose Hill	919	Skyland	704	Sylva	704			Wilmington Beach	919
Rosman	704	Sligo	919					Wilson	919
Rougemont	919	Smithfield	919			Waco	704	Wilsons Mills	919
Rowland	919	Smyrna	919	Tabor City	919	Wade	919	Windom	704
Roxboro	919	Sneads Ferry	919	Tapoca	704	Wadesboro	704	Windsor	919
Roxobel	919	Snowden	919	Tarboro	919	Wagram	919	Winfall	919
Ruffin	919	Snow Hill	919	Taylorsville	704	Wakefield	919	Wingate	704
Rural Hall	919	Sophia	919	Teacheys	919	Wake Forest	919	Winnabow	919
Rutherfordton	704	South Crowders Creek	704	Terrell	704	Walkertown	919	Winston-Salem	919
		Southern Pines	919	Thomasville	919	Wallace	919	Winterville	919
		South Mills	919	Thurmond	919	Wallburg	919	Winton	919
		Southmont	704	Tillery	919	Walnut	704	Wise	919
St. Helena	919	Southport	919	Timberlake	919	Walnut Cove	919	Wood	919
St. Pauls	919	South River	919	Toast	919	Walstonburg	919	Woodland	919
Salemburg	919	Sparta	919	Tobaccoville	919	Wananish	919	Woodlawn	704
Salisbury	704	Speed	919	Toluca	704	Wanchese	919	Woodleaf	704
Salter Path	919	Spencer	704	Tomotla	704	Warne	704	Woodsdale	919
Saluda	704	Spindale	704	Topsail Island	919	Warren Plains	919	Woodville (Bertie Co.)	919
Salvo	919	Spot	919	Topton	704	Warrenton	919	Woodville
Sanatorium	919	Spray	919	Trenton	919	Warsaw	919	(Perquimans Co.)	919
Sandy Ridge	919	Spring Creek	704	Triangle	704	Washington	919	Worthville	919
Sanford	919	Spring Hope	919	Trinity	919	Watauga	704	Wrightsboro	919
Sapphire	704	Spring Lake	919	Trotville	919	Waterlily	919	Wrightsville Beach	919
Saratoga	919	Spruce Pine	704	Troutman	704	Waterville	704	
Saxapahaw	919	Stacy	919	Troy	919	Watha	919	
Scotland Neck	919	Staley	919	Trust	704	Waves	919	
Scotts	704	Stanfield	704	Tryon	704	Waxhaw	704	
Scotts Hill	919	Stanhope	919	Tuckaseegee	704	Waynesville	704	
Scottville	919	Stanley	704	Turkey	919	Weaverville	704	
Seaboard	919	Stanleyville	919	Turnersburg	704	Webster	704	
Seagrove	919	Stantonsburg	919	Tuxedo	704	Weeksville	919	Yadkin	704
Sealevel	919	Star	919	Tyner	919	Welch	919	Yadkinville	919
Seaside	919	Startown	704			Welcome	704	Yanceyville	919
Sedalia	919	State Road	919			Weldon	919	Youngsville	919
Selma	919	Statesville	704			Wendell	919	
Semora	919	Stedman	919			Wentworth	919	
Seven Springs	919	Stella	919			Wesser	704	
Severn	919	Stokes	919			West End	919	
Sevier	704	Stokesdale	919	Unaka	704	Westfield	919	
Seymour Johnson Air		Stoneville	919	Union Grove	704	West Jefferson	919	Zebulon	919
Force Base	919	Stonewall	919	Union Mills	704	Whispering Pines	919	Zephyr	919
						Whitakers	919	

ALL POINTS—AREA CODE 701

OHIO
Aberdeen—Collinsville

Place Name	Area Code	Place Name	Area Code	Place Name	Area Code	Place Name	Area Code	Place Name	Area Code
Aberdeen	513	Bailey Lakes	419	Big Prairie	216	Brunswick	216	Ceylon	419
Ada	419	Baileys Mills	614	Big Springs	513	Bryan	419	Ceylon Junction	419
Adams Mills	614	Bainbridge (Geauga Co.)	216	Birds Run	614	Buchtel	614	Chagrin Falls	216
Adamsville	614	Bainbridge (Ross Co.)	614	Birmingham	216	Buckeye Lake	614	Chalfants	614
Adario	419	Bairdstown	419	Blackfork	614	Buckland	419	Chambersburg	614
Addison	614	Bakersville	216	Black Lick	614	Bucyrus	419	Champion (Heights)	216
Addyston	513	Baltic	216	Blackrun	614	Buena Vista	614	Chandler	614
Adelphi	614	Baltimore	614	Bladen	614	Buffalo	614	Chandlersville	614
Adena	614	Bangs	614	Bladensburg	614	Buford	513	Chardon	216
Aid	614	Bannock	614	Blaine	614	Burbank	216	Charlestown	216
Akron	216	Bantam	513	Blakeslee	419	Burghill	216	Charm	216
Albany	614	Barberton	216	Blanchard	419	Burgoon	419	Chatfield	419
Alexandria	614	Barlow	614	Blanchester	513	Burkettsville	513	Chatham	216
Alger	419	Barnesville	614	Blissfield	614	Burlington	614	Chauncey	614
Allensville	614	Barnhill	216	Bloomdale	419	Burr Oak	614	Chautauqua	513
Alliance	216	Barrs Mills	216	Bloomingburg	614	Burton	216	Cherry Fork	513
Alpha	513	Bartlett	614	Bloomingdale	614	Burton Station	216	Cherry Valley	216
Alta	419	Barton	614	Bloomingville	419	Businessburg	614	Chesapeake	614
Alton	614	Bascom	419	Bloomville	419	Butler	419	Cheshire	
Alvada	419	Basil	614	Blue Ash	513	Butlerville	513	(Delaware Co.)	614
Alvordton	419	Batavia	513	Blue Creek	513	Byesville	614	Cheshire (Gallia Co.)	614
Amanda	614	Batesville	614	Blue Rock	614	Byhalia	513	Cheshire-Center	614
Amberly	513	Bath	216	Bluffton	419			Chester	614
Amelia	513	Bayard	216	Boardman	216			Chesterfield	419
Amesville	614	Baybridge	419	Bolivar	216			Chesterhill	614
Amherst	216	Bay Village	216	Bono	419	Cable	513	Chesterland	216
Amlin	614	Beach City	216	Booth	419	Cadiz	614	Chesterville	419
Amsden	419	Beachwood Village	216	Boston Heights	216	Cadiz Junction	614	Cheviot	513
Amsterdam	614	Beallsville	614	Botkins	513	Cairo	419	Chickasaw	419
Andover	216	Beaver	614	Boughtonville	419	Caldwell	614	Chili	614
Ankenytown	614	Beavercreek	513	Bourneville	614	Caledonia	419	Chillicothe	614
Anna	513	Beaverdam	419	Bowerston	614	Cambridge	614	Chilo	513
Ansonia	513	Bedford	216	Bowersville	513	Camden	513	Chippewa Lake	216
Antioch	614	Bedford Heights	216	Bowling Green	419	Cameron	614	Christiansburg	513
Antrim	614	Beebe	614	Bowlusville	513	Campbell	216	Cincinnati	513
Antwerp	419	Belden	216	Braceville	216	Campbellstown	513	Circleville	614
Apple Creek	216	Belfast	513	Bradford	513	Camp Dennison	513	Claiborne	614
Arabia	614	Bellaire	614	Bradley	614	Camp Perry	419	Claridon	
Arcadia	419	Bellbrook	513	Bradner	419	Canal Fulton	216	(Geauga Co.)	216
Arcanum	513	Belle Center	513	Brady Lake	216	Canal Winchester	614	Claridon	
Archbold	419	Bellefontaine	513	Branch Hill	513	Canfield	216	(Marion Co.)	614
Arlington		Belle Valley	614	Bratenahl	216	Canton	216	Clarington	614
(Hancock Co.)	419	Bellevue	419	Brecksville	216	Carbondale	614	Clark	216
Arlington		Bellville	419	Bremen	614	Carbon Hill	614	Clarksburg	614
(Montgomery Co.)	513	Belmont	614	Brewster	216	Cardington	419	Clarksfield	419
Arlington Heights	513	Belmore	419	Brice	614	Carey	419	Clarkson	216
Armstrongs Mills	614	Beloit	216	Briceton	419	Carlisle (Noble Co.)	614	Clarksville	513
Arthur	419	Belpre	614	Bridgeport	614	Carlisle (Warren Co.)	513	Clay	419
Ashland	419	Bentleyville	216	Briggsdale	614	Carpenter	614	Clay Center	419
Ashley	614	Benton	216	Brighton	216	Carroll	614	Claysville	614
Ashtabula	216	Benton Ridge	419	Brilliant	614	Carrollton	216	Clayton	513
Ashville	614	Bentonville	513	Brimfield	216	Carrothers	419	Cleveland	216
Assumption	419	Berea	216	Brinkhaven	614	Carthagena	419	Cleveland Heights	216
Athalia	614	Bergholz	614	Bristol	614	Casstown	513	Cleves	513
Athens	614	Berkey	419	Bristolville	216	Castalia	419	Clifton	513
Atlanta	614	Berlin	216	Broadacre	614	Castine	513	Climax	419
Attica	419	Berlin Center	216	Broadview Heights	216	Catawba	513	Clinton	216
Atwater	216	Berlin Heights	419	Broadway	513	Catawba Island	419	Cloverdale	419
Auburn	216	Berne	614	Broadwell	614	Cecil	419	Clyde	419
Augusta	216	Berwick	419	Brookfield	216	Cedar Point	419	Coalburg	216
Aultman	216	Bethany	513	Brooklyn (Heights)	216	Cedarville	513	Coal Grove	614
Aurora	216	Bethel	513	Brook Park	216	Celina	419	Coal Run	614
Austin	614	Bethesda	614	Brookside	614	Centerburg	614	Coalton	614
Austinburg	216	Bettsville	419	Brookville	513	Centerton	419	Coldwater	419
Austintown	216	Beulah Beach	216	Broughton	419	Centerville		Colebrook	216
Ava	614	Beverly	614	Brownhelm	216	(Belmont Co.)	614	Colerain	614
Avery	419	Bexley	614	Brownsville		Centerville		College Corner	513
Avon	216	Bidwell	614	(Licking Co.)	614	(Gallia Co.)	614	Collins	419
Avon Lake	216	Big Island	614	Brownsville		Centerville		Collinsville	513
Ayersville	419			(Monroe Co.)	614	(Montgomery Co.)	513		

TELEPHONE AREA CODE DIRECTORY

Place Name	Area Code	Place Name	Area Code	Place Name	Area Code	Place Name	Area Code	Place Name	Area Code
Colton	419	Deer Park	513	East Springfield	614	Foraker	419	Gordon	513
Columbiana	216	Deersville	614	East Townsend	419	Forest	419	Gore	614
Columbia Park	513	Defiance	419	Eastwood	513	Fort Ancient	513	Goshen	513
Columbia Station	216	De Graff	513	East Woodburn	419	Fort Hayes Garrison	614	Grafton	216
Columbus	614	Delaware	614	Eaton	513	Fort Jefferson	513	Grand Rapids	419
Columbus Grove	419	Delhi	513	Edenton	513	Fort Jennings	419	Grand River	216
Commercial Point	614	Dellroy	216	Edgerton	419	Fort Loramie	513	Grandview	614
Concord	216	Delphos	419	Edinburg	216	Fort Recovery	419	Grandview Heights	614
Condit	614	Delta	419	Edison	419	Fort Seneca	419	Grants	419
Conesville	614	Dennison	614	Edon	419	Foster	513	Granville	614
Congress	419	Derby	614	Elba	614	Fostoria	419	Gratiot	614
Congress Lake	216	Derwent	614	Eldorado	513	Fowler	216	Gratis	513
Conneaut	216	Deshler	419	Elgin	419	Frank	419	Graysville	614
Connorville	614	Deweyville	419	Elida	419	Frankfort	614	Graytown	419
Conotton	614	Dexter	614	Elizabethtown	513	Franklin	513	Green Camp	614
Conover	513	Dexter City	614	Elkton	216	Franklin Furnace	614	Greene	216
Constitution	614	Diamond	216	Ellsworth (Ellsworth		Frazeysburg	614	Greenfield	513
Continental	419	Dilles Bottom	614	Station)	216	Fredericksburg	216	Greenford	216
Convoy	419	Dillonvale—		Elm Grove	614	Fredericktown	614	Greenhills	513
Coolville	614	Mount Pleasant	614	Elmira	419	Freeburg	216	Greensburg	216
Cooney	419	Dixon	419	Elmore	419	Freedom	216	Green Springs	419
Cooperdale	614	Dodson	513	Elmwood Place	513	Freeport	614	Greentown	216
Copley	216	Dola	419	Elroy	513	Fremont	419	Greenville	513
Corning	614	Donnelsville	513	Elyria	216	Fresno	614	Greenwich	419
Cortland	216	Dorset	216	Emmett	419	Friendship	614	Grelton-Malinta	419
Corwin	513	Dover	216	Empire	614	Frost	614	Grove City	614
Coshocton	614	Downington	614	Englewood	513	Fulton	419	Groveport	614
Cove	614	Doylestown	216	Enon	513	Fultonham	614	Grover Hill	419
Covington	513	Dresden	614	Enterprise	614			Guernsey	614
Cozaddale	513	Dublin	614	Epworth Heights	513			Gustavus	216
Craig Beach	216	Duffy	614	Era	614			Gutman	513
Creola	614	Dunbridge	419	Erhart	216			Guyan	614
Crescent	614	Duncan Falls	614	Erie Ordnance Depot	419	Gahanna	614	Guysville	614
Crestline	419	Dundas	614	Erlin	419	Galena	614	Gypsum	419
Creston	216	Dundee	216	Etna	614	Galion	419		
Cridersville	419	Dunglen	614	Euclid	216	Gallipolis	614		
Cromers	419	Dunkirk	419	Evansport	419	Galloway	614		
Crooksville	614	Dupont	419	Evendale	513	Gambier	614	Hackney	614
Croton	614	Durant	614	Ewington	614	Garfield	216	Hageman	513
Crown City	614	Duvall	614	Excello	513	Garfield Heights	216	Halls Corners	
Crystal Lake	513	Dwyer	513			Garrettsville	216	Village	216
Crystal Spring	216					Gates Mills	216	Hallsville	614
Cuba	513					Geauga Lake	216	Hambden	216
Cumberland	614					Geneva	216	Hamden	614
Curtice-Oregon	419			Fairborn	513	Geneva-on-the-Lake	216	Hamersville	513
Custar	419	Eagleport	614	Fairfax	513	Genoa	419	Hamilton	513
Cutler	614	Earlville	216	Fairfield	513	Georgetown	513	Hamler	419
Cuyahoga Falls	216	East Cadiz	614	Fairhaven	513	Gerald	419	Hamlet	513
Cuyahoga Heights	216	East Canton	216	Fairpoint	614	Germano	614	Hammondsville	216
Cygnet	419	East Claridon	216	Fairport	216	Germantown	513	Hanford	614
Cynthiana	614	East Cleveland	216	Fairview	614	Gettysburg	513	Hanging Rock	614
		East Danville	513	Fairview Park	216	Ghent	216	Hannibal	614
		East Fairfield	216	Farmdale	216	Gibisonville	614	Hanover	614
		East Fultonham	614	Farmer	419	Gibson	614	Hanoverton	216
		East Greenville	216	Farmersville	513	Gibsonburg	419	Harbor Hills	614
Dalton	216	East Harbor	419	Fayette	419	Gilboa	419	Harbor View	419
Dalzell	614	Eastlake	216	Fayetteville	513	Girard	216	Hardin	513
Damascus	216	East Lewistown	216	Feesburg	513	Glandorf	419	Harlem Springs	216
Danbury	419	East Liberty		Felicity	513	Glass Rock	614	Harmon	216
Danville		(Logan Co.)	513	Fernald	513	Glencoe	614	Harpster	614
(Highland Co.)	513	East Liberty		Flat	216	Glendale	513	Harriettsville	614
Danville (Knox Co.)	614	(Summit Co.)	216	Fincastle	513	Glen Echo	614	Harrisburg	
Darbydale	614	East Liverpool	216	Findlay	419	Glenford	614	(Franklin Co.)	614
Darbyville	614	East Monroe	513	Firebrick	614	Glenkarn	513	Harrisburg	
Darrowville	216	East Monroeville	419	Flat Rock	419	Glenmont	216	(Stark Co.)	216
Darrtown	513	East New Corydon	419	Fleming	614	Glenmore	419	Harrison	513
Dart	614	Easton	216	Fletcher-Lena	513	Glenroy	614	Harrisonville	614
Dawn	513	East Orwell	216	Flint	614	Glenwillow Village	216	Harrisville	614
Dayton	513	East Palestine	216	Floodwood	614	Glouster	614	Harrod	419
Deavertown	614	East Richland	614	Florence	216	Gnadenhutten	614	Hartford	
Decatur	513	East Richmond	513	Florida	419	Golf Manor	513	(Licking Co.)	614
Decliff	614	East Rochester	216	Flushing	614	Gomer	419	Hartford	
Deerfield	216	East Sparta	216	Fly	614	Good Hope	614	(Trumbull Co.)	216

Place Name	Area Code	Place Name	Area Code	Place Name	Area Code	Place Name	Area Code	Place Name	Area Code
Hartland	419	Indian Lake	513	Kingston	614	Liberty	513	Malvern	216
Hartland Station	419	Ingomar	513	Kingsville	216	Liberty Center	419	Manchester	
Hartville	216	Irondale	216	Kingsway	419	Lilly Chapel	614	(Adams Co.)	513
Harveysburg	513	Ironton	614	Kinnikinnick	614	Lima	419	Manchester	
Haskins-Tontogany	419	Irwin	614	Kinsman	216	Lima Ordnance Depot	419	(Summit Co.)	216
Havana	419	Isle St. George	419	Kipling	614	Limaville	216	Mansfield	419
Haverhill	614	Isleta	614	Kipton	216	Lime City	419	Mantua	216
Haviland	419	Ithaca	513	Kirby	419	Limestone	419	Mantua Center	216
Haydenville	614			Kirkersville	614	Lincoln Heights	513	Mantua Corners	216
Hayesville	419			Kirkwood	513	Lindsey	419	Maple Grove	419
Heath	614			Kirtland	216	Linworth	614	Maple Heights	216
Hebron	614			Kirtland Hills	216	Lippincotts	513	Maplewood	513
Helena	419	Jackson	614	Kitts Hill	614	Lisbon (Clark Co.)	513	Marathon	513
Hemlock	614	Jacksonburg	513	Knoxville	614	Lisbon		Marble Cliff	614
Hemlock Grove	614	Jackson Center	513	Kunkle	419	(Columbiana Co.)	216	Marblehead	419
Hendrysburg	614	Jacksontown	614	Kyger	614	Litchfield	216	Marengo	419
Hepburn	419	Jacksonville				Lithopolis	614	Maria Stein	419
Hicksville	419	(Adams Co.)	513			Little Hocking	614	Mariemont	513
Higby	614	Jacksonville				Lockbourne	614	Marietta	614
Higginsport	513	(Athens Co.)	614			Lockbourne Air Force		Marion	614
Highland	513	Jacobsburg	614	Lacarne	419	Base	614	Marion Engineer	
Highland Heights	216	Jaite	216	Ladd	614	Lockington	513	Depot	614
Highland Park	216	Jamestown	513	Lafayette	419	Lockland	513	Mark Center	419
Hillcrest	216	Jasper	614	Lafferty	614	Lockville	614	Marlboro	216
Hill Grove	513	Jefferson		LaGrange	216	Lockwood	216	Marne	614
Hilliard	614	(Ashtabula Co.)	216	Lakeline	216	Lodi	216	Marseilles	614
Hilliards	614	Jefferson		Lake Milton	216	Logan	614	Marshall	513
Hillsboro	513	(Wayne Co.)	216	Lakemore	216	London	614	Marshallville	216
Hills & Dales	216	Jeffersonville	614	Lakeside	419	Londonderry	614	Martel	419
Hinckley	216	Jenera	419	Lakeview	513	Long Bottom	614	Martin	419
Hiram	216	Jeromesville	419	Lakeville		Lorain	216	Martinsburg	614
Hobson	614	Jerry City	419	(Ashtabula Co.)	216	Lordstown	216	Martins Ferry	614
Hockingport	614	Jerseyville	614	Lakeville (Holmes Co.)	419	Lordstown Ordnance		Martinsville	513
Holgate	419	Jerusalem	614	Lakewood	216	Depot	216	Marysville	513
Holland	419	Jewell	419	Lamartine	216	Lore City	614	Mason	513
Hollansburg	513	Jewett	614	Lancaster	614	Loudonville	419	Massieville	614
Hollister	614	Johnsons	216	Landeck	419	Louisville	216	Massillon	216
Holloway	614	Johnston	216	Langsville	614	Loveland	513	Masury	216
Holmesville	216	Johnstown	614	Lansing	614	Lowell	614	Maud	513
Homer	614	Johnsville		La Rue	614	Lowellville	216	Maumee	419
Homerville	216	(Montgomery Co.)	513	Latham	614	Lower Salem	614	Mayfield	216
Homeworth	216	Johnsville		Latty	419	Loyal Oak	216	Mayfield Heights	216
Hooven	513	(Morrow Co.)	419	Laura	513	Loydsville	614	May Hill	513
Hopedale	614	Junction	419	Laurelville	614	Lucas	419	Maynard	614
Hopetown	614	Junction City	614	Lawrenceville	513	Lucasville	614	McArthur	614
Hopewell	614	Justus	216	Lawshe	513	Luckey	419	McClure	419
Horatio	513			Leavittsburg	216	Ludlow Falls	513	McComb	419
Houston	513			Lebanon		Lykens	419	McConnelsville	614
Howard	614			(Monroe Co.)	614	Lynchburg	513	McCuneville	614
Howenstine	216			Lebanon		Lyndhurst	216	McCutchenville	419
Hoytville	419	Kalida	419	(Warren Co.)	513	Lyndon	513	McDermott	614
Hubbard	216	Kanauga	614	Lecta	614	Lynx	513	McDonald	216
Hudson	216	Kansas	419	Leesburg	513	Lyons	419	McDonaldsville	216
Hume	419	Keene	614	Lees Creek	513	Lytle	513	McGuffey	419
Huntington	216	Kelleys Island	419	Leesville				McLuney	614
Hunting Valley	216	Kensington	216	(Carroll Co.)	614			Meade	614
Huntsburg	216	Kent	216	Leesville				Mechanicsburg	513
Huntsville	513	Kenton	419	(Crawford Co.)	419			Mechanicstown	216
Huron	419	Kenwood	513	Leetonia	216			Medina	216
Hyatts	614	Kerr	614	Leipsic	419	Macedonia	216	Medway	513
		Kessler	513	Lemert	614	Macksburg	614	Melbern	419
		Kettering	513	Lemoyne	419	Macon	513	Melmore	419
		Kettlersville	513	Lena	513	Madeira	513	Melrose	419
		Key	614	Leonardsburg	614	Madison	216	Melvin	513
		Kidron	216	Leroy (Lake Co.)	216	Madison Mills	614	Mendon	419
Iberia	419	Kieferville	419	Leroy (Medina Co.)	216	Magnetic Springs	513	Mentor	216
Idaho	614	Kilbourne	614	Le Sourdsville	513	Magnolia-		Mentor-on-the-Lake	216
Ilers	419	Kilgore	216	Letart Falls	614	Waynesburg	216	Mercer	419
Independence		Kilbuck	216	Lewisburg	513	Maineville	513	Mercerville	614
(Cuyahoga Co.)	216	Kimball	419	Lewis Center	614	Malaga	614	Mermill	419
Independence		Kimbolton	614	Lewistown	513	Malinta	419	Mesopotamia	216
(Defiance Co.)	419	Kings Creek	513	Lewisville	614	Mallet Creek	216	Metals Park	216
Indian Hill	513	Kings Mills	513	Lexington	419	Malta	614	Metamora	419

OHIO
Meyers Lake–Quincy

Place Name	Area Code	Place Name	Area Code	Place Name	Area Code	Place Name	Area Code	Place Name	Area Code
Meyers Lake	216	Moulton	419	New Harrisburg	216	Oak Harbor	419	Peoria	513
Miamisburg	513	Mount Blanchard	419	New Haven	419	Oak Hill	614	Pepper Pike	216
Miamisburg-West		Mount Carmel	513	New Holland	614	Oak Shade	419	Perintown	513
Carrollton	513	Mount Cory	419	Newhope	513	Oakwood		Perry	216
Miamitown	513	Mount Eaton	216	New Jasper	513	(Montgomery Co.)	513	Perrysburg	419
Miamiville	513	Mount Ephriam	614	New Knoxville	419	Oakwood		Perrysville	
Middle Bass	419	Mount Gilead	419	New Lebanon	513	(Paulding Co.)	419	(Ashland Co.)	419
Middle Bass Island	419	Mount Healthy	513	New Lexington	614	Oakwood Village	216	Perrysville	
Middlebranch	216	Mount Holly	513	New London	419	Oberlin	216	(Carroll Co.)	216
Middleburg	513	Mount Hope	216	New Lyme	216	Obetz	614	Petersburg	216
Middleburgh Heights	216	Mount Liberty	614	New Madison	513	Oceola	614	Pettisville	419
Middlefield	216	Mount Orab	513	New Marshfield	614	Octa	614	Phalanx	216
Middle Point	419	Mount Perry	614	New Matamoras	614	Ohio City	419	Phillipsburg	513
Middleport	614	Mount Pleasant		New Miami	513	Okeana	513	Philo	614
Middleton	216	(Hocking Co.)	614	New Middletown	216	Okolona	419	Phoneton	513
Middletown	513	Mount Pleasant		New Milford	216	Old Fort	419	Pickerington	614
Midland	513	(Jefferson Co.)	614	New Moorefield	513	Old Washington	614	Piedmont	614
Midvale	216	Mount Pleasant		New Paris	513	Olena	419	Pierpont	216
Midway	614	(Vinton Co.)	614	New Philadelphia	216	Olmsted Falls	216	Piketon	614
Mifflin	419	Mount Sterling	614	New Plymouth	614	Omega	614	Pikeville	513
Milan	419	Mount Vernon	614	Newport	614	Oneida	216	Pine Lake	216
Milford	513	Mount Victory	513	New Richland	513	Ontario	419	Piney Fork	614
Milford Center	513	Mount Washington	513	New Richmond	513	Orange Village	216	Pioneer	419
Millbury	419	Mowrystown	513	New Riegel	419	Orangeville	216	Piqua	513
Milledgeville	614	Moxahala	614	New Rome	614	Oregon	419	Pisgah	513
Miller	614	Mulberry	513	New Rumley	614	Oregonia	513	Pitchin	513
Miller City	419	Munroe Falls	216	New Salem	614	Oreton	614	Pitsburg	513
Millersburg	216	Munson	216	New Springfield	216	Orient	614	Plain City	614
Millersport	614	Murray City	614	New Straitsville	614	Orland	614	Plainfield	614
Millersville	419	Mutual	513	Newton Falls	216	Orrville	216	Plainville	513
Millfield	614			Newtonsville	513	Orwell	216	Plankton	419
Millville	513			Newtown	513	Osgood	419	Plattsburg	513
Millwood	614			New Vienna	513	Ostrander	614	Pleasant Bend	419
Milton Center	419			New Washington	419	Otsego	614	Pleasant City	614
Milton Lake	216			New Waterford	216	Ottawa	419	Pleasant Corners	614
Miltonsburg	614	Nankin	419	New Weston	513	Ottawa Hills	419	Pleasant Hill	513
Mineral	614	Napoleon	419	New Winchester	419	Ottokee	419	Pleasant Plain	513
Mineral City	216	Nashport	614	Ney	419	Ottoville	419	Pleasant Valley	614
Mineral Ridge	216	Nashville	216	Niles	216	Otway	614	Pleasantville	614
Minersville	614	Navarre	216	North Auburn	419	Outville	614	Plymouth	419
Minerva	216	Neapolis	419	North Baltimore	419	Overpeck	513	Poasttown	513
Minerva Park	614	Neffs	614	North Bass Island	419	Owens	614	Point Pleasant	513
Minford-Stockdale	614	Negley	216	North Bend	513	Owensville	513	Poland	216
Mingo	513	Nellie	614	North Benton	216	Oxford	513	Polk	419
Mingo Junction	614	Nelsonville	614	North Bloomfield	216			Pomeroy	614
Minster	419	Nevada	614	North Canton	216			Poplargrove	513
Mitiwanga	216	Neville	513	North College Hill	513			Portage	419
Mogadore	216	New Albany		North Creek	419			Portage Lakes	216
Moline	419	(Franklin Co.)	614	North Eaton	216	Painesville	216	Port Clinton	419
Monclova	419	New Albany		North Fairfield	419	Palestine	513	Porterfield	614
Monroe	513	(Mahoning Co.)	216	Northfield	216	Palmyra	216	Port Homer	614
Monroeville	419	New Alexandria	614	North Georgetown	216	Pandora	419	Port Jefferson	513
Monterey	513	Newark	614	North Hampton	513	Paris	216	Portland	614
Montezuma	419	New Athens	614	North Industry	216	Parkertown	419	Portsmouth	614
Montgomery	513	New Baltimore	513	North Jackson	216	Parkman	216	Port Washington	614
Montpelier	419	New Bavaria	419	North Kenova	614	Parkview	216	Port William	513
Montrose		New Bedford	216	North Kingsville	216	Parma	216	Potsdam	513
(Cuyahoga Co.)	216	New Bloomington	614	North Lewisburg	513	Parma Heights	216	Pottersburg	513
Montrose		New Boston	614	North Lima	216	Parral	216	Powell	614
(Summit Co.)	216	New Bremen	419	North Madison	216	Pataskala	614	Powhatan Point	614
Montville	216	Newburgh Heights	216	North Olmsted	216	Patterson	419	Proctorville	614
Moorefield	614	New Burlington		North Perry	216	Patterson Field	513	Prospect	614
Moraine City	513	(Clinton Co.)	513	North Ridgeville	216	Pattersonville	216	Prout	419
Moran	216	New Burlington		North Robinson	419	Paulding	419	Provident	614
Moreland Hills	216	(Hamilton Co.)	513	North Royalton	216	Pavonia	419	Pulaski	419
Morenci	419	Newbury	216	North Star	419	Payne	419	Put-in-Bay	419
Morges	216	New Carlisle	513	Northup	614	Pearl	614		
Morning Sun	513	Newcomerstown	614	Norwalk	419	Peebles	513		
Morral	614	New Concord	614	Norwich	614	Pemberton	513		
Morristown	614	New Cumberland	216	Norwood	513	Pemberville	419		
Morrow	513	New Dover	513	Nova	419	Peninsula	216		
Moscow	513	New Franklin	216	Novelty	216	Pennsville	614	Quaker City	614
Moss Run	614	New Hampshire	419	Nutwood	216	Peoli	614	Quincy	513

Place Name	Area Code	Place Name	Area Code	Place Name	Area Code	Place Name	Area Code	Place Name	Area Code
Racine	614	Rushtown	614	Silica	419	Swanders	513	U. S. Government Dam	
Radcliff	614	Rushville	614	Silver Lake	216	Swanton	419	No. 17	614
Radnor	614	Russell	216	Silverton	513	Sycamore	419	U. S. Government Dam	
Ragersville	216	Russells Point	513	Simons	216	Sycamore Valley	614	No. 37	513
Rainsboro	513	Russellville	513	Sinking Spring	513	Sylvania	419	Unity	216
Randolph	216	Russia	513	Slate Mills	614	Syracuse	614	University Heights	216
Rarden	614	Rutland	614	Smithfield	614			Upper Arlington	614
Rathbone	614	Rye Beach	419	Smithville	216			Upper Sandusky	419
Ravenna	216			Solon	216			Urbana	513
Ravenna Arsenal	216			Somerdale	216			Urbancrest	614
Rawson	419			Somerset	614			Utica	614
Rayland	614			Somerton	614				
Raymond	513	Sabina	513	Somerville	513	Tacoma	614		
Reading	513	Sagamore Hills	216	Sonora	614	Tallmadge	216		
Redhaw	419	St. Bernard	513	South Amherst	216	Tama	419		
Reedsville	614	St. Clairsville	614	South Bloomfield	614	Tedrow	419		
Reesville	513	St. Henry	419	South Bloomingville	614	Temperanceville	614		
Reily	513	St. James	419	South Charleston	513	Terrace	216	Valley City	216
Reinersville-Hackney	614	St. Johns	419	South Euclid	216	Terrace Park	513	Valley Junction	216
Rendville	614	St. Louisville	614	South Lebanon	513	Terre Haute	513	Valley View	216
Reno	614	St. Martin	513	South Newbury	216	Thackery	513	Vanatta	614
Republic	419	St. Marys	419	South Olive	614	The Plains	614	Van Buren	419
Resaca	614	St. Paris	513	South Point	614	Thompson	216	Vandalia	513
Reynoldsburg	614	Salem	216	South Russell	216	Thornville	614	Vanlue	419
Richfield	216	Salesville	614	South Salem	513	Thorps	513	Van Wert	419
Richfield Center-		Salineville	216	South Solon	513	Thurston	614	Vaughnsville	419
Berkey	419	Sandusky	419	South Vienna	513	Tiffin	419	Venedocia	419
Richmond	614	Sandy Lake	216	South Webster	614	Tiltonsville	614	Venice	419
Richmondale	614	Sandyville	216	South Zanesville	614	Tipp City	513	Vermilion	216
Richmond Heights	216	Santa Fe	419	Spargursville	614	Tippecanoe	614	Vermilion-on-	
Richville	216	Sarahsville	614	Sparta	419	Tippecanoe City	513	the-Lake	216
Richwood	614	Sardinia	513	Speidel	614	Tiro	419	Verona	513
Ridgeville Corners	419	Sardis	614	Spencer	216	Tobasco	513	Versailles	513
Ridgeway	513	Sargents	614	Spencerville	419	Toboso	614	Vickery	419
Rimer	419	Savannah	419	Springboro	513	Toledo	419	Victory	216
Rinard Mills	614	Savona	513	Springfield	513	Toledo Municipal		Vienna (Clark Co.)	513
Rio Grande	614	Saybrook	216	Springfield Lake	216	Airport	419	Vienna	
Ripley	513	Schumm	419	Spring Valley	513	Tontogany	419	(Trumbull Co.)	216
Risingsun	419	Scio	614	Stafford	614	Torch	614	Vigo	614
Rittman	216	Scioto Furnace	614	Stafford Lake	216	Toronto	614	Vincent	614
Riverlea	614	Sciotoville	614	Standley	419	Trebein	513	Vinton	614
Riverside	513	Scott	419	Stanleyville	614	Tremont City	513		
Roads	614	Scottown	614	Starr	614	Trenton	513		
Robertsville	216	Seaman	513	Stelvideo	513	Trimble	614		
Robyville	614	Sebring	216	Sterling	216	Trinity	216	Wabash	419
Rochester	216	Sedalia	614	Steubenville	614	Trinway	614	Wade	614
Rockbridge	614	Selma	513	Stewart	614	Trotwood	513	Wadsworth	216
Rock Creek	216	Senecaville	614	Stillwater	614	Troy	513	Wainwright	614
Rockford	419	Seven Hills	216	Stillwater Junction	513	Trumbull	216	Waite Hill	216
Rockland	614	Seven Mile	513	Stockdale	614	Tunnel Hill	614	Wakefield	614
Rocky Ridge	419	Seville	216	Stockport	614	Tuppers Plains	614	Wakeman	216
Rocky River	216	Shade	614	Stone Creek	216	Tuscarawas	614	Walbridge	419
Rodney	614	Shadyside	614	Stony Ridge	419	Twin Lakes	216	Waldo	614
Rogers	216	Shaker Heights	216	Stoutsville	614	Twinsburg	216	Walhonding	614
Rome (Adams Co.)	513	Shalersville	216	Stow	216			Walnut	614
Rome		Shandon	513	Strasburg	216			Walnut Creek	216
(Ashtabula Co.)	216	Shanesville	216	Stratton	614			Wapakoneta	419
Rootstown	216	Sharon (Noble Co.)	614	Streetsboro	216	Uhrichsville	614	Warner	614
Roscoe	614	Sharon		Strongsville	216	Union	513	Warnock	614
Roseville	614	(Trumbull Co.)	216	Struthers	216	Union City	513	Warren	216
Rosewood	513	Sharon Center	216	Stryker	419	Union Furnace	614	Warrensville	216
Ross	513	Sharonville	513	Suffield	216	Unionport	614	Warrensville Heights	216
Rossburg	513	Sharpsburg	614	Sugarcreek	216	Uniontown	216	Warrenton	614
Rossford	419	Shawnee	614	Sugar Grove	614	Unionvale	614	Warsaw	614
Rossmoyne	513	Sheffield	216	Sugar Ridge	419	Unionville	216	Warwick	216
Roswell	614	Sheffield Lake	216	Sugar Tree Ridge	513	Unionville Center	614	Washington Court	
Roundhead	513	Shelby	419	Sullivan	419	Uniopolis	419	House	614
Roxabell	614	Sherrodsville	614	Sulphur Springs	419	U. S. Government Dam		Washingtonville	216
Roxbury	614	Sherwood	419	Summerfield	614	No. 10	614	Waterford	614
Rudolph	419	Shiloh	419	Summit Station	614	U. S. Government Dam		Waterloo	614
Ruggles Beach	419	Short Creek	614	Summitville	216	No. 14	614	Watertown	614
Rush Run	614	Shreve	216	Sunbury	614	U. S. Government Dam		Waterville	419
Rushsylvania	513	Sidney	513	Superior	614	No. 15	614	Wauseon	419
								Waverly	614
								Wayland	216

Place Name	Area Code	Place Name	Area Code	Place Name	Area Code	Place Name	Area Code	Place Name	Area Code
Wayne	216	Westlake	216	Whipple	614	Windsor	216	Xenia	513
Wayne-Bradner	419	West Lebanon	216	White Cottage	614	Winesburg	216		
Waynesburg	216	West Leipsic	419	Whitehall	614	Wingett Run	614		
Waynesfield	419	West Liberty	513	Whitehouse	419	Winona	216		
Waynesville	513	West Manchester	513	Wickliffe	216	Winterset	614		
Weilersville	216	West Mansfield	513	Wilberforce	513	Wintersville	614	Yale	216
Wellington	216	West Middletown	513	Wilkesville	614	Withamsville	513	Yankee Lake	216
Wellston	614	West Millgrove	419	Wilkins Air Force		Wolf	614	Yellow Springs-	
Wellsville	216	West Milton	513	Depot	419	Wolf Creek	614	Clifton	513
Wengerlawn	513	Westminster	419	Willard	419	Woodington	513	York Center	513
West Alexandria	513	Weston	419	Williamsburg	513	Woodlawn	513	Yorkshire	419
West Austintown	216	West Point	216	Williamsfield	216	Woodsfield	614	Yorkville	614
West Bedford	614	West Portsmouth	614	Williamsport	614	Woodside	419	Youngstown	216
Westboro	513	West Richfield	216	Williamstown	419	Woodstock	513		
West Carrollton	513	West Rushville	614	Williston	419	Woodville	419		
West Chester	513	West Salem	419	Willoughby	216	Wooster	216		
West Elkton	513	West Union	513	Willowick	216	Worthington	614		
Westerville	614	West Unity	419	Willshire-Wren	419	Wren	419		
West Farmington	216	Westview	216	Wilmer	419	Wright Field	513	Zaleski	614
Westfield Center	216	Westville	513	Wilmington	513	Wright-Patterson		Zanesfield	513
Westhope	419	Weyers	419	Wilmot	216	Air Force Base	513	Zanesville	614
West Jefferson	614	Wharton	419	Winchester	513	Wrightsville	614	Zoar	216
West Lafayette	614	Wheelersburg	614	Windham	216	Wyoming	513	Zoarville	216

Place Name	Area Code	Place Name	Area Code	Place Name	Area Code	Place Name	Area Code	Place Name	Area Code
Achille	405	Bokoshe	918	Clarita	405	Eagle City	405	Gracemont	405
Ada	405	Boley	918	Clayton	918	Eagletown	405	Graham	405
Adair	918	Booker	405	Clearlake	405	Eakly	405	Grainola	918
Adams	405	Boswell	405	Clearview	405	Earlsboro	405	Grandfield	405
Addington	405	Bowlegs	405	Clebit	405	Eddy	405	Granite	405
Afton	918	Boynton	918	Clemscot	405	Edmond	405	Grant	405
Agra	918	Bradley	405	Cleo Springs	405	Edna	918	Gray	405
Albert	405	Braggs	918	Cleveland	918	Eldorado	405	Greenfield	405
Albion	918	Braman	405	Clinton	405	Elgin	405	Griggs	405
Alderson	918	Bray	405	Clinton-Sherman		Elk City	405	Grove	918
Alex	405	Breckinridge	405	Air Force Base	405	Elmer	405	Guthrie	405
Alfalfa	405	Bridgeport	405	Clyde	405	Elmore City	405	Guymon	405
Aline	405	Brinkman	405	Coalgate	405	Elmore-West	405		
Allen	405	Bristow	918	Colbert	405	Elmwood	405		
Alluwe	918	Britton	405	Colcord	918	El Reno	405		
Alma	405	Broken Arrow	918	Coleman	405	Enid	405	Haileyville	918
Alsuma	918	Broken Bow	405	Collinsville	918	Enterprise	918	Hallett	918
Altoona	405	Bromide	405	Colony	405	Erick	405	Hammon	405
Altus	405	Bryan's Corner	405	Comanche	405	Eufaula	918	Hanna	918
Alva	405	Buffalo	405	Commerce	918	Eva	405	Hardesty	405
Amber	405	Buffalo Valley	918	Concho	405			Harmon	405
America	405	Bunch	918	Connerville	405			Harrah	405
Ames	405	Burbank	918	Cookson	918			Hartshorne	918
Amorita	405	Burlington	405	Cooperton	405	Fairfax	918	Haskell	918
Anadarko	405	Burneyville	405	Copan	918	Fairland	918	Hastings	405
Antlers	405	Burns Flat	405	Cordell	405	Fairmont	405	Hawley	405
Apache	405	Butler	405	Corn	405	Fairview	405	Haworth	405
Arapaho	405	Byars	405	Council Hill	918	Fallis	405	Hayward	405
Arcadia	405	Byron	405	County Line	405	Fanshawe	918	Headrick	405
Ardmore	405			Covington	405	Fargo	405	Healdton	405
Ardmore Air Park	405			Coweta	918	Faxon	405	Heavener	918
Arkoma	918			Cox City	405	Fay	405	Helena	405
Arnett	405	Cache	405	Coyle	405	Featherston	918	Hendrix	405
Arpelar	918	Caddo	405	Craterville Park	405	Felt-Wheeless	405	Hennepin	405
Asher	405	Calera	405	Crescent	405	Fittstown	405	Hennessey	405
Ashland	918	Calumet	405	Cromwell	405	Fitzhugh	405	Henryetta	918
Atoka	405	Calvin	405	Crowder	918	Fletcher	405	Hickory	405
Atwood	405	Camargo	405	Crusher	405	Floris	405	Higgins	405
Avant	918	Cameron	918	Cushing	918	Foraker	918	Hillsdale	405
Avard	405	Canadian	918	Custer City	405	Forgan	405	Hinton	405
		Caney	405	Cyril	405	Fort Cobb	405	Hitchcock	405
		Canton	405			Fort Gibson	918	Hitchita	918
		Canute	405			Fort Sill	405	Hitchland	405
Balko	405	Capron	405	Dacoma	405	Fort Supply	405	Hobart	405
Banner	405	Cardin	918	Dale	405	Fort Towson	405	Hochatown	405
Barnsdall	918	Carmen	405	Darrouzett	405	Foss	405	Hockerville	918
Baron	918	Carnegie	405	Davenport	918	Foster	405	Holdenville	405
Bartlesville	918	Carney	405	Davidson	405	Fox	405	Hollis	405
Battiest	405	Carrier	405	Davis	405	Foyil	918	Hollister	405
Beaver	405	Carter	405	Dawson	918	Francis	405	Holly Creek	405
Beggs	918	Cartwright	405	Deer Creek	405	Frederick	405	Homestead	405
Bengal	918	Cashion	405	Delaware	918	Freedom	405	Hominy	918
Bennett	918	Castle	405	Delhi	405			Hooker	405
Bennington	405	Catoosa	918	Depew	918			Hopeton	405
Berlin	405	Cedar Crest	918	Devol	405			Howe	918
Bernice	918	Cedar Lake	405	Dewar	918	Gage	405	Hugo	405
Bessie	405	Cedars	918	Dewey	405	Gans	918	Hulbert	918
Bethany	405	Cement	405	Dibble	405	Garber	405	Hunter	405
Big Cabin	918	Centrahoma	405	Dill City	405	Garvin	405	Hydro	405
Billings	405	Centralia	918	Disney	918	Gate	405		
Binger	405	Century	918	Dodson	405	Geary	405		
Bison	405	Cestos	405	Dougherty	405	Gene Autry	405		
Bixby	918	Chandler	405	Douglas	405	Geronimo	405	Idabel	405
Bixby North	918	Chattanooga	405	Dover	405	Gerty	405	Indiahoma	405
Blackburn	918	Checotah	918	Dow	405	Glencoe	405	Indianola	918
Blackwell	405	Chelsea	918	Driftwood	405	Glenpool	918	Inola	918
Blair	405	Cherokee	405	Drummond	405	Glover	405	Isabella	405
Blanchard	405	Chester	405	Drumright	918	Golden	405		
Blanco	918	Cheyenne	405	Duke	405	Goltry	405		
Blocker	918	Chickasha	405	Dunbar	918	Goodwell	405		
Blue	405	Chilocco School	405	Duncan	405	Gore	918	Jay	918
Blue Jacket	918	Choctaw	405	Durant	405	Gotebo	405	Jefferson	405
Boise City	405	Chouteau	918	Durham	405	Gould	405	Jenks	918
Bokchito	405	Claremore	918	Dustin	918	Gowen	918	Jennings	918

OKLAHOMA
Jester—Tyrone

Place Name	Area Code	Place Name	Area Code	Place Name	Area Code	Place Name	Area Code	Place Name	Area Code
Jester	405	Manitou	405	Oak Hill	405	Ralston	918	South Dearing	918
Jet	405	Mannford	918	Oaks	918	Ramona	918	South Edna	918
Jones	405	Mannford East	918	Oakwood	405	Randlett	405	South Elgin	918
		Mannsville	405	Ochelata	918	Ratliff City	405	South Elkhart	405
		Maramec	918	Oglesby	918	Rattan	405	South Englewood	405
		Marble City	918	Oilton	918	Ravia	405	South Hardtner	405
Kansas	918	Marietta	405	Okarche	405	Redden	405	South Haven	405
Kaw City	405	Marland	405	Okeene	405	Red Oak	918	South Hewins	918
Keefeton	918	Marlow	405	Okemah	918	Red Rock	405	South Meade	405
Kellyville	918	Marshall	405	Oklahoma City	405	Reed	405	South Tyro	918
Kemp	405	Martha	405	Okmulgee	918	Renfrow	405	South Waldron	405
Kendrick	918	Maud	405	Olustee	405	Reydon	405	South West City	918
Kenefic	405	May	405	Omega	405	Richard's Spur	918	Sparks	918
Kenton	405	Maysville	405	Oney	405	Ringling	405	Spaulding	405
Kenwood	918	Mazie	918	Oologah	918	Ringwood	405	Spavinaw	918
Keota	918	McAlester	918	Optima	405	Ripley	918	Spencer	405
Ketchum	918	McCurtain	918	Orienta	405	Rocky	405	Sperry	918
Keyes	405	McLoud	405	Orlando	405	Roff	405	Spiro	918
Keystone	918	McMillan	405	Osage	918	Roger Mills	405	Springer	405
Kiefer	918	Mead	405	Oscar	405	Roland	918	Sterling	405
Kildare	405	Medford	405	Owasso	918	Roosevelt	405	Stigler	918
Kingfisher	405	Medicine Park	405			Rosedale	405	Stillwater	405
Kingston	405	Meeker	405			Rosston	405	Stilwell	918
Kinta	918	Meno	405			Rufe	405	Stonewall	405
Kiowa	918	Meridian	405			Rush Springs	405	Strang	918
Knowles	405	Merrick	405	Paden	405	Russett	405	Stratford	405
Konawa	405	Miami	918	Panama	918	Ryan	405	Stringtown	405
Krebs	918	Midwest City	405	Paoli	405			Strong City	405
Kremlin	405	Milburn	405	Paradise	405			Stroud	918
		Milfay	918	Pauls Valley	405			Stuart	918
		Mill Creek	405	Pawhuska	918			Sulphur	405
		Millerton	405	Pawnee	918	St. Louis	405	Summerfield	918
Lahoma	405	Minco	405	Pearson	405	Salina	918	Summit	918
Lamar	405	Moffett	918	Peckham	405	Sallisaw	918	Sweetwater	405
Lamont	405	Moho	918	Peggs	918	Sand Springs	918	Swink	405
Langley	918	Monroe	918	Pensacola	918	Sapulpa	918	
Langston	405	Moon	405	Perkins	405	Sasakwa	405	
Laverne	405	Moore	405	Pernell	405	Savanna	918	
Lawton	405	Mooreland	405	Perry	405	Sawyer	405	
Leach	918	Moorewood	405	Perryton	405	Sayre	405	
Leedey	405	Morris	918	Picher	918	Schulter	918	Tabler	405
Leflore	918	Morrison	405	Piedmont	405	Scipio	918	Tahlequah	918
Lehigh	405	Mounds	918	Pierce	918	Seiling	405	Talala	918
Lenapah	918	Mountain Fork	405	Pike City	405	Selman	405	Talihina	918
Leon	405	Mountain Park	405	Pittsburg	918	Seminole	405	Taloga	405
Leonard	918	Mountain View	405	Platter	405	Sentinel	405	Tamaha	918
Lexington	405	Moyers	405	Pocasset	405	Seward	405	Tecumseh	405
Limestone Gap	918	Muldrow	918	Pocola	918	Shady Point	918	Temple	405
Lindsay	405	Mulhall	405	Ponca City	405	Shamrock	918	Terlton	918
Loco	405	Muse	918	Pond Creek	405	Sharon	405	Terral	405
Locust Grove	918	Muskogee	918	Pontotoc	405	Shattuck	405	Texhoma	405
Logan	405	Mustang	405	Pooleville	405	Shawnee	405	Texola	405
Lone Grove	405	Mutual	405	Porter	918	Shidler	918	Thackerville	405
Lone Wolf	405			Porum	918	Skedee	918	Thomas	405
Longdale	405			Poteau	918	Skeeter Lease	918	Tiff City	918
Longtown	918			Prague	405	Skiatook	918	Tinker Air Force Base	405
Lookeba	405	Nardin	405	Preston	918	Slick	918	Tipton	405
Loveland	405	Nash	405	Proctor	918	Smithville	405	Tishomingo	405
Lovell	405	Nashoba	918	Producers	918	Snug Harbor	918	Tom	405
Loyal	405	Nelagoney	918	Prue	918	Snyder	405	Tonkawa	405
Lucien	405	Newalla	405	Pryor	918	Soper	405	Tribbey	405
Lugert	405	Newcastle	405	Purcell	405	Southard	405	Trousdale	405
Luther	405	New Home	918	Putnam	405	South Arkansas City	405	Tryon	918
		Newkirk	405			South Bartlett	918	Tullahassee	918
		New Lima	405			South Baxter Springs	918	Tulsa	918
		Newport	405			South Bluff City	405	Tupelo	405
Macomb	405	Nicoma Park	405			South Caldwell	405	Turpin	405
Madill	405	Noble	405			South Caney	918	Tushka	405
Madison	405	Norge	405	Quapaw	918	South Chetopa	918	Tuskahoma	918
Manchester	405	Norman	405	Quinlan	405	South Coffeyville	918	Tuttle	405
Mangum	405	Nowata	918	Quinton	918	South Coldwater	405	Tyrone	405

Place Name	Area Code	Place Name	Area Code	Place Name	Area Code	Place Name	Area Code	Place Name	Area Code
Uncas	405	Wagoner	918	Watts	918	Westville	918	Wright City	405
Union City	405	Wainwright	918	Waukomis	405	Wetumka	405	Wyandotte	918
Utica	405	Wakita	405	Waurika	405	Wewoka	405	Wynnewood	405
		Walters	405	Wayne	405	Wheatland	405	Wynona	918
		Wanette	405	Waynoka	405	Wheelock Academy	405		
		Wann	918	Weatherford	405	Whiteoak	918		
Valliant	405	Wapanucka	405	Webb City	918	Wilburton	918		
Velma	405	Wardville	918	Webbers Falls	918	Willow	405		
Vera	918	Warner	918	Welch	918	Wilson	405	Yale	918
Verden	405	Warwick	405	Weleetka	405	Wirt	405	Yarhola	405
Vian	918	Washington	405	Wellston	405	Wister	918	Yeager	405
Vici	405	Washita	405	West Fort Smith	918	Woodford	405	Yewed	405
Vinita	918	Washunga	405	West Seneca	918	Woodville	405	Yuba	405
Vinson	405	Watonga	405	West Uniontown	918	Woodward	405	Yukon	405

ALL POINTS—AREA CODE 503

Place Name	Area Code	Place Name	Area Code	Place Name	Area Code	Place Name	Area Code	Place Name	Area Code
Aaronsburg	814	Aniline Village	215	Avondale		Bedford	814	Big Run	
Abbottstown	717	Anise	215	(Delaware Co.)	215	Bedford Springs	814	(Jefferson Co.)	814
Aberdeen	717	Annandale	412	Avonmore	412	Bedford Valley	814	Bigspring	717
Abington	215	Annville	717			Bedminster	215	Billmeyer	717
Academia	717	Ansonia	717			Beech Creek	717	Bino	717
Achenbach Hill	215	Ansonville	814	Bachmanville	717	Beecherstown	717	Birchardville	717
Ackerly	717	Antes Fort	717	Bacontown	717	Beech Glen	717	Birchrunville	215
Ackermanville	215	Antrim	717	Baden	412	Beech Grove	717	Bird-in-Hand	717
Acme	412	Apollo	412	Bainbridge	717	Beechview	412	Birdsboro	215
Acmetonia	412	Appenzell	717	Bair	717	Beegletown	814	Birmingham	814
Acosta	814	Aquashicola	215	Bairdford	412	Beisels Corners	717	Bishop	412
Adah	412	Aqueduct	717	Bakers Summit	814	Belden	814	Bittersville	717
Adamsburg	412	Ararat	717	Bakerstown	412	Belfast	215	Bittinger	717
Adamsdale	717	Arcadia	814	Bala-Cynwyd	215	Belin Village	717	Bitumen	717
Adamstown	215	Archbald	717	Bald Mount	717	Bellaire	717	Bixler	717
Adamsville	412	Arcola	215	Balliettsville	215	Bellaire Park	717	Black	717
Addison	814	Ardara	412	Balls Mills	717	Bellbank	717	Black Creek	717
Admire	717	Ardmore	215	Bally	215	Bellefonte	814	Black Gap	717
Airville	717	Ardsley	215	Bangor	215	Bellegrove	717	Black Lick	412
Aitch	814	Arendtsville	717	Bannerville	717	Bellemont	717	Black Moshannon	814
Akersville	814	Argentine	412	Barbara	814	Belle Vernon	412	Blacktown	412
Akron	717	Argus	215	Barbours	717	Belleville	717	Black Walnut	717
Aladdin	412	Aristes	717	Bard	814	Bellevue	412	Blackwell	717
Alba	717	Armagh	814	Bardwell	717	Bellwood	814	Blain	717
Albany	215	Armbrust	412	Baresville	717	Belsano	814	Blainsport	215
Albert	717	Armenia	717	Bareville	717	Beltzhoover	412	Blairs Mills	717
Albion	412	Arnold	412	Barking	412	Belvidere	215	Blairsville	412
Albrightsville	717	Arnold City	412	Barlow	717	Ben Avon	412	Blairton	412
Alburtis	215	Arnot	717	Barnesboro	814	Ben Avon Heights	412	Blakely	717
Aldan (Delaware Co.)	215	Arona	412	Barnesville	717	Bendersville	717	Blakeslee	717
Alden (Luzerne Co.)	717	Arters Station	717	Barnitz	717	Bendertown	717	Blanchard	717
Aldenville	717	Asaph	717	Barree	814	Benezette	814	Blandburg	814
Alderson	717	Asbury	717	Barville	717	Benfer	717	Blandon	215
Aleppo	412	Ashcom	814	Bart	717	Bennett Creek	717	Blawnox	412
Alexandria	814	Asherton	717	Barto	215	Bensalem	215	Bloomfield	814
Alford	717	Ashfield	215	Bartonsville	717	Benscreek	814	Bloomingdale	
Alinda	717	Ashland		Bartville	717	Bentley Creek	717	(Carbon Co.)	717
Aline	717	(Clearfield Co.)	814	Basket	215	Bentleyville	412	Bloomingdale	
Aliquippa	412	Ashland		Bastress	717	Benton	717	(Luzerne Co.)	717
Allegheny	412	(Schuylkill Co.)	717	Bath	215	Benvenue	717	Blooming Glen	215
Allen	717	Ashley	717	Batts Switch	215	Bergey	215	Blooming Grove	717
Allenport	412	Ashmore	717	Baumgardner	717	Berkley	215	Bloomington	814
Allensville	717	Ashton	215	Baxter	814	Berlee	717	Blooming Valley	814
Allentown		Ashville	814	Baylors Lake	717	Berlin	814	Bloomsburg	717
(Lehigh Co.)	215	Askam	717	Beach Haven	717	Berlin Junction	717	Bloserville	717
Allentown–Bethlehem		Aspers	717	Beach Lake	717	Bermudian	717	Blossburg	717
Airport	215	Aspinwall	412	Beading	412	Bernice	717	Blue Ball	
Allenwood	717	Atco	717	Beallsville	412	Bernville	215	(Clearfield Co.)	814
Allis Hollow	717	Atglen	215	Bear Creek	717	Berrysburg	717	Blue Ball	
Allison	412	Athens	717	Bear Gap	717	Berrytown	717	(Lancaster Co.)	717
Allison Park	412	Athol	215	Bear Lake		Berwick	717	Blue Bell	215
Allport	814	Atlantic	814	(Luzerne Co.)	717	Berwick Heights	717	Blue Knob	814
Almedia	717	Atlas	717	Bear Lake		Berwindale	814	Blue Ridge Summit	717
Alpha	215	Atlasburg	412	(Warren Co.)	814	Berwyn	215	Blue Spring	717
Alpine	717	Auburn	717	Beartown	717	Bessemer	412	Blytheburn	717
Altenwald	717	Auburn Center	717	Beaumont	717	Bethany	717	Blythedale	412
Altoona	814	Auburn Four Corners	717	Beaver	412	Bethayres	215	Boalsburg	814
Alum Bank	814	Aucheys	717	Beaver Brook	717	Bethel (Berks Co.)	717	Boardman	814
Alverda	814	Audenried	717	Beaverdale	814	Bethel (Sullivan Co.)	717	Bobtown	412
Alverton	412	Audubon	215	Beaver Falls	412	Bethel Hill	717	Bodines	717
Amaranth	717	Augustaville	717	Beaver Lake	717	Bethel Park	412	Bohemia	717
Ambler	215	Aula	717	Beaver Meadows	717	Bethesda	717	Boiling Springs	717
Ambridge	412	Aultman	412	Beaver Run Valley	215	Bethlehem	215	Bolivar	412
Amity	412	Austin	814	Beaver Springs	717	Beulah	814	Boltz	814
Amity Hall	717	Austin Heights	717	Beavertown (Blair Co.)	814	Beverly	717	Bonneauville	717
Amityville	215	Austinville	717	Beavertown		Beyer	412	Bonny Brook	717
Analomink	717	Avalon	412	(Snyder Co.)	717	Big Cove Tannery	717	Bon View	717
Anchor	717	Avella	412	Beavertown		Bigdam	717	Booth Corner	215
Andalusia	215	Avery	717	(York Co.)	717	Bigler	814	Boothwyn	215
Andersonburg	717	Avis	717	Beccaria	814	Biglerville	717	Bordnerville	717
Andreas	717	Avoca	717	Bechtelsville	215	Big Mount	717	Bossardsville	717
Andrews Bridge	717	Avon	717			Big Pond	717	Boston	412
Angels	717	Avondale				Big Run (Dauphin Co.)	717	Boswell	814
		(Chester Co.)	215						

TELEPHONE AREA CODE DIRECTORY

Place Name	Area Code	Place Name	Area Code	Place Name	Area Code	Place Name	Area Code	Place Name	Area Code
Bovard	412	Brookside		Cabot	412	Centerport	215	Churchville	
Bowman Hollow	717	(Schuylkill Co.)	717	Cadis	717	Center Square	215	(Bucks Co.)	215
Bowmansdale	717	Brookville	814	Cadogan	412	Center Valley	215	Circleville	412
Bowmanstown	215	Broomall	215	Cains	717	Centerville		Cisna Run	717
Bowmansville	215	Broughton	412	Cairnbrook	814	(Bradford Co.)	717	Clairton	412
Boyds Mills	717	Browndale	717	Caledonia	717	Centerville		Clapper Hill	717
Boyers	412	Brownfield	412	California	412	(Crawford Co.)	814	Clappertown	814
Boyertown	215	Browns Mills	717	Callensburg	814	Centerville		Clarence	814
Boynton	814	Brownstown		Callery Junction	412	(Cumberland Co.)	717	Claridge	412
Brackenridge	412	(Lancaster Co.)	717	Callicoon	717	Centerville		Clarington	814
Brackney	717	Brownsville	412	Calumet	412	(Washington Co.)	412	Clarion	814
Braddock	412	Browntown		Calvert	717	Central	717	Clark	412
Bradenville	412	(Bradford Co.)	717	Camargo	717	Central City	814	Clarksburg	412
Bradford	814	Browntown		Cambra	717	Centralia	717	Clarks Green	717
Bradford Woods	412	(Luzerne Co.)	717	Cambridge Springs	814	Centre Hall	814	Clarks Mills	412
Brady	717	Bruceton	412	Cameron	814	Cessna	814	Clarks Summit	717
Bradys Bend	412	Bruckharts	717	Cammal	717	Chadds Ford	215	Clarkstown	717
Braeburn	412	Bruin	412	Campbelltown	717	Chalfant Borough	412	Clarks Valley	717
Branch Dale	717	Brumbaugh	814	Camp Hill	717	Chalfont	215	Clarksville	
Branchton	412	Brumbaugh Crossing	814	Camptown	717	Chalkhill	412	(Greene Co.)	412
Brandonville	717	Brunnerville	717	Canadensis	717	Chalybeate	814	Clarksville	
Brandtsville	717	Brush Run	717	Canadohta Lake	814	Chambersburg	717	(Mercer Co.)	814
Brandy Camp	814	Brushtown	717	Canby	717	Chambersville	412	Clay	717
Brave	412	Brush Valley	412	Canebrake	717	Champion	412	Clay Hill	717
Breezewood	814	Brushville	717	Canonsburg	412	Chanceford	717	Claysburg	814
Breinigsville	215	Bryantown	717	Canton	717	Chaneysville	814	Claysville	412
Brentwood	412	Bryn Athyn	215	Caprivi	717	Chapman	717	Clayton	215
Bressler	717	Bryn Mawr	215	Carbon	412	Chapman Lake	717	Clearfield	814
Briar Creek	717	Brysonia	717	Carbondale	717	Chapmans Run	814	Clear Ridge	814
Brickerville	717	Buchanan Valley	717	Cardale	412	Charleroi	412	Clear Spring	717
Bridgeport		Buck	717	Carley Brook	717	Charlesville	814	Clearville	814
(Montgomery Co.)	215	Buck Hill Falls	717	Carlisle	717	Charmian	717	Cleona	717
Bridgeport		Buckhorn	717	Carlisle Junction	717	Chase	717	Cleversburg	717
(Perry Co.)	717	Buckingham	215	Carlisle Springs	717	Chatham	215	Clifford (Snyder Co.)	717
Bridgeville	412	Buckman Village	215	Carlton	814	Cheesetown	717	Clifford	
Bridgewater		Buck Mountain	717	Carmichaels	412	Cheltenham	215	(Susquehanna Co.)	717
(Beaver Co.)	412	Bucksville	215	Carnegie	412	Cherry Mills	717	Cliftmont	717
Bridgewater		Buck Run	717	Carney Flats	717	Cherry Ridge	717	Clifton	717
(Delaware Co.)	215	Buck Valley	717	Carnwath	814	Cherrytown	814	Clifton Heights	215
Brier Hill	412	Buena Vista	412	Carrick	412	Cherry Tree	814	Climax	814
Briggsville	717	Buena Vista Spring	717	Carrolltown	814	Cherry Valley	412	Clinton	
Brillharts	717	Buffalo	412	Carsonville	717	Cherryville		(Allegheny Co.)	412
Brior Ridge	717	Buffalo Mills	814	Carversville	215	(Northampton Co.)	215	Clinton	
Brisbin	814	Buffalo Springs	717	Carverton	717	Cherryville		(Armstrong Co.)	412
Bristol	215	Bulger	412	Cascade	717	(Schuylkill Co.)	717	Clintondale	717
Broad Top	814	Bunches	717	Cashtown	717	Chester	215	Clintonville	814
Broad Top City	814	Bunker Hill		Cassandra	814	Chesterfield	814	Clovercreek	814
Broadway		(Lebanon Co.)	717	Casselman	814	Chester Heights	215	Cly	717
(Franklin Co.)	717	Bunker Hill		Cassville	814	Chester Springs	215	Clyde	412
Broadway		(Luzerne Co.)	717	Castanea	717	Chestnut Hill	215	Clymer	412
(Luzerne Co.)	717	Bunkertown	717	Castle Shannon	412	Chestnut Level	717	Coal Center	412
Brockport	814	Bunnell Hill	717	Catasauqua	215	Chestnut Ridge	412	Coal City	814
Brockton	717	Bunnelltown	717	Catawissa	717	Chest Springs	814	Coaldale	
Brockway	814	Bunola	412	Cave Hill	717	Cheswick	412	(Bedford Co.)	814
Brodbecks	717	Burgettstown	412	Cecil	412	Cheyney	215	Coaldale	
Brodheadsville	717	Burholme	215	Cedar Grove	717	Chickies	717	(Schuylkill Co.)	717
Brogue	717	Burlington	717	Cedar Lane	717	Chickies Park	717	Coalmont	814
Brommerstown	717	Burnham	717	Cedarridge	717	Chicora	412	Coalport	814
Brookdale	717	Burning Bush	814	Cedar Run	717	Childs	717	Coal Run	717
Brook Haven	215	Burnside	814	Cedars	215	Chinchilla	717	Coatesville	215
Brookline		Burnt Cabins	717	Cedar Springs	717	Chippewa	412	Cobblesville	717
(Allegheny Co.)	412	Burnwood	717	Cementon	215	Choconut	717	Coburn	814
Brookline		Burtville	814	Centennial	717	Christiana	215	Cocalico	215
(Delaware Co.)	215	Bushkill	717	Center (Beaver Co.)	412	Church Hill	717	Cochranton	814
Brooklyn	717	Bustleton	215	Center		Churchtown		Cochranville	215
Brookside		Butler	412	(Cumberland Co.)	717	(Cumberland Co.)	717	Cocolamus	717
(Franklin Co.)	717	Butztown	215	Center (Juniata Co.)	717	Churchtown		Codorus	717
Brookside		Buyerstown	717	Center (Perry Co.)	717	(Lancaster Co.)	215	Cogan House	717
(Lackawanna Co.)	717	Byberry	215	Center Mills	717	Churchville		Cogan Station	717
Brookside		Byrnedale	814	Center Moreland	717	(Bedford Co.)	814	Cogan Valley	717
(Lycoming Co.)	717			Center Point	215			Cokeburg	412

Place Name	Area Code	Place Name	Area Code	Place Name	Area Code	Place Name	Area Code	Place Name	Area Code
Cold Run	215	Covedale	814	Dale (Berks Co.)	215	Donegal		Eagleville	
Cold Spring	717	Cove Gap	717	Dale (Cambria Co.)	814	(Lancaster Co.)	717	(Montgomery Co.)	215
Colebrook	717	Covington	717	Daleville	717	Donegal		Earlington	215
Colebrookdale	215	Cowan	717	Dallas	717	(Westmoreland Co.)	412	Earlston	814
Colemanville	717	Cowanesque	814	Dallastown	717	Donerville	717	Earlville	215
Coleraine	717	Cowansville	412	Dalmatia	717	Donnally Mills	717	East Athens	717
Coleville	814	Coxeville	717	Dalton	717	Donora	412	East Bangor	215
Collamer	215	Coxton	717	Damascus	717	Doolittle Hill	717	East Berlin	717
Collegeville	215	Crabtree	412	Danboro	215	Dora	814	East Brady	412
Colley	717	Crafton	412	Danielsville	215	Dormont	412	East Branch	814
Collingdale	215	Craig	717	Danville	717	Dornsife	717	East Butler	412
Collins	717	Craighead	717	Darby	215	Dorrance	717	East Earl	215
Collinsburg	412	Craigsville	412	Darling	215	Dorseyville	412	East Falls	215
Collinsville	717	Craley	717	Darlington		Dott	717	East Freedom	814
Collomsville	717	Cramer	814	(Beaver Co.)	412	Doubling Gap	717	East Greenville	215
Colmar	215	Cranberry		Darlington		Douglassville	215	East Hickory	814
Colonial Park	717	(Luzerne Co.)	717	(Delaware Co.)	215	Dover	717	East Lansdowne	215
Columbia	717	Cranberry		Darragh	412	Downingtown	215	East Lemon	717
Columbia Cross Roads	717	(Venango Co.)	814	Dauberville	215	Doylesburg	717	East Liberty	412
Columbus	814	Cranesville	814	Dauphin	717	Doyles Mills	717	East McKeesport	412
Colver	814	Cream	717	Davidsburg	717	Doylestown	215	East Millsboro	412
Colwyn	215	Creamery	215	Davidsville	814	Dravosburg	412	East Norriton	215
Colyer	814	Creekside	412	Davistown	412	Drehersville	717	Easton	215
Comly	717	Creighton	412	Davisville	215	Dresher	215	East Palestine	412
Commodore	412	Cresco	717	Dawson	412	Drexelbrook	215	East Petersburg	717
Compass	717	Cresson	814	Daylesford	215	Drexel Hill	215	East Pittsburgh	412
Conashaugh	717	Cressona	717	Dayton		Drifting	814	East Prospect	717
Concord	717	Criders Corners	412	(Armstrong Co.)	814	Drifton	717	East Smithfield	717
Concordville	215	Croft	814	Dayton (Dauphin Co.)	717	Driftwood	814	East Springfield	814
Conemaugh	814	Crooked Creek	717	Deegan	412	Dromgold	717	East Stroudsburg	717
Conestoga Center	717	Crosby	814	Deep Valley	412	Drumore	717	East Texas	215
Conewago	717	Cross Creek	412	Deer Lake	717	Drumore Center	717	East Vandergrift	412
Conewago Chapel	717	Cross Fork	717	Defiance	814	Drums	717	East Waterford	717
Confluence	814	Crossgrove	717	Deiblers	717	Drurys Run	717	Eastwick	215
Congo	215	Crossings	814	Delabole	215	Dry Gap	814	Eatonville	717
Conneaut Lake	814	Cross Keys	717	DeLancey	814	Dry Run	717	Eau Claire	412
Conneaut Lake Park	814	Crossroads	717	Delano	717	Dryville	215	Ebenezer	717
Conneautville	814	Crothers	412	Delaware Water Gap	717	Dublin	215	Ebensburg	814
Connellsville	412	Crowl	717	Delmont	412	Dublin Mills	814	Eberlys Mill	717
Connoquenessing	412	Crown	814	Delroy	717	DuBois	814	Ebervale	717
Conshohocken	215	Croydon	215	Delta	717	Duboistown	717	Ebys	717
Constitution	717	Crucible	412	Demunds	717	Dudley	814	Echo Lake	
Conway	412	Crum Lynne	215	Denbo	412	Duffield	717	(Monroe Co.)	717
Conyngham	717	Crystal Lake	717	Denholm	717	Duke Center	814	Echo Lake	
Conyngham-Drums	717	Crystal Spring	814	Denver	215	Dunbar	412	(Northampton Co.)	215
Conyngham Pass	717	Cuba Mills	717	Deodate	717	Duncannon	717	Eckley	717
Cooksburg	814	Culbertson	717	Derrick City	814	Duncansville	814	Eckville	215
Cooks Mills	814	Culmerville	412	Derrs	717	Dundaff	717	Eddington	215
Coolspring	814	Cumberland Park	717	Derry	412	Dundore	717	Eddystone	215
Coon Hill	717	Cumbola	717	Derry Church	717	Dunkard	412	Edella	717
Coopersburg	215	Cummingston	717	Devault	215	Dunlevy	412	Edenville	717
Cooperstown		Curllsville	814	Devitt Home	717	Dunlo	814	Edgegrove	717
(Butler Co.)	412	Curry	412	Devon	215	Dunmore	717	Edgely	215
Cooperstown		Curryville	814	Dewart	717	Dunns Station	412	Edgemere	717
(Venango Co.)	814	Curtin (Centre Co.)	814	De Young	814	Dunnstown	717	Edgemont	215
Coplay	215	Curtin (Dauphin Co.)	717	Diamond	814	Dupont	717	Edgewood	
Coral	412	Curtis Valley	717	Dickerson Run	412	Duquesne	412	(Allegheny Co.)	412
Coraopolis	412	Curtisville	412	Dickinson	717	Durell	717	Edgewood (Bucks Co.)	215
Cordelia	717	Curwensville	814	Dickson City	717	Durham	215	Edgewood	
Core	412	Custer City	814	Dilliner	412	Durlach	717	(Luzerne Co.)	717
Cork Lane	717	Cyclone	814	Dillinger	215	Duryea	717	Edgeworth	412
Cornwall	717	Cynwyd	215	Dillsburg	717	Dushore	717	Edinboro	814
Cornwells	215	Cypher	814	Dilltown	814	Dutch Hill	717	Edinburg	412
Cornwells Heights	215			Dimock	717	Dyberry	717	Edinger Hill	717
Corry	814			Dingmans	717	Dysart	814	Edison	215
Corsica	814			Dingmans Ferry	717			Edmon	412
Coudersport	814	Daggett	717	Distant	814			Edwardsville	717
Coulter	412	Daguscahonda	814	Dixmont	412			Effort	215
County Line	717	Dagus Mines	814	Dixon	717	Eagle (Chester Co.)	215	Egypt	215
Coupon	814	Daiseytown		Dixonville	412	Eagle (Delaware Co.)	215	Ehrenfeld	814
Courtdale	717	(Cambria Co.)	814	Dolington	215	Eagles Mere	717	Eichelbergertown	814
Courtney	412	Daisytown		Donaldson	717	Eagleville		Eighty-four	412
Cove	717	(Washington Co.)	412			(Centre Co.)	717	Elbon	814

PENNSYLVANIA
Elco—Glassport

Place Name	Area Code	Place Name	Area Code	Place Name	Area Code	Place Name	Area Code	Place Name	Area Code
Elco	412	Euclid	412	Fay Extension	814	Forestville	412	Fulton House	717
Elders Ridge	412	Eureka	215	Feasterville	215	Forks	717	Furlong	215
Eldersville	412	Evans City	412	Felton (Delaware Co.)	215	Forkston	717	Furniss	717
Elderton	412	Evans Falls	717	Felton (York Co.)	717	Forksville	717		
Eldred	814	Evansville (Berks Co.)	215	Feltonville	215	Fortenia	717		
Elgin	814	Evansville		Fenelton	412	Fort Hill	814		
Elimsport	717	(Columbia Co.)	717	Fern	814	Fort Hunter	717		
Elizabeth	412	Evendale	717	Fern Brook	717	Fort Littleton	717		
Elizabethtown	717	Everett	814	Ferndale (Bucks Co.)	215	Fort Loudon	717	Gablesville	215
Elizabeth Township	412	Evergreen	717	Ferndale		Fort Ritchie	717	Gaines	814
Elizabethville	717	Everson	412	(Cambria Co.)	814	Fort Robinson	717	Galeton	814
Elkdale	717	Ewardtown	717	Ferndale		Fortuna	215	Galilee	717
Elkins Park	215	Excelsior	717	(Schuylkill Co.)	717	Fort Washington	215	Gallatin	412
Elk Lake		Exchange		Fern Glen	717	Forty Fort	717	Gallitzin	814
(Susquehanna Co.)	717	(Montour Co.)	717	Fernridge	717	Fossilville	814	Ganister	814
Elk Lake (Wayne Co.)	717	Exchange (North-		Fern Rock	215	Foundryville	717	Ganoga Lake	717
Elkland	814	umberland Co.)	717	Fernville	717	Fountain Dale	717	Gap	717
Elk View	717	Exeter Boro	717	Fernwood	215	Fountain Hill	215	Gap Road	717
Ellenton	717	Export	412	Fertigs	814	Fountain Springs	717	Gapsville	814
Elliott	412	Exton	215	Fetterville	717	Fountainville	215	Garards Fort	412
Elliottsburg	717	Eyers Grove	717	Fiddle Lake	717	Foustown	717	Garden City	215
Elliottson	717	Eynon	717	Fields Station	717	Foxburg	412	Garden View	717
Ellisburg	814			Filbert	412	Fox Chapel	412	Gardenville	215
Ellis Hill	717			Finch Hill	717	Fox Chase	215	Gardners	717
Ellsworth	412			Finleyville		Fox Gap	215	Garfield	215
Ellsworth Hill	717	Factoryville	717	(Bedford Co.)	814	Frackville	717	Garrett	814
Ellwood City	412	Fairbank	412	Finleyville		Franconia	215	Garrettford	215
Elm	717	Fairchance	412	(Washington Co.)	412	Frank	412	Garrett Hill	215
Elmhurst	717	Fairdale	717	Fisher	814	Frankford	215	Garrison	412
Elmora	814	Fairfield (Adams Co.)	717	Fishers Ferry	717	Frankford Arsenal	215	Gastonville	412
Elrama	412	Fairfield		Fishertown	814	Franklin	814	Gatchellville	717
Elroy	215	(Lancaster Co.)	717	Fisherville	717	Franklin Center	215	Gatesburg	814
Elstonville	717	Fairfield Center	717	Fishing Creek		Franklindale	717	Geeseytown	814
Elton	814	Fairhope		(Columbia Co.)	717	Franklin Forks	717	Geigertown	215
Elverson	215	(Fayette Co.)	412	Fishing Creek		Franklin Furnace	717	Geistown	814
Elwyn	215	Fairhope		(Lancaster Co.)	717	Franklintown	717	Gelatt	717
Elysburg	717	(Somerset Co.)	814	Fishing Creek Valley	717	Franklinville	814	Genesee	814
Emaus	215	Fairland	717	Fiveforks	717	Frazer	215	Geneva	814
Embreeville	215	Fairless Hills	215	Five Points	717	Frear Hill	717	George School	215
Emeigh	814	Fairmount	717	Fivepointsville	215	Frederick	215	Georgetown	
Emerald	215	Fairmount City	814	Fleetwood	215	Fredericksburg		(Adams Co.)	717
Emerickville	814	Fairmount Springs	717	Fleming	814	(Blair Co.)	814	Georgetown	
Emigsville	717	Fairoaks	412	Flemington	717	Fredericksburg		(Beaver Co.)	412
Emlenton	412	Fairview (Butler Co.)	412	Flicksville	215	(Lebanon Co.)	717	Georgetown	
Emmaus	215	Fairview (Erie Co.)	814	Flinton	814	Fredericksville	215	(Lancaster Co.)	717
Emmaville	814	Fairview		Flintville	717	Fredericktown	412	Georgetown	
Emporium	814	(Luzerne Co.)	717	Floradale	717	Fredonia	412	(Luzerne Co.)	717
Emsworth	412	Fairview Lake	717	Floreffe	412	Freeburg	717	Georgeville	412
Endeavor	814	Fairview Village	215	Florence	412	Freedom	412	German Hill	717
Enders	717	Fallbrook	717	Florin	717	Freeland	717	Germansville	215
Englesville	215	Fallen Timber	814	Florinel	717	Freemansburg	215	Germantown	215
English Center	717	Falling Springs	717	Flourtown	215	Freeport	412	Gettysburg	717
Enhaut	717	Falls	717	Fogelsville	215	Freeport Mills	717	Ghent	717
Enola	717	Falls Creek	814	Folcroft	215	Fremont	717	Gibraltar	215
Enon Valley	412	Fallsington	215	Folsom	215	French Creek	215	Gibson	717
Enterline	717	Falls of Schuylkill	215	Folstown	717	Frenchtown	717	Gibsonia	412
Entlerville	717	Fallston	412	Foltz	717	Frenchville	814	Gifford	814
Entriken	814	Falmouth	717	Fombell	412	Freysville	717	Gilbert	215
Ephrata	717	Fannettsburg	717	Fontaine	215	Friedens	814	Gilberton	717
Equinunk	717	Farmers Mills	814	Fontana	717	Friedensburg		Gilbertsville	215
Erdenheim	215	Farmersville	717	Footedale	412	(Berks Co.)	215	Gillespie	412
Erdman	717	Farmington	412	Forbes Road	412	Friedensburg		Gillett	717
Erie	814	Farragut	717	Force	814	(Schuylkill Co.)	717	Ginter	814
Erly	717	Farrandsville	717	Ford City	412	Friendsville	717	Gipsy	814
Ernest	412	Farrell	412	Ford Cliff	412	Friesville	814	Girard	814
Erwinna	215	Farr Hollow	717	Forest City	717	Fritztown	215	Girardville	717
Eshbach	215	Farview	717	Forest Grove	215	Frostburg	814	Glade Mills	412
Espy	717	Farwell	717	Forest Hills	412	Frosty Valley	717	Glades	717
Espyville	412	Fassett	717	Forest Lake		Frugality	814	Gladwyne	215
Essington	215	Fawn Grove	717	(Pike Co.)	717	Fruitville	215	Glasgow (Beaver Co.)	412
Estella	717	Faxon	717	Forest Lake		Fryburg	814	Glasgow	
Etna	412	Fayette City	412	(Susquehanna Co.)	717	Frystown	717	(Cambria Co.)	814
Etters Post Office	717	Fayetteville	717	Forest Park	717	Fullerton	215	Glassmere	412
								Glassport	412

Place Name	Area Code	Place Name	Area Code	Place Name	Area Code	Place Name	Area Code	Place Name	Area Code
Glatfelters Station	717	Greeley	717	Hamburg	215	Heckscherville	717	Hockersville	
Gleason	717	Greenawald	215	Hametown	717	Hecla	717	(Dauphin Co.)	717
Gleasonton	717	Greenbank	717	Hamilton		Hecla Park	814	Hoffer	717
Glenburn	717	Greenbrier	717	(Jefferson Co.)	814	Hegins	717	Hoffmansville	215
Glen Campbell	814	Greenburr	717	Hamilton (North-		Heidelberg	412	Hogestown	717
Glencoe	814	Greencastle	717	umberland Co.)	717	Heidlersburg	717	Hokendauqua	215
Glendale		Greene	717	Hamlin (Lebanon Co.)	717	Heilmandale	717	Holbrook	412
(Luzerne Co.)	717	Greenfield	717	Hamlin (Wayne Co.)	717	Heilwood	814	Holicong	215
Glendale		Green Grove	717	Hammersley Fork	717	Heiser	717	Holland	215
(Wyoming Co.)	717	Green Hills	215	Hampton	717	Helfenstein	717	Hollars Hill	717
Glendenville	717	Green Lane	215	Hancock	215	Helixville	814	Hollenback	717
Glendon	215	Greenmount	717	Hannah	814	Hellam	717	Hollidaysburg	814
Glenfield	412	Greenock	412	Hannastown	412	Hellertown	215	Hollisterville	717
Glen Hope	814	Greenpark	717	Hanover (Luzerne Co.)	717	Hendersonville	412	Hollywood Heights	717
Glen Iron	717	Green Point	717	Hanover (York Co.)	717	Hendricks	215	Holmes	215
Glenloch	215	Green Ridge		Hanover Junction	717	Henningsville	215	Holsopple	814
Glen Lyon	717	(Delaware Co.)	215	Harborcreek	814	Henrietta	814	Holtwood	717
Glen Manor	717	Green Ridge (North-		Harding	717	Henryville	717	Home	412
Glen Mawr	717	umberland Co.)	717	Harford	717	Hensel	717	Homer City	412
Glen Mills	215	Greensboro	412	Harkness	717	Hepburnia	814	Homestead	412
Glenmoore	215	Greensburg	412	Harlansburg	412	Hepburnville	717	Hometown	717
Glenolden	215	Greens Landing	717	Harleigh	717	Hepler	717	Homets Ferry	717
Glen Richey	814	Green Spring	717	Harleysville	215	Hereford	215	Homewood	
Glen Riddle	215	Greenstone	717	Harmarville	412	Herman	412	(Allegheny Co.)	412
Glen Rock	717	Greentown	717	Harmonsburg	814	Herminie	412	Homewood	
Glenshaw	412	Greentree		Harmony	412	Herndon	717	(Beaver Co.)	412
Glenside	215	(Allegheny Co.)	412	Harnedsville	814	Herrick	717	Honesdale	717
Glen Summit	717	Green Tree		Harpers Tavern	717	Herrick Center	717	Honey Brook	
Glenville	717	(Lancaster Co.)	717	Harrisburg	717	Herrickville	717	(Chester Co.)	215
Glenwillard	412	Green Village	717	Harrison	814	Herrs Island	412	Honey Brook	
Glenwood	717	Greenville	412	Harrison City	412	Hershey	717	(Mifflin Co.)	717
Globe Mills	717	Greenwood		Harrison Valley	814	Heshbon	412	Honey Creek	717
Glyde	412	(Columbia Co.)	717	Harrisonville	717	Hess	717	Honey Grove	717
Goff	412	Greenwood		Harristown	717	Hessdale	717	Honeyhole	717
Golden Hill	717	(Franklin Co.)	717	Harrisville	412	Hess Station	717	Honey Pot	717
Goldsboro	717	Greshville	215	Harrity	215	Hesston	814	Hooker	412
Goodspring	717	Greythorne	717	Harrow	215	Hewitt	814	Hookstown	412
Goodville	215	Grier City	717	Hartleton	717	Hibbs	412	Hoovers Island	717
Goodyear	717	Grier Point	717	Hartstown	814	Hickory	412	Hooversville	814
Gordon	717	Griesemersville	215	Hartsville	215	Hickory Bottom	814	Hop Bottom	717
Gordonville	717	Grimville	215	Harveys	412	Hickory Corners	717	Hopeland	717
Goshen		Grindstone	412	Harveys Lake	717	Hickory Grove	717	Hopewell	
(Clearfield Co.)	814	Grindstone Hill	717	Harveyville	717	Hickory Ridge	717	(Beaver Co.)	412
Goshen		Grists Flats	717	Harwick	412	Hickory Run	717	Hopewell	
(Lancaster Co.)	717	Groffdale	717	Harwood	717	Hickorytown	717	(Bedford Co.)	814
Gouldsboro	717	Grovania	717	Hastings	814	Hicks Ferry	717	Hopwood	412
Gowen City	717	Grove City	412	Hatboro	215	Highland Park		Hornbrook	717
Graceton	412	Grover	717	Hatch Hill	717	(Cumberland Co.)	717	Horsham	215
Graceville	814	Groveton	412	Hatfield	215	Highland Park		Host	215
Gradyville	215	Guernsey	717	Hauto	717	(Delaware Co.)	215	Hostetter	412
Graeffenburg	717	Guilford Siding	717	Haverford	215	Highlands	717	Houserville	814
Grampian	814	Guilford Springs	717	Havertown	215	Highmount	717	Houston	412
Grand Valley	814	Guldens	717	Hawk Run	814	Highrock	717	Houtzdale	814
Granite	717	Gulf Mills	215	Hawley	717	Highspire	717	Howard	814
Grantham	717	Gulph Mills	215	Hawthorn	814	Hill Church	215	Hubers	717
Grantville	717	Guys Mills	814	Haycock Run	215	Hill End	717	Hublersburg	814
Granville	717	Gwynedd	215	Hays	412	Hiller	412	Hudson	717
Granville Center	717	Gwynedd Valley	215	Hays Grove	717	Hilliards	412	Hudsondale	717
Granville Summit	717			Haysville	412	Hill Road	717	Huey	814
Grapeville	412			Hazelhurst	814	Hillsdale	814	Huff	412
Grassflat	814			Hazelwood	412	Hillsgrove	717	Huffs Church	215
Graterford	215			Hazen	814	Hillside	717	Hughes	814
Gratz	717	Haafsville	215	Hazlebrook	717	Hillsville	412	Hughestown	717
Gravel Pitt	814	Haas	717	Hazleton	717	Hilltown (Adams Co.)	717	Hughesville	717
Gravel Pond	717	Hacklebernie	717	Hazleton Heights	717	Hilltown (Bucks Co.)	215	Hulmeville	215
Gravity	717	Hadley	412	Heart Lake		Hinkletown	717	Hummelstown	717
Gray	814	Hahnstown	717	(Lackawanna Co.)	717	Hiveleys	717	Hummels Wharf	717
Graybill	717	Haleeka	717	Heart Lake		Hoadleys	717	Hungerford	717
Grays Landing	412	Halfville	717	(Susquehanna Co.)	717	Hobart	717	Hunkers	412
Graysville	412	Halifax	717	Heathville	814	Hobbie	717	Hunlock Creek	717
Greason	717	Hallowell	215	Hebe	717	Hoblitzell	814	Hunters Run	717
Great Bend	717	Halls	717	Heberlig	717	Hockersville		Hunterstown	717
Greble	717	Hallstead	717	Hebron	717	(Cumberland Co.)	717	Huntersville	717
		Hallton	814						

PENNSYLVANIA
Huntingdon—Lees Cross Roads

Place Name	Area Code
Huntingdon	814
Huntingdon Furnace	814
Huntingdon Valley	215
Huntington Mills	717
Huntsdale	717
Huntsville	717
Husband	814
Hustontown	717
Hyde	814
Hyde Park	412
Hydetown	814
Hyndman	814
Hynemansville	215
Hyner	717
Ickesburg	717
Idaville	717
Idetown	717
Imler	814
Imlertown	814
Imperial	412
Independence (Beaver Co.)	412
Independence (Snyder Co.)	717
Independence (Washington Co.)	412
Indiana	412
Indian Head	412
Indian Hill	717
Indianola	412
Indian Orchard	717
Indian Springs	814
Indiantown Gap Military Reservation	717
Industry	412
Inglenook	717
Inglesmith	814
Ingomar	412
Ingram	412
Inkerman	717
Intercourse	717
Inwood	717
Iola	717
Iona	717
Irish Hill	717
Irishtown	717
Irish Valley	717
Iron Springs	717
Ironton	215
Ironville	717
Irvona	814
Irwin	412
Isabella (Chester Co.)	215
Isabella (Fayette Co.)	412
Iselin	412
Island Park (Northampton Co.)	215
Island Park (Northumberland Co.)	717
Ithan	215
Ivyland	215
Ivywood	412
Jacks Mountain	717
Jackson (Luzerne Co.)	717
Jackson (Susquehanna Co.)	717
Jackson Center	412
Jackson Summit	717
Jackson Valley	717
Jacksonville (Centre Co.)	814
Jacksonville (Cumberland Co.)	717
Jacksonville (Lebanon Co.)	717
Jacksonville (Lehigh Co.)	215
Jacobs Creek	412
Jacobs Mills	717
Jacobus	717
James City	814
James Creek	814
Jamestown (Carbon Co.)	215
Jamestown (Mercer Co.)	412
Jamison	215
Jamison City	717
Janesville	814
Japan	717
Jarrettown	215
Jaynes Bend	717
Jeanesville	717
Jeannette	412
Jefferson (Greene Co.)	412
Jefferson (Schuylkill Co.)	717
Jefferson (York Co.)	717
Jenkintown	215
Jenks	717
Jenners	814
Jennerstown	814
Jenningsville	717
Jermyn	717
Jerome	814
Jersey Mills	717
Jersey Shore	717
Jerseytown	717
Jessup	717
Jim Thorpe	717
Joanna	215
Jobs Corners	717
Joffre	412
Johnsonburg	814
Johnsonville	215
Johnstown	814
Johnsville	215
Joliett	717
Jollytown	412
Jones Mills	412
Jonestown (Columbia Co.)	717
Jonestown (Lebanon Co.)	717
Jordan Hollow	717
Jorytown	215
Josephine	412
Julian	814
Junedale	717
Juniata	814
Juniata Bridge	717
Justus	717
Kaiserville	717
Kane	814
Kantner	814
Kantz	717
Kapp Heights	717
Karns City	412
Karthaus	814
Kasiesville	717
Kaska	717
Kasson Brook	717
Kato	814
Kauffmans Station	717
Kaylor	412
Kearney	814
Keating	717
Kecksburg	412
Keelersburg	717
Keewaydin	814
Keffers	717
Kegg	717
Kehler	717
Keiser	717
Keisters	412
Keisterville	412
Kelayres	717
Kellers Church	215
Kellettville	814
Kelleytown	814
Kellogg	717
Kelly Cross Roads	717
Kelly Point	717
Kelly Station	412
Kelton	215
Kemblesville	215
Kempton	215
Kenhorst	215
Kenmar	717
Kennard	412
Kennerdell	814
Kennett Square	215
Kent	412
Kerrmoor	814
Kersey	814
Keys	717
Keystone	717
Killinger	717
Kimberton	215
Kimbles	717
Kimmerlings	717
Kinderhook	717
King	814
King of Prussia	215
Kings Bridge	717
Kingsdale	717
Kingsley	717
Kingston	717
Kingsville	814
Kingwood	814
Kinkora	717
Kintnersville	215
Kinzers	717
Kipps Run	717
Kirby	412
Kirklyn	215
Kirks Mills	717
Kirkwood	717
Kishacoquillas	717
Kiskiminetas Junction	412
Kisselhill	717
Kissimme	717
Kistler	717
Kittanning	412
Klahr	814
Kleinfeltersville	717
Klines Corner	215
Klines Grove	717
Klinesville (Berks Co.)	215
Klinesville (Lancaster Co.)	717
Klingerstown	717
Knobel's Grove	717
Knob Mountain	717
Knobsville	717
Knousetown	717
Knowlton	215
Knox	814
Knoxdale	814
Knoxlyn	717
Knoxville (Allegheny Co.)	412
Knoxville (Tioga Co.)	814
Kobuta	412
Koonsville	717
Koontzville	814
Koppel	412
Kossuth	814
Kralltown	717
Kratzerville	717
Kreamer	717
Kregar	412
Kresgeville	215
Krumsville	717
Kulpmont	717
Kulpsville	215
Kunkle	717
Kunkletown	215
Kutztown (Berks Co.)	215
Kutztown (Lebanon Co.)	717
Kylertown	814
Kyleville	717
La Belle	412
La Bott	717
Laceyville	717
Lackawaxen	717
Laddsburg	717
Lafayette Hill	215
Lafayetteville	814
Laflin	717
La Grange	215
Lahaska	215
Lairdsville	717
LaJose	814
Lake Ariel	717
Lake Carey	717
Lake City	814
Lake Como	717
Lake Harmony	717
Lake Lynn	412
Lakemont	814
Lake Paupack	717
Lake Shehawken	717
Lake Sheridan	717
Lakeside (Schuylkill Co.)	717
Lakeside (Susquehanna Co.)	717
Lake Silkworth	717
Lake Teedyuscung	717
Laketon	717
Lakeville	717
Lake Wallenpaupack	717
Lake Wesauking	717
Lake Winola	717
Lakewood (Schuylkill Co.)	717
Lakewood (Wayne Co.)	717
Lamar	717
Lamartine	814
Lambert	412
Lamberton	412
La Mott	215
Lampeter	717
Lancaster	717
Lancaster Junction	717
Landenberg	215
Landingville	717
Landisburg	717
Landis Store	215
Landisville	717
Lanesboro	717
Langdondale	814
Langeloth	412
Langhorne	215
Lansdale	215
Lansdowne	215
Lanse	814
Lansford	717
Laplume	717
Laporte	717
Lapps	717
Larchmont	215
Large	412
Larimer	412
Larksville	717
Larrys Creek	717
Larryville	717
Larue	717
Lathrop	717
Latimore	717
Latrobe	412
Lattimer	717
Laughlintown	412
Laurel (Cumberland Co.)	717
Laurel (York Co.)	717
Laureldale	215
Laurella	717
Laurel Lake	717
Laurel Run	717
Laurelton	717
Laurys Station	215
Laurytown	717
Lawn	717
Lawnton	717
Lawrence	412
Lawrence Park	814
Lawrenceville	717
Lawsville	717
Lawton	717
Layfield	215
Layton	412
Leacock	717
Leaman Place	717
Leamersville	814
Leatherwood	814
Lebanon	717
Leck Kill	717
Leckrone	412
Lecontes Mills	814
Lederach	215
Ledy	717
Lee	717
Leechburg	412
Lee Park	717
Leeper	814
Leesburg	717
Lees Cross Roads	717

Place Name	Area Code	Place Name	Area Code	Place Name	Area Code	Place Name	Area Code	Place Name	Area Code
Leesport	215	Linden Grove	215	Lovely	814	Manchester		Maynard Hill	717
Leetsdale	412	Linden Hall	814	Lowber	412	(York Co.)	717	Maysville	717
Lehigh Gap	215	Line Lexington	215	Lowellville	412	Mandata	717	Maytown	717
Lehighton	215	Linesville	814	Lower Askam	717	Manheim	717	Mayview	412
Lehman	717	Linfield	215	Lower Burrell	412	Manns Choice	814	Maze	717
Lehmasters	717	Linglestown	717	Lowhill	215	Mannsville	717	Mazeppa	717
Leiperville	215	Linstead	215	Loyalhanna	412	Manoa	215	McAdoo	717
Lemon	717	Linwood	215	Loyalsock	717	Manor	412	McAlevys Fort	814
Lemont	814	Linwood Park	215	Loyalton	717	Manor Hill	814	McAlisterville	717
Lemont Furnace	412	Lionville	215	Loyalville	717	Manorville	412	McCall Ferry	717
Lemoyne	717	Lisburn	717	Loysburg	814	Mansfield	717	McCartys Ridge	717
Lenape	215	Listie	814	Loysville	717	Mantzville	717	McClellandtown	412
Lenhartsville	215	Listonburg	814	Lucerne	412	Maple Glen	215	McClure	717
Lenkerville	717	Litchfield	717	Lucinda	814	Maplehill	717	McConnellsburg	717
Lenni	215	Lithia Springs	717	Lucknow	717	Maple Ridge	814	McConnellstown	814
Lenni Mills	215	Lithia Valley	717	Ludlow	814	Mapleton Depot	814	McCoysville	717
Lennox Park	215	Lititz	717	Lumber City		Mapletown	412	McCrea	717
Lenover	215	Little Britain	717	(Clearfield Co.)	814	Maplewood	717	McCullocks Mills	717
Lenoxville	717	Little Gap	215	Lumber City		Marble	814	McDonald	412
Leola	717	Little Marsh	717	(Mifflin Co.)	717	Marburg	717	McElhattan	717
Leolyn	717	Little Meadows	717	Lumberville	215	Marchand	412	McEwensville	717
Leona	717	Little Oley	215	Lundys Lane	814	Marcus Hook	215	McGees Mills	814
Le Raysville	717	Littlestown	717	Lungerville	717	Marianna	412	McGrann	412
LeRoy	717	Little Weavertown	717	Lurgan	717	Marienville	814	McIlhaney	717
Lester	215	Liverpool	717	Lutherland	215	Marietta	717	McIntyre	412
Letort	717	Livonia	814	Luthersburg	814	Marion	717	McKean	814
Letterkenny		Llanerch	215	Luthers Mills	717	Marion Center	412	McKeansburg	717
Ordnance Depot	717	Llewellyn	717	Lutzville	814	Marion Heights	717	McKees Half Falls	717
Levittown	215	Lloyd	717	Luxor	412	Markelsville	717	McKeesport	412
Lewisberry	717	Lloydell	814	Luzerne	717	Markes	717	McKees Rocks	412
Lewisburg	717	Loag's Corner	215	Lycippus	412	Markle	412	McKnightstown	717
Lewis Run	814	Lobachsville	215	Lykens	717	Marklesburg	814	McMurray	412
Lewistown		Lobato	717	Lyles	717	Markleton	814	McSherrystown	717
(Mifflin Co.)	717	Lock Haven	717	Lymanville	717	Marklesburg	412	McSparran	717
Lewistown		Lockport	717	Lyndell	215	Mar Lin	717	McVeytown	717
(Schuylkill Co.)	717	Locksley	215	Lyndora	412	Mars	412	Meadowbrook	215
Lewisville		Lockville	717	Lynn	717	Marsh	215	Meadow Brook Park	717
(Chester Co.)	215	Locust Gap	717	Lynnport	215	Marshalls Creek	717	Meadow Lands	412
Lewisville		Locust Grove		Lynnville	215	Marsh Creek	717	Meadville	814
(Potter Co.)	814	(Lancaster Co.)	717	Lyons	215	Marsh Creek Heights	717	Mechanic Grove	717
Lexington	717	Locust Grove		Lyon Station	215	Mars Hill	717	Mechanicsburg	
Liberty		(York Co.)	717	Lyonsville	717	Marsh View	717	(Cumberland Co.)	717
(Allegheny Co.)	412	Locust Level	717	Lyon Valley	717	Marsteller	814	Mechanicsburg	
Liberty (Tioga Co.)	717	Locust Run	717			Marstown	717	(Lancaster Co.)	717
Liberty Corners	717	Locust Summit	717			Martha Furnace	814	Mechanicsburg Naval	
Liberty Square	717	Locust Valley				Martic Forge	717	Supply Depot	717
Library	412	(Lehigh Co.)	215			Marticville	717	Mechanicsville	
Lickdale	717	Locust Valley				Martin	412	(Bucks Co.)	215
Licking Creek	717	(Schuylkill Co.)	717	Macdonaldton	814	Martindale	215	Mechanicsville	
Lickingville	814	Logan (Columbia Co.)	717	Macedonia	717	Martinsburg	814	(Lehigh Co.)	215
Light Street	717	Logan		Mackeyville	717	Martins Creek	215	Mecks Corner	717
Ligonier	412	(Philadelphia Co.)	215	Macungie	215	Martinsville	717	Meckville	717
Lilly	814	Loganton	717	Maddensville	814	Marwood	412	Media	215
Lily Lake	717	Loganville	717	Madera	814	Maryd	717	Meeker	717
Lima	215	Lonepine	412	Madison	412	Marysville	717	Mehoopany	717
Lime Hill	717	Long Branch	412	Madisonburg	814	Mascot	717	Meiserville	717
Limekiln	215	Long Level	717	Madisonville	717	Mason & Dixon	717	Melcroft	412
Limeport	215	Long Pond	717	Madley	814	Masontown	412	Melrose	215
Limerick	215	Long Ridge	717	Mahaffey	814	Masten	717	Melrose Park	215
Lime Ridge	717	Longsdorf	717	Mahanoy City	717	Mastersonville	717	Menchtown	814
Lime Rock	717	Longspond	717	Mahoning	412	Matamoras		Mendenhall	215
Limestone	814	Longstown	717	Mahoningtown	412	(Dauphin Co.)	717	Menges Mills	717
Limestoneville	717	Longswamp	215	Maiden Creek	215	Matamoras (Pike Co.)	717	Mentcle	814
Limeville	717	Lookout	717	Mainesburg	717	Mather	412	Mercer	412
Lincoln	717	Lopez	717	Mainland	215	Mattawana	717	Mercersburg	717
Lincoln Borough	412	Lorane	215	Mainville	717	Matterstown	717	Mercur	717
Lincoln Falls	717	Lords Valley	717	Malta	717	Mattie	814	Meridian	412
Lincoln Park	215	Loretto	814	Malvern	215	Mauch Chunk	717	Merion	215
Lincoln Place	412	Loschs	717	Mammoth	412	Mausdale	717	Merriam	717
Lincoln University	215	Loshs Run	717	Mamont	412	Maxatawny	215	Merrittstown	412
Lincolnville	814	Lost Creek	717	Manada Gap	717	May	717	Merryall	717
Lindaville	717	Loupurex	412	Manatawny	215	Mayfair	215	Mertztown	215
Linden	717	Lovelton	717	Manayunk	215	Mayfield	717	Merwin	412
				Manchester (Erie Co.)	814				

Place Name	Area Code	Place Name	Area Code	Place Name	Area Code	Place Name	Area Code	Place Name	Area Code
Meshoppen	717	Millville	717	Morrisville		Mount Wolf	717	Newberry	717
Metal	717	Millway	717	(Greene Co.)	412	Mount Zion		Newberrytown	717
Mexico	717	Millwood	717	Morton	215	(Cumberland Co.)	717	New Bethlehem	814
Meyers Crossing	215	Milmont		Mortonville	215	Mount Zion		New Bloomfield	717
Meyersdale	814	(Delaware Co.)	215	Morwood	215	(Lebanon Co.)	717	New Boston	
Meyersville	215	Milnesville	717	Morysville	215	Mount Zion		(Luzerne Co.)	717
Mickleys	215	Milnor	717	Moscow	717	(York Co.)	717	New Boston	
Middleburg		Milport		Moselem	215	Mowersville	717	(Schuylkill Co.)	717
(Franklin Co.)	717	(Lancaster Co.)	717	Moselem Springs	215	Mowry	717	New Bridgeville	717
Middleburg		Milroy	717	Moshannon	814	Moxie	717	New Brighton	412
(Snyder Co.)	717	Milton	717	Mosherville	717	Moyers Station	717	New Britain	215
Middlebury	717	Milton Grove	717	Mosserville	215	Moylan	215	New Buena Vista	814
Middlebury Center	717	Milwaukee	717	Mossville	717	Muddy Creek Forks	717	New Buffalo	717
Middlecreek	717	Mineral Point	814	Mount Aetna	717	Muhlenburg	717	Newburg	
Middle Creek Dam	717	Mineral Springs	814	Mountain	215	Muir	717	(Cumberland Co.)	717
Middleport	717	Minersville	717	Mountaindale	814	Mummasburg	717	Newburg	
Middlesex	717	Mines	814	Mountain Grove	717	Muncy	717	(Huntingdon Co.)	814
Middle Spring	717	Mingoville	814	Mountainhome	717	Muncy Creek	717	New Castle	412
Middleswarth	717	Minisink Hills	717	Mountaintop	717	Muncy Station	717	New Castle Junction	412
Middletown		Minooka	717	Mount Airy		Muncy Valley	717	New Centerville	814
(Blair Co.)	814	Miola	814	(Lancaster Co.)	717	Mundys Corner	814	New Chester	717
Middletown		Miquon	215	Mount Airy		Munhall	412	New Columbia	717
(Dauphin Co.)	717	Mocanaqua	717	(Philadelphia Co.)	215	Munson	814	New Columbus	717
Middletown		Modena	215	Mount Bethel	717	Munster	814	New Cranberry	717
(Luzerne Co.)	717	Mohnton	215	Mount Braddock	412	Murdocksville	412	New Cumberland	717
Middletown Air		Mohrsville	215	Mount Carmel	717	Murraytown	717	New Derry	412
Material Area	717	Molino	717	Mount Dallas	814	Murrell	412	New Eagle	412
Middletown Center	717	Molltown	215	Mount Gretna	717	Murrysville	412	Newell	412
Middle Village	717	Monaca	412	Mount Holly Springs	717	Muse	412	New Enterprise	814
Midland	412	Monessen	412	Mount Hope		Myersburg	717	New Era	717
Midvalley	717	Mongul	717	(Adams Co.)	717	Myerstown	717	New Florence	412
Midway (Adams Co.)	717	Monocacy	215	Mount Hope		Myo Beach	717	Newfoundland	717
Midway		Monocacy Station	215	(Lancaster Co.)	717			New Franklin	717
(Washington Co.)	412	Monongahela	412	Mount Jackson	412			New Freedom	717
Mifflin	717	Monroe	814	Mount Jewett	814			New Freeport	412
Mifflinburg	717	Monroe Mills	717	Mount Joy	717			New Galilee	412
Mifflintown	717	Monroeton	717	Mount Lebanon	412	Nacetown	717	New Geneva	412
Mifflinville	717	Monroeville	412	Mount Morris	412	Naginey	717	New Germantown	717
Milan	717	Mont Alto	717	Mount Nebo	717	Nanticoke	717	New Grenada	814
Milanville	717	Montandon	717	Mount Oliver	412	Nanty Glo	814	New Holland	717
Mildred	717	Mont Clare	215	Mount Penn	215	Naomi Pines	717	New Hope	215
Milesburg	814	Montdale	717	Mount Pisgah	717	Napier	814	New Jerusalem	215
Milford	717	Montello	215	Mount Pleasant		Narberth	215	New Kensington	412
Milford Square	215	Monterey		(Adams Co.)	717	Narrowsburg	717	New Kingstown	717
Millbach	717	(Franklin Co.)	717	Mount Pleasant		Narvon	717	New Lebanon	412
Millbach Springs	717	Monterey		(Berks Co.)	215	Nashville	717	New London	215
Mill City	717	(Lancaster Co.)	717	Mount Pleasant		Natalie	717	New Mahoning	717
Millcreek (Erie Co.)	814	Montgomery	717	(Franklin Co.)	717	Natrona	412	Newmanstown	215
Mill Creek		Montgomery Ferry	717	Mount Pleasant		Natrona Heights	412	New Market	717
(Huntingdon Co.)	814	Montgomeryville	215	(Juniata Co.)	717	Nazareth	717	New Milford	717
Millersburg	717	Montoursville	717	Mount Pleasant		Neath	717	New Millport	814
Millers Mill	717	Montrose	717	(Lebanon Co.)	717	Needmore	717	New Milltown	717
Millerstown		Montsera	717	Mount Pleasant		Neelyton	814	New Oxford	717
(Blair Co.)	814	Monument	717	(Mifflin Co.)	717	Neffs	215	New Paris	814
Millerstown		Moon Run	412	Mount Pleasant		Neffs Mills	814	New Park	717
(Perry Co.)	717	Moon Street	717	(Westmoreland Co.)	412	Neffsville	717	New Philadelphia	717
Millersville	717	Moores	215	Mount Pleasant		Neiman	717	Newport	717
Millerton	717	Mooresburg	717	(York Co.)	717	Nekoda	717	Newport Center	717
Mill Grove		Mooresville	814	Mount Pleasant Mills	717	Nelson	717	Newportville	215
(Columbia Co.)	717	Mooretown	717	Mount Pocono	717	Nemacolin	412	New Providence	717
Millgrove (Erie Co.)	814	Moosic	717	Mount Rock		Nescopeck	717	New Ringgold	717
Mill Hall	717	Moosic Lakes	717	(Adams Co.)	717	Neshaminy	215	Newry	814
Millheim	814	Mooween	412	Mountrock ·		Neshaminy Falls	215	New Salem	412
Millmont (Union Co.)	717	Morann	814	(Cumberland Co.)	717	Nesquehoning	717	New Smithville	215
Millport (Potter Co.)	814	Moravia	412	Mount Royal	717	Nether Providence	215	New Stanton	412
Millrift	717	Morea	717	Mount Tabor	717	Nettleton	814	New Street	717
Mill Run	412	Morgan Run	814	Mount Top	717	Neville Island	412	Newton	717
Mills	814	Morgantown	215	Mount Union	814	New Albany	717	Newton Hamilton	814
Millsboro	412	Morris	717	Mount Vernon	717	New Alexandria	412	Newton Lake	717
Milltown	717	Morrisdale	814	Mountville	717	New Baltimore	814	Newtown (Bucks Co.)	215
Millvale	412	Morris Run	717	Mount Washington	412	New Bedford	412	Newtown	
Millview	717	Morrisville		Mount Wilson	717	New Berlin	717	(Lancaster Co.)	717
Mill Village	814	(Bucks Co.)	215			New Berlinville	215		

Place Name	Area Code	Place Name	Area Code	Place Name	Area Code	Place Name	Area Code	Place Name	Area Code
Newtown Square	215	Oakbottom	717	Orwin	717	Penbrook	717	Plainfield	717
New Tripoli	215	Oakbourne	215	Osborne Borough	412	Penfield		Plains	717
Newville		Oakdale		Osceola	814	(Clearfield Co.)	814	Plainsville	717
(Cumberland Co.)	717	(Allegheny Co.)	412	Osceola Mills	814	Penfield		Platea	814
Newville		Oakdale (Luzerne Co.)	717	Oshanter	814	(Delaware Co.)	215	Pleasant Corner	717
(Lancaster Co.)	717	Oakford	215	Osterburg	814	Penllyn	215	Pleasant Gap	814
New Wilmington	412	Oak Grove	717	Osterhout	717	Pen Mar	717	Pleasant Grove	
Niagara	717	Oak Hall Station	814	Oswayo	814	Pen Mar Park Station	717	(Lancaster Co.)	717
Niantic	215	Oak Hill		Ottawa	717	Penn	412	Pleasant Grove	
Nicholson	717	(Bradford Co.)	717	Ottsville	215	Penn Avon	717	(York Co.)	717
Nickel Mines	215	Oak Hill		Ott Town	814	Pennbrook	215	Pleasant Hall	717
Nickleville	814	(Lancaster Co.)	717	Oval	717	Penndel	215	Pleasant Hill	
Nicktown	814	Oakland	717	Overbrook	215	Pennersville	717	(Lebanon Co.)	717
Nimble	717	Oakland Mills	717	Overlook	717	Penn Hall	814	Pleasant Hill	
Ninepoints	717	Oak Lane	215	Overshot	717	Penn Hill	717	(York Co.)	717
Nineveh	412	Oakmont		Overton	717	Penn Hills	412	Pleasant Hills	
Nisbet	717	(Allegheny Co.)	412	Oxford	215	Penn Run	412	(Allegheny Co.)	412
Nittany	814	Oakmont		Oyster Point	717	Pennsburg	215	Pleasant Mount	717
Nixon	412	(Delaware Co.)	215			Penns Cave	814	Pleasant Unity	412
Noble	215	Oakryn	717			Penns Creek	717	Pleasant Valley	
Noblestown	412	Oaks	215			Pennsdale	717	(Bucks Co.)	215
Nook	717	Oak Shade	717	Packerton	215	Penns Park	215	Pleasant Valley	
Nordmont	717	Oakville	717	Palace	717	Pennsylvania Furnace	814	(Lycoming Co.)	717
Normal Square	717	Obelisk	215	Palm	215	Penn Valley	215	Pleasant Valley	
Normalville	412	Oberlin	717	Palmdale	717	Pennville	717	(Schuylkill Co.)	717
Norristown	215	Obold	215	Palmer	412	Penn Wynne	215	Pleasant Valley	
Northampton	215	Ogden	215	Palmerton	215	Penobscot	717	(Westmoreland Co.)	412
North Bangor	215	Ogdensburg	717	Palmyra	717	Penryn	717	Pleasant View	717
North Belle Vernon	412	Ogletown	814	Panther Valley	717	Pequea	717	Pleasantville	
North Bend	717	Ohiopyle	412	Paoli	215	Perdix	717	(Bedford Co.)	814
North Bessemer	412	Ohio View	412	Paradise (Adams Co.)	717	Perkasie	215	Pleasantville	
North Bingham	814	Ohioville	412	Paradise		Perkiomenville	215	(Berks Co.)	215
Northbrook	215	Oil City	814	(Lancaster Co.)	717	Perryopolis	412	Pleasantville	
North Charleroi	412	Oklahoma	412	Paradise		Perrysville	412	(Venango Co.)	814
North East	814	Olanta	814	(Schuylkill Co.)	717	Perryville	717	Pleasureville	717
North Eaton	717	Old Boston	717	Paradise Furnace	814	Perulack	717	Plowville	215
North Flat	717	Old Concord	412	Pardeesville	717	Petersburg	814	Plumsteadville	215
North Heidelberg	215	Old Forge	717	Pardoe	717	Petrolia	412	Plumville	412
North Hills	215	Old Port	717	Paris	412	Philadelphia	215	Plymouth	717
North Hopewell	717	Old Zionsville	215	Park Crest	717	Philipsburg	814	Plymouth Meeting	215
North Huntingdon	412	Oley	215	Parker	412	Phillipston	412	Pocono	717
North Lake	717	Oliphant Furnace	412	Parker Ford	215	Phillipsville	814	Pocono Lake	717
North Mehoopany	717	Oliveburg	814	Parkersglen	717	Philmont	215	Pocono Manor	717
Northpoint	814	Oliver	412	Parkers Landing	412	Phoenixville	215	Pocono Pines	717
North Springfield	814	Olivers Mills	717	Parkesburg	215	Picture Rocks	717	Pocono Summit	717
Northumberland	717	Olmsted Air		Parkhill	814	Pikes Creek	717	Pocopson	215
North Vandergrift	412	Force Base	717	Parkland	215	Pikesville	717	Point	814
North Wales	215	Olney	215	Park Place	717	Piketown	717	Point Breeze	717
North Washington		Olyphant	717	Parkside	215	Pillow	717	Point Marion	412
(Butler Co.)	412	Oneida	717	Parkview	717	Pine Bank	412	Point Pleasant	215
North Washington		Ono	717	Parkville	717	Pine Creek	717	Point View	814
(Westmoreland Co.)	412	Opp	717	Parkwood	412	Pine Forge	215	Poland	412
North York	717	Orange	717	Parnassus	412	Pine Glen	814	Polk	814
Norvelt	412	Orangeville	717	Parryville	215	Pine Grove	717	Pomeroy	215
Norway Ridge	717	Orbisonia	814	Parsons	717	Pine Grove Furnace	717	Pompeii	215
Norwood		Orefield	215	Parvin	717	Pine Grove Mills	814	Pond Bank	717
(Delaware Co.)	215	Oregon	717	Patterson Heights	412	Pine Station	717	Pond Creek	717
Norwood		Ore Hill	814	Patton	814	Pine Summit	717	Pond Hill	717
(Lancaster Co.)	717	Oreland	215	Paupack	717	Pine Swamp	215	Portage	814
Nottingham	215	Oriental	717	Pavia	814	Pine View	717	Port Allegany	814
Noxen	717	Oriole	717	Paxinos	717	Pineville	215	Port Blanchard	717
Nuangola	717	Ormsby	814	Paxtang	717	Pinola	717	Port Carbon	717
Nuangola Station	717	Orrstown	717	Paxtonia	717	Pipersville	215	Port Clinton	215
Numidia	717	Orrtanna	717	Paxtonville	717	Pitcairn	412	Porter	814
Nu Mine	412	Orson	717	Peach Bottom	717	Pitman	717	Porter Road	717
Nuremberg	717	Orvilla	215	Peach Glen	717	Pittock	412	Porters	717
Nyesville	717	Orviston	717	Peck's Grove	717	Pittsburgh	412	Portersville	412
		Orwell	717	Peckville	717	Pittston	717	Port Griffith	717
		Orwigsburg	717	Pen Argyl	215	Plain Grove	412	Port Kennedy	215

PENNSYLVANIA
Portland—Sells Station

Place Name	Area Code	Place Name	Area Code	Place Name	Area Code	Place Name	Area Code	Place Name	Area Code
Portland	717	Ranshaw	717	Ridgway	814	Roulette	814	Salisbury	
Portland Mills	814	Ransom	717	Ridley Park	215	Roundtown	717	(Somerset Co.)	814
Port Matilda	814	Raubsville	215	Riegelsville	215	Rouseville	814	Salix	814
Port Royal	717	Rauchtown	717	Rienze	717	Rouzerville	717	Salladasburg	717
Port Trevorton	717	Rauschs	717	Rife	717	Rowenna	717	Sally Ann Furnace	215
Port Vue	412	Ravine	717	Rileyville	717	Rowland	717	Salona	717
Potetown	814	Rawlinsville	717	Rillton	412	Roxborough	215	Saltillo	814
Potters Creek	814	Rays Hill	814	Rimersburg	814	Roxbury	717	Saltsburg	412
Pottersdale	814	Raystown Dam	814	Ringgold	814	Royal	717	Salunga	717
Potters Mills	814	Rea	412	Ringtown	717	Royalton	717	Saluvia	717
Potterville	717	Reading	215	Rinley	717	Royer	814	Sanatoga	215
Pottsgrove	717	Reamstown	215	Rising Springs	814	Royersford	215	Sanbourn	814
Pottstown	215	Rebersburg	814	Riverside	717	Ruchsville	215	Sandbeach	717
Pottsville	717	Rebuck	717	Riverton	215	Ruffs Dale	412	Sand Hill	
Powder Glen	717	Rector	412	Rixford	814	Ruggles	717	(Dauphin Co.)	717
Powder Valley	215	Redbank	412	Roaring Branch	717	Rummerfield	717	Sand Hill	
Powell	717	Red Bridge	717	Roaring Creek	717	Rupert	717	(Lebanon Co.)	717
Powys	717	Red Cross	717	Roaring Spring	814	Rural Ridge	412	Sand Patch	814
Poyntelle	717	Red Hill	215	Robertsdale	814	Rural Valley	412	Sandts Eddy	215
Prescott	717	Red Lion	717	Robesonia	215	Rush	717	Sandy Lake	412
Presque Isle Coast		Red Rock	717	Robinson	412	Rushboro	717	Sandy Ridge	814
Guard Sta. No. 236	814	Redrun	717	Robinson Extension	814	Rushland	215	Sandy Run	
Presto	412	Reed	717	Rochester	412	Rushtown	717	(Bedford Co.)	814
Preston Park	717	Reeders	717	Rochester Mills	412	Rushville	717	Sandy Run	
Pricedale	412	Reeds Gap	717	Rock	717	Russell	814	(Luzerne Co.)	717
Pricetown	215	Reed Station	717	Rock Glen	717	Russell Hill	717	Sankertown	814
Primos	215	Reedsville		Rockhill Furnace	814	Russellton	412	Sarah Furnace	412
Princeton	412	(Mifflin Co.)	717	Rockingham	814	Russellville	814	Sarver	412
Pringle	717	Reedsville		Rock Lake	717	Rutan	412	Sassamansville	215
Proctor	717	(Schuylkill Co.)	717	Rockland	814	Rutherford	717	Satterfield	717
Progress	717	Refton	717	Rockledge	215	Rutland	717	Saulsburg	814
Prompton	717	Register	717	Rockport	717	Rutledge	215	Saville	717
Prospect	412	Rehrersburg	717	Rockton	814	Rutledgedale	717	Saxonburg	412
Prospect Hill	717	Reidsburg	814	Rockview	814	Rydal	215	Saxton	814
Prospect Park	215	Reinerton	717	Rockville	717	Ryot	814	Saybrook	814
Prospectville	215	Reinholds	215	Rockwell Hill	717			Sayles	717
Prosperity	412	Reistville	717	Rockwood	814			Saylorsburg	717
Pughtown	215	Renfrew	412	Rocky Forest	717			Saylors Lake	717
Pulaski	412	Rennerdale	412	Rocky Glen	717			Sayre	717
Punxsutawney	814	Reno	814	Rockygrove	814			Scalp Level	814
Purcell	814	Renovo	717	Rodman	814	Sabinsville	814	Scarlets Mill	215
Puseyville	717	Renton	412	Roeders	717	Sacramento	717	Scenery Hill	412
Putneyville	814	Republic	412	Roedersville	717	Sadsburyville	215	Schaefferstown	717
		Retreat	717	Roelofs	215	Saegertown	814	Schanno	717
		Retta	717	Roger Hollow	717	Safe Harbor	717	Schellsburg	814
		Revere	215	Rogersville	412	Sagamore	412	Schenley	412
Quakake	717	Revloc	814	Rohrerstown	717	Sagon	717	Schnecksville	215
Quaker Lake	717	Rew	814	Rohrsburg	717	St. Benedict	814	Schocks Mills	717
Quakertown	215	Reward	717	Rolling Green	717	St. Boniface	814	Schoeneck	215
Quarryville	717	Rexmont	717	Rome	717	St. Charles	814	Schultzville	717
Queen	814	Reynolds	717	Ronco	412	St. Clair	717	Schuyler	717
Queen Junction	412	Reynoldsdale	814	Ronks	717	St. Clairsville	814	Schuylkill Haven	717
Quehanna	814	Reynoldsville	814	Rook	412	St. Davids	215	Schwenksville	215
Quentin	717	Rhawnhurst	215	Roscoe	412	St. Johns	717	Sciota	717
Quicks Bend	717	Rheems	717	Rosedale		St. Joseph	717	Scotch Valley	717
Quiggleville	717	Rices Landing	412	(Allegheny Co.)	412	St. Lawrence		Scotland	717
Quincy	717	Riceville	814	Rosedale		(Berks Co.)	215	Scotrun	717
		Richardsville	814	(Chester Co.)	215	St. Lawrence		Scottdale	412
		Richboro	215	Rosemont	215	(Cambria Co.)	814	Scottsville	717
		Richeyville	412	Roseto	215	St. Leonard	215	Scranton	717
Racine	412	Richfield	717	Rose Valley	215	St. Marys	814	Seanor	814
Radnor	215	Richland	717	Roseville	717	St. Michael	814	Sebastopol	717
Rahns	215	Richlandtown	215	Roslyn	215	St. Nicholas	717	Secane	215
Railroad Borough	717	Richmond		Ross Common	215	St. Peters	215	Seek	717
Rainsburg	814	(Northampton Co.)	215	Rossiter	814	St. Petersburg	412	Seelyville	717
Ralpho Township	717	Richmond (York Co.)	717	Rosslyn	412	St. Thomas	717	Seiberlingsville	215
Ralphton	814	Richmondale	717	Rosslyn Farms	412	Salem	717	Seipstown	215
Ralston	717	Richmond Furnace	717	Rossmoyne	717	Salemville	814	Seisholtzville	215
Ramey	814	Rickertsville	215	Rosston	412	Salford	215	Seitzland	717
Ramola	814	Ricketts	717	Rossville	717	Salfordville	215	Selinsgrove	717
Ramsey	717	Riddlesburg	814	Rote	717	Salina	412	Sellersville	215
Rankin	412	Ridgebury	717	Rothsville	717	Salisbury		Sells Station	717
						(Lancaster Co.)	717		

Place Name	Area Code	Place Name	Area Code	Place Name	Area Code	Place Name	Area Code	Place Name	Area Code
Seltzer City	717	Shoemakersville	215	Snow Shoe	814	Sproul	814	Stowell	717
Seminole	814	Shohola	717	Snyders	717	Spruce Creek	814	Stoystown	814
Seneca	814	Shope Garden	717	Snydersburg	814	Spruce Hill	717	Strabane	412
Sergeant	814	Short Mountain	814	Snydersville	717	Spry	717	Strafford	215
Seven Points	717	Shraders	717	Snydertown	717	Square Corners	717	Strasburg	717
Seven Springs	814	Shrewsbury	717	Solebury	215	Squirrel Hill	412	Strattanville	814
Seven Stars		Shumans	717	Somerset	814	Stahlstown	412	Strausstown	215
(Adams Co.)	717	Shunk	717	Somerton	215	Stairville	717	Strawberry Ridge	717
Seven Stars		Shupp Hill	717	Sonestown	717	Stalker	717	Strawbridge	717
(Juniata Co.)	717	Shy Beaver	814	Sonman	814	Standing Stone		Stricklerstown	717
Seven Valleys	717	Siddonsburg	717	Soudersburg	717	(Bradford Co.)	717	Strinestown	717
Seward	814	Sideling Hill	717	Souderton	215	Standing Stone		String Town	814
Sewickley	412	Sideling Hill Tunnel	814	Southampton	215	(Huntingdon Co.)	814	Strobleton	814
Sewickley Heights	412	Sidman	814	South Auburn	717	Stanton	717	Strong	717
Shade Gap	814	Sigel	814	South Bend	412	Starford	412	Strongstown	814
Shadle	717	Siglerville	717	South Canaan	717	Star Junction	412	Stroudsburg	717
Shadow Brook	717	Sigmund	215	South Connellsville	412	Starkville	717	Strouptown	717
Shadygrove	717	Silvara	717	Southdale	717	Starlight	717	Sturgeon	412
Shamokin	717	Silver Brook	717	South Danville	717	Starners	717	Sturges	717
Shamokin Dam	717	Silver Creek	717	South Eaton	717	Starrucca	717	Sugar Creek	717
Shamrock		Silverdale	215	South Fork	814	Starview	717	Sugar Grove	814
(Berks Co.)	215	Silver Lake	717	South Gibson	717	State College	814	Sugar Hill	717
Shamrock (North-		Silver Lake Terrace	215	South Greensburg	412	State Line		Sugar Hollow	717
umberland Co.)	717	Silver Spring		South Heights	412	(Bedford Co.)	814	Sugar Lake	814
Shanesville	215	(Cumberland Co.)	717	South Montrose	717	State Line		Sugarloaf	717
Shanksville	814	Silver Springs		South Mountain	717	(Franklin Co.)	717	Sugar Notch	717
Shannon Hill	717	(Lancaster Co.)	717	South Sterling	717	State School	717	Sugar Run	717
Sharon	412	Simpson	717	Southview	412	Steam Valley	717	Sugartown	215
Sharon Hill	215	Sinking Spring	215	South Waverly	717	Stearns Station	717	Sullivan Park	717
Sharpsburg		Sinnamahoning	814	Southwest	412	Steckman	814	Sulphur Spring	
(Allegheny Co.)	412	Sipesville	814	South Williamsport	717	Steelton	717	(Perry Co.)	717
Sharpsburg (Blair Co.)	814	Six Mile Run	814	Spangler	814	Steelville	215	Sulphur Springs	
Sharpsville	412	Skinners Eddy	717	Spangsville	215	Steene	717	(Bedford Co.)	814
Shartlesville	215	Skippack	215	Spartansburg	814	Steinsville	215	Summerdale	717
Shavertown	717	Skytop	717	Speeceville	717	Stemlersville	215	Summerhill	
Shawanese	717	Slabtown	717	Speers	412	Stenger	717	(Cambria Co.)	814
Shawnee	717	Slatedale	215	Spinnerstown	215	Sterling	717	Summer Hill	
Shawnee-on-the-		Slateford	717	Split Rock	717	Sterling Run	814	(Columbia Co.)	717
Delaware	717	Slate Hill	717	Sporting Hill	717	Sterretts Gap	717	Summerville	814
Shawville	814	Slate Run	717	Spraggs	412	Stevens	215	Summit Hill	717
Sheakleyville	412	Slatington	215	Sprankle Mills	814	Stevenson	717	Summit Station	717
Sheatown	717	Slaymakertown	717	Springboro	814	Stevens Point	717	Sumneytown	215
Sheffield	814	Slickville	412	Springbrook	717	Stevensville	717	Sunbury	717
Shellsville	717	Sligo	814	Spring Church	412	Stewartstown	717	Sunnyburn	717
Shellytown	814	Slippery Rock	412	Spring City	215	Stier	717	Sunny Side	412
Shelocta	412	Slocum	717	Springdale	412	Stifflertown	814	Sunset	717
Shenandoah	717	Slovan	412	Springfield		Stiles	215	Sunshine	717
Shenandoah Heights	717	Smethport	814	(Bradford Co.)	717	Stillwater	717	Suplee	215
Shenango	412	Smicksburg	814	Springfield		Stines Corner	717	Surveyor	814
Shepherdstown	717	Smithdale	412	(Cumberland Co.)	717	Stockdale	412	Suscon	717
Sheppton	717	Smithfield		Springfield		Stockertown	215	Susquehanna	717
Sherersville	215	(Fayette Co.)	412	(Delaware Co.)	215	Stockton	717	Sutersville	412
Sheridan		Smithfield		Spring Garden	717	Stoddartsville	717	Suttons Creek	717
(Lebanon Co.)	215	(Huntingdon Co.)	814	Spring Glen	717	Stoneboro	412	Swamp Brook	717
Sheridan		Smith Gap	215	Spring Grove	717	Stone Church	215	Swarthmore	215
(Schuylkill Co.)	717	Smith Hill	717	Springhill	717	Stonecrest	717	Swartzville	215
Sherman	717	Smithmill	814	Springhope	814	Stonehenge	717	Swatara Station	717
Shermans Dale	717	Smiths Crossing	814	Spring House	215	Stonersville	215	Swedeland	215
Sheshequin	717	Smiths Ferry	412	Spring Lake	717	Stoney Point	717	Sweet Arrow Lake	717
Shickshinny	717	Smith Station	717	Springmeadow	814	Stonington	717	Sweet Valley	717
Shickshinny Valley	717	Smithton		Spring Mills		Stony Hill	717	Swengel	717
Shillington	215	(Westmoreland Co.)	412	(Centre Co.)	814	Stony Run	215	Swiftwater	717
Shiloh	717	Smithtown		Spring Mount	215	Stoopville	215	Swineford	717
Shimerville	215	(Bucks Co.)	215	Spring Run	717	Stormstown	814	Swissvale	412
Shinglehouse	814	Smithville	717	Springs	814	Stormville	717	Switzer	215
Shintown	717	Smock	412	Springtown	215	Stouchsburg	215	Swoyersville	717
Shippensburg	717	Smokerun	814	Springvale	717	Stoufferstown	717	Sybertsville	717
Shippenville	814	Smoketown	717	Springville		Stoughstown	717	Sycamore	412
Shippingport	412	Smyrna	215	(Lancaster Co.)	717	Stoverdale	717	Sykesville	814
Shiremanstown	717	Smysers Mill	717	Springville		Stoverstown	717	Sylvania	717
Shirleysburg	814	Snedekerville	717	(Susquehanna Co.)	717	Stowe	215	Sylvan Lake	717
								Syner	717

PENNSYLVANIA
Table Rock—Westtown

Place Name	Area Code	Place Name	Area Code	Place Name	Area Code	Place Name	Area Code	Place Name	Area Code
Table Rock	717	Transue	717	Uniontown (North-		Vintondale	814	Webster	412
Tafton	717	Trappe	215	umberland Co.)	717	Virginia Mills	717	Webster Mills	717
Talmage	717	Trauger	412	Unionville		Virginville	215	Weedville	814
Tamanend	717	Trees Mills	412	(Centre Co.)	814	Voganville	717	Weigh Scales	717
Tamaqua	717	Treichlers	215	Unionville		Volant	412	Weir Lake	215
Tamiment	717	Tremont	717	(Chester Co.)	215	Vosburg	717	Weisenberg	215
Tanguy	215	Trenton	717	Union Water Works	717	Vose	717	Weiser Park	215
Tank	717	Tresckow	717	United	412			Weissport	215
Tanners Falls	717	Treveskyn	412	U. S. Army				Welcome Lake	717
Tannersville	717	Trevorton	717	Philadelphia				Wellersburg	814
Tarentum	412	Trevose	215	Signal Depot	215	Waddle	814	Wells	717
Tarrs	412	Trexler	215	U. S. Naval Air		Wagontown	215	Wellsboro	717
Tatamy	215	Trexlertown	215	Station,Willow		Wakefield	717	Wells Tannery	814
Tatesville	814	Trooper	215	Grove	215	Walheim	717	Wellsville	717
Taxville	717	Trough Creek	814	Unity	412	Walker Lake	717	Welsh Hill	717
Taylor	717	Trout Run	717	Unityville	717	Walkers Mills	412	Welsh Run	717
Tayloria	717	Troutville	814	Universal	412	Wall	412	Wendel	412
Taylorstown		Troxelville	717	University Park	814	Wallace	717	Wenksville	717
(Greene Co.)	412	Troy	717	Upland	215	Wallaceton	814	Werleys Corner	215
Taylorstown		Truce	717	Upper Askam	717	Wallenpaupack	717	Wernersville	215
(Washington Co.)	412	Trucksville	717	Upper Bern	215	Waller	717	Wernersville Heights	215
Taylorsville	717	Truemans	814	Upper Black Eddy	215	Wallingford	215	Wertz	814
Telford	215	Trumbauersville	215	Upper Darby	215	Wallis Run	717	Wescosville	215
Temple	215	Tryonville	814	Upper Lehigh	717	Wallsville	717	Wesley	814
Templeton	412	Tuckerton	215	Upper Strasburg	717	Walnut	717	Wesleyville	814
Tenmile	412	Tullytown	215	Upton	717	Walnut Bottom	717	Wessnersville	215
Terre Hill	215	Tulpehocken	215	Urban	717	Walnutport	215	West Abington	717
Terrytown	717	Tunkhannock	717	Uriah	717	Walnuttown	215	West Alexander	412
Texas	717	Tunnelhill	717	Ursina	814	Walston	814	West Aliquippa	412
Tharptown	717	Tunnelton	412	Uswick	717	Waltersburg	412	Westbrook	717
The Pines	717	Turbotville	717	Utahville	814	Waltz's Mills	412	West Brownsville	412
Thomasville	717	Turkey City	814	Utica	814	Wampum	412	West Chester	215
Thompson	717	Turkey Foot	717	Uwchland	215	Wanamakers	215	Westcolang	717
Thompsontown	717	Turrell Corners	717			Wanamie	717	West Conshohocken	215
Thornburg	412	Turtle Creek	412			Wapwallopen	717	West Decatur	814
Thorndale	215	Turtlepoint	814			Warburton Hill	717	West Elizabeth	412
Thornhurst	717	Tuscarora				Ward	215	West Fairfield	412
Thornton	215	(Juniata Co.)	717	Valencia	412	Wardan Place	717	West Fairview	717
Three Springs	814	Tuscarora		Valentine Hill	717	Warfordsburg	717	Westfield	814
Three Tuns	215	(Schuylkill Co.)	717	Valier	814	Warminster	215	West Finley	412
Throop	717	Tusseyville	814	Valley Forge	215	Warren	814	Westford	412
Thurston Hollow	717	Tweedale	717	Valley Glen	717	Warren Center	717	West Grove	215
Tidioute	814	Twilight	412	Valley View		Warrendale	412	West Hanover	717
Timblin	814	Twin Lakes	717	(Centre Co.)	814	Warrensville	717	West Hazleton	717
Tingley Lake	717	Twin Oaks	215	Valley View		Warrington	215	West Hickory	814
Tinicum	215	Twin Rocks	814	(Schuylkill Co.)	717	Warriors Mark	814	West Homestead	412
Tioga	717	Two Taverns	717	Van	814	Warwick	215	Westland	412
Tionesta	814	Tyler Hill	717	Vancamp	717	Washington	412	West Lawn	215
Tipton	814	Tyler Lake	717	Vanderbilt	412	Washington Boro	717	West Leisenring	412
Tire Hill	814	Tylersburg	814	Vandergrift	412	Washington Crossing	215	Westline	814
Titusville	814	Tylersport	215	Vandling	717	Washingtonville	717	West Mayfield	412
Tivoli	717	Tylersville	717	Vandyke	717	Waterfall	814	West Middlesex	412
Tobyhanna	717	Tyre	412	Van Meter	412	Waterford	814	West Middletown	412
Todd	814	Tyrell Hill	717	Vanport	412	Waterloo	717	West Mifflin	412
Tohickon	215	Tyrone	814	Van Voorhis	412	Waterside	814	West Milton	717
Toland	717			Van Wert	412	Water Street	814	Westminster	717
Tolna	717			Varden	717	Waterton	717	Westmont	814
Tomhicken	717			Venango	814	Waterville	717	West Monterey	412
Tompkinsville	717	Uhlerstown	215	Venetia	412	Watrous	814	Westmoreland City	412
Tomstown	717	Uledi	412	Venus	814	Watsontown	717	West Nanticoke	717
Topton	215	Ulster	717	Vera Cruz	215	Wattsburg	814	West Newton	412
Torrance	412	Ulysses	814	Verdilla	717	Watts Station	717	West Oak Lane	215
Torresdale	215	Unicorn	717	Vernfield	215	Waverly	717	Weston	717
Toughkenamon	215	Union	717	Vernon	717	Wawa	215	Westover	814
Towanda	717	Union City	814	Verona	412	Waymart	717	West Pittsburgh	412
Tower City	717	Union Dale	717	Versailles	412	Wayne	215	West Pittston	717
Town Hill	717	Union Deposit	717	Vestaburg	412	Waynecastle	717	West Point	215
Townline	717	Union Grove	215	Vian	717	Wayne Heights	717	Westport	717
Townville	814	Union Hill	215	Vici	717	Wayne Junction	215	West Reading	215
Trachsville	215	Uniontown		Vicksburg	717	Waynesboro	717	West Salisbury	814
Trafford	412	(Fayette Co.)	412	Village Green	215	Waynesburg	412	West Springfield	814
Trainer	215	Uniontown		Villa Maria	412	Weatherly	717	West Sunbury	412
Transfer	412	(Indiana Co.)	814	Villanova	215	Weaverland	215	Westtown	215
				Vintage	717	Weavertown	717		

Place Name	Area Code	Place Name	Area Code	Place Name	Area Code	Place Name	Area Code	Place Name	Area Code
West Valley	717	White Rock	717	Willow Hill	717	Woodland (Clearfield Co.)	814	Yardley	215
West View	412	Whites Crossing	717	Willow Street	717	Woodland (Mifflin Co.)	717	Yatesboro	412
Westville	814	Whites Ferry	717	Wills Creek	814	Woodlyn	215	Yatesville	717
West Whiteland	215	Whites Valley	717	Wilmerding	412	Woodrow	412	Yeadon	215
West Willow	717	Whitford	215	Wilmington Junction	412	Woodruff	412	Yeagertown	717
West Winfield	412	Whitney	412	Wilmore	814	Woodside	215	Yellow Creek	814
Westwood	412	Whitsett	412	Wilmot	717	Woodstock	717	Yellow House	215
West York	717	Wick	412	Wilpen	412	Woodstown	717	Yellow Springs	814
Wetona	717	Wickhaven	412	Wilson	412	Woodville	412	Yocumtown	717
Wexford	412	Wicks Station	412	Wilson Borough	215	Woodward	814	Yoders Heights	215
Weyant	814	Wiconisco	717	Wilsonville	717	Woolrich	717	Yoe	717
Wheatland	412	Widnoon	412	Winburne	814	Worcester	215	York	717
Wheelerville	717	Wila	717	Windber	814	Worleytown	717	York Furnace	717
Whitaker	412	Wilawana	717	Wind Gap	215	Worman	215	York Haven	717
White	412	Wilburton	717	Windham	717	Wormleysburg	717	York New Salem	717
White Deer	717	Wilcox	814	Windham Center	717	Worthington	412	York Road Station	717
White Hall (Adams Co.)	717	Wildwood (Allegheny Co.)	412	Wind Ridge	412	Worthville	814	York Springs	717
Whitehall (Allegheny Co.)	412	Wildwood (Bradford Co.)	717	Windsor	717	Woxall	215	Youngdale	717
Whitehall (Lehigh Co.)	215	Wilkes-Barre	717	Winfield	717	Wrighter's Lake	717	Youngstown	412
Whitehall (Mifflin Co.)	717	Wilkes-Barre, Wyoming Valley Airport	717	Wingate	814	Wrightsdale	717	Youngsville	814
White Hall (Montour Co.)	717	Wilkinsburg	412	Winterdale	717	Wrightstown	215	Youngwood	412
White Haven	717	William Penn	717	Winterstown	717	Wrightsville	717	Yount	814
White Hill	717	Williamsburg	814	Wintersville	717	Wyalusing	717	Yukon	412
White Horse	717	Williams Grove	717	Winton	717	Wyano	412		
Whiteland	215	Williamson	717	Wireton	412	Wycombe	215		
Whitemarsh	215	Williamsport	717	Wissahickon	215	Wyncote	215	Zelienople	412
White Mills	717	Williamstown	717	Wissinoming	215	Wyndmoor	215	Zenith	717
White Oak	717	Willock	412	Witmer	717	Wynnefield	215	Zerbe	717
White Oak Borough	412	Willow Grove (Bedford Co.)	814	Wolfdale	412	Wynnewood	215	Zieglerville	215
White Pine (Franklin Co.)	717	Willow Grove (Columbia Co.)	717	Wolfsburg	814	Wyoanna	717	Zion	814
Whitepine (Lycoming Co.)	717	Willow Grove (Montgomery Co.)	215	Womelsdorf	215	Wyoming	717	Zion Grove	717
				Wood	814	Wyomissing	215	Zionsville	215
				Woodbine	717	Wyomissing Hills	215	Zora	717
				Woodbourne	215	Wysox	717	Zullinger	717
				Woodbury	814				
				Woodbush	814				
				Woodcock	814				

ALL POINTS—AREA CODE 401

ALL POINTS—AREA CODE 803

ALL POINTS—AREA CODE 605

Place Name	Area Code	Place Name	Area Code	Place Name	Area Code	Place Name	Area Code	Place Name	Area Code
Adams-Cedar Hill	615	Bonicord	901	Collinwood	615	Elbridge	901	Greenfield	901
Adamsville	901	Booneville	615	Columbia	615	Elgin	615	Green Grove	615
Aetna	615	Boonshill	615	Conasauga	615	Elizabethton	615	Gruetli	615
Afton	615	Boyds Creek	615	Concord	615	Elkmont	615	Guild	615
Alamo	901	Braden	901	Cookeville	615	Elkton	615	Guys	901
Alcoa	615	Bradford	901	Cookeville South	615	Elk Valley	615		
Alexandria	615	Bradyville	615	Copperhill	615	Ellendale	901		
Algood	615	Brazil	901	Copper Basin	615	Elora	615		
Allisona	615	Brentwood	615	Cordova	901	Emory Gap	615	Habersham	615
Alnwick	615	Briceville	615	Cornersville	615	Englewood	615	Haley	615
Altamont	615	Brick Church	615	Corryton	615	Enville	901	Halls	901
Andersonville	615	Brighton	901	Cortner	615	Erin	615	Halls Cross Roads	615
Anes	615	Bristol	615	Cottagegrove	901	Erwin	615	Hampshire	615
Antioch	615	Brownfield	901	Cottontown	615	Estill Springs	615	Hampton	615
Apison	615	Brownsville	901	Counce	901	Ethridge	615	Hardisons Mills	615
Ardmore	615	Bruceton	901	Covington	901	Etowah	615	Harriman	615
Arlington	901	Brush Creek	615	Cowan	615	Evensville	615	Harrison	615
Armona	615	Brushy Mountain		Crawford	615			Harrogate	615
Arnold Air		Mines	615	Crockett Mills	901			Hartford	615
Force Station	615	Buford	615	Cross Plains-Orlinda	615			Hartsville	615
Arp	901	Bulls Gap	615	Crossville	615	Fairfield	615	Heiskell	615
Arrington	615	Bumpus Mills	615	Culleoka	615	Fairview	615	Helenwood	615
Arthur	615	Burns	615	Cumberland City	615	Falcon	901	Henderson	901
Ashburn	615	Butler	615	Cumberland Furnace	615	Fall Branch	615	Henderson Springs	615
Ashland City	615	Byington	615	Cumberland Gap	615	Fall Creek Falls	615	Hendersonville	615
Ashport	901	Byrdstown	615	Cunningham	615	Farmington	615	Henning	901
Aspen Hill	615			Curve	901	Fayetteville	615	Henry	901
Athens	615			Cypress	901	Finger	901	Henryville	615
Atoka	901	Cades	901			Finley	901	Hermitage	615
Atwood	901	Calderwood	615			Flat Creek	615	Hickman	615
Auburntown	615	Calhoun	615	Daisy-Soddy	615	Flintville	615	Hickory Valley	901
		Camden	901	Dancyville	901	Fordtown	615	Hickory Withe	901
		Campbell's Station	615	Dandridge	615	Forest Hill	901	Highcliff	615
		Campbellsville	615	Dante	615	Forked Deer	901	Highland	615
Bacchus	615	Carpenter's		Darden	901	Fork Ridge	615	Hillsboro	615
Baileyton	615	Camp Ground	615	Dayton	615	Fort Pillow	901	Hillsdale	615
Bakerville	615	Carters Creek	615	Decatur	615	Fosterville	615	Hixson	615
Ball Play	615	Carthage	615	Decaturville	901	Fountain City	615	Hodges	615
Barren Plains	615	Caryville	615	Decherd	615	Fowlkes	901	Hohenwald	615
Barretville	901	Catletts	615	Deer Lodge	615	Frankewing	615	Hollow Rock	901
Baxter	615	Catlettsburg	615	Defeated	615	Franklin	615	Holmes Road	901
Bean Station	615	Cedar Grove	901	Delina	615	Fredonia	615	Hornbeak	901
Beech Grove		Cedar Hill	615	Dellrose	615	Friendship	901	Hornsby	901
(Anderson Co.)	615	Celina	615	Denmark	901	Friends Station	615	Howell	615
Beech Grove		Centennial Island	901	Denver	615	Friendsville	615	Humboldt	901
(Coffee Co.)	615	Centertown	615	Detroit	901	Fruitland	901	Huntersville	901
Beech Hill	615	Centerville	615	Devonia	615	Fruitvale	901	Huntingdon	901
Beech Springs	615	Central	901	Dibrell	615			Huntland	615
Beersheba	615	Chapel Hill	615	Dickson	615			Huntsville	615
Belfast	615	Charleston	615	Dixie Lee Junction	615			Hurdlow	615
Bell Buckle	615	Charlotte	615	Dixon Springs	615	Gadsden	901	Huron	901
Bellevue	615	Chattanooga	615	Donelson	615	Gainesboro	615	Hurricane Mills	615
Bells	901	Chestnut Mound	615	Dossett	615	Gainesville	901		
Belmont	615	Chilhowee	615	Dover	615	Gallatin	615		
Belvidere	615	Christiana	615	Dowelltown	615	Galloway	901		
Bemis	901	Chuckey	615	Doyle	615	Gates	901	Indian Mound	615
Benton	615	Church Hill	615	Dresden	901	Gatliff	615	Indian Springs	615
Berlin	615	Clairfield	615	Drummonds	901	Gatlinburg	615	Iron City	615
Bethel Springs	901	Clarkrange	615	Duck River	615	Georgetown	615	Island 26	901
Bethesda	615	Clarksburg	901	Ducktown	615	Germantown	901		
Bethpage	615	Clarksville	615	Dukedom	901	Gibson	901		
Bigbyville	615	Claxton	615	Duncan	615	Gladeville	615		
Big Rock	615	Cleveland	615	Dunlap	615	Gleason	901	Jacksboro	615
Big Sandy	901	Clifton	615	Durhamville	901	Glendale	615	Jacks Creek	901
Birchwood	615	Clinchport	615	Dyer	901	Glenmary	615	Jackson	901
Blaine	615	Clinton	615	Dyersburg	901	Goodlettsville	615	Jamestown	615
Blanche	615	Coalfield	615			Goodluck	901	Jasper	615
Blountville	615	Coalmont	615			Gordonsville	615	Jefferson City	615
Bluff City	615	Coker Creek	615	Eads	901	Grand Junction	901	Jellico	615
Bodenham	615	Colby	615	Eagan	615	Grant	615	Jewell	901
Bold Spring	615	Collegedale	615	Eagleville	615	Granville	615	Joelton	615
Bolivar	901	College Grove	615	Eaton	901	Graysville	615	Johnson City	615
Bolton	901	College Station	615	Eatons Cross Roads	615	Greenback	615	Johnsonville	615
Bon Aqua	615	Collierville	901	Edith	901	Greenbrier	615	Jonesboro	615
						Greeneville	615		

TENNESSEE
Keeling—Tusculum

Place Name	Area Code	Place Name	Area Code	Place Name	Area Code	Place Name	Area Code	Place Name	Area Code
Keeling	901	Masseyville	901	Nine Mile	615	Powell Valley	615	Shellmound	615
Keiser	615	Maury City	901	Niota	615	Pressmens Home	615	Sherwood	615
Kelso	615	Maynardville	615	Nolensville	615	Prospect	615	Shiloh	901
Kenton	901	McBurg	615	Norene	615	Pruden	615	Shouns	615
Kerrville	901	McCains	615	Norma	615	Pulaski	615	Sidonia	901
Kimball	615	McDonald	615	Normandy	615	Puryear	901	Signal Mountain	615
Kimmins	615	McEwen	615	Northern Field	615			Slayden	615
Kingsport	615	McGhee-Tyson		Norris	615			Smithville	615
Kingston	615	Airport	615	North Springs	615			Smyrna	615
Kingston Springs	615	McKenzie	901	Nunnelly	615			Sneedville	615
Kinzel Springs	615	McLemoresville	901					Soddy-Daisy	615
Knoxville	615	McMinnville	615			Raleigh	901	Somerville	901
Kyles Ford	615	McNairy	901			Rally Hill	615	South Fulton	901
		Meadow	615			Ramer	901	South Guthrie	615
		Medina	901	Oakdale	615	Readyville	615	South Hazel	901
		Medon	901	Oakfield	901	Reagan Station	615	South Oak Grove	615
		Memphis	901	Oak Grove	615	Red Boiling Springs	615	South Pittsburg	615
Laager	615	Mentor	615	Oakland	901	Riceville	615	Southport	615
Lafayette	615	Mercer	901	Oak Ridge	615	Richard City	615	Southside	615
La Follette	615	Michie	901	Oakville	901	Richland	615	Sparta	615
La Grange	901	Middlecreek	615	Obion	901	Rickman	615	Speedwell	615
Lake City	615	Middleton	901	Ocoee	615	Riddleton	615	Spencer	615
Lancaster	615	Midland	615	Old Hickory	615	Ridgely	901	Spring City	615
Lancing	615	Midtown	615	Old Zion	615	Ridgetop	615	Springfield	615
Laneview	901	Milan	901	Olivehill	901	Ridgeville	615	Spring Hill	615
Lascassas	615	Milledgeville	901	Oliver Springs	615	Ridley	615	Statesville	615
Latham	901	Milligan College	615	Oneida	615	Ripley	901	Stanton	901
Laurel	615	Millington	901	Ooltewah	615	Rives	901	Stella	615
Lavergne	615	Milton	615	Ore Springs	901	Roan Mountain	615	Strawberry Plains	615
Lawrenceburg	615	Minor Hill	615	Orlinda	615	Robbins	615	Sugar Tree	615
Lea Lakes	615	Miser Station	615	Orysa	901	Rockford	615	Sullivan Gardens	615
Lebanon	615	Mitchellville	615	Ostella	615	Rock Island	615	Sulphur Springs	615
Lenoir City	615	Mohawk	615	Oswego	615	Rockvale	615	Summertown	615
Lenox	901	Monoville	615	Ovoca	615	Rockwood	615	Summitville	615
Leoma	615	Monsanto	615	Ozone	615	Rogers Springs	901	Sunbright	615
Lewisburg	615	Monteagle	615			Rogersville	615	Surgoinsville	615
Lexington	901	Monterey	615			Rosemark	901	Sweetwater	615
Liberty	615	Montezuma	901			Roseville	615	Sylvia	615
Limestone	615	Montvale	615			Rossville	901		
Linden	615	Mooresburg	615	Palmer	615	Rover	615		
Livingston	615	Mooresville	615	Palmersville	901	Rugby	615		
Lobelville	615	Morley	615	Palmetto	615	Russellville	615		
Lone Mountain	615	Morrison	615	Palmyra	615	Rutherford	901		
Longtown	901	Morristown	615	Paris	901	Rutledge	615	Taft	615
Lookout Mountain	615	Moscow	901	Parksville	615			Talbott	615
Loretto	615	Mosheim	615	Parrottsville	615			Tallassee	615
Loudon	615	Moss	615	Parsons	901			Tansi	615
Louisville	615	Mountain City	615	Pegram	615			Tarpley	615
Lowland	615	Mountain Home	615	Pelham	615	St. Bethlehem	615	Tate Springs	615
Lucy	901	Mountairy	615	Perryville	901	St. Joseph	615	Tazewell	615
Luray	901	Mount Carmel	615	Persia	615	Sale Creek	615	Telford	615
Luttrell	615	Mount Juliet	615	Petersburg	615	Salem	615	Tellico Plains	615
Lyles	615	Mount Pleasant	615	Petros	615	Saltillo	901	Temperance Hall	615
Lynchburg	615	Mulberry	615	Philadelphia	615	Samburg	901	Tennessee City	615
Lynnville	615	Munford	901	Phillippy	901	Sango	615	Tennessee Ridge	615
		Murfreesboro	615	Pickwick Dam	901	Santa Fe	615	Thompsons Station	615
				Pigeon Forge	615	Sardis	901	Thorn Hill	615
				Pikeville	615	Saulsbury	901	Tigrett	901
				Piney Flats	615	Savannah	901	Tiprell	615
Macon	901			Pinson	901	Sawdust Valley	615	Tiptonville	901
Madison	615	Nashville	615	Pittman Center	615	Scotts Hill	901	Toone	901
Madisonville	615	Neapolis	615	Pleasant Grove	615	Selmer	901	Townsend	615
Malesus	901	Neptune	615	Pleasant Hill	615	Sequatchie	615	Tracy City	615
Manchester	615	Neva	615	Pleasant Shade	615	Sevierville	615	Trade	615
Marion	615	Newbern	901	Pleasant Valley	615	Sewanee	615	Trenton	901
Martha	615	Newcomb	615	Pleasant View	615	Shady Grove	615	Trezevant	901
Martin	901	New Johnsonville	615	Pocahontas	901	Shady Valley	615	Tri-City Airport	615
Maryville	615	New Market	615	Portland	615	Sharon	901	Trimble	901
Mascot-Strawberry		New Middleton	615	Port Royal	615	Sharps Chapel	615	Triune	615
Plains	615	Newport	615	Pottsville	615	Shawanee	615	Troy	901
Mason	901	New Providence	615	Powder Springs	615	Shelby Forest	901	Tullahoma	615
Mason Hall	901	New Tazewell	615	Powell	615	Shelbyville	615	Tusculum	615

Place Name	Area Code	Place Name	Area Code	Place Name	Area Code	Place Name	Area Code	Place Name	Area Code
Unaka Springs	615	Vasper	615	Wartburg	615	White House	615	Woodbury	615
Unicoi	615	Verona	615	Wartrace	615	White Pine	615	Woodland	615
Union City	901	Viola	615	Washburn	615	Whitesburg	615	Woodland Mills	901
Unionville	615	Vonore	615	Washington College	615	Whites Creek	615	Woodlawn	615
U. S. Naval Air Station	901	Vose	615	Watauga	615	Whiteville	901	Woodville	901
U. S. Naval Air Technical Training Center	901			Watertown	615	Whitlock	901	Wooldridge	615
				Watts Bar	615	Whitwell	615	Wrigley	615
U. S. Naval Hospital	901	Waco	615	Waverly	615	Wildwood	615		
		Wadeville	615	Waynesboro	615	Williamsport	615		
		Wales	615	Westbourne	615	Williston	901		
		Walland	615	Westmoreland	615	Winchester	615		
Vanleer	615	Walterhill	615	West Point	615	Winchester Springs	615	Yell	615
		Warren	901	Wheel	615	Windrock	615	Yokeley	615
				White Bluff	615	Winfield	615	Yorkville	901

Place Name	Area Code	Place Name	Area Code	Place Name	Area Code	Place Name	Area Code	Place Name	Area Code
Abbott	817	Avinger	214	Big Valley	915	Brownwood	915	Center Point	512
Abernathy	806	Avoca	915	Big Wells	512	Bruceville	817	Centerville	214
Abilene	915	Axtell	817	Birthright	214	Bruni	512	Central	713
Ackerly	915	Azle	817	Bishop	512	Bryan	713	Chandler	214
Acton	817			Bivins	214	Bryan Air Force Base	713	Channelview	713
Acuff	806			Black	806	Bryson	817	Channing	806
Adamsville	512			Blackwell	915	Buchanan Dam	512	Chapman Ranch	512
Addison	214	Babcock	512	Blanchard	713	Buckeye	713	Chappell Hill	713
Adkins	512	Bacliff	713	Blanco	512	Buckholts	817	Charco	512
Adrian	806	Bagwell	214	Blanket	915	Buda	512	Charlie	817
Afton	806	Bailey	214	Bledsoe	806	Buena Vista	512	Charlotte	512
Agua Dulce	512	Baird	915	Bleiblerville	713	Buffalo (Harris Co.)	713	Chatfield	214
Airline	713	Balcones	512	Blessing	512	Buffalo (Leon Co.)	214	Cheapside	512
Alamito	915	Ballinger	915	Blewett	512	Buffalo Gap	915	Cherokee	915
Alamo	512	Balmorhea	915	Bloomburg	214	Bula	806	Chester	713
Alanreed	806	Bammel	713	Blooming Grove	214	Bullard	214	Chico	817
Alba	214	Bandera	512	Bloomington	512	Bulverde	512	Childress	817
Albany	817	Bangs	915	Blossom	214	Buna	713	Chillicothe	817
Albert	512	Banquete	512	Blue Grove	817	Bunkerhill	806	Chilton	817
Aldine	713	Bardwell	214	Blue Ridge		Burkburnett	817	China	713
Aledo	817	Barker	713	(Collin Co.)	214	Burkett	915	China Spring	817
Alexander	817	Barksdale	512	Blue Ridge		Burkeville	713	Chireno	713
Alice	512	Barnhart	915	(Fort Bend Co.)	713	Burleson	817	Christine	512
Alief	713	Barnum	713	Bluffdale	817	Burlington	817	Christoval	915
Allen	214	Barry	214	Blum	817	Burnet	512	Churchill	713
Allison	806	Barstow	915	Boerne	512	Burton	713	Cibolo	512
Alpine	915	Bartlett	817	Bogata	214	Bushland	806	Cisco	817
Altair	713	Bartonville	817	Boling-New Gulf	713	Byers	817	Clairemont	806
Alta Loma	713	Bastrop	512	Bomarton	817	Bynum	817	Clairette	817
Alto	713	Batesville	512	Bonham	214			Clarendon	806
Alvarado	817	Batson	713	Bonita	817			Clarksville	214
Alvin	713	Bay City	713	Bon Wier	713			Clarkwood	512
Alvord	817	Bayside	512	Booker	806	Cactus	806	Claude	806
Amarillo	806	Baytown	713	Boonsville	817	Caddo	817	Clayton	214
Amherst	806	Beach City	713	Booth	713	Caddo Mills	214	Cleburne	817
Anahuac	713	Bean	806	Borden	713	Calallen	512	Clemville	713
Anderson	713	Beasley	713	Borger	806	Calamity Creek	915	Cleo	915
Andrews	915	Beaumont	713	Boston	214	Caldwell	713	Cleta	806
Angleton	713	Bebe	512	Bovina	806	Calliham	512	Cleveland	713
Anna	214	Beckville	214	Bowie	817	Calvert	713	Clifton	817
Annarose	512	Bedford	817	Boyd	817	Camden	713	Clint	915
Annona	214	Bedias	713	Boys Ranch	806	Cameron	817	Clute-Lake Jackson	713
Anson	915	Bee Caves	512	Bracken	512	Campbell	214	Clyde	915
Antelope	817	Bee Creek	512	Brackettville	512	Campbellton	512	Coahoma	915
Anthony	915	Beeville	512	Bradshaw	915	Camp Wood	512	Coldspring	713
Anton	806	Belle Plain	806	Brady	915	Canadian	806	Coldwater	806
Apollo	713	Bellevue	817	Brandon	817	Canton	214	Coleman	915
Apple Springs	713	Bells	214	Brashear	214	Canutillo	915	Collegeport	512
Aquilla	817	Bells-Savoy	214	Brazoria-Churchill	713	Canyon	806	College Station	713
Aransas Pass	512	Bellville	713	Brazos	817	Caprock	806	Collinsville	214
Arcadia	713	Belmont	512	Brazos Santiago Coast		Caradan	915	Colmesneil	713
Archer City	817	Belton	817	Guard Sta. No. 222	512	Carbon	817	Colorado City	915
Arcola	713	Ben Arnold	817	Breckenridge	817	Carey	817	Columbus	713
Argyle	817	Benavides	512	Bremond	817	Carlsbad	915	Comanche	915
Arlington	817	Ben Bolt	512	Brenham	713	Carlton	817	Combes	512
Arnett	806	Benbrook	817	Bridge City	713	Carmine	713	Combine	214
Arp	214	Benchley	713	Bridgeport	817	Carrizo Springs	512	Comfort	512
Art	915	Bend	915	Briggs	512	Carrollton	214	Commerce	214
Artesia Wells	512	Ben Franklin	214	Bristol	214	Carta Valley	512	Como	214
Arthur City	214	Ben Hur	817	Broaddus	713	Carthage	214	Comstock	512
Asherton	512	Benjamin	817	Bronson	713	Cash	214	Concan	512
Aspermont	817	Ben Wheeler	214	Bronte	915	Cason	214	Concepcion	512
Atascosa	512	Berclair	512	Brooke Army Medical		Castell	915	Concord	713
Aten	806	Bergheim	512	Center	512	Castroville	512	Cone	806
Athens	214	Bertram	512	Brookeland	713	Catarina	512	Connally, James Air	
Atlanta	214	Bettie	214	Brookesmith	915	Cayuga	214	Force Base	817
Aubrey	817	Big Bend National		Brooks Air Force		Cedar Hill	214	Conroe	713
Ausborne	806	Park	915	Base	512	Cedar Park	512	Cookville	214
Austin	512	Big Canyon	915	Brookshire	713	Cedar Valley	512	Coolidge	817
Austonio	713	Big Foot	512	Brookston	214	Cee Vee	817	Cooper	214
Austwell	512	Big Lake	915	Brownfield	806	Celeste	214	Copeville	214
Avalon	214	Big Sandy	214	Brownsboro	214	Celina	214	Coppell	214
Avery	214	Big Spring	915	Brownsville	512	Center	713	Copperas Cove	817

TEXAS
Corpus Christi—Hargill

Place Name	Area Code	Place Name	Area Code	Place Name	Area Code	Place Name	Area Code	Place Name	Area Code
Corpus Christi	512	Detroit	214	Elkins	806	Forest	713	Gladebranch	214
Corrigan	713	Devers	713	Ellinger	713	Forestburg	817	Gladewater	214
Corsicana	214	Devine	512	Ellington	713	Forney	214	Glazier	806
Cost	512	Dewalt	713	Ellington Air Force		Forreston	214	Glen Cove	915
Cotton Center	806	Deweyville	713	Base	713	Forsan	915	Glen Flora	713
Cotulla	512	D'Hanis	512	Elm Creek	512	Fort Bliss	915	Glen Rose	817
County Line	806	Dialville	214	Elm Mott	817	Fort Davis	915	Glidden	713
Coupland	512	Diboll	713	Elmendorf	512	Fort Hancock	915	Gober	214
Courtney	713	Dickens	806	Elmo	214	Fort Hood	817	Godley	817
Covington	817	Dickinson	713	El Paso	915	Fort McKavett	915	Golden	214
Coyanosa	915	Dike	214	Elsa	512	Fort Sam Houston	512	Goldsboro	915
Coy City	512	Dilley	512	El Sauz	512	Fort Stockton	915	Goldsmith	915
Crandall	214	Dime Box	713	Elysian Fields	214	Fort Worth	817	Goldthwaite	915
Crane	915	Dimmitt	806	Emhouse	214	Fort Worth-		Goliad	512
Cranes Mill	512	Dodd City	214	Emory	214	Wedgwood	817	Gonzales	512
Cranfills Gap	817	Dodge	713	Encinal	512	Foster	512	Good Fellow	
Crawford	817	Dodson	806	Encino	512	Fowlerton	512	Air Force Base	915
Creedmoor	512	Donie	817	Energy	817	Francitas	512	Goodlett	817
Cresson	817	Donna	512	Engle	713	Frankel City	915	Goodnight	806
Crews	915	Doole	915	Enloe	214	Franklin	713	Goodrich	713
Crockett	713	Dorchester	214	Ennis	214	Frankston	214	Good Springs	214
Crosby	713	Doss	512	Enochs	806	Fratt	512	Gordon	817
Crosbyton	806	Double Bayou	713	Eola	915	Fredericksburg	512	Gordonville	214
Cross Plains	817	Doucette	713	Estelline	806	Fredonia	915	Goree	817
Crowell	817	Dougherty	806	Etoile	713	Freeport	713	Gorman	817
Crowley	817	Douglassville	214	Euless	817	Freer	512	Gouldbusk	915
Crystal City	512	Driftwood	512	Eureka	214	Freestone	817	Graford	817
Cuero	512	Dripping Springs	512	Eustace	214	Fresno	713	Graham	817
Culebra	512	Driscoll	512	Evadale	713	Friendswood	713	Granbury	817
Cumby	214	Dry Creek	214	Evant	817	Frio	806	Grandfalls	915
Cuney	214	Dryden	915	Evergreen	713	Friona	806	Grand Prairie	214
Cushing	713	Dry Lake	806	Everman	817	Frisco	214	Grand Saline	214
Cypress	713	Dublin	817			Fritch	806	Grandview	817
Cypress Springs	214	Duffau	817			Frost	214	Granger	512
		Dumas	806			Fruitvale	214	Granite Shoals	512
		Duncanville	214			Fuller Springs	713	Grapeland	713
		Dundee	817	Fabens	915	Fulshear	713	Grapevine	817
Daingerfield	214	Dunlay	512	Fairfield	214	Fulton	512	Grayburg	713
Daisetta	713	Dunn	915	Fairlie	214			Greenville	214
Dale	512			Fairmount	713			Greenwood	817
Dale Robertson	214			Falcon Heights	512			Greggton	214
Dalhart	806			Falfurrias	512			Gregory	512
Dallas	214			Falls City	512	Gail	915	Grit	915
Dallas-Ft. Worth		Eagle Lake	713	Fannett	713	Gainesville	817	Groesbeck	817
Airport	214	Eagle Mountain Lake	817	Fannin	512	Gallatin	214	Groom	806
Damon	713	Eagle Pass	512	Farmers Branch	214	Galveston	713	Grosvenor	915
Danbury	713	Earth	806	Farmersville	214	Ganado	512	Gruver	806
Danciger	713	East Bernard	713	Farnsworth	806	Garciaville	512	Guadalupe Peak	915
Danevang	713	Easterly	713	Farwell	806	Garden City	915	Gunter	214
Danieldale	214	East Glenrio	806	Fashing	512	Garden Valley	214	Gurley	806
Darrouzett	806	East Hobbs	915	Fate	214	Garfield	512	Gustine	915
Dawn	806	East Houston	713	Fayetteville	713	Garland	214	Guthrie	806
Dawson	817	Eastland	817	Fentress	512	Garner	817	Guy	713
Dayton	713	Easton	214	Ferris	214	Garrett	214	Guymon	806
Deadwood	214	Ector	214	Field Creek	915	Garrison	713	
Deanville	713	Edcouch	512	Fieldton	806	Garvin Store	512	
De Berry	214	Eddy	817	Fife	915	Garwood	713	
Decatur	817	Eden	915	Fisk	915	Gary	214	
Deer Park	713	Edgecliff	817	Flat	817	Gary Air Force Base	512	Hackmont	806
DeKalb	214	Edgewood	214	Flatonia	512	Gatesville	817	Hale Center	806
De Leon	817	Edinburg	512	Flat Rock	512	Gause	713	Halfway	806
Dell City	915	Edmondson	806	Fletcher Carter	806	Gay Hill	713	Hallettsville	512
Del Rio	512	Edna	512	Flint	214	Geneva	713	Hallsburg	817
Del Valle	512	Edom	214	Flomot	806	Georgetown	512	Hallsville	214
Delwin	806	Edroy	512	Florence	512	George West	512	Hamby	915
Denison	214	Egypt	713	Floresville	512	Geronimo	512	Hamilton	817
Denton	817	Elbert	817	Florey	915	Geronimo Creek	512	Hamlin	915
Denver City	806	El Campo	713	Flour Bluff	512	Gholson	817	Hamshire	713
Deport	214	Eldorado	915	Floyd	214	Giddings	713	Hancock	512
Derby	512	Electra	817	Floydada	806	Gilchrist	713	Hankamer	713
Dermott	915	Elgin	512	Fluvanna	915	Gillett	512	Happy	806
Desdemona	817	Eliasville	817	Flynn	713	Gilmer	214	Happy Union	806
Desert Haven	915	El Indio	512	Foard City	817	Girard	806	Hardin	713
De Soto	214	Elkhart	214	Follett	806	Girvin	915	Hargill	512

Place Name	Area Code	Place Name	Area Code	Place Name	Area Code	Place Name	Area Code	Place Name	Area Code
Harleton	214	Hutchins	214	Kelly Air Force Base	512	Lampasas	512	London	915
Harlingen	512	Hutto	512	Kelton	806	Lancaster	214	Lone Grove	915
Harper	512	Huxley	713	Keltys	713	Lane City	713	Lone Oak	214
Harrold	817	Hye	512	Kemah	713	Laneville	214	Lone Star	214
Hart	806			Kemp	214	Langham Creek	713	Long Mott	512
Hartley	806			Kempner	512	Langtry	512	Longview	214
Haskell	817	Iago	713	Kenberg	512	La Porte	713	Longworth	915
Haslet	817	Idalou	806	Kendalia	512	La Pryor	512	Loop	806
Hatch	806	Imperial	915	Kendleton	713	Laredo	512	Loraine	915
Hatchel	915	Indian Creek	512	Kenedy	512	Lariat	806	Lorena	817
Hawkins	214	Indian Gap	817	Kennard	713	Larue	214	Lorenzo	806
Hawley	915	Industry	713	Kennedale	817	La Salle	512	Los Angeles	512
Hearne	713	Inez	512	Kerens	214	Lasara	512	Los Fresnos	512
Heath	214	Ingleside	512	Kermit	915	Latexo	713	Los Indios	512
Heath Canyon	915	Ingram	512	Kerrick	806	Lautz	806	Lott	817
Hebbronville	512	Iola	713	Kerrville	512	Lavernia	512	Louise	713
Hedley	806	Iowa Park	817	Kildare	214	La Villa	512	Lovelady	713
Heidenheimer	817	Ira	915	Kilgore	214	Lavon	214	Loving	817
Helotes	512	Iraan	915	Killeen	817	La Ward	512	Loyola Beach	512
Hemphill	713	Iredell	817	Kingsbury	512	Lawn	915	Lubbock	806
Hempstead	713	Ireland	817	Kingsland	915	Lawson	214	Luckenbach	512
Henderson	214	Irene	817	Kings Mill	806	Lazbuddie	806	Lueders	915
Henly	512	Irving	214	Kingsville	512	Leaday	915	Lufkin	713
Henrietta	817	Italy	214	Kingwood-Porter	713	League City	713	Luling	512
Hensley Field U. S.		Itasca	817	Kirbyville	713	Leakey	512	Lumberton	713
Air Force	214	Ivanhoe	214	Kirkland	817	Leander	512	Luther	915
Hereford	806			Kirvin	214	Leary	214	Lyford	512
Hermleigh	915			Kleberg	214	Leesburg	214	Lyons	713
Hewitt	817			Klondike	214	Leesville	512	Lytle	512
Hext	915			Knickerbocker	915	Lefors	806	Lytton Springs	512
Hico	817	Jacksboro	817	Knippa	512	Leggett	713	
Hidalgo	512	Jackson	214	Knott	915	Legion	512	
Higginbotham	915	Jacksonville	214	Knox City	817	Lehman	806	Mabank	214
Higgins	806	Jal	915	Koon Kreek	214	Lela	806	Macdona	512
High	214	Jarratt	512	Kopperl	817	Lelia Lake	806	Madisonville	713
Highbank	817	Jarrell	512	Kosciusko	512	Leming	512	Magnolia	713
High Hill	713	Jasper	713	Kosse	817	Lenorah	915	Malakoff	214
High Island	713	Jayton	806	Kountze	713	Leona	214	Malone	817
Highlands	713	Jean	817	Kress	806	Leonard	214	Manchaca	512
Hillister	713	Jefferson	214	Krum	817	Leon Springs	512	Manor	512
Hillsboro	817	Jermyn	817	Kurten	713	Leroy	817	Mansfield	817
Hilltop Lakes	713	Jersey Village	713	Kyle	512	Levelland	806	Manvel	713
Hitchcock	713	Jewett	713			Levita	817	Maple	806
Hochheim	512	Jim Hogg	214			Lewisville	214	Marathon	915
Hockley	713	Joaquin	713			Lexington	713	Marble Falls	512
Holland	817	Johnson City	512	La Belle	713	Liberty	713	Marfa	915
Hollandville	806	Joinerville	214	La Blanca	512	Liberty Hill	512	Marietta	214
Holliday	817	Jolly	817	Lackland	512	Lillian	817	Marion	512
Hondo	512	Jollyville	512	Lackland Air Force		Lindale-Swan	214	Markham	713
Honey Grove	214	Jonah	512	Base	512	Linden	214	Marlin	817
Hooks	214	Jonesboro	817	Lacoste	512	Lindsay	817	Marquez	214
Hoover	806	Jonesville	214	Ladonia	214	Lingleville	817	Marshall	214
Hostyn	713	Joplin	817	La Feria	512	Linn	512	Marshall Ford	512
Houston	713	Josephine	214	La Grange	713	Lipan	817	Mart	817
Howe	214	Joshua	817	Laguna	817	Lipscomb	806	Martindale	512
Hub	806	Jourdanton	512	Lake Arrowhead	817	Lissie	713	Martinez	512
Hubbard	817	Joy	817	Lake Brownwood	915	Little Elm	214	Martins Mills	214
Huckabay	817	Judson	214	Lake Coleman	915	Littlefield	806	Maryneal	915
Hudson		Junction	915	Lake Creek	214	Little River	817	Mason	915
(Angelina Co.)	713	Juno	512	Lake Dallas	817	Liverpool	713	Masterson	806
Hudson		Justin	817	Lakehills	512	Livingston	713	Matador	806
(Cherokee Co.)	214			Lake Houston	713	Llano	915	Matagorda	713
Huffman	713			Lake Jackson	713	Locker	915	Matagorda Coast Guard
Hufsmith	713			Lake Kemp	817	Lockhart	512	Light Sta.	512
Hughes Springs	214	Kamay	817	Lake Kickapoo	817	Lockney	806	Matagorda Island Air
Hull	713	Karnack	817	Lake Palestine East	214	Loco	806	Force Base	512
Humble-South Humble	713	Karnes City	512	Lakeside Village	817	Lodi	214	Mathis	512
Hungerford	713	Katemcy	915	Lake Travis	512	Logan	806	Maud	214
Hunt	512	Katy	713	Lakeview	806	Lohn	915	Mauriceville	713
Huntington	713	Kaufman	214	Lake Whitney	817	Lolita	512	Maxwell	512
Huntsville	713	Keene	817	Lake Worth	817	Loma Alta	512	May	817
Hurlwood	806	Keller	817	La Marque	713	Lomax	915	Maydelle	214
Hurst	817	Kellerville	806	Lamesa	806	Lometa	512	Maypearl	214
				Lamkin	817			McAdoo	806

Place Name	Area Code	Place Name	Area Code	Place Name	Area Code	Place Name	Area Code	Place Name	Area Code
McAllen	512	Montgomery		Nolan	915	Palo Alto	512	Porter Heights	713
McCamey	915	(Montgomery Co.)	713	Nolanville	817	Palo Pinto	817	Port Isabel	512
McCauley	915	Monthalia	512	Nome	713	Paluxy	817	Portland-Gregory	512
McCook	512	Moody	817	Noodle	915	Pampa	806	Port Lavaca	512
McCoy	512	Moore	512	Nordheim	512	Pandora	512	Port Mansfield	512
McDade	512	Moran	915	Normangee	713	Panhandle	806	Port Neches	713
McGregor	817	Moravia	713	Normanna	512	Panola	214	Port O'Connor	512
McKinney	214	Morgan	817	North Cowden	915	Pantex	806	Possum Kingdom	
McLean	806	Morgan's Mill	817	Northfield	817	Paradise	817	Lake	817
McLeod	214	Morse	806	North Mesquite	214	Paris	214	Post	806
McNeil	512	Morton	806	North Richland Hills	817	Parmer	806	Postoak	817
McQueeney	512	Moscow	713	Northrup	713	Parnell	806	Poteet	512
Meadow	806	Mosheim	817	North Zulch	713	Pasadena	713	Poth	512
Medicine Mound	817	Moulton	512	Norton	915	Patricia	806	Potosi	915
Medina	512	Mound	817	Notrees	915	Pattonville	214	Potranco	512
Medina Lake	512	Mountain Home	512	Novice	915	Pawnee	512	Pottsboro	214
Megargel	817	Mount Calm	817	Nubia	915	Payne Springs	214	Pottsville	817
Melissa	214	Mount Enterprise	214	Nursery	512	Peacock	806	Powderly	214
Melvin	915	Mount Pleasant	214			Pearland	713	Powell	214
Memorial Point	713	Mount Selman	214			Pearsall	512	Poynor	214
Memphis	806	Mount Sylvan	214			Pear Valley	915	Prairie Hill	817
Menard	915	Mount Vernon	214			Peaster	817	Prairie Lea	512
Mentone	915	Mozelle	915	Oak Hill	214	Pecan Gap	214	Prairie View	713
Mercedes	512	Muenster	817	Oakhurst	713	Pecos	915	Premont	512
Mercury	915	Muldoon	512	Oak Island	512	Pendleton	817	Presidio	915
Mereta	915	Muleshoe	806	Oakland	214	Penelope	817	Price	214
Meridian	817	Mullen	915	Oakville	512	Penitas	512	Priddy	915
Merit	214	Mumford	713	Oakwood	214	Pennington	713	Princeton	214
Merkel	915	Munday	817	O'Brien	817	Pep	806	Pritchett	214
Merrell	806	Murchison	214	Odell	817	Percilla	713	Proctor	817
Mertens	214	Myra	817	Odem	512	Perrin	817	Progreso	512
Mertzon	915	Myrtle Springs	214	Odessa	915	Perrin Air Force Base	214	Prosper	214
Mesquite	214			O'Donnell	806	Perry	817	Punkin Center	806
Mexia	817			Oenaville	817	Perryton	806	Purdon	214
Meyersville	512			Oglesby	817	Petersburg	806	Purmela	817
Miami	806			Oilton	512	Petrolia	817	Putnam	915
Mico	512	Nacogdoches	713	Oklahoma Lane	806	Pettit	806	Pyote	915
Middlewater	806	Naples	214	Oklaunion	817	Pettus	512	Pyote Army Air Base	915
Midfields	512	Nash	214	Olden	817	Petty	214		
Midkiff	915	Nassau Bay	713	Old Glory	817	Pflugerville	512		
Midland	915	Natalia	512	Old Ocean	713	Pharr	512	Quail	806
Midlothian	214	Navasota	713	Olmito	512	Phelps	713	Quanah	817
Midway	713	Nazareth	806	Olney	817	Phillips	806	Queen City	214
Milam	713	Neches	214	Olton	806	Pickton	214	Quemado	512
Milano	512	Nederland-		Omaha	214	Pierce	713	Quinlan	214
Mile High	915	Port Neches	713	Onalaska	713	Pilot Point	817	Quitaque	806
Miles	915	Needmore	806	Orange	713	Pine Acres	214	Quitman	214
Milford	214	Needville	713	Orangefield	713	Pine Forest	214		
Miller Grove	214	Negley	214	Orange Grove	512	Pine Hill	214		
Millersview	915	Nelms	806	Orchard	713	Pinehurst	713		
Millett	512	Nemo	817	Ore City	214	Pineland	713	Rainbow	817
Millican	713	Nevada	214	Orla	915	Pine Mills	214	Ralls	806
Millsap	817	Newark	817	Orth	817	Pipe Creek	512	Randolph	214
Milo Center	806	New Baden	713	Osage	817	Pittsburg	214	Randolph Air Force	
Mims	214	New Boston	214	Osceola	817	Placid	915	Base	512
Minden	214	New Braunfels	512	Ottine	512	Plains	806	Ranger	817
Mineola	214	Newburg	915	Otto	817	Plainview	806	Rankin	915
Mineral	512	New Caney	713	Ovalo	915	Plano	214	Ransom Canyon	806
Mineral Wells	817	Newcastle	817	Overton	214	Plantersville	713	Ratcliff	713
Mingus	817	New Deal	806	Owentown	214	Pleasanton	512	Ravenna	214
Mirando City	512	New Gulf	713	Ozona	915	Pledger	713	Rayburn	713
Mission	512	New Home	806			Plum	713	Raymondville	512
Missouri City	713	New London	214			Point	214	Raywood	713
Mobeetie	806	Newport	817			Point Comfort	512	Reagan	817
Moffat	817	Newsome	214			Pollok	713	Reagan Wells	512
Monahans	915	New Summerfield	214	Padre Island	512	Ponder	817	Realitos	512
Montague	817	Newton	713	Paducah	806	Ponta	214	Redford	915
Montalba	214	New Ulm	713	Paige	512	Pontotoc	915	Redmon	806
Mont Belvieu	713	New Waverly	713	Paint Rock	915	Poolville	817	Red Oak	214
Montell	512	Nixon	512	Palacios	512	Port Alto	512	Red Rock	512
Montgomery		Nobility	214	Palestine	214	Port Aransas	512	Red Springs	
(Bexar Co.)	512	Nocona	817	Palmer	214	Port Arthur	713	(Baylor Co.)	817
						Port Bolivar	713	Red Springs	
								(Smith Co.)	214

Place Name	Area Code	Place Name	Area Code	Place Name	Area Code	Place Name	Area Code	Place Name	Area Code
Redwater	214	Sabina	512	Seven Points	214	Sterling City	915	Timpson	713
Reese Air Force Base	806	Sabinal	512	Seymour	817	Stevens	806	Tioga	817
Refugio	512	Sabine	713	Shafter	915	Stillman	512	Tivoli	512
Reklaw	713	Sabine Pass	713	Shallowater	806	Stinnett	806	Tokio	806
Renner	214	Sachse	214	Shamrock	806	Stockdale	512	Tolar	817
Reno	817	Sacul	713	Shavano	512	Stonewall	512	Tomball	713
Rhome	817	Sadler	214	Sheffield	915	Stowell	713	Tom Bean	214
Rice	214	Sagerton	817	Shelbyville	713	Stratford	806	Tool-Seven Points	214
Richards	713	Saginaw	817	Sheldon	713	Strawn	817	Tow	915
Richardson	214	St. Hedwig	512	Shepherd	713	Streeter	915	Toyah	915
Richland	214	St. Jo	817	Sheppard Air Force		Streetman	214	Travis	817
Richland Springs	915	St. Lawrence	915	Base	817	Sublime	512	Trent	915
Richmond-Rosenberg	713	Salado	817	Sheridan	713	Sudan	806	Trenton	214
Riesel	817	Saltillo	214	Sherley	214	Sugar Land	713	Trinidad	214
Ringgold	817	Saluria Coast Guard		Sherman	214	Sullivan City	512	Trinity	713
Rio Frio	512	Sta. No. 220	512	Sherwood	915	Sulphur Bluff	214	Troup	214
Rio Grande City	512	San Angelo	915	Shiloh	713	Sulphur Springs	214	Troy	817
Rio Hondo	512	San Antonio	512	Shiner	512	Summerfield	806	Trumbull	214
Rio Medina	512	Sanatorium	915	Shiro	713	Sumner	214	Truscott	817
Rio Vista	817	San Augustine	713	Sidney	817	Sundown	806	Tucker	214
Rising Star	817	San Benito	512	Sierra Blanca	915	Sunnyside	806	Tuleta	512
Riverside	713	Sanderson	915	Silsbee	713	Sunnyvale	214	Tulia	806
Riviera	512	Sandia	512	Silver	915	Sunray	806	Turkey	806
Roane	214	San Diego	512	Silver Creek	817	Sunset	817	Turnersville	817
Roanoke	817	Sand Springs	915	Silverton	806	Sutherland Springs	512	Turnertown	214
Roan's Prairie	713	Sandy (Blanco Co.)	512	Simms	214	Swan	214	Tuscola	915
Roaring Springs	806	Sandy		Simonton	713	Sweeny	713	Twitty	806
Robert Lee	915	(Limestone Co.)	817	Singleton	713	Sweet Home	512	Tye	915
Robstown	512	Sandy Creek	214	Sinton	512	Sweetwater	915	Tyler	214
Roby	915	Sandy Hills	512	Sisterdale	512	Sweetwater West	806	Tynan	512
Rochelle	915	San Elizario	915	Six Shooter	915	Sylvester	915		
Rochester	817	San Felipe	713	Skellytown	806				
Rockdale	512	San Gabriel	512	Skidmore	512				
Rock Island	713	Sanford	806	Slaton	806				
Rockland	713	Sanger	817	Slidell	817				
Rockport	512	San Isidro	512	Slocum	214	Taft	512	Umbarger	806
Rocksprings	512	San Juan	512	Smiley	512	Tahoka	806	Uncertain	214
Rockwall	214	San Marcos	512	Smithers Lake	713	Talco	214	Union	806
Rockwood	915	San Miguel	512	Smithfield	817	Talpa	915	U.S. Naval Air	
Roganville	713	San Perlita	512	Smith Point	713	Tanglewood	512	Station	214
Rogers	817	San Saba	915	Smithson's Valley	512	Tarpley	512	Universal City	512
Roma	512	Santa Anna	915	Smithville	512	Tarzan	915	Utopia	512
Romero	806	Santa Maria	512	Smyer	806	Tatum	214	Uvalde	512
Roosevelt	915	Santa Rosa	512	Snook-Tunis	713	Tawakoni	214		
Ropesville	806	Santo	817	Snyder	915	Taylor	512		
Rosanky	512	Saragosa	915	Somerset	512	Teague	817		
Roscoe	915	Saratoga	713	Somerville	713	Tehuacana	817	Valentine	915
Rosebud	817	Sarita	512	Sonora	915	Telegraph	915	Valera	915
Rosenberg	713	Satin	817	Sour Lake	713	Telephone	214	Valley Lodge	713
Rosenthal	817	Satsuma	713	South Bend	817	Tell	817	Valley Mills	817
Rosewood	214	Sattler	512	South Bosque	817	Temple	817	Valley Spring	915
Rosharon	713	Saturn	512	South Hardesty	806	Tenaha	713	Valley View	817
Ross	817	Savoy	214	Southland	806	Tennessee Colony	214	Valley View East	817
Rosser	214	Sayers	512	Southmayde	214	Tennyson	915	Van	214
Rosston	817	Schertz	512	South Plains	806	Terlingua	915	Van Alstyne	214
Rotan	915	Schulenburg	713	Southton	512	Terminal	915	Vancourt	915
Round Mountain	512	Schwertner	817	South Vidor	713	Terrell	214	Vanderbilt	512
Round Rock	512	Scotland	817	Spade	806	Texarkana	214	Vanderpool	512
Rowena	915	Scottsville	214	Spanish Fort	817	Texas City-		Van Horn	915
Rowlett	214	Scranton	817	Spearman	806	La Marque	713	Van Vleck	713
Roxton	214	Scroggins	214	Spicewood	512	Texline	806	Vega	806
Royalty	915	Scurry	214	Splendora	713	Texon	915	Venus	214
Royse City	214	Seabrook	713	Spofford	512	Thalia	817	Vera	817
Ruby	713	Seadrift	512	Spring	713	Tharp	806	Verbena	806
Rule	817	Seagoville	214	Springlake	806	Thelma	512	Vernon	817
Runaway Bay	817	Seagraves	806	Springtown	817	Thomaston	512	Victoria	512
Runge	512	Sealy	713	Spur	806	Thompsons	713	Vidor	713
Rusk	214	Sebastian	512	Spurger	713	Thorndale-Thrall	512	View	915
Rye	713	Segno	713	Stafford	713	Thornton	817	Vigo Park	806
Rylie	214	Seguin	512	Stamford	915	Thrall	512	Village Mills	713
		Selman City	214	Stanton	915	Three Rivers	512	Vincent	915
		Seminole	915	Star	915	Throckmorton	817	Vinegarroon	512
				Stephenville	817	Tilden	512	Vivian	214

Place Name	Area Code	Place Name	Area Code	Place Name	Area Code	Place Name	Area Code	Place Name	Area Code
Voca	915	Webberville	512	West Reydon	806	Wichita Falls	817	Wolters Air Force	
Von Ormy	512	Webster	713	West Roger Mills	806	Wickett	915	Base	817
		Wedgwood	817	West Stanton	915	Wiergate	713	Woodlake	713
		Weimar	713	Westway	806	Wildorado	806	Woodlawn	214
		Weinert	817	Wetmore	512	Wildwood	713	Woodrow	806
		Weir	512	Wharton	713	Willis	713	Woodsboro	512
Waco	817	Welch	806	Wheatland	817	Willow City	512	Woodson	817
Waelder	512	Weldon	713	Wheatley	806	Wills Point	214	Woodville	713
Waka	806	Welfare	512	Wheeler	806	Wilmer	214	Wortham	817
Walburg	512	Wellington	806	Wheelock	713	Wilson	806	Wrightsboro	512
Wall	915	Wells	713	White City-Odell	817	Wimberley	512	Wylie	214
Waller	713	Weslaco	512	White Deer	806	Winchester	713	Wynne	214
Wallis	713	West	817	Whiteface	806	Windom	214		
Wallisville	713	Westbrook	915	Whiteflat	806	Windthorst	817		
Walnut Springs	817	Westbury	713	Whitehouse	214	Winfield	214	Yancey	512
Warren	713	West Columbia	713	White Oak	214	Wingate	915	Yantis	214
Warrenton	713	Westfield	713	White River	806	Wink	915	Yoakum	512
Washington	713	Westhoff	512	Whitesboro	214	Winkler	214	Yorktown	512
Waskom	214	West Lakes	806	White Settlement	817	Winnie	713		
Water Valley	915	Westland	817	Whitewright	214	Winnsboro	214		
Waterwood	713	West Llano	915	Whitharral	806	Winona	214	Zabcikville	817
Waxahachie	214	Westminster	214	Whitney	817	Winters	915	Zapata	512
Weatherford	817	Weston	214	Whitsett	512	Wolfe City	214	Zavalla	713
Weaver	214	West Point	713	Whitt	817	Wolfforth	806	Zephyr	915

ALL POINTS—AREA CODE 801

ALL POINTS—AREA CODE 802

Place Name	Area Code	Place Name	Area Code	Place Name	Area Code	Place Name	Area Code	Place Name	Area Code
Abingdon	703	Atlee	804	Bethel		Browns Store	804	Catharpin	703
Accomac	804	Augusta Springs	703	(Fauquier Co.)	703	Browntown	703	Catlett	703
Achilles	804	Austinville	703	Bethel (Prince		Brucetown	703	Catoctin	703
Acorn	804	Avalon	804	William Co.)	703	Bruington	804	Cauthornville	804
Ada	703	Avon	703	Bethia	804	Brutus	804	Cave Spring	703
Adamsville	804	Axton	703	Beulahville	804	Bryant	804	Cedar Bluff	703
Aden	703	Aylett	804	Beverly Mills	703	Buchanan	703	Cedar Creek	703
Adner	804	Aylor	703	Beverlyville	804	Buck Hall	703	Cedar Forest	804
Adria	703			Big Island	804	Buckingham	804	Cedar Grove	804
Advance Mills	804			Big Meadows	703	Buckland	703	Cedarville	703
Afton	703			Big Prater	703	Buckner	703	Cedon	804
Agricola	804	Bachelors Hall	804	Big Rock	703	Buckroe Beach	804	Centenery	804
Airpoint	703	Back Bay	804	Big Stone Gap	703	Buena Vista	703	Center Cross	804
Alberene	804	Bacons Castle	804	Birchleaf	703	Buffalo Forge	703	Central Hill	804
Alberta	804	Bacova	703	Birdsnest	804	Buffalo Junction	804	Central Plains	804
Aldie	703	Baden	703	Biscoe	804	Buffalo Ridge	703	Central Point	804
Alexandria	703	Bagby	804	Bishop	703	Buffalo Station	804	Centreville	703
Alfonso	804	Balcony Falls	703	Blackford	804	Bull Run	703	Ceres	703
Algoma	703	Baldwin	703	Blackridge	804	Bumpass	703	Chalk Level	804
Alleghany	703	Ballard	703	Blacksburg	703	Bundick	804	Champlain	804
Alleghany Spring	703	Balty	804	Blackstone	804	Burgess Store	804	Chance	804
Allens Creek	804	Banco	703	Blackwood	703	Burke	703	Chancellor	703
Alliance	804	Bandy	703	Blairs	804	Burkes Garden	703	Chancellorville	703
Allmondsville	804	Bane	703	Blakes	804	Burketown	703	Chantilly	703
Allnut	703	Banner	703	Bland	703	Burkeville	804	Charles City	804
Allwood	804	Barbours Creek	703	Blantons	804	Burks Fork	703	Charlotte Court House	804
Alma	703	Barboursville	703	Blowing Rock	703	Burnleys Station	804	Charlottesville	804
Alps	804	Barhamsville	804	Bloxom	804	Burnsville	703	Chase City	804
Altavista	804	Barnesville	804	Bluefield	703	Burnt Chimney	703	Chatham	804
Alto	804	Barnett	703	Blue Grass	703	Burwells Bay	804	Chatham Hill	703
Alton	804	Barrett Heights	703	Bluemont	703	Bushy	804	Cheapside	804
Alum Ridge	703	Bartlett	804	Blue Ridge	703	Butylo	804	Check	703
Alvarado	703	Bartlick	703	Bluff City	703	Buzzard Roost	703	Cheriton	804
Amburg	804	Baskerville	804	Bohannon	804	Byrdton	804	Cherry Hill	703
Amelia Court House	804	Bassett	703	Boissevain	703			Chesapeake	804
Amherst	804	Bastian	703	Bon Air	804			Chesconessex	804
Amissville	703	Basye	703	Bondtown	703			Chester	804
Ampthill	804	Batestown	703	Bonsack	703	Callands	804	Chesterfield	804
Amsterdam	703	Batesville	804	Boones Mill	703	Callao	804	Chestnut Hill	703
Andersonville	804	Battery Park	804	Boonsboro	804	Callaway	703	Chilesburg	804
Andover	703	Bavon	804	Boston	703	Calverton	703	Chilhowie	703
Annandale	703	Bayford	804	Bowlers Wharf	804	Cambria	703	Chincoteague	804
Antioch		Baynesville	804	Bowling Green	804	Cameron	703	Chippokes	804
(Fluvanna Co.)	804	Bayside	804	Boyce	703	Campbell	804	Christ Church	804
Antioch (Prince		Bay Side Wharf	804	Boydton	804	Camp Peary	804	Christiansburg	703
William Co.)	703	Bayview	804	Boykins	804	Camp Pickett	804	Chuckatuck	804
A. P. Hill Military		Baywood	703	Bracey	804	Cana	703	Chula	804
Reservation	804	Bealeton	703	Braddock	703	Caney Ridge	703	Churchland	804
Appalachia	703	Beaverdam	804	Bradley Forest	703	Capahosic	804	Church Road	804
Appomattox	804	Beaverlett	804	Bradshaw	703	Cape Charles	804	Church View	804
Ararat	703	Bedford	703	Branchville	804	Cape Charles Coast		Churchville	703
Arcadia		Beechwood	804	Brandy Station	703	Guard Light Sta.	804	Cifax	703
(Botetourt Co.)	703	Belfast	703	Brandywine	804	Capeville	804	Cismont	804
Arcadia		Bellamy	804	Brays	804	Capron	804	Claraville	804
(Spotsylvania Co.)	703	Belle Haven	804	Bremo Bluff	804	Carbo	703	Claremont	804
Arcola	703	Belle Meade	703	Brentsville	703	Cardinal	804	Clarksville	804
Ark	804	Bellevue	703	Bridges	804	Cardwell	804	Claudville	703
Arlington	703	Bells Valley	703	Bridgetown	804	Caret	804	Clay Bank	804
Aroda	703	Bellwood	804	Bridgewater	703	Carrollton	804	Clayville	804
Arrington	804	Belmont	703	Brights	804	Carrsville	804	Clear Brook	703
Arvonia	804	Belroi	804	Brightwood	703	Carson	804	Clear Fork Valley	703
Ashburn	703	Belspring	703	Bristersburg	703	Carters Bridge	804	Cleveland	703
Ashland	804	Belvoir	703	Bristol	703	Carters Grove	804	Clifford	804
Assateague	804	Bena	804	Bristow	703	Cartersville	804	Clifton	703
Assateague Beach		Benhams	703	Broadford	703	Carterton	703	Clifton Forge	703
Coast Guard		Benns Church	804	Broad Run	703	Carthage	703	Climax	804
Sta. No. 150	804	Bensley	804	Broadwater	804	Carysbrook	804	Clinchburg	703
Assateague Coast		Bent Creek	804	Broadway	703	Casanova	703	Clinchco	703
Guard Light Sta.	804	Bent Mountain	703	Brodnax	804	Cascade	804	Clinchfield	703
Assateague Seaplane		Bentonville	703	Brokenburg	703	Cash	804	Clinchport	703
Anchorage	804	Berea	703	Brooke	703	Cashville	804	Clintwood	703
Assawoman	804	Bergton	703	Brookneal	804	Castleton	703	Clover	804
Atkins	703	Berryville	703	Brook Vale	804	Castlewood	703	Cloverdale	703
Atlantic	804	Berton	703	Brosville	804	Catawba	703	Clover Hollow	703
		Bertrand	804	Brownsburg	703	Catawba Sanatorium	703	Cluster Springs	804

VIRGINIA
Coatesville–Hallwood

Place Name	Area Code	Place Name	Area Code	Place Name	Area Code	Place Name	Area Code	Place Name	Area Code
Coatesville	804	Dalbys	804	Dunn Loring	703	Falls Church	703	Georges Tavern	804
Cobb Island Coast Guard Sta. No. 156	804	Dale City	703	Dunnsville	804	Falls Mills	703	Gera	703
Cobbs	804	Daleview	703	Dutton	804	Falmouth	703	Gether	804
Cobbs Creek	804	Daleville	703	Dwale	703	Fancy Gap	703	Gholsonville	804
Cobham	804	Damascus	703	Dwight	703	Farmers	804	Gibson Station	703
Cody	804	Dam Neck	804	Dwina	703	Farmers Fork	804	Gillaspie	703
Coeburn	703	Danieltown	804			Farmville	804	Gilmore	703
Coke	804	Dante	703			Farnham	804	Gladehill	703
Colemans Falls	804	Danville	804	Eagle Mountain	703	Featherstone	703	Glade Spring	703
Coles Point	804	Dare	804	Eagle Rock	703	Fentress	804	Gladstone	804
Collierstown	703	Darlington Heights	804	Earlehurst	703	Ferrum	703	Gladys	804
Collinsville	703	Darwin	703	Earlysville	804	Fieldale	703	Glamorgan	703
Cologne	804	Daugherty	804	East Falls Church	703	Fife	804	Glasgow	703
Colonial Beach	804	Davenport	703	East Stone Gap	703	File	804	Glass	804
Colonial Heights	804	Davis Wharf	804	Eastville	804	Fincastle	703	Glebe Point	804
Columbia	804	Dawn	804	Ebony	804	Fine Creek Mills	804	Glen Allen	804
Columbia Furnace	703	Dawsonville	804	Eclipse	804	Finney	703	Glendale	804
Comers Rock-Elk Creek	703	Dayton	703	Edgehill	703	Fishers Hill	703	Glenlyn	703
Comorn	703	Decatur	703	Edinburg	703	Fishersville	703	Glenns	804
Concord	804	Decca	804	Edom	703	Fitchetts	804	Glen Wilton	703
Conicville	703	Deep Creek (Accomac Co.)	804	Edwardsville	804	Five Forks	804	Glenwood	804
Cooper	804	Deep Creek (Norfolk Co.)	804	Eggleston	703	Five Mile Fork	703	Gloucester	804
Copper Creek	703	Deerfield	703	Elberon	804	Flatridge	703	Gloucester Point	804
Copper Hill	703	De Jarnette	804	Eley's Ford	703	Fleeton	804	Golansville	804
Copper Valley	703	Delaplane	703	Elk Creek	703	Flint Hill	703	Goldvein	703
Corbin	703	Deltaville	804	Elk Garden	703	Floris	703	Goochland	804
Corn Valley	703	Denbigh	804	Elk Hill	804	Floyd	703	Goode	703
Cornwall	703	Dendron	804	Elko	804	Folly	804	Goodview	703
Coulwood	703	Detrick	703	Elkrun	703	Fontaine	703	Gordonsville	703
Courtland	804	Dewitt	804	Elkton	703	Ford	804	Gore	703
Covesville	804	Dickensonville	703	Elkwallow	703	Fordwick	703	Goshen	703
Covington	703	Dickinson	703	Elkwood	703	Forest	804	Grafton	804
Cowart	804	Diggs	804	Ellerson	804	Forestville	703	Graham	703
Coyners Springs	703	Dillwyn	804	Elliston	703	Forks of Buffalo	804	Granite	804
Crab Orchard	703	Dinwiddie	804	Elm	703	Fork Union	804	Grant	703
Craddockville	804	Disputanta	804	Elmont	804	Fort Belvoir	703	Grassland	703
Cradock	804	Ditchley	804	Elmwood	703	Fort Blackmore	703	Gravel Lick	703
Craig Springs	703	Dixie	804	Elon	804	Fort Chiswell	703	Graves Mill	703
Craigsville	703	Doe Hill	703	Elsom	804	Fort Defiance	703	Graysontown	703
Cranes Nest	703	Dogue	703	Emmerton	804	Fort Eustis	804	Great Bridge	804
Creeds	804	Dolphin	804	Emory	703	Fort John Custis	804	Great Falls	703
Cresthill	703	Doran	703	Emporia	804	Fort Lee	804	Greenbackville	804
Crewe	804	Dorchester	804	Endicott	703	Fort Mitchell	804	Green Bay	804
Cricket Hill	804	Doswell	804	Enfield	804	Fort Monroe	804	Greenbush	804
Criglersville	703	Dovesville	804	Engleside	703	Fort Myer	703	Greendale	703
Crimora	703	Downings	804	Eppes Fork	804	Fort Story	804	Greenfield	804
Cripple Creek	703	Dragonsville	804	Epworth	804	Foster	804	Greenlee	703
Crittenden	804	Drakes Branch	804	Erica	804	Fosters Falls	703	Green Spring Depot	703
Critz	703	Dranesville	703	Esmont	804	Fox	703	Greenville	703
Croaker	804	Draper	703	Esserville	703	Foxwells	804	Greenwich	703
Crockett	703	Drewrys Bluff	804	Ethel	804	Franconia	703	Greenwood	703
Crocketts Cove	703	Drewryville	804	Etlan	703	Franklin	804	Gressitt	804
Crockett Springs	703	Drill	703	Ettrick	804	Franklin City	804	Gretna	804
Cross Junction	703	Driver	804	Everett's Bridge	804	Franktown	804	Grimes	703
Cross Roads	703	Dry Branch	703	Evergreen	804	Fredericksburg	703	Grimstead	804
Croxton	804	Dryden	703	Evergreen Mills	703	Fredericks Hall	703	Grit	804
Crozet	804	Dry Fork (Buchanan Co.)	703	Evington	804	Freeport	804	Grottoes	703
Crozier	804	Dry Fork (Pittsylvania Co.)	804	Ewing	703	Free Union	804	Grundy	703
Crystal Hill	804	Dry Fork (Tazewell Co.)	703	Exmore	804	Fremont	703	Guilford	804
Cuckoo	703	Duane	804			Fries	703	Guinea	804
Cullen	804	Dublin	703	Faber	804	Front Royal	703	Gum Fork	804
Culpeper	703	Duffield	703	Fairfax	703			Gum Spring	804
Cumberland	804	Dugspur	703	Fairfax Station	703	Gainesboro	703	Gum Tree	804
Cumberland Gap	703	Dulles	703	Fairfield (Henrico Co.)	804	Gainesville	703	Gwynn	804
Cumnor	804	Dumbarton	804	Fairfield (Rockbridge Co.)	804	Gala	703		
Curdsville	804	Dumfries	703	Fairlawn	703	Galax	703		
Curles Neck	804	Dunbrooke	804	Fair Port	804	Galveston Mills	804	Hacksneck	804
		Dundas	804	Fairview	804	Gardners	703	Haden	703
Dahlgren	703	Dungannon	703	Fairview Beach	703	Garfield Estates	703	Hadensville	804
Dahlgren, Naval Weapons Laboratory	703			Fairystone Park	703	Garrisonville	703	Hague	804
						Gasburg	804	Halifax	804
						Gate City	703	Hallieford	804
						Georges Fork	703	Hallsboro	804
								Hallwood	804

Place Name	Area Code	Place Name	Area Code	Place Name	Area Code	Place Name	Area Code	Place Name	Area Code
Hamilton	703	Howardsville	804	Kenbridge	804	Limeton	703	Marionville	804
Hamlin	703	Howertons	804	Kendall Grove	804	Lincoln	703	Markham	703
Hampden Sydney	804	Huddleston	703	Kennard	804	Linden	703	Marksville	703
Hampton	804	Hudgins	804	Kents Store	804	Linville	703	Marlboro Point	703
Hampton Roads Port		Huffville	703	Kentuck	804	Lithia	703	Marshall	703
of Embarkation	804	Hume	703	Keokee	703	Little Creek	804	Martinsville	703
Hanging Rock	703	Huntly	703	Kerrs Creek	703	Little Plymouth	804	Marumsco Village	703
Hanover	804	Hunton	804	Keswick	804	Littleton	804	Marye	703
Hansonville	703	Hurley	703	Keysville	804	Litwalton	804	Maryus	804
Harborton	804	Hurricane	703	Kidds Fork	804	Lively	804	Mascot	804
Hardings	804	Hurt	804	Kilmarnock	804	Lloyds	804	Massanetta Springs	703
Hardware	804	Hustle	804	Kimball	703	Locklies	804	Massanutten	703
Hardy	703	Hyacinth	804	Kimballton	703	Locust Dale	703	Massaponax	703
Hardyville	804	Hylas	804	King and Queen	804	Locust Grove		Massies Mill	804
Harman	703			King and Queen		(Floyd Co.)	703	Mathews	804
Harmony	804			Courthouse	804	Locust Grove		Matoaca	804
Harmony Village	804			King George	703	(Orange Co.)	703	Mattaponi	804
Harris	703	Iberis	804	King William	804	Locust Hill	804	Mattoax	804
Harrisonburg	703	Ida	703	Kino	804	Locustville	804	Maurertown	703
Harriston	703	Independence	703	Kinsale	804	Lodge	804	Maxie	703
Harryhogan	804	Independent Hill	703	Kiptopeke	804	Londonbridge	804	Max Meadows	703
Hartfield	804	Index	703	Koehler	703	Lone Fountain	804	Maxwell	703
Hartwood	703	Indian	703	Konnarock	703	Loretto	804	Mayland	703
Hat Creek	804	Indian Creek	703			Lorne	804	Maytown	703
Hayes	804	Indian Neck	804			Lorton	703	Maywood	703
Hayfield	703	Indian Rock	703			Lottsburg	804	McClung	703
Haymakertown	703	Indian Valley	703	Laban	804	Louisa	703	McClure	703
Haymarket	703	Ingram	804	Lacey Spring	703	Lovettsville	703	McCoy	703
Haynesville	804	Iron Gate	703	Lackey	804	Lovingston	804	McDowell	703
Haysi	703	Ironto	703	La Crosse	804	Lowesville	804	McGaheysville	703
Haywood	703	Irving	703	Ladysmith	804	Lowmoor	703	McHenry	703
Healing Springs	703	Irvington	804	Lafayette	703	Lowry	804	McKenney	804
Healys	804	Irwin	804	Lahore	703	Lucketts	703	McLean	703
Heathsville	804	Island Ford	703	Lake	804	Lunenburg	804	Meadows of Dan	703
Hebron	804	Isle of Wight	804	Lake Jackson	703	Luray	703	Meadowview	703
Henry	703	Isom	703	Lake of the Woods	703	Luttrellville	804	Mears	804
Herald	703	Ivanhoe	703	Lambsburg	703	Lyells	804	Mechanicsville	804
Herndon	703	Ivondale	804	Lanahan	703	Lynchburg	804	Mechum River	804
Hewlett	804	Ivor	804	Lancaster	804	Lynch Station	804	Meherrin	804
Hickory	804	Ivy Depot	804	Laneview	804	Lyndhurst	703	Melfa	804
Hickory Grove	703			Lanexa	804	Lynnhaven	804	Melrose Gardens	703
Hicks Wharf	804			Langley	703	Lynnwood		Meltons	703
Highland Springs	804			Langley Air Force		(Rockingham Co.)	703	Meridithville	804
Hightown	703	Jacobs Fork	703	Base	804	Lynwood (Prince		Merrifield	703
Hill Grove	804	Jamaica	804	Lantz Mills	703	William Co.)	703	Merrimac Mines	703
Hillsboro	703	James Store	804	Lauraville	804			Merry Point	804
Hillsville	703	Jamestown	804	Laurel	804			Messick	804
Hilton	703	Jamesville	804	Laurel Fork	703			Messongo	804
Hinton	703	Jarratt	804	Laurel Grove	804	Machipongo	804	Metomkin Inlet Coast
Hiwasee	703	Java	804	Lawrenceville	804	Machodoc	804	Guard Sta. No. 152	804
Hoadly	703	Jefferson	804	Lawyers	804	Macon	804	Mew	703
Hobson	804	Jeffersonton	703	Leaksville	703	Madison	703	Michaux	804
Hockley	804	Jeffs	804	Leatherwood	804	Madison Heights	804	Middlebrook	703
Hodges Ferry	804	Jenkins Bridge	804	Lebanon	703	Madison Mills	703	Middleburg	703
Hoges Store	703	Jennings Ordinary	804	Lebanon Church	703	Madison Run	703	Middletown	703
Hog Island Coast		Jerome	703	Lecato	804	Madisonville	804	Midland	703
Guard Light Sta.	804	Jersey	703	Leck	703	Maggie	703	Midlothian	804
Hog Island Coast		Jetersville	703	Lee	703	Magotha	804	Midvale	703
Guard Sta. No. 155	804	Jewell Ridge	703	Lee Hall	804	Magruder	804	Midway (Augusta Co.)	804
Holcomb Rock	804	Jewell Valley	703	Leemont	804	Maidens	804	Midway
Holdcroft	804	John's Creek	703	Leesburg	703	Makemie Park	804	(Stafford Co.)	703
Holland	804	Johnsontown	804	Leesville	804	Manakin	804	Mila	804
Hollins	703	Jonesville	703	Lenah	703	Manassas	703	Miles Store	804
Holston	703	Jordon Mines	703	Lennig	804	Mangohick	804	Milford	703
Homeville	804			Leon	703	Mannboro	804	Millard	703
Honaker	703			Lerty	804	Manquin	804	Millboro	703
Honeyville	703			Lewisetta	804	Mansion	804	Millenbeck	804
Hopeton	804	Kearns	703	Lewis Mountain	703	Manteo	804	Millers Tavern	804
Hopewell	804	Kecoughtan	804	Lewiston	703	Maple Grove	804	Mill Gap	703
Hopkins	804	Keeling	804	Lexington	703	Mapleton	703	Millwood	703
Horntown	804	Keene	804	Liberty Furnace	703	Mappsville	804	Mineral	703
Horse Head	804	Keezletown	703	Lick Fork	703	Marengo	804	Mine Run	703
Horsey	804	Keller	804	Lightfoot	804	Marine Corps		Minneville	703
Hot Springs	703	Kelso	703	Lignum	703	Base, Quantico	703	Minor	804
Houchins	703	Kempsville	804	Lillian	804	Marion	703	Mint Spring	703

Place Name	Area Code	Place Name	Area Code	Place Name	Area Code	Place Name	Area Code	Place Name	Area Code
Miskimon	804	New Glasgow	804	Paces	804	Potts Creek	703	Riceville	804
Mitchells	703	New Hope	703	Paeonian Springs	703	Pound	703	Richardsville	703
Mobjack	804	Newington	703	Paint Bank	703	Pounding Mill	703	Rich Creek	703
Moccasin	703	New Kent	804	Painter	804	Powcan	804	Richlands	703
Modest Town	804	Newland	804	Palmer	804	Powhatan	804	Richmond	804
Mollusk	804	New Market	703	Palmer Springs	804	Prilliman	703	Rich Valley	703
Monaskon	804	New Point	804	Palmyra	804	Prince George	804	Ridgeway	703
Moneta	703	Newport	703	Pampa	804	Princess Anne	804	Rileyville	703
Monroe	804	Newport News	804	Pamplin	804	Proffit	804	Riner	703
Monroe Hall	804	New River	703	Panorama	703	Prospect	804	Ringgold	804
Montague	804	Newsoms	804	Paris	703	Providence Forge	804	Rio Vista	804
Montebello	804	Newtown	804	Parker	703	Pulaski	703	Ripplemead	703
Monterey	703	New Upton	804	Parksley	804	Pungo	804	Riverton	703
Montevideo	703	Nickelsville	703	Parramore Beach Coast		Pungoteague	804	River View	703
Monticello	804	Nimmo	804	Guard Sta. No. 154	804	Purcellville	703	Riverville	804
Montpelier	804	Nimrod Hall	703	Parrott	703	Purdy	804	Rixeyville	703
Montpelier Station	703	Ninde	703	Parsonage	703			Roanes	804
Montross	804	Noel	804	Partlow	804			Roanoke	703
Montvale	703	Nokesville	703	Passing	804			Robley	804
Moon	804	Nola	703	Patrick Springs	703			Rochelle	703
Moores	804	Nomini Grove	804	Pauls Cross Roads	804	Quantico	703	Rockbridge Baths	703
Morattico	804	Nora	703	Paytes	703	Quantico, Marine		Rock Castle	804
Morrison City	703	Norfolk	804	Peaceful Valley	703	Corps Base	703	Rockfish	804
Morrisville	703	Norge	804	Peaks	804	Quarry	703	Rockingham	703
Moseleys Junction	703	North	804	Pearisburg	703	Quicksburg	703	Rockland	703
Moss	703	North Garden	804	Peary	804	Quinby	804	Rockville	804
Moss Neck	804	North Holston	703	Pedlar Mills	804	Quinque	804	Rocky Gap	703
Motley	804	North Tazewell	703	Pemberton	804	Quinton	804	Rocky Mount	703
Motorun	804	Northwest	804	Pembroke	703			Rocky Point	703
Mountain Grove	703	Norton	703	Pendleton	703			Rollins Fork	703
Mountain Lake	703	Norwood	804	Penhook	703			Rosedale	703
Mountain View	703	Nottoway	804	Penicks	703			Rose Hill	703
Mount Airy	804	Nuttall	804	Peninsula	804	Radford	703	Roseland	804
Mount Clinton	703	Nuttsville	804	Pennington Gap	703	Radio U. S. Naval		Roseville	703
Mount Crawford	703			Penn Laird	703	Radio Station	703	Rosslyn	703
Mount Cross	804			Penola	804	Rainswood	804	Round Hill	703
Mount Gilead	703			Perrin	804	Randolph	804	Roxbury	804
Mount Holly	804	Oak Grove	804	Perrowville	804	Raphine	804	Ruark	804
Mount Jackson	703	Oak Hall	804	Petersburg	804	Rapidan	703	Ruby	703
Mount Landing	804	Oak Hill	804	Phenix	804	Rappahannock		Ruckersville	804
Mount Laurel	804	Oak Level	703	Philomont	703	Academy	804	Rue	804
Mount Meridian	703	Oak Park	703	Phoebus	804	Raven	703	Rumford	804
Mount Olive	703	Oakton	703	Pilot	703	Rawlings	804	Rural Retreat	703
Mount Pleasant	804	Oakwood	703	Pinero	804	Ray	804	Rushmere	804
Mount Sidney	703	Occoquan	703	Pinetta	804	Reba	804	Rustburg	804
Mount Solon	703	Occupacla	804	Piney River	804	Rectortown	703	Ruther Glen	804
Mount Vernon	703	Oceana	804	Pisgah	703	Rectory	703	Ruthville	804
Mouth of Wilson	703	Ocran	804	Pittsville	804	Redart	804	
Mulch	804	Odd	804	Plains	703	Red Ash	703	
Munden	804	Old Church	804	Plain View	804	Red Hill	804	
Mundy Point	804	Oldhams	804	Plasterco	703	Red House	804	Sabot	804
		Old Point Comfort	804	Pleasantgap	804	Red Lawn	804	St. Brides	804
		Omaha	703	Pleasant Ridge	804	Red Oak	804	St. Charles	703
		Omega	804	Pleasant Valley	703	Redwood	703	St. Davids Church	703
		Onancock	804	Pleasantview	804	Reedville	804	St. Paul	703
Nace	703	Onemo	804	Pleasant Village	703	Regent	804	St. Stephens Church	804
Nahor	804	Onley	804	Poages Mill	703	Regina	804	St. Stone	804
Naola	804	Ontario	804	Pocahontas	703	Rehoboth Church	804	Salem	703
Narrows	703	Opal	703	Poindexter	703	Reids Ferry	804	Salem Heights	703
Naruna	804	Oranda	703	Pole Green	804	Reliance	703	Salem Road	804
Nasons	703	Orange	703	Pons	804	Remington	703	Saltville	703
Nassawadox	804	Orbit	804	Popes Island Coast		Remlik	804	Saluda	804
Natural Bridge	703	Orchid	804	Guard Sta. No. 149	804	Remo	804	Samos	804
Navy	703	Ordinary	804	Poplar Hill	703	Renan	804	Sampsons Wharf	804
Naxera	804	Oriskany	703	Poquoson	804	Republican Grove	804	Sandbridge Beach	804
Naylors	804	Orkney Springs	703	Port Haywood	804	Rescue	804	Sandidges	804
Nealy Ridge	703	Orlean	703	Port Republic	703	Reston	703	Sand Lick	703
Neenah	804	Oronoco	804	Port Richmond	804	Retreat	703	Sandston	804
Negro Foot	804	Ottoman	804	Port Royal	804	Retz	804	Sandy Bottom	804
Nellys Ford	804	Overall	703	Portsmouth	804	Reusens	804	Sandy Hook	804
Nelsonia	804	Owens	703	Post Oak	703	Reva	703	Sandy Level	804
Newbern	703	Owenton	804	Potomac	703	Revis	804	Sandy Point
New Canton	804	Oxford	703	Potomac Beach	804	Rexburg	804	(Charles City Co.)	804
New Castle	703	Oyster	804	Potomac Mills	804	Rhoadsville	703	Sandy Point
New Church	804	Ozeana	804			Rice	804	(Westmoreland Co.)	804

Place Name	Area Code	Place Name	Area Code	Place Name	Area Code	Place Name	Area Code	Place Name	Area Code
Sandy River	804	South Norfolk	804	Syringa	804	U. S. Army Signal		Waterfall	703
Sanford	804	Spainville	804			Corps, Vint Hill		Waterford	703
Sarah	804	Sparta	804			Farms	703	Water View	804
Sassafras	804	Speedwell	703			U. S. Naval Air		Watson	703
Saumsville	703	Spencer	703			Station–Oceana	804	Wattsville	804
Savageville	804	Sperryville	703	Tabb	804	University	804	Waugh	804
Saxe	804	Splashdam	703	Tabernacle	804	Upperville	703	Waverly	804
Saxis	804	Spotsylvania	703	Tabscott	804	Upright	804	Waverly Village	703
Schley	804	Spottswood	804	Tacoma	703	Upshaw	804	Waynesboro	703
Schoolfield	804	Spout Spring	804	Tangier	804	Urbanna	804	Weber City	703
Schuyler	804	Spring City	703	Tappahannock	804			Webster	703
Scotland	804	Spring Creek	703	Tarpon	703			Weedonville	703
Scottsburg	804	Springfield	703	Tasley	804			Weems	804
Scottsville	804	Spring Garden	804	Taylors Store	703	Valentines	804	Weirwood	804
Scruggs	703	Spring Grove	804	Taylorstown	703	Valley View	703	Wellford	804
Seaford	804	Springville	703	Taylor Valley	703	Varina	804	Wellington Villa	703
Sealston	703	Springwood	703	Tazewell	703	Vera	804	Wellville	804
Seaview	804	Spruce Run	703	Temperanceville	804	Verdon	804	West Falls Church	703
Sedley	804	Stafford	703	Templeman	804	Vernon Hill	804	West Fork	804
Selden	804	Staffordsville	703	Tenso	703	Verona	703	Westland	804
Selma	703	Stanardsville	804	Tenth Legion	703	Vesta	804	Westmoreland	804
Senora	804	Stanley	703	Terrys Fork	703	Vesuvius	703	West Norfolk	804
Seven Mile Ford	703	Stanleytown	703	Tetotum	703	Victoria	804	West Point	804
Severn	804	Stapleton	804	Thaxton	703	Vienna	703	Weyers Cave	703
Shackelfords	804	Starkey	703	The Plains	703	Viewtown	703	Whaleyville	804
Shadow	804	State Farm	804	Thomas Town	703	Village	804	Wheeler	703
Shadwell	804	Staunton	703	Thompsons Park	703	Villamont	703	Whitacre	703
Shadyside	804	Steeleburg	703	Thompsons Valley	703	Vint Hill Farms	703	White Gate	703
Shanghai	804	Steeles Tavern	804	Thornburg	703	Vinton	703	White Hall	804
Sharps	804	Steinman	703	Thoroughfare	703	Virgilina	804	White Marsh	804
Shawsville	703	Stephens City	703	Thoroughfare Gap	703	Virginia Beach	804	White Plains	804
Shawver Mill	703	Stephenson	703	Threeway	804	Virginia City	703	White Post	703
Shenandoah	703	Sterling	703	Tibitha	703	Virginia Mineral		Whites	804
Shenandoah National		Sterling Park	703	Tidemill	804	Springs	703	White Shop	804
Park	703	Stevensburg	703	Tidewater	804	Volens	804	White Stone	804
Shenandoah Park	703	Stevensville	804	Tidwells	804	Volney	703	White Sulphur	
Sheppards	804	Stewartsville	703	Timberlake	804			Springs	703
Sherando	703	Stingray Point	804	Timber Ridge	703			Whitetop	703
Shiloh	703	Stonega	703	Timberville	703			Whitmell	804
Shipman	804	Stone House	703	Tiptop	703			Whitten Mills	703
Shipps Corner	804	Stone Mountain	703	Toano	804	Wachapreague	804	Wicomico	804
Short Lane	804	Stonewall	804	Toms Brook	703	Wachapreague Coast		Wicomico Church	804
Short Pump	804	Stony Creek	804	Toms Creek	703	Guard Sta No. 153	804	Widewater	703
Shumansville	703	Stony Point	804	Topping	804	Waddell	703	Wilder	703
Sigma	804	Stormont	804	Toshes	804	Waidsboro	804	Wilderness	703
Signpine	804	Strasburg	703	Totuskey	804	Wake	804	Williamsburg	804
Silver Leaf	703	Stratford (Hall)	804	Townsend	804	Wakefield		Williams Mill	703
Simmonsville	703	Stratton	703	Trammel	703	(Sussex Co.)	804	Williamsville	703
Simonson	804	Stuart	703	Trenholm	804	Wakefield		Williams Wharf	804
Simpsons	804	Stuarts Draft	703	Trevilians	703	(Westmoreland Co.)	804	Willis	703
Singers Glen	703	Studley	804	Triangle	703	Wakenva	703	Willis Wharf	804
Sinking Creek	703	Suffolk	804	Trigg	703	Walker Ford	804	Wilmington	804
Skeetrock	703	Sugar Grove	703	Triplet	804	Walkerton	804	Wilson	804
Skippers	804	Sumerduck	703	Trone	703	Wallace	703	Wilton	804
Skipwith	804	Sun	703	Troutdale	703	Wallaceton	804	Winchester	703
Skyland	703	Sunbright	703	Troutville	703	Wallops Beach Coast		Windsor	804
Slate Mills	703	Sunnybank	804	Truhart	804	Guard Sta. No. 151	804	Windsor Shades	804
Smithfield	804	Sunset Hills	703	Tucker Hill	804	Wallops Island	804	Winginia	804
Smith Island Coast		Supply	804	Tumbez	703	Walmsley	804	Winston	703
Guard Sta. No. 157	804	Surry	804	Tunstall	804	Walnut Point	804	Winterham	804
Smoky Ordinary	804	Susan	804	Turbeville	804	Walters	804	Winterpock	804
Smoots	804	Sussex	804	Turpin	804	Wan	804	Wirtz	703
Snell	703	Sutherland	804	Tye River	804	Wardtown	804	Wise	703
Snowden	804	Swansonville	804	Tyro	804	Ware Neck	804	Wisharts Point	804
Snowflake	703	Sweet Briar	804			Wares Wharf	804	Withams	804
Snow Hill	804	Sweet Chalybeate	703			Warfield	804	Wolftown	703
Snowville	703	Sweet Hall	804			Warminster	804	Woodberry Forest	703
Somers	804	Swift Run	703			Warm Springs	703	Woodbridge	703
Somerset	703	Swoope	703	Union	703	Warner	804	Woodford	804
Sontag	703	Swords Creek	703	Union Hall	703	Warren	804	Woodlawn	703
South Boston	804	Sycamore	804	Union Level	804	Warrenton	703	Woodrum Field	703
South Brunswick	804	Sydnorsville	703	Unionville	703	Warsaw	804	Woods Cross Roads	804
South Clinchfield	703	Sylvatus	703	U. S. Amphibious		Warwick	804	Woodstock	703
South Hill	804	Syria	703	Base–Little Creek	804	Washington		Woodville	703
						(Rappahannock Co.)	703		

Place Name	Area Code	Place Name	Area Code	Place Name	Area Code	Place Name	Area Code	Place Name	Area Code
Woodway	703	Wyndale	703	Yancey Mills	804	Yorktown	804	Zanoni	804
Woolsey	703	Wytheville	703	Yellow Sulphur				Zepp	703
Woolwine	703			Springs	703			Zion	804
Wylliesburg	804	Yale	804	Yorkshire	703	Zacata	804	Zuni	804

Place Name	Area Code	Place Name	Area Code	Place Name	Area Code	Place Name	Area Code	Place Name	Area Code
Aberdeen	206	Brewster	509	Creosote	206	Fairfield	509	Hatton	509
Acme	206	Bridgeport	509	Creston	509	Fall City	206	Hay	509
Addy	509	Brinnon	206	Crystal Mountain	206	Farmington	509	Hazeldell	206
Adna	206	Brownsville	206	Curlew	509	Felida	206	Holmes Harbor	206
Adrian	509	Brush Prairie	206	Curtis	206	Felts Field	509	Hoodsport	206
Albion	509	Bryant	206	Cusick	509	Ferndale	206	Hoquiam	206
Alderton	206	Bryn Mawr	206	Custer	206	Fletcher Bay	206	Humptulips	206
Alderwood Manor	206	Buckley	206			Forks	206	Hunters	509
Alger	206	Bucoda	206			Fort Flagler	206	Huntsville	509
Allyn	206	Burley	206			Fort George Wright	509	Husum	509
Almira	509	Burlington	206	Dabob	206	Fort Lawton	206		
Amber	509	Burton	206	Dalkena	509	Fort Lewis	206		
Amboy	206	Bush Point	206	Dallesport	509	Fort Simcoe	509		
American Lake	206			Danville	509	Fortson	206		
Anacortes	206			Darrington	206	Fort Worden	206	Ilwaco	206
Anatone	509			Dash Point	206	Foster	206	Independence	206
Anderson Island	206	Camano Island	206	Davenport	509	Four Lakes	509	Index	206
Annapolis	206	Camas	206	Dayton	509	Fox Island	206	Indian Island	206
Arden	509	Camp McDonald	206	Deep River	206	Frances	206	Indianola	206
Ardenvoir	509	Camp Murray	206	Deer Harbor	206	Freeland	206	Indian Prairie	509
Ariel	206	Cape Disappointment		Deer Lake	509	Freeman	509	Ione	509
Arletta	206	Coast Guard Sta.	206	Deer Park	509	Friday Harbor	206	Irby	509
Arlington	206	Cape Flattery Coast		Deming	206	Fruitland	509	Issaquah	206
Army Hdqrs. of		Guard Light Sta.	206	Denison	509				
Ninth Army Corps	206	Carlsborg	206	Des Moines	206				
Ashford	206	Carnation	206	Diablo Dam	206	Galvin	206		
Asotin	509	Cashmere	509	Diamond Lake	509	Gardena	509	Jared	509
Attalia	509	Castle Rock	206	Dieringer	206	Gardiner	206	Jerry	509
Auburn	206	Cathcart	206	Dishman	509	Garfield	509	Joyce	206
Austin	206	Cathlamet	206	Dixie	509	Garrison	509	Juanita	206
Azwell	509	Cedar Falls	206	Dockton	206	Gate	206		
		Center	206	Doty	206	Gedney Island	206		
		Centralia	206	Douglas	509	George	509		
		Chattaroy	509	Dryad	206	Gig Harbor	206	Kahlotus	509
Bainbridge Island	206	Chehalis	206	Dryden	509	Gilberton	206	Kalama	206
Baker Lake	206	Chelan	509	Duckabush	206	Glacier	206	Kapowsin	206
Bald Hills	206	Chelan Falls	509	Dungeness	206	Gleed	509	Kelso	206
Bangor	206	Cheney	509	Dupont	206	Glenoma	206	Kenmore	206
Baring	206	Chesaw	509	Duvall	206	Glenwood	509	Kennewick	509
Barberton	206	Chewelah	509			Gold Bar	206	Kennydale	206
Basin City	509	Chico	206			Goldendale	509	Kent	206
Battle Ground	206	Chimacum	206	Eagledale	206	Gorge Dam	206	Kettle Falls	509
Bay Center	206	Chinook	206	Eagle Harbor	206	Graham	206	Key Center	206
Bayview		Clallam Bay	206	Earlington	206	Grand Coulee	509	Keyport	206
(Island Co.)	206	Clarkston	509	East Farms	509	Grand Mound	206	Keyport Torpedo	
Bay View		Clayton	509	Easton	509	Grandview	509	Station	206
(Skagit Co.)	206	Clear Lake	206	Eastsound	206	Granger	509	Kingston	206
Beaver	206	Clearview	206	East Stanwood	206	Granite Falls	206	Kiona	509
Beebe	509	Clearwater	206	Eatonville	206	Grapeview	206	Kirkland	206
Belfair	206	Cle Elum	509	Edgecomb	206	Grayland	206	Kitsap Lake	206
Bellevue	206	Clinton	206	Edison	206	Grays Harbor Coast		Kittitas	509
Bellingham	206	Cloverland	509	Ediz Hook Coast Guard		Guard Light Sta.	206	Klaber	206
Benge	509	Cohassett	206	Light Sta.	206	Grays Harbor Coast		Klickitat	509
Benton City	509	Colbert	509	Edmonds	206	Guard Sta.	206	Kosmos	206
Beverly	509	Colfax	509	Edwall-Tyler	509	Grays River	206		
Beverly Park	206	College Place	509	Eglon	206	Greenbank	206		
Bickleton	509	Colman Dock Coast		Elbe	206	Green Bluff	509		
Big Lake	206	Guard Light Sta.	206	Elk	509	Grotto	206	La Center	206
Bingen	509	Colton	509	Ellensburg	509	Guemes Island	206	Lacey	206
Birch Bay	206	Columbia	509	Elma	206			La Conner	206
Black Diamond	206	Columbia Beach	206	Eltopia	509			Lacrosse	509
Blaine	206	Colville	509	Endicott	509			La Grande	206
Blakely Island	206	Conconully	509	Entiat	509	Hadlock	206	Lake Ballinger	206
Blanchard	206	Concrete	206	Enumclaw	206	Halls Lake	206	Lakebay	206
Blue Creek	509	Connell	509	Ephrata	509	Hamilton	206	Lake Crescent	206
Boeing Field	206	Conway	206	Eureka	509	Hanford	509	Lake Cushman	206
Boisfort	206	Cook	509	Everett	206	Hansville	206	Lake Quinault	206
Bordeaux	206	Copalis	206	Everson	206	Harper	206	Lake Sammamish	206
Bothell	206	Cosmopolis	206	Ewan	509	Harrah	509	Lakeside	509
Boundary Bay	206	Cougar	206			Harrington	509	Lake Stevens	206
Bow	206	Coulee City	509			Harstine Island	206	Lake Sutherland	206
Bremerton	206	Coulee Dam	509			Hartford	206	Lakeview	206
Bremerton U. S. Naval		Coupeville	206	Fairchild Air Force		Hartline	509	Lake Wenatchee	509
Radio Sta.	206	Cowiche	509	Base	509	Hat Island	206	Lakewood	206

Place Name	Area Code	Place Name	Area Code	Place Name	Area Code	Place Name	Area Code	Place Name	Area Code
Lamona	509	Mesa	509	Omak	509	Randle	206	Snohomish County	
Lamont	509	Metaline Falls	509	Onalaska	206	Ravensdale	206	U. S. Naval Radio	
Langley	206	Methow	509	Opportunity	509	Raymond	206	Sta.	206
La Push	206	Mica	509	Orcas	206	Reardan	509	Snoqualmie	206
Larson Air Force Base	509	Midlakes	206	Orchards	509	Redmond	206	Snoqualmie Falls	206
Latah	509	Midway	206	Orient	509	Renton	206	Snoqualmie Pass	206
Lauderdale	509	Millwood	509	Orillia	206	Republic	509	Soap Lake	509
Laurel	206	Mineral	206	Orondo	509	Retsil	206	Soldiers Home	206
Laurier	509	Minnehaha	206	Oroville	509	Rice	509	South Beach	206
Leavenworth	509	Moab	509	Orting	206	Richardson	206	South Bellingham	206
Lebam	206	Moclips	206	Oso	206	Richland	509	South Bend	206
Lester	206	Molson	509	Othello	509	Richmond Beach	206	South Colby	206
Lewisville	206	Monitor	509	Otis Orchards	509	Ridgefield	206	South Prairie	206
Liberty Lake	509	Monroe	206	Outlook	509	Rimrock	509	South Tacoma	206
Lind	509	Monse	509	Oysterville	206	Ritzville	509	South Whidbey	206
Little Rock	206	Montesano	206			Riverside	509	Southworth	206
Locke	509	Morgan Park	509			Roche Harbor	206	Spanaway	206
Long Beach	206	Morton	206			Rochester	206	Spangle	509
Longbranch	206	Moses Lake	509	Pacific Beach	206	Rockford	509	Spokane	509
Longmire	206	Moses Lake Air Base	509	Packwood	509	Rockport	206	Sprague	509
Longview	206	Mossyrock	509	Palisades	509	Rolling Bay	206	Springdale	509
Loomis	509	Mountlake Terrace	206	Palouse	509	Ronald	509	Stanwood	206
Loon Lake	509	Mount Vernon	206	Parkland	206	Roosevelt	509	Starbuck	509
Lopez	206	Moxee	509	Parkwater	509	Rosalia	509	Startup	206
Lowden	509	Mukilteo	206	Pasco	509	Rosburg	206	Steilacoom	206
Lowell	206	Mukilteo Coast Guard		Pateros	509	Roslyn	509	Steptoe	509
Lummi Island	206	Light Sta.	206	Paterson	509	Ross Dam	206	Stevenson	509
Lyle	509			Pe Ell	206	Roy	206	Stevens Pass	206
Lyman	206			Peshastin	509	Royal City	509	Sultan	206
Lyman-Hamilton	206			Pinehurst	206	Ruby	509	Sumas	206
Lynden	206	Naches	509	Pioneer	509	Ryderwood	206	Sumner	206
Lynnwood	206	Nahcotta	206	Plaza	509			Sunnyside	509
		Napavine	206	Plymouth	509			Sunnyslope	206
		Naselle	206	Point Roberts	206			Suquamish	206
		National	206	Point Wells	206	St. John	509	Synarep	509
		Navy Hdqrs. of		Pomeroy	509	St. Mary's Mission	509		
Mabton	509	Thirteenth Naval		Portage	206	Salkum	206		
Machias	206	District	206	Port Angeles	206	Sammamish	206	Tacoma	206
Mae	509	Navy Radio		Port Blakely	206	Sand Point Naval		Tatoosh Island	206
Malaga	509	Bainbridge	206	Port Discovery	206	Air Station	206	Tekoa	509
Malden	509	Neah Bay	206	Port Gamble	206	Sappho	206	Tenino	206
Malott	509	Neppel	509	Port Ludlow	206	Sara	206	Thornton	509
Maltby	206	Nespelem	509	Port Madison	206	Saratoga	206	Thorp	509
Manchester	206	New Dungeness Coast		Port Orchard	206	Satsop	206	Tieton	509
Manitou Park	206	Guard Light Sta.	206	Port Stanley	206	Sauk	206	Tillicum	206
Mansfield	509	Newman Lake	509	Port Townsend	206	Seabeck	206	Tokeland	206
Manson	509	Newport	509	Potlatch	206	Seabold	206	Toledo	206
Manzanita	206	Nile	509	Poulsbo	206	Seattle	206	Tonasket	509
Maple Falls	206	Nine Mile Falls	509	Prescott	509	Seattle Heights	206	Toppenish	509
Maple Valley	206	Nooksack	206	Preston	206	Seattle U. S. Naval		Touchet	509
Marblemount	206	Nordland	206	Priest Rapids	509	Radio Sta.	206	Toutle	206
Marcus	509	Norma Beach	206	Priests Point	206	Seaview	206	Tracyton	206
Marietta	206	North Bend	206	Prosser	509	Sedro Woolley	206	Trentwood	509
Marlin	509	North Bonneville	509	Puget Island	509	Sekiu	206	Trinidad	509
Marshall	509	North Cove Coast		Puget Sound Navy		Selah	509	Trout Lake	509
Marysville	206	Guard Sta.	206	Yard	206	Sequim	206	Tulalip	206
Mason City	509	North Fort Lewis	206	Pullman	509	Shaw	206	Tum Tum	509
Mathews Corner	509	Northport	509	Purdy	206	Shelton	206	Tumwater	206
Matlock	206			Puyallup	206	Silvana	206	Twisp	509
Mattawa	509					Silverdale	206	Tyler	509
Maxwelton	206					Silver Lake			
Mayview	509					(Cowlitz Co.)	206		
McChord Air Force		Oakesdale	509	Quilcene	206	Silver Lake			
Base	206	Oak Harbor	206	Quinault	206	(Snohomish Co.)	206	Underwood	509
McCleary	206	Oakville	206	Quincy	509	Sims Corner	509	Union	206
McKenna	206	Ocean City	206			Skamokawa	206	Union Gap	509
McMurray	206	Ocean Park	206			Skykomish	206	Uniontown	509
McNeil Island	206	Ocean Shores	206			Slip Point Coast Guard		U. S. Navy Yard	206
Mead	509	Ocosta	206			Light Sta.	206	U. S. Penitentiary	206
Medical Lake	509	Odessa	509	Rainier	206	Snohomish	206	Useless Bay	206
Medina	206	Okanogan	509	Rainier National Park	206	Snohomish County		Usk	509
Megler	206	Olalla	206	Ralston	509	Airport	206	Utsalady	206
Mercer Island	206	Olympia	206						

Place Name	Area Code	Place Name	Area Code	Place Name	Area Code	Place Name	Area Code	Place Name	Area Code
Vader	206	Wallula	509	Westport	206	Willada	509	Woodland	206
Vail	206	Wanapum	509	Westport Coast		Willapa	206	Woodway Park	206
Valley	509	Wapato	509	Guard Sta.	206	Willapa Bay Coast			
Valleyford	509	Warden	509	West Richland	509	Guard Light Sta.	206		
Vancouver	206	Warm Beach	206	Westwood	206	Willapa Bay Coast			
Vantage	509	Washington Veterans		Wheeler	509	Guard Sta.	206	Yacolt	206
Van Zandt	206	Home	206	Whidbey City	206	Willard	509	Yakima	509
Vashon	206	Washougal	206	Whidbey Island Naval		Wilson Creek	509	Yale	206
Vaughn	206	Washtucna	509	Air Station	206	Wing Point	206	Yelm	206
Venice	206	Waterman	206	White Salmon	509	Winlock	206	Yeomalt	206
Verlot	206	Waterville	509	White Swan	509	Winona	509		
View	206	Wauna	206	Whitstran	509	Winslow	206		
		Waverly	509	Wickersham	206	Winthrop	509		
		Wenatchee	509	Wilbur	509	Wishram	509		
Waitsburg	509	Westpoint Coast Guard		Wiley City	509	Withrow	509	Zenith	206
Walla Walla	509	Light Sta.	206	Wilkeson	206	Woodinville	206	Zillah	509

ALL POINTS—AREA CODE 304

Place Name	Code	Place Name	Code	Place Name	Code	Place Name	Code	Place Name	Code
Abbotsford	715	Bayfield	715	Burlington	414	Conrath	715	Eden	414
Abrams	414	Bayside	414	Burnett	414	Cooksville	608	Edgar	715
Ackerville	414	Bear Creek	715	Busseville	608	Coomer	715	Edgerton	608
Adams	608	Beaver	414	Butler	414	Coon Valley	608	Edmund	608
Adell	414	Beaver Dam	414	Butte des Morts	414	Cooperstown	414	Egg Harbor	414
Afton	608	Beetown	608	Butternut	715	Cornell	715	Eland	715
Albany	608	Beldenville	715			Cornucopia	715	Elcho	715
Albion	608	Belgium	414			Cottage Grove	608	Elderon	715
Algoma	414	Bell Center	608	Cable	715	Couderay	715	El Dorado	414
Allen Grove	414	Belleville	608	Cadott	715	Crandon	715	Eleva	715
Allenton	414	Bellevue	414	Caledonia	414	Cranmoor	715	Elk Creek	715
Allenville	414	Belmont	608	Calumet Harbor	414	Crescent Lake	715	Elkhart Lake	414
Alma	608	Beloit	608	Calvary	414	Crivitz	715	Elkhorn	414
Alma Center	715	Benet Lake	414	Cambria	414	Cross Plains	608	Elk Lake	715
Almena	715	Bennett	715	Cambridge	608	Cuba City	608	Elk Mound	715
Almond	715	Benoit	715	Cameron	715	Cudahy	414	Ellis	715
Altoona	715	Benton	608	Campbellsport	414	Cumberland	715	Ellison Bay	414
Amberg	715	Bergen	414	Camp Douglas	608	Cushing	715	Ellsworth	715
Amery	715	Berlin	414	Camp Lake	414	Custer	715	Elm Grove	414
Amherst	715	Big Bend	414	Canton	715	Cylon	715	Elmhurst	715
Amherst Junction	715	Big Cedar Lake	414	Caroline	715			Elmwood	715
Angus	715	Big Falls	715	Caryville	715			El Paso	715
Aniwa	715	Big Suamico	414	Cascade	414			Elroy	608
Anson	715	Birchwood	715	Casco	414	Dairyland	715	Elton	715
Antigo	715	Birnamwood	715	Cashton	608	Dale	414	Embarrass	715
Appleton	414	Biron	715	Cassville	608	Dallas	715	Emerald	715
Arbor Vitae	715	Black Creek	414	Cataract	608	Dalton	414	Emerald Grove	608
Arcadia	608	Black Earth	608	Catawba	715	Danbury	715	Endeavor	608
Arena	608	Black Hawk	608	Cavour	715	Dancy	715	Enterprise	715
Argonne	715	Black River Falls	715	Cayuga	715	Dane	608	Ephraim	414
Argyle	608	Blackwell	715	Cazenovia	608	Danville	414	Esdaile	715
Arkansaw	715	Blair	608	Cecil	715	Darien	414	Ettrick	608
Arlington	608	Blanchardville	608	Cedarburg	414	Darlington	608	Eureka	414
Armstrong Creek	715	Blenker	715	Cedar Creek	414	Deerbrook	715	Evansville	608
Arnott	715	Bloom City	608	Cedar Grove	414	Deerfield	608	Excelsior	608
Arpin	715	Bloomer	715	Cedar Lake	414	Deer Park	715	Exeland	715
Ashippun	414	Bloomingdale	608	Center	608	De Forest	608		
Ashland	715	Bloomington	608	Center Valley	414	Delafield	414		
Astico	414	Blue Mounds	608	Centerville	608	Delavan	414		
Athelstane	715	Blue River	608	Centuria	715	Denmark	414	Fairchild	715
Athens	715	Bluff Siding	608	Chaseburg	608	De Pere	414	Fairplay	608
Atlas	715	Boardman	715	Chelsea	715	Deronda	715	Fairwater	414
Auburndale	715	Boaz	608	Chenequa	414	De Soto	608	Fall Creek	715
Augusta	715	Bohners Lake	414	Chetek	715	Devils Lake	608	Fall River	414
Aurora	715	Boltonville	414	Chili	715	Diamond Bluff	715	Falun	715
Aurorahville	414	Bonduel	715	Chilton	414	Dickeyville	608	Fargo	608
Avalon	608	Boscobel	608	Chippewa Falls	715	Dodge	608	Fennimore	608
Avoca	608	Boulder Junction	715	City Point	715	Dodgeville	608	Fenwood	715
		Bowler	715	Clam Falls	715	Donald	715	Ferryville	608
		Boyceville	715	Clam Lake	715	Dorchester	715	Fifield	715
		Boyd	715	Clarno	608	Dousman	414	Fillmore	414
Babcock	715	Branch	414	Clayton	715	Downing	715	Fish Creek	414
Badger Ordnance	608	Brandon	414	Clear Lake	715	Downsville	715	Fitchburg	608
Bagley	608	Brantwood	715	Clearwater Lake	715	Doylestown	414	Florence	715
Baileys Harbor	414	Bridgeport	608	Cleghorn	715	Dresser	715	Fond Du Lac	414
Baileys Harbor Coast Guard Sta. No. 289	414	Briggsville	608	Cleveland	414	Drummond	715	Fontana	414
Baldwin	715	Brill	715	Clinton	608	Dunbar	715	Footville	608
Balsam Lake	715	Brillion	414	Clintonville	715	Dundas	414	Forest Junction	414
Bancroft	715	Bristol	414	Clyman	414	Duplainville	414	Forestville	414
Bangor	608	Brodhead	608	Cobb	608	Durand	715	Fort Atkinson	414
Baraboo	608	Brookfield	414	Cochrane	608	Duvall	715	Fort McCoy	608
Barksdale	715	Brooklyn	608	Coddington	715	Dyckesville	414	Fountain City	608
Barnes	715	Brooks	608	Colby	715			Foxboro	715
Barneveld	608	Brown Deer	414	Coleman	414			Fox Creek	715
Barnum	608	Brown's Lake	414	Colfax	715			Fox Lake	414
Barre Mills	608	Brownsville	414	Colgate	414	Eagle	414	Fox Point	414
Barron	715	Browntown	608	College Camp	414	Eagle Point	715	Francis Creek	414
Barronett	715	Bruce	715	Collins	414	Eagle River	715	Franklin	414
Barton	414	Brule	715	Coloma	715	East Bristol	608	Frederic	715
Basco	608	Brussels	414	Columbus	414	Eastman	608	Fredonia	414
Bass Lake	715	Bryant	715	Combined Locks	414	East Troy	414	Freedom	414
Bateman	715	Buffalo City	608	Comstock	715	Eaton	414	Fremont	414
Bay City	715	Burke	608	Conover	715	Eau Claire	715	Friendship	608
		Burkhardt	715			Eau Galle	715	Friesland	414

Place Name	Area Code	Place Name	Area Code	Place Name	Area Code	Place Name	Area Code	Place Name	Area Code
Friess Lake	414	Hersey	715	Kenosha	414	London	608	Middleton	608
Fulton	608	Hertel	715	Kenosha Coast Guard		Lone Rock	608	Midway	608
		High Bridge	715	Sta. No. 282	414	Long Lake		Mifflin	608
		Highcliff	414	Keshena	715	(Chippewa Co.)	715	Mikana	715
		Highland	608	Kewaskum	414	Long Lake		Milladore	715
Galesville	608	Hilbert	414	Kewaunee	414	(Florence Co.)	715	Mill Center	414
Galloway	715	Hiles	715	Kewaunee Coast Guard		Long Lake		Millston	715
Garfield	715	Hillpoint	608	Sta. No. 287	414	(Washburn Co.)	715	Milltown	715
Gays Mills	608	Hillsboro	608	Kiel	414	Loraine	715	Milton	608
Genesee	414	Hillsdale	715	Kieler	608	Loretta (Sauk Co.)	608	Milton Junction	608
Genoa	608	Hillside	608	Kimberly	414	Loretta (Sawyer Co.)	715	Milwaukee	414
Genoa City	414	Hintz	414	King	715	Louis Corners	414	Milwaukee Coast Guard	
Germania	414	Hixton	715	Kingston	414	Lowell	414	Sta. No. 284	414
Germantown	414	Holcombe	715	Klevenville	608	Loyal	715	Milwaukee U. S. Naval	
Gile	715	Hollandale	608	Knapp	715	Luck	715	Radio Sta.	414
Gillett	414	Hollandtown	414	Knowles	414	Luxemburg	414	Mindoro	608
Gillingham	608	Holmen	608	Knowlton	715	Lyndhurst	715	Mineral Point	608
Gills Landing	414	Holy Hill	414	Kohler	414	Lyndon Station	608	Minocqua	715
Gills Rock	414	Horicon	414	Krakow	414	Lynxville	608	Minong	715
Gilman	715	Hortonville	414			Lyons	414	Mirror Lake	608
Gilmanton	715	Houlton	715					Mishicot	414
Gleason	715	Howards Grove	414					Modena	715
Glenbeulah	414	Hubertus	414	Lac du Flambeau	715	Mackville	414	Monches	414
Glendale	414	Hudson	715	La Crosse	608	Madeline Island	715	Mondovi	715
Glen Flora	715	Humbird	715	Ladysmith	715	Madison	608	Monico	715
Glenhaven	608	Humboldt	414	La Farge	608	Magnolia	608	Monroe	608
Glenmore	414	Hurley	715	La Grange	414	Maiden Rock	715	Monroe Center	608
Glenwood City	715	Hustisford	414	Lake Beulah	414	Malone	414	Mont du Lac	715
Glidden	715	Hustler	608	Lake Delavan	414	Manawa	414	Montello	414
Goodman	715	Hyde	608	Lake Delton	608	Manchester	414	Monterey	414
Gordon	715			Lake Geneva	414	Manitowish	715	Montfort	608
Gotham	608			Lake Keesus	414	Manitowish Waters	715	Monticello	608
Grafton	414			Lake Lawn	414	Manitowoc	414	Montreal	715
Grandmarsh	608	Independence	715	Lake Mills	414	Maple	715	Moquah	715
Grandview	715	Indianford	608	Lake Nebagamon	715	Mapleton	414	Morgan	414
Grange Hall	715	Ino	715	Lake Ripley	608	Maplewood	414	Morrison	414
Granton	715	Iola	715	Lake Tomahawk	715	Marathon	715	Morrisonville	608
Grantsburg	715	Irma	715	Lake Waubesa	608	Marengo	715	Mosel	414
Gratiot	608	Iron Belt	715	Lakewood	715	Marinette	715	Mosinee	715
Green Bay	414	Iron Ridge	414	Lamartine	414	Marion	715	Mountain	715
Greenbush	414	Iron River	715	Lancaster	608	Markesan	414	Mount Calvary	414
Greendale	414	Ironton	608	Land O'Lakes	715	Marquette	414	Mount Hope	608
Greenfield	414	Ithaca	608	Langlade	715	Marshall	608	Mount Horeb	608
Green Lake	414	Ixonia	414	Lannon	414	Marshfield	715	Mount Sterling	608
Greenleaf	414			Laona	715	Martell	715	Mount Tabor	608
Greenvalley	715			La Pointe	715	Martintown	608	Mount Vernon	608
Greenville	414			Larsen	414	Marytown	414	Mount Zion	608
Greenwood	715	Jackson	414	Lauderdale Lake	414	Mason	715	Mukwonago	414
Gresham	715	Jacksonport	414	La Valle	608	Mason Lake	715	Muscoda	608
		Janesville	608	Lawton	715	Mather	608	Muskego	414
		Jefferson	414	Leadmine	608	Mattoon	715		
		Jefferson Junction	414	Lebanon	414	Mauston	608		
Hager City	715	Jennings	715	Lena	414	Mayville	414		
Hales Corners	414	Jewett	715	Leopolis	715	Mazomanie	608	Nabob	414
Hamburg	715	Jim Falls	715	Le Roy	414	McAllister	715	Nagawicka Lake	414
Hammond	715	Johnsburg	414	Lewis	715	McFarland	608	Namekagon Lake	715
Hancock	715	Johnson Creek	414	Leyden	414	McNaughton	715	Nashotah	414
Hannibal	715	Johnsonville	414	Liberty Pole	608	Medford	715	Navarino	715
Hanover	608	Johnstown	608	Lily	715	Medina	414	Necedah	608
Harmony	715	Juda	608	Lima Center	414	Mellen	715	Neenah	414
Harrisville	608	Jump River	715	Lime Ridge	608	Melrose	608	Neillsville	715
Harshaw	715	Junction City	715	Lincoln	414	Menasha	414	Nekoosa	715
Hartford	414	Juneau	414	Linden	608	Mendota	608	Nelson	715
Hartland	414			Lindsey	715	Menomonee Falls	414	Nelsonville	715
Hatley	715			Little Cedar Lake	414	Menomonie	715	Neopit	715
Haugen	715			Little Chute	414	Mequon	414	Neosho	414
Hawkins	715	Kaukauna	414	Little Kohler	414	Mercer	715	Neshkoro	414
Hawthorne	715	Kegonsa Village	608	Little Sturgeon	414	Merrill	715	Neva	715
Hayward	715	Kekoskee	414	Little Suamico	414	Merrillan	715	Newald	715
Hazel Green	608	Kellnersville	414	Livingston	608	Merrimac	608	New Auburn	715
Hazelhurst	715	Kelly Lake	414	Lodi	608	Merton	414	New Berlin	414
Heafford Junction	715	Kempster	715	Loganville	608	Middle Inlet	715	Newburg	414
Helenville	414	Kendall	608	Lohrville	414	Middle River		New Diggings	608
Herbster	715	Kennan	715	Lomira	414	(Sanitorium)	715	New Franken	414

Place Name	Area Code	Place Name	Area Code	Place Name	Area Code	Place Name	Area Code	Place Name	Area Code
New Glarus	608	Perkinstown	715	Rice Lake	715	Sheridan	715	Taycheedah	414
New Holstein	414	Peshtigo	715	Richfield	414	Sherwood	414	Taylor	715
New Lisbon	608	Pewaukee	414	Richland Center	608	Shiocton	414	The Island	715
New London	414	Pewaukee Lake	414	Richmond	608	Shopiere	608	Theresa	414
New Richmond	715	Phelps	715	Ridgeland	715	Shorewood	414	Thiensville	414
New Rome	715	Phillips	715	Ridgeville	608	Shullsburg	608	Thorp	715
Newry	608	Phlox	715	Ridgeway	608	Silver Lake		Three Lakes	715
Newton	414	Pickerel	715	Rio	414	(Kenosha Co.)	414	Tiffany	608
Newtonburg	414	Pickett	414	Rio Creek	414	Silver Lake		Tigerton	715
Niagara	715	Pigeon Falls	715	Ripon	414	(Washington Co.)	414	Tilleda	715
Nichols	414	Pike Lake	414	River Falls	715	Sinsinawa	608	Tipler	715
Norrie	715	Pilsen	414	River Hills	414	Siren	715	Tisch Mills	414
North Antioch	414	Pine Knob	608	Roberts	715	Sister Bay	414	Tomah	608
North Apple River	608	Pine Lake	414	Rochester	414	Slinger	414	Tomahawk	715
North Clayton	608	Pittsville	715	Rockbridge	608	Slovan	414	Tony	715
Northfield	715	Plain	608	Rockdale	608	Sobieski	414	Townsend	715
North Freedom	608	Plainfield	715	Rock Elm	715	Soldiers Grove	608	Trade Lake	715
North Lake	414	Plainville	608	Rock Falls	715	Solon Springs	715	Trego	715
North Prairie	414	Platteville	608	Rockfield	414	Somers	414	Trempealeau	608
North Winslow	608	Pleasant Prairie	414	Rockland		Somerset	715	Trevor	414
North York	715	Pleasantville	715	(La Crosse Co.)	608	Soo Lake	715	Tripoli	715
Norwalk	608	Plover	715	Rockland		Soperton	715	Trout Lake	715
Nye	715	Plum City	715	(Manitowoc Co.)	414	South Milwaukee	414	Troy Center	414
		Plum Island Coast		Rock Springs	608	South Range	715	Truax Field (U. S.	
		Guard Sta. No. 290	414	Romance	608	South Wayne	608	Army Air Forces)	608
		Plymouth	414	Rome	608	Sparta	608	Truesdell	414
		Polar	715	Rosendale	414	Spencer	715	Tunnel City	608
Oak Creek	414	Polonia	715	Rosholt	715	Spider Lake	715	Turtle Lake	715
Oakdale	608	Poplar	715	Rosiere	414	Spooner	715	Tustin	414
Oakfield	414	Popple River	715	Rothschild	715	Sprague	608	Twin Bluffs	608
Oconomowoc	414	Portage	608	Roxbury	608	Spread Eagle	715	Twin Bridge	715
Oconto	414	Port Edwards	715	Royalton	414	Springbrook	715	Twin Lakes	414
Oconto Falls	414	Porterfield	715	Rubicon	414	Springfield	414	Two Rivers	414
Odanah	715	Port Washington	414	Rudolph	715	Spring Green	608	Two Rivers Coast	
Ogdensburg	715	Port Wing	715	Rush Lake	414	Spring Lake		Guard Sta. No. 286	414
Ogema	715	Poskin	715			(St. Croix Co.)	715		
Okauchee	414	Potosi	608			Spring Lake			
Okee	608	Potter	414			(Waushara Co.)	414		
Oliver	715	Pound	414			Springstead	715	Underhill	414
Omro	414	Powers Lake	414	Sabin	608	Spring Valley	715	Union	715
Onalaska	608	Poynette	608	St. Cloud	414	Stanley	715	Union Center	608
Oneida	414	Poy Sippi	414	St. Croix Falls	715	Stanton	715	Union Grove	414
Ontario	608	Prairie du Chien	608	St. Francis	414	Starlake	715	Unity	715
Oostburg	414	Prairie du Sac	608	St. Germain	715	Star Prairie	715	Upson	715
Oregon	608	Prairie Farm	715	St. John	414	Stephensville	414	Utica	608
Orfordville	608	Prentice	715	St. Lawrence	414	Stetsonville	715		
Orihula	414	Prescott	715	St. Michaels	414	Steuben	608		
Osceola	715	Presque Isle	715	St. Nazianz	414	Stevens Point	715		
Oshkosh	414	Princeton	414	Salem	414	Stiles	414		
Osseo	715	Prospect	414	Salmo	715	Stitzer	608	Valders	414
Otsego	414	Pulaski	414	Salvatorian Center	414	Stockbridge	414	Valley	608
Owen	715	Pulcifer	715	Sanborn	715	Stockholm	715	Van Dyne	414
Oxford	608			Sand Creek	715	Stockton	715	Verona	608
				Sarona	715	Stoddard	608	Vesper	715
				Sauk City	608	Stone Lake	715	Victory	608
		Racine	414	Saukville	414	Stoughton	608	Viola	608
		Racine Coast Guard		Saxon	715	Stratford	715	Viroqua	608
Packwaukee	608	Sta. No. 283	414	Saylesville	414	Strum	715	Volk Field	608
Paddock Lake	414	Radisson	715	Sayner	715	Sturgeon Bay	414		
Palmyra	414	Randolph	414	Scandinavia	715	Sturgeon Bay Canal			
Paoli	608	Random Lake	414	Schofield	715	Coast Guard Sta.			
Pardeeville	608	Rankin	414	Schoolhill	414	No. 288	414	Wabeno	715
Park Falls	715	Readfield	414	Seneca	608	Sturtevant	414	Waino	715
Parkside	414	Readstown	608	Sextonville	608	Suamico	414	Waldo	414
Parrish	715	Redgranite	414	Seymour	414	Sugar Bush	414	Wales	414
Patzau	715	Red Mound	608	Sharon	414	Sugar Camp	715	Walsh	715
Pearson	715	Reedsburg	608	Shawano	715	Sullivan	414	Walworth	414
Pelican Lake	715	Reedsville	414	Sheboygan	414	Summit Lake	715	Wanderoos	715
Pell Lake	414	Reeseville	414	Sheboygan Coast		Sun Prairie	608	Warrens	608
Pembine	715	Retreat	608	Guard Sta. No. 285	414	Superior	715	Washburn	715
Pence	715	Rewey	608	Sheboygan Falls	414	Suring	414	Washington Island	414
Peninsula Center	414	Rhinelander	715	Sheldon	715	Sussex	414	Waterford	414
Pensaukee	414	Rib Falls	715	Shell Lake	715	Sylvan	608	Waterloo	414
Pepin	715	Rib Lake	715	Shennington	608	Symco	414	Watertown	414
								Waubeka	414

TELEPHONE AREA CODE DIRECTORY

Place Name	Area Code	Place Name	Area Code	Place Name	Area Code	Place Name	Area Code	Place Name	Area Code
Waucousta	414	West Allis	414	Whitehall	715	Winnebago	414	Wrightstown	414
Waukau	414	West Bend	414	White Lake	715	Winneconne	414	Wyeville	608
Waukesha	414	West Bloomfield	414	Whitelaw	414	Winter	715	Wyocena	608
Waumandee	608	Westboro	715	Whitewater	414	Wiota	608		
Waunakee	608	Westby	608	Whittlesey	715	Wisconsin Dells	608		
Waupaca	715	West De Pere	414	Wild Rose	414	Wisconsin Rapids	715		
Waupun	414	Westfield	608	Willard	715	Withee	715		
Wausau	715	West Lima	608	Williams Bay	414	Wittenberg	715		
Wausaukee	715	West Milwaukee	414	Wilmot	414	Witwen	608	Yellowlake	715
Wautoma	414	Weston	715	Wilson	715	Wonewoc	608	Yuba	608
Wauwatosa	414	West Prairie	608	Wilton	608	Wood	414		
Wauzeka	608	West Salem	608	Winchester		Woodford	608		
Waverly	715	Weyauwega	414	(Vilas Co.)	715	Woodland	414		
Wayside	414	Weyerhauser	715	Winchester		Woodman	608		
Webb Lake	715	Wheatland	414	(Winnebago Co.)	414	Woodruff	715	Zachow	715
Webster	715	Wheeler	715	Wind Lake	414	Woodville	715	Zenda	414
Wentworth	715	Whitefish Bay	414	Windsor	608	Woodworth	414	Zittau	414

ALL POINTS—AREA CODE 307

ALL POINTS—AREA CODE 403

ALL POINTS—AREA CODE 604

ALL POINTS—AREA CODE 204

ALL POINTS—AREA CODE 506

ALL POINTS—AREA CODE 709

ALL POINTS—AREA CODE 403

ALL POINTS—AREA CODE 902

Place Name	Area Code	Place Name	Area Code	Place Name	Area Code	Place Name	Area Code	Place Name	Area Code
Aberarder	519	Ariss	519	Barrie Island	705	Birdsall Station	705	Brechin	705
Aberdeen	519	Arkell	519	Bar River	705	Bird's Creek	613	Brentha	705
Aberfeldy	519	Arkona	519	Barry's Bay	613	Birkendale	705	Brentwood	705
Aberfoyle	519	Armadale	416	Barryvale	613	Birnam	519	Breslau	519
Actinolite	613	Armitage	416	Bartonville	416	Birr	519	Brethour	705
Acton	519	Armow	519	Barwick	807	Bishop's Mills	613	Brewer's Mills	613
Adastral Park	519	Armstrong	807	Batawa	613	Bissett	613	Brewster	519
Addison	613	Arner	519	Batchawana Bay	705	Bissett Creek	613	Bridgenorth	705
Adelaide	519	Arnold Farms	416	Bath	613	Blackbridge	705	Bridgeport	519
Admaston	613	Arnprior	613	Bathurst Station	613	Blackhawk	807	Brigden	519
Admiralty Islands	613	Aroland	807	Batteaux	705	Blackheath	416	Bright	519
Adolphustown	613	Arnstein	705	Battersea	613	Black Sands Park	807	Brighton	613
Agincourt	416	Arthur	519	Baxter	705	Blackstock	416	Bright's Grove	519
Ahmic Lake	705	Arva	519	Bayfield	519	Blackwater	705	Brightside	613
Ailsa Craig	519	Ash	416	Bayham	519	Blackwell	519	Brinsley	519
Airy	705	Ashburn	416	Bay Ridges	416	Blair	519	Brinston	613
Ajax	416	Ashdad	613	Bayside	613	Blairton	705	Britannia	
Alban	705	Ashdod	613	Baysville	705	Blake	519	(Carleton Co.)	613
Alberton (Rainy		Ashgrove	416	Beachburg	613	Blakeney	613	Britannia	
River Dist.)	807	Ash Rapids	807	Beachville	519	Blandford	519	(Muskoka Dist.)	705
Alberton		Ashton	613	Beamsville	416	Blantyre	519	Britannia (Peel Co.)	416
(Wentworth Co.)	416	Aspdin	705	Bear Brook	613	Blenheim	519	Britt	705
Albion	416	Astorville	705	Beardmore	807	Blezard's	705	Britton	519
Albuna	519	Athens	613	Bear Lake	705	Blezard Valley	705	Brock Road	416
Alcona	705	Atherley	705	Bear Line	519	Blind River	705	Brock's Beach	705
Alderdale	705	Atikokan	807	Beaumaris	705	Bloomfield	613	Brockville	613
Aldershot	416	Attercliffe	416	Beaverton	705	Bloomingdale	519	Brodhagen	519
Alderwood	416	Atwood (Perth Co.)	519	Becher	519	Bloomsburg	519	Bromley	613
Alexandria	613	Atwood (Rainy		Becker	807	Blount (Dufferin Co.)	519	Bronson	613
Alexandria Island	807	River Dist.)	807	Beckett	613	Bluevale	519	Bronte	416
Alfred	613	Auburn	519	Bedell	613	Bluewater	705	Brooke	613
Algoma Mills	705	Aurora	416	Bedford Mills	613	Blyth	519	Brooklin	416
Algonquin	613	Avening	705	Beeton	416	Blytheswood	519	Brooksdale	519
Algonquin Park	705	Avon	519	Bekanon	705	Bobcaygeon	705	Brougham	416
Alice	613	Avonbank	519	Belfast	519	Bogartown	416	Brown Hill	416
Allanburg	416	Avonmore	613	Belfountain	519	Bognor	519	Browning Island	705
Allandale	705	Avonton	519	Belgrave	519	Bolingbrook	613	Brown's Corners	416
Allan Park	519	Aylmer	519	Belhaven	416	Bolsover	705	Brownsville	519
Allenford	519	Ayr	519	Bellamy	613	Bolton	416	Brucefield	519
Allensville	705	Ayton	519	Belle Ewart	705	Bon Air	705	Bruce Lake	807
Allenwood	705	Azilda	705	Belle River	519	Bonar Law	705	Bruce Mines	705
Allisonville	613			Belle Vallee	705	Bona Vista	705	Brudenell	613
Alliston	705			Belleville	613	Bond Head	416	Brule Lake	705
Alma	519	Baden	519	Bell's Corners	613	Bond Lake	416	Brunner	519
Almira	416	Badjeros	519	Belmont	519	Bon Echo	613	Brussels	519
Almonte	613	Bailieboro	705	Belmore	519	Bonfield	705	Bryanston	519
Alsfeldt	519	Bainsville	613	Belton	519	Bonnechere	613	Buckham Bay	613
Alton	519	Baird	807	Belwood	519	Bonville	613	Buckhorn	705
Altona	416	Bala	705	Benmiller	519	Borden-Angus	705	Bulger's Corners	613
Alvinston	519	Balaclava	519	Bennington	519	Bornholm	519	Bullock's Corners	416
Amaranth	519	Balderson	613	Bensfort	705	Boskung	705	Bunessan	519
Amaranth Station	519	Baldwin	416	Bent River	705	Boston	519	Burford	519
Ameliasburg	613	Ballantrae	416	Bergland	807	Boston Creek	705	Burgessville	519
Amherstburg	519	Ballinafad	416	Berkeley	519	Bosworth	519	Burk's Falls	705
Amulree	519	Ballycroy	416	Bervie	519	Bothwell	519	Burleigh	705
Ancaster	416	Ballydown Beach	705	Berwick	613	Bouck's Hill	613	Burleigh Falls	705
Ancona Point	705	Ballymote	519	Bethany	705	Boulter	613	Burlington	416
Anderson	519	Balm Beach	705	Bethesda	416	Bourget	613	Burnhamthorpe	416
Annan	519	Balmertown	807	Beverley Isles	416	Bourkes	705	Burnstown	613
Ansonia	705	Balsam	416	Bewdley	416	Bowmanville	416	Burnt River	705
Anten Mills	705	Balsam Creek	705	Bexley	705	Boxall	519	Burridge	613
Antrim	613	Balsam Lake	705	Bickford	519	Box Grove	416	Burritt's Rapids	613
Appin	519	Baltimore	416	Bicroft	613	Boyne	416	Burtch	519
Appleby	416	Bamberg	519	Big Bay Point	705	Bracebridge	705	Burwash	705
Apple Hill	613	Bancroft	613	Big Cedar Point	705	Brackenrig	705	Buttermilk Falls	705
Appleton	613	Bankfield Mine	807	Big Lake	705	Bradford	416	Buttonville	416
Apsley	705	Banks	705	Big Point	519	Bradley	519	Byng Inlet	705
Apto	705	Bannockburn	613	Bigwin Inn	705	Bradshaw	519	Byron	519
Arbor Vitae	807	Baptiste	613	Bigwood	705	Braemar	519	
Arden	613	Barclay	705	Billing's Bridge	613	Braeside	613	
Ardendale	613	Barkway	705	Binbrook	416	Bramalea	416	
Ardoch	613	Barrie	705	Birch Cliff	416	Brampton	416	Cache Bay	705
Ardtrea	705	Barriefield	613	Birch Island	705	Branchton	519	Caesarea	416
Argyle	705			Birch Point	705	Brantford	519	Cainsville	519

TELEPHONE AREA CODE DIRECTORY

Place Name	Area Code	Place Name	Area Code	Place Name	Area Code	Place Name	Area Code	Place Name	Area Code
Caintown	613	Cedar Grove	416	Clute	705	Crosshill	519	Dinorwic	807
Cairngorm	519	Cedar Hill	613	Clyde Forks	613	Crossland	705	Dixie	416
Cairo	519	Cedarhurst	705	Coatsworth	519	Croton	519	Dixon's Corners	613
Caistor Center	416	Cedar Point	705	Cobalt	705	Crowe's Landing	705	Dobbinton	519
Caistorville	416	Cedar Springs	519	Cobden	613	Crow Lake	613	Doe Lake	705
Calabogie	613	Cedar Valley	416	Coboconk	705	Crowland	416	Dog Hole Bay	807
Caledon	519	Cedarville	519	Cobourg	416	Crown Hill	705	Doherty	705
Caledon East	416	Centralia	519	Cochenour	807	Crow Rock	807	Dokis	705
Caledonia	416	Central Patricia	807	Cochrane	705	Crozier	807	Domville	613
Caledonia Springs	613	Centreton	416	Cockburn Island	705	Crumlin	519	Donald	705
Callander	705	Centreville (Addington Co.)	613	Codrington	613	Crysler	613	Donegal	519
Calton	519	Centreville (Northumberland Co.)	705	Coe Hill	613	Crystal Beach	416	Dongola	705
Camborne	416			Colborne	416	Culloden	519	Don Mills	416
Cambridge	519	Centreville (Waterloo Co.)	519	Colchester	519	Cultus	519	Doon	519
Camden East	613	Ceylon	519	Cold Springs	416	Cumberland	613	Dorchester	519
Camel Chute	613	Chaffey's Locks	613	Coldstream	519	Cumnock	519	Dorion	807
Camelot Beach	416	Chalk River	613	Coldwater	705	Cundles	705	Dorking	519
Cameron	705	Chamberlain	705	Colebrook	613	Curran	613	Dorland	613
Cameron Falls	807	Chambers Corners	416	Coleraine	416	Curtis Township	705	Dornoch	519
Camilla	519	Chandos	705	Colgan	416	Curve Lake	705	Dorset	705
Camlachie	519	Chantler	416	Collingwood	705	Cutler	705	Douglas	613
Campbellcroft	416	Chantry	613	Collins Bay	613	Cyrville	613	Douglas Point	519
Campbellford	705	Chapleau	705	Columbus	416			Douro	705
Campbell's Cross	416	Charing Cross	519	Colwell	705			Dover Centre	519
Campbellville	416	Charlemont	519	Comber	519			Downer's Corners	705
Campden	416	Charleston Lake	613	Combermere	613	Dack	705	Downeyville	705
Camperdown	519	Charleville	613	Commanda	705	Dacre	613	Downsview	416
Camp Robinson	807	Charlton	705	Concord	416	Dalhousie Mills	613	Drayton	519
Canaan	613	Chartrand	613	Conestogo	519	Dalkeith	613	Dresden	519
Canboro	416	Chatham	519	Coniston	705	Dalmeny	613	Drew	519
Canfield	416	Chatsworth	519	Conn	519	Dalrymple	705	Dromore	519
Cannamore	613	Cheapside	416	Consecon	613	Dalston	705	Drumbo	519
Cannifton	613	Chelmsford	705	Constance Bay	613	Damascus	519	Drummond Centre	613
Cannington	705	Cheltenham	416	Conway	613	Dance	807	Drumquin	416
Canoe Lake	705	Cheminis	705	Cookstown	705	Dane	705	Dryberry Lake	807
Canton	519	Chepstowe	519	Cooksville	416	Danforth	416	Dryberry River	807
Cape Croker	519	Cherry Valley	613	Cooper	613	Darlington	416	Dryden	807
Cape Rich	519	Cherrywood	416	Cooper's Falls	705	Dartford	705	Drysdale	519
Capreol	705	Chesley	519	Copetown	416	Dashwood	519	Duart	519
Caradoc	519	Chesterville	613	Copleston	519	Dawn Mills	519	Dublin	519
Cardiff	613	Chikopi	705	Coppell	705	Dawn Valley	519	Dubreuilville	705
Cardinal	613	Chippawa	416	Copper Cliff	705	Day Mills	705	Duclos Point	705
Cargill	519	Chippewa Hill	519	Corbett	519	Decew's Falls	416	Dugwal	705
Caribou Falls	807	Chiswick	705	Corbetton	519	Decewsville	416	Dunbarton	416
Carleton Place	613	Christie Lake	613	Corbyville	613	Deep River	613	Duncan	519
Carley	705	Christina	519	Cordova Mines	705	Deer Falls	807	Dunchurch	705
Carlingford	519	Chub Lake	705	Corinth	519	Deerhurst	416	Dundalk	519
Carlisle	416	Churchill	705	Corkery	613	Degrassi Point	705	Dundas	416
Carlow	519	Churchville	416	Cormac	705	Delamere	705	Dundonald	416
Carlsbad Springs	613	Chute a Blondeau	613	Cornell	519	Delaware	519	Dunedin	705
Carlsruhe	519	Clachan	519	Cornwall	613	Delhi	519	Dungannon	519
Carluke	416	Clandeboye	519	Corunna	519	Delmer	519	Dunkeld	519
Carmunnock	519	Clappison's Corners	416	Corwhin	519	Deloro	613	Dunlop	519
Carnarvon	705	Clara Belle Junction	705	Cottam	519	Delray	705	Dunn	416
Carp	613	Claraday	705	Cottesloe	705	Delta	613	Dunnet Corners	705
Carr	705	Claremont	416	Coulson	705	Demorestville	613	Dunn's Valley	705
Carrying Place	613	Clarence	613	Courtice	416	Denbigh	613	Dunnville	416
Carsonby	613	Clarence Creek	613	Courtland	519	Denfield	519	Dunrobin	613
Carterton	705	Clarina	705	Courtright	519	Departure Lake	705	Dunsford	705
Carthage	519	Clarke	416	Craighurst	705	Depot Harbor	705	Duntroon	705
Cartier	705	Clarksburg	519	Craigleith	705	Dereham Centre	519	Dunvegan	613
Cartwright	416	Clarkson	416	Crampton	519	Derryville	705	Durham	519
Cashel	416	Clavering	519	Cranbrook	519	Derry West	416	Dutton	519
Casselman	613	Clayton	613	Crediton	519	Desaulniers	705	Dwight	705
Castleford	613	Clear Creek	519	Creemore	705	Desbarats	705	Dwyer Hill	613
Castlemore	416	Clear Lake	705	Creighton Mine	705	Desboro	519	Dyment	807
Castleton	416	Clearwater Bay	807	Creswell	705	Deseronto	613		
Cataract	519	Cliff Lake	807	Crewson's Corners	519	Des Joachims	613		
Cataraqui	613	Clifford	519	Crinan	519	Desmond	613	Eady	705
Cathcart	519	Clinton	519	Cromarty	519	Detlor	613	Eagle	519
Cavan	705	Cloyne	613	Crombies	519	Devizes	519	Eagle Lake	705
Cayuga	416			Crooked Bay	705	Devlin	807	Eagle River	807
Cedarbrae	416			Crookston	613	Devonshire	705	Ear Falls	807
Cedardale	416			Crosby	613	Dexter	519		

Place Name	Area Code	Place Name	Area Code	Place Name	Area Code	Place Name	Area Code	Place Name	Area Code
Earlscourt	416	Erin	519	Flower Station	613	Genier	705	Grand Valley	519
Earlton	705	Erindale	416	Folden's Corners	519	Georgetown	416	Granite Lake	807
Eastbourne	416	Erinsville	613	Foleyet	705	Geraldton	807	Granton	519
East Linton	519	Ernestown	613	Fonthill	416	Germania	705	Grant's Corners	613
East Loon	807	Escott	613	Foote's Bay	705	Germanicus	613	Grassie's	416
Easton's Corners	613	Espanola	705	Fordwich	519	Gesto	519	Grassmere	705
East Oro	705	Esquesing	416	Forest	519	Gibraltar	613	Grassy Narrows Lake	807
East Windsor	519	Essa	705	Forester's Falls	613	Gilbert Lake	807	Gratton	613
Eastwood	519	Essex	519	Forest Hill	416	Gilchrist	705	Gravenhurst	705
East York	416	Essonville	705	Forest Mills	613	Gilford	705	Graystock	705
Eau Claire	705	Estaire	705	Forestville	519	Gillies Depot	705	Greely	613
Eberts	519	Ethel	519	Forfar	613	Gilmour	613	Greenbank	416
Echo Bay	705	Etobicoke	416	Forks of Credit	519	Giroux Lake	705	Greenbush	613
Echo Lake	613	Ettrick	519	Formosa	519	Gladstone	519	Greenfield	613
Eden	519	Etwell	705	Fort Erie	416	Glammis	519	Greenhurst	705
Eden Grove	519	Eugenia	519	Fort Frances	807	Glanford	416	Greenock	519
Eden Mills	519	Eugenia Falls	519	Forthton	613	Glanford Station	416	Green River	416
Edenvale	705	Eva Lake	807	Fort Stewart	613	Glanworth	519	Greensville	416
Edgar	705	Evansville	705	Fort William	807	Glasgow	613	Green Valley	613
Edgeley	416	Evanturel	613	Fournier	613	Glen Alda	613	Greenwood	416
Edville	416	Evelyn	519	Fowler's Corners	705	Glen Allan	519	Gregory	705
Edwards	613	Everett	705	Foxboro	613	Glen Buell	613	Gretna	613
Effingham	416	Eversley	416	Foxmead	705	Glencairn	705	Griffith	613
Eganville	613	Everton	519	Fox Point	705	Glencoe	519	Grimsby	416
Egbert	705	Exeter	519	Foymount	613	Glen Cross	519	Grove Park	705
Egerton	519			Franconia	416	Glen Gordon	613	Guelph	519
Egmondville	519			Frankford	613	Glen Huron	705	Guelph Junction	416
Elba	519			Franklin Beach	416	Glen Major	416	Guild's	519
Elder	519	Fairfield	613	Franktown	613	Glen Meyer	519	Guilletville	705
Eldon Station	705	Fairfield East	613	Frankville	613	Glen Morris	519	Gull Bay	807
Eldorado	613	Fairground	519	Franz	705	Glenmount	705	Gun Lake	
Electric	519	Fairport Beach	416	Fraserburg	705	Glennevis	613	(Minaki Dist.)	807
Elford	519	Fairview	519	Fraserville	705	Glen Norman	613	Guthrie	705
Elfrida	416	Fairview Island	705	Fraxa Junction	519	Glenora	613	Guysboro	519
Elgin	613	Falconbridge	705	Frederickhouse	705	Glen Orchard	705		
Elginburg	613	Falkenburg	705	Freeland	613	Glen Rae	519		
Elginfield	519	Fallbrook	613	Freelton	416	Glen Robertson	613		
Elgin Mills	416	Fallowfield	613	Freeman	416	Glen Roy	613	Hagar	705
Elia	416	Falls View	416	Freeport	519	Glen Sandfield	613	Hagerman's Corners	416
Elimville	519	Fanshawe	519	French Hill	613	Glenshee	519	Hagersville	416
Elizabeth	807	Faraday	613	French Lake	807	Glen Tay	613	Haileybury	705
Elizabethville	416	Farringdon	519	French River	705	Glenvale	613	Hainsville	613
Elk Lake	705	Fassifern	519	Frogmore	519	Glenville	416	Haldane Hill	705
Ellesmere	416	Featherstone Point	416	Frome	519	Glen Walter	613	Haley Station	613
Elliot Lake	705	Fells	705	Frood Mine	705	Glen Williams	416	Haliburton	705
Elliott	613	Fenella	416	Froomfield	519	Glenwood Station	519	Haliburton Lake	705
Ellwood	613	Fenelon Falls	705	Fruitland	416	Gloucester	613	Hallebourg	705
Elma	613	Fenwick	416	Fullarton	519	Gobles	519	Halloway	613
Elmira	519	Fergus	519	Fulton	416	Goderich	519	Hall's Glen	705
Elmstead	519	Ferguson Falls	613			Godfrey	613	Hall's Lake	705
Elmvale	705	Fergusonvale	705			Godolphin	705	Hallville	613
Elmwood	519	Fermoy	613			Gogama	705	Hamilton	416
Elora	519	Ferndale	705	Gadshill	519	Goldenburg	705	Hammertown	416
Elsinore	519	Fern Glen	705	Galeton	705	Golden Lake	613	Hammond	613
Embro	519	Fernleigh	613	Galetta	613	Golden Valley	705	Hampshire Mills	705
Embrun	613	Feronia	705	Gallingerton	613	Goldstone	519	Hampton	416
Emerald	613	Ferris	705	Galt	519	Gooderham	705	Hanbury	705
Emery	416	Fesserton	705	Gamebridge	705	Goodwood	416	Hanmer	705
Emeryville	519	Feversham	519	Gameland	807	Gordon	519	Hanna	705
Emo	807	Field	705	Gananoque	613	Gordon Bay	705	Hannah Bay	
Emsdale	705	Finch	613	Garafraxa	519	Gordon Lake		Goose Camp	705
Enchanted Island	807	Fingal	519	Garden Hill	416	(Algoma Dist.)	705	Hannon	416
Englehart	705	Finland	807	Garden Island	613	Gordonville	519	Hanover	519
Ennett	519	Finmark	807	Garden Lake	705	Gore Bay	705	Harcourt	705
Enniskillen	416	Fisherville	416	Garden River	705	Gore's Landing	416	Harcourt Park	705
Ennismore	705	Fitzroy Harbor	613	Gardenville	613	Gormley	416	Hardrock	807
Ennottville	519	Flamboro Centre	416	Garnett	416	Gorrie	519	Harlem	613
Enterprise	613	Flamboro Station	416	Garson	705	Goudreau	705	Harley	519
Epsom	416	Flesherton	519	Gas Line	416	Goulais	705	Harlowe	613
Eramosa	519	Fletcher	519	Gatchell	705	Gowanstown	519	Harmony	416
Erbsville	519	Flint	807	Gateway	705	Goward	705	Harold	613
Erieau	519	Flinton	613	Geco Mine	807	Grace Anne 11	807	Harper	613
Erie Beach	416	Floradale	519	Gelert	705	Grafton	416	Harper's Corners	416
Erieview	519	Florence	519	Geneva Park	705	Grand Bend	519	Harpley	519

Place Name	Area Code	Place Name	Area Code	Place Name	Area Code	Place Name	Area Code	Place Name	Area Code
Harrietsville	519	Holt	416	Janetville	705	Kinglake	519	Limoges	613
Harrington	519	Holtyre	705	Jarratt Corners	705	Kingsbridge	519	Lincoln	416
Harrisburg	519	Holyrood	519	Jarvis	519	Kingscourt	519	Lindsay	705
Harrison's Corners	613	Homer	416	Jasper	613	Kingsdale	519	Linwood	519
Harriston	519	Honey Harbour	705	Jeannette's Creek	519	Kingsford	613	Lisle	705
Harrow	519	Honeywood	705	Jefferson	416	Kingsmill	519	Listowel	519
Harrowsmith	613	Hope	416	Jellyby	613	Kingston	613	Little Britain	705
Harstone	807	Hopetown	613	Jermyn	705	Kingsville	519	Little Current	705
Hartford	519	Hopeville	519	Jerseyville	519	Kingsway	705	Little Rapids	705
Hartington	613	Hornby	416	Jessopville	519	Kinloss	519	Lively	705
Harty	705	Hornepayne	807	Jocelyn	705	Kinmount	705	Livingston	705
Harwich	519	Horning's Mills	519	Johnstown	613	Kinsale	416	Lloydtown	416
Harwood	416	Horseshoe Bay	705	Jones Falls	613	Kintail	519	Lobo	519
Hastings	705	Horton Township	613	Joques	705	Kintore	519	Lobstic Bay	807
Hatchley	519	Houghton	519	Jordan	416	Kippen	519	Lochalsh	705
Haultain	705	Housey's Rapids	705	Joyceville	613	Kirkfield	705	Lochiel	613
Havelock	705	Howdenvale	519	Juddhaven	705	Kirkland Lake	705	Lochlin	705
Havilah Mine	705	Howe Island	613	Judge	705	Kirkton	519	Loch Winnoch	613
Hawkesbury	613	Hoyle	705	Juniper Island	705	Kishkutena	807	Lockerby	705
Hawkestone	705	Hudson	807			Kitchener	519	Locksley	613
Hawkesville	519	Hugel	705			Kitigan	705	Locust Hill	416
Hawthorne	613	Humber Bay	416			Kleinburg	416	Lombardy	613
Hawtrey	519	Humberstone	416	Kagawong	705	Kohler	416	Londesborough	519
Hay	519	Humber Summit	416	Kahshe	705	Komoka	519	London	519
Hay Bay	613	Humphrey	705	Kakabeka Falls	807	Krugerdorf	705	Long Beach	416
Haycroft	519	Huntley	613	Kaladar	613	Kukatush	705	Longbow Lake	807
Haysville	519	Huntsville	705	Kaministiquia	807	Kurtzville	519	Long Branch	416
Hazeldean	613	Hurdville	705	Kanata	613			Longford Mills	705
Headford	416	Hurkett	807	Kapuskasing	705			Longlac	807
Head Lake	705	Huron Park	519	Kars	613			Long Lake	613
Healy Falls	705	Huttonville	416	Katrine	705	Lafontaine	705	Long Point	519
Hearst	705	Hybla	613	Kawartha Park	705	Laird	705	Long Sault	613
Heaslip	705	Hyde Park	519	Keady	519	Lakefield	705	Longwood	519
Heathcote	519	Hymers	807	Kearney	705	Lakehurst	705	Lonsdale	613
Heckston	613	Hyndford	613	Kearns	705	Lakelet	519	Loon Lake	807
Heidelberg	519			Keemle Lake	807	Lakeport	416	Loretto	705
Hekkla	705			Keene	705	Lakeside	519	L'Orignal	613
Henderson	613			Keewatin	807	Lakeview	416	Lorne Park	416
Hendrie	705	Ida	705	Keldon	519	L'Amable	613	Lorneville	705
Hensall	519	Ignace	807	Kelso (Halton Co.)	416	Lambeth	519	Loughborough	613
Hepworth	519	Ilderton	519	Kelvin	519	Lambton	416	Lovering	705
Heron Bay	807	Ilfracombe	705	Kemble	519	Lanark	613	Lovett	613
Herron's Mills	613	Indian River	705	Kemptville	613	Lancaster	613	Lowther	705
Hespeler	519	Ingersoll	519	Kenabeek	705	Lancelot	705	Lucan	519
Hesson	519	Ingleside	613	Kendal	416	Langstaff	416	Lucknow	519
Heyden	705	Inglewood	416	Kenilworth	519	Langton	519	Lunds Bay	705
Hickson	519	Ingoldsby	705	Kenmore	613	Lansdowne	613	Lunenburg	613
High Falls	705	Ingolf	807	Kenney	705	Lansing	416	Lyn	613
Highgate	519	Inkerman	613	Kennicott	519	La Passe	613	Lynden	519
Highland Creek	416	Innerkip	519	Kennisis Lake	705	Larchwood	705	Lyndhurst	613
Highland Grove	705	Innisville	613	Kenogami Lake	705	Larder Lake	705	Lynedoch	519
Highland Point	705	Inverary	613	Kenora	807	La Salle	519		
Hilliardton	705	Inverhuron	519	Kent Bridge	519	Latchford	705		
Hillier	613	Inwood	519	Kent Centre	519	Laurin	705		
Hillsburgh	519	Iona	519	Kentvale	705	La Vallee	807	Maberly	613
Hillsdale	705	Ipperwash	519	Kerr Lake	705	Lavant	613	MacDiarmid	807
Hills Green	519	Iron Bridge	705	Kerwood	519	Lavigne	705	Mackenzie	807
Hillside		Iroquois	613	Keswick	416	Lawrence Station	519	Maclennan	705
(Muskoka Dist.)	705	Iroquois Falls AP	705	Kettleby	416	Leamington	519	MacTier	705
Hillview	705	Iroquois Falls NT	705	Key River	705	Leaside	416	Madawaska	705
Hilton	613	Isbester	705	Khiva	519	Leaskdale	416	Madoc	613
Hilton Beach	705	Island Grove	416	Kilbride	416	Lebel	705	Madsen	807
Hinchinbrook	613	Islington	416	Killaloe	613	Leeburn	705	Magnetawan	705
Hoard's Station	705	Ivanhoe	613	Killarney	705	Lee Valley	705	Maidstone	519
Hockley	519	Ivy	705	Killean	519	Lefaivre	613	Maitland	613
Holbrook	519	Ivy Lea	613	Kilmarnock	613	Lefroy	705	Mallorytown	613
Holland	705			Kilmaurs	613	Leith	519	Malone	613
Holland Centre	519			Kilsyth	519	Leitrim	613	Malton	416
Holland Landing	416			Kilworthy	705	Lemieux	613	Malvern	416
Holland Marsh	416	Jack's Lake	705	Kimball	519	Leonard	613	Mandaumin	519
Holly	705	Jackson	519	Kimberley	519	Lepage	705	Manilla	705
Hollywood	416	Jackson's Point	416	Kinburn	613	Leskard	416	Manitouwadge	807
Holmesville	519	Jaffray-Melick	807	Kincardine	519	Levack	705	Manitowaning	705
Holstein	519	Jamot	705	King City	416	Limerick Forest	613	Manotick	613

Place Name	Area Code	Place Name	Area Code	Place Name	Area Code	Place Name	Area Code	Place Name	Area Code
Manotick Station	613	Millbridge	613	Mount St. Patrick	613	Northbrook	613	Oxbow Park	705
Mansewood	416	Millbrook	705	Mount Salem	519	North Bruce	519	Oxdrift	807
Mansfield	519	Millgrove	416	Mount Vernon	705	North Buxton	519	Oxenden	519
Manvers	705	Millhaven	613	Muirkirk	519	North Cobalt	705	Oxford Centre	519
Maple	416	Milliken	416	Mull	519	Northcote	613	Oxford Mills	613
Maple Lake	705	Milton	416	Mulmur	705	Northfield Station	613	Oxtongue Lake	705
Mar	519	Milverton	519	Muncey	519	Northgate Point	705		
Marathon	807	Mimico	416	Munro	519	North Gower	613		
Marden	519	Mimosa	519	Murillo	807	North Keppel	519		
Marionville	613	Minahico	807	Murvale	613	Northmount	416	Paincourt	519
Mariposa	705	Minaki	807	Muskoka Beach	705	North Osgoode	613	Painswick	705
Markdale	519	Mindemoya	705	Muskoka Falls	705	Northport	613	Paisley	519
Markham	416	Minden	705	Musselman's Lake	416	Northwood	519	Pakenham	613
Markstay	705	Miner's Bay	705	Myrtle Station	416	North York	416	Palermo	416
Marlbank	613	Minesing	705			Norval	416	Palgrave	416
Marmora	613	Minet's Point	705			Norwich	519	Palmer Rapids	613
Marter	705	Minett	705			Norwood	705	Palmerston	519
Martintown	613	Minnitaki	807	Nahma	705	Nottawa	705	Palmyra	519
Marvelville	613	Missanabie	705	Nairn	519	Nottawa Beach	705	Pamour	705
Maryhill	519	Mississauga	416	Nairn Centre	705	Nottawaga Beach	705	Pancake Bay	705
Marysville	613	Mitchell	519	Nakina	807	Novar	705	Panmure	613
Massey	705	Mitchell's Bay	519	Nanticoke	519			Paquette	519
Matachewan	705	Moffat	416	Napanee	613			Parham	613
Matawatchan	613	Moira	613	Narrowlock	613			Paris	519
Matheson	705	Molesworth	519	Nashville	416	Oak Lake	705	Parker	519
Mattawa	705	Monck	519	Nassagaweya	416	Oakland	519	Parkhead	519
Maxville	613	Monckland Station	613	Nassau Lake	705	Oak Ridges	416	Parkhill	519
Maxwell	519	Monck Township	705	Naughton	705	Oakview	705	Parkinson	705
Maynooth	613	Monetville	705	Navan	613	Oakville	416	Parry Sound	705
McAlpine	613	Mongolia	416	Nelles Corners	416	O'Connor		Pass Lake	807
McCool	705	Monkton	519	Nellie Lake	705	(Thunder Bay Dist.)	807	Payne's Mill	519
McCrackens Landing	705	Mono Centre	519	Nephton	705	Oconto	613	Peacock Point	416
McDonald's Corners	613	Mono Mills	519	Nestleton	705	Odessa	613	Pearl	807
McFarlane Lake	705	Mono Road	416	Nestor Falls	807	Ohsweken	519	Pearson	705
McGaw	705	Monteagle Valley	613	Nestorville	519	Oil City	519	Pefferlaw	705
McGregor	519	Monticello	519	Neustadt	519	Oil Springs	519	Peffers	519
McIntosh	807	Montreal River		Newboro	613	Ojibway	519	Pelee Island	519
McKellar	705	Harbour	705	Newboyne	613	Oldcastle	519	Pelham	416
McKenzie Island	807	Montreal River Mouth	705	Newburgh	613	Oliphant	519	Pelham Centre	416
McKenzie Portage	807	Moonbeam	705	Newbury	519	Omagh	416	Pellatt	807
McKerrow	705	Moonstone	705	New Canaan	519	Omemee	705	Pembroke	613
McMurrich	705	Moorefield	519	Newcastle	416	Onaping	705	Pendleton	613
Meadowvale	416	Mooretown	519	New Dundee	519	Oneida	416	Penetanguishene	705
Meaford	519	Moor Lake	613	New Hamburg	519	One Sided Lake	807	Pen Lake	705
Medina	519	Moose Creek	613	Newington	613	Onondaga	519	Perkinsfield	705
Medonte	705	Moose Factory	705	New Liskeard	705	Ophir	705	Perrault Falls	807
Melancthon	519	Moosonee	705	New Lowell	705	Orangeville	519	Perry Station	416
Melbourne	519	Morewood	613	Newmarket	416	Orient Bay	807	Perth	613
Meldrum Bay	705	Morgan's Point	416	New Osnaburg	807	Orillia	705	Perth Road	613
Melissa	705	Morganston	416	New Sarum	519	Oriole	416	Petawawa	613
Melville	519	Morinus	705	Newton	519	Orland	613	Peterborough	705
Merivale	613	Morpeth	519	Newton Brook	416	Orleans	613	Petersburg	519
Merlin	519	Morrisburg	613	Newton Robinson	705	Ormond	613	Petrolia	519
Merrickville	613	Morriston	519	Newtonville	416	Ormsby	613	Phelpston	705
Merritton	416	Morson	807	New Toronto	416	Oro	705	Philipsburg	519
Metcalfe	613	Mortimer's Point	705	New Wasaga Beach	705	Orono	416	Philipsville	613
Meyersburg	705	Morton	613	Niagara Falls	416	Orr Lake	705	Pickerel Lake	705
Mica Bay	705	Mosborough	519	Niagara on the Lake	416	Orrville	705	Pickering	416
Michipicoten	705	Moscow	613	Nilestown	519	Orton	519	Pickering Beach	416
Micksburg	613	Mossley	519	Niobe Lake	807	Osgoode	613	Pickle Crow	807
Middlemarch	519	Motherwell	519	Nipigon	807	Osgoode Station	613	Pickle Lake	807
Middlemiss	519	Mountain Grove	613	Nipissing	705	Oshawa	416	Picton	613
Middleport	416	Mountain View	613	Nipissing Junction	705	Osnabruck Centre	613	Pikangikum	807
Middleville	613	Mount Albert	416	Nixon	519	Oso	613	Pinegrove	416
Midhurst	705	Mount Brydges	519	Nobel	705	Osseo	705	Pine Orchard	416
Midland	705	Mount Carmel	519	Nobleton	416	Ossossane Beach	705	Pinewood	807
Milberta	705	Mount Dennis	416	Noelville	705	Ostrander	519	Pinkerton	519
Mildmay	519	Mount Elgin	519	Nolalu	807	O'Sullivan's Corners	416	Plainfield	613
Miles Bay	807	Mount Forest	519	Norembega	705	Ottawa	613	Plainville	416
Mile 212	705	Mount Hope	416	Norham	705	Otter Lake	705	Plantagenet	613
Milford	613	Mount Irwin	705	Norland	705	Otterville	519	Plattsville	519
Milford Bay	705	Mount Joy	416	Normandale	519	Overbrook	613	Pleasant Park	519
Milford Haven	705	Mount Julian	705	North Augusta	613	Owen Brook	705	Pleasant Point	705
Millbank	519	Mount Pleasant	519	North Bay	705	Owen Sound	519	Plevna	613

ONTARIO, CAN.
Plum Hollow—Sunderland

Place Name	Area Code	Place Name	Area Code	Place Name	Area Code	Place Name	Area Code	Place Name	Area Code
Plum Hollow	613	Quadeville	613	Rosebank	416	Sapawe	807	Southampton	519
Plummer	705	Queensboro	613	Rosedale	705	Sarnia	519	South Bay	807
Point Alexander	613	Queenston	416	Rosegrove	705	Sarsfield	613	South Bay Mouth	705
Point Anne	613	Queensville	416	Roseland	519	Sauble Beach	519	South Cayuga	416
Pointe au Baril	705	Queenswood	613	Rosemount	705	Sault Ste. Marie	705	South Gillies	807
Point Edward	519	Quibell	807	Roseneath	416	Sawpit Bay	705	South March	613
Point Pelee	519			Rose Point	705	Scarborough	416	South Mindoka	705
Poland	613			Roslin	613	Schomberg	416	South Monaghan	705
Pontypool	705	Raglan	416	Rossclair	705	Schreiber	807	South Mountain	613
Poole	519	Rainy River	807	Rosseau	705	Schumacher	705	South Parry	705
Poplar	705	Rama	705	Rosslyn	807	Science Hill	519	South Porcupine	705
Poplar Dale	705	Ramore	705	Rossport	807	Scotia Junction	705	South River	705
Poplar Hill		Ramsayville	613	Rostock	519	Scotland	519	Southwold Station	519
(Kenora Dist.)	807	Randall	705	Rostrevor	705	Scottsville	519	Sowerby	705
Poplar Hill		Ranger Lake		Rothsay	519	Scugog Island	519	Spanish	705
(London Dist.)	519	(Algoma Dist.)	705	Rouge Hill	416	Seaforth	519	Sparrow Lake	705
Porquis	705	Rankin	613	Rough Rock Lake	807	Sebright	705	Sparta	519
Portage Bay	807	Rathburn	705	Round Lake Centre	613	Sebringville	519	Spencerville	613
Port Albert	519	Raven Lake		Rowan Lake	807	Seeley's Bay	613	Spragge	705
Port Alma	519	(Lindsay Dist.)	705	Ruby	613	Seguin Falls	705	Springbank	519
Port Anson	705	Ravenna	519	Rupert's Harbour	705	Selby	613	Spring Bay	705
Port Arthur	807	Ravenscliffe	705	Ruscom	519	Selkirk	416	Springbrook	613
Port Bolster	705	Ravenshoe	416	Russell	613	Sellars	807	Spring Creek	705
Port Bruce	519	Ravenswood	519	Russell Landing	705	Separation Lake	807	Springfield	519
Port Burwell	519	Raymond	705	Rutherford	519	Serpent River	705	Springford	519
Port Carling	705	Reaboro	705	Rutherglen	705	Sesekinika	705	Spring Hill	613
Port Carmen	705	Read	613	Ruthven	519	Severn Bridge	705	Springhurst Beach	705
Port Colborne	416	Red Bay	519	Rutter	705	Severn Falls	705	Springtown	613
Port Credit	416	Redbridge	705	Ryckman's Corners	416	Shabaqua	807	Springvale	416
Port Cunnington	705	Red Lake	807	Rydal Bank	705	Shakespeare	519	Sprucedale	705
Port Dalhousie	416	Red Lake Road	807	Ryland	705	Shallow Lake	519	Staffa	519
Port Davidson	416	Rednersville	613			Shannonville	613	Stafford	613
Port Dover	519	Red Rock	807			Shanty Bay	705	Stamford Centre	416
Port Elgin	519	Redwater	705	Sadowa	705	Sharbot Lake	613	Stanley	807
Port Franks	519	Redwing	519	St. Agatha	519	Sharon	416	Stanleyville	613
Port Granby	416	Redwood	705	St. Albert	613	Sharps Corners	613	Staples	519
Port Hope	416	Reeves Township	705	St. Andrews West	613	Shawanaga	705	Starkville	416
Port Lambton	519	Renabie	705	St. Anne de Prescott	613	Shebandowan	807	Stayner	705
Portland	613	Renfrew	613	St. Ann's	416	Shedden	519	Steelton	705
Portlock	705	Rennison	705	St. Bernardin	613	Sheguiandah	705	Steenburg	613
Port Loring	705	Renton	519	St. Catharines	416	Shelburne	519	Steep Rock Mine	807
Port Maitland	416	Restoule	705	St. Charles	705	Shelter Bay	807	Stella	613
Port McNicoll	705	Rexdale	416	St. Clair Beach	519	Sheridan	416	Stephens Bay	705
Port Nelson	416	Riceville	613	St. Clements	519	Sherkston	416	Stevensville	416
Port Perry	416	Richard's Landing	705	St. Columban	519	Shillington	705	Still River	705
Port Robinson	416	Richmond	613	St. Davids	416	Shipka	519	Stirling	613
Port Rowan	519	Richmond Hill	416	St. Eugene	613	Shoal Lake	807	Stittsville	613
Port Ryerse	519	Richvale	416	St. George	519	Shrewsbury	519	Stoco	613
Port Sandfield	705	Richwood	519	St. Isidore de Prescott	613	Shuniah	807	Stonecliff	613
Port Severn	705	Rideau Ferry	613	St. Jacobs	519	Silver Centre	705	Stoneleigh	705
Portsmouth	613	Ridgetown	519	St. Joachim	519	Silver Creek	807	Stoney Creek	
Port Stanley	519	Ridgeville	416	St. Joseph	519	Silverdale Station	416	(Kenora Dist.)	807
Port Stanton	705	Ridgeway	416	St. Joseph Island	705	Silver Hill	519	Stoney Creek	
Port Sydney	705	Ringwood	416	St. Marys	519	Silverwater	705	(Wentworth Co.)	416
Port Union	416	Ripley	519	St. Ola	613	Simcoe	519	Stoney Point	519
Port Weller	416	River Canard	519	St. Onge	613	Simcoe Point	705	Stouffville	416
Port Whitby	416	Riverside	519	St. Paschal Baylon	613	Singhampton	705	Straffordville	519
Potter	705	River Valley	705	St. Paul's	519	Sioux Lookout	807	Strange	416
Powassan	705	Riverview	519	St. Raphael West	613	Sioux Narrows	807	Stratford	519
Prairie Siding	519	Roblin	613	St. Thomas	519	Sistonens Corners	807	Strathcona	613
Prescott	613	Roche's Point	416	St. Williams	519	Skead	705	Strathroy	519
Presqu'ile Point	613	Rockcliffe	613	Salem	519	Skibo	705	Stratton	807
Preston	519	Rockland	613	Salford	519	Slate River	807	Streetsville	416
Priceville	519	Rocklyn	519	Sand Banks	613	Sleeman	807	Stroud	705
Prince Albert	416	Rockport	613	Sand Bay	613	Smithfield	613	Sturgeon Bay	705
Princeton	519	Rock Springs	613	Sandfield	705	Smiths Falls	613	Sturgeon Falls	705
Prospect	613	Rockton	519	Sand Point	613	Smithville	416	Sturgeon Point	705
Proton	519	Rockwood	519	Sandwich	519	Smooth Rock Falls	705	Sudbury	705
Providence Bay	705	Roddis Gate	705	Sandwich South	519	Snake River	613	Sulphide	613
Puce	519	Rodney	519	Sandwich West	519	Snelgrove	416	Summerstown	613
Purbrook	705	Rolphton	613	Sandy Beach	807	Snug Harbour	705	Summerville	416
Puslinch	519	Romford	705	Sandy Lake	807	Sombra	519	Sunbury	613
Putnam	519	Romney	519	Sanford Lake	807	Sonya	705	Suncrest Island	807
						Soperton	613	Sunderland	705

Place Name	Area Code	Place Name	Area Code	Place Name	Area Code	Place Name	Area Code	Place Name	Area Code
Sundridge	705	Tincap	613	Varna	519	Watford	519	Wilfrid	705
Sunnidale Corners	705	Tiverton	519	Varney	519	Watson's Corners	613	Wilkesport	519
Sunnyside	705	Todmorden	416	Vars	613	Waubaushene	705	Williamsburg	613
Sunshine	807	Toledo	613	Vasey	705	Waupoos	613	Williamsford	519
Sutton	416	Toronto	416	Vennachar	613	Wavell	705	Williamstown	613
Sutton Bay	705	Torrance	705	Vermilion Bay	807	Waverley	705	Willisville	705
Sutton West	416	Tory Hill	705	Verner	705	Wawa	705	Willowdale	416
Swansea	416	Tottenham	416	Vernon	613	Wawbewawa	705	Wilno	613
Swastika	705	Townsend Centre	519	Vernonville	416	Webbwood	705	Wilsonville	519
Swords	705	Trafalgar	416	Verona	613	Welcome	416	Wilton	613
Sydenham	613	Trenton	613	Viamede	705	Welland	416	Wilton Grove	519
Sylvan Lake	807	Trent River	705	Victoria	416	Wellandport	416	Winchester	613
		Triple Bay	705	Victoria Harbour	705	Wellesley	519	Windermere	705
		Trout Creek	705	Victoria Road	705	Wellington	613	Windham Centre	519
		Trout Mills	705	Vienna	519	Wellman's Corners	613	Windsor	519
Talbotville	519	Trowbridge	519	Villa Nova	519	Wemyss	613	Windy Lake	705
Tamworth	613	Troy	519	Vine	705	Wendake Beach	705	Wingham	519
Tara	519	Tully Township	705	Vineland	416	Wendover	613	Winona	416
Tarzwell	705	Tunis	705	Vinemount	416	Weslemkoon	613	Winterbourne	519
Tatlock	613	Tupperville	519	Virgil	416	West Bay	705	Wolfe Island	613
Taunton	416	Turbine	705	Virginia	705	Westbrook	613	Wolverton	519
Tavistock	519	Turkey Point	519	Virginiatown	705	West Flamboro	416	Woman River	807
Tecumseh	519	Turners	519	Vittoria	519	West Guilford	705	Woodbridge	416
Teeswater	519	Tweed	613			West Hill	416	Woodford	519
Teeterville	519	Twin Elm	613			West Huntingdon	613	Woodham	519
Tehkummah	705					West Lincoln	416	Woodington	705
Temagami	705			Waba	613	West Lorne	519	Woodland Beach	705
Tempo	519			Wabigoon	807	Westmeath	613	Woodlawn	613
Tenby Bay	705	Udney	705	Wagarville	613	Westminster	519	Woods	705
Terrace Bay	807	Udora	705	Wahnapitae	705	West Monkton	519	Woodslee	519
Terra Cotta	416	Uffington	705	Wainfleet	416	West Montrose	519	Woodstock	519
Terra Nova	705	Ufford	705	Waldemar	519	Westmount	416	Woodville	705
Teston	416	Uhthoff	705	Waldhof	807	Weston	416	Wooler	613
Tetu Lake	807	Ullswater	705	Walford Station	705	Weston Derry	416	Worthington	705
Thamesford	519	Underwood	519	Walker's	519	West Plain	613	Wroxeter	519
Thamesville	519	Union	519	Walkerton	519	Westport	613	Wyebridge	705
Thedford	519	Uniondale	519	Walkerville	519	Westwood	705	Wyevale	705
Thessalon	705	Unionville	416	Wallaceburg	519	Wexford	416	Wylie	613
Thistletown	416	Uno Park	705	Wallacetown	519	Wharncliffe	705	Wymbolwood Beach	705
Thomasburg	613	Uphill	705	Wallenstein	519	Wheatley	519	Wyoming	519
Thompsonville	705	Uplands Airport	613	Walsingham	519	Whitby	416		
Thorah Township	705	Upsala	807	Walters Falls	519	Whitechurch	519		
Thornbury	519	Uptergrove	705	Walton	519	White Dog	807		
Thorndale	519	Utopia	705	Wanstead	519	White Dog Island	807	Yarker	613
Thornhill	416	Utterson	705	Wardsville	519	Whitefish	705	Yarmouth Centre	519
Thornloe	705	Uxbridge	416	Warkworth	705	Whitefish Falls	705	Yonge's Mills	613
Thornton	705			Warren	705	White Lake	613	York (Haldiman Co.)	416
Thorold	416			Warsaw	705	White River	807	York (York Co.)	416
Thunder Bay	807			Warwick	519	Whiteside	705	Young's Harbour	416
Thunder Bay Beach	705	Valentia	705	Wasaga Beach	705	Whitevale	416	Young's Point	705
Thurlow	613	Val Rita	705	Washago	705	Whitney	705	Yuil	613
Thurstonia Park	705	Vandorf	416	Washburn	613	Wiarton	519		
Tichborne	613	Vanessa	519	Washburn's Island	705	Wicklow	416		
Tilbury	519	Vanier	613	Waterdown	416	Wikwemikong	705		
Tillsonburg	519	Vankleek Hill	613	Waterford	519	Wilberforce	705	Zephyr	416
Timmins	705	Vankoughnet	705	Waterloo	519	Wilcox Lake	416	Zurich	519

ALL POINTS—AREA CODE 902

Place Name	Area Code	Place Name	Area Code	Place Name	Area Code	Place Name	Area Code	Place Name	Area Code
Abbotsford	514	Barrette	819	Bougainville	418	Causapscal	418	Cote St. Luc	514
Abenaquis	418	Barriere De Stoneham	418	Bourlamaque	819	Cavignac	514	Cote St. Paul	514
Abercorn	514	Barrington	514	Bras d'Apic	418	Cazaville	514	Cote St. Pierre	819
Abord a Plouffe	514	Barville	819	Brasset	418	Cedars	514	Cote St. Therese	514
Acton Vale	514	Baskatong Lake	819	Breakeyville	418	Chaleurs	418	Courcelles	418
Adamsville	514	Batesville	819	Brebeuf	819	Chambly	514	Courville	418
Adderley	418	Batiscan	418	Breche a Manon	418	Chambord	418	Cowansville	514
Adstock	418	Beaconsfield	514	Breckenridge	819	Champigny	418	Crabtree	514
Aeroport Bagotville	418	Bearn (Abitibi Co.)	819	Brennan's Hill	819	Champion Siding	418	Craig's Road	418
Ahuntsic	514	Beattyville	819	Bridgeville	418	Champlain	819	Cranberry	418
Albanel	418	Beauce Jonction	418	Brigham	514	Champneuf	819	Cranbourne	418
Albertville	418	Beauceville	418	Bristol	819	Chandler	418	Cross Point	418
Alcove	819	Beauchastel	819	Broadlands	418	Chapais	819	Croydon	514
Aldermac	819	Beaudry	819	Brome	514	Chapeau	819	Cullens Brook	418
Allumette Island	819	Beauharnois	514	Bromont	514	Charette	819	Cushing	514
Alma	418	Beaulac	514	Bromptonville	819	Charlemagne	514		
Amos	819	Beaulieu	418	Brookline	514	Charlesbourg	418		
Amqui	418	Beaumont	418	Brossard	514	Charny	418		
Ancienne Lorette	418	Beauport	418	Brownsburg	514	Charteris	819		
Ange Gardien de		Beaupre	418	Bruchesi	514	Chartierville	819	Daaquam	418
Rouville	514	Beaurepaire	514	Brunet	819	Chateauguay	514	D'Aiguillon	418
Angeline	418	Beaurivage	418	Bryson	819	Chateau Richer	418	Dalembert	819
Angers	819	Beaver	514	Buckingham	819	Chaudiere Basin	418	Dalesville	514
Anjou	514	Becancour	819	Buckland	418	Chaudiere Station	418	Dalquier	819
Anse a Fougeres	418	Bedard	819	Bugeaud	418	Chazel	819	Danby	819
Anse a Giles	418	Bedford	514	Bulwer	819	Chelsea	819	Danville	819
Anse a Mercier	418	Beebe	819	Bury	819	Chemin des Buttes	418	Daveluyville	819
Anse a Valleau	418	Beech Grove	819			Cheneville	819	Davengus	819
Anse St. Jean	418	Belair	418			Chenier	819	Davidson	819
Aresville	514	Belcourt				Chertsey	514	Deauville	819
Armagh	418	(Abitibi Co.)	819			Chesham	819	De Beaujeu	514
Armstrong	418	Belle Anse	418	Cabano	418	Chesterville	819	Defoy	819
Arntfield	819	Bellecombe	819	Cacouna	418	Chibougamau	819	De Grasse	418
Arseneault	418	Belle Plage	514	Cadillac	819	Chicoutimi	418	Deleage	819
Arthabaska	819	Bellerive		Campbell's Bay	819	Choisy	514	Delson	514
Arundel	819	(Beauharnois Co.)	514	Canatiche Station	418	Chomedey	514	Desbiens	418
Arvida	418	Bellerive (Labelle Co.)	819	Candiac	514	Christieville	514	Deschaillons	819
Asbestos	819	Belle Riviere	514	Cannes des Roches	418	Chute a Caron	418	Deschambault	418
Ascot	819	Bellevue		Canrobert	514	Chute a Panet	418	Deschenes	819
Aston Junction	819	(Chateauguay Co.)	514	Cantic	514	Chute aux Outardes	418	Des Ormeaux	819
Aston Station	819	Bellevue		Cantley	819	Chute St. Philippe	819	Despinassy	819
Athelstan	514	(Richelieu Co.)	514	Canton Begin	418	Cite des Deux-		Destor	819
Aubrey	514	Beloeil	514	Cap a la Baleine	418	Montagnes	514	Dewittville	514
Auclair	418	Bergeronnes	418	Cap a la Branche	418	Clairvaux	514	Dijon	418
Audet	819	Bergerville	418	Cap a L'Aigle	418	Clapperton	819	Dimock Creek	418
Aurigny	418	Bernieres	418	Cap au Renard	418	Clarenceville	514	Disraeli	418
Austin	819	Bernierville	418	Cap aux Meules (Iles		Clarke City	418	Dixville	819
Authier	819	Berthier en bas	418	de la Madeleine)	418	Clemville	418	Dock	418
Avoca	819	Berthier en Haut	514	Cap aux Oies	418	Clericy	819	Dolbeau	418
Ayer's Cliff	819	Berthierville	514	Cap aux Os	418	Clermont		Dollard des Ormeaux	514
Ayersville	514	Bevcon	819	Cap Chat	418	(Abitibi Co.)	819	Donnacona	418
Aylmer	819	Bic	418	Cap de la Madeleine	819	Clermont		Dorion	514
		Biencourt	418	Cap d' Espoir	418	(Charlevoix Co.)	418	Dorval	514
		Bienville	418	Cap des Rosiers	418	Clerval	819	Dosquet	418
		Birchton	819	Cape Cove	418	Cloridorme	418	Douglastown	418
Bagotville	418	Biron	418	Capelton	819	Cloutier	819	Douville	514
Baie Carrierre	819	Bishopton	819	Caplan	418	Coaticook	819	Dragon	514
Baie Comeau	418	Black Cape	418	Caplan River	418	Coleraine	418	Drapeau	418
Baie des Bacons	418	Black Lake	418	Cap Rouge	418	Collinsville	819	Drummondville	819
Baie des Rochers	418	Black Pool	514	Cap St. Ignace	418	Colombiere	819	Dubois	819
Baie des Sables	418	Blanche	819	Cap St. Martin	514	Colonbourg	819	Dubuisson	819
Baie d'Urfe	514	Boileau	819	Cap Sante	418	Colonie Fourniere	819	Duchesnay	418
Baie Laval	418	Boischatel	418	Cap Saumon	418	Como	514	Duclos	819
Baie Mississiquoi	514	Bois de Filion	514	Cap Tourmente	418	Compton	819	Dudswell Junction	819
Baie St. Catherine	418	Bois Franc	819	Carey's Hill	418	Contrecoeur	514	Dufresne Lake	418
Baie St. Ludger	418	Boisville	418	Carignan	819	Cookshire	819	Duhamel	819
Baie St. Paul	418	Bolton Centre	514	Carillon	514	Corner of the Beach	418	Dunany	514
Baie Shawinigan	819	Bonaventure	418	Carleton	418	Corriveau	418	Duncan	819
Baie Trinite	418	Bondville	514	Caron	819	Cortereal	418	Dundee	514
Barachois	418	Bonsecours	514	Cartierville	514	Coteau du Lac	514	Dunham	514
Barkmere	819	Bouchard		Cascades	819	Coteau Landing	514	Dunkin	514
Barnston	819	(Terrebonne Co.)	514	Casey	819	Coteau Station	514	Dupuy	819
Barraute	819	Boucherville	514	Castagnier	819	Cote St. Catherine	514	Duret	418
		Bouchette	819	Caughnawaga	514	Cote St. Louis	514	Duvernay	514

Place Name	Area Code	Place Name	Area Code	Place Name	Area Code	Place Name	Area Code	Place Name	Area Code
Eardley	819	Gardenvale	514	Henrysburg	514	La Baie	514	Lac Sergent	418
East Aldfield	819	Garneau Junction	819	Henryville	514	La Baleine	418	Lac Simon	819
East Angus	819	Garthby	418	Heppel	418	La Barriere	514	Lac Superieur	819
East Broughton	418	Gascons	418	Herouxville	418	Labelle	819	Lac Tremblant	819
East Clifton	819	Gaspe	418	Hervey Junction	418	La Butte	418	Lac Trois Saumons	418
East Farnham	514	Gatineau	819	Highwater	514	Lac a Beauce	819	Lac Victoria	819
East Greenfield	514	Gentilly	819	Hillhurst	819	L'Acadie	514	La Cyr	418
East Hereford	819	Georgeville	819	Hinchenbrooke	514	Lac a Foin	514	La Dore	418
Eastman	514	Giffard	418	Holton	514	Lac a la Tortue	819	La Durantaye	418
East Pinnacle	514	Girard Station	514	Honfleur	418	Lac au Saumon	418	Ladysmith	819
East Templeton	819	Girardville	418	Hopetown	418	Lac aux Sables	418	Laferme	819
Eastray	514	Glen Almond	819	Howick	514	Lac Beauport	418	Laferte	819
Eaton Corner	819	Glendyne	418	Huberdeau	819	Lac Bleu	418	Lafleche	514
Elgin Road	418	Glen Eagle	819	Hudson	514	Lac Blouin	819	Lafontaine	418
Emberton	819	Glenelm	514	Hull	819	Lac Bouchette	418	La Gabelle	819
Emileville	514	Glen Sutton	514	Hunter's Point	819	Lac Brule	819	La Glaciere	514
Entry Island	418	Godbout	418	Huntingdon	514	Lac Carre	819	La Gorgendiere	418
Escoumins	418	Gore	819			Lac Castagnier	819	La Guadeloupe	418
Escuminac	418	Gould	819			Lac Castor	819	Lakefield	514
Esprit-Saint	418	Gracefield	819	Iberville	514	Lac Charlebois	514	Lakeside	514
Estcourt	418	Granada	819	Ile aux Coudres	418	Lac Connolly	514	Lake View	819
Esterel	514	Granby	514	Ile aux Grues	514	Lac Cooper	819	L'Alverne	418
Etang des Caps	418	Grand Bernier	514	Ile aux Noix	514	Lac Cornu	819	La Macaza	819
Etang du Nord	418	Grand Cascapedia	418	Ile Bizard	514	Lac Delage	418	La Malbaie	418
Evain	819	Grande Baie	418	Ile Cadieux	514	Lac des Aigles	418	La Martine	418
		Grande Entree (Iles		Ile du Grand Calumet	819	Lac des Ecorces	819	Lambton	418
		de la Madeleine)	418	Ile Maligne	418	Lac Desert	819	La Miche	418
Fabreville	514	Grande Greve	418	Ile Perrot	514	Lac des Iles	819	La Minerve	819
Falardeau	418	Grande Ligne	514	Ile Perrot North	514	Lac des Loups	819	La Montee	418
Farewell Cove	418	Grande Riviere	418	Ile Perrot South	514	Lac des Plages	819	Lamorandiere	819
Farmborough	819	Grandes Bergeronnes	418	Ile Perrot Village	514	Lac des Seize Iles	514	La Motte	819
Farm Point	819	Grandes Piles	819	Ile St. Therese	514	Lac Drolet	819	Lamy	418
Farnham	514	Grande Vallee	418	Ilets Jeremie	418	Lac du Cerf	819	Landrienne	819
Farnham Centre	514	Grand'Mere	819	Inverness	418	Lac du Domaine	819	L'ange Gardien	418
Farrelton	819	Grand Metis	418	Irishtown	418	Lac Echo	514	Languedoc	819
Fassett	819	Grand Remous	819	Iron Hill	514	Lac Edouard	819	L'Annonciation	819
Father Point	418	Grand Ruisseau	418	Island Brook	819	Lac Etchemin	418	Lanoraie	514
Fatima	418	Grand St. Esprit	819	Isle Nepawa	819	Lac Fiedmont	819	Lanoraie Station	514
Fauvel	418	Graniteville	819	Issoudun	418	Lac Francais	819	L' Anse au Beaufils	418
Ferland	418	Greenfield Park	514	Ivry	819	Lac Frontiere	418	L' Anse aux Cousins	418
Ferme Neuve	819	Greenlay	819			Lac Gauvin	819	L' Anse du Cap	418
Fermont	418	Grenville	819			Lac Grosleau	819	Lanthier	819
Fiedmont	819	Grondines	418			Lac Guindon	514	La Patrie	819
Figuery	819	Gros Cap	418	Jacola	819	Lachenaie	514	La Plaine	514
Fire Lake	418	Gros Morne	418	Joannes	819	Lachevrotiere	418	La Pocatiere	418
Fitch Bay	819	Grosse Ile (Iles de la		Joliette	514	Lachine	514	Laprairie	514
Fitzpatrick	819	Madeleine)	418	Joly	418	Lac Humqui	418	La Presentation	514
Fleurant	418	Grosse Ile		Jonquiere	418	Lachute	514	La Providence	514
Fleuriot	418	(Montmagny Co.)	418	Joutel	819	Lac l'Achigan	514	La Redemption	418
Flodden	514	Grosses Roches	418			Lac la Peche	819	Larouche	418
Fontainebleau	819	Guenette	819			Lac Lemoyne	819	Larrimac	819
Fontenelle	418	Guyenne	819			Lac Malartic	819	La Salle	514
Forestville	418			Kamouraska	418	Lac Marois	514	La Sarre	819
Fort Chambly	514			Kanasuta	819	Lac Masson	514	Lascelles	819
Fort Coulonge	819			Kateville	418	Lac Megantic	819	L'Ascension	
Fortierville	819	Hadlow	418	Kazabazua	819	Lac Mercier	819	(Labelle Co.)	819
Fort William	819	Haldimand	418	Kempt Road	418	Lac Millette	514	L'Ascension	
Foster	514	Halet	819	Kenogami	418	Lac Noir	514	(Lac St. Jean Dist.)	418
Fourteen Island Lake	819	Ham Nord	819	Kenogevis	819	Lacolle	514	L'Assomption	514
Fox River	418	Hampstead	514	Kiamika	819	La Conception	819	Laterriere	418
Frampton	418	Ham Sud	819	Kiamika Reservoir	819	La Corne	819	La Tuque	819
Franklin Centre	514	Harrington	819	Kimberley	418	Lacoste	819	Launay	819
Franquelin	418	Hartwell	819	Kingsbury	819	Lac Ouareau	819	Laurel	514
Frelighsburg	514	Hatley	819	Kingscroft	819	Lac Pauze	514	Laurier Station	418
Freniere	514	Hauterive	418	Kingsey	819	Lac Quevillon	819	Laurierville	819
Frost Village	514	Havelock	514	Kingsey Falls	819	Lac Quinn	514	Lauzon	418
Fulford	514	Havre Aubert (Iles		Kingsmere	819	Lac Saguay	819	Laval des Rapides	514
		de la Madeleine)	418	Kinnear's Mills	418	Lac St. Charles	418	Laval-Est	514
		Havre aux Maisons (Iles		Kipawa	819	Lac St. Denis	514	Laval Ouest	514
Gagne	418	de la Madeleine)	418	Kirkland	514	Lac St. Joseph	418	Laval sur le Lac	514
Gagnon	418	Havre St. Pierre	418	Kirk's Ferry	819	Lac St. Marie	819	Lavaltrie	514
Gallichan	819	Hebertville	418	Knob Lake	418	Lac St. Paul	819	L'Avenir	819
		Hebertville Station	418	Knowlton	514	Lac St. Remi	819	La Verniere	418
		Hemmingford	514					La Visitation	514

Place Name	Area Code	Place Name	Area Code	Place Name	Area Code	Place Name	Area Code	Place Name	Area Code
Lawrenceville	514	Mal Bay	418	Mont Carmel	418	Notre Dame		Parc des Laurentides	418
Lebel sur Quevillon	819	Mancebourg	819	Montcerf	819	de la Paix	819	Parc du Mont	
Leclercville	819	Manche d'Epee	418	Montebello	819	Notre Dame de la		Tremblant	
Leeds	418	Manicouagan 2	418	Montfort	514	Salette	819	(Lac Chat)	819
Lejeune	418	Manicouagan 3	418	Mont Gabriel	514	Notre Dame de L'Ile		Parc du Mont	
Le Martinet	418	Manicouagan 5	418	Montgay	819	Perrot	514	Tremblant	
Lemesurier	418	Maniwaki	819	Mont Joli	418	Notre Dame		(Lac Lauzon)	819
Lemieux	819	Mann	418	Mont Laurier	819	de L'Isle-Verte	418	Parc du Mont	
Lennoxville	819	Manneville	819	Mont Louis	418	Notre Dame de		Tremblant (Petit	
Lepage	514	Mann Settlement	418	Montmagny	418	Lourdes (Joliette		Lac Monroe)	819
L'Epiphanie-		Manseau	819	Montmorency	418	Co.)	514	Parent	819
L'Assomption	514	Mansonville	514	Montpellier	819	Notre Dame de Lourdes		Parisville	819
Le Pre	418	Maple Grove		Montreal	514	(Megantic Co.)	819	Parker	819
Lesage	514	(Beauharnois Co.)	514	Montreal East	514	Notre Dame de		Pascalis	819
Les Becquets	819	Maple Grove		Montreal Sud	514	Pierreville	514	Paspebiac	418
Les Boules	418	(Megantic Co.)	418	Mont Rolland	514	Notre Dame de		Patricktown	418
Les Caps	418	Marbleton	819	Mont St. Gregoire	514	Pontmain	819	Pellegrin	418
Les Capucins	418	Maria	418	Mont St. Hilaire	514	Notre Dame des		Pelletier Station	418
Les Cedres	514	Marieville	514	Mont St. Michel	819	Anges	418	Peninsula	418
Les Eboulements	418	Marsboro	819	Mont St. Pierre	418	Notre Dame des Bois	819	Pentecote	418
Les Ecureuils	418	Marsoui	418	Mont Tremblant	819	Notre Dame des		Perce	418
Les Escoumins	418	Martindale	819	Moose Bay		Laurentides	418	Peribonka	418
Les Etrolts	418	Martin River	418	(Wolfe Co.)	418	Notre Dame des		Perkins	819
Les Forges	819	Martinville	819	Morehead	819	Monts	418	Perron	819
Les Gres	819	Maryland	819	Morin Heights	514	Notre Dame		Petit Cap	418
Les Greves	514	Mascouche	514	Morisset	418	des Sept Douleurs	418	Petite Anse	418
Les Hauteurs	418	Mascouche Heights	514	Morris	418	Notre Dame de		Petite Matane	418
Leslie	418	Masham's Mills	819	Morrison	819	Stanbridge	514	Petite Riviere au	
Les Mechins	418	Maskinonge	819	Moulin a Scie	418	Notre Dame		Renard	418
Les Saules	418	Massawippi	819	Moulin Caron	819	d' Issoudun	418	Petite Riviere	
L'Etape	418	Masson	819	Moulin Valliere	819	Notre Dame du Bon		St. Francois	418
Levis	418	Massueville	514	Mount Royal	514	Conseil	819	Petites Bergeronnes	418
Ligny St. Flochel	418	Mastal	819	Mount Wright	418	Notre Dame du Lac	418	Petite Tourelle	418
Limbour	819	Matagami	819	Murdochville	418	Notre Dame du Laus	819	Petite Vallee	418
Lime Ridge	819	Matane	418	Murray Bay	418	Notre Dame du		Petit Lac Long	819
Limoilou	418	Matapedia	418	Mystic	514	Portage	418	Petit Metis	418
Lingwick	819	Mattawin	819			Notre Dame du		Petit Saguenay	418
Lisbourg	514	Mayo	819			Rosaire	418	Phillipsburg	514
Lisgar	819	McKee	819			Notre Dame du Sacre		Piedmont	514
L'Islet	418	McLeod Crossing	819	Namur	819	Coeur	819	Pierrefonds	514
L'Isle-Verte	418	McMasterville	514	Nantel	819	Nouvelle	418	Pierreville	514
Lithium	819	McWatters	819	Nantes	819	Nouvelle Ouest	418	Pike River	514
Little Gaspe	418	Meach Lake	819	Naplerville	514	Noyan	514	Pincourt	514
Lochaber Bay	819	Mechins	418	Naudville	418			Pine Beach	514
Longue Pointe de		Megantic	819	Neubols	418			Pine Hill	514
Mingan	418	Melbourne	819	Neufchatel	418			Pintendre	418
Longueuil	514	Melocheville	514	Neuville	418	Oak Bay	418	Piopolis	819
L'Oranger	819	Mercier	514	Newago	514	Obaska	819	Plaisance	819
Loretteville	418	Messines	819	New Carlisle	418	O'Connell Lodge	819	Plessisville	819
Lorraine	514	Metabetchouan	418	New Glasgow	514	Odanak	514	Point Comfort	819
Lost River	819	Metis Beach	418	New Ireland	418	Oka	514	Pointe a Bois Vert	418
Lotbiniere	418	Micoua	418	New Liverpool	418	Old Chelsea	819	Pointe a la Garde	418
Louiseville	819	Miguasha	418	Newport	418	Old Harry	418	Pointe au Loup	418
Lourdes	819	Milan	819	New Richmond	418	Omerville	819	Pointe au Pere	418
Louvicourt	819	Mille Iles	514	Nicolet	819	Onslow Corners	819	Pointe au Pic	418
Low	819	Millerand	418	Nipisso	418	Opemiska	819	Pointe aux Anglais	418
Lucerne	819	Milles Vaches	418	Nitro	514	Orford Lake	819	Pointe aux Outardes	418
Luceville	418	Millstream	418	Nominingue	819	Ormstown	514	Pointe aux Trembles	514
Luskville	819	Milnikek	418	Noranda	819	Orsainville	418	Pointe Basse	418
Lussier	819	Milot	418	Norbestos	819	Otterburn Park	514	Pointe Bleue	418
Lyster	819	Mingan	418	Normandin	418	Otter Lake	819	Pointe Bourg	418
Lytton	819	Mirabel-Aeroport	514	Normetal	819	Outremont	514	Pointe Calumet	514
		Mirabel St. Augustin	514	North Ham	819			Pointe Claire	514
		Mirabel-Ste.		North Hatley	819			Pointe de Moulin	514
		Scholastique	514	North Stukely	514			Pointe des Cascades	514
Macamic	819	Mission St. Louis	418	Norway Bay	819	Pabos	418	Pointe des Monts	418
Macaza	819	Mistassini	418	Notre Dame		Packington	418	Pointe du Lac	819
Maddington Falls	819	Mohr	819	Auxiliatrice	418	Padoue	418	Pointe Fortune	514
Madeleine Centre	418	Moisie	418	Notre Dame de Grace	514	Palmarolle	819	Pointe Jaune	418
Magog	819	Monk	819	Notre Dame de Ham	819	Panet	418	Pointe Lebel	418
Magpie	418	Mont Albert	418	Notre Dame de La		Papinachois	418	Pointe Navare	418
Mai	418	Mont Apica	418	Dore	418	Papineauville	819	Pointe Noire	418
Maillard	418	Montauban les Mines	418	Notre Dame de la		Paquetteville	819	Poirier	819
Malartic	819	Montbrun	819	Merci	819	Parc de la Verendrye	819	Poltimore	819

Place Name	Area Code	Place Name	Area Code	Place Name	Area Code	Place Name	Area Code	Place Name	Area Code
Ponsonby	819	Riviere au Renard	418	St. Adele	514	St. Anne des Monts	418	St. Camille	
Pontbriand	418	Riviere au Tonnerre	418	St. Adelphe	418	St. Anne de Sorel	514	(Bellechasse Co.)	418
Pontiac	819	Riviere aux Chiens	418	St. Adelme	418	St. Anne des Plaines	514	St. Camille	
Pont Rouge	418	Riviere aux Pins	418	St. Adolphe	418	St. Anne du Lac	819	(Wolfe Co.)	819
Pont Viau	514	Riviere aux Rats	819	St. Adolphe de		St. Anselme	418	St. Canut	514
Portage de la Nation	819	Riviere Beaudette	514	Dudswell	819	St. Antoine	514	St. Casimir	418
Portage du Cap	418	Riviere Bersimis	418	St. Adolphe		St. Antoine Abbe	514	St. Catherine de	
Portage du Fort	819	Riviere Blanche	418	d' Howard	819	St. Antoine de		Quebec	418
Portage St. Helier	418	Riviere Bleue	418	St. Adrien de Ham	819	Pontbriand	418	St. Cecile de Levrard	819
Port Alfred	418	Riviere Bonaventure	418	St. Adrien d'Irlande	418	St. Antoine des		St. Cecile de Masham	819
Port au Persil	418	Riviere des Prairies	514	St. Agapit	418	Laurentides	514	St. Cecile de Milton	514
Port aux Quilles	418	Riviere du Loup	418	St. Agathe	819	St. Antoine de Tilly	418	St. Cecile de Whitton	819
Port Cartier	418	Riviere du Moulin	418	St. Agathe de		St. Antoine sur		St. Celestin	819
Port Daniel	418	Riviere Eperlans	418	Lotbiniere	418	Richelieu	514	St. Cesaire	514
Port Lewis	514	Riviere Eternite	418	St. Agnes de		St. Antonin	418	St. Charles Borromee	418
Portneuf	418	Riviere Hatee	418	Charlevoix	418	St. Apollinaire	418	St. Charles de	
Portneuf Sur Mer	418	Riviere Heva	819	St. Agnes de Dundee	514	St. Apolline de		Bellechasse	418
Potton	514	Riviere Jaune	418	St. Agricole	819	Patton	418	St. Charles de Caplan	418
Poupore	819	Riviere Mailloux	418	St. Aime	514	St. Armand Station	514	St. Charles de	
Precieux Sang	819	Riviere Mingan	418	St. Aime des Lacs	418	St. Arsene	418	Mandville	514
Prefontaine	819	Riviere Nouvelle	418	St. Alban	418	St. Athanase	418	St. Charles Garnier	418
Preissac	819	Riviere Ouelle	418	St. Albert	819	St. Aubert	418	St. Charles sur	
Premio	418	Riviere Ouelle Station	418	St. Alexandre		St. Augustin (Lac		Richelieu	514
Prevel	418	Riviere Pontecote	418	(Kamouraska Co.)	418	St. Jean Dist.)	418	St. Christine	418
Preville	514	Riviere Portneuf	418	St. Alexandre		St. Augustin		St. Christine d' Acton	819
Prevost	514	Riviere Rouge	514	(Matapedia Co.)	418	(Portneuf Co.)	418	St. Chrysostome	514
Price	418	Riviere St. Jean	418	St. Alexandre		St. Augustin (Two		St. Claire de	
Primeauville	514	Riviere St. Marguerite	418	d'Iberville	514	Mountains Co.)	514	Colombourg	819
Princeville	819	Riviere Trois Pistoles	418	St. Alexis de		St. Aurelie	418	St. Claire de	
Privat	819	Riviere Verte	418	Matapedia	418	St. Barbe	514	Dorchester	418
Proulxville	418	Riviere Yamaska	514	St. Alexis de		St. Barnabe	819	St. Claude	418
		Rivington	819	Montcalm	514	St. Barnabe Sud	514	St. Clement	418
		Robertsonville	418	St. Alexis des Monts	819	St. Barthelemy	514	St. Cleophas	418
		Roberval	418	St. Alexis Station	418	St. Basile de		St. Cleophas de	
Quebec	418	Robitaille	418	St. Alphonse de		Portneuf	418	Brandon	514
Quevillon	819	Rochebaucourt	819	Caplan	418	St. Basile le Grand	514	St. Clet	514
Quyon	819	Rockburn	514	St. Alphonse de		St. Beatrix	514	St. Clothilde de	
		Rock Forest	819	Granby	514	St. Benjamin	418	Beauce	418
		Rock Island	819	St. Alphonse de		St. Benoit	514	St. Clothilde de	
		Rockway Valley	819	Rodriguez	514	St. Benoit de		Chateauguay	514
Racine	514	Roquemaure	819	St. Amable	514	Matapedia	418	St. Clothilde	
Radstock	514	Rosaire	418	St. Ambroise de		St. Benoit de		de Horton	819
Ragueneau	418	Rosebridge	418	Chicoutimi	418	Packington	418	St. Coeur de Marie	418
Rameau	418	Rosemere	514	St. Ambroise		St. Benoit du Lac	819	St. Colomban	514
Randborough	819	Rosenburger's	514	de Kildare	514	St. Benoit Labre	418	St. Come	514
Rapide Beaumont	819	Ross Bay Junction	418	St. Anaclet	418	St. Bernard de		St. Come de	
Rapide Blanc	819	Rougemont	514	St. Anastasie de		Dorchester	418	Kennebec	418
Rapide Danseur	819	Rouge Valley	819	Lyster	819	St. Bernard de		St. Constant	514
Rapide des Cedres	819	Routhierville	418	St. Andre	418	Michaudville	514	St. Croix (Lac	
Rapide Deux	819	Rouyn	819	St. Andre Avellin	819	St. Bernard des Lacs	418	St. Jean Dist.)	418
Rapide Sept	819	Roxboro	514	St. Andre		St. Bernard Sud	514	St. Croix	
Rapid Lake	819	Roxton Falls	514	d'Argenteuil	514	St. Bernard sur Mer	418	(Lotbiniere Co.)	418
Rat River	819	Roxton Pond	514	St. Andre de		St. Blaise	514	St. Cuthbert	514
Rawdon	514	Ruisseau a la Loutre	418	Restigouche	418	St. Blandine	418	St. Cyprien	
Red Mills	819	Ruisseau Arbour	418	St. Andre Est	514	St. Bonaventure		(Dorchester Co.)	418
Renaud	514	Ruisseau Castor	418	St. Andrews East	514	d'Upton	819	St. Cyprien (Riviere du	
Renault	819	Ruisseau Le Blanc	418	St. Angele de Laval	819	St. Boniface de		Loup Co.)	418
Repentigny	514	Ruisseau St. Georges	514	St. Angele de Merici	418	Shawinigan	819	St. Cyprien de	
Restigouche	418	Ruisseau Vert	514	St. Angele de Monnoir	514	St. Brigitte de Laval	418	Napierville	514
Riceburg	514	Rupert	819	St. Angele de		St. Brigitte des		St. Cyr	819
Richardville	418	Russeltown	514	Premont	819	Saults	819	St. Cyrille de L'Islet	418
Richelieu	514			St. Anges	418	St. Bruno		St. Cyrille de	
Richmond	819			St. Anicet	514	(Chambly Co.)	514	Wendover	819
Rigaud	514			St. Anne de Beaupre	418	St. Bruno (Lac St.		St. Damase	
Rimouski	418	Sabrevois	514	St. Anne de Bellevue	514	Jean Dist.)	418	(Matapedia Co.)	418
Ripon	819	Sacre Coeur		St. Anne de la		St. Bruno de		St. Damase	
Rivele St. Marguerite	418	(Rimouski Co.)	418	Perade	418	Kamouraska	418	(St. Hyacinthe Co.)	514
River Bend	418	Sacre Coeur		St. Anne de la		St. Cajetan		St. Damase de	
Riverfield	514	(Saguenay Co.)	418	Pocatiere	418	(Bellechasse Co.)	418	L'Islet	418
Riviere a Claude	418	Sacre Coeur de Marie	418	St. Anne de la		St. Cajetan		St. Damien de	
Riviere a la Truite	418	Sagard	418	Rochelle	514	(Gatineau Co.)	819	Bellechasse	418
Riviere-a-Martre	418	Saguenayville	418	St. Anne de Portneuf	418	St. Calixte de		St. Damien de	
Riviere a Pierre	418	St. Adalbert	418	St. Anne de		Kilkenny	514	Brandon	514
		St. Adelaide	418	Roquemaure	819			St. Daniel	418

Place Name	Area Code	Place Name	Area Code	Place Name	Area Code	Place Name	Area Code	Place Name	Area Code
St. David	514	St. Famille d'Aumond	819	St. Gerard Magella	514	St. Jean de Cherbourg	418	St. Leonard de Portneuf	418
St. David de Falardeau	418	St. Famille d'Orleans	418	St. Germain de Grantham	819	St. Jean de Dieu	418	St. Leon de Chicoutimi	418
St. David de l'Auberiviere	418	St. Faustin	819	St. Germain de Kamouraska	418	St. Jean de la Lande (Beauce Co.)	418	St. Leon de Frontenac	819
St. Denis	514	St. Felicien	418	St. Germaine	418	St. Jean de la Lande (Temiscouata Co.)	418	St. Leon de Standon	418
St. Denis de la Bouteillerie	418	St. Felicite	418	St. Germaine de Boule	819	St. Jean de Matha	514	St. Leon le Grand	418
St. Didace	514	St. Felicite de L'Islet	418	St. Gertrude (Abitibi Co.)	819	St. Jean de Matapedia	418	St. Liboire	514
St. Dominique	514	St. Felix de Dalquier	819	St. Gertrude (Nicolet Co.)	819	St. Jean Deschaillons	819	St. Liguori	514
St. Dominique de Bagot	514	St. Felix de Kingsey	819	St. Gervais	418	St. Jean des Piles	819	St. Lin	514
St. Dominique du Rosaire	819	St. Felix de Valois	514	St. Gilbert	418	St. Jean de Vianney	819	St. Lin Junction	514
St. Donat de Montcalm	819	St. Felix d'Otis	418	St. Gilles	418	St. Jean Eudes	418	St. Louis de Blandford	819
St. Donat de Rimouski	418	St. Felix du Cap Rouge	418	St. Godfroi	418	St. Jean Ile d'Orleans	418	St. Louis de France	819
St. Dorothee	514	St. Ferdinand d'Halifax	418	St. Gregoire de Nicolet	819	St. Jeanne d'Arc	418	St. Louis de Gonzague	514
St. Dunstan du Lac Beauport	418	St. Fereol	418	St. Gregoire le Grand	514	St. Jeanne d'Arc de Clerval	819	St. Louis de Masham	819
St. Edmond (Abitibi Co.)	819	St. Fidele (Bonaventure Co.)	418	St. Guillaume	819	St. Jean Port Joli	418	St. Louis de Richelieu	514
St. Edmond (Gaspe Co.)	418	St. Fidele (Charlevoix Co.)	418	St. Guillaume Nord	514	St. Jean sur Lac	819	St. Louis de Terrebonne	514
St. Edmond les Plaines	418	St. Firmin	418	St. Guy	418	St. Jerome	514	St. Louis du Ha! Ha!	418
St. Edouard	819	St. Flavie	418	St. Hedwidge	418	St. Jerome du Lac St. Jean	418	St. Louise de L'Islet	418
St. Edouard de Frampton	418	St. Flavien	418	St. Helene de Bagot	514	St. Joachim	514	St. Luc (Champlain Co.)	819
St. Edouard de Lotbiniere	418	St. Flore	819	St. Helene de Chester	819	St. Joachim de Courval	819	St. Luc (Dorchester Co.)	418
St. Edouard de Napierville	514	St. Florence de Beaurivage	418	St. Helene de Kamouraska	418	St. Joachim de Montmorency	418	St. Luc (St. Johns Co.)	514
St. Edwidge	819	St. Fortunat de Wolfestown	819	St. Helene de la Croix	418	St. Joachim de Shefford	514	St. Luc de Matane	418
St. Eleuthere	418	St. Foy	418	St. Helene de Mancebourg	819	St. Joachim Les Tourelles	418	St. Luce	418
St. Elie de Caxton	819	St. Francois (Montmagny Co.)	418	St. Helier	418	St. Jogues	418	St. Lucie de Beauregard	418
St. Elie d'Orford	819	St. Francois d'Assise	418	St. Henedine	418	St. Johns	514	St. Lucie de Doncaster	819
St. Elizabeth	514	St. Francois de Masham	819	St. Henri de Levis	418	St. Joseph d'Alma	418	St. Lucien	819
St. Elizabeth de Warwick	819	St. Francois de Sales (Lac St. Jean Dist.)	418	St. Henri de Taillon	418	St. Joseph de Beauce	418	St. Ludger	819
St. Eloi	418	St. Francois de Sud	418	St. Hermas	514	St. Joseph de Ham Sud	819	St. Ludger de Milot	418
St. Elphege	514	St. Francois du Lac	514	St. Hermenegilde	819	St. Joseph de Kamouraska	418	St. Madeleine	514
St. Elzear (Bonaventure Co.)	418	St. Francoise	418	St. Hilaire	514	St. Joseph de la Rive	418	St. Magloire	418
St. Elzear (Temiscouata Co.)	418	St. Francoise Romaine	819	St. Hilaire de Dorset	418	St. Joseph de Lepage	418	St. Malachie	418
St. Elzear de Beauce	418	St. Francois Xavier	418	St. Hilarion	418	St. Joseph de Levis	418	St. Malo	819
St. Emelie de l'Energie	514	St. Francois Xavier de Brompton	819	St. Hippolyte	514	St. Joseph de Sorel	514	St. Marc (Temiscouata Co.)	418
St. Emile de Montcalm	514	St. Francois Xavier de Viger	418	St. Honore (Beauce Co.)	418	St. Joseph du Lac	514	St. Marc (Vercheres Co.)	514
St. Emile de Quebec	418	St. Frederic de Tring	418	St. Honore (Chicoutimi Co.)	418	St. Jovite	819	St. Marc de Figuery	819
St. Emile de Suffolk	819	St. Fulgence	418	St. Honore (Temiscouata Co.)	418	St. Jude	514	St. Marc des Carrieres	418
St. Emmelie	819	St. Gabriel	418	St. Hubert	514	St. Jules de Beauce	418	St. Marcel de L'Islet	418
St. Ephrem de Beauce	418	St. Gabriel de Brandon	514	St. Hubert Audet	819	St. Jules de Maria	418	St. Marcel de Richelieu	514
St. Esprit	514	St. Gabriel de Portneuf	418	St. Hugues	514	St. Julie de Somerset	418	St. Marcellin de Rimouski	418
St. Etienne de Beauharnois	514	St. Gabriel de Rimouski	418	St. Hyacinthe	514	St. Julie de Vercheres	514	St. Marcelline	514
St. Etienne de Bolton	514	St. Gabriel Lallement	418	St. Ignace de Loyola	514	St. Julien de Wolfestown	418	St. Marguerite	514
St. Etienne des Gres	819	St. Gedeon	418	St. Ignace de Stanbridge	514	St. Julienne	514	St. Marguerite de Dorchester	418
St. Eugene	418	St. Gedeon de Beauce	418	St. Ignace du Lac	514	St. Juste du Lac	418	St. Marguerite de Matapedia	418
St. Eugene de Chazel	819	St. Genevieve	514	St. Irene	418	St. Justin de Maskinonge	819	St. Marguerite du Lac Masson	514
St. Eugene de Grantham	819	St. Genevieve de Batiscan	418	St. Irenee	418	St. Justine	418	St. Marguerite Station	514
St. Eugene de L'Islet	418	St. Georges de Beauce	418	St. Isidore	418	St. Justine de Newton	514	St. Marie de Beauce	418
St. Eulalie	819	St. Georges de Champlain	819	St. Isidore d'Auckland	819	St. Lambert	514	St. Marie de Blandford	819
St. Euphemie	418	St. Georges de Windsor	819	St. Isidore de Laprairie	514	St. Lambert de Lauzon	418	St. Marie Salome	514
St. Eusebe	418	St. Gerard	819	St. Jacques	514	St. Laurent	514	St. Marthe	514
St. Eustache	514	St. Gerard de Berry	819	St. Jacques le Majeur	418	St. Laurent de Gallichan	819	St. Marthe de Gaspe	418
St. Evariste	418	St. Gerard des Laurentides	819	St. Jacques le Mineur	514	St. Laurent d'Orleans	418	St. Marthe sur le Lac	514
St. Fabien de Panet	418	St. Gerard d'Yamaska	514	St. Janvier	514	St. Lazare	514	St. Martin	514
St. Fabien de Rimouski	418			St. Janvier de Chazel	819	St. Lazare de Bellechasse	418	St. Martin de Beauce	418
				St. Jean	514	St. Leandre	418	St. Martine (Chateauguay Co.)	514
				St. Jean Baptiste de Rouville	514	St. Leon	819	St. Martine (Frontenac Co.)	418
				St. Jean Baptiste de Vianney	418	St. Leonard d'Aston	819		
				St. Jean Chrysostome	418	St. Leonard de Port Maurice	514		

Place Name	Area Code	Place Name	Area Code	Place Name	Area Code	Place Name	Area Code	Place Name	Area Code
St. Martyrs	418	St. Patrice de		St. Roch de		St. Thomas Didyme	418	South Bolton	514
St. Mathias	514	Beaurivage	418	Richelieu	514	St. Thuribe	418	South Durham	819
St. Mathias de		St. Patrick	418	St. Roch des Aulnaies	418	St. Timothee		South Roxton	514
Bonneterre	819	St. Paula	418	St. Romain	418	(Beauharnois Co.)	514	South Stukely	514
St. Mathieu		St. Paul		St. Romuald		St. Timothee		Springfield Park	514
(Abitibi Co.)	819	d'Abbotsford	514	d'Etchemin	418	(Champlain Co.)	418	Squatteck	418
St. Mathieu		St. Paul de Joliette	514	St. Rosaire	819	St. Tite	418	Stanbridge East	514
(Rimouski Co.)	418	St. Paul de la Croix	418	St. Rosalie	514	St. Tite des Caps	418	Standon	418
St. Mathieu		St. Paul de		St. Rose	514	St. Ubalde	418	Stanfold	819
(St. Maurice Co.)	819	Montminy	418	St. Rose de Lima	819	St. Ulric	418	Stanhope	819
St. Mathieu de		St. Paul du Nord	418	St. Rose de Poularies	819	St. Urbain	418	Stanstead	819
Laprairie	514	St. Paulin	819	St. Rose de Watford	418	St. Urbain de		Staynerville	514
St. Maurice	819	St. Paulin Dalibaire	418	St. Rose du Nord	418	Chateauguay	514	Stoke	819
St. Maurice de		St. Paul l'Ermite	514	St. Rose Ouest	514	St. Ursule	819	Stoneham	418
Dalquier	819	St. Perpetue	418	St. Sabine		St. Valentin	514	Stornoway	819
St. Maxime	418	St. Perpetue de		(Iberville Co.)	514	St. Valere	819	Stratford	418
St. Medard	418	Nicolet	819	St. Sabine de		St. Valerien		Strathmore	514
St. Melanie	514	St. Petronille	418	Bellechasse	418	(Rimouski Co.)	418	Sullivan	819
St. Methode	418	St. Philemon	418	St. Sabine Station	418	St. Valerien		Sully	418
St. Methode de		St. Philibert	418	St. Samuel de Horton	819	(Shefford Co.)	514	Sutton	514
Frontenac	418	St. Philippe	514	St. Samuel Station	819	St. Vallier	418	Sweetsburg	514
St. Michel	514	St. Philippe		St. Sauveur	514	St. Veronique de			
St. Michel de		d'Argenteuil	514	St. Sebastien		Turgeon	819		
Bellechasse	418	St. Philippe de		(Frontenac Co.)	819	St. Vianney	418		
St. Michel de		Laprairie	514	St. Sebastien		St. Viateur d'Anjou	514		
Napierville	514	St. Philippe de Neri	418	(Iberville Co.)	514	St. Victoire	514	Tadoussac	418
St. Michel des Saints	514	St. Philomene de		St. Seraphine	819	St. Victor de Beauce	418	Tapani Farm	819
St. Michel de		Fortierville	819	St. Severe	819	St. Vincent de Paul	514	Taschereau	819
Wentworth	514	St. Pie	514	St. Severin	418	St. Vital de		Tee Lake	819
St. Modeste	418	St. Pie de Guire	514	St. Severin de Beauce	418	Clermont	819	Temiscaming	819
St. Moise	418	St. Pierre Baptiste	418	St. Severin de		St. Wenceslas	819	Tenaga	819
St. Monique de		St. Pierre de		Beaurivage	418	St. Yvon	418	Terrace Vaudreuil	514
Honfleur	418	Broughton	418	St. Simeon		St. Zacharie	418	Terrebonne	514
St. Monique de		St. Pierre de		(Bonaventure Co.)	418	St. Zenon	514	Tewkesbury	418
Nicolet	514	Montmagny	418	St. Simeon		St. Zenon du Lac		Thetford Mines	418
St. Monique des Deux		St. Pierre de		(Charlevoix Co.)	418	Humqui	418	Thivierge	418
Montagnes	514	Wakefield	819	St. Simon de Bagot	514	St. Zephirin	514	Thorne	819
St. Narcisse de		St. Pierre d'Orleans	418	St. Simon de		St. Zotique	514	Three Rivers	819
Beaurivage	418	St. Pierre les		Rimouski	418	Salaberry	418	Thurso	819
St. Narcisse de		Becquets	819	St. Sixte	819	Salaberry de		Tiblemont	819
Champlain	418	St. Placide		St. Sophie de		Valleyfield	514	Tika	418
St. Narcisse de		(Charlevoix Co.)	418	Lacorne	514	Saraguay	514	Tingwick	819
Rimouski	418	St. Placide (Two		St. Sophie de Levrard	819	Sault au Mouton	418	Tobin	418
St. Nazaire		Mountains Co.)	514	St. Sophie de		Sawyerville	819	Tomifobia	819
(Bagot Co.)	819	St. Polycarpe	514	Megantic	819	Sayabec	418	Tonkas	418
St. Nazaire (Lac		St. Praxede	418	St. Stanislas	418	Schefferville	418	Tourelle	418
St. Jean Dist.)	418	St. Prime	418	St. Stanislas de		Scotstown	819	Tourville	418
St. Nazaire de Berry	819	St. Prosper de		Champlain	418	Scott Jonction	418	Tracy	514
St. Nazaire de		Champlain	418	St. Stanislas de		Seal Cove	418	Tring Jonction	418
Buckland	418	St. Prosper de		Kostka	514	Seigniory Club	819	Trinite des Monts	418
St. Neree	418	Dorchester	418	St. Sulpice	514	Selby Lake	514	Trinity Bay	418
St. Nicephore	819	St. Raphael d'Aston	819	St. Sylvere	418	Sellarsville	418	Trois Pistoles	418
St. Nicolas	418	St. Raphael de		St. Sylvestre	418	Senneterre	819	Trois Rivieres	819
St. Nil	418	Bellechasse	418	St. Telesphore	514	Senneville	514	Trois Saumons	418
St. Noel	418	St. Raymond	418	St. Tharsicius	418	Sept Iles	418	Trottier Mills	819
St. Norbert		St. Redempteur	514	St. Thecle	418	Seven Islands	418	Trout Lake	819
(Berthier Co.)	514	St. Redempteur de		St. Theodore d'Acton	514	Shawbridge	514	Two Mountains	514
St. Octave de		Levis	418	St. Theodore de		Shawinigan	819		
l'Avenir	418	St. Regis	514	Chertsey	514	Shawville	819		
St. Octave de Metis	418	St. Remi	514	St. Theodosie	514	Sheenboro	819		
St. Octave Dosquet	418	St. Remi d'Amherst	819	St. Theophile	418	Sheldrake	418		
St. Odilon de		St. Remi de Tingwick	819	St. Therese	514	Shelter Bay	418	Ulverton	819
Cranbourne	418	St. Remi du Lac		St. Therese de		Shenley East	418	Upton	514
St. Omer		au Sable	418	Gaspe	418	Sherbrooke	819		
(Bonaventure Co.)	418	St. Rene de Beauce	418	St. Therese de		Sherrington	514		
St. Omer (L'Islet Co.)	418	St. Rene Goupil	418	Gatineau	819	Shigawake	418		
St. Onesime	418	St. Rita	418	St. Therese du		Shiphaw	418	Val Alain	418
St. Ours	514	St. Robert	514	Colombier	418	Sillery	418	Val Barrette	819
St. Pacome	418	St. Robert Bellarmin	418	St. Thomas d'Aquin	514	Silver Yard	418	Val Brillant	418
St. Pamphile	418	St. Roch de		St. Thomas de Caxton	819	Siscoe	819	Valcartier	418
St. Pascal	418	Bellechasse	819	St. Thomas de		Sixteen Island Lake	514	Val Clermont	819
St. Pascal Baylon	418	St. Roch de		Cherbourg	418	Solomon	418	Valcourt	514
		L'Achigan	514	St. Thomas de		Sorel	514	Val David	819
		St. Roch de Mekinac	819	Joliette	514	South Beach	418	Val des Bois	819

Place Name	Area Code	Place Name	Area Code	Place Name	Area Code	Place Name	Area Code	Place Name	Area Code
Val d' Espoir	418	Vaucluse	514	Ville de Tracy	514	Wakeham	418	Wickham	819
Val d'Or	819	Vaudreuil	514	Ville de Vimont	514	Waltham	819	Wilson's Corners	819
Vale Perkins	514	Vendee	819	Ville Esterel	514	Warden	514	Windsor	819
Val Laflamme	819	Venise en Quebec	514	Ville Jacques Cartier	514	Warwick	819	Woburn	819
Vallee Jonction	418	Venosta	819	Ville Le Moyne	514	Waterloo	514	Wolf Lake	819
Valleyfield	514	Vercheres	514	Villemontel	819	Waterville	819	Woodlands	514
Val Limoges	819	Verdun	514	Villeneuve	418	Way's Mills	819	Woodside	418
Val Morin	819	Versailles	514	Villeroy	819	Wedding River	819	Wotton	819
Valois	514	Vianney	418	Ville St. Pierre	514	Weedon	819	Wright	819
Val Quesnel	819	Victoriaville	819	Vimy Ridge	418	Weir	819	Wychwood	819
Val Racine	819	Vien	819	Vincennes	819	West Brome	514	Wyman	819
Val St. Gilles	819	Vigneau	418	Vinoit	819	Westmount	514		
Val St. Michel	418	Ville d'Anjou	514			West Shefford	514		
Val Senneville	819	Ville d'Auteuil	514			Weygand	418	Yamachiche	819
Varennes	514	Ville de Belair	418			White Head	418	Yamaska	514
Vassan	819	Ville Degelis	418	Waco	418	White's	514	Yarm	819
Vauban	418	Ville de Lery	514	Wakefield	819	Whitworth	418	York	418

ALL POINTS—AREA CODE 306

ALL POINTS—AREA CODE 403

MEXICO
Ciudad Morelos—Tijuana

Place Name	Area Code	Place Name	Area Code	Place Name	Area Code	Place Name	Area Code	Place Name	Area Code
*Ciudad Morelos	903	*Las Palomas	903	Osimaga	903	*San Luis Rio Colorado	903	*Tecate	903
*Ensenada	903	*Los Algodones	903			*Sonoyta	903	*Tijuana	903
Guadalupe	903	Luis B. Sanchez	903	*Rosarito	903				
		*Mexicali	903						

*Information service for this place can be obtained by calling your long distance operator.

Place Name	Area Code	Place Name	Area Code	Place Name	Area Code	Place Name	Area Code	Place Name	Area Code
Abaco	809	Current	809	Harbour	809	Mayaguana	809	Roses	809
Arthurs Town	809			Harbour Island	809	Moores Island	809	Rudder Cut Cay	809
Autec	809	Deadman's Cay	809	Hatchet Bay	809	Moor Mgo	809	Rum Cay	809
		Delaporte	809	High Rock	809	Morgan's Bluff	809		
Bering Point	809	Diamond Town	809	Hope Town	809			Sandy Point	809
Bimini	809							San Salvador	809
Black Point	809			Inagua	809			Simms	809
Blanket Sound	809	Eight Mile Rock	809			Nassau	809	Spanish Wells	809
Bluff	809			James Cistern	809	Nichollas Town	809	Spring City	809
Bogue	809							Spring Point	809
Bright	809	Farmers Hill	809	Kemps Bay	809			Stafford Creek	809
Bullocks Harbour	809	Foxtown	809					Staniard Creek	809
		Freeport	809					Stella Maris	809
		Fresh Creek	809	Lucaya	809	Paradise Island	809	Sugar Mill	809
Campertown	809							Sugar Site	809
Cat Cay	809								
Cedar Harbour	809	George Town	809					Tarpum Bay	809
Cherokee Sound	809	Governors Harbour	809	Mangrove Cay	809			Treasure Cay	809
Church Grove	809	Grand Clay	809	Man-O-War Cay	809				
Clarence Town	809	Green Turtle Cay	809	Mars Bay	809	Ragged Island	809	Water Cay	809
Coopers Town	809	Gregory Town	809	Marsh Harbour	809	Rock Sound	809	West End	809
Crooked Island	809	Guana Cay	809	Mastic Point	809	Rolleville	809	Windermere Island	809

Place Name	Area Code	Place Name	Area Code	Place Name	Area Code	Place Name	Area Code	Place Name	Area Code
Hamilton	809								

Place Name	Area Code	Place Name	Area Code	Place Name	Area Code	Place Name	Area Code	Place Name	Area Code
Azua	809	Jarabacoa	809	Mella	809	San Cristobal	809	Santiago	809
				Moca	809	San Francisco de		Santo Domingo	809
						Macoris	809	Sosua	809
						San Juan de la			
Bani	809	La Romana	809			Maguana	809		
Barahona	809	La Vega	809	Neyba	809	San Pedro de			
Boca Chica	809					Macoris	809	Valverde Mao	809
Bonao	809								
				Puerto Plata	809				

Place Name	Area Code	Place Name	Area Code	Place Name	Area Code	Place Name	Area Code	Place Name	Area Code
Annotto Bay	809	Falmouth	809	Mandeville	809	Pembroke	809	Santa Cruz	809
				May Pen	809	Port Antonio	809	Savanna-La-Mar	809
				Montego Bay	809	Port Maria	809	Spanish Town	809
				Montrose	809			Stony Hill	809
Balaclava	809	Harbour View	809	Morant Bay	809				
Black River	809	Highgate	809						
Brown's Town	809					Reading	809		
						Red Hills	809	Tower	809
		Irish Town	809	Negril	809	Rose Hall	809	Tryall	809
Carlton	809					Runaway Bay	809		
Chapelton	809								
Christiana	809							Vere	809
Claremont	809	Kingston	809	Ocho Rios	809				
				Old Harbour	809	St. Ann's Bay	809		
				Oracabessa	809	San San	809		
Discovery Bay	809	Linstead	809					Williamsfield	809
Duncans	809	Lucea	809						

Place Name	Area Code	Place Name	Area Code	Place Name	Area Code	Place Name	Area Code	Place Name	Area Code
Adjuntas	809	Cidra	809	Humacao	809	Naguabo	809	San Jose	809
Aguadilla	809	Coamo	809	Humacao Playa	809	Naranjito	809	San Juan	809
Aguas Buenas	809	Comerio	809	Hyde Park	809			San Lorenzo	809
Aibonito	809	Condado	809					San Patricio	809
Altamesa	809	Consumo	809					San Rosa	809
Altamira	809	Corcega	809	Isabela	809	Orocovis	809	San Sebastian	809
Anasco	809	Corozal	809	Isla Verda	809			Santa Isabel	809
Aquada	809	Corral Viejo	809					Santa Maria	809
Aquirre	809	Cotto Laurel	809					Santana	809
Arecibo	809	Country Club	809					Santa Teresita	809
Arroyo-Patillas	809	Culebra	809	Jayuya	809	Park Boulevard	809	Santurce	809
		Cupey Alto	809	Juana Diaz	809	Pasto Viejo	809	Suchville	809
Bajadero	809			Juncos	809	Penuelas	809	Summit Hills	809
Baldrich	809	Dorado-Toa Baja	809			Ponce	809		
Barceloneta	809					Pueblo Viejo	809		
Barranquitas	809			La Alhambra	809	Puerto Nuevo	809		
Barrio Coqui	809	El Comandante	809	Lajas-San German	809	Punta Arenas	809		
Barrio Guaraguao	809	El Rosario	809	La Parguera	809	Punta Las Marias	809	Toa Alta	809
Barrio Oberero	809	El Vigia	809	La Rambla	809			Trujillo Alto	809
Bayamon	809	El Yunque	809	Lares	809				
Bay View	809			La Riviera	809				
Boca de Cangrejos	809			Las Croabas	809	Quebradillas	809		
Buchanan	809			Las Lomas	809			Utuado	809
Buena Vista	809	Fajardo	809	Las Marias	809				
Buen Consejo	809	Florida	809	Las Piedras	809				
		Fort Allen	809	Levittown	809	Ramey Air Force			
				Loiza	809	Base	809		
Cabo Rojo	809			Loiza Aldea	809	Reparto		Vega Alta	809
Caguas	809	Garden Hills	809	Los Angeles	809	Metropolitano	809	Vega Baja	809
Camuy-Hatillo	809	Guajataca	809	Luquillo	809	Rincon	809	Vieques	809
Cantera	809	Guanajibo	809			Rio Grande	809	Villalba	809
Caparra	809	Guanica-Ensenada	809			Rio Piedras	809	Villamar	809
Caparra Heights	809	Guayama	809					Villa Nevarez	809
Caparra Terrace	809	Guayanilla	809	Manati	809				
Capetillo	809	Guaynabo	809	Maricao	809				
Carolina	809	Gurabo	809	Maunabo	809				
Catano	809			Mayaguez	809				
Cayey	809	Hato Rey	809	Miramar	809	Sabana Grande	809	Yabucoa	809
Ceiba	809	Hato Tejas	809	Moca	809	Salinas	809	Yauco	809
Ciales	809	Hormigueros	809	Morovis	809	San Augustin	809		

Place Name	Area Code	Place Name	Area Code	Place Name	Area Code	Place Name	Area Code	Place Name	Area Code
Charlotte Amalie, St. Thomas	809	Christiansted, St. Croix	809	Frederiksted, St. Croix	809	St. John Island	809	Tutu	809